D0398797

58953

HQ 809.3 .G7 L39 1988

Lawson, Annette.

Adultery

D|

FEB 9 1990		
APR 1 9 1999		
NO NEWER 3/2012		

COMMUNITY COLLEGE
OF DENVER
RED ROCKS CAMPUS

ADULTERY

ADULTERY

An Analysis of Love and Betrayal

ANNETTE LAWSON

Basic Books, Inc., Publishers

NEW YORK

RED ROCKS
COMMUNITY COLLEGE

58953

HQ
809.3
G7
L39
1988

Library of Congress Cataloging-in-Publication Data

Lawson, Annette.
  Adultery: an analysis of love and betrayal.

  Bibliography: p. 411.
  Includes index.
  1. Adultery—Great Britain. 2. Adultery. I. Title.
HQ809.3.G7L39 1988   306.7'36 88–47685
ISBN 0–465–00075–4

Copyright © 1988 by Annette Lawson
Printed in the United States of America
Designed by Vincent Torre
88 89 90 91 RRD 9 8 7 6 5 4 3 2 1

For

David, Emily, Ralph, and George

and

in memory of

C.P.D.

RED ROCKS
COMMUNITY COLLEGE

CONTENTS

ACKNOWLEDGMENTS

How, I wonder, can one adequately thank family, friends, and colleagues in two countries and three universities over far too many years for all the support that has gone into the making of this book? Let me begin with my children.

When I began to work on *Adultery*—not an easy topic to understand or explain to one's schoolmates or teachers—my children were not even teenagers. Now even the youngest is nearly out of school and the other two are in universities. It was the youngest who told me I should dedicate the book to them since, "after all, we are the ones who lost our mother"! Clearly, even in (as I like to think) enlightened homes, us working mums must suffer the slings and arrows of outrageous children. And he need not have worried, for my children deserve much more than a dedication: their love sustains me and their conviction that it would be finished (*must* be finished) has ensured that it was finished. All three helped in practical ways, too, Emily with referencing, Ralph organizing footnotes into endnotes on the computer, and George working with me on the proofs.

In order to accomplish all that has gone into this book, we have had to have a household in London that runs reasonably smoothly and that continues to do so when we are not living in it but in Berkeley, California. Looking after all of us, including cats and fish, has been "Nanny," the person who cared for me as a child and who returned to live with us since 1972. Although now retired, she remains a constant resource, effectively helped by Bernie Hayes. At all times, too, our office, which is in our house in London, has been administered by Vivienne Clark. Her efficiency and loyal support have been of immeasurable importance throughout these years. Although she is employed mainly as my husband's personal assistant, she has searched for questionnaires for me, ordered my work for me, and generally helped us remain sane in times of upheaval.

Then there are my friends—people who, at various times throughout the long years of this study, have been there when I needed them—and some of the times, especially early on, would have been insupportable without them. Among them, in England, Katrin, Camilla, Richard, Charles, Enid, Margot, Sue and Mac, Dennis and Rachel, the Tackaberrys, and my sister-in-law, Penny Tillett, have played important parts, but I thank all my friends—each is precious to me.

In Berkeley we were privileged to live on Tamalpais Road, in the Schorer house—the same Mark Schorer whose work on William Blake I had already discovered and decided to quote before I found myself in his house. Tamalpais Road is a friendly and fascinating place full of interesting people, including academic visitors to Berkeley and their families. There we made new friends and were particularly lucky to have Liza and Ned Goldwasser living right next door for two years, while Mary Ann Mason and Paul Ekman lived up the hill. A little further afield, in Marin County, were Ann and Phil Murphy and Bob and Judy Wallerstein. And, up in the Napa Valley, Tony Cartlidge and Sarah Forni together taught me to relax in Calistoga's hot springs and opened the doors to the sybaritic pleasures of massage and mud baths.

Others forwarded the study. Peta Levi, both friend and free-lance journalist, provided me with the opportunity to obtain a sample from the London *Sunday Times*. The publicity that followed this and a later article by Polly Toynbee in the *Guardian*, led to financial support from a publishing house and a television production company which enabled me to employ research assistants. In addition, the Nuffield Foundation funded the development of the questionnaire; and for the year 1984–85, I was awarded the "Thank-offering to Britain" fellowship of the British Academy. These awards enabled me to take two separate years of leave from my faculty post at Brunel, the University of West London.

My colleagues and the secretarial staff (especially Margaret and Norma) in the department of sociology there, as well as in other branches of the social sciences, were also supportive of my work. Keith Hopkins (now professor of ancient history at the University of Cambridge) supported the early phases with departmental funds, Salvador Giner (now professor of sociology at the University of Barcelona in Spain) was always ready to offer theoretical explanation, and others—including those deeply critical of such research techniques—even filled out pilot questionnaires. The research itself was carried forward with the help of many different assistants, usually working on specific tasks. David Mingay worked full time on the questionnaire, while Clare Bakes, Anna Wynne, Terri Walker, and George Berguno—all then graduate students in sociology or psychology at Brunel—attended groups, helped transcribe interviews and group discussions, developed the coding frame for the questionnaire, and carried out the coding itself. In 1983, Carole Ilett, a graduate of the sociology department, became my research assistant and continued for about two years. She was responsible for supervising almost all the coding, for the bulk of the analysis, and for writing important summary reports. She remained steady and unruffled even when faced with quite overwhelming amounts of paper to analyze. She worked closely with Dave Guppy of the University of London Computing Center who put the material onto the mainframe computer, obtained all the tables we wanted, and attended meetings where we tried to understand what all those reams of paper meant, sometimes late into the night well fortified by appropriate refreshment. Alison Lyons joined us for a few months, and her excellent sociological mind was a real spurt to further analysis.

I remained unconvinced by my efforts to explain my data, however. Even my year away with the British Academy award did not lead to clarification. During that year, Alex Zwerdling, a friend and professor of English at the University of California at Berkeley, was on leave in London. He liked my work and suggested he show something I had written to certain colleagues in Berkeley. The idea grew that I might go to Berkeley or to Stanford for a year, especially since my husband was in partnership producing wine in the Napa Valley. I have Alex to thank for his introductions to Berkeley that led to an invitation from Professor Guy Swanson to come as visiting scholar to the Institute of Human Development. Ed Swanson treated me most generously, as did Professor Paul Mussen who succeeded Ed as director for the year 1988–89, providing office space, stationery, and mainframe computer time. The staff, too, were consistently kind and helpful.

Few people have read the manuscript, but I want to thank Alex Zwerdling again for his early reading of five chapters and the great boost he gave to my morale through his pleasure in it. All his detailed comments have been incorporated in the text. In the year before he and his wife, Florence Elon, left to live (temporarily) in Washington, they found us our house in Berkeley, introduced us to their friends, and generally acted as "gatekeepers" to Berkeley for us.

Meanwhile, through Keith Hopkins, I had been introduced to Lenore Weitzman at Stanford University, who proposed my affiliation to what was then known as CROW, the Center for Research on Women at Stanford University (now the Institute for Research on Women and Gender), to which, by invitation of Marilyn Yalom, I also became a visiting and, later, an affiliated scholar. There, my welcome was warm—in part especially due to the continuing presence of Lorraine Macchello, who keeps the whole place running in its pleasant way. When I arrived in Berkeley, Lenny also invited me to participate in the Berkeley Faculty Women's Research Seminar—a group of scholars drawn from universities around the San Francisco Bay area. We met once a month in one another's homes and discussed a member's current research or a topic of general interest to feminist scholars. From all the members of that wonderful group, organized by Karen Eriksen, Gloria Bowles, and Ruth Dixon-Mueller, I learned much and spent many thoroughly enjoyable evenings in their company. Judith Stacey, whom I met there, I count among my many Berkeley friends.

It was not until I reached the West Coast of America that I found the theoretical structure I needed to interpret my data. The major differences I had found were always between the women and the men, complicated by generation and by the timing of the affair. Beyond stating them, how could these differences be explained? Those theories with which I was familiar as a sociologist (especially deviancy theory) seemed helpful but inadequate. Biological difference, economic determinism, psychoanalysis, and political change were relevant, but nothing pulled it all together. Then I gave the opening scholar's seminar at Stanford in October 1985.

Just let me set the scene. Serra House, where the institute has its home, is a delightful small house, on a human scale. It was once the president's house. You go in and you see flowers, carpets, a friendly receptionist. The seminars are held in a calm French-windowed conference room—once, I imagine, the library or dining room of the house. The room was crowded, and I began. Not with theory or figures or information about my sample, but about myself. I made my study make logical sense in the context of who I was and from whence I came. I cannot now say why I did this—only that it seemed appropriate. The whole time I never once felt, as I had always previously done, that I was "on show," that I was giving a "performance" (these are the words used), and that everyone was waiting, not constructively to criticize or help, but to show off their own brilliance. Words like the "cutting edge" of knowledge come to mind. Most academic seminars consist of people listening impatiently for question and discussion time so they can tell the speaker (with enormous tact, of course) that, *if* they had had those ideas or had done that study (which they did not because neither the ideas nor the study were worthy of them), they would have had the ideas and done the study differently—and far better. In this case, the attention was quiet, concentrated, and supportive. I felt buoyed up, as if I were on a water bed.

When I finished speaking, comments and questions were made in a way that was completely unthreatening and wholly constructive. Yet these scholars were not blindly obsequious; serious problems that I needed to address were raised, and new lines for analysis proposed. Various authors whose names I had not known were suggested; one of these was Carol Gilligan. Later that day, I went to the library at Stanford and took out her *In a Different Voice*. It was on two-hour loan. I curled up in an armchair there in Green Library and read the whole book. It was a major turning point. My findings began to fall into place. I read more and more, nearly everything now by feminist scholars, many of whom I was now meeting in one or another of the various groups to which I belonged. They were all concerned to explore gender roles in history, in pre-literate and industrialized societies, at the present time, in both the inner and outer worlds. Some of these were members of faculty at the two universities or at the University of California at Davis, and some I met through the Faculty Research Seminar and through two other groups: the Association for Women in Psychology and Sociologists for Women in Society. I presented my work to all these groups, and from each I gained new insights as well as emotional support from their remarkable members.

At the same time, within the University of California at Berkeley, I became a member of a faculty seminar on family dynamics held each month in the Institute of Human Development under the auspices of professors Philip and Carolyn Cowan from the psychology department. There I met still other scholars, both women and men, drawn from the departments of education, sociology, and anthropology as well as from psychology. From my participation in this group, too, I learned a great deal, each month hearing about another intriguing study on marriage, children, and the family. When I presented my own work, I was invited to circulate a chapter, and I am most grateful for all the comments I received.

Everywhere I experienced a generous welcome, and my whole intellectual life advanced once more. Among those whose work was particularly important to me were Nancy Chodorow, Ravenna Helson, Arlie Hochschild, Kristin Luker, Lillian Rubin, Nancy Scheper-Hughes, Arlene Skolnick, and Ann Swidler. Now I knew I was not the classic "exceptional woman," content to succeed in a man's world that in the end proved inhospitable, but just another woman for whom mainstream academic explanatory systems were not enough. In sociology we speak of a person's "master status"—the position that best defines her or him, let us say as teacher, mother, carpenter, doctor, son, and so forth; writing *Adultery*, my "mistress status" has shifted from sociologist to feminist scholar.

Meanwhile, some of the scholars' group at the institute in Stanford met regularly to work on a project analyzing and expanding the argument put by Betty Friedan in the Sunday *New York Times* in November 1985 about the best ways forward for the women's movement. I became firmer friends with and more influenced by the thinking of members of the institute there. Among them—some only there for a year, others longer—were the anthropologists Gina Holloman and Jean Davison; the historians Karen Offen, Edie Gelles, and Mollie Rosenhan; the literary scholar Brit Sundquist; the playwright Elisabeth Roden; and the sociologists Mary du Quinn, Karen Skold, and Pamela Eakins. Marilyn Yalom published her *Maternity, Mortality and the Literature of Madness*. Autumn Stanley completed *Mothers of Invention*. The directors of my respective institutes changed: Deborah Rhode took over at Stanford, ably assisted by Sherri Matteo; and Paul Mussen, at Berkeley.

Soon after I arrived in Berkeley, and through another considerable scholar and past director of the Institute of Human Development, John Clausen, I met Colin Samson, a young English sociologist and a doctoral candidate on a fellowship from the National Institute of Mental Health. Colin became my research assistant, sometimes working intensively, sometimes just for the odd hour here and there. He was invaluable. Together, we learned how to access and use the mainframe computer. Colin has become a good friend; life in Berkeley would have been emptier without him and my work less expertly analyzed and referenced. Neil Smelser, professor at the University of California, despite his crowded schedule, read and liked my work and also took the time to read and comment on a paper written with Colin.

Several people have helped at times when I have been stuck: my office-mate in Berkeley, Sharon Jenkins, and next-door-neighbor there, Dorothy Field, helped with statistics (never my forte) and were also just friendly companions. With Arlene and Jerome Skolnick's minds at work, over dinner at the Cafe Pastoral accompanied by Stratford wine, I was able to develop my ideas about "this telling business," and about the "masculinization of sex" and the "feminization of love." Autumn Stanley read various drafts and did a rapid editing job that was most helpful, and Margot Levy pulled me from the Slough of Despond in London with her own brilliant editing skills. Peggy Thoits, while she was at the institute at Berkeley, suggested typologies and offered to read the entire manuscript—something I have not inflicted on her until after publication.

My deep thanks go, then, to all those scholars, mainly but not only women, whose support, ideas, and writings have moved me on and helped me find my own voice.

Without, however, the voices of those who generously participated in this study, men and women, this book could not, would not have been written. I have, of course, jealously guarded their confidence (and that of others—friends and colleagues who told me their stories). All names have been changed; indeed, I cannot even remember some of their real names. Some have a first name only; others, a surname. This reflects not my feelings for them nor about them, but my relationship to them. In real life I do not call everyone by their first name, and nor did I in this study. But each main character is marvelously familiar to me. Because each social fact—date of a marriage, number of children, type of job—is an important facet of the analysis, I have changed them as rarely as is consistent with protecting the confidentiality of my study participants. They told their dramatic life stories with feeling and often with difficulty. I hope I have done them justice. If they recognize themselves or think they do, and especially if you, my reader, recognize yourself in their stories, I will be reassured, for while each was unique, their stories also follow patterns and it is these patterns I have attempted to elucidate. These are the people to whom I now say "thank you."

Throughout the years, librarians in each of the universities where I worked have been more than helpful, willingly pursuing my strangest requests and often intrigued with my topic. I also spent valuable hours in the British Library in the British Museum in London—required, as often as not, to sit at the "dirty books" table under the watchful eyes of the North Library librarians in case reading books on marriage and the family proved too stimulating!

A book has to be produced. I am proud to be published by Basic Books and grateful to my editor, Steven Fraser, and to Phoebe Hoss, developmental editor, who proposed changes, carried out all the detailed editing, and helped pull the book into shape. Their insistence that I rewrite a substantial amount in a very short period of time, stressful as it was, has resulted in a much better book. Being English, I am, perhaps, more cavalier with the language than they; I use the third-person plural after the collective noun just as everyone does happily in everyday speech and think it important that writers print such desirable changes so that they become accepted usage. Thus, any lapses of grammar are undoubtedly mine and not to be blamed on my meticulous editors or their publishing house.

Finally, how can I thank a husband for helping me write a book about adultery? David, from the beginning, believed in me and believed in the project. Whatever difficulties he experienced about my topic, he kept, as is his wont (even when I would rather he did not follow his wont), to himself. Believing I had quite enough editors already, he has read only bits and pieces. He has, however, taken over the shopping—often the cooking, too—plied me with necessary glasses of excellent wine, and collected endless cups of cold coffee from around the house. And although it was David who kept me equipped with regularly updated computers and software, he has called himself a "computer widow" as I have sat hunched over my word processor, my eyes giddy with flickering green light. Perhaps now the book is in print, David will read it all. If he does I hope he will find it to his liking.

Berkeley, California
June 1988

ADULTERY

לֹא תִנְאָף

Thou shalt not commit adultery.

Prologue

Inside-out

1976

At a dinner in London, my friend Jan, whom I'd known for more than twenty years, said to me out of the blue: "There's something I have to tell you. Charlie and I—our marriage, I mean—it's on the rocks. . . . And that"—she pointed to a man some twenty years older than us—"is the man I am involved with."

I was stunned. Of all the couples I knew, Jan and Charlie seemed among the happiest and most secure. They had been married nearly twenty years. They and my husband and I were contemporaries, all English, all of us celebrating (if such a word can describe how at least one of us felt) our fortieth birthdays that year, and close friends. Marrying some ten years later than Jan and Charlie, I had remained close to them, shared some of their joys and tribulations, and, in the early years of their marriage, taken my own partners to visit them. Their third child, named after me, was a kind of honorary goddaughter to me. I loved both Jan and her husband, an attractive and intelligent man. What does she prefer in this man? I wondered. What does he feel? What does Charlie feel? What on earth has brought this about? And why must it threaten their marriage? Couldn't she just have had an affair with the man? After all, he's married, too.

Over the years, the four of us had joined in jokey conversations, in which Jan and Charlie in particular seemed, if not explicitly, nonetheless clearly to be granting each other permission to step outside the boundaries of marital sexual exclusivity. But never had anyone hinted that such a step might end the marriage. Furthermore, those two marriages involved six children.

In the weeks following the dinner, I became the confidante not only of Jan but also of Charlie. I learned that he, too, had had an affair that summer. This woman also was married and had three children. That brought the toll to nine children. Perhaps her husband and his wife were also "carrying on," and then there would be . . . It was beginning to sound like the "Ten Green Bottles" song that ends with none standing on the wall, only this was in reverse. But soon I learned that there was an adult victim as well. The husband of Charlie's mistress (lover? girlfriend? what *was* the right word for Sheila?) was quite seriously ill. If she left him, he would be desolated. There was no one else in his life.

These had been secret affairs. It had been Charlie who had broken silence and had told Jan of his involvement, because, he said, he wanted to leave her and live with Sheila. However, Sheila had not finally decided to leave her unwell husband and was afraid she would lose her children. In the confessional, Jan had admitted her own affair. Charlie was devastated. It was one thing for him to be having this relationship. Quite another for Jan, especially as she had not intended to tell him. He said, "I would never have known anything about it if I hadn't told her about me." "But you only told Jan, Charlie, because you wanted to leave her," I replied. "She wasn't going to leave you. Indeed, she had been feeling badly about her neglect of you and the children. She was worried that you were working too hard [his major excuse for absence was 'work'], and Jake [their son] in particular was suffering, she thought, because you were so little at home. She blamed herself. And so she was about to try to put things right."

One thing was made clear to me by both friends. Their marriage had been happy. Each confirmed that they had created together what Donald Winnicott, the English psychoanalyst, might have called a "good enough" marriage.[1] Although Charlie was talking of going to live with Sheila—"just to try it and see what happened"—neither really wished the marriage to end. Rather, it seemed the many dinner-party conversations about possible "other relationships" had been taken seriously by each as a permission to explore, to engage in affairs. Not that any express permission had been sought or granted by either, but each had sensed and accepted a permissiveness, conditional on the preservation of what each perceived as a strong and good marriage. The boundaries set, however, had not withstood the strength of the new relationships. The control each thought he or she could exercise over the course of any affair was a mirage. The "good" marriage had been undermined by the "good" adulterous relationship. As confidante, I also felt and heard the guilt and the fury, the sadness and the pain. Each felt profoundly betrayed by the other. Yet, objectively, each was equally guilty. Charlie, describing his feelings, said, "It's such a mess, isn't it? Last summer I thought anything and everything was possible. I felt fantastic. Now——" While Jan said, "Last summer I was feeling really bad about Sam, and I made up my mind to make it up to Charlie and to try to be a really 'good wife' over the holidays. We were all going away together to Scotland, and I was determined to concentrate on the family and that we would all have a great time together. In the end, Charlie was working so hard, he couldn't come for a whole month and then, when he was there, he had to keep dashing off to 'emergencies.' Some emergencies! It never—not for one moment—occurred to me *he* might have someone else."

I began to piece together the puzzle. Clearly, each had kept special secrets—sexual secrets—from the other. It was talk and telling that had brought matters to such a pitch. Thus secrecy and telling were important sections of the puzzle. The affairs were certainly not explicable in terms only of an unhappy marriage. On the other hand, at that stage in their marriage—with children becoming less dependent, with both working, Jan at a new career, Charlie at the top of his profession but also beginning to appreciate that dreams he had had of greatness at twenty-five might need to be given up at forty—perhaps they were restless, seeking to fill gaps in experience that they could not (or so they felt) enjoy with one another. Having focused for so long on one another and on their children, perhaps they now felt a wider view was desirable. I wondered whether they had felt that these excursions into self-fulfillment outside the confines of their marital relationship could be kept in properly labeled compartments and not impinge on sacred areas within the marriage. After all, countless liaisons had been managed in this way through the centuries. Now, however, these boundaries had been breached; powerful emotions could not be held at bay or kept in the box marked "profane."

Control thus seemed another part of the puzzle. What, I wondered, was its importance? Had Jan and Charlie experienced life as chaotic and *disordered* in some way so that they needed to take control of it again—that is, of their own lives or, perhaps, of one another? Or was life *too* ordered, too predictable? Did it lack chaos and excitement, the sense of living dangerously that imparts a sense of living at all? Could they be attempting to *reorder* the world according to their own desired pattern? Or was it, perhaps, as popular wisdom might have said, a desire to act irresponsibly, to deny or stave off approaching middle age, to forget the mortgage and the family? Was it an attempt to make up for having married so young? To be free and single and out at work?

Yet, I was struck by the disorder, by the chaos that seemed to have replaced regular and comprehensible patterns. This was certainly not the first marriage to have included affairs in its story, and, it seemed, not all marriages foundered in such circumstances. Indeed, some, it was said, flourished especially because of such relationships. And, despite the sorrow that their marriage might end, Jan and Charlie rejoiced in their affairs; neither was saying, "It wasn't worth it."

As I listened both to Jan and, even more, to her husband, I recognized not just sympathy for their misery but also envy at the excitement of their lives, at their power to attract others and their daring to engage in new relationships outside their marriage. I also recognized fear—fear that the admired structure of a stable marriage could be so fragile in the face of additional (alternative? again, what *was* the right way to describe these third parties intruding on the pair?) intimate relationships. In other words, this happened to be "them." But it could as well have been "us."

Both these adulterous liaisons had begun through meetings at work. It seemed possible that experiences at work would provide another piece of the puzzle. Having been, for the immediately preceding ten years at home bearing and rearing my own three children, I had, just that year, returned to full-time work—paid work. Even though, unlike Jan, I had had several years of work before leaving to look after my children, I experienced the return as violent in its impact. It was a real culture shock. I was the only woman in the sociology department of my small university near London that year, older than all but two of my male colleagues, yet junior to them in status. I, like so many women of my class and generation, had at thirty-nine re-entered at a level lower than I had achieved at twenty-nine. I recall sitting in the concourse of the dining building, waiting for someone or something, I forget who or what. At eye level were the crotches of hundreds of young men and tens of young women, all identically clad, in their more or less tight blue jeans.

To me, who had never possessed a pair of jeans in my life, this overtly sexual challenge (as I felt) went along with an intellectual one. In my ten-year absence, there had been many changes in sociology. During these first two terms back in full-time employment, it is no exaggeration to say that there was not a single day, including Christmas Day and New Year's Eve, when I did not do some work, even if it was only to fall asleep with an article or a chapter of some academic tome in my hands. I certainly brought my work home; the whole family was involved, willy-nilly, in my job, and my husband had books in the bed.

There is, I know, nothing unique about this experience. Nor did I regret my decision, strongly supported by my husband, to return to work. I rapidly became caught up in teaching and enjoyed my students and my colleagues. I was given considerable administrative responsibility and loved the intellectual stimulation. Other women, not as lucky as I was in obtaining a higher education or a good job, have nonetheless followed similar patterns, perhaps taking a degree, specific courses to equip then for today's market, or some other educational route when their children were old enough. Others have gone back to part-time work or struggle with full-time jobs at the same time as their maternal responsibilities have scarcely reduced. All have left the tight circle of hearth and home and all that that means—its values and its patterns which they understand—and are moving in a man's world. This world is not only often sexually exciting and challenging but is also run in ways that are barely comprehensible to women. We make mistakes because we read the signals wrongly or, rather, not in the way the men who send them intend them to be read. Perhaps, too, our signals are misread, in their turn perceived as wrong.[2]

Traumatic as it was, this experience of mine is just one tiny part of a huge social change—the return of women, particularly married women into the marketplaces. In England and Wales, in 1971, fewer than one half of married women were working; but by 1981, nearly 60 percent were.[3] Since many married women still take time off work when their children are very small, this average hides the fact that over two thirds are working of those aged forty-five to fifty-four.[4] It seemed to me then—a perception confirmed in this study as well as in others[5]—that the relationships between home and work, work and love, domesticity and economic public activity are currently being renegotiated—a process entailing for me and Jan, as for many women, considerable conflict.

Certainly Jan and her new love seemed plagued by problems. And, as I heard more and confronted my own conflicting feelings at home and at work, I knew I wanted to try to understand what was going on. I wanted to understand for my own sake but not only from the inside. That is, I wanted to understand my own experience, Jan's experience, and the experience of thousands of others, women and men, as they became involved or perhaps avoided becoming involved in these classic triangles. As a sociologist, though, concerned with examining groups of people, whole institutions, whole societies and attempting to grasp why they are shaped as they are, what changes have occurred or are now taking place, why the people within them are behaving as they do, I wanted to understand adultery as a social phenomenon—from the outside.

Outside-in

How, then, was this to be done? There are, of course, well-recognized sociological research methods, but this subject remains relatively taboo. Indeed, there is almost no academic work by historians, sociologists, or anthropologists that focuses on adultery and no book with the word *Adultery* as its title. Rather, people have written of the "affair," of "playing around," or of "extramarital relations," of the "extra-sex factor" or the "extramarital connection."[6] These seem to me synonyms without stigma, words and phrases developed to minimize the sense of sin and guilt, crime and shame, that pervades "adultery" with its long foundations in Church and Law. They also mask the fact that adultery has long been a much worse problem when committed by the married woman than by her husband for the penalties for her have been much greater. When I was given leave to pursue this research, I was asked by my university not to disclose publicly what the topic of my study was; I did not think the large-scale funding that would be needed for taking representative or random samples would be forthcoming.

My own preferred way of working in social science is to use every source of knowledge available to me that seems relevant and appropriate to the topic to be studied. Eventually, knowing that I wanted both quantitative and qualitative material—figures and stories—I chose survey methods and in-depth interviews, together with small-group discussions. Three national, major British newspapers published articles about my work, each article ending with an appeal to those seriously interested in participating in the study to come forward. From these sources, 579 people completed questionnaires that have provided the statistical data, and about 100 were interviewed or participated in the small-group discussions. Both on their questionnaires and in these tape-recorded and transcribed conversations, people told their stories; these have provided the rich accounts that give meaning to the numbers. This was the formally gathered information. Informally, I gained much from constant "people watching," from literary texts and drama—both stage and film—and from the experience of others; as well as painstaking introspection.

Clearly, the people in my study were all volunteers—volunteering, moreover, to speak about something still relatively taboo; still, if not felt as sin or acted upon as crime, an illicit relationship that breaches powerful social norms. This relationship is often also still kept secret, especially from the spouse. How reliable these accounts were must, therefore, be of legitimate concern.

The reasons for accepting the information offered me as worth the reliance I give it are detailed in appendix B, together with a full description of the sample: there were, for example, more women than men (60:40); and sample members were overwhelmingly middle-class, highly educated, and white. This, too, is explained in appendix B, where I also describe my methods; the questionnaire itself is in appendix A. Here, suffice it to say that people came from a whole variety of stances: "faithful" and "unfaithful" (more of the latter than the former, 73:27), "conforming to the marriage vows" and "denying the relevance of marriage vows," "tempted but not (yet) succumbed" and "victim." They came also for a variety of reasons: to help in what they perceived as useful social science—dealing with a problem affecting so many and yet barely touched by academics; because they were puzzled by their own feelings and actions and thought they might learn while contributing; to ensure I would "get it right, since sociologists always get it wrong"; because they felt they had valid and relevant experiences to relate; because, adultery being so taboo, they could speak of it to no one. They came, in other words, to confess. Some perhaps, though I think very few, came to boast.

Yet I do not think them weird exhibitionists but reliable witnesses of their own experience and representative of others like themselves who did not come forward. This I base primarily on two facts. First, their premarital sexual experience is almost exactly as would be expected when compared with information derived from representative national samples. This is important both because premarital and postmarital sexual behavior are said to be related; and because, if the accounts given of this sexual behavior— which, although relatively acceptable now, has only recently become so— were unrepresentative and/or inaccurate, it would be much more likely that accounts of adultery also would be unreliable.

Second, a "snowball" sample—that is, people approached by the volunteers and who then agreed to participate—differ significantly from the other sample members in only one respect: they do not talk to others about such personal matters. For example, they discussed sexual matters rarely even with their own spouses; they went hardly ever to professional counselors; and they less frequently had confidantes.

Thus, the accounts given by sample members of another recently illicit aspect of their sexual behavior appear accurate, and the stories of others who did not initially volunteer, but who have been involved in these adulterous triangles, do not differ in outline (though, of course, each is unique) from those told by the study volunteers. Finally, these stories tally, too, with those told elsewhere—among friends, on trains, in bars, or in countless novels.[7]

I collected, then, a mass of computer-analyzed data and transcripts of interviews. Another social event prompted ideas useful to the task of analysis.

In the winter of 1984, we were invited with our children to a party by an old friend, one of a group whom we had got to know more than twenty years earlier. All the guests, like ourselves, were middle-class couples—mostly Jewish—with teenage families living in London, and we had originally been brought together at the sort of party our parents gave for their young to meet other "suitable" young people. Courtship, sexual, and marriage patterns have changed so much that a two-generation party where our children could meet suitable partners had become an unusual event. But someone noticed an odd phenomenon: there appeared to be few divorced or separated people on their own, and no remarried couples. Thirty, or even twenty, years ago, it was not the absence but the presence of divorced people that would have been the subject of comment.

It is hard now to recall that divorce was accessible only to the relatively well off; and that, even for the rich, divorce carried social ostracism in its wake. (Divorced people were not admitted to the Royal Enclosure at Ascot,[8] for example; and, following his divorce and subsequent marriage to Happy, Nelson Rockefeller failed to win the support he needed to run for president.) Someone had to be "guilty," or "at fault," of having caused the divorce, and no one could assume that a mother would obtain custody even of her very young children if she were the guilty party. The "fault" most commonly employed was adultery.

Over centuries of Western culture, divorce has been tied to adultery, for a long time practically the only ground on which a man could divorce his wife.[9] Adultery breaches *the* rule of marriage—the sexual exclusivity rule—that each must "forsake all others," cleaving from the wedding day forward only to one another. This rule not only requires partners in a marriage to be sexually faithful to one another, it also positively enjoins them to have sex together. A marriage may be annulled if it remains unconsummated, if sex does not take place between the couple. It contains a right—to the body of the other (for the procreation of children, if for no other purpose)[10]— and, at the same time, sets firm, high, and impermeable boundaries around the availability of the marriage partners to anyone else.

But in the Western world today these boundaries are no longer fixed and certain. Indeed, changes have extended beyond what kind of party you can give and for whom, beyond what may be ingested, sniffed, or smoked and how, beyond table manners and the extravagances of dress and hair about which the confused person may appeal to Miss Manners as arbiter, to the facts of sexual behavior. These facts are surprisingly unknown. For example, it is not possible to say what the rates of adultery are, nor how they have changed. We do not even know with any certainty whether adultery is an experience of the minority or majority of married people. I say "surprisingly," for it seems as if there is endless talk about sex. Books and articles proliferate, some schools in some places have sex education, films are increasingly explicit, pamphlets (especially since the AIDS crisis) arrive by mail,[11] and the very essence of the sexual and loving relationship is felt to lie in confession—in self-disclosure.

It is no longer at all clear what is private and what public, what may be spoken and what left unsaid, what kept secret and from whom. The boundaries of both sexual behavior and sexual secrets are elastic. People at this party, knowing the publicity my work had received, and linking adultery with divorce, suggested that because I knew "all about adultery," I should explain marital breakdown and marital endurance. But in their questioning I sensed another but apprehensive expectation: that I would speak my own sexual secrets and that I might have hidden access to theirs, an anxiety that the boundaries of what had once been a private, illicit, and secret relation might be breached.

This very ordinary social transaction confirmed the extraordinary paradox that had emerged from my reflections about Jan and Charlie: that while honesty and openness are held to be modern moral goals, individuals need jealously to guard their own secrets, especially their sexual secrets. Adultery is a relationship that is in essence secret though its consequences may become public.

Adultery is, indeed, firmly tied to marital breakdown. It undermines the social order. It may also be a sordid, mundane affair, meaningless and empty. But it is often more than this. Much more. It is a great myth: as Denis de Rougemont long ago told us, as he struggled to understand the unspeakable events that loomed over Europe and wrote of love and war, adultery is often "an atmosphere beyond good and evil, and a drama, either lofty or dreadful; in short a drama—a *romance*."[12] Hence, adultery has to be set in context, both as the underside, the breach of marriage, an undercover institution with its own secret rules, and as a narrative—an adventure and a story—that pulls people constantly to it with the promise of dangerous passion.

Introduction

The Story of Adultery

> My lords, if you would hear a high tale of love and death, here is
> that of Tristan and Queen Iseult; how to their full joy, but to their
> sorrow also, they loved each other, and how, at last, they died of
> that love together upon one day; he by her and she by him.
> —Joseph Bedier, *The Romance of Tristan and Iseult*

> Isolde, Queen of Cornwall. See Iseult.
> Iseult, Queen of Cornwall. See Tristan.
> —The British Library, London, Main Catalogue

Legends opening with words like these, irresistible to listeners everywhere,
and long ago forming the backbone of ballads sung by roving troubadours,
told of the love of a knight for a lady who was always already betrothed or
married to another—a lord, often one to whom the knight owed allegiance.
The knight was doubly bound by the code of honor that sustained chivalry
and by the Christian ethic, forbidding the consummation of any love but
that between married couples. As part of his knightly duties, he had to un-
dergo all manner of trials of his strength and his wits, pitting good against
evil, but also to demonstrate to his lady how deserving he was of her love.
To succeed in this goal of love was a moral—a virtuous—goal. He had to
prove himself worthy of her and overcome many obstacles to gain her. But,
if he was successful, if he did capture her, and if their love was consummated, death—since it was adulterous, passionate love—would surely
follow.[1]

The ballad epitomizing such fatal love is that of Tristan and Isolde—the
"great European myth of adultery."[2] This myth remains firmly lodged in
Western consciousness, running—as such stories must—underground, not

immediately accessible and not known in all its parts but appearing in dreams and influencing everyone through modern versions on film, in novels and plays, or sung by poets and lived—lived out in daily life by hundreds and thousands of ordinary knights and princesses, confidantes and kings. Tristan and Isolde's story is important not only for its influence on so much of Western culture but because it is paradoxically woven into the cloth of the modern ideal of married love.

Let me briefly outline the story—using Joseph Bedier's version translated by Hilaire Belloc,[3] whose words head this introduction—not to analyze it, nor to point to the many features it shares with other great myths, nor to consider detailed meanings such as the extent to which Tristan might be perceived as attempting to replace his lost parents in the triangle he creates, but to notice its toxicity, the absolute necessity for the lovers to act secretly and with deception especially of those they love and honor, the sense they have that they are without responsibility for their feelings and can do nothing about them, and, above all, the difference in the roles of the two heroes, for it is not Isolde's story that leads us into the tale and takes us to its tragic end, but Tristan's. I will then examine the durability of the story, consider the nature of a myth, and show how people, using the adulterous tale—that is, by living and relating this story—"renarrativize" their own lives.[4] I follow the capturing of the adulterous love story by marriage and the emergence of two new great myths that merge and compete: these I call the *Myth of Romantic Marriage* and the *Myth of Me*. I suggest that these mythologies serve as boundaries and goals within which modern women and men set their own limits and aspirations. I outline important social changes in sexual behavior and in talk and telling and indicate the shape of the book.

Tristan and Isolde

Blanchefleur, sister to King Marc of Cornwall, mourns the death of her husband, King of Lyonesse and, having given birth to a son whom she names Tristan for *tristesse* because she is so sad, herself dies. The orphaned baby is taken in and hidden as his own son by Rohalt, trusted friend of Tristan's father. Tristan grows up to be an extraordinarily gifted young man. Eventually he goes to Cornwall where, his birth origins unknown, he wins the king's heart with his charm, his talented playing of the lyre, and his hunting prowess. Rohalt informs the king of Tristan's origins, and Tristan becomes the king's beloved foster son as well as his nephew.

Morholt, brother to the Queen of Ireland, has come to Cornwall to collect Cornwall's three-yearly tribute of six hundred young women and men. Tristan challenges Morholt to single combat and kills him but is poisoned by a splinter from Morholt's sword. Mortally sick, Tristan persuades King Marc to let him be placed in a boat with his lyre, for no one in Cornwall can cure him. He drifts to Ireland and is rescued by fishermen who take him to the court where the queen and her daughter, Isolde the Fair, not knowing this is the knight who has slain their kinsman, tend him and cure him with their magical potions.

Tristan leaves Ireland and returns to Cornwall where jealous barons and knights plot against him: they persuade King Marc he must have an heir. Marc says he will marry the woman whose hair matches a strand of gold dropped by swallows. Tristan recognizes the hair as Isolde's and, despite the danger he knows he faces in returning to Ireland, sets out to win her for his uncle-father. In Ireland, he kills a monster dragon terrorizing the countryside but is wounded again. Again, he is tended by Isolde, who does not recognize him. However, by matching the splinter of her uncle's sword to his weapon, Isolde discovers that this is the knight who killed her uncle and, with Morholt's sword, nearly kills Tristan as he takes a bath. However, Tristan, suggesting his deep interest in her, persuades her to spare him. Isolde's reward is to be given by her father as tribute to Tristan, but Tristan accepts her not for himself but for his uncle, Marc.

The Queen of Ireland prepares a love potion for her daughter to drink with King Marc on their wedding night and entrusts it to Brangien, Isolde's nurse and companion. (Bedier's version describes Isolde's deep hurt and anger at being deceived by Tristan in this way, but Wagner goes further and has her hating him so deeply that she prepares, as well as the love potion, a death potion with which she tries to cause his death and her own.) On the ship carrying them from Ireland to Cornwall, they are becalmed. It is very hot, and a young maid, not realizing what she offers, brings them the potion to drink. They are immediately lost to perpetual and dangerous enchantment of one another:

> She had found not wine—
> But Passion and Joy most sharp,
> And Anguish without end,
> And Death.[5]

Returning to solid land and the normal order of the society, Marc and Isolde are married, but Brangien takes Isolde's place on the wedding night, presumably because Tristan and Isolde are now lovers and her betrayal will be discovered.[6] Thereafter, Tristan and Isolde meet in ever-increasing danger and are betrayed by the jealous courtiers. After numerous tests and trials, they eventually flee to the forest, where they live many months in a hut and without comfort. On a certain occasion Marc discovers them sleeping there, Tristan's unsheathed sword between them. Marc replaces Tristan's weapon with his own. After this episode, their homeless and rough life as outcasts palls; Tristan returns Isolde to Marc and leaves for France—but not before she has given him a green jasper ring telling him if he needs her to send the ring and she will come.

Tristan, after some years, marries another Isolde—of the White Hands— but he remains "faithful" to Isolde the Fair and refuses to consummate the marriage: it remains white. Tristan for the third time is wounded and, dying, sends the ring to Isolde. She is to hoist a white sail if she is in the returning ship. She comes but, jealous of their love, Isolde of the White Hands tells her husband the ship has black sails; Tristan dies. When Isolde lands and finds him dead, she, too, dies. They are buried, and from their graves two briars grow and wrap around each other.

The Goddess of Love

The legend of Tristan and Isolde, together with other such love myths altered to take account of Christianity, probably originated in ancient stories based on the worship and love of the Goddess of Love. Deep in the ancient tales was hidden a view of woman as the possessor of wisdom and great powers. And there was a vital secret: these powers might be obtained by her lover if he could learn *drudaria*, or *coitus reservatus*. In achieving this (a great skill requiring the most demanding trial asked of any knight—that he should conquer his own desire), the lover would be serving his lady and love, giving her pleasure without thought of his own, but he would win his lady's heart and gain her wisdom and power. This, it appears, was derived from tantrism, the Indian system of yoni worship, or female-centered worship, particularly of the Goddess Shiva or *She* (*Tristan* is *Tantrist* reversed). The gypsies might have brought this belief system, and the practice of what in tantrism was called *maithuna*, into southern Europe and up to Provence;[7] while de Rougemont suggests the troubadours probably learned of it in the Manichaean tradition among the Cathars of Provence whose writings contain much that is similar to the ancient Buddhist and Hindu texts which had been translated and brought to the West via Persia.[8] Indeed, courtly love honored the same restraints: the art of love was to withhold, to give pleasure; delight was in the chase of the heart, not the conquest of the body, for the latter was a *profanation* of love only redeemed by death.[9] The woman's sexuality was unbounded; the man's closely controlled. In this way would the greatest ecstasy be achieved.

With this deep origin, it is scarcely surprising that the adulterous love story was so subversive. In a Christian world, it overturned the "natural" heterosexual relationship where the husband (as the "head of the wife," as Paul instructed in Ephesians 5:23) was on top both mentally and physically, pleasure becoming sinful and intercourse permitted only for procreation. Thus, indeed, the secrets of *drudaria* had to be hidden. The man's pleasure was now specifically not to be controlled; the woman's, bounded or even unimportant. Furthermore, Christianity preached that the greatest ecstasy was to be found not in the love of man for man (nor for woman) but in the love of God—of *Him*, not of *She*. Nor could this love be achieved in this life on earth but only after death. Thus, poets and minstrels ("minnesingers," or singers of the Goddess Minne whose name was a synonym for love) were denied the sacrament of communion by the Church before the thirteenth century, and their romantic poetry remained heretical.

Yet the legend does not give prominence to Isolde. Even now, libraries, like the British Library in the epigraph to this chapter, direct the reader who searches for Isolde to Tristan.

The legend is Tristan's. It is a tale of conquest, a tale of male heroism where women are beautiful and desirable, difficult to obtain unless guile (even deceit) is used and battles are fought, and possessed of the traditional and magical skills of healing. Men and women are alike in their capacity to deceive and dishonor those men to whom they owe deep duty whether as husband, ruler, uncle-father, or God; but the woman waits on the man's desires. She is passive, having to be invited to meet her lover dangerously at night, rather than initiating such meetings. Even her medicinal skills lie dormant until summoned to Tristan's service. In earlier versions—the Icelandic saga, for example—Isolde had powers of the intellect, of knowledge, the voice, or the word, that is, as well as her powers of herbal and medicinal healing; she could cast spells.[10]

A French dramatist, Agnes Verlet, in her 1977 play, *Yseult et Tristan*, has returned to this idea, making Yseult cast a spell on Tristan for disdaining her, leading her *comme une esclave*—"like a slave"—to his uncle-father. She curses him to love her *éperdument*—"hopelessly, as one for ever lost."[11] Wagner has Isolde attempting to kill Tristan who has dishonored her by killing the man she loves, and it is Isolde, even in earlier versions, who arranges for Tristan, disguised as a boatman or a beggar, to carry her across water so that she can truthfully claim to have lain only in the arms of her husband and of the poor man who had just carried her across the water. But these are rare moments when Isolde's emotions, skills, and intelligence are central, for she does not, for example, mix an antidote to her mother's love potion or return home to learn greater skills. Indeed, she lives her secret and intriguing life always at the behest of others: it is her father who sends her to Marc, and her mother mixes the potion that continues to control her, her destiny determined now by her lover and her husband. Even in death, Tristan takes the lead. He dies. Without him, she dies, too.

The drama is not about the time they spend together but about separation and meeting, about Tristan's enduring great danger to be a worthy knight, someone whom Isolde could scarcely resist even had she never drunk the love potion. After drinking it, she is completely lost. He, on the other hand, does not even attempt to woo her for himself. It is only the potion that makes him love her. In other words, although she has great gifts of healing, Isolde is never in control of her life or her emotions. She discovers real joy when she abandons herself to her lover's passion. He loses control only through magic—women's magic. Afterward, the tale continues with many trials of their love. Thus, passionate love is never calm and ordered but intense with suffering (de Rougemont points out that happy love has no history, no story).[12] "Happy ever after" in this tale is "happy after death."

The Adulterous Myth in Modern Times

In modern times, certain elements retain a particular importance (among them, even the love that is never consummated): the continuing heroism in overcoming obstacles for love and the longing to possess the unobtainable; pleasure in the illicit and secret (not only in the secret, forbidden relationship but also, perhaps, in the deeper secrets of tantrism and goddess worship); the drama of meeting and separation; the feeling of being overtaken by emotion and yet powerful; the suffering and the deep betrayal that is always involved of an Other and sometimes of an Ideal; the challenge to social order together with the possibility of punishment and exclusion from civil society; and the fact that adultery has no place of its own. As Tony Tanner, in his analysis of three of the greatest nineteenth-century novels of adultery, has written:

> If society depends for its existence on certain rules governing what may be combined and what should be kept separate, then adultery, by bringing the wrong things together in the wrong places (or the wrong people in the wrong beds), offers an attack on those rules, revealing them to be arbitrary rather than absolute.[13]

In chapter 1, "What Is Adultery?" I pursue these elements and, throughout the book, they recur in the stories of individuals.

For the man, much remains unchanged. The would-be lover can still feel the thrill of embarking on a quest for good. In achieving his quest, he conquers another man's wife or, perhaps, another woman who is forbidden him because he already has a wife. All manner of boundaries are breached; he is a rebel, choosing people, places, and moments that might minimize danger and yet meet deeply felt psychological needs. He wins her because of his own potency; he *merits* her. He may win her because of his high status relative to her, because of his charm, his looks, his sense of humor, his flattery of her, his money, or for many other reasons. He *feels* it is entirely his own achievement. In modern times, people gain much of their sense of self-worth from their work—indeed, the identity of men may be so bound up with their occupation that when they are unemployed, they cannot say who they are; but in this relationship the lover is not dependent on his employer for congratulations and rewards—only on the lady for affirmation of his worth. When a man chooses a brother's or a best friend's wife as his adulterous partner, we see again the drama of double betrayal—the male bond undermined in deadly rivalry. In book II, chapters 6 and 7, I relate these experiences.

However, in most cases, the lover is not betraying the woman's husband but his own wife. The myth depicts Tristan's wife, Isolde of the White Hands, as barely relevant to his feelings: she is the subservient and suffering yet nurturant wife, denied even the joy of children. Her part is scarcely one many modern women desire or happily fulfill; yet many women in history and even now bide their time, not free to leave, unwilling to fight until opportunity beckons when they may strike with deadly force. In times of greater freedom for women and in a world where egalitarianism is an ideal (if not a fact), similar double betrayal and rivalry occur between wives and "other women"; but there have yet to be established bonds of sisterhood in this arena to match the brotherhood of men.[14] And there is a particular conflict for modern women in Isolde's story: longing still for the conquering lover who woos them with such finesse and bravery, they also desire autonomy and control. They want simultaneously to be magically transported and to determine their own fate. Throughout my book, women speak of these two desires. It is by no means clear, however, that women desire an unobtainable man or one more powerful than her husband; nor that for women obstruction is necessary to erotic desire as Freud thought it was for men.[15] That she may still enjoy rebellion in the face of severe constraint is, however, clear in the stories of modern women. As Shulamith Firestone some time ago suggested, even love may be "complicated, corrupted, or obstructed by an unequal balance of power."[16]

The myth of adulterous love remains ubiquitous: the story is hard to avoid. Pick up almost any novel, go to almost any film or play, listen to a popular song, and the chances are high that it will deal centrally with adultery. Simultaneously, over many months in London between 1982 and 1984, full houses attended a number of plays by serious playwrights: Peter Nichol's *Passion Play*, about a happily married middle-aged couple whose life is destroyed when the husband is seduced by a "siren-girl"; Tom Stoppard's *The Real Thing*, about various adulterous liaisons in plays and among the actors playing the characters in the plays; and Harold Pinter's *Betrayal*, about a wife's love affair with her husband's good friend.[17] In 1984, Wagner's opera of *Tristan and Isolde* was played in five capitals of Europe; and even more recently, in 1987 and 1988, it is being produced in several major cities of the United States. In 1984, the Booker Prize for literature went to Anita Brookner's *Hotel du Lac*, a story of a woman trying to break away from her adulterous lover and failing to find true happiness in marriage. Three years later, one critic attending the Booker Prize dinner was heard to mutter, "I want Chinua Achebe's book to win because it's the only damned book *not* about adultery." In Boston, Camerata, a musical group, has returned to early sources of both music and text to develop a new musical version of Tristan and Isolde; they will take it in 1988 to the Far East and Europe.[18]

Less elevated and typical of so many inexpensive novels, dramas, and comic strips, and reaching at least as wide and a very differently constituted audience, *Jackie*, a British teenage girls' comic magazine, in 1983 published the "Last Fairy Tale" depicting a prince who rescues a maiden hidden deep in a forest and about to marry the ugly troll who has stolen her kingdom.

The prince is given the magic "word" that, when used, weakens the troll and enables him to fight the creature with bare hands.[19] In this modern tale, it is, however, the princess who picks up her suitor's sword and kills the troll. Alas, she is not permitted public recognition but acquiesces to her lover's request that she keep this brave act secret: the triumph will be his alone. She, once more, gains a conquering hero. Films, too—from *Brief Encounter* of some forty years ago (where the lovers part and the would-be adulterous married woman returns to the protective love of her husband) to *Fatal Attraction* launched in 1987 (where the "dangerous," modern professional and single woman seduces the married man, only to be murdered by his devoted wife)—continue to focus on the ancient conflict, working it around contemporary anxieties, and reach an audience of millions covering the whole social spectrum.

We are as obsessed with the adulterous liaison as ever the nineteenth century was. That century produced, with *Anna Karenina* and *Madame Bovary*, just to mention two, some of the greatest literature of all time to focus on this topic.[20]

But our obsession is justified for this is not only a story: it is a myth.

The Power of the Myth

"Myths," wrote Mark Schorer, "are the instruments by which we continually struggle to make our experience intelligible to ourselves. A myth is a large, controlling image, that gives philosophical meaning to the facts of ordinary life, that is, which has organizing value for experience. . . . Without such images, experience is chaotic, fragmentary and merely phenomenal. It is the chaos of experience that creates [myths] and they are intended to rectify it."[21] Myths are *necessary* for human existence (Schorer wrote of the "Necessity of Myth") because they delineate and explore fundamental "constant relations" that have become unrecognized and unspeakable perhaps because they are in opposition to contemporary rules of conduct or beliefs. The myth permits us "to become aware at a glance" of these relations and "to disengage them from the welter of everyday appearances."[22] Emile Durkheim thought myth suggested the sacred rather than the profane, but this does not mean myths deal only with what is specifically considered religious in any given society; rather, myths deal with human feeling and experience: they may also narrate the search for good and attempt to bound evil. For the Jungian Joseph Campbell, the myth "is the secret opening through which the inexhaustible energies of the cosmos pour into human cultural manifestation. [Even] the very dreams that blister sleep boil up from the basic, magic ring of myth."[23]

Schorer stresses both meaning and control. The myth has power. De Rougemont thought, indeed, that the "most profound characteristic [of the symbolic fable] is the power it wins over us, usually without our knowing," even when this power is exercised only in our dreams.[24] We need myths, then, and they control us; yet they remain narratives, dramas, adventures. Myths help us make sense of our experience, yet they also contain guiding principles to new experience. Above all, the myth is not false. Quite the reverse, for it expresses hidden truth. To denigrate something as "mere myth" reflects the anxiety that what has been symbolically said may indeed be really true.

The myth speaks, then, of "constant relations" or continuities that are true. But each historical period has a dynamic and structure that varies and will select from the fable those aspects—those continuities—that illuminate its particular struggles. Furthermore, in stratified societies, not all social classes share the same myths, nor would the same truths apply. In Tristan and Isolde, according to de Rougemont's analysis, feudal rule, the Christian Church, Manichaean heresies, the laws of chivalry and courtly love all did battle within its drama. Clearly, so too did the relations of power between men and women of that particular noble élite. When the myth surfaces in our own times, we may be sure our own divisions and struggles will be reflected there. Again, throughout this book, I notice both change and continuities traced to modern upheavals in structural and cultural arrangements.

Adultery as Story

In a concrete way, Phyllis Rose, in her analysis of five literary marriages in nineteenth-century England, has employed the idea of the myth as "imaginative patterns—(or) mythologies"[25] to explain how a marriage may be experienced as happy or miserable. For Rose, marriages, which she calls "parallel lives," are not so much objectively measurable as happy or miserable but share or fail to share a story. Sharing an imaginative construct or story line, the marriage that from the outside appears quite disjointed may be experienced as smooth and unruffled. Thus, the marriage of John Stuart Mill and Harriet Taylor—whom, in traditional courtly fashion, he had had to win, overcoming the obstacle of her first marriage—was, "objectively" speaking, far from happy, yet they clearly shared an "imaginative construct" of the rights of women which both believed they were truly *creating* and *living* together.[26]

To create and live one's own story appears impossible. Despite social upheavals of great magnitude that permit a florid pluralism of dress, behavior, and manners, particularly to the young, there remain powerful constraining forces—material and cultural. Intimate relations and personal life, however, offer an adventure that *appears* unrestricted even as it deliberately and consciously breaches powerful norms. In a democratic age, no one need be a real princess or knight but may *live* this story for themselves. Each can have an adventure (in Italian, *l'avventura* also means "the future") that seems invented spontaneously but springs from the source of the adulterous love myth which for centuries has taught that the pursuit of passionate love is noble. Further, in a historical moment when the goal of self-

knowledge is itself morally good—even a moral imperative—passion promises the power of self-awareness in a way that is qualitatively different from
other paths to such enlightenment because we think we shall discover "real
life." According to de Rougemont, however, this real life is impossible to
know: "Suffering and understanding are deeply connected; death and self-
awareness are in league."[27] The modern story maker, excising death from
the calculation, nonetheless recognizes these deep connections. It becomes
worthwhile to risk pain and suffering in order to live this story, especially
since it is in living this story that so many in my sample felt, sometimes for
the first time, that they were "really alive" and, even, *why* they were alive.[28]
Adultery "renarrativizes" lives that have come to feel empty of meaning
without a sense of moving forward purposefully—lacking story.

Phyllis Rose puts strongly the need of human beings to create narratives
that give coherence and meaning to their lives: she argues that it is not facts
that give rise to the story, but vice versa; the story gives rise to the "facts."[29]
Similarly, the novelist-heroine of *Hotel du Lac*, describing her approach to
her love affair, "sometimes thought that the time spent working out the
plots of her novels had prepared her for this, her final adventure, her story
come to life."[30] Thus I understand adultery *as* story, a particular drama
central to Western culture, but always, because it is a story, available for
creative rewriting. The participants in this study created, lived, and narrated
their own stories.

I have said that each historical period has a dynamic and a structure of
its own, and that what is true for one class (or gender) within any one society
may not be true for another. Clearly, to speak of Western culture also masks
the divisions of nationality and language. In the twentieth century, television has become a major carrier of mass culture reaching into the living
room of almost every household—and many bedrooms, too—simultaneously and paradoxically diffusing a "florid pluralism" and a small number
of dominant, or—as Antonio Gramsci, the great Italian philosopher-
revolutionary, called them—hegemonic ideologies that are powerful at every level, for both women and men and, I believe, across the Western
world.[31] One of the most important of the narratives told by television is
again, according to Roland Barthes, the story of adultery—not, he suggests,
just in fictional, dramatic form but also in talk shows and interviews. Describing an interview with an actor, Barthes wrote, "The interviewer *wants*
the good husband to be unfaithful: this excites him, he *demands* an ambiguous phrase, the seed of a story."[32] Television programs are sold from one
nation to another; travel is no longer limited to the élite few; and in many
hotels all over Europe and the English-speaking world, it is often difficult
to know where one has landed. International and supranational corporations and institutions provide working environments that are more similar
than dissimilar whether they are located in Rome, New York, or London.
Often the same films are seen and books read in Paris as in San Francisco
and Madrid. I do not wish to imply there are no differences for there are—

profound ones—but with respect to the place in culture of the Myth of Romantic Marriage which embraces so much of the adulterous love story, and the Myth of Me, the two mythologies central to my thesis, I emphasize what is shared.[33]

I choose the term *mythology* or *myth*, rather than *ideology* or *value* or *belief system*, because in everyday thinking *ideology*'s marxist connotations might imply *false* political belief, while the functionalist and consensus connotation of *value system* fails to take account of the considerable conflict that is experienced as people employ the myths in competition as both justification and explanation for their actions, particularly in adultery. But especially I wish to capture the idea of adultery as story, and a myth is, above all, a narrative.

The Myth of Romantic Marriage and the Myth of Me

Romantic love, instead of being an accident to marriage, . . . [is] the basis on which all marriages must be built.
—Kenneth Walker, 1957

I remember consciously thinking, "I am thirty-five—that's half way to threescore years and ten. What have you done with your life? I've got teenage kids. I've been married seventeen years. There must be more to life than this. What had I done so far? What had I achieved?" . . . I think I was very much aware of being my parents' daughter; my husband's wife; my children's mother—but who was I? There must be more in it, I felt, for *me*.
—Fanny, study participant

Medieval courtly love had separated marriage and love: they were seen as in complete contradiction.[34] Scholars argue whether and, if so, when this essentially dark and dangerous passion became enclosed within the safety of conventional and institutionalized marriage, an arrangement that is expected to be creative and life giving. All agree that if the partners do not choose for themselves, romantic, passionate love cannot be the basis of marriage. C. S. Lewis, for example, noting that in past times many had little say in the choice of their marital partners, wrote that "where marriage does not depend on the free will of the married, any theory which takes love for a noble form of experience must be a theory of adultery."[35] He was perhaps thinking of the kind of family depicted in 1818 by the writer Susan Ferrier in her novel *Marriage*. Her seventeen-year-old heroine was roundly scolded by her father, Lord Courtland, when she timidly suggested she might be allowed to choose a "man of her heart," for it was her obligation "to marry for the purposes for which matrimony was ordained amongst people of birth—that is, for the aggrandizement of her family, the extending of political influence—for becoming, in short, the depository of their mutual interest."[36] Certainly this passage suggests that the landed gentry and aristocracy in early nineteenth-century England might desire romantic love within marriage but would not be free to choose it—especially where daughters were concerned.

The American historian of English love and marriage Lawrence Stone has traced four stages (that may not apply equally to all social classes, and that overlap to some extent) in the development of free choice by marriage partners:

> In the first, marriage was arranged by the parents with relatively little reference to the wishes of children; in the second, parents continued to arrange the marriage, but granted children the right of veto; in the third, the children made the choice but the parents retained the power of veto; in the fourth—which was only reached in this century—the children arrange their own marriages, with little open reference to—but under a good deal of subtle influence from—their parents.[37]

For Stone, marriage, instead of being founded upon rational choices not always or exclusively made by the two partners, became in the twentieth century a question of falling in love and marrying on the basis of that desire. In fact before the wedding, parents now may barely know the person their children have chosen: a student writing to her professor, Laurence Lerner, told him she was engaged "to a young man I was introduced to by my father: seems rather quaint in this day and age."[38]

Meanwhile Alan Macfarlane has recently argued that England is a special case: just as, according to his earlier work, individualism developed much sooner in England than in the rest of Europe,[39] so English people—whether propertied or propertyless—have always (the period examined is 1300 to 1840) been relatively free of parental control in making marriage choices and have based them on a balancing of the desire for a long-lasting loving relationship of deep friendship and companionship with economic considerations.[40] This is because in England parents had much less control over their children and were separated from them through apprenticeship, tutoring, and domestic service from an early age, while the legal-economic structures expected and enabled the establishment of separate households by young couples. Macfarlane acknowledges, however, that he has few women's reports on which to base his analysis; yet their choices are likely to have been much less free than those of men.

In America, Ellen Rothman finds that while people have perhaps always hoped for love in marriage, from around the mid-eighteenth century "Americans were beginning to make love between men and women a necessary rather than a desirable precondition for marriage."[41] De Rougemont indeed, thought that "in America the terms 'love' and 'marriage' are practically equivalent; that when one 'loves' one must get married instantly."[42] Perhaps this is somewhat exaggerated, yet it captures the *necessity* for marriage as well as the solid link between love and marriage made by Rothman: it is really only in very recent times—over the last two decades—that marriage *itself* may be relatively freely chosen or rejected, whether or not individuals make the choice largely unfettered (overtly) by parents. Particularly for women, few alternatives for economic advancement and security have been available; and for men who must work outside known communities and often far from families, marriage, too, has been not only their best choice for nurturance and security but even the "haven in a heartless world."[43]

Furthermore, it was in England that Kenneth Walker, whose words appear in the first epigraph to this section, somewhat unexpectedly for a medical writer emphasized romantic love as the "basis for marriage."[44] And even Macfarlane seems to feel there has been something of a qualitative shift since love—or knowledge of it—became in the eighteenth century "instituted irrationality" at the heart of marriage.[45] Culture was turned into nature: that is, the most unnatural willed decision became felt as the most natural and most profound bond. This natural and most profound bond is inescapable as a moral goal for the modern person. Especially for women, to love and to be in love is to become the good and whole person, a hero.[46] To base a decision to marry on the feeling of love is part of the moral goal, while love has undeniably become the only publicly acceptable reason for marriage—or, indeed, for any long-term committed equivalent relationship.

While some of the people Macfarlane quotes wrote that, for the successful marriage, passion was necessary as well as esteem and affection, few stressed the passionate and erotic forms of love. Thus, it seems, the kind of love earlier generations hoped for in marriage was generally *agape*, creative and life-giving love, not much infused with *eros*, the dangerous passion (dark and of the night) that is adulterous love.

But eros and agape are not now divided into separate spheres: both are desired. As Robert Sternberg has suggested, the decision to marry is based on both passion and intimacy coupled with commitment: these are the points of the triangle of the romantic love that provides the basis for marriage.[47] No longer is it praiseworthy to yearn for another lady who is someone else's wife, but this ideal soulmate should be one's *own* wife. Romantic love has become the most desired experience of life—the fantasy of the West. Thus an ideal of Romantic Love has been bounded by the conventional form of marriage and a great modern myth—the Myth of Romantic Marriage—has been created.

Central to the Myth of Romantic Marriage is thus an ideal of a love for one other person—and only one—which will last. But for how long? Once

the answer was clear: as long as both live. Now permanence cannot be separated from the ideal of love: permanence means as long as love lasts—until
the death, we might say, not of the body but of the soul. It is the quality
of the relationship that must carry the weight of marriage; this is valued,
not the solidity of the institution itself. Hence, the reasoning of those who
choose not to marry, and see the contract as one only between two freely
acting individuals more or less detached from families, communities, workplaces, religious and political institutions. Indeed, the institution of marriage has lost much of its solidity—the high divorce rate is proof enough of
that. Nonetheless, those marrying (and the vast majority of people still
spend at least part of their lives married) expect and hope for permanence:
they do not, as they enter marriage, intend a temporary relationship.

Sexual exclusivity and permanence are the linchpins of the myth. Thus,
at the broad, dominant cultural level, people are *expected* to find—that is,
they *should* find—a love story within their marriages. This love story begins
with an expectation that the relationship will be one of partnership between
equals, not one of domination and subordination—one variously termed
"companionate," "egalitarian," and "symmetrical."[48] "Happy ever after"
is thus a phrase containing whole sets of ideas and images about a future,
patterned not randomly but according to expectations and fantasies. This
is a commonly shared, if rather rough outline story because it is not unique
to each person. Each of us brings to a partnership an idea of how the story
of our lives together will go that has unique elements but it is set within
these broad outlines.[49] It is the way in modern times to experience oneself
as *good*—that is, as morally worthwhile. Loving and being loved, being "in
love," are virtuous conditions—the "proper" goal for every adult and particularly for every woman. In this sense, the story is a "public morality," as
described by Margaret Voysey explaining the ways families with handi-
capped children cope: they use accounts publicly well rehearsed but *not*
false, ideas about what a happy or normal family *ought* to be like.[50] These
"public moralities" appear to be spread much more widely across social
class and ethnic lines than ever before. Certainly the desire for romance—
which is, after all, a love story—is by no means the property of any one
class.

The Myth of Romantic Marriage receives powerful support from a whole
range of social institutions, many benefits, both economic and social accruing to the married[51] and the message being powerfully broadcast in all the
media. In particular, news stories of the ideal romances of real, living
princes and princesses such as the Prince and Princess of Wales and the
Duke and Duchess of York—romances that fascinate nations throughout
the world—serve to perpetuate and enhance the mythology. Even rumors
that suggest all is not well imply how important it is that these marriages
survive. Similarly, gossip about the rich and famous—politicians or stars of
rock, film and stage, for example—who are seen with people other than
their spouses also serves to support the mythology of the permanent and

sexually exclusive marriage, for gossip, even as it indicates ambivalence about a rule, is simultaneously a technique of rule enforcement. It has often worked through its effect on the *reputation* of those who are the subject of gossip; indeed, the cuckolding of men (something the adulterous woman did *to* men) was one way that women exercised power over men. In the seventeenth and eighteenth centuries in England, thousands of cases of *criminal conversation* (sexual intercourse) were brought in the courts both to protect the reputation of husbands by obtaining an adultery payment or fine from the wife's lover to compensate him for the damage he had suffered, and to obtain the necessary grounds to proceed to the ecclesiastical court for a divorce. I explore these ideas and consider the influence of the myth on modern women and men in chapter 2, "Marriage Lines," and chapter 8, "This Telling Business."

Once marriage became the place where love and sexual fidelity were linked, successful consummation and expression of this love was supposed to lead not to death but to creative life—the marriage providing the source of nurturance, both for the partners to it and for their children. Within marriage, therefore, a journey is now promised during which both wife and husband should find fulfillment. At marriage, the hope and expectation is that through this love the partners will grow together in such a way that they can and will help each other on the path to self-fulfillment: thus marriage should also provide for the fulfillment of the self, an ideal of its own.

The Myth of Me is the story of the development of the self throughout life. Although at the outset encompassed within the Myth of Romantic Marriage, this adventure, while encouraging interrelatedness, requires no one Other: it is a journey of and for the Self. The goal, requiring that each person risk the loss of secure and known positions for the danger of new and exciting challenges, is to achieve the peak of self-actualization[52]—the height of maturity. The myth is not new but it has achieved new prominence in recent times; indeed, it was a modern writer, Tom Wolfe, who coined the phrase the "me generation" to describe the young most affected by the turbulent late 1960s and early 1970s. In the search for true self-knowledge, people must explore all facets of themselves, including their sexuality.

Self-development *need* not lead to estrangement from the chosen Other, for the strongest relationships may well be those that permit autonomy to each partner while encouraging a way of loving that Francesca Cancian has termed *interdependent* rather than *independent*;[53] but, alas, for many, and particularly for women, the pursuit of selfhood often does involve conflict since their self-interest is so frequently "at odds"[54] with the interests of their family members—both husband and children. Thus, it may become difficult to achieve the Myth of Romantic Marriage ideal while embracing a program to develop the self, for the exploration of one's many facets is unlikely to be accomplished with just one other life partner. If this life partner, too, is simultaneously engaged in the same quest, the chances of fitting facets becomes remote indeed, particularly since, in the West, life expectancy for both men and women is so improved that death is most unlikely to intervene to shorten the marriage as once it did.[55] While such long lives lived with one other life partner may develop with various new themes and shared adventures, they may also become devoid of this necessary sense of "story": a life lacking narrative, the sense of moving through time purposefully, of adventure and of knowing that one is alive.

Marriage tames adventure to a journey involving hard work but little play, a space well if not impenetrably bounded against invaders, with little opportunity for heroism or rebellion, excitement or danger. Indeed, the only heroism may be in overcoming obstacles in making the marriage work and endure—still no playground. Hence, the Myth of Me, instead of being encompassed within the marriage story, may, as in a Venn diagram, slip out from under and then compete with the Myth of Romantic Marriage. Perhaps it still overlaps in parts with the marriage story, but it may also offer a justification for breaching the boundaries of marriage and for living a different story, the story of adulterous love where, perhaps because it is a theme of such importance in the West, it seems to the adventurer that the self may best be found. Some of the study members who most strongly espoused the Myth of Me are described in chapter 3, "Changing the Contract"; while the myth itself is further explored in chapter 4, "Keeping Faith."

In chapter 5, "The Debate," the way individuals shift adherence from the Myth of Romantic Marriage to the Myth of Me, and manage conflict as they contemplate a first adulterous liaison, is addressed. Fanny's words—the preamble to her first liaison—in the epigraph to this section indicate the importance the Myth of Me has had, particularly for women as, supported by newer humanistic psychologies and the women's movement, they have begun to feel entitled to pursue self-development even when to do so presents the conflicts I have outlined. Returning in such large numbers to paid employment outside the home, women have attended closely to such reasoning.

However, the appeal is not limited to women. Despite the profound narcissism implied in the Myth of Me, it couples quite comfortably with the notion of "openness." People who value this notion must be unrestrained, honest with one another at all costs for a proper flowering of their personalities. Maturity requires the ability to face unpleasant or difficult truths, "working through" them and not—to continue the jargon, "acting out." These ideas thus fit with the current stress on "communication," a catchword describing a general panacea. We live in a culture where talk seems the solution to all problems. But the necessary content of that talk and of that communication has been left ill defined. Nor is sufficient attention paid to the listener. What will the response be? What can be heard and taken in? Whose need is being met? What might be the speaker's underlying motives? People search for a sense of wholeness, of belonging, of being not jagged at the edges but rounded as a circle.

To become profoundly intimate with another person in both "body and soul"—that is, in a sexual and an intellectual embrace—is a way, perhaps the most satisfying way of all, to attain that rounded wholeness. The Myth of Romantic Marriage is by no means opposed to this wholeness, but it should be achieved not by breaching the boundaries but by maintaining them and bringing into the marriage the talk, the honesty, the "integrity," and hence the "trust" which both those in traditional, sexually exclusive and those in the permissive, open marriage say they have.

The partners in the open marriage, expressing their feelings in chapter 3, recognize that passion declines over time and, perhaps, that obstacles are necessary to passion. In any event, by permitting the flame to be rekindled in new relationships, they seek to ensure that dwindling passion does not interfere with their long-term commitment to and intimacy between one another. But there is a difficulty. Love cannot generally be perceived as packaged in this way, and is seldom experienced as divisible. A new falling-in-love, then, becomes the justification for transgression of that marriage. "I couldn't help myself—I fell in love," becomes sufficient reason for divorce, even if the infidelity itself is not condemned.

Two or more loves at a time does not seem an easy or a much desired pattern for many people, and particularly not for many women, perhaps because the very concept of love includes sexual exclusivity. Tristan, remember, was faithful to his love for Isolde the Fair in his refusal to consummate his marriage to Isolde of the White Hands. Certainly people in this study (albeit more women than men) repeatedly explained, like Janet, a young woman in a northern industrial town, that "if you really love someone, you don't never want anyone else, never mind you go and sleep with them." Monogamy is preferred, and hence the serial monogamy of the person who will have no affairs but six marriages. Those who do manage more than one affair at a time seem to stress the "purely physical" over the emotional gains; they separate sex and psychology. Men, perhaps, have been frequent users of this theme, enjoying the bawdy house "for the sex" and claiming they have to have extramarital affairs to satisfy their sexual appetites, as if there were no relationship between the enjoyment of sex and the feelings engendered. This "scientific" and masculine argument that sex is a "drive" or "need," which must be "gratified" lest it erupt in violence, has been left in place, while another gentler idea of sex as sensuous pleasure, good for recreation and enjoyment and for the delight of the participants, has surfaced.[56] These different ideas of sex have an important function in defining the adulterous liaison: the various types of adultery I have identified are described in chapter 1. These are: *parallel* (to the marriage, often condoned), *traditional* (secret and potentially threatening to the marriage), and *recreational* (for the pleasure and enjoyment of participants, rarely perceived as a serious breach of the marriage). Each may be *supportive, dangerous,* or *transitional*—that is, serving to help the individual leave the marriage; there are no clear boundaries between them, and any one relationship may change as it proceeds.

The "Sexual Revolution" and the
Masculinization of Sex

The idea that sex might be enjoyed purely for pleasure has permitted women as well as men to claim that sexual relationships can be enjoyed separately from profound (intimate) love and from any durable commitment. And women, too, have begun more often to use another argument stressing similarity rather than difference between the sexes: women, like men, have sexual needs to be satisfied, separately from any emotions they may have.

Indeed, the so-called sexual revolution was a revolution of—if not for—women. It is women's sexual behavior that has changed over recent decades. Women used (often) to be virgins at marriage. Now they are not, and they have sex with a greater variety of partners than once they did. Fewer married women used to have adulterous liaisons than married men; now the proportion who have such liaisons may nearly equal that of men. And those women who had liaisons, had many fewer than men (see chapter 2). Women still restrict the number of their lovers but, as can be seen in chapter 6, "The *When*, the *Where*, the *How*, and the *Who*," women married in the 1970s seem to be "catching up," perhaps even overtaking men in the speed with which they have their affairs. The earlier a person begins to have affairs, the more (generally) he or she will have. Thus, if this generation of women stay married (and many, of course do not), they may well have more liaisons than their older sisters and, perhaps, more than men of the same generation. Women used not to have "casual affairs" or "one-night stands"—this was male behavior. Now men describe their liaisons less often in this way; women more (see chapter 7, "Pleasures and Pains"). These changes are emphasized in the choice of partner—most being met through work—and in the feelings women and men have about intimacy in the workplace. Yet the liaison is generally conducted according to traditional expectations of, for example, who pays and where they may make love (see chapter 6).

There have also been some important changes in attitudes to fidelity, some general, some dependent on marital experience. Women, for example, who have been divorced and remarried adhere at least as firmly to sexual fidelity second time around as they did at the outset of their first marriages, and those who stay married to a first spouse but have at least one affair think fidelity unimportant; but men's attitudes do not vary with these experiences. Similarly, there has been a substantial increase in the numbers entering marriage with agreements that they may each have other sexual partners, but this is a much more important shift in opinion for women than for men since so few women ever agreed to *in*fidelity in the past. In chapter 2, these changes are explored and analyzed in terms of the differential structural and emotional consequences for women as compared with those for men of adultery and divorce.

In chapter 7, women make it clear they have gained a great deal from a feeling that they are entitled to make decisions affecting their own bodies for themselves. Clearly, too, sex is often enormously pleasurable to women, and a sense of who they are and of their own value is gained from their sexual relationships. But the trends I have outlined seem, at the least, to make them appear *like* men and, in some cases, *as if* they were men. Certainly these changes appear to conform to male rather than female models of heterosexuality and to meet the needs and desires of men better than those of women, which have yet to be thoroughly and separately explored. Women have thus appropriated behaviors previously perceived as male. I therefore call this pattern, which I describe in chapter 7, the *masculinization of sex.*[57]

The "Talking Revolution," This Telling Business, and the Feminization of Love

In the "open" marriage, the act of sexual intercourse, meaning both sexual passion and pleasure, and the gratification of sexual needs, is removed from the center and in its place is put the importance of talk and telling. In this arrangement (whether reached after years of a traditional marriage, or agreed at the outset) it seems as if intimacy, real intimacy, will be achieved through the sharing of secrets, the "knowing" of the intellect. The phrase *carnal knowledge* takes on new meaning in this context. What seems to be happening here, then, is that new boundaries are being created to replace those felt to be outmoded and constraining. This particular contract fits well with the explosion of information technology when information has become central and more widely available to more people than ever before, while the broad cultural trend is to value communication and speech. Symptomatic of these broad changes is the fact that, whereas almost no couples in this study sample marrying before 1960 discussed the possibility of extramarital sexual relationships or their feelings about fidelity before they married, few did *not* do so if they married in or after 1970. I call this general change the *talking revolution* and that between couples, the *telling business*, for it seems to me that knowledge has become the new commodity of exchange between intimate partners.

Once, men vied for possession of a woman's body in order to gain her reproductive and her productive labor. Her virginity was to be protected, gained, and taken, and her chastity jealously guarded. The code according to which these exchanges were conducted was a code of honor. It is now information rather than the woman's body that is to be exchanged—secrets are valued; and the code of conduct is a code, not of honor, but of honesty.

Women have always valued speech, talk, and communication as the way to intimacy. Thus, just as men had less far to go in the sexual revolution because their starting point was different, so women have had fewer changes to make in the talking revolution. In any event, men seem to have changed more than women in this respect and are talking and telling more. After all, men are accustomed to dealing and would wish to master a new currency. With Cancian, I think this trend is well termed the *feminization of love*.[58] These ideas are elaborated in chapter 8, "This Telling Business."

This search for truth, for the sharing of sexual secrets, is not limited to the open marriage; it merely appears in its purest form there. Nor, although the rule to tell is a strong mechanism of control and a fierce boundary, is it an end in itself. Rather, access to information is intended to increase or to create intimacy between couples. Obviously, those who know nothing about one another, nothing about the other's thoughts and feelings, ideas and activities, can share little intimacy. If they are a circle, it cannot be a very rich or full one.

Those who seek "openness" often also assume a political equality between the partners. *Non-exploitation* is, indeed, the keyword for some couples (particularly those in open marriages and those who live in a long-term and committed relationship deliberately eschewing marriage because it has traditionally exploited women). In this sample, no one seriously believed any more that a man should possess a woman in order to exert power over her, owning her as he would any material object (or of they did, they did not express it); but in the struggle for more equality, access to knowledge has become real power. Yet no one person can know everything about another. Always choices must be made about what is to be said and what withheld, if only because there is neither time nor interest in all of another's activities or thoughts. In reality, few couples are politically equal, and it is hard to accept that greater intimacy is achieved when everyone sits round in a family circle discussing the affair, and the miscreant, having fulfilled the telling obligation, can return, reassured, to the lovers' bed, there to "feel alive."[59] Adultery is a particular relationship that is transformed when no longer secret. Make extramarital sex permissible, and require that what might otherwise have been kept secret be told, then this becomes the rule that will in turn be broken. Illicit sex becomes secret sex, and we are back where we started.

Perhaps some who give their spouses information about illicit relationships genuinely seek to reduce their own power and enhance equality, since it is true that many do experience a sense of power as they hug their secret to themselves and say (to themselves), "I've got a lover, I've got a lover, and *you* don't know that." Yet the motive for telling may not be so altruistic; rather, it may be a way not to give up power but to employ it against the spouse, at the same time perhaps relieving guilty feelings. In either case, this is an emotional power, not real and concrete political power, not the kind of power that grants a woman economic independence, a real sharing of household responsibilities and child-caring tasks and seriously thought-out decision sharing. I address the issues of power and control in chapter 9. Emotional and political power are not identical; their elision is dangerous.

However, adultery can be a relationship where one or the other partner does gain real power, and it seems to me that it has, unlike marriage, often afforded women power. Women have been able to begin and end relationships, to refuse and reject advances, to set the pace of involvement, to gain material advantage, to achieve status, to travel, to expand the boundaries of their lives, and to know the extent of their powers of attraction. They have been able, on occasion, to exercise control over their marriages through their adulterous liaison. Maintaining a triangle and refusing to become a couple is also a form of power. These powers have not, of course, always been held by every married woman in an adulterous liaison, and they are often held by men. The situation is very different, too, for the woman who is not married but who forms the apex of her married lover's triangle.[60] But if marriage, as the legal and conventional form of the relationship between men and women, has generally reflected a society where men have held greater power than women, so adultery, as the breach of marriage and as the illicit form, has been able to turn these relations around. As equality within marriage grows, perhaps there will be greater power sharing in adultery, too.

There is another sense, too, in which power is hoped for but not always exercised in adultery: people begin their liaisons convinced they can control the outcome, but the experience, like that of Tristan and Isolde, often controls them. The "good" adultery becomes one where surrender to feeling is complete and the individual feels out of control.

At the end of the book, I assess the extent to which adultery remains toxic. If death or banishment is less often the outcome, divorce is more frequent and both women and men suffer still at the same time as they experience great joy in these relationships—pleasures and pains that arise at least in part from the very triangular structure of adultery.

Throughout I make it clear that adultery has always been a more serious problem for the adulterous married woman than for the adulterous married man, her punishment being greatly more severe than his. And throughout I stress substantial gender differences in behavior and feelings about both adultery and marriage. Yet there is also much overlap, much that is similar. Indeed, a *convergence* between women and men is apparent. Finding *both* change and continuity permits me to question underlying biological premises that argue for an unchanging and universal imperative in the differences between women and men, and to assert the overriding salience of

dynamic economic and social conditions that permeate—even construct—
the unconscious as well as the more accessible desires and wishes of modern
people as they continue to enact their adulterous dramas.

There remains a profound confusion about the shape and content of
relations between women and men. This is seen in the confusion about what
marriage is or ought to be; about the rules that should or should not be
followed; about what consequences will flow from what action. Adultery is
all about the setting, breaking, or maintaining and the creation of boundaries. It is about breaching the social order, about transgression. It is, as
Tanner says, about "the wrong people in the wrong beds."[61] In the breach
of a rule is the rule made clear: by studying adultery, what names it is called
and why; what feelings it engenders; what place it holds in our society, marriage may better be understood. Yet adultery is about much more than
marriage. It is about relations between women and men—indeed, it is
about the nature of the whole society.

BOOK I

WHAT IS ADULTERY?

1

What Is Adultery?

What is adultery? I mean, what do you *mean*?
　　　　—Group Discussion, Brunel University, January 1983

I, for having imitated [my husband] once, for having done with
the most handsome man in Lisbon what he did every day with
impunity with the most idiotic strumpets of the court and town,
have to answer at the bar before licentiates each of whom would
be at my feet if we were alone together in my closet; have to endure at the court the usher cutting off my hair which is the most
beautiful in the world and being shut up among nuns who have
no common sense, deprived of my dowry and my marriage cove-
nants, with all my property given to my coxcomb of a husband to
help him seduce other women and to commit fresh adulteries.
　　　　—Voltaire's "Countess of Arcira," pleading her case
　　　　　　　　　　　　　　　before the junta of Portugal

What Is Adultery?

Conjuring desire and lust, shame and punishment, sin and secrets, the very
word *adultery* reminds the atheist of damnation and the devout of the holi-
ness of marriage, a sacrament requiring the absolute sexual exclusivity of
the marriage partners who, at least in this life, must cleave to one another
and only to one another. Yet it is by no means clear to many in today's world
what adultery means. The term strikes people as archaic and stern, full of
condemnation, but what it is and who it is that is condemned remain
obscure.

　　Does it, participants in the study asked, apply to unmarried people who
have affairs with married people, and what about before you are married

or if you are not married at all but committed to someone in a long-term and stable relationship? Does it count if you just sleep with someone for one night, and what if you don't even know their name? What if you love someone but you don't actually have sex with them? "What do you mean?" they asked. "What do you *mean?*"

In modern times, few people speak of "committing adultery," though nearly one third of the study participants had used phrases including the word *adultery*, and about one half felt the term had applied to them. One man explained, "It's a strong term—adultery. I think that's what I'm in at the moment." A married couple who had remained faithful for years, focusing on their two children and one another, reached a point where both wanted to "grow" and by placing advertisements in *Forum*, a contact magazine, had found other couples with whom to "swing." This couple had always known about one another's affairs and hence, so they said, "we never thought of what we were doing as adultery. Never. We always knew, you see." A young woman, trying to understand herself, said with a note of desperation, "Well, I suppose I am having an affair. I just don't know what is an affair, what is a relationship, what is anything particularly."

Adultery is, it seems, something strong, something of which the spouse is ignorant, and a "relationship." In America, one attorney said adultery was the word used by her clients when they were "going to sue for adultery," while another said, "Adultery is a broken promise, any promise you make to your mate." A professor thought, too, that adultery was a broken promise, an important broken promise—to be sexually faithful—but it was also about deception. Adulterers may deceive their mates (or the person they're having an affair with) by feigning deep feelings as well as by lying or by remaining silent. A divorce consultant said firmly that, "while sex is a necessary component for an affair to be adulterous, not all extramarital affairs are adultery. I do not count a one-night fling." From the point of view of those going through her office, she felt "most people consider adultery as a *substantial* involvement with someone else." Hence, according to these people interviewed for a newspaper article, adultery threatens the central aspect of modern marriage—the relationship—just as it once threatened it for other reasons.[1]

Adultery *spoils* the marriage, said one young woman study participant, describing how she felt about her husband's adultery. "I still feel now [some seven years later] that it spoilt our relationship. It spoilt it, just spoilt it."

The adulterous spouse, by bringing a third into the marital pair, does not, it seems, simply add another person, as when a child is born (and although having a child often *defines* family and is a highly desired goal, even this new threesome may be difficult to negotiate) but—as the dictionary definition of "to adulterate" has it—"despoils, dilutes, poisons, pollutes or debases"[2] with the addition of a substance, thing, or person.

Derived from the Latin *adulter(i)um*—perhaps from *ad + alter*, meaning different, or *adulter*, "to defile," and *adulterat(us)*, "altered"—the word *adultery* may also mean "going off to somebody *other* than one's husband; or, possibly, wife."[3] This link arises from medieval French versions which have included *advoultre* and *avoutire*, with later derivations in *voltare*, or *volte-face* meaning to "move away quickly" or a "jump away from."[4] Although similar in English, the word *adult* has an entirely different root— *adult(us)*, meaning "grown"; or *adolere*, "to make grow."

The adulterous spouse—usually the wife is intended—"turns away" from the husband (or wife) and "goes off" to a third person, thus "diluting" or even "debasing" the marriage whether the other spouse knows of the relationship or not, making possible another whole dimension of emotions, coalitions, and power struggles which are immediately of a different (and it is implied damaging) quality from any struggles occurring between the two of the marital couple. She or he breaks the boundary around them—both the social circle placed around this particular heterosexual pair set apart in the institution of marriage, and the magical circle or sense of wholeness which is desired, and perhaps experienced, when two people become one couple. There are now three where there were two—the classic triangle. Not everyone, however, thinks there is such a magical encircling of the couple, nor does everyone desire it. Indeed, many feel the couple to be claustrophobic, and marriage an undesirable and exploitative state. Most people, however, do feel like this; that is, there exists still a broad consensus about the desirability of the intimate relationship with one Other, to be "a couple," across class and ethnic lines. Lesbian and homosexual couples, even when they reject traditional roles within their relationship, also often desire a form of marriage.

Because adultery offers a threat to the couple, it remains strongly linked with divorce in people's minds, and the notion of "fault" dies hard. To the believer, adultery is still a sin and, although rarely prosecuted, it remains on the statute books as a crime in various parts of the Western world; while in Islam and elsewhere it is still severely punished—even by death, although the sinners (especially the married woman) are more likely to be stoned or to have their hands or genitals cut off.[5]

In both church and law, adultery is technically sexual intercourse between a married woman or man and someone who is not at that time their spouse. A single person who has sex with a married person commits not adultery but the lesser sin of fornication, ranked eighth by the Christian writer Cassian and coupled with mere greed.[6] But for the adulterer, sex with an unmarried person is technically speaking *single*, while sex with another married person is *double*, adultery. (Usually only intercourse with someone of the opposite sex is intended, but people in my sample included liaisons with same-sex persons as adulterous.)

In addition to sexually consummated liaisons, over 40 percent of study participants reported a relationship that they considered adulterous even though they and their partners had "never made love."[7] These adulteries of the heart lacked the sin of carnal knowledge but were an emotional gain, in a sense a thieving of a benefice to which they had no entitlement because they were already married, or, perhaps, because the partner in the relationship was already married—secular interpretations of "spiritual" or "interpretative" adultery that once applied to any marriage seen as "improper," to the worshiping of idols, and to the enjoyment by anyone of a benefice during the lifetime of the legal incumbent.

The longing and the fantasy is to breach the boundaries of the marriage, the proper place for the enjoyment of the benefice and to translate not, as was once intended, a bishop from one see to another, but the status of husband to that of lover, of wife to that of mistress. The Christian fathers, following Matthew's gospel, also condemned the man who lusted after another man's wife even if only in thought. (In our own times, perhaps Jimmy Carter's chances in the United States presidential elections in 1980 might have been improved had he not admitted that he had sinned, lusting in his heart after other women.)

In the church, if a man "put away" his wife—something he might do if she were barren, for example—both he and his wife became adulterers, for marriage was for life, indissoluble, a permanent relationship.[8] Indeed, Voltaire's dictionary entry for *adultery*, which includes the Countess of Arcira's story quoted in the epigraph to this chapter, includes the tale of "a senior magistrate in a French town in about 1764" whose wife was persistently unfaithful and whom he left.[9] Not permitted to divorce or remarry, he became an adulterer if he had a sexual relationship with anyone else. Thus, even within the Church, the term has been used to encompass quite a wide range of actions well beyond the technical definition. Among ordinary people the variation in meaning is much greater.

In my study, those who felt they had "committed adultery," or actually used those terms to describe their own actions, were more religious than others, believed strongly in sexual exclusivity, and were also among the strongest adherents of the Myth of Romantic Marriage.[10] However, even some who were in "open," sexually free marriages also used these terms; and although such people had normally both agreed the other could be sexually free, they still commonly spoke of being "faithful" or "unfaithful." (For this reason, among others, I have found it acceptable to write of fidelity and infidelity, of the faithful and the unfaithful without feeling I take a moralistic stance. See appendix B, pages 352–53, for further discussion of these problems.)

Both women and men in the study sample generally described their liaisons as "serious affairs" or used the word *relationship* either on its own or in *extramarital relationship*; but women, much less often than men, said their liaisons were "one-night stands," "brief encounters," or "casual affairs." The women who did describe their affairs in these terms were—at the time they first married—the most permissive—that is, the most committed to the Myth of Me; they had more and a greater variety of liaisons. By contrast, it was the most traditional men—those most strongly adhering to the Myth of Romantic Marriage—who spoke of their liaisons in this way. In other words, "casual affairs," were what highly permissive women but highly traditional men, recalling their feelings when they married, had. They indicate the continuing greater breach implied by a wife's adultery compared with that of a husband; she commits adultery generally only when her feelings are deeply involved or likely to become so—the risks are too great for her to play as he can—while he is entitled to his "bit on the side."

Studying people having affairs in America in 1969, Morton Hunt similarly found that—while both genders used more serious terms for the more emotionally involving extramarital relationships, and men, like women, thought it not "real" infidelity to have sex with "a call girl while away on business," feeling they needed to care for another woman, see a good deal of her, and "spend part of the family income on her" for this to amount to infidelity—women required a certain depth of feeling to classify something as an "affair," preferring more pejorative terms such as *cheating* or *running around* for the swift, spontaneous sexual encounter: "A third to a half more men than women classify as an extra-marital affair a situation in which two married strangers meet at a party, swiftly develop emotional rapport, and have sexual relations that same night.'"[11]

Now (that is, at the time of completing the questionnaire in 1982), there is less difference between women and men in my study because men have reduced the number of their "casual affairs" while women have become readier to engage in them. This change is especially marked among the most traditional men—those who remained strongly committed to the Myth of Romantic Marriage. "Casual affair" has dropped from the repertoire of these men without entering the repertoire of the equally committed women. It seems that such men are now less sure that a casual relationship, perhaps seen as an escape valve (as Kinsey suggested), and carried out alongside or *parallel* with their marriage, is acceptable. Instead, the Myth of Me and a general permissiveness must play a greater part in the thinking of both genders for these relationships to be acceptable.

It might be said that women have simply learned to speak as men once did—that is, to speak of "casual affairs" without shame but without having increased the number of such affairs—a change in rhetoric and style but not in behavior. Indeed, there have been many such changes, women learning to use four-letter words where once they eschewed them, a further instance, perhaps, of liberation that ends by conforming to a male model that offers only trivial freedoms to women. In this case, given the evidence of many behavioral changes, it seems to me that both practice and language usage have recently changed.

It is not only whether you are male or female and what your beliefs are that matters in the naming business, but whether you have had an affair yourself, and how many. To Hunt's question whether a married person having sexual relations with someone picked up in a bar would constitute an extramarital affair, half of the "faithful" did think so while only a third of those who had been "unfaithful" thought it did; by devaluing the experience—that is, by saying it does not "count"—the unfaithful can feel less guilty and reaffirm the inconsequential nature of such recreational or, as this terminology suggests, trivial activity. In my study, this pattern is reflected in the fact that the more liaisons people had, the greater variety they reported.

People in my study considered single people could commit adultery. They could do so as the third party but even a remembered premarital sexual encounter was sometimes included as it continued to impinge on the marriage. Thus Janet, the young woman who spoke of the spoiling of the marriage, recalled an incident before she and her husband were married, both studying and living in a student hostel. Her boyfriend (as he then was) "went off and slept with" another student. Even at the time of interview, many years later, having forgiven him in accordance with her profound Christianity, become engaged, and then married and with a baby, she still thinks about it. It meant he did not really love her. Hence, for Janet, adultery breaches the love between two committed people, whenever it occurs.[12] The underlying idea is that two people in a committed and loving relationship may *take for granted* that they will be faithful: for the majority, this belief provides the basis for the "trust" they place in their relationship; hence, the importance placed by some on the alteration of this "contract" to permit sexual freedom. For such people are no longer "unfaithful" and cannot, it would seem, "commit adultery."[13] Similarly, the knowledge spouses have of one another's intentions is critical in determining what will and will not count as adultery.

In British courts during divorce actions at a time when fault had to be proved, Michael Freeman notes:

> In *Barnacle v. Barnacle* in 1948, it transpired that one petitioner thought adultery involved illicit connection between two unmarried persons with the consequent production of a child. Others had thought it was not adultery "during the daytime," or it was "drinking with men in public houses"; yet another averred that it was not adultery if the woman was "over 50."[14]

Even legal definitions have been broad:

> Adultery in English law connotes voluntary or consensual sexual intercourse between a married person and a person (whether married or unmarried) of the opposite sex not being the other's spouse. . . . Acts which do not constitute adultery in England have been held to do so in other systems. In New York sodomy constitutes adultery. . . . In New Zealand an attempt by a father to have sexual intercourse with his 9-year-old daughter was held to constitute adultery. In England sexual familiarity or masturbation is not adultery. Insemination with the semen of a third

party donor is probably not adultery according to English law. It is in Canada, though it has been held not to be in Scotland.[15]

In these two examples, the possibility that a child might be born, either by artificial insemination or even to an unmarried couple, suggests adultery; while the woman over fifty, being unlikely to conceive, will not "count" as an adulterous partner. She is defined—from the man's point of view—as nonsexual, not really a woman.

In law for centuries, adultery was defined only as the act of a married woman. There were two main reasons: that she was the property of her husband, and that she might bear another man's child whom she would "pass" as his—a cuckoo in his nest.

Adultery Is Theft

"Whom God hath joined together let no man put asunder."

"No man."[16] These words from the Anglican marriage service invoke the possibility that another man might invade the marital pair and "take" the wife: it is the married woman's adultery that would be such a damaging breach of the marital boundary. Thus, in Hebraic law, despite the fact that the seventh commandment[17]—"Thou shalt not commit adultery"—does not distinguish between men and women, adultery was committed only by or with a married woman. As explained in Leviticus 20:10, a man's act became punishable only if he had sex with another man's *wife*:

And the man that committeth adultery with another man's wife, even he that committeth adultery with his neighbour's wife, the adulterer and the adulteress shall surely be put to death.

The implication was that a man steals another man's property; he "possesses" what is not his to "take," even if the woman "gives" herself to him, for she does not own her own self, not even her body. He owns her and can—indeed, sometimes must—punish her, even kill her. The very phrase *man and wife*, not *husband and woman* or *woman and husband*, provides a clue to the unequal relationship between the married partners. Modern theologians defend Augustine's separation of wives from a man's other possessions in altering the order of the Ten Commandments to that still followed by Catholics and Lutherans: thus, he made the seventh into the sixth by uniting the beginning verses about the nature of God and the forms of permissible worship (to have no strange gods, to make no graven images), and expanding the last verse into two ("Thou shalt not covet thy neighbour's wife, nor his house, nor his maidservant, nor manservant . . ."). They say it is morally right that a man's wife should be considered separately from his servants, animals, and material objects (thus not recognizing servants as human beings), but the wife nonetheless remains a possession.

In Roman law also, adultery was an act of the married woman: should her husband discover her with her lover in his—that is, the husband's—house, he was under an obligation to kill both his wife and her lover.[18] Under the Justinian sixth-century code, the adulterous wife was subject to exile or death; and her lover could be decapitated if he was a free man or burned if a slave, yet a slave could obtain a pardon if he denounced his mistress.[19] Before this period, under the *lex de adulteriis*, neither the infidelity of a fiancée nor that of a female slave was punished but a concubine could, if she had the status of matron, be accused of adultery.[20] If she changed her status to that of prostitute, she could avoid the accusation. It was thus both gender and social status that marked the boundary to the offense: the nearer a woman was to being a full wife, the nearer she came to being able to commit the crime of adultery: a prostitute might be "possessed" by a man and paid for by a man, but she could not commit adultery.

Adultery as an act only of the married woman could, however, be qualified by the place where the *husband's* extramarital sex occurred and by repeated flaunting of his sexual encounters. As the Emperor Justinian wrote:

> A man could repudiate his wife if she committed adultery, but a wife might repudiate her husband if he took a woman to live in the same house with her, or if he persisted in frequenting any other house in the same town with any woman after being warned more than once by his wife or her parents or other persons of respectability.[21]

These rules are the recognizable ancestors of the French penal code that, up until a mere decade ago, permitted a husband who killed his wife in the act of adultery to be "excused," making him liable only to imprisonment, while a husband's adultery was punishable only by a fine and then only if he kept a "concubine" in the marital home.[22] This distinction was made clear by the use of two different Latin words to describe the actions of wives and husbands: a wife's adultery was *adulterio*; and a husband's, *concubinato*. Only in 1975 did France reform this code and its divorce law, making the fact of adultery no longer a sufficient cause; the ideas that adultery might be tolerated or that one spouse might condone it or connive in it became relevant to gaining a divorce.[23] French women, despite believing it is as serious if men are unfaithful as if women are, are also more forgiving of a husband's adultery, particularly if it is not a long-term affair.[24]

Even in modern America, a legal commentator has recently noted that some states "have restricted [adultery as an unlawful act] only to the woman, provided she is the one who has a spouse." There is considerable variation among the states, "some courts [finding] that the act is unlawful only when committed openly and notoriously or lewdly, or that it is unlawful only for the married party."[25] In America now, there are but five states

(Arkansas, Louisiana, Nevada, New Mexico, and Tennessee) in which adultery and two related concepts—"criminal conversation" and "alienation of a spouse's affections"—are *not* still crimes on the books. Three of these, together with California and Indiana, hold adultery indictable only as "lewd and lascivious cohabitation"—that is, living with someone when one or both of the parties is married to a third person. Because the couple is living together, they display publicly their sin. Instead of the secrecy normally associated with illicit acts, they force others to notice. Thus, it is a criminal offense to engage in *both* adultery and lewd cohabitation in the majority of states. Four states (Delaware, Iowa, Pennsylvania, and South Dakota) and Washington, D.C., have penalties for adultery but not for lewd cohabitation. The fact that no state makes it unlawful only for the man suggests, again, that the woman is the more to be controlled and punished.[26] Of course, to have adultery on the books as a crime does not mean it is prosecuted. Yet, even in the 1980s, cases have surfaced across the states, and the courts have been more likely to uphold than to abandon the constitutionality of the prosecution.[27] Indeed, in Georgia, in 1984, the court extended the definition of adultery to include extramarital homosexual as well as heterosexual relations—a definition fitting the way people spoke of it in my study.[28]

In England until the present century, the doctrine of unity prevailed: that at marriage man and wife became one, and he was it. A married woman did not even own the property she brought with her to the marriage. Indeed, her value was something that could be worked out in money: in England—and similar laws applied in America—husbands bringing actions of "criminal conversation" against a wife's lover could gain an adultery payment—a fine from him—for the wrong they had suffered.[29] Furthermore, if the husband then gained a divorce, he might also gain the material benefits of the house, matrimonial property, and, in the case of wealthy women, any wealth she had brought to him when they married. This, too, is somewhat like an adultery payment, albeit confiscated from the wife and not from her lover. The possession of a woman by a man, thus, is not something merely sensed: it has, in the vast preponderance of societies around the world, brought tangible benefits of wealth to men. In many societies the "punishment" for adultery still takes the form of adultery payments. The lover must give the husband oxen or other goods that represent compensation for his loss.

The late Victorians introduced—with the Married Woman's Property Acts in 1870, 1874, and, especially, 1882 (and earlier in 1839, with Mississippi leading the way, in the United States)—the major shift in a woman's economic position in England, permitting married women to own property. This act made little difference to the vast majority of women who did not have any property worth fighting about, but it was nonetheless significant for the change in attitude it represented about the *capacity* of women to be perceived as separate and identifiable persons in law, for until this time, the married woman was not a proper legal subject.[30] Subsequently, however, the married woman was enabled to protect her own property, even to the extent that she could sue her husband;[31] and a husband could no longer (legitimately) say with Petruchio in *The Taming of the Shrew*:

> I will be master of what is mine own.
> She is my goods, my chattels; she is my house,
> My household stuff, my field, my barn,
> My horse, my ox, my ass, my any thing."[32]

That it was a considerable change, this opinion from the great eighteenth-century legal commentator Sir William Blackstone, about the inferiority of the wife and hence her inability to act independently, makes clear: "The inferior hath no kind of property in the company, care, or assistance of the superior as the superior is held to have in those of the inferior; and therefore the inferior can suffer no loss or injury."[33]

Because of this, the eighteenth-century married man might "with impunity" commit many adulteries "every day . . . with the most idiotic strumpets of the court and town," while his wife who did so "once with the most handsome man in all Lisbon" was banished from society, her property confiscated and her hair cut off. It was this injustice that so distressed Voltaire's Countess.[34]

Thus, the married woman was not merely her husband's possession—his "any *thing*"; she was his inferior and subordinate, one who could be chastised and beaten at his will and who owed him conjugal rights. Nor have these attitudes wholly disappeared. In 1935 a legal scholar could write, "It is not immorality which is punished but theft. As the act of the wife, adultery is a revolt against the husband's property rights";[35] and in the study sample both women and men complained of experiencing their spouse's adultery as if it were theft. One faithful man felt "as if someone had pinched some*thing* of mine" [my italics]; and another woman who herself had had several affairs, when she discovered her husband had been having an affair with her best friend, said, "Until this time [I] had believed that although flirtatious and despite faults, he was faithful. It felt like a double theft. Very isolating experience." A faithful married woman put it the other way about, reminding us that she was cared for by her husband—the contract was not one way—but emphasized honesty in the relationship, too: "I cannot reconcile infidelity with an honest outlook on life. . . . I think it's dishonest to live under a man's roof—to be kept by him [and yet] to be open to offers from other men."

A shift has occurred so that, whereas women were the property and subordinates of men, and this was true in a serious material sense (nor have these conditions wholly disappeared), now each regards the other as belonging to her or him in an ideological and emotional sense that has consequences often quite as serious and as practical.

Adultery Threatens the Lineage

> A wife might without any loss of caste, and possibly without reference to the interests of her children, or even of her husband, condone an act of adultery on the part of the husband; but a husband could not condone a similar act on the part of a wife. No one would venture to suggest that a husband could possibly do so, and for this, among other reasons . . . that the adultery of the wife might be the means of palming spurious offspring upon the husband, while the adultery of the husband could have no such effect with regard to the wife.
> —Lord Cranworth, 1857

Wives were the property of men and so were children. The legal guardian was the father; and in England right up until the Second World War, a mother could not count on obtaining custody of even her very young children especially if she was the "guilty party," for divorce could be obtained only on the grounds of fault: someone had to be guilty, the other presumed innocent of causing the marriage to break down. The major cause of divorce has for centuries been adultery—again, however, adultery of the married woman, not of her husband. In the two centuries before the passage of the first act in England in 1857 to permit divorce in the civil as opposed to the ecclesiastical courts and an expensive special act of Parliament, there were about two hundred and sixty divorces for men and but four for women.[36] In the debate preceding the act from which this section's epigraph is drawn, Lord Cranworth, the Lord Chancellor, enunciated the values of his age, stressing the dangers for a man whose wife, having committed adultery, then introduces "spurious offspring" into his household, thieving from his *own* children what is rightfully theirs.[37]

The act in its final form permitted husbands to divorce their wives on the ground of adultery alone, but a wife had to prove additional grounds, such as bestiality or incest.[38] Clearly, illegitimacy and adultery were so closely identified that, at this time, one could not be understood without reference to the other.

Inheritance in the Western world passes through the male line: it is patrilineal. (Sometimes, and for some social groups, countries have stressed primogeniture—the passing of the major portions of land and wealth to the first-born son only; others have divided wealth among the sons or among all the children.)[39] Establishing the fact that children (especially sons) are the biological offspring of the father is thus critically important for a whole range of property relations. But fathers can never be certain of their paternity in the same way that mothers can be certain of their maternity (that is, until mothers go into hospital for childbirth and—albeit rarely—their babies are switched!). Even a woman may be uncertain who is the father of her child. She certainly knows she is the mother. Fairy stories and dramas that

tell of changelings, and of infants removed at birth to be brought up by
another (usually to escape death in a battle over inheritance and to be rescued by a much poorer family), indicate the deep anxiety aroused by paternal uncertainty. In Shakespeare's *The Winter's Tale*, for example, which is
based on an earlier legend, the king (Leontes) comes to believe that his wife
has been unfaithful with his friend, Polixenes, and that his baby daughter,
Perdita, is not his own. The king tries to kill Polixenes and imprisons his
wife, who later dies. He also orders Perdita's death, but a shepherd finds
her abandoned on a shore and raises her. In adult life, she falls in love with
Polixenes' son who flees his father's wrath, taking Perdita to her father's
court where her origins become known, her mother is discovered to be
alive, and eventually everyone is reconciled.

Such anxiety has nurtured different attitudes toward the adultery of husbands, as compared with wives, which can be found to this day. The historian Keith Thomas, discussing this double standard, noted the acceptability,
even necessity, for men of high social status to have many mistresses and
the contrary deep condemnation of their wives:

> From Henry I to George IV most of the Kings of England kept mistresses
> and their examples were followed by many of their subjects. At the court
> of Charles II, where debauchery was a proof of loyalty, Francis North,
> Lord Guildford, was seriously advised to "keep a whore" because, we are
> told, "he was ill looked upon for want of doing so." But on the other
> hand if a woman once fell from virtue her recovery might be impossible.[40]

The free husband and the rarely straying wife (like the "Countess of Arcira") in fact provide the common historical picture at least among the powerful and élite classes whose lives are best documented. Georges Duby's
description of the life of Count Baldwin of the House of Guines in twelfth-
century France illustrates the style of most men of power and prestige at
many other periods of history.[41] Baldwin, it appears, was devoted to his wife
who bore him many children. She, as was proper, had her bedroom in the
center of the house, symbolizing the centrality of her role in ensuring the
continuity of the lineage. And when she died, her husband was, we are told,
stricken with melancholy—quite inconsolable. Their relationship, it appears, did not stop with the formal contract and alliance and the birth of
heirs; it was a loving and emotionally important one, too. Yet the men of
the time were proud of their sexual exploits (while women were kept strictly
cloistered especially until marriage), and Baldwin had many concubines and
young women to satisfy "his hot loins . . . which were stirred by the intem-
perance of an impatient libido."[42] The offspring of these illicit amours were
not denied and were brought up within the household, serving, perhaps, to
people it with companions and sexual partners for the legitimate descen-
dants and to provide allies for the future.

Whether his wife also had lovers, the account does not say. In a world where the virginity and chastity of young women were prizes to be guarded, given or taken by fathers, brothers, and husbands, some women saw marriage as the opportunity to begin a life of love making not only with the husband selected for her, but also with those lovers chosen and invited by her. But if the countess did have lovers, it is unlikely that her relationships would have been condoned and accepted in the same way as her husband's, and she would have exercised great discretion.

Lawrence Stone confirms that, in the Middle Ages in England and among the aristocracy, lovers were commonplace and bastards not hidden. Stone believes that the taking of mistresses and the having of bastard children made arranged marriages "tolerable."[43] Whether the taking of lovers also made arranged marriages more tolerable for wives is unclear, but a wife who did not wish to be discovered would have to continue to have sex even with an intolerable husband. Later there were changes among "the divines and the bourgeoisie" which were taken up by the aristocracy not only because by the sixteenth century they were obsessed "with patrilineal and primogeniture inheritance, but also to suit the social, ethical and religious conditions of the modern world."[44] During the second half of the sixteenth and first part of the seventeenth century, "public opinion began to object to the number of breakdowns of marriages and the reluctance to mention bastards in wills."[45] Even so, to the austere Protestant ethics of Samuel Johnson, a husband's affairs were "mere lapses from saintliness in the sight of God. Socially they were petty derelictions which a sensible wife would ignore."[46] And Lord Carlisle in mid-Victorian times is said to have blamed the gout on the fact that he was "living too chaste, not," as he said, "a common fault with me." "Nor," evidently, "was it a common fault with any of them."[47]

Beyond the Victorian era and in modern times, public leaders—especially presidents and politicians—have commonly kept mistresses and "committed many adulteries" no different in style from their powerful predecessors—again, as for the ministers of King Charles II, practically required behavior if they wished to continue as men of rank and prestige. Most recently, as values have changed and powerful men are no longer immune from public scrutiny of their "private" lives, scandals have erupted in Britain about Cecil Parkinson and Jeffrey Archer, and in America, about Gary Hart and Jimmy Bakker, demonstrating that, even if no longer positively sanctioned or even expected behavior, ruling-class adultery is still not uncommon: Cecil Parkinson was a member of Margaret Thatcher's cabinet and, like Jeffrey Archer, had been chairman of the Conservative party; Gary Hart was a candidate for the presidential nomination, and Jimmy Bakker a leading television evangelist controlling an enormous following and a wealthy empire. All were accused of adultery, albeit of rather different varieties. Nor has this been limited to men of high rank: in certain working-class communities, male adultery has similarly been virtually required social behavior, perhaps both to maintain male bonds beyond marriage, signaling to other men that marriage has not tamed nor trapped them, and uphold self-esteem in a hostile world.[48]

Edvard Westermarck, the philosopher-sociologist who wrote extensively in the 1930s about marriage, and agreeing that adultery had been almost *exclusively* a problem for married woman, cited three writers: the first expressing the problem of "spurious offspring" as the reason for the greater condemnation of the wife who committed adultery compared with the husband who did so; and the second two employing arguments that posit deep and unchanging biological and emotional differences between the sexes as sufficient explanation:

> The adulterous wife unquestionably commits a more inconsiderate [!] and blameworthy act than the adulterous husband, for the former deceives doubly by fathering upon her husband the children of another man. (Michels, *Sexual Ethics*, 1914)

> The difference between infidelity in the two sexes is so real, that a woman of passion may pardon it, while for a man that is impossible. (Stendhal, in *De l'Amour*, 1915)

> While the adultery of the husband is in many cases a purely sensual act, which need not spoil the marriage, that of the wife is in no case a mere bodily attachment. (Hedrig Wega)[49]

And Kinsey wrote that

> most societies recognize the necessity for accepting some extramarital coitus as an escape valve for the male, to relieve him from the pressures put on him by society's insistence on stable marital relationships. These same societies, however, less often permit it for the female.[50]

Yet such biological explanation—a "sensual act," "relieving" the man of "pressure," but "no mere bodily attachment" for the woman—is inadequate to account for the variety of behaviors and customs found even within any one society: men can be serious and committed and find it quite impossible and unthinkable to dally elsewhere and women may be promiscuous and easy in their affections.[51] Prostitutes often claim to feel "nothing" in their work. Around the world anthropologists describe enormous variation in different societies in type of marriage and in sex-role behavior—that is, in what is considered *appropriate* behavior for women and men—indicating that there is little of universal validity in the idea of unalterable biological differences in sex drives, needs or behavior.[52] Indeed they point to societies where women have many husbands or lovers as well as to those where men have more than one wife and perhaps concubines and mistresses, too; they show that who is forbidden as a sexual partner, when sexual partners may be taken and where they may be taken, the numbers of partners, and the feelings about all these relationships cannot be predicted either from the animal kingdom where ethologists have noted—even among primates—females acting in ways regarded by Westerners as typically male and males acting in ways believed to be female, or from Western ideas of marriage and adultery. In fact, Western conceptions of "feminine" and "masculine" have probably led to faulty interpretations of animal behavior![53] Rather, the social conditions, prevailing customs, and belief systems determine what it is "normal" for both a man and a woman to need and to feel. Even if we accept the basic biological premise that it is imperative for the male to impregnate as many females as possible in order to stand the best chance of handing on his genes, while the female needs to find fewer (because of the time she takes to gestate and lactate) but the "best" males, the resolution will vary according to social conditions. Robin Fox argues, for example, that there is one basic triangular pattern, the resolution of which in sexual politics in societies is extremely varied. The three groups forming the triangle are: powerful males, females and their young, and peripheral (younger) or aspiring males. He points out that a "polygyny of the powerful," where older men have control over desirable females, is the commonest form of marriage in human society (75 percent) and that even when there is ostensible monogamy, such men continue to have easy access to other women.[54]

In these conditions, such sexual arrangements come to seem "natural" and hence, "right." In Greece, for example, even in modern times, men's extramarital sex is thought to be " 'normal' and attributable to the 'polygamous nature' of men" while a woman's is a deliberate insult to her husband on whom she brings shame. Although adultery is no longer (since 1982) a crime in Greece, a husband who takes revenge on his wife or her lover remains unlikely to be actively pursued, prosecuted, or severely punished.[55] Thus, where property is to be passed down to the blood heirs of the married couple, a married man may "express" his sexual needs with relative impunity, but his wife endangers these property relations. To behave in this way and to believe in the pattern as "natural" and hence as permanent has protected marriage and has helped to preserve male and female roles within it as well as outside it.[56]

Keith Thomas argued convincingly that it was the "desire of men for absolute property in women" rather than "the fact of childbirth and elaborations thereon," that best explained the insistence in England on the fidelity of women.[57] However, these ideas are intimately related. Men wish to control women *both* because they desire absolute property in them *and* because women can always know their maternity in a way that men can never be sure of their paternity.

Adultery Encourages Male Competition and Risks the Expression of Female Sexual Power: The Vagina Dentata

> Magical women, "by arousing sexual desire seek to devour whom they wish."
>
> —*The Women's Encyclopedia of Myths and Secrets*

There is a further reason for men to feel that women's sexuality needs to be bounded and controlled: a woman (it is thought) is capable of insatiable appetites that she would (if free) pursue with many men who threaten the legal husband not only by possibly fathering infants that he might assume were his own, but also by pleasuring her more than he can. The threat is to his fundamental security—both emotional and practical; it reflects deep needs.

In the widespread myth of the *vagina dentata*, men's terror of women's untrammeled sexuality is clear.[58] The vagina is everywhere likened to a mouth. It has lips (labia) and a moist and dark interior with a passage leading to a stomachlike cavity. It is but a minor step to imagine this mouthlike vagina must be ringed with teeth. Let loose, woman will devour man. Freud thought that a man's fear of death in the act of sex was connected with his terror of being castrated by the woman: even the sight of the vagina would be enough to terrify him.[59] Perhaps her vagina was toothed to bite off the penis. It is more likely that the fear does not stop here. Rather, she who can give life can surely take it away again. He will return to the cavern whence he came, wholly devoured by the vagina that comes to represent the *whole* woman. Miró's three paintings entitled *Woman* attest to the continuing influence of this idea in modern times. In one the entire center consists of a great oval slash—the vagina; and just above it are fangs from a gaping mouth. Both holes occupy almost the whole canvas. Miró also indicates, with his little splash of fiery red or orange, sexual desire.[60] There is, thus, a paradox in that the man may also long to be encompassed and enveloped: both a nightmare and a dream. Hence the elision of sex and death.[61]

This fear and its opposite, this longing, are found at all times and in very different societies. Among many pre-literate peoples—as, for example, among the !Kung of the Kalahari desert in Africa, described by Marjorie Shostak—the same words are used for making love, having sex, and eating. Here, the life-giving and life-withholding powers of women are stressed by Nisa, the woman whose story Shostak tells:

> Women are strong; women are important. Zhun/twa (real people) men say that women are the chiefs, the rich ones, the wise ones. Because women possess something that enables men to live: their genitals. . . . A woman can bring a man to life, even if he is almost dead. She can give him sex and make him alive again. If she were to refuse, he would die! If

there were no women around, their semen would kill men. Did you know that? If there were only men, they would all die. Women make it possible for them to live. Women have something so good that if a man takes it and moves about inside it, he climaxes and is sustained.[62]

In Ancient Greece, the idea of ejaculation as a life force, producing food that was eaten by a woman, was also found; *sema* ("semen") means both seed and food. To consummate is, thus, for the man, to be consumed:

According to Philostratus, magical women, "by arousing sexual desire seek to devour whom they wish." To the patriarchal Persians and Moslems, this seemed a distinct possibility. Viewing women's mouths as either obscene, dangerous, or overly seductive, they insist on veiling them. Yet men's mouths, which look no different, were not viewed as threatening.[63]

Indeed, it is in the most patriarchal of societies that this idea flourishes. Thus, the Yanomamo Indians in southern Venezuela—known as the "fierce people"[64] because they are, indeed, among "the most aggressive, warlike and male-oriented societies in the world"[65]—brutally rape and seduce women and beat their wives, holding them in complete submission. "If a wife is suspected of infidelity she will be seriously injured, perhaps killed."[66] They also wound one another ferociously and yet exaggerate the competition among themselves by so denigrating females that women kill their infant daughters, thus producing a society with a great many more men than women. They believe in the *vagina dentata*, expressly saying it will cut off their penises, and are deeply fearful of extermination.[67] Among the Malekula in Melanesia, another strongly patriarchal society, the men, "having overthrown the matriarchate, were haunted by a yonic spirit called, 'that which draws us to It so that It may devour us.' "[68] In other words, where men restrict women most, holding them in greatest subjection, that is where women are also most feared and need to be most carefully controlled. Possession, in both a sexual and a material sense, is the way to exercise maximum control—to stay on top and alive.

Types of Adultery

Exercising such control over wives has led to two types of adultery—one more commonly pursued by men, the other by women—and to a third that has been more typical of men but is now appealing to women.

Parallel Adultery

An affair at any historical period, with a concubine or a mistress whose relationship to the husband is well known and even accepted by the wife— as in the case of Nelson and Lady Hamilton; or "the king's whore" (as Nell Gwynn called herself) and her royal sponsor, Charles II; or a later king, Edward VII and Mrs. Keppel who was invited, so it is said, by Queen Alexandra to the king's bedside before he died[69]—is well described as *parallel adultery*. Similar examples in America are the well known and accepted or condoned relationships of many presidents from F. D. Roosevelt to L. B. Johnson, whose wife Lady Bird, is reported as saying "My husband loved all people, and half the world's people are women."[70] Rather than being perceived as a serious breach of the marriage vows or of the marital relationship, it becomes simply another and parallel relationship, sometimes mirroring quite closely the marriage.

Edna Salaman, writing of the "kept woman" in the 1980s, notes that mistresses use the "excuse" of being "in love" in the same way as people explain getting married. They also remember important anniversaries (the first meeting, the first time they made love with their lover) as bench marks of the relationship, just as married couples celebrate wedding anniversaries, birthdays, particularly of their children, and so on. The lovers, like husbands, were less good at this.[71] Most of the "kept" women she interviewed were not wholly dependent on their lovers, just as most married women are no longer (at least not for the entire period of their marriages) wholly dependent on their husbands; but she says that "this did not generally deter them from identifying as kept women."[72] The man may provide housing and financial support and may even require that the mistress remains sexually bound to him—exclusively his. It is this mirroring of the public face of marriage in the secret and illicit relationship which allows us to see adultery as telling us more about the *general* relations between women and men than simply providing for the exotic and curious needs of a perhaps rather special and small number of idiosyncratic people.

Parallel adultery is usually known to the wife who may condone it by her silence even if she does not approve or enjoy it. Lady Nelson, for example, did eventually become estranged from her husband. Sometimes the wife does approve and even enjoys her husband's adultery; it may leave her with greater freedom to lead her own adventurous life, or, perhaps, to ensure she is "bothered less"—an important way, at least in past times, to render herself less likely to bear another child, risking death with each birth.

Traditional Adultery

Parallel adultery is to be distinguished from the traditional form where the relationship, while similar in many ways, *is* considered a breach of the marriage. This, the illicit relationship *par excellence* is usually, at least at first, kept secret. Great pains are taken to ensure the spouse is not told, although mutual friends or relations may know about it. This is the *traditional adultery* which wives have most commonly enjoyed. Where material life is dependent on marriage, discretion must cover the illicit relationship.

For historical reasons, then, just as it is possible to understand marriage, as Jessie Bernard said, only by dividing it into "his" marriage and "hers,"[73] so adultery is *hers* and *his*. Marriage has denoted quite different roles to husbands and to wives: in particular men have held the power and women have been required to serve and nurture them (see chapter 2, pages 85–87).[74]

It may be that in the adulterous affair this relationship of power is reversed, the straying wife initiating her affairs and controlling their progress, including the decision whether and, if so, when they should end. Again, this is not a modern development, for Lyle Koehler, writing of the search for power by the "weaker sex" in seventeenth-century New England, tells us:

> In adultery, many women inverted the proper feminine role by extending sexual overtures to men who were not their mates. . . . Despite the subservient role that women in Calvinist New England were expected to assume, in 60 per cent of the cases where adultery was actually committed, the woman served as the "seducer." . . . Cuckoldery was something women did to men.[75]

Among study participants, Keith, a truck driver and delivery man, felt strongly that the "bored" housewives who invited him to "go upstairs" with them held all the cards; although he could have rejected their offers, he would, he felt, "have been mad to do so" because it was fun and dangerous. They took him and discarded him, however, at their pleasure, not his. In taking him as a lover, these women cuckolded their husbands—an exercise of power of a kind even if the men remained ignorant of it.

For the mistress who was herself not married or married to someone less powerful than her lover, adultery often opened doors to wealth, travel, and freedoms impossible to achieve on her own. For many women, the invitation to open these doors remains enticing.

No relationship remains stable, however. Always it is in dynamic process of change and development; in adultery this arises as a result of changes from within the particular relationship itself, from the marriage, and from external circumstances. Thus what has been parallel may become traditional and *vice versa*. When a wife's traditional and secret liaison is discovered, for example, she may persuade her husband to accept it, or a man's long-term (and condoned) mistress may demand a divorce, bringing the two women into open conflict.[76] A husband may decide to leave, a job may change, a child become sick. Maintaining a balance is often difficult: there is always a *frisson* of danger. Yet each type may be experienced as *supportive* rather than *dangerous*: that is, not so much a risk-taking venture but a way to make up the "gaps," as one man said, in the marital relationship, or to reassure the individual of her or his worth.

Recreational Adultery

Finally, there is a third type—one that satisfies a desire to play: *recreational* adultery. Havelock Ellis, the turn-of-the-century writer on sexual matters, arguing strenuously for greater liberation of the sensual and sexual, thought "nothing . . . so full of play as love," and described a woman transformed in looks and behavior by her sexual awakening to the erotic delights of sexual play. Indeed, she would be a better mother as a result![77] Since this type of adultery is generally aimed at pleasure and seeks to avoid the moral dilemma or sidestep it, players often wish to expand the parameters further and invite additional players making "gang-bangs" and "sandwiches," or simply threesomes, thus including rather than excluding spouses. In this sample, as in Peter Nichol's *Passion Play*, when it is the husband who seeks to play in this way, it was men rather than women who expressed this desire.[78]

This, too, may move readily into the parallel or traditional forms, but these I characterize as having a certain solidity and endurance, whereas recreational adultery is brief, a way to live dangerously but not to risk everything valuable, to manage the moral dilemma by insisting on the division between sex only and sex with love. It is, as its name implies, lighthearted, not serious or committed, but for *fun, joie de vivre*, filling empty moments rather than hours, time away from normal family and working environments, a leisure activity like an excellent meal with a good bottle of wine, a hedonistic adventure of the flesh rather than of the spirit though it is the spirit that may be enchanted. May be, for even though this adultery may be undertaken to satisfy "the caprices of sexual appetite (which are by no means incompatible with a perfectly sincere devotion to a spouse who has become a lifelong friend and partner)," it may also "be the culminating expression of a fixed detestation by one spouse of the other accompanied by every kind of cruelty and treachery."[79]

Indeed, the variation in motive affects the way each is experienced, one woman, for example, being disgusted that her husband had, within three weeks of their marriage, "gone to a whore" to satisfy "certain sexual needs" that he would not, he said, even wish his wife to meet. Each may, for example, be used as a stepping stone out of the marriage; in this sense it may be supportive or dangerous but also *transitional*—that is, it is like a way station, serving also as an emotional transition.

It is clear that adultery has had very different meanings with markedly different outcomes depending, first of all, on whether it was committed by a wife or a husband. This is not the end of the problem of what is to count as adultery, however; and, despite the fact that in modern times conditions have altered—no longer are women the mere chattels of men; equality is a powerful ideal (if not a fact); adultery is condemned equally for both men and women (over 80 percent of people in survey after survey consider extra-marital sexual relations to be "wrong," as I explore in chapter 2); and possession has come to mean something much more to do with belonging as part of loving and much less to do with material ownership—yet powerful feelings are still aroused by adultery, and its meaning, although quite varied, remains marked by continuities that are striking and worth further exploration. In particular, the widespread trust in fidelity, like the difference in attitude to the adultery of wives and husbands, has a long history. Although neither Judaic law nor Christian doctrine can tell us what "actually happened [or happens] between lover and lover, man and wife,"[80] the sense of serious transgression, of "the unforgivable"—or as "something which was basically wrong," as two women saw it—has been handed down over centuries[81] and is not easily discarded.

Adultery Is "Basically Wrong" and Threatens the Group

The sense of a profound wrong in the betrayal of the single-minded monogamous relationship is given lyrical justification by Philo, a first-century Alexandrian Jew perhaps writing to impress on the Romans the strength of the Judaic case:

> In the first place adultery has its source in the love of pleasure which enervates the bodies of those who entertain it, relaxes the sinews of the soul and wastes away the means of subsistence, consuming like an unquenchable fire all that it touches and leaving nothing wholesome in human life. Secondly, it persuades the adulterer not merely to do the wrong but to teach another to share the wrong by setting up a partnership in a situation where no true partnership is possible. For when the frenzy has got the mastery, the appetites cannot possibly gain their end through one agent only, but there must necessarily be two acting in common, one taking the position of teacher, and the other of pupil whose aim is to put on a firm footing the vilest of sins, licentiousness and lewdness. We cannot even say that it is only the body of the adulteress which is corrupted, but the real truth is that her soul rather than her body is habituated to estrangement from the husband, taught as it is to feel complete aversion and hatred for him.
>
> And the matter would be less terrible if the hatred were shown openly,

since what is conspicuous is more easily guarded against, but in actual
fact it easily eludes suspicion and detection, shrouded by artful knavery
and sometimes creating by deceptive wiles the opposite impression of
affection. Indeed it makes havoc of three families: of that of the husband
who suffers from the breach of faith, stripped of the promise of his marriage vows and his hopes of legitimate offspring, and of two others, those
of the adulterer and the woman, for the infection of the outrage and
dishonor and disgrace of the deepest kind extends to the family of both.
And if their connexions include a large number of persons through inter-
marriages and widespread associations the wrong will travel all round and
affect the whole State.[82]

Philo's triangle consists of a married woman betraying her husband (who
appears innocent) with a lover who is also married. Three families (the wider
kin of husband and wife and the adulterer's family) will be "infected" by
the poison of the adulterer, which he will spread through his actions which
"teach" the adulteress wickedness. The root cause is seen as hedonism—
the pleasures of the flesh demanding expression against the force of the
moral law. The whole order of the state is undermined because each family's
orderly life is diseased, particularly because the certain knowledge that
these are the legitimate children of the marriage becomes uncertain. Indeed, all knowledge is uncertain because everything is secret. Chaos threatens. This chaos is both a personal and emotional crisis and a structural one
affecting the taken-for-granted relationships between everyone—husbands
and wives, parents and children, children with their brothers and sisters,
grandparents, and all the ramifications of polluted and muddled relations.

Working on reports about the Ashanti and Tallensi of Africa, Jack Goody
noticed that the most severe punishments were meted out on those who had
sex with forbidden members of their own clan. Indeed, *mogyadie* (to "eat
up one's own blood") described illicit sex with someone from the maternal
or matri-clan and was punishable by death, while sex with a willing married
woman was called by a different name (*di obi yere*) and was punishable only
by an adultery payment. Since the Ashanti had a cult of the earth, it was
also a serious matter to defile the wild places. Hence, sex, even with one's
own wife *in the bush*, was ridiculed and was serious if done with other partners. Such differences, Goody argued, can be explained only if "one introduces the system of descent as a variable." The descent group must be protected, not so much because of lawful or unlawful offspring, but because it
needs group solidarity to survive.[83] It is common to find that intercourse
with the sisters of a wife is particularly forbidden. This is as true of England
("incestuous adultery")[84] as it is of the Nuer and many African societies:
"these prohibitions are to be seen as preventing a confusion of kinship statuses, a disruption of the solidarity of the sororal group."[85] So, in modern
times in the Western world, we cannot explain the continuing powerful

emotions and private, if lesser public, punishment without introducing the idea of group solidarity.

Although families now take many different forms, they have not ceased to need solidarity and to feel threatened by the alien or stranger invading from "outside." Rather, the very fluidity of family shape and family membership across the life cycle might mean (since there are fewer structural constraints) that even stronger emotional responses and punishing reactions will be produced by the intruding third.[86] The greater the necessity for the group to depend on close relationships among the members for its effective functioning, the greater the need for those relationships to remain unthreatened by the particular strength and, hence, the potential disruption of a sexual relationship. Roger Libby has argued that one reason Americans still view "extra-marital sex as adultery and therefore as morally bankrupt" is that they fear the expanding of the "erotic and emotional parameters." The strength of this sense of danger in a possible expansion of boundaries both of the self and of the marriage is expressed when someone says, "I'd kill him (or her) if I caught them 'playing around' suggesting a justification to feel the spouse is no longer fit even to live!"[87]

Indeed, for this same reason it is not only the family in modern times, but also the work group, that requires protection. Thus, Karen, one of only two women in her department at work, described her male colleagues—"those men"—as "taboo" and did not permit herself even to fantasize about them, for if she could not keep her relationship with them "purely professional, . . . it would be just too difficult." It is wiser to keep the barriers and the boundaries high and relatively impermeable in order to avoid the chaos of which Philo wrote.

While most people are not articulate about the sense of order threatened by the adulterous affair, one man, Ross Ash, wrote an article about his experience in the London *Sunday Times* in 1981. Ash left his wife for another woman. He suffered the threat of his wife's suicide, the temporary loss of his children, two beatings-up, and one pursuit through darkened streets with murderous threats as well as the more usual loss of financial stability, loss of home, and increase in debts. He wrote:

> What we had done . . . was to damage the fabric of society. Society may be tolerant and flexible enough to cope with most eventualities: but it seemed we pushed too hard. We were to be, at any cost, cajoled or wrenched back to our proper positions. If we refused to be persuaded, and we did refuse, society would do without us.[88]

The pursuers of Ross Ash were people with a particular and personal interest in the outcome. But the wider society of which he speaks in the shape of its legitimized defenders—social workers, doctors, and so on, whose personal stake in the affair is not great—exerted considerable pressure on a study participant, Dan, a manager in his mid-thirties. Dan, like Ross Ash, had also fallen in love with another woman and prepared to leave his wife and family for her. He similarly found the social pressures dramatic and, in his case, overwhelming:

> My children were very young then. I knew it was highly dangerous and I knew it was, to say the least, irresponsible, but it seemed to be the only alternative open at the time. . . . Somehow our intentions got around. Before I could say "knife," we were being visited by social workers from County Hall and so forth. And I suddenly realized what tremendous pressure there is to make you conform. Didn't matter whether what you have is true and right or . . . or not, you know. You've made your bed and you must lie on it—this is the advice you get from professionals—social workers, doctors, G.P.'s, and so on.

The social services began to call on him, and his lover became ill. He and his wife moved house to "start again." The very words Dan chose to describe these events indicate the destruction he experienced—a "knife," perhaps, should be employed to "slice the thing off" before his marriage is broken and his children damaged and lost to him.

Thus, "the overlords who see their property threatened, the lawmakers apprehensive of the undermining of the social order, and the church leaders excoriating the souls who deviate from the conjugal path to heaven," described by Judith Armstrong writing about the novel of adultery, have not ceased to function, although the particular roles occupied by the guardians of morality may change.[89]

Ross Ash and Dan were speaking of the "serious affair," the adulterous liaison that leads to another monogamous coupling and threatens to or actually does break up a marriage (and at least one family with children), and not about the liaison that does not extend so far along a breach of order. In this study, about a quarter of those reporting at least one liaison (28 percent of the men and 23 percent of the women) had had one that ended in a divorce from their first spouse and in a new marriage to the adulterous partner. Since most people in the sample were reporting more than one affair amounting, in total, to about two thousand five hundred liaisons between them (the men averaging five or six; and the women, three or four each), few liaisons end either in divorce or a new marriage.[90] Thus, the order that is breached by most people is not so much that of the marriage but the social or moral code. Peter Rivière has argued that "marriage [is an] expression or statement about the order of things."[91] Because marriage itself takes so many different forms, from woman-woman marriage described by Evans-Pritchard among the Nuer[92] to forms with no permanency where the woman moves from one husband to another, as among the Irigwe of the Benue-Plateau state in Nigeria, so marriage is itself simply "an expression of some deep underlying structure. . . . The ordering principle of this deep structure . . . is the universal distinction to be drawn between male and female."[93]

In a society where egalitarianism is, at least on the surface as demonstrated in the law, a value to be pursued and upheld, the distinction between male and female cannot be grounded in the power of the male over the female in the institution of marriage. In the minds of modern women and men, a partnership between equals is desired and expected[94]—this despite oft-repeated evidence in their own experience and that of their families of origin, to the contrary. Hence, the ordering principle of the deep structure that is recognized is one not of distinction but of sameness, sameness of *feeling* between male and female, which brings them together in a marriage.

Elaine, who had never had an affair and contributed to the study as a counselor concerned about marital problems, identified the essential relationship between woman and man in marriage as one of "true love." For her this is the order broken by adultery: "From my observations, . . . adultery is the termination of true love between husband and wife. It does inflict the worst kind of domestic misery and unhappiness and is the major source of marital breakdown in modern times." Thus, the order that is threatened by the "invitation to passion" of the adulterous liaison is the order of marriages based on feeling: adultery is destructive of that feeling. Still, Armstrong reminds us, the adulteress remains the "underlying menace": "From having been first the traitor who betrayed the family religion, then the cuckoo threatening to deprive the true offspring of their rightful inheritance, she is now seen to be the invitation to passion, death, and the destruction of society."[95]

Adultery, it seems, breaches evident power structures or, at the least, attacks a subjectively experienced sense of ban. What if this sense of ban is removed—the spouse knowing about and consenting to such relationships?

Adultery Without the Knowledge or Consent of the Spouse

> Now then, would you like to know how many women I have known since I have been married?
> —Bernard, study participant

Making the assumption that adultery relates only to sexual experiences postdating his marriage and using *known* in the sense of "carnal knowledge," this sixty-seven-year-old man, who had had many relationships during his marriage, caught the Biblical connotations precisely with his question. Yet he differentiated among his many relationships, of which he kept a tally like the notches on the staff of Don Juan. Wife swapping, for example was not adultery in the same way as was a relationship kept secret from his wife. The openness of sexual relationships that he and his wife shared with other couples did not constitute adultery. There was no ban. It was permitted through the active participation of consenting adults in private. Further distinctions had sometimes to be made, as he described in explaining the end of one relationship: "It was a romantic thing, which is out. You see, you can't fall in love with your foursome. That is out. Totally." He set out clearly the necessity for participation by him and his wife *together*: to see even the other known and accepted partners alone was not within their rules, but would constitute adultery or, if the word itself was avoided (he preferred "infidelities"), its impact would be serious—unpleasant and undesired consequences flowing from it:

> Interestingly enough, in that sort of relationship it didn't matter so long as we knew, but what was wrong, what she [his wife] didn't like me doing was going to see Liza unknown to her, and I didn't like her here with Tim when I was away. That constituted infidelity. If it was done openly without subterfuge—this was all right.

This ability to condone adultery, or not to view an act of sexual intercourse with a third party as adultery when there is both knowledge and consent from the spouse, is not new though it does have new importance in a world where honesty and integrity are the linchpins of what is considered a healthy and mature relationship. If for Philo, the secret damaged the husband because he could not "guard against" what he did not know, for the modern betrayed spouse the problem is this elevation of honesty to a prime moral value within marriage. Sexual betrayal and deceit are two distinct wrongs, and often the latter is stressed over the former. It is this that makes the *illicit* quality central in defining what does and does not count as an adulterous relationship. One respondent, Chris, a thirty-seven-year old lecturer in architecture, said that, even if the spouse knew about the affair, it would still be hidden from others:

> It has its own internal dynamics, its own internal excitement. Maybe it's partly to do with it being an illicit relationship—being one that hasn't got a bed of its own, if you like. And is hiding, if not from the husbands and wives, at least from other people—from neighbors and children and whoever else.

Even within the Church, when both spouses have known about a possible adulterous act and when the nonparticipating[96] spouse has given permission for it to take place, adultery has had elastic boundaries.

Lord Lyndhurst, appealing in 1857 in the House of Lords for the equal treatment of wives and husbands in the proposed bill to permit, in the civil courts, suits for divorce on the grounds of adultery, cited even Augustine in his Sermon on the Mount,[97] as having been unwilling to condemn a wife as an adulteress in the following story:

> A man from Antioch lay in gaol for the non-payment of his taxes. On the morrow he would die. A rich man offers the prisoner's wife a bargain: If she will spend the night with him, he will pay all her husband's debts. The wife goes to the gaol and tells her husband of this offer and asks what she should do. Her husband gives her "permission" to accept the bargain and she does so. Augustine is asked: "And is this adultery?"

Augustine, recognizing the principle enunciated by Paul that "the husband has no power over his person but the wife, and the wife has no power over her person but the husband," chose not to rule on the question, saying that it must be a matter for the conscience of the individual.[98] Considering the strength of the ban and the condemnation and the punishment to be meted out to offenders, Augustine's element of doubt, leaving some room for maneuver, is surprising. According to Leviticus 20:10, after all, those who commit adultery are to die. Even after death, they will not find peace since then they have no hope of being in the kingdom of God—as Augustine said, quoting Paul to the Galatians:

> Now the works of the flesh are manifest which are these: adultery, fornication, uncleanness, lasciviousness, idolatry, witchcraft, hatred, variance, emulations, wrath, strife, seditions, heresies, envying, murders, drunkeness, revellings and such like . . . as I have also told you in time past . . . they which do such things shall not inherit the kingdom of God.[99]

It is clear that the "situation ethics" employed by Augustine center both on the principle that each of the husband and wife has dominion over the body of the other *and* on knowledge of and consent to the act. This makes the act under the control of will and reason, for it was lust that was so condemned and feared by the early Christian Fathers. In the Antioch tale, the rich man is depicted as lusting after the married woman, but she (it appears) has no desire for him. Carefully, the married couple work out a decision; that is, they use reason and will. The contrast is drawn between acting as a rational being—Will—and as an irrational being—Lust. Augustine describes remarkable feats of will as "wiggling the ears" and "sweating at will." He refers to lust as "the war in our members which wars against the law of our mind."[100] (We might recall the ancient myth and the way Tristan and Isolde are portrayed as unable to act with will or reason because of the magic love potion that induces lust. Similarly people in the sample spoke of "being carried away," of not being able to "do anything about it.")

The story of Jesus and the woman taken in adultery who was about to be stoned for her sin, and Jesus' invitation to him who was without sin to cast the first stone, is not much present in these earlier writings. This might be because Jesus refuses to *hear* the ban or to recognize the rule—faced with the elders representing ban, he keeps his head down and draws in the sand with a stick—but insists on the individual problem: that is, the woman is not merely any woman, a categorical object, but, as Tony Tanner has suggested, *this* woman before them.[101] We can see this personalizing of the problem in the much more modern setting of the famous film *Casablanca*, in which the young Bulgarian girl asks the hero (played by Humphrey Bogart) whether it would really be so wicked if she were to "do something bad": that is, she would have sex with the French chief of police in return for exit visas desperately needed in wartorn Europe for herself and her husband of eight weeks, and keep this bad thing from her husband. Bogart's distinctly unhelpful answer is "Go back to Bulgaria"; but then, in more practical vein, he helps the husband win enough money on his (Bogart's) gaming table, so that the young man can pay the police chief in cash, thus making his wife's sexual favors unnecessary to the bargain. Here, the lady is insisting on secrecy and on the fact that she commits adultery for love of her husband—not for love, or even desire, of another. From her point of view, it is, again, an act of deliberation and of her will—not a passionate moment where she could claim to have lost control of herself and her emotions. In Bogart's response, however, we see a confirmation that *sexual fidelity itself* is the clue to the badness of the act: not whether the spouse shares the knowledge, nor whether consent has been obtained; not even whether money, or other desirable or even essential goods such as the release of two innocents from the prison of Europe, is the reward. Ban is recognized, but it is also personalized and a specific way found to avoid the conflict.

Thus, to avoid the ban, individuals have to change the rules, for marriage remains built on sexual exclusivity that is interpreted in modern times as part of the very structure of love.

2

Marriage Lines

Before you are joined in matrimony I must remind you of the solemn and binding nature of the vows you are about to make. Marriage, according to the law of this country, is the union of one man and one woman, entered into freely, to the exclusion of all others, for life.
> —Registrar's words at civil marriage ceremony

The terms "love" and "marriage" are practically equivalent; that when one "loves" one must get married instantly; and, further, that "love" should normally overcome all obstacles, as is shown every day in films, novels and comic strips.
> —Denis de Rougemont, 1983

If you love someone, really love them, then you don't never *want* someone else—never mind you go and sleep with them.
> —Janet
> Study participant

Love—as Emma Goldman, the great turn-of-the-century anarchist and exponent of free love, was to experience in her passionate affair with the philandering Ben Reitman—can mean both life and death: "Do you know, lover mine, that . . . love stands over me, like a mighty spectre, and that it has both life and death for me?"[1] To be so passionately absorbed in an Other can lead both to a feeling of ecstasy and simultaneously to annihilation. Georg Simmel expressed it thus: "Passion seeks to tear down the borders of the ego and to absorb 'I' and 'thou' in one another";[2] while Max Weber wrote, "eroticism . . . rests upon the possibility of a communion which is felt as complete unification, as a fading of the 'thou.' "[3] In other words, two wholes become as one. This, however, is also an ideal for marriage. Two of my students described their images: One felt she was as if only half complete and longed to find someone to love and marry who, as the everyday expression has it, would be her "other half." Her goal, with Simmel and Weber (who also thought this erotic love was experienced, as in marriage, "as a sacrament"[4]), was the meeting of two halves to make a whole. The other student felt she, herself, had to be a complete whole. In her relations with an Other, it would be the coming together of two wholes in marriage that would be ideal (though she doubted the possibility of achieving this).

Thus, the very same toxic passion that caused Emma Goldman (who had believed jealousy was something to be conquered) to write in despair that her lover's ceaseless escapades "tear at my very vitals, . . . turn me into something foreign to myself," is the basis for marriage.[5] Love and marriage "go together like a horse and carriage," after all; or, as de Rougemont thought, writing especially about America some years ago, "the terms love and marriage are practically equivalent" (even if nowadays the one no longer follows, as he wrote, "instantly" upon the other);[6] and, for very many people whose feelings are expressed in the epigraph to this chapter by Janet (the twenty-six-year-old woman living with her husband and baby on a municipal housing development in northern England, and described in chapter 1, page 36)—the meaning of love itself is deeply embedded in sexual fidelity. Hence, adultery becomes interpreted as a statement about the love that the straying spouse feels for his or her marital partner; indeed, the underlying motivation for the affair may lie in a desire to make such a statement.

Other people might emphasize premarital infidelity less than Janet, but sexual exclusivity remains at the center of marital vows, even when, as the registrar's words also used in the epigraph here show, secular marriage is chosen.

In this chapter, I explore changing patterns in attitudes and beliefs about love and sexual fidelity and in sexual behavior both before and after marriage, and suggest that these changes and some important variations between women and men in their marriage lines can best be understood as arising from the different scripts[7] that they are expected to follow but that they, themselves, creatively employ and refashion in attempting to pursue the Myth of Romantic Marriage.

Love

Difference and Similarity in Scripts for Women and Men

In our culture, the intimacy between a couple that is considered true love (and that may be most successfully expressed by both men and women during courtship) is an intimacy based on talking, self-disclosure, and self-expression. Sex within this context is a major, but not the only, way that love is demonstrated and experienced. After marriage, women continue to desire and experience love—active loving—in this way. But men express and experience love in more practical ways. Looking after his wife by (for example) cleaning her car, earning money, or doing a share of household chores—what Francesca Cancian calls "instrumental" and "masculine" loving—together with making love, constitutes a man's idea of love.[8] Except when a sacrifice is called for because the spouse is sick or particularly vulnerable, neither men nor women seem to perceive the everyday material caring that women do—washing, ironing, cooking, cleaning—as constituting love. For women, the verbal expression of feeling and ideas remain central to love. This "feminine" or "expressive" version is the ideal in the wider culture. Men are urged to talk more, to reveal more of their inner selves, and to demonstrate their affection in these ways; indeed, one married man in Cancian's sample was told by the marriage counselor he and his wife were seeing that washing her car was an inadequate way for him to demonstrate his love for his wife; he had to learn to express these feelings verbally.[9] Lillian Rubin similarly considers that the "reciprocal expression of feeling and thought" has come actually to define intimacy—that is, love.[10] There does, indeed, appear to have been a widespread *feminization of love* in our society: it seems that psychological bonds of empathy and affection characterize the whole version of loving: both partners share erotic bonds, but the social and legal aspects of loving have been diminished or even play very little part in the ideal of long-term loving.[11]

This feminization of love is accompanied by a widespread stress on acknowledging and, in intimate matters, pursuing *feeling*. Thus, in Sweden, those who are in love are *entitled* to a sexual relationship:[12] people believe in love.

At the outset, during courtship, the ideas held by men as well as women, while varying somewhat by social class, focus nonetheless on intimacy through the sharing of activities and verbal communication—the unwrapping of each other's lives, wishes, and desires—as well as sexual intimacy. Before marriage, thus, the ideas of love held by women and men are more alike than perhaps at any other time. The courting couple shares more, we might say, of the script and speaks more of the same lines than does the marital pair when roles become so much more firmly divided. Hence, to feel and assert that love is the prerequisite for marriage does not bring the pair into conflict.

Throughout life one is continually in process of learning one's role, of knowing how to act in daily life: there are *scripts* to be learned and followed, appropriate to the particular situation. These scripts are not fixed, because each individual also creates variations on the theme or story line at the same time as social conditions change, rendering some lines, and even some parts, archaic.

Gender roles are among the most carefully, although not consciously, taught. It is not that anyone says, "Now I must explain to little Eve how she should be as a female person and to little Adam how he must be as a male person." Rather, from the moment the cry, "It's a girl!" or "It's a boy!" is heard, others respond to the child accordingly. Baby boys are physically bounced and handled more; baby girls are talked to more. Girls and boys have different toys, wear different clothes, and are subject to different expectations about many, many aspects of their behavior. And this is just the beginning. Over the whole of the early and adolescent years, boys learn to be boys and girls, girls in preparation for the adult drama. These gender scripts are also *sexual scripts*. The sexual script details when and with what kind of person sexual behavior, experimentation, and relations should occur, how one should behave during such encounters, what happens in and after marriage, and so forth; that is, there is a right and a wrong way to perform sexually and right and wrong people to have sexual feelings about or to approach sexually. In a society where heterosexuality is nearly "compulsory," as Adrienne Rich, the feminist scholar and poet, has written, getting to know and follow a homosexual script is much harder—but not impossible.[13]

It is possible to work out even quite refined details of the script—who will initiate what and when and where, for example.[14] Before marriage, men have been permitted considerable laxity, while women have had to protect their reputations against being deemed "whores," "slags," or "easy lays." Nor has this wholly disappeared: Sue Lees, in her work on young people in Britain, recounts receiving copies of essays written by young male teenagers in school acknowledging they used such terms but explaining they meant nothing by them—ignoring, of course, the import and consequences for the girls! As one girl said: "If you don't like them, then they'll call you a tight bitch. If you go with them they'll call you a slag afterwards."[15]

At marriage, both men and women have been required to remain faithful, but men have been well trained to follow a conquering script and have often not ceased to follow it.

Love and Marriage

> Happy, socially acceptable love—the lace-and-velvet-hearted valentines which lead to marriage and families.
>
> —Jacqueline Sarsby (1983)

> I promised myself to him when I was fourteen and adored him, really adored him when we got married.
>
> —Mrs. Waterford
> Study participant

I return to the analysis of changing scripts later in this chapter, for on one thing the genders are not divided: love is, indeed, the generally accepted prerequisite for marriage in the West, and almost every bride and groom considers that she or he was "in love" when they first married (about 96 percent of Americans;[16] over 80 percent of those marrying for the first time and over 90 percent of those marrying on a second or later occasion in my sample). Similarly, when they are in love, "The vast majority of the Dutch population—in 1968, 94%—want to spend their lives married . . . (or in a committed but non-formal marriage) . . . and in more recent surveys (reported in 1970 and 1975) it has been found that the younger generation hardly differ in their views.'"[17]

To say that romantic love and personal choice form the basis for marital choice, and that love is expected to continue to provide that gentle base, is not to say that economic or political considerations are unimportant. Even our most personal choices do not ignore such elements as social background and religious affiliation. Choices take account of compatibility of intelligence, social status (past or likely to be achieved), as well as such individual characteristics as beauty, attractiveness, strength, a sense of humor, and shared interests.[18] William Goode puts it this way:

> In the advanced nations young people try to do as well as they can in their love relationships, and young people gravitate towards persons of a similar class background just the same. That is their best market choice.
> . . . In such a market one is likely to receive only about as much as one can offer: thus homogamy remains the typical outcome even when parents do not control their children's mate choices much.[19]

Thus, all the qualities Goode listed—whether of class, ethnic background, or personality—are simply encapsulated, wrapped up in one package that makes a particular person desirable, makes them the person with whom one is "in love," and unique. Indeed, however many other reasons there may be for choosing this person, love is the only *publicly* acceptable reason that can be voiced.

People, however, recognize the idealism involved: in my study, about one third felt they would have disagreed to some extent with the statement that "love is the *only* good reason for marriage" even when they first married, and *now*, over 40 percent disagree. Also, as a marriage progresses, the partners put less emphasis on this romantic notion of love. Thus, a poll commissioned by the London *Sunday Times*[20] found that over 60 percent of the younger people, 35 percent of the late thirty-year-olds, and a higher proportion again of older people rated "being in love" as important for marriage. People thus simultaneously recognize the more prosaic facts of daily existence and hold to an ideal of love on which most hope to base a decision to marry. As Ann Swidler[21] has shown, and as she together with Robert Bellah and others have recently elaborated,[22] this ideal and this experience give focus and meaning as a moral goal to the lives of many people, particularly to women: to love is to be mature and good. It is, indeed, *the* proper goal to which, in the West, each should aspire. It is not simply that love and marriage "go together like a horse and carriage" but that they *should* do so—a moral imperative: "Thou shalt fall in love and marry," or, altered slightly to take account of the antipathy among some people to the institutional bonds of marriage: "Thou shalt fall in love and live together."

In line with these broad cultural values, teenagers of different social class backgrounds in England think "being in love" is, by a very substantial amount, the most important reason for marriage. These same young people also give high priority to faithfulness.[23] Georg Simmel pointed out that faithfulness was necessary to all social relationships—that is, a necessary dependability is entailed;[24] but the "forsaking of all others" in marriage demands more: not just the closure of the bodily boundaries to all others but also the building of new emotional and social boundaries within which will be contained secrets—both the everyday and the more vital kinds that forge a person's sense of identity. Indeed, the vast majority of people expect to be faithful themselves when they marry and expect that their wives and husbands will be faithful to them.

Love and Sexual Fidelity

INTERVIEWER: I know you are married, is he your first husband?
MRS. CROWBOROUGH: Yes, and it's the only one I intend to have as well!
MR. CROWBOROUGH: I had absolutely no intention, and it hadn't occurred to me that there was any question of breaking marriage vows. I mean, as far as I'm concerned, marriage is once and for all and that is that.
—Study interview

Despite the so-called sexual revolution, this vast majority in both the United States and Britain is convinced not only that sexual exclusivity is part and parcel of marriage but that adultery remains wrong. For example, even in the liberal San Francisco Bay area of the United States, in a representative sample of adults polled late in 1986, over 80 percent believed extramarital sex to be wrong. In Britain, Roger Jowell and Colin Airey show that "marriage . . . once entered into . . . is certainly seen by the great majority of the population to be an *exclusive* relationship for men and women equally." Only 14 percent of these respondents thought an extramarital relationship was "sometimes, rarely or not wrong at all."[25] Similarly, the London *Sunday Times*, in a representative quota sample of 1,069 adults ages eighteen and over interviewed face to face in fifty-one constituencies throughout Great Britain, found that

at least two people in every three [the graph actually shows nearer three quarters] deplore the notion of married people sleeping with anyone other than their proper legal partners—bachelors and spinsters almost as firmly as married couples, Tories only slightly ahead of Labour, Liberal and SDP [Social Democratic Party] voters, the Midlands only marginally less vehemently than the North and South, boiler suit as aggressively (indeed slightly more aggressively) than flowery hat and rolled umbrella.[26]

In my study, over 90 percent of women and over 80 percent of men intended to remain sexually faithful at the point of their first marriage and expected their spouses to behave in the same way. Study participants were asked to think back to the time when they first married and to indicate the extent of their agreement or disagreement then with the very strong statement:

> When you are married sexual relationships outside marriage are always wrong.

Only 21 percent of the women and 29 percent of the men indicated *any* disagreement with the statement, and over one third of women and over one quarter of the men *strongly agreed* with it. These beliefs about sexual fidelity rested on little discussion of the issue. Three fifths had *never* discussed the possibility of infidelity with one another. This despite the fact that some were realistic enough to accept that they might *want* a sexual relationship with someone else. Only about 40 percent of the men and about half of the women thought they would "never want a sexual relationship with anyone else" when they first married. Even at the time of this first marriage, nearly one third of young husbands were clear that they might want another sexual relationship at some time. Their wives were much less inclined to this view, only half as many (15 percent) expecting that they might want to have another relationship.

Kate, engaged to be married in 1981 and having had a considerable number and variety of lovers in the past, stumbled as she expressed what for her were difficult new ideals:

> I'd said for a long time that I didn't think marriage was for me. I didn't think I could actually live with anybody because I find it very hard to accept that one man can fulfill all your needs and I still think that is true. . . . I've been with Ned since the time we decided to get married and— er—I'm sure I want to get married this time. I'm really sure now— umm—we've discussed it endlessly—sexual fidelity, I mean, because we're both very sexually active and umm—we have come to the joint decision that neither of us wants to be unfaithful, and—umm—now that he's free, he supplies the sufficiency of my needs for me to be happy, and sex is an important one.

Thus even Kate, a 1970s person, accustomed to fulfilling her own desires and to a great deal of freedom, with much of her sense of her own self-worth derived from her several lovers and from good sexual experiences, thinks long-term commitment and sexual exclusivity belong together. Ear-lier she had said that "it was obvious the relationship wasn't working if I was starting to have affairs." Just like her older sisters in the sample, Kate has a deep belief that many sexual liaisons indicate "something not right" with the principal relationship. It is not true love.

To Kate, it would have seemed absurd not to have sex with the person she loved and intended to marry—but for her older sisters and some broth-ers in the sample, it was not so.

Changing Attitudes and Behavior: Premarital Sex

STEVEN: I was brought up to believe that one saved oneself for marriage.
BETH: We had sex long before we were married and there again, this just served to emphasize in my mind that this was the thing, and I had to go through with it. I mean, having committed myself physically, that was it.

Sex was either something you did not do before marriage, or, if you did, you were already as good as married. But the script has changed. Whereas men have always had greater freedom for sexual conquest and experimenta-tion before marriage (although the chaste young man, as for Steven, whose words appear in the epigraph to this section, was also an ideal for some) women were expected to remain unsullied and inexperienced—to save themselves for their husbands. Men and women of all social classes are now most commonly no longer virgins when they marry, although it may be that the change is exaggerated by an increased readiness to admit to premarital sexual experience (over the last ten years alone, there has been a 14-percent increase—26 percent to 40 percent—in the proportions prepared to say that premarital sex is "not wrong at all").[27] Indeed, it may be embarrassing now to admit to virginity. There is little doubt that many women, particu-larly working-class women whose capacity to bear children was an important economic consideration for marriage, had in past times to become pregnant before they were married.[28] Changes in reporting are, however, unlikely to account for the shifts among *both* men and women. When the Marriage Guidance Council recommended in 1984 that couples assess carefully their sexual relationship *prior* to marriage by trial and error, there was a rather generally heard shout of mirth. Who, it was asked was *not* trying it out?[29] Much has changed since Peter, a thirty-eight-year-old social worker, pre-pared for his first marriage. Looking back, he said that sex "was crossing my mind every second of the day, but I did not have enough security or drive to overcome the barriers of religion, of class—that whole ethos that you should remain a virgin until you gave yourself to the one and only."

My sample fits well with others[30] that show not only that fewer people are now entering marriage as virgins but also that they have a greater variety of lovers and many more of them than in the past. Of the women in the adultery sample, for example, 44 percent had had sex not only with their future husbands but also with other people. Most included only other single persons, but as many as 17 percent of the total had had sex with married men or with other women (3 percent) as well. Over half of the men had a variety of single partners, and a quarter had experience with married women and their own sex (4 percent) too. This change has been in fact less revolutionary than the phrase "permissive *revolution*" indicates, since the pattern is discernible from quite early in the century. Thus Paul Gebhard, one of the authors of the Kinsey reports, describes the "progressive increase in premarital coitus in the USA and in northern and western Europe" as "simply the continuation of a trend visible since the beginning of this century. For example, the Kinsey data reveal that 8 percent of the females born before 1900 had had premarital coitus by age 20 and this percentage gradually rose until among women born between 1910–19 some 23 percent had had premarital coitus by age 20." Similar trends were evident both in work Gebhard conducted himself in 1967 and in Vance Packard's 1968 study, when 33 percent of the unmarried college females were no longer virgins by age twenty.[31]

Study participants nonetheless show marked changes, so that the oldest who married before 1960 were often still virgins and the youngest marrying in the 1970s, rarely were.[32] Given that the contraceptive pill became widely available to women of all social classes only in the 1960s, this change should not surprise us: it is also among women that the biggest changes have occurred.[33]

Using studies conducted during the 1970s by *Psychology Today*, *Playboy*, and *Redbook*,[34] Gebhard shows that the proportion of women reporting premarital sex rose from around 31 percent (women aged fifty-five or over) to about 81 percent (the "youngest group").[35] The change apparent in these figures is also reflected in the drop in academic interest in premarital sex. Only a generation ago, many academics wrote about premarital behavior.[36] Now few do. Similarly, guidance counselors, therapists, and advice columnists showed considerable concern. It was considered, as adultery still is for most people, deviant sexual behavior. At the outset of most marriages, as the figures given earlier in the chapter about attitudes to sexual fidelity clearly show, this is still how adultery is viewed.

Changing Attitudes During Marriage: Sexual Fidelity

During their marriages, however, people generally have become more tolerant and less insistent on the centrality of sexual fidelity. Sixty percent of the men and nearly as many women *now* (that is, at the time of the study) disagree to some extent with the strong statement that sexual relations outside marriage are *always* wrong, and over 60 percent of both men and women are tolerant of one another's adultery "in certain circumstances." People now generally place less emphasis on the need to remain sexually faithful in marriage. Rather more than 60 percent of both husbands and wives now think they *should* be faithful, whereas about 90 percent had believed this to be necessary when first they married. As one man said:

> Sex wasn't great, but the idea of sleeping with anyone else was nowhere around. Now it's just different. I don't know if it'll last, but for now we're happier than we've been for years. We both go our own way and that's agreed.

This overall change, however, masks major differences between those who have stayed married to one spouse, between women and men, between the divorced and remarried and others, and between those who have had at least one liaison and the faithful. It is those who have stayed married to one spouse (like the man just quoted) who no longer place a high value on sexual fidelity—indeed, who may make new specific agreements to be sexually free; while those who have been divorced and remarried are, perversely (since they have usually had at least one liaison themselves), much more traditional in their views, both than those who have stayed married to the same person or than those who have not remarried following a separation and divorce.

Only about one half of women and men who remained married to the same spouse thought either they or their spouse should now be faithful, as shown in figure 2.1, but around *90 percent* of the remarried women thought both should, and 71 percent of remarried men thought their wives should be faithful, although slightly fewer believed this for themselves.[37]

These differences need further unraveling, however, for, among people in first marriages, it is those *who have had at least one liaison themselves who no longer place an emphasis on sexual fidelity*; the faithful still do so. Thus, a mere quarter of women who have had an affair think fidelity central to their marriages. Janet, the young woman so disturbed by her husband's single act of premarital infidelity, provides the example of the faithful woman who maintains her belief in fidelity: "I couldn't sleep with anyone now I'm married. It would seem dirty to me." But for her "unfaithful" sisters, an accommodation seems to be made: they have had or have a lover as well as a husband, have maintained their marriages, and are no longer committed to sexual fidelity. In this they are quite *unlike* all other "unfaithful" women, of whom *80 percent* believe still in fidelity.

Men also vary in this way but with much less difference between those who have stayed married and those who have divorced—40 percent of the former and about 55 percent of the latter still being committed to fidelity.[38] In summary, the faithful still adhere strongly to a belief that they should remain so; it is among those who have themselves had at least one liaison that infidelity is condoned, but *not* if they have been divorced. In particular, if women divorce, and even more if they remarry, they are most unlikely to condone infidelity.

FIGURE 2.1
Belief in Fidelity for Self and Marital Career
(Proportions saying they *should* be faithful)

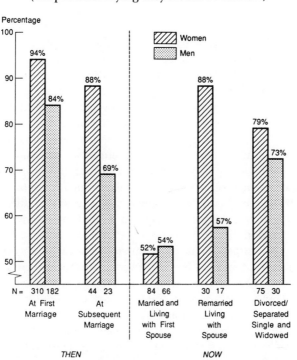

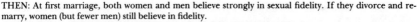

THEN: At first marriage, both women and men believe strongly in sexual fidelity. If they divorce and re-marry, women (but fewer men) still believe in fidelity.

NOW: That is, in 1982–83 when completing the questionnaire—those still married to a first spouse believe in fidelity least, while remarried women but *not* remarried men, remain strongly committed to fidelity. The remainder of the sample who have not remarried occupy an intermediate position on fidelity.

Similar events—that is, adultery, divorce, and remarriage—are, it seems, somewhat different experiences for women and men, leading them to hold dissimilar beliefs. Having experienced the trauma of divorce, its dislocation, and impoverishing effects—recently shown to be worse for women than for men[39]—and the difficulties of managing effectively as a single parent, anxious about her prospects should the second attempt fail in a "couples" world that values very differently men's increasing age to her own, a woman's investment in a new marriage is greater than a man's. I return to these issues at the end of the book.

It is normally assumed that fidelity and infidelity are opposite ends of a continuum, but there is a considerable difference in believing that one must be faithful and asserting that one should not be—in seeking a sexually free marriage. In order to reach these more dramatic differences, I asked study participants to say whether they thought they *should* be sexually faithful, whether their spouse should be, and whether they and their spouse *should not* be faithful (see question 17(g) in appendix A). Indeed, there is a striking increase over time in the numbers who say that they should *not be sexually faithful* to one another. Of husbands still married to their first wives, as many as 40 percent believe they should not be sexually faithful, and nearly as many believe the same for their wives. More women similarly consider infidelity desirable but, again, *not* if they have been married more than once: these women remain strongly opposed to sexual infidelity.

It is mainly those who have had at least one liaison who think sexual freedom or infidelity is desirable (that is, only one of thirty men and five of sixty women who had remained faithful believed now they could be sexually free), and this attitude is more marked among men. Thus, at remarriage, twice the proportions of both women and men believed that they could be sexually "unfaithful": 6 percent to 12 percent of women and 16 percent to 31 percent of men—that is, nearly a third of men (more than double the proportion of women) reporting a particular commitment to a *non*sexually exclusive, "free," or "open" marriage. Again, the gender difference in beliefs suggest that what objectively appear similar events are in fact quite differently experienced.

It is not only that people have become more permissive over the period of their marriages; there has been a general cultural shift, and it is women who are most affected. Whereas over 80 percent of women marrying for the first time before 1960 agreed (thinking back to when they married) that "sexual relations outside marriage were always wrong," less than half of 1970s brides thought so. Now a mere quarter of 1970s brides and grooms (23 percent of women and 27 percent of men) agree with the statement. It is also striking that the *gap* between men and women in their attitudes on this matter has substantially narrowed. In my sample, men are consistently more liberal in their stated attitudes to the sexual behavior of both themselves and their wives than women—*until* the 1970s, when there has been a shift: women have recently become more liberal than men both at the point of marriage and *now*. Since the gap was greatest between women and men marrying before 1960, the biggest leap has been made among that group, with well above half (54 percent) of those women becoming more permissive during their marriages. *Now* women and men express similar attitudes to this question: that is, they are more like than unlike one another when they are divided according to the year when first they married. In this sense, then, the old double standard that insisted extramarital sex for men was tolerable, when it was not for women, has weakened. As egalitarian ideas reach further through the social spectrum, and as women increasingly work alongside men (though still generally in less well rewarded and more subordinate positions), attitudes to the more private and most intimate aspects of life also change.

During Marriage: Changing Sexual Patterns

It is clear that attitudes to fidelity have changed. What about extramarital behavior? Only just over one quarter of those responding to the adultery study had not themselves "committed adultery." These people were responding as victims of another's affair, or as faithful and contented, or, perhaps, as faithful and not contented; others, although tempted, had not so far succumbed. About 10 percent of the sample never began a marriage committed to sexual exclusivity. The 73 percent who had at least one "adulterous liaison" in any marriage represents, to judge by other studies, a high proportion. In their first marriages, 66 percent of women and 68 percent of men—and in the most recent marriage, 39 percent of women and 42 percent of men—in this sample reported at least one liaison. Moreover (including the faithful and those not yet forty when the data were collected), over half the men and 60 percent of the women had a liaison by the time they were forty. Indeed, the commonest age for a first affair was twenty-four for women and twenty-five for men, while the average was around thirty for both. But arriving at a good general estimate is fraught with difficulty, for different ways of counting extramarital sex have been employed. For example, some researchers have asked about the number of sexual outlets; others, about the number of partners; some, about nonmonogamy, others, about extramarital sex. Some have been concerned to take into account duration of marriage; and others, the age of the respondents. Few have been concerned to consider which marriage the respondents refer to. Hence, it should not surprise us that estimates vary from 3 percent (Geoffrey Gorer in England in 1971 for women) to Shere Hite's recent American figure of over 70 percent for both men and women after five years of marriage.[40] Thus, as I said in my prologue, we cannot even say whether this is a behavior of the majority or the minority of married people.

Nonetheless, the various researchers arrive at a general consensus (at least for women since, as we might expect, there are more studies of female than male adultery) suggesting that above one quarter to about one half of married women have at least one lover after they are married in any given marriage. Given the history of adultery, married men probably still stray more often than married women—perhaps from 50 percent to 65 percent by the age of forty.[41]

In *American Couples*, the sociologists Philip Blumstein and Pepper Schwartz examined "nonmonogamy" among married and unmarried heterosexual couples and among homosexual male and female couples. They found, in 1983, only one quarter of married couples reporting *any* nonmonogamy at any time during their current marriages (slightly more husbands than wives, as we would expect). Couples had been married for varying lengths of time, and between 7 percent (wives married less than two years or more than ten) and 12 percent (husbands married more than ten years) had had sex with at least one other person within the preceding year. (The rates for cohabiting heterosexual, lesbian female, and gay male couples were progressively higher, reaching 83 percent for male homosexuals.)[42]

These figures for married couples tally well with a study carried out in 1973 by Robert Bell and Dorthyann Peltz, who found 26 percent of over two thousand well-educated married women, with a mean age of thirty-five years and of marriages lasting thirteen years, reported having "engaged in extramarital coitus."[43] Because their sample was younger than Kinsey's (who estimated around one quarter of married women and one half of married men would have had at least one extramarital relationship by the age of forty),[44] and the highest rates were reported for women in the 26–30 age group (34 percent having had extramarital sex), they predicted that by the age of forty, about 40 percent of married women in the United States would have had such relationships. More recently Diane Grosskopf and Shere Hite have reported higher estimates.[45]

Grosskopf, the executive editor of *Playgirl*, found almost half of the 1,207 women surveyed (questionnaires were sent out via doctors, nurses, and health-care workers in Ohio, Washington, D.C., California, and North Carolina) were then having or had had an affair, but these could have been in any marriage.[46] Apart from difficulties with her samples, Hite similarly apparently achieved her high figure of 70 percent by adding together everyone who ever had any affairs in any marriage, so long as they had been married for at least five years when they completed her questionnaires.[47]

In England, surveys conducted by two women's magazines, *Woman* and *Woman's World*, in 1983 and 1985, found about 30 percent to 38 percent of readers saying they had had "at least one lover since they married" and "having had affairs," respectively; while 10 percent of the *Woman* survey were currently involved in "an affair."[48] (Although the seven thousand reader-respondents were said to be representative of all women in Britain according to age and region, *Woman* is read by more working than middle-class women.)

Earlier British studies have reported very much lower figures. Geoffrey Gorer, for example, using a stratified and representative sample of English people, and conducting his study by formal and standardized interview in 1969, found only 8 percent admitted to having ever "made love to anybody other than your wife/husband since marriage." Furthermore, only about two thirds of these (5 percent of the total sample) agreed they had gone "all the way." Indeed, Gorer's figures vary according to the words used, indicating again considerable variation in meaning: 3 percent reported some "extra-marital sexual experience"; 5 percent, "extra-marital intercourse"; 11 percent, an "extra-marital love affair"; and 22 percent had "seriously kissed" someone other than their spouse since marriage.[49] That these are somewhat minimal figures is suggested by the results of a study carried out for quite different purposes—to examine the formation of antibodies in the blood—in England in the early 1970s. Through the analysis of blood samples, it was noted that no less than 30 percent of the men *could not* have been the fathers of their children—a minimum, not a maximum, since the test can demonstrate only the absence and not the presence of a biological link between father and child.[50]

Clearly, to cite any figure is dangerous. Is one speaking of people married six months, or six or sixty years? Is there a difference between first and later marriages? In my sample, people are more faithful in later than in earlier marriages. Does one put an age limit on the calculation, as has become *de rigueur* since Kinsey? If the couple has separated, albeit briefly, is an affair during that period to be counted? And, as I have pointed out in the introduction and elsewhere, and as Gorer's study reiterates, what counts for one person does not count for another. Thus, how are the questions to be asked? What words can be employed? And since people may have liaisons in one but not in another marriage, perhaps my overall figure (and Hite's) is not as outrageous as it first appears. More interesting is the *pattern* of adultery— different as it is for women and men.

Patterned Differences Between Women and Men

Since Kinsey's two reports in 1948 and 1953, all the provisos notwithstanding, and according to best estimates, it appears that women are having more affairs than they did at that time. One way of explaining this change (since repeated studies have found premarital experience to be highly correlated ...ital behavior)[51] is to point to the increase in premarital sexual ... Indeed, in my study, premarital sexual experi- ...ways to postmarital behavior, the faithful more often being inexperi... before marriage and the most adulterous the most experienced. For example, of those who remained faithful, 60 percent had had sex only with their future spouses or had remained virgins until marriage; and the opposite was true of those who had had many liaisons (that is, only 40 percent of those reporting at least four affairs had been virgins or had had sex only with a future spouse at marriage). Furthermore, the greater the variety of lovers before marriage, the more likely it was that people would have affairs following marriage. In particular, none of those reporting any premarital sexual relationship with someone of their own sex (about 4 percent) remained faithful after marriage.[52] Yet, it seems there is also much creative rewriting of the lines of any given script, since many who had various lovers before marriage have none thereafter, and some who were "virgins" at marriage have many lovers later. Furthermore, whereas men's postmarital behavior is strongly correlated with their premarital behavior, the links are much weaker for women.

In particular, the age and year of marriage makes a considerable difference for both women and men. Thus, the striking increase in sexual experience before marriage over the earlier and later decades of the period covered by this study does not explain the differences between the faithful and the adulterous, for the younger people marrying in the 1970s or later have reported *fewer* liaisons overall (perhaps because their marriages are of shorter duration), yet they have had much more premarital experience *and* wait much less time before a first liaison than did those marrying in earlier decades. It is in general the older people whose premarital experience remains related to their postmarital behavior—especially, those men marrying before 1960 who were virgins remained the most faithful, and those who were most experienced before marriage, the most adulterous subsequently.

Thus, during the period covered by the study, men have begun (statistically speaking) to "look like" women, and vice versa. This is not the only trend to lead me to this conclusion. We will see in book II that the basis of the decision to go ahead with a liaison (chapter 5), the choice of partner, the place of meeting, the type and duration of liaison, and the number of liaisons are all more similar for the youngest men and women than for the older people in the sample. Where once rigorously separate roles were to be played by men and women with different scripts to follow, more flexible and more similar parts may be being created. Yet one fact remains unchanged: women have fewer lovers than men.

Now, thinks Gebhard, about one third of married women have liaisons, the proportion of men remaining relatively stable. Of this one third, about half, he believes, have only one; and the other half, two to five liaisons.[53] Men, by contrast, rarely restrict themselves, once the first hurdle is crossed, to these numbers. This patterned difference is strongly supported by Blumstein and Schwartz in their American sample; and, in my study, in a virtually identical way, the women also have fewer and the men more affairs.[54]

From the outset I have assumed that adulterous liaisons differ in meaning and value for the people who engage in them, and that the words used to describe them indicate some of these differences. Yet, regardless whether a liaison is one night with a stranger or a ten-year love affair of fundamental emotional importance, the mere number of liaisons people say they have had turns out to differentiate between women and men quite clearly. *Only 15 percent of men but one quarter of women have had just one liaison; half of the women but one third of men have had between one and three; while 40 percent of men have had at least four liaisons, but only one quarter of women have had as many as four* (see figure 2.2).[55]

This consistent finding suggests that the script that permitted and even rather encouraged the male in premarital experience still also, while proposing that at marriage he should stop, nonetheless remains fairly lenient and flexible, the lines relatively easily altered and transgressed. In certain instances (particularly, as I have suggested, perhaps among élite and powerful men and among working-class men), the script even encourages a *continuation* of sexual conquest after marriage. For women, *pre*marital sexual relations have only recently entered the permitted script: a woman is certainly not expected to continue to have other sexual relationships once she is mar-

FIGURE 2.2
Number of Adulterous Liaisons for Women and Men

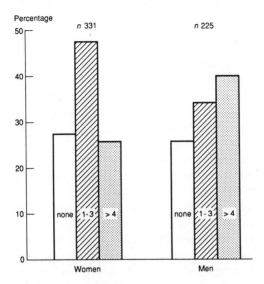

ried, even though, like men, she is now accustomed to gaining a sense of who she is and of renewal from the relatively free expression of her sexuality. Still, therefore, if he has a postmarital sexual relationship, it is likely to be *parallel* with his marriage, while hers remains likely to threaten the marriage and be *traditional*.

In the limited number of lovers that women generally take compared with men, the strength of these scripts remains apparent.

Changing the Pattern: Educational Discrepancy

This basic pattern is very hard indeed to disturb. There is no variation, for example, according to the year when people were married. It also makes no difference what educational level had been achieved by the individual respondents; the pattern is, however, affected by the *difference* in the educational level achieved by husbands and wives. While the numbers are small when the groups are divided too many ways, there is a suggestion that men who are married to women with the same or a lower level of education than their own "look like" other men in the number of liaisons they have. That is, when the husband (educationally speaking) is in the traditionally superior or equal relationship to his wife, he has no more and no fewer liaisons than is typical of other men. But the man whose wife is better educated than he is, tends to reduce the number of liaisons he has, while she increases hers. In other words, when the expected patterns of dominance are reversed in educational level, the extramarital sexual lives of the spouses are also reversed.[56]

There are emotional as well as social consequences for marital partners whose achievements fail to follow expected patterns. A woman of high achievement relative to her husband is likely to be employed or to be making contacts outside her home that are, at least intellectually, more satisfying to her than those her husband offers. She may also be exposed to greater opportunities through her work or through her education, or because, like Mrs. Inkerman, a nurse married to a security officer and living in Scotland, she decides to pursue her capacities yet further through an extramural university course. Indeed, Mrs. Inkerman, tired of all the *dependency*, was well aware that she was "stepping outside a bit." She said, "They all depend so much." For her, it is the excitement of the books and the people—as her mind, rather than her body, is "turned on"—that enables her to continue at all with a husband who insists on watching television—and then nothing she would enjoy—while she retires to the "lavatory to read Plato."

A husband with such a wife is likely to feel insecure—as, indeed, Mr. Inkerman did, objecting as forcefully as he could to her extramural course which was giving her the power to argue with him (see pages 111–12). As women traditionally have done, such a man clings to the known base of his marriage and family, not risking outside liaisons with their toxic possibilities for loss; indeed, he feels a sense of loss already, a lack of self-esteem in the face of his wife's capacities. He is, it might be said, now in the feminine role, subordinate to her; and she, in the masculine. Hence it may be that the script is written for people occupying particular roles normally associated with one rather than the other gender, than with being male or female.

Changing the Pattern: Occupation and Gender

These patterns are reversed in another way that lends further and more substantial credence to this idea. When I divided the sample according not simply to whether people were working, but to their occupational and professional qualifications, I found that those men who were in the traditionally male-dominated professions (business, accountancy, law, for example) and those women who were in typically female-dominated occupations (nursing, social work, teaching) had the same number of liaisons as expected. This holds also for those who had qualifications that entitled them to enter occupations normally dominated by their own gender: for example, women who had qualified as hairdressers, men as electrical engineers, followed the typical female and male patterns, respectively, in the number of liaisons they had. When, however, we looked at the men who had entered the "female" professions or occupations and the women who had entered the "male" spheres, then these women "looked like" men and these men "looked like" women in the number of their liaisons (see figure 2.3).

One could argue that these differences are due to greater opportunities

FIGURE 2.3

Number of Adulterous Liaisons, Occupational Qualifications, and Sex

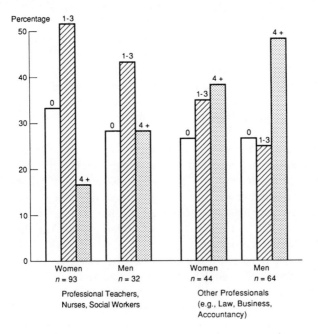

for illicit sex in some professions; and, indeed, women, entering a world with many more men available to them and opportunities for late meetings, travel, and so forth, do have more liaisons than other women. But this does not explain why men, exposed to a greater number of women with whom they could form liaisons and just as much freedom to do so as in male-dominated occupations, *reduce* the number of their affairs. Indeed, a social worker illustrated how easy it was to conduct a secret affair because she was always able "to plead emergency case meetings," and was worried about how she would be able to continue her long-standing affair if she gave up her job; her male colleagues do not appear to make use of these opportunities as frequently as they might.

Another possibility is that the kind of man who becomes a nurse or a social worker—who, in other words, goes into the "caring" professions—is a different sort of person from one who becomes a businessman or lawyer—that is, more "feminine" (nurturant, caring). Similarly, those women who compete in the worlds of business or law with men might be different, more "masculine" (assertive, ambitious). But these people had often been in "ordinary" jobs—that is, ones typical of their gender—at an earlier stage of life. Thus, Jack, who became a social worker and had two affairs, had begun his career in business. Besides, although I have termed teachers, nurses, and social workers traditionally female-dominated, men have, in fact, outnumbered women in secondary boys' and in tertiary education.

For them, entering teaching or lecturing would not have the same symbolic meaning as might be implied in the decision to become a nurse or a primary schoolteacher. Rather, the possible effects of the occupation itself, the nature of the work and its culture need to be examined.

The training for these occupations consists, in part, of advanced learning of the practical skills and of a body of specialized knowledge. Another part consists in the emphasis on commitment, the importance of doing the work through the relationships established with clients, patients, children, and students. The ability to impose discipline and be disciplined, and the importance of serious relationships, not trivial and temporary contact, are central aspects of the assumptions about what constitutes a good teacher, social worker, or nurse. There would, it seems to me, be some inconsistency in holding beliefs such as these and, at the same time, leading a personal life that implicitly contradicts them. This is not, of course, to say that it is impossible: substantial numbers of both women and men with these qualifications reported at least four liaisons. Moreover, this is a measure only of number and not of the quality or meaning of the relationship. Yet the pattern is shown in the numbers alone.

I did not use any personality tests, but the scores for traditional or permissive stance—that is, adherence to the two myths—might help in the resolution of this conundrum. That is, if people are attracted into occupations best suited to their personalities as more "masculine" or "feminine," we would expect those people with the highest number of liaisons to be the most permissive at the outset; and vice versa, those with the least, to be the most traditional.

In the past—that is, using the measure relating to the time of first marriage—women in the most "female" occupations were, indeed, more traditional and less permissive than were those women in other occupations. But men who entered the nursing, teaching, and social work professions, were *less* traditional and *more* permissive than those men entering other occupations. Now—that is, in 1982—while men in the "female" occupations have become more traditional, they have not, however, changed at all in their "own" professions. Women have become slightly more permissive in every profession. Teachers, nurses, and social workers, regardless of gender, are more permissive and less traditional than both women and men in other occupations. This means attitudes have shifted for these individuals as they have worked in their jobs—a trend supporting (but not proving, for they might change for quite other reasons) my claim that the work itself exerts important influences.[57] Thus Ruth, a woman in a "male" profession who had many liaisons, often with colleagues, was exhilarated as she contemplated all the men around her at a meeting and gloated that she "had slept with nearly all of them, and they [that is, the others] did not know it." She was competitive, perhaps in the same way men in these professions and business often are, and delighted in her power, at least over their emotional lives.

In other words, people's attitudes seem to flow from the daily experience of being in particular work settings and in responding to particular conditions and expectations. Again, the idea of scripts followed by people in particular gender roles is useful, for it explains how a social worker may find it difficult to have many lovers without commitment, since the ethos of such occupations rests on ideas about the importance of nurturing and caring relationships, about responsibility and help. Usually, too, obtaining promotion in such jobs is unlikely to depend on an assertive, strong personality that is competitive rather than cooperative in relation to colleagues. The opposite, on the other hand, is likely to be true of business or the law.

Marriage

The Modern Contract

Clearly, both attitudes toward extramarital sex and extramarital behavior are changing: while not perhaps as substantially as premarital sex has changed, there is greater permissiveness.[58] However, certain aspects of marriage lines remain relatively unaltered, and it is these that continue to play havoc when one spouse commits adultery or has an affair. First, some people emphasize the fact that at marriage a contract is made, and made in public, that cannot be altered merely at the whim of one partner. Such people also recognize that marriage is not only about the two of the marital pair disturbed by the intruding third, but about making alliances and forging families. This is something often recognized all too late by the couple who has lived together for years but who finds on marriage that their status in relation to, for example, their in-laws, has so altered that their couple relationship cannot survive. Second, within marriage, the roles of men and women are neither equal nor the same: wives and husbands have different scripts *within* the marriage still, and these affect the feelings when one, rather than the other, breaches the contract. Finally, as we saw at the beginning of this chapter, love is the focus of marriage, and the sense of possession, so long the real material as well as an emotional fact, now rests much more on the feeling that he or she belongs to me as, say, my leg or arm does rather than my picture or the chair. Yet this "emotional contract" is also often not equal.[59]

The Public Contract

We had a good sound moral background . . .
— Woman, study participant

But she has breached a contract. That's what I just *cannot* accept. A contract made in public with witnesses in church. You can't

take the bits of it you like and discard those you don't. It's not
tolerable.

—Tarquin
Study participant

Tarquin, a man of fifty-eight, came to a group discussion and repeatedly
spoke of his great distress at his wife's breach of their contract of marriage.
There followed a furious argument between him and Louise who believed
this contract could change:

LOUISE: You do keep harking back to your original contract. . . . The mar-
    riage itself is an ongoing contract, and because we are two people
    who are changing, then we can change the contract. We can change
    the contract to a situation that suits us. We don't have to keep hark-
    ing back to the original contract which may be meaningless to us
    now.
TARQUIN: Well, but that's a contract made in front of other people. What
    happens to the promises you make? You can't, you can't in any con-
    tract you make, you can't say, "I'll have this term and that term and
    reject that term and that term." You take the package as a contract.
LOUISE: You can write your own contract.
TARQUIN: Well. O.K. Do so, but don't hide behind another contract and
    quietly elide a couple of the clauses. . . . It's absurd. Unless the thing
    is done *in front* of somebody with witnesses, you're talking about skat-
    ing on thin ice because there is no guarantee, no proof of it. You
    can't change the rules of the game at whim. You've got to agree them
    somehow or other. . . .

His wife's adultery was, Tarquin felt, particularly intolerable since he had
had a relationship (never consummated) some years before with a woman
whose company he had very much enjoyed. When his wife had asked him
to stop seeing this woman, he had done so. Now his wife had first denied
her own involvement, and then, having admitted it, refused to give up her
affair—and hers was a fully sexual relationship. Tarquin felt that the couple
was at the pinnacle of a pyramid of relationships. Only one other person
could be accommodated at the top of this pinnacle: a third meant one had
to fall. Marriage, this publicly made contract, provided the support for this
structure, and you had to be prepared to give up any relationship (as he had
been) that might entail the collapse of the structure and of the couple. For
Tarquin's wife, this notion of a public contract was not, it seemed, central:
"I don't see why one shouldn't have two men in one's life."
    Louise understood Tarquin's idea about the pyramid but stressed the
feeling rather than the public accountability:

I think it's to do with threatening your position as the most loved one.
Because if my husband had come home and told me, "Yes, last night I

slept with this girl I met in the bar of a hotel and we just quickly went to bed and I regret it and it was all awful and you, know, it happened," I would have been stunned but I'd have felt: "It's happened," and I could have recovered that much more easily because I wouldn't have felt *my* position threatened. As it was, he came home and said, "And I still want to go on seeing her because I've become extremely fond of her." And I thought: "Hello! This is it, you know. Bye-bye marriage." And so it wasn't actually sex that was important; it was the feeling that I, myself, was being replaced by someone else—a younger model.

Tarquin continued to insist on the public and legal aspects of marriage, refusing to be drawn too close to the pain of the broken relationship. But the couple does, indeed, enter a new estate on marriage for, when they marry, new expectations are placed on each of them: to be a husband or to be a wife is to fulfill social roles, not merely to continue to relate to one another in a particular way. Marriage realigns social groups and extends a family into a kin group through in-laws. Having an intimate, sexual relationship does none of these things.[60] A woman's magazine interviewed a series of couples who had all lived together for some time before marrying. Several—both men and women—complained that the new expectations of mothers-in-law or of other relations led to their divorce. As one woman said:

We had been in that flat for seven years, and all that time I had not been expected to have John's parents to dinner. Suddenly I was, and suddenly, too, John expected me to do the shopping and the cooking for it. Before, when we had people in, we used to share all that.

And one young man in Penny Mansfield's 1982 study of newly married couples, said:

My parents—I think they still love me as much as they did but they definitely treat me as a married man. They know Sue comes first now, not them, and it is completely different. They still want to help whenever they can and offer advice, financial support, and everything else—yes my parents treat me like a married man. They sometimes ask my advice now.[61]

These status changes announced in the public ceremony are particularly sought even by those couples who change the traditional rules of marriage to permit sexual freedom, as we will see in the next chapter.

His Marriage and Hers

While for centuries men have been told—by other men—that marriage is no bed of roses, a necessary evil, a noose, a desperate thing, a field of battle, a curse, . . . it is men who thrive on mar-

riage. Despite all the jokes about marriage in which men indulge,
all the complaints they lodge against it, it is one of the greatest
boons of their sex.

—Jessie Bernard, 1972

Both these young people in the examples just given recognize, too, that
each has a particular role to fill. Wives are expected to shop and cook still,
while men go out to work and are supposed to take responsibility for their
wives; offering help has to be done with greater tact, for the son now holds
the same social status as his father: both are husbands.

Marriage is expected to offer a certain security—both material and emotional; but it remains women, generally earning less and normally still caring
more for the children than does the husband, whose need is greater. Hence,
getting married for a woman who is financially independent may become
less attractive. Gae Exton, who has lived with the actor Christopher Reeve
for many years and has two children with him, said in an interview: "It's
funny but I really don't need security."[62] Indeed, she does not, because she
can and does earn her own living. For most women, however, such economic independence, particularly during the years of childbearing and
rearing, is wholly unrealistic. Rather, the woman's place, psychologically
speaking (though she is present physically in the marketplaces of work in
ever-increasing numbers) is still the home.[63] Among others, it is this fact that
led Jessie Bernard, in her well-known *The Future of Marriage*,[64] to describe
marriage in two quite distinct ways—"his" and "hers"; for the experience
of marriage for husbands is profoundly different from (and much better
than) that of wives. Thus married men have better mental health either than
their wives or than single men. The reason men remarry following divorce
with great rapidity has as much to do with the fact that his marriage is better
for him than hers is for her, as with the numbers of single women available
to him compared with the paucity of single men available to her, or the
greater value placed on youth for women than for men.

Every study examining who actually does what within families demonstrates that, where both spouses are present, it remains the woman who
holds the "maps" in her head of the household day.[65] She knows about and
arranges for the children's activities; she seeks her husband's permission,
but he informs her of his movements—sometimes (otherwise, he may simply
go out without information); she will take the responsibility for providing
food and clothing and for preparing meals as well as for the housecleaning.
Many, many studies have explored the division of household and child-care
tasks assuming that when women worked outside the home, men would participate more. Joseph Pleck, in a recent review of this literature and a new
analysis finds that, indeed, most recently married men are participating
more in these ways and that this is true of those men whose wives do not, as
well as of those who do, have paid work away from home.[66] However, by far
the greater burden is still carried by women who put in very long hours and

do not receive the reciprocal help at home that they might expect given their own contribution to the family finances.

A vivid example of this imbalance in ordinary marital relations was recently provided by a woman talking on television in Britain about plans she and her women colleagues at work had made to hire a bus for a Saturday's excursion. About a week after the bus had been hired and the details arranged, first one woman and then another came into work saying, "I can't go. We had a terrible row about it. My husband won't let me. He won't have the kids all day by himself. . . . It practically led to a divorce in my family." As she said, it seemed grossly unfair to her that these women could not have one day on their own without having to provide meals, iron shirts, and answer the perennial, "Mu-um, where's my scarf?" and "Mu-um, please can I have some ice cream?" and "When's dinner?"[67]

Given responses such as these to the efforts of working and married women to make independent arrangements, we might ask of what are their husbands really afraid? A better answer than changing the baby's diaper might be "sex": perhaps she will, as men in similar circumstances might, "get laid." She is "my" wife. "That's not going to happen."

It is clear that roles are by no means shared. In addition, there is a necessary emotional labor to marriage; and it is women, more than men, who do this work. The sustaining of the relationship and of the children, of contacts with in-laws and other friends and relations are, in nine out of ten cases, the responsibility of the wife. Women are deeply interested in this work and do it without necessarily even becoming aware of what they do and of its vital importance in keeping the whole family running reasonably smoothly; indeed, part of what they do may be confrontational, but it is also their task to resolve confrontation. As time passes, however, they may become more aware of the unequal burden they have shouldered, and harbor resentment, especially when they are also helping to earn the daily bread. This kind of unhappiness was voiced repeatedly in Shere Hite's recent study, and her term—the unequal emotional contract—is apposite. This part of the marital script has, it seems, changed but little.

Love and Possession

> Her liaison was unbearable from the lies point of view and unbearable from the point of view where she was possibly going to have sex. . . . I had to earn the money to support her and the children even though I didn't feel that they were "my" children and "my" wife. It was an obligation. It was like . . . saving up for something and some guy just comes along and takes it away and you say, "Bugger off," you know, "That's mine. You're not having it. I am going to fight you for it."
>
> —Dick, study participant

Dick's misery about his wife Fanny's "affair of the heart" illustrates both his firm sense of his marital and paternal role and the considerable confusion that exists in the minds of both women and men about the meaning of possession. Men might put much less importance on virginity as a prime quality of their brides, and appreciate they do not own their wives' bodies, while women have decided for the first time they are in charge of their own bodies and no longer care whether the hymen is intact when they marry; but the confusion is deep seated and not only because property laws have changed or because contraception can prevent unwanted pregnancy and a possible "pollution" of the male line. Rather, the imagery of possession is deeply embedded in our conceptions of sex—similar to the descriptions of passion with which I began this chapter. When people speak of "my" wife or "her" husband, they do more than merely and practically differentiate this couple from that one. In intercourse the physical boundaries of two people are dissolved: two become literally one. In this way, he is an extension of me and she of him. The imagery conjured is closer to that of "my" arm or "his" leg than to that of "my house" or "her picture."

Hence, for many people, marriage entails a relationship that may not—cannot—be shared. Unlike Tarquin's wife, many feel that a desire to have two at once denies the fact that love is often experienced as diminished when shared: for most people—and despite the lover-spouse's cry "But I want you both!" and "I love you both—why not?"—it does not seem that a spouse's capacity for love can grow to encompass another, only that when another lover is found, the uninvolved husband or wife suffers the slicing off of a part of his or her own share. They are like the child expected by its parents to share their love with the new baby and unlike the parent whose love seems able to grow to encompass many children—to expand without diminishing effect.

Indeed, the increasing independence of women (even as they continue to perform traditional roles) places a greater burden on the *quality* of the relationship: it must be more valuable than any other relationship and different from all others. As women gain the freedom, always owned by men, to decide whether to stay within the traditional boundaries of marriage, so belonging gains in potency and meaning. Meanwhile, it is clear that, at the outset of marriage, love and sexual exclusivity are profoundly enmeshed.

3

Changing the Contract

But let there be spaces in your togetherness. Fill each other's cup
but drink not from one cup.

—Kahlil Gibran, *The Prophet*

Open Marriage

Some are not prepared from the moment they marry to forsake all others.
They acknowledge that, were they to attempt to live by the rules of monogamous marriage, they would fail. They are not prepared to give up on what
they perceive as the potential for *life*. They want to continue to pursue *eros*
and *agape*, whether expressed in sexual relations or not. They will also pursue other sexual relationships, and these may have very little or nothing at
all to do with love. Their morality has nothing to do with sexual activity and
everything to do with honesty. Their commandment reads not,

Thou shalt not commit adultery,

but,

Thou shalt tell thy spouse of any other sexual relationship thou hast.

This commandment involves a heavy burden—changing as it does ideas
about love, possession, and jealousy—and those who adhere to it do not
believe any less strongly in their chosen ideal than the more conventionally
religious, but they do remove the inherent conflict in, for example, being a
devout Christian and also adulterous. Nor are beliefs changed merely so as
to justify adultery—that is, adultery is not necessarily followed by a change
in belief—rather a change in belief may precede adultery. Belief acts in this
way both as motivation for and justification of adultery: "emotional work"

is undertaken that reduces conflict and pain.[1] Indeed, these people celebrate an alternative but still powerful emotional contract.

In this chapter, I describe three couples who have developed open marriages differing in certain ways but each adhering strongly to the telling
commandment. Their stories are set in the context of the range of pacts
or agreements about sexual fidelity made by the whole sample and of the
powerful association that still exists between religious belief and adultery
more generally. They all illustrate the continuing importance of knowledge
and consent in defining and managing adultery by removing the sense of
ban (see chapter 1, pages 59–62).

Clearly, to be required to tell one's spouse about any extramarital involvement turns traditional adultery on its head. It is the illicit quality that makes
adultery necessarily secret; especially, it must be kept a secret from the betrayed spouse. Indeed, it is the husband or wife who so often says despair-
ingly: "I knew nothing. I was completely shattered. I just had no idea. It
seems I was the last to know. Everyone else had known for months."

Not all spouses remain ignorant of the adultery of their partner; and
some say that spouses always know, if not consciously, then at a deeper level.
At the level of conscious awareness, less than half of spouses in this study
never discovered it, according to their straying partner's report. Of the remainder, two thirds were told by their own husbands or wives, for honesty
is not a value limited to the open marriage. Indeed, almost everyone—men
and women alike and those entering the study from whatever source, believed "honesty was the cornerstone of a good marriage" (83 percent at first
marriage, 77 percent "now"). Only those men who were most adulterous
(that is, reporting four or more liaisons of whatever kind) showed significantly less agreement with this ideal. Those who adhered most strongly to a
traditional-romantic view of marriage were also those who reported most
frequently their belief in honesty as an ideal; yet "permissiveness" was a
measure on which all open marriage couples scored highly. It appears that
the deceit involved in a liaison for those who are traditional does, to some
extent, prevent them from having one.[2]

One woman explained that the sexual relationship between her husband
and herself had been disastrous for virtually the whole of their fifteen years
together. (Indeed, 44 percent of both men and women said their sexual
needs were unmet in their marriages.) This couple had intercourse on very
few occasions, even at the beginning—just enough for her to conceive and
carry two children. It was extremely painful for her and devastating for her
husband who felt impotent to help his wife and, indeed, became sexually
impotent as time went on and matters did not improve. They sought and
received expert advice, but to no avail. During the marriage despite the
misery she experienced and her knowledge that sex could be very different
(for she had had a successful love affair before her marriage), Diana never
looked for or was invited to begin another relationship—not even a one-
night stand or something "purely physical." Only after she and her husband

separated did other men suddenly become "available," and did she then begin to have satisfying sexual experiences. She said:

> I suppose the opportunities were always there in a way. But as far as I was concerned, they were not. I mean, the man I'm now with was around for ages. We even worked together but it never occurred to me. I mean, it never entered my head. No way would I have ever done anything about it so long as we were together. I don't believe in that. That would be dishonest. Either you are married and you stick to that or you are not—in which case, then, you're free.

It seems, then, that while honesty is an ideal for most people—and, in general, being deceitful is an unattractive option—to guide one's life by this ideal when it is coupled with sexual permissiveness is a particular combination of some interest. This is the way thirty-five-year-old Bud, who ran a small store, expressed the agreement he had with his wife, Lee, a journalist thirty-three years old. It had been operating since they lived together (five years before they actually were married in church in 1979):

> It was fine if one of us wanted to go and sleep with somebody else, but the rule was you had to tell the other person and that has always stood. It is just part of the honesty, and there is nothing to hide, and I can't remember all the rest behind it but it was agreed and it seemed logical.

Bud and Lee reaffirmed this by commenting on the attitude of friends:

> Some friends of ours have a similar attitude. She once said, "It would be much more important to me that he doesn't tell me something he is thinking about and he would talk about it with his friends in the pub, than if he slept with somebody, which he would tell me about anyway."

Given this attitude, one wonders, Why the wedding ceremony? And why in a church? For civil ceremonies, although the "rules" are similar, carry neither the solemnity nor the sanctity of a religious ceremony. Church ceremonies are often, too, more public than a registry office, more guests being invited: the former is a bigger declaration in every sense. Bud, indicating the way marriage still realigns social groups and publicly links kin, explained:

> My parents had just been visiting here for a holiday, and I think they found it a bit difficult although they would never say so, and Lee's parent's certainly found it difficult to handle. . . . Lee was going on about it—well, not a pushy sort of thing but . . . I was in the position I didn't really care whether I was physically married or not. As far as I was concerned I was married in a sense.

and Lee, stressing the relationship, said:

> I began to feel that if we weren't married we were *not* being honest be-
> cause we were saying that we were committed to each other indefinitely,
> for life, which is indefinitely and if we weren't being married, then we
> weren't really meaning what we said. I suddenly decided that we were
> living a lie if we weren't married because everything that we said and
> committed ourselves to *was* being married as I understand it. So if we
> weren't, either Buddy was holding out on me or I was holding out on
> him.

Honesty was thus part of the reason for the marriage as well as providing
the rules to which the couple would adhere. Asked how they squared the
"no lying" with the undertaking to forsake all others, Bud said: "I don't
feel badly about that because, I mean, omnipresent God is there and He
knows how I think and what my views are." Because God knew and Bud's
wife knew, any implied deceit was unimportant. The quality of what they
had together was much more important to both of them and was not threatened by sex with others—*unless* the vow of telling was betrayed.

In similar ways, Harry and Maisie, a couple married in 1975 and unortho-
dox in many ways, stress this openness and their feelings about one another.
Much older than she (when interviewed in 1981, he was fifty and she was
twenty-five), Harry had already been married once before and had had another long relationship with someone, which had lasted over ten years. This
was for him like a third marriage. For Maisie it was her first. They had met
when she came to "temp" for him (do typing and other secretarial tasks,
temporarily) at his house (he worked at home), and he felt "an animal attraction" that over the next few days rapidly deepened. She "had a premoni-
tion" as soon as he opened the door to her (then aged eighteen) that he was
going to be very important in her life: "I just knew straight away." It became
clear to them that they belonged together.

Maisie had had a tempestuous adolescence and even a "sort of a breakdown," and had been influenced by the humanistic psychologies that emphasize the flowering of the personality that must open to others and grow.
Both she and Harry were completely committed to this ideal of personal
growth and also to the idea that marriage should be experienced not as a
constraining but as an enabling relationship. It was not possible for one's
marital partner to satisfy all one's needs, whether sexual or of other kinds.
These were to be met through an engagement with others.[3] For Harry, this
was self-evident in that since he was bi-sexual he would, he said, always need
sexual contact with other men from time to time. For this couple, too, *telling*
the other was central to their understanding. Sex could be had with anyone
and with any number of people, but you had to tell your spouse that this was
happening. Harry had found marriage itself not a rewarding relationship,
particularly as his first wife's participation in the women's movement had

caused ideological clashes between them: finding new ways of relating had simply proved impossible for both.

Harry, like Bud, would not have minded if he and Maisie had simply continued to live together. For Maisie, however, this arrangement was unsatisfactory; and, like Bud's, her reasons were social: "It was silly things—like the milkman not knowing what to call me and not taking my word for the order. And I want children—lots of children—and I do think they need a proper marriage to be born into."

They had done a great deal of research to find the right person to marry them (a Unitarian minister) and the right words to say at their marriage. In the end, both were delighted with the wedding service and felt it had a profound importance in their lives. Furthermore, they recognized the importance it had as a public act of commitment for their families and friends. And they wanted to marry in church but were opposed to any ceremony that failed to make clear to everyone what commitment it was they were making. According to Maisie:

> What we said was, "I come to you in marriage, loving and respecting you and hoping to go through life at your side. I pledge my . . . trust, friendship, comfort and support for as long as our union is a source of strength and guidance to us both." . . . We never said we were going to do it for ever.

Harry clarified the commitment involved:

> What we are saying to the world is, 'look! here we are, together as a married couple *for as long as we love each other*' [my italics]. If either of us get to a point where somebody else is more important, and we say, 'look, I'm sorry love, I want to make the rest of my life with that person,' then that is the end of this marriage. And that would be a matter of great sadness to us both.

Feeling for one another is so important, however, that no one else need be involved.

> MAISIE: Or it might not have anything to do with another person, one of us might just decide we had grown apart.
> HARRY: Or we don't want this any more, you see. That is why we are not prepared to make this church statement, you know—the Christian establishment statement of what a marriage is about.

Harry and Maisie thus achieve the benefits of public ceremony but take the loving relationship between them as the only and finite reason for becoming or staying married. Next, they remove the barrier to openness beyond their own relationship:

HARRY: We think that we have built-in security because *we have removed from our marriage the usual threats to marriage* [my italics].

MAISIE: Yes and the temptations of illicit affairs . . .

HARRY: You see, we are completely open and honest with each other about absolutely everything about our own sexuality and everything else. There is really, as far as we are concerned, nothing that can really threaten our marriage. Certainly there is no case of sexual jealousy upsetting it or anything like that.

Clearly, they now intend to continue with sexual relationships of many kinds; these are not to be *excluding* but *including* (they had group experiences, too). It is not at all that they fail to share the values of others emphasizing the *quality* of the marital relationship; but rather that they believe the way to an enduring relationship based on love and trust and commitment is to be achieved by *removing* the boundary that creates the obstacle, the temptation, and the breakdown. If there is no rule, it cannot be broken; hence the marriage is stronger, not weaker. Similarly, it is strengthened by bringing things back into the marriage from "other relationships." As Harry said, "There is a delight in the other fulfilling themselves by bringing something back into our marriage—a very real thing for both of us."

Harry and Maisie were also clear that if there was "something of a relationship," it might deepen and the involvement become too great for the security of their own feelings for one another. Harry appreciated that they tried to ensure their outside relationships did not impinge in this way; yet: "We would be very sad if that happened—very sad. But those are the grounds of our marriage. If one of us loves someone else so much more that we want to share our life with that person rather than with each other, then we will have to abide by that."

They tried to separate the concepts of love and sex, even though they were currently having a "passionate sexual relationship" with one another. Describing her father's affair which had apparently nearly brought her parent's marriage to an end, Maisie said:

It was a sexual attraction. I think that was aggravated because he had been brought up in a pattern which said that when you are married, you are faithful to your partner and if you are attracted to somebody else, it must be because you love somebody else. He couldn't separate the sex and the love. To him, it was the same thing. . . . I think they are very different things and when they combine they are lovely. That's a very lucky and happy situation, but I don't think they *have* to combine at all.

Harry and Maisie believed in the corollary, too—that one may, and often does, love deeply without sexual attraction—and foresaw a time when their own relationship (especially given their age discrepancy) might have little sexual expression but be unharmed, in a sense taking out an insurance policy.

Clearly, this couple combined the Myth of Me and the Myth of Romantic Marriage. Through the development of the self, however, they give the upper hand to romance, for love (of another) may destroy the marriage.

Lee and Bud also separated out love and sex. Lee preferred any sexual encounters she had to lack involvement. She had always had many sexual partners. Like Maisie, who had described herself as having been through a "very promiscuous phase" that she had surpassed, needing now "something of a relationship" in every sexual encounter, Lee also described herself as "promiscuous," though without condemnation; while Bud had had fewer relationships and felt "bad" when, on occasion, he had had sex with someone else while apparently committed to another. Before her marriage to Bud, Lee had had two very serious relationships: neither had required sexual exclusivity, and in both she had continued to have other sexual partners. She explained that this was agreed during one because she and her partner were divided by distance. During the second, she had come to feel the relationship was doomed; yet both for herself and for her partner, *telling* about other sexual encounters acted as a "turn-on" and gave the relationship a little longer life. (Harry said, when speaking of the need for him and Maisie to tell one another about their sexual relationships with others, that they should *not* tell the details: To get one's "kicks that way would be sick.")

Neither Bud nor Lee had any doubt about the profundity and seriousness of their feelings for one another, and both took great delight in their sexual relationship. Lee was beginning to find the imperative to continue sexual relations with others something of a burden. One reason was:

> I just have a much better time in bed with Bud. I certainly don't feel the need for more sex than I'm getting or anything like that, but what does happen from time to time is I am presented with a situation where somebody is terribly attractive and what's to stop me?

Lee's question hits the same note, but from another direction, as Harry did when he pointed out that, if sexual relationships are not limited to the marriage, the traditional boundaries are removed. Although Lee had no limits to her encounters, she was not enjoying them as once she had done. Perhaps her need was for obstacles, for her husband to say, "Stop. I love you too much to have you screwing anyone else." Indeed, she said that on one occasion he had been very angry when she had sex with a "yobbo" she met at a party. She liked her husband's anger. But now Bud was *requiring* her to continue in order, as he saw it—again, like Harry—to forestall later possible difficulties. Bud wanted both of them to continue always to have other sexual partners for two reasons: to leave a gateway open to later sex when, as he said, "Who knows—I *might* want someone and that would create havoc if it wasn't normal and acceptable"—his insurance policy; and because he both loved sex and considered it far too trivial to damage something as durable as their relationship:[4]

> The reason I think the way I do is I have never really believed that it was that important—that a purely physical act could somehow destroy a whole relationship. . . . I just thought there was more to a marriage than that. There should be and that can destroy the whole thing and I think that's where this thing about telling the other comes in.

While Lee, like Maisie, has always had the romantic ideal that she would marry, have children, and live happily ever after, Bud, unlike Harry, who already had two children from his first marriage and was happy to have another three, if not five, with Maisie, has not wanted children. Bud had specifically avoided the possibility of marriage, which he had seen as a real threat, by setting himself the age of twenty-eight before which he would not settle down. Until then, he had traveled the world. To him, marriage did form part of an imagined future, but not before that age. This difference of view also affected Lee's feelings about continuing to have other sexual relationships. She is, in a sense, bored with *recreational* adultery. She wants to stop "playing around" for a while, to feel secure in her relationship with Bud, and to have children: indeed, to "settle down." By contrast, Bud seeks to retain their rules as an insurance against such unmentioned and (as he feels) potentially stifling intimacy.

Both Bud and Lee cared about the politics of equality. Bud complained about the way men he knew expected their wives to wait on them, to remain sexually faithful, and yet for the men to feel entirely free, as he put it, "to fuck whenever they please." They were less interested in or influenced by "growth" philosophies, spiritual experiences or, indeed, *experience* as a good in itself than were Harry and Maisie. Rather, Bud and Lee stressed the "honesty" and the "telling" that had to be at the center of all their actions. Not that this would ensure absence of jealousy. Both were plagued by such feelings (although since their marriage, neither have had many other lovers). Their jealous feelings are related to specific situations and problems. For Lee, it was intolerable that, first, her husband was not "straight" with her when he intended to spend the night with another man's wife, and then did so while she was in the same house and left her to pass the night talking to the woman's equally unsettled husband. (It might have been better had Lee and this man "fancied" one another and also had sex, but they did not.) For Bud, it was bad that she had sex casually with a drunken stranger, met at a party. She should have sex only with friends—people who were "good," not just anyone.

This split between having sex with known people where there is a good chance of loving feelings was continually compared by many people in the sample with having sex "casually" or with a "one-night stand." Thus, one couple were at loggerheads because the husband had "gone to a whore" six weeks after he and his wife were married—something that deeply shocked his wife; while she was having an affair with a colleague that involved rather more talk than sex—something that her husband felt undermined the basic trust he had in their marital relationship. He tried to split sex and love, going to the prostitute for "certain sexual needs" he would not wish his wife to meet; while she felt the combination of sex and loving feelings excused her affair. They thus defined adultery according to its seriousness—the extent to which it involved or failed to involve a commitment—beyond the sexual encounter. When adultery is defined according to these parameters, jealous feelings also vary. Thus, jealousy is felt only when certain conditions are met. For Bud, jealousy was experienced only when there was *no* emotional involvement; but for most others, precisely the opposite was true. For Lee, the quick "five-minute fling" was much to be preferred to any deeper arrangement (although it could be lovely if it was for "five hours if you're lucky") because she would not want anything more. She was (in spite of two or so very difficult years, owing to pressures at work and her desire for children and for a rather more settled existence) happy in her marriage. The feelings she had when Bud had sex while she was in the same house related directly to her *exclusion*. She wanted to be *in*cluded, either through full knowledge and being "in the same bed and sharing the sexual relationship"—or else be far enough away not to *feel* excluded.

Lee's feelings are like another woman whose husband, away from her all week, lived with another man, with whom he had a homosexual relationship. Jessica valued her marriage and was determined that her husband should stay married to her and help her rear their two small children. They, too, had an agreement that each could have other lovers, but Jessica knew the security of her marriage was threatened if both did so simultaneously. She decided to invite her husband's lover home—and into their matrimonial bed—and thus ensured her inclusion and avoided continuing painful exclusion. She and her husband shared a lover.

The third couple, Jay and Sacha, are quite different. Married young, in 1969, they had two children, aged twelve and ten. Although Sacha was thirty-five, she looked about twenty-seven—something like Twiggy, so thin was she. Her husband also seemed much younger than his chronological age, being fresh-faced and blond, with what seemed a "normal" haircut until he turned around to reveal a tiny pigtail. They came to a group in jeans, Sacha looking androgynous wearing a man's shirt and basketball boots. Although every group was supplied with refreshments, these were limited to tea or coffee and sandwiches. This couple produced a can of beer and a joint which they shared (but did not pass round). He was a teacher, and she had not worked outside the family but was now studying for a degree. Although their private contract, too, permitted co-marital relationships, they also found these difficult because it was so easy to slip into traditional male-dominant and female-subservient roles. Or just to get more from the relationship than either could give, quite simply because they were committed to one another:

> JAY: I gave up this girl because I could see that she was leaning on me in a dependent way and I even enjoyed that and I really didn't want to get into that kind of thing.
>
> SACHA: I really liked this guy I was having a relationship with but I could see that it would have been wrong to continue because I've got Jay and he had only me and it was getting to be really heavy. I couldn't give him what he wanted and needed.

Jay and Sacha were much more concerned with the politics of monogamy. They were trying, in all their relationships, to avoid exploitation, to engage in a socialist-feminist praxis. Sacha wanted to find a way of being a woman that did not always relate her to men or to a man. As if the normal is male, and the only way of describing a woman is to say in what ways she is unlike a man. Jay shared her ideals of non-exploitation, rejecting monogamy for its male-dominated characteristics. This attitude extended to the details of their own relationship. They had moved out of their double room (something that did cause a certain amount of "hassle" when different lovers were brought home) and into the children's rooms, each having a double bed. The children (a boy and a girl) were sharing their parents' ex-matrimonial bedroom. Jay and Sacha each, in this way, owns a "space" into which the other (and any other friend or lover) might be invited—but *only* by invitation. The claim was that the children were not disturbed by this move.

As far as Jay and Sacha could see, difficulties for the children, despite the fact that the faces at breakfast might change from time to time, would arise only from school or from other settings where different values held sway. They were open with their children, too, it seemed, by talking about these things with them. Apparently, this couple had surrounded themselves with like-minded friends so that there was some degree of cultural homogeneity for them. However, they had grossly underestimated the power of "school" and "other social settings." For the children, these would constitute at least as much their concrete daily experience as the alternative values and practices of their parents and of their parents' friends. Jay and Sacha were perhaps missing the fact that they might have been exploiting their own children. Life was, not surprisingly, a terrible struggle. Sacha felt she was old at thirty-five. She felt she was "going to die quite soon," and, at the time I saw them, she was leading a celibate life—both in relation to her husband and in relation to anyone else.

The emphasis was different for these three "open marriage" couples in that both Bud and Lee, and Harry and Maisie, seemed rather to be ensuring a varied sex life with many partners—a denial of the sexual boredom of much monogamy; while Jay and Sacha were making a political statement that—for Sacha, at any rate—had less to do with sex than with other facets of the relationships between women and men. Jay and Sacha were troubled by jealousy too. Both were sure that what mattered were the feelings you had about yourself. If you felt jealous, that was because you were insecure in your feelings about yourself; and the task was to look inside and to "grow" in maturity through that self-exploration so that jealousy would be vanquished.

Jealousy was to be frowned on, too, because it was so closely linked to possession, which easily slips into exploitation—one partner exercising rights of possession over the other. Harry and Maisie cared about this too, but without identifying it as specifically a political concern:

> This is where the religious bit comes in . . . and all the other ideas we have. You see, neither of us have ever actually thought that anyone can ever *own* anybody else anyway. So you see, the whole idea of possessiveness— I don't just mean sexual possessiveness—I mean the idea you can have any rights over any other person, proprietorial rights of any kind, is alien to both of us.

And Maisie echoed him: "I think there are two forms of belonging. You can say you belong to someone without saying that they own you. Belonging is part of love in a way, but that is when you *choose* to belong."

Overtly political or not, the problem of possession underpins the emotion of jealousy, and these couples were living an alternative life style that attempted to avoid the pitfalls of ownership of bodies or souls. Indeed, they echo the issues raised in one month's special edition (in 1981) of a journal with the very name *Alternative Lifestyles*.[5] They echo, too, a general acknowledgment and understanding of jealousy as an expected if undesirable response to the loss of a loved person to another. Taking their cue from humanistic psychologies that emphasize personal growth, jealousy becomes an immature personal response.[6] The couples attempt, in fact, to deal with two strands I have already identified that have such long histories in Western culture: possession and the exclusivity of *love*. But they ignore the strength of culture.

In societies where different ideas have held sway about the meaning of sexual relationships outside marriage, the feeling of jealousy appears also to vary. An anthropologist, L. J. Henriques, has pointed out that, among the Marquesan islanders of the Pacific where extramarital sex is common, jealousy is met with ridicule; and among the Todas people of southern India, it is considered not only bad form to "begrudge" one's wife to another, but such begrudging will make it more difficult to enter the next world after death.[7] In a lengthy discussion of the meaning of a "group wife"—that is, one who is sexually available to men other than her husband, often other kin—and of the operation of the hospitality rule in certain tribes as among the Inuit people, the renowned anthropologist Lucy Mair has observed that such nonmonogamous relationships are primarily not for the provision of sexual variety and quantity for men, but for material advantage.[8] Nonetheless, whatever the function of these arrangements, jealousy may still be felt. Even among the Nuer, a Nilotic people of the Sudan where co-wives were permitted, adultery was frequent (that is, with someone not legitimately recognized as a wife), quarrels about it infrequent, and divorce rare (because it would be so expensive, the husband forfeiting his bride-wealth), there is one word—*nyak*—to describe *both* a co-wife *and* jealousy. Furthermore, although the lovers were not ashamed of their acts, they were "scared of being caught and risked being speared or clubbed or having to pay compensation to the husband."[9]

Lucy Mair also points out that the rules for the marriage partners (the rules not only of sexual conduct but about the proper forms of address, the preparation of food, and of dwelling) may be as much to prevent divisions between spouses—and, hence, in the family structure—as for reasons of property. In our culture, remarked Mair, "what holds it [the family] together now is sentiment rather than necessity and sentiment is weaker than necessity in restraining individual interests."[10] In this context, jealousy, as the *feeling* (or sentiment) that restrains, has—however destructive and powerful it may be—a very useful function. Hence, the feeling Mrs. Long, a study participant, expressed—knowing her lover must be having sex with his wife and fearing he might have other women, too—that "if you truly care for someone, I suppose you want to be exclusively theirs and they exclusively yours. I think that still counts nowadays."

While Harry and Maisie did not subscribe to the idea of *sexual* exclusivity, they shared one rule with couples in traditional marriages—an unwritten rule whose breaching, they said, *would* make them feel jealous. Thus, Christmas, birthdays, anniversaries, or St. Valentine's Day—days of special significance to them as individuals or of general symbolic importance—were to be spent together. When challenged about the ritual nature of this rule, they argued that their jealousy was comprehensible because, if one of them preferred to spend those days with someone else, their own love would be shown to be less central, and hence the marriage would be really threatened. To protect against this possibility, there was a further unwritten rule to tell: this time, however, the telling was to the *lover*—he or she must know "from the beginning that I was married and loved my husband very much and wanted to stay with him and had no intention whatever of leaving him and I would make it plain that Harry knew all about any other relationship I had."

Harry and Maisie claim a success in their marriage denied others trying similar experiments. They both feel that they have changed and "grown out of all recognition really" and are very, very happy. Above all, they "feel themselves":

HARRY: I am myself at last, you see, and that's marvelous.

MAISIE: "I think I am myself. I feel very privileged to have such a good relationship with myself. I think I understand the person I am and my capabilities and needs and where I am going and what I am doing very, very well and I feel lucky about that. I have grown enormously in the time I have known Harry."

Jay and Sacha were, on the other hand, not "themselves." They were insecure and struggling. In a discussion group, they were at loggerheads with another couple who attended the same group, a faithful and middle-class, middle-aged pair. The husband was an ex-army officer; and his wife, a marriage guidance counsellor and sex therapist. Both were quite clear that temptation was something they knew all about; and James, at any rate, found flirting delightful and would not be prepared to give it up. It was, however, quite harmless. To go beyond the flirtation to the bed would be to destroy the "trust" he and his wife had, which was so important to both of them.

"But I trust Jay," said Sacha softly. "I trust Jay. I trust him with my life."

It is not necessarily the name of the ingredient which differs. It is the meaning that name has."

Pacts and Agreements

While each of these couples had begun marriage with a commitment to lead their sexual lives free from the taboos normally associated with marriage, others came to such arrangements over time. Fanny and her husband, Dick, were married when they were very young because Fanny was pregnant. They married, despite the alternatives offered by Fanny's parents (both abortion and the "passing" of Fanny's baby as the parents') because it seemed the right thing to do and because they believed they were in love with one another. But sex was never good between them, and they were constantly worried about money and housing. Not that they ever quarreled about these things, and Fanny found Dick a most supportive and loving father. Later, as she and her children grew older, Fanny began to feel frustrated—but not because she was ignored or kept out of her husband's life; indeed, she worked with him in his business. When she fell for the most handsome man and the best player at her local sports club, Dick was beside himself ("eaten up," he said, and he lost a great deal of weight) with jealousy. Fanny left home, and the whole family was in a state of great distress. But they began to meet and to talk: "We talked and talked. Every weekend, we'd get in the

FIGURE 3.1

Spouses' Agreements and the Number of Adulterous Liaisons

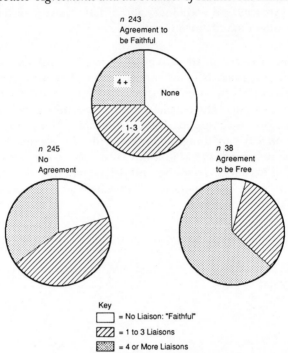

Key
= No Liaison: "Faithful"
= 1 to 3 Liaisons
= 4 or More Liaisons

car and drive to Southbay where we kept the boat. We'd park the car and take the dingy out and we'd not come in all weekend. And we talked. About anything. And everything." Fanny moved back home; and when I saw both her and Dick, they had, they said, a new agreement—one permitting each to pursue other relationships. They felt much happier and both had, in fact, subsequently had brief sexual affairs (though neither saw these as relationships of any importance, whereas Fanny's first liaison had been one "of the heart only" but centrally and profoundly important—after two hours of conversation in which I heard the drama unfold, she had announced, "Of course, I never slept with him . . ."). Alas, their newly discovered way of living did not last; and a year later, Fanny wrote to say (though without any explanation) that they were getting divorced.

I asked people in the study to say whether they felt they had any agreement about sexual fidelity with their spouses at the time they were first married; and if so, whether this was implicit or explicit, informal or written down, and what the agreement was. I then asked them to say whether this changed; and if it did so, in what direction. Many (both men and women) did not answer this question. Although they perhaps believed the answer "Yes, that they should be faithful," to be obvious, I have not assumed any *specific* agreement, especially since most people (59 percent of the sample, or 200 women and 134 men) did not discuss their feelings about extramarital relationships at the time of their (first) marriages. Over half the men (52 percent, or 117) and slightly more women (58 percent, or 197) said they did think they had a specific agreement with their husbands and wives at the time.[12] Of those who did consider they had an agreement—implicit, if not explicit—with their spouses when they married, most, not surprisingly, believed they should be sexually faithful; but some began with an agreement that they could be "free," and others came to this arrangement as time passed. A few began with an open arrangement and later became insistent on monogamy, generally as a result of unsuccessful affairs.

There was a clear relationship between belief and action: thus, even though there were many who "should" be "faithful" and were not, and some who could be "free" and remained monogamous, by far the most liaisons occurred among people who had agreed they could be "free," and the least among those who had agreed to remain "faithful" (see figure 3.1).[13] Since the people in the study themselves drew the distinction between fidelity and infidelity, and since this strong correlation holds, it seems unnecessary to continue to enclose the words *faithful* and *unfaithful* or *free* in quotation marks. Indeed, it is striking that even those who were "open" in their marriage still reported that they thought of themselves as "adulterers" or as having "committed adultery," albeit with less frequency than did those in the "closed" marriages. That is, half those couples examined in detail who were in closed marriages and who had at least one liaison described themselves this way, while 20 percent of those in the "open" marriages did so.

These figures support the idea that sexual relationships, in addition to a marriage or outside its boundaries, present people with conflict that they manage through beliefs that reduce anxiety and guilt. As one wife said: "Everyone has to find a way of managing their guilt. Either you do so or you stop the affair. You cannot continue unless you find a resolution to that." Thus, it is intriguing to examine any *change* in the agreements reached between spouses over time and to see whether they "fit" with the number of liaisons reported.

There has, since the time of their first marriages, been a considerable reduction overall in the numbers feeling they have an agreement to be sexually faithful (whether implicit or explicit) and a corresponding increase in the numbers granting each other freedom. The largest proportion of the non-adulterous is still found among those believing in sexual exclusivity; and the largest proportion of those having four or more liaisons, among those permitted them. Those who feel they have no particular agreement (265 people) are also those who are neither particularly adulterous nor particularly faithful. While there are people who show no exact "fit"—that is, who believe they may be free but choose not to have other sexual partners, and those who think they should be sexually faithful and who have not merely one but four or more liaisons—the *pattern* of fit with belief and

behavior is statistically very strong.[14] Of the seventy-five people who now
believe they may be free, half came to this decision over time. Perhaps the
fact each is permitting the other such freedom reduces the need to engage
with others, as Lee has already suggested (see page 95). And like Lee, the
writer Ingrid Bengis believed, for a brief period, that

> selective promiscuity was a means of resolving some of the conflicts of
> love. [But] the issue of multiple relationships is not a moral one: it is an
> emotional one . . . as well as a practical one. . . . Even if society was to
> declare that I was entitled to go fifty-fifty with a man on the number of
> love affairs we were allowed to indulge in simultaneously, I would never
> make use of my share. . . . because sex is a deeply revealing matter and I
> prefer not to reveal myself that much to that many people. [For some
> women the] only workable solution was to remain faithful themselves . . .
> and adapt to the diversity of attachments to which the men they loved
> were inclined.[15]

The fact both these examples are women is not, I think, coincidence. In
this as in every other study, women find multiple sexual partners more
difficult as a pattern to sustain than do men. This difficulty is seen in its
most extreme form in the attempt to live as an open marriage couple but
the fact that women who make no pretense of believing in sexual freedom
tend to have fewer sexual relationships than do men with similar attitudes
(as in this study where the majority of adulterous women had between one
and three liaisons, and the men four or more) allows the problem to be
interpreted as a more general one of women's sexuality and feeling. (To do
so by no means leads to a conclusion that this is a universal difference related to biological imperatives, for cultural experience is no "mere" surface
appearance. Centuries of history and years of daily learning, together with
the structural facts of marriage, child rearing, and work are robust enough
reasons for the profundity of these differences between women and men,
as I argued in chapter 1, pages 48–49.)

During the 1970s, the people who participated in this study were all exposed to considerable change, but some were more influenced than others,
and indeed, were more exposed than others. Thus, Justin and Edith, who
came together as an adulterous pair, both worked in the "media business,"
as did Justin's first wife. He reported ten liaisons during his first marriage,
the first within two weeks of his wedding. Although he had never intended
to be faithful to his wife, he expected her to be faithful to him. At one level
this is, of course, a traditional pattern, but it was an untraditional marriage
in that he, marrying at twenty-five, was much younger than his wife who had
already been married once and brought two children to this marriage. The
world of film and television, he said, is a world where considerable time is
spent apart from spouses and in intimate and creative contact with "intelligent and attractive" people. Justin also said that for him adultery had never

been a question of rational thought but of feeling: "Adultery wasn't a 'thinking' function: it was an intimate and feeling one. . . . A part of that is temperament, in that I'm incapable of casual fucking."

Given the number of his partners and the rapidity with which he began, after marriage, to have them, his view of himself as incapable of "casual fucking" sounds strange. Yet, for him, each liaison arose in situations (particularly at work) and with women for whom he had warm feelings; he regarded none as lacking serious meaning. Justin's last liaison was with Edith, his present wife, whom he met through their work. Only her husband had *not* played a part in this media world. Her attitude to sexual fidelity has not changed; a virgin when she married for the first time, sexual fidelity was necessary in that marriage and is necessary to her now. Her meeting with Justin was, as he said, "the love of their lives" and is the only affair she has ever had. Having been through a painful divorce during which many children suffered, they have now agreed to permit no other sexual relationships. They feel this would damage what they have together, which is immensely precious to both.

This couple was also influenced by much of literature, drama, and everyday conversation—so much so, in fact, that they could select little from it of particular importance; but many people, and especially those in open marriages, listed Nena and George O'Neill's book *Open Marriage* (1972) (although it does not deal explicitly with sexually open relationships, but concentrates on opening opportunities for other kinds of relationship outside a marriage) as having offered the kind of example and information they needed as a spur to exploration of other forms of marital contract and arrangements.[16] Feminist writers such as Germaine Greer and Betty Friedan were also commonly mentioned; but among the most frequently mentioned authors and sources were Marilyn French's *The Women's Room*,[17] all of D. H. Lawrence's novels and short stories, and both women's magazines and sex manuals or those magazines like *Forum* that enable people to make contacts that could be overtly sexual or offered the possibility of sexual contact. Women listed "women's authors" such as Margaret Drabble and Shere Hite, Fay Weldon (*Three Women*) and Rosamund Lehmann, as well as humanistic psychologists such as Carl Rogers; while men, sharing the women's feelings about the importance of D. H. Lawrence, listed more frequently Freud and Jung, Alvin Toffler's *The Third Wave* and *Future Shock*, Dostoevsky, and writers on sexual matters such as Havelock Ellis and Albert Ellis,[18] as well as the popular magazines and manuals.

Rarely did people consider their own behavior to be directly the result of early influence; but Justin believed that his own father's "philandering," despite the fact he had sworn never to follow this pattern in his life, had neurotically affected his own first marriage. Another husband, Peter, blamed his lack of understanding of women on his years in the traditional upper-middle- and upper-class British boarding school which, he felt, had

FIGURE 3.2

Importance of Religion to Respondents and Number of Adulterous Liaisons

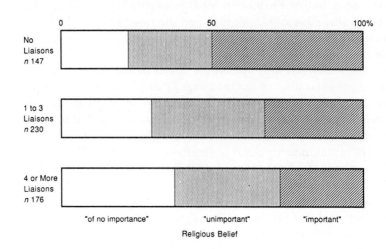

seriously undermined his emotional development, leaving him heavily defended against deep feeling and grossly "immature."

Peter's first marriage began without discussion of feelings about sexual fidelity but with an assumed code of Christian morality and a strong adherence to the Myth of Romantic Marriage. As the marriage began to feel increasingly empty of meaning for him, especially when the babies were small, he had sex with a prostitute and came away "in a haze of Somerset Maugham guilt"—conjuring a class-ridden image. His response was to alter the agreement he felt existed and to attempt to persuade his wife to permit more open arrangements precisely because he could not tolerate his own guilt and yet was satisfied that his "needs" constituted an imperative that had to be pursued, his scientific version of the Myth of Me. The new agreement did not permit the survival of the marriage because he fell in love with another partner and wanted to live with her. He had thought he could control the strength of any other relationship, that it would not threaten his marriage. He, like so many others, was wrong. The emotions are not within conscious control, and sexual bonds are difficult to alter, break, and resume. Leaving "spaces in your togetherness" and drinking from many cups, as the sage advises in the epigraph to this chapter, is not easy.[19]

If there is one message to be drawn from the analysis of how people make and change their contracts with one another, and how they breach them, it is that these arrangements are never static. Needs change, and so do the circumstances of people's lives. Today's contract may be tomorrow's waste paper—not because agreements are not taken seriously but because emotions demand action; and action in conflict with belief demands a change in the latter or, at a minimum, in the importance of that belief and hence of its salience in daily life. Religious belief provides a further way to examine the relationship between belief and action.

In the study sample as a whole, there was a clear and predictable shift away from a belief during childhood and young adulthood in some form of religion or guiding and organized belief system. Thus, only 8 percent of both women and men said they had been brought up without a belief, but 56 percent of men and 47 percent of women said that now they believed in "none" (see appendix A, questions 5 and 6; and appendix B, page 359, and notes 13–15, pages 407–8). Since all the Christian denominations, Judaism, and Islam forbid adultery, particularly of the woman, one would expect that those who wanted to reduce conflict between beliefs and actions would work at resolving such conflict in proportion to the importance to them of their religious belief. (Very few people—slightly over 6 percent—in this sample had been brought up as "humanists" or described themselves as belonging to any of the small sects that do not subscribe to the sexual-exclusivity rule of marriage.) This expectation was supported by the extremely close relationship found between the importance of religion in people's lives and the *number* of liaisons they reported,[20] whether a ten-year devoted affair or an hour or two with a prostitute. Those for whom religion was the most important are also those who remained most frequently faithful; and, vice versa, those for whom religion was of no importance were also those who had the most liaisons (see figure 3.2). Thus, of those who had no liaison, 50 percent said religion was important (or very important) to them; while of those who had four or more liaisons, religion was either of no importance at all or unimportant for nearly three quarters of them. Among people whose belief system was important, and had some or many liaisons, were the "open marriage" couples, along with a substantial number who had, in adult life, become atheists, or subscribed to no religious belief (221), and humanists (55). There were also people for whom religion was of no importance but who remained faithful.

It appears that, while the relationship between belief and action is extremely close, it is not perfect. There is a gap for some people between ideal and action; changing beliefs is one way to deal with the considerable pressures everyone entering a committed relationship must face. The faithful, however, are more likely to avoid dangerous action than dangerous belief.

4

Keeping Faith

QUESTION: A man stands on a river bank. Two women—one his wife, the other his mistress—are drowning. He can save only one. Which is it to be?
ANSWER: His mistress; his wife wouldn't understand.

—A riddle

Culture is best seen . . . as plans, recipes, rules, instructions (what computer engineers call "programs")—for the governing of behavior.

—Clifford Geertz, 1973

Mrs. Crowborough wrote that she never took part in surveys of any kind normally, but since "sociologists usually got it wrong" she wished to be included—to demonstrate that there were "ordinary middle-class, middle-aged, contented married couples still." When I visited her, Mr. Crowborough was also at home and joined in the interview. They lived in a not at all grand house in the country,¹ having recently moved there in preparation for Mr. Crowborough's retirement and in order to have somewhere smaller as their children began leaving home. Mrs. Crowborough's difficult and cantankerous father lived with them. The house was full of dogs, and the atmosphere was friendly. For a while, Mrs. Crowborough talked freely about her early life and about the way in which she and her husband had eloped when he was teaching art and she was barely out of school, aged seventeen:

My mother had unrealistic ideas about my future. We sort of lived in a private dream world where she saw me flaunting myself on the stage and my father had not bothered to think about anything at all. So I had catapulted myself away from home altogether by the age of seventeen. . . . This teacher at the school—art he taught—was just what I needed to take care of me and be bohemian and creative, perhaps like a real dream. I was very much taking my cue from him and was very happy to do so. I mean, he was rather sophisticated compared to any other man that I had ever known and very kind.

And Mr. Crowborough was responsive to her: "Having been brought up with a widowed mother, I think I probably got some certain insight into the feminine point of view."

> MRS. CROWBOROUGH: He was certainly very sympathetic to the way that a feminine mind worked; that I did know and could express.
> MR. CROWBOROUGH: You know, I am really proud [of the elopement]. We are both proud of it. You know, when you do something in the teeth of opposition and you can turn around and say, 'Well, it worked!' then you start to feel pleased. But it is a lousy way to start. You know, the lack of people's blessings and approval is miserable, really and truly.

The lack of any "proper wedding," she explained—both for religious reasons and because it meant they had few material possessions, no presents to provide the basis of necessary household requirements and comforts—had been a real disadvantage. Yet, the rebellion against a mother who held fantastic ideas and a father who held none, and the drama and romance of the elopement with this understanding and sophisticated man (clearly more desirable than her father), were important in a continuing way and perhaps met any need either might have felt to rebel and commit adultery now; it was a victory for young love. They both felt that a belief in "ethical" if not religious values was important, as Mrs. Crowborough said:

> I would have preferred a church wedding. I went on for years feeling that I would have preferred a church wedding. . . . I believe in God. I don't believe altogether in a lot of religion, I don't worship the Church. . . . [but] I mean, you know, as far as I'm concerned, marriage is once and for all and that is that.

Even if they did not now profess any particular religious faith, the faithful people in the sample were much more likely than the others to report that religion or some moral belief system played a part, often an important part, in their lives (see page 107). Mr. and Mrs. Crowborough were clearly no exception. "The whole idea of marriage was that the acid test was that if you went out with a girl, or if you were attracted to a girl, you said to yourself, do I want to spend the rest of my life with this one?" as he said. They had had their full share of troubles, including a "difficult" child with learning and school problems, little money, and an impossible mother-in-law (Mr.

Crowborough's mother), who muddled up their everyday lives and their inheritance, leading them into litigation against their own family. This had been emotionally a profoundly traumatic experience and was also extremely costly. Mrs. Crowborough felt under considerable pressure from the family rows, and the problems they were having with their child worried her.

Nor was she exempt from feelings similar to those expressed by people in open marriages who thought it centrally important to grow in maturity, to move outside the home, to find new aspects of the self, to join in the movement for self-discovery, and to be open and honest about everything. She also felt entitled, as the family was growing up, to pursue her own interests, to do something for herself. Mrs. Crowborough went back to college and took a course that included some psychology. She felt she had changed but only within clear limits. "I feel I have grown into a very different person and I have had to re-assess a lot of ideas . . . but there are certain basic essentials which are still as good as they were. They are unalterable." Nonetheless, her husband most certainly did not enjoy her venture into further education:

> I noticed that she started nearly all her sentences in the first-person singular—you know, "*I* am going to do this" and "So and so occurred to *me*," and so on. They were encouraged to do this on that course. . . . There was altogether too much "me." I used to hear plenty of "we," but not when she was at that college. It was all "I" and "me." Bad for her and bad for us. Very bad for the children.

Objectively speaking, Mrs. Crowborough clearly wished to expand her own horizons, explore undiscovered "intelligent life in there," as Mrs. Inkerman, another woman who felt constrained by everyone's heavy *dependence* on her, described it. This desire led Mrs. Crowborough to change in ways unacceptable to her husband, who controlled this development and forced her to give up her course. Yet she said she *did not mind*. Some might call this 'false consciousness,' but because Mrs. Crowborough shared her husband's point of view, she was not unhappy. Perhaps, too, because suffering and love are also so frequently tied together in a culture dominated by Christian ideas about the relationship of sacrifice and suffering to the gaining of great love, then Mrs. Crowborough may actually have gained from painfully giving up something *for* her husband, but she gave me no inkling that she had then or was now suffering from his dislike of her course. Indeed, she praised her husband and was grateful to him for having encouraged her to take a "part-time job"—his compromise offer. This compromise was offered as part of *his* determination of *her* life and as a result of *his* judgment of what was the right way for a mother to bring up *her* children (not *our* children). He also could not tolerate her new "knowingness": "If I said, 'why on earth didn't you ask me about something?' she would say, 'Oh well,' in a rather superior voice, 'I didn't ask you because I knew what your reaction was going to be.' " Mrs. Crowborough agreed this had happened: "If I ever thought I knew what the psychological process was that was going on in his mind—it was that which peeved him."

The crucial factor was Mrs. Crowborough's *acceptance* of her husband's point of view. His lead, his idea of the proper way for their life (rather than lives, perhaps) to be led was *shared* by his wife. By her compliance, Mrs. Crowborough differs from Mrs. Inkerman who also knew her husband detested her taking an academic course, but who took money from the housekeeping to buy books and read Plato in the lavatory rather than comply with her husband's terror of her self-advancement.

Mrs. Inkerman had, she wrote, "discovered autonomy at forty-one." "Tempted but not succumbed," she had been brought up, as she put it, in "a feminine household" so poor that she did not think they had "even achieved working-class status." By this she meant a family consisting of her mother and maternal grandmother "rocking" in the corner, her sister, brother, and herself, their father having abandoned them when Mrs. Inkerman was five. Always showing "guts," always needing and taking "just that wee bit of independence," Mrs. Inkerman had won but been unable (because of poverty) to take up a scholarship at the local grammar school. Indeed, she had spent two years "in care" away from home. Her mother wrote regularly to her; and, by the time she was sixteen, Mrs. Inkerman was earning two salaries and giving all her money to her mother, keeping nothing— not even enough to buy a pair of dancing shoes so that she could go with other young people to local dances.

She "lost her virginity" to a married man and decided she "had to get away. I think I always knew I deserved better somehow." She borrowed the money for a bus ticket and went to Scotland where she "felt it was like home" because she knew a grandfather came from there. She became a nurse and was engaged several times, including once to an upper-class young man training to be a doctor whose family she shocked by being unable to handle the silverware at dinner "properly." During this time, Mrs. Inkerman thought she was "very promiscuous" and seeking "to belong" and to enjoy sex. "I never had an orgasm until I married, you know. I think a lot of it was approval seeking, too." She chose a security officer to marry. Like Mrs. Crowborough, she could be dominated—that is, led—by him as well as protected and cared for: "He was so sure of his ground. He was so . . . now I see it as authoritarian and bigoted but at that time, he seemed to be just a tower of strength."

Even when her children were quite small, Mrs. Inkerman had always worked to help stretch the family finances. But, continuing her own family's practice, she never kept any of her earnings for herself; they all went to the housekeeping. Her family pressed on her:

> They all depend so much and I got a bit tired of this, so I started stepping outside the home a bit and discovered there is intelligent life in there

somewhere [because she was accepted on an extramural course at Aberdeen University], and I have had a wonderful time."

Again, like Mrs. Crowborough, she loves her course. Indeed, it is like a drug to her: "I am in a dream. Just now, during the holidays, I feel bereft. I am suffering from separation anxiety and withdrawal symptoms! I am lost without it. I did, I got lost the other day just at the end of our road and I've lived here fifteen years nearly!" But it is the ideas that Mrs. Inkerman loves. She is "turned on" by them, finding it all "terribly exciting," and, again like Mrs. Crowborough, has learnt to argue with her husband. Above all, Mrs. Inkerman knows she is somebody:

> Nobody ridicules you. Everything you say is listened to. Like I spent a whole hour saying 'Goth', you know and it wasn't until afterwards that someone told me it was 'Goethe'. I've learned I have a point—I am a part of society. What I have to say matters.

But Mr. Inkerman was terrified. He suspected that she was going to go in for "hanky-panky"; and, indeed, Mrs. Inkerman had been pursued by her "dishy sociology tutor." He wished she would give up the course, and she feels forced to lie about using money from the housekeeping to buy books and to accept her family's choice of television programs that did not interest her. Her husband wished he could just "board her up": "If he could board us up and keep us all inside, he would. But he realizes he can't do this to me."

Mrs. Inkerman has her own reasons—she called them "hangups"—for not having an affair:

> How do you take your 'all-in-one' off in front of a stranger? How do you put on your [slinky] underwear, kiss the children good-bye in the morning and spend the afternoon with your lover? Besides, semen do not feed the ego.

But it is less these considerations that keep her from actually having an affair and more her feeling that she does not really need one. She has a good sexual relationship with her husband ("he's a good lover and I always feel, you know, that an orgasm in the marital bed is worth any amount of fumbling around"), and she feels "not guilt—that has very little place in my life right now, but a sense of responsibility and compassion for my husband."

In addition, Mrs. Inkerman's needs for growth and change are being met by her educational course. Before the course, she asked herself, "Who the hell am I?" and felt she "had no identity. I was not anyone. If I lost my husband, my children, and my job, would I have had an identity? . . . *Now* I have so much identity, it's enough for ten!"

Where Mrs. Inkerman quietly rebelled, Mrs. Crowborough loved, honored, and obeyed. She admired her husband, and what he said she felt was right. When I put it to her that another woman, forced like her to give up her course, might have gone looking for another man, she said, "No. Never. No. Why? But he understands. When I'm dreadful, he understands." This remark sharpens the irony of the time-honored excuse of the married man to his potential mistress—that his wife does not "understand" him—and makes us wish we had not laughed (if we did) at the riddle that opens this chapter.[2]

"Understanding" is a shorthand way of describing a profound and valued intimacy that, for the Crowboroughs, came not from broadcasting feelings but from a capacity to share them with just one other person. Honesty was essential but only between the two of them; openness was essential but only to one another. Mr. and Mrs. Crowborough had a *private life* that was a central core to their relationship which could scarcely be approached by an outsider, never mind invaded. Early in the interview, Mrs. Crowborough had replied to my question whether they were happy "physically" together:

> I know it dates me, but it is a very important part of the fabric of this relationship. . . . it's private. If you want to know the sort of marriage I've got, one of the most essential things about this is that when it comes to intimate matters, Bob and I have always talked about them between the two of us, building this up to the point over the years where we can sort out things which are intimate and sexual and we have never discussed this with anybody else—not professionals, not family, not friends. It is ours and it is very private. *We* talk. We talk and talk and talk.

They seem to have been successful. As Mr. Crowborough observed:

> You know, a man must be generous [as a lover]. If he can be generous so can she; his rewards will be ten times greater than he imagined when he took that extra care. I feel sorry for the men I hear shouting their mouths off in the pub about the five or six women they've laid in the week. They don't know what they're missing.

Far from the openness of the couples who change the rules away from sexual exclusivity to open talk—not just to one another (though that is crucial) but to others such as potential lovers, too—this couple hold their intimacy close. With these comments—and, indeed, throughout the interview—Mrs. Crowborough and her husband demonstrate what Phyllis Rose has called the happiness of marriage based on *shared* "imaginative projections":[3] that is, on the fact that they *share the idea of their lives together*. *The couple shares a story*, even though a struggle for autonomy and independence has been abandoned.

Distinguishing the "Faithful"

The Crowboroughs felt they had a contented marriage and were faithful to their beliefs and to one another. They had found ways of managing difficulties that worked for them. They scored low on marital conflict (see note 21 to chapter 6, page 390, for this measure). But the faithful in general are distinguished not so much by the absence of conflict—that is, by a rough and ready measure of marital misery—as much as by their strong beliefs. Karen Horney has written about the "obsession" of fidelity, when unconscious sexual guilt for betraying the parents is concealed behind conventional prohibitions. For, she argues, marriage based on romantic love revives infantile wishes "to monopolize the father or mother."[4] Some did, indeed, seem obsessed in this way. It would have torn such couples apart to breach the fidelity rule. But for the most part, these people were strong believers in ideals that supported them and made their marriages more contented than otherwise they might have been. In other words, the marriage was "good enough," to use D. W. Winnicott's phrase,[5] not only because they were less troubled and happier, but because their way of life was integrated with their values. There is less need of compartmentalization, less need to keep things in clearly demarcated boxes, hidden from the Other.

Thus, it is not only that the faithful generally held more strongly to religious or ethical belief systems; they also emerge as strongly committed to the marriage vows and hence to the contract they have undertaken. They value the love they have, and think it can last with the appropriate input. The faithful are in significant disagreement with others in supporting the strong statements "When you are married, sexual relations outside of marriage are always wrong" and "True love is the only good reason for marriage." They believe problems can be solved if both partners work at it, and that marriage should last until the death of one of them. They do not agree that it is important to develop as an adult even if the marriage suffers, and they do believe that "in a good marriage all needs can be met within it." They also tend to think that if one spouse has an affair, the marriage is over.[6]

Even before the wedding, they faithful felt differently about marriage itself. Thus, they were relatively less sexually experienced and less likely to have lived together before marriage. Those that had done so felt it was a qualitatively different experience from the later marriage. Even when they had been divorced and married more than once, the faithful differed from their brothers and sisters in this respect, still feeling that "living together" is not equivalent to the marriage itself. Less than 10 percent of the non-adulterous but more than twice as many (over 20 percent) of the adulterous felt they were not "in love" when they married—a substantial difference; and they held attitudes in line with these feelings about sexual infidelity.[7] Because of these strong beliefs, more of the faithful also felt they had been "victims" of a spouse's adultery than did those who were themselves adulterous—a feeling, though, by no means limited to the faithful. Dramatic differences exist as well between these two groups in their feelings about the need to change and develop as a person even at the expense of the marriage. Under one third agreed and 38 percent disagreed with this idea among the faithful, but over 40 percent agreed and only one quarter disagreed if they had had four or more liaisons; in both instances, those reporting one to three liaisons held an intermediate position.

On the other hand, the faithful and those who had at least one liaison agreed that it is possible to stay in love for many years, and similar proportions of both groups thought it was "important to be true to oneself even if the marriage suffers," around 40 percent agreeing and 30 percent disagreeing at the time of first marriage.

As with the Crowboroughs and the Inkermans, it is not that the ideal of self-fulfillment is absent among the faithful but that it plays a less insistent role compared with other values, or is interpreted in other than sexual ways, or is more readily given up if the spouse requires it. (In fact, several wives related similar tales; but that there was no husband whose desires for growth were thwarted by his wife suggests that it is only the more powerful male, unaccustomed to sacrificing his own goals and outside commitments for his family, who can set this agenda.)[8] In other words, the faithful adhered more strongly to the Myth of Romantic Marriage and were less influenced by the Myth of Me, than were those who had had at least one adulterous liaison. Even the faithful, however, as the stories of Mrs. Crowborough and Mrs. Inkerman illustrate, are not *un*influenced by the Myth of Me; it exerts pressure and may be employed by faithful and unfaithful alike.

The Myth of Me

The Myth of Me is, as I pointed out in the introduction (see pages 25–26), a mythology in the same sense as is the Myth of Romantic Marriage. It is not false, it has profound consequences for the lives of individual women and men, it operates at a mass cultural level but is employed by particular people in their everyday reasoning and in their feelings about themselves; it is an adventure story, a way to live life in a purposeful way. Furthermore, this story begins *within* the Myth of Romantic Marriage but comes to compete with it. It offers an alternative dream and, in this sense, is one of the pressures exerted on the married.

The Myth of Me, like the Myth of Romantic Marriage, details how a person may become morally worthwhile. In this case, however, becoming a *good* human being is achieved by setting goals to explore all the talents that may be found within the self and by pursuing this self-fulfillment, here, within an allotted lifetime. This accomplishment is not dependent on finding an Other but is an accomplishment of the Self.[9] Nor are there any clear limits to the expansion of this self. The imagery is of mountain climbing, the peak is known as the pinnacle of self-actualization. Can more than one person stand (never mind, lie) on a pinnacle? *Tarquin* thought maybe two could, but not three. Certainly there is little in the literature that expects there to be regularly two within the program for self-actualization or that a goal of the program is to become committed as well as passionately involved with a specific Other.

Self-actualization was the last and the most difficult of the stages set out in 1968 by the acknowledged leader of the "human potential movement," Abraham Maslow, in his famous *Toward a Psychology of Being*.[10] Indeed, most would never achieve it. In other words, life, like the heroic journey, presents a series of trials to be accomplished with ever harder barriers to be overcome. However, unlike the old adulterous tale of love, there is no toxicity to this accomplishment. It seems safe enough to try, and there are no specific sex roles: the attempt may be made by both women and men. The endeavor does, nevertheless, entail risk.

In this growth concept of maturity, the mature person does not have to settle for any one particular, socially defined role. He, or she, is *entitled* to discover the real "me." In the search for maturity, both she and he are enjoined to seek out all possible routes to "self-actualization." Though Maslow did not spell this out himself, this search might lead to the forsaking of wife or husband and child in favor of the freedom to explore one's sexuality in new areas. If you have only limited sexual relationships, how can you know what your true potential for growth is? The potential is not something to be denied but to be courted and explored, for it is a denial of the self to ignore the profound expression of sexuality. Any risk lies in the possible giving up or loss of known relationships.

The idea that denial has no intrinsic moral worth, and that the pursuit of pleasure is legitimate, is a natural ally to the Myth of Me. And hedonism, like the ideal of personal growth, has also increasingly flourished. It, too, exerts pressure on the married.

Cultural Pressures

Hedonism—the grasping of pleasure because tomorrow may be too late—is no longer an unacceptable philosophy. Furthermore, ideas change about what pleasure is, and leave much room for hedonism to remain legitimate. Thus, now, people seek to be beautiful and fit, even though the necessary denial of food and insistence on exercise may be painful, in order to live longer and more fully in the interim. Hedonism flourishes where there is little belief in divine retribution or in the promise of better things to come. If there is no life after death, what is wrong with making the most of it here, on earth, in earthly pursuits? There has, in the Western world, been a considerable drift away from formal religious beliefs that emphasized life after death, that taught the avoidance of earthly pleasures, especially pleasures of the flesh, for the greater gain of that ecstasy which could be obtained only after suffering and after death. In my sample those who were most adulterous were also, as we have seen, those for whom traditional religious belief was least important, though they might hold to other values extolling love of other humans and the importance of leading the good life here on earth.[11] Hedonism flourishes, too, where economic life is easy and money is relatively plentiful, for the pursuit of pleasure may (though not always does) cost money. Paradoxically, it also prevails when substantial numbers of people need to fill hours made empty by unemployment. The work ethic, linked to Protestantism and to capitalism,[12] is difficult to maintain when so many have no work, or when so many are "enjoying" retirement after a long life at work. Leisure time is growing and with it, the idea that pleasure may, legitimately, be sought. Indeed, Marilyn French, author of *The Women's Room*, the most influential book for the women in this study, has recently, in *Beyond Power*, appealed for the goal of power to be set aside so that pleasure may be the most valued experience in the world.[13]

The idea that one who chooses to pursue pleasure is a mature and well-adjusted person who is, quite properly, expanding the boundaries of the self, learning and growing throughout adulthood, has received substantial institutionalized support from psychology. This support extends through the many counseling services and therapies which attempt to apply psychological theories to the miseries and everyday problems of ordinary people, and beyond to social work and advice bureaus, to television and radio talk shows and phone-ins. Hedonism is, thus, part of the fertile environment that has sustained the ideal of personal growth thrust forward as an appealing mythology by psychology.

Barbara Ehrenreich, in her *Hearts of Men*, traced the effects of the "Human Potential Movement" on American men, claiming that it gave them justification for their "flight from commitment."[14] In the past, men believed they had a responsibility to protect and provide for their wives and children; and, according to much research, it is this fact that has provided the emotional strength of feeling among men for their families. Mothers provided daily nurturance and, in the doing of those tasks, loved; fathers provided the means and the shelter for those tasks and, in so doing, loved.[15] But the new psychologies have exhorted them to pursue their own needs for self-actualization, even if that means abandoning these commitments to others. In a time of massive growth in consumption (mirroring the expansion of self that was promised and sought), the goods offered by the movement were to be bought and taken in whatever the cost to existing ties and human relationships. This is how Ehrenreich describes it:

> Everyone was a potential candidate for growth, and everyone was a potential winner in the therapies, encounters, exercises and guided experiences that offered, not the painful introspection of classical psychoanalysis, but "joy and more joy." It helped that the Human Potential Movement, with its emphasis on spontaneity and the goodness of impulses, echoed the hedonistic message of the consumer culture. What was no less important to its success, the new psychology offered its own cri-

tique of the consumer culture: It was right to want "something more out of life," and that "something more" could itself be purchased as one of many commoditized therapeutic experiences, including, by the late sixties, Gestalt therapy, nude therapy, encounter groups, primal scream therapy and transactional analysis, plus their combinations and improved versions. At its peak, as Joel Kovel (1976) has written, the new psychology [the "Maslovian Revolution"] was both an industry and a kind of secular religion, enlisting hundreds of thousands of middle-class Americans in the project of self-improvement through psychological growth.[16]

Even as these new psychologies were spreading the word of the importance of the self, the women's movement was gathering momentum. If men could legitimately pursue the self and its pleasures, and, in so doing, abandon their commitment to their families, what of women who have always been prepared to sacrifice self-interest to that of their family members? For women, the strong backing of a movement determined that they should be freed from shackles not experienced by men, and from being enclosed in the private and excluded from the public domain, has been a necessary concomitant to their sense of an entitlement to explore the self. Women have attained their sense of who they are first from their fathers (daughter of a doctor, a railwayman, a manager) and then from their husbands (Mrs. Jack Smith, a goldsmith's wife). Social class, for example, is still determined for women according not to their own educational or occupational achievements and skills, but to those of the significant men in their lives. Such a public approach to resolving who a woman is reflects in a profound way on her inner sense of self. It is scarcely surprising, therefore, that women, given the support of feminism, have responded strongly to the message of the new psychologies, particularly as women work outside the home in increasing numbers and feel themselves to "be" something other than and in addition to the daughters and wives and mothers of men. Now, it seems to me, and certainly in this sample, the Myth of Me is of greater importance for women than for men, whose freedom to explore themselves and the world has always been greater.

Of course, it *need* not follow that therapy encourages egotism rather than altruism, the pursuit of self *at the expense* of others rather than in relation to others. Earlier in her book, Ehrenreich details the differences between the approaches of various theories of psychology, arguing that only this late movement had these effects, for psychoanalysis and the derivative ego psychologies, developed by (among others) Erich Fromm, Erik Erikson, and Heinz Hartmann,[17] required painful introspection and internal adaptation between competing aspects of the unconscious or between the self and the outside world. Even Lise and Michael Wallach—who suggested in the very title of their book, *Psychology's Sanction for Selfishness*,[18] that *all* psychology was to blame for its insistence on the priority of the self over relations with others, for egotism as opposed to altruism—did not consider this the inevitable or logical result of psychology's teaching. Similarly, Cancian points out that therapy *need* not lead to a lack of connection and relatedness to others, especially since what one learns has essentially to do with feelings about an Other—in this case, the ever welcoming and uncritical therapist.[19] The trouble is that in the real world, beyond the therapist's consulting room, others are not always uncritical or accepting; demands are made, and the relationship has constantly to be negotiated and renegotiated. The paradox seems to be that, in the attempt to learn about the self and to heal the self, often undertaken because there is a sense of failure in the capacity to relate in profound and meaningful ways to others, a greater isolation and superficiality to relationships may nonetheless result. This may be the surface appearance or something more profound, but it arises where the demand for talk is so insistent.

An essential ingredient to any therapy is talk. The prerequisite for these therapeutic groups and encounters is that patients and clients *tell*, that they delve into the recesses of their minds and hearts and express what they find—both anger and love, despair and joy—something I explore further in chapter 8. Any emotion is appropriate in the consulting room and essential to treatment. When picked up and developed into a rule for all *normal* relationships between people wherever they are, it may be called the rule of "psychobabble."[20] In saying, "I know it dates me" about her unwillingness to discuss "sexual and intimate" matters with anyone other than her husband, Mrs. Crowborough indicated awareness of the pressures to *communicate*, even when it seems inappropriate to speak.

In fact, the Crowboroughs appeared to share a belief in the need for reticence and discretion. The feeling was that certain things are better left *unsaid* except in carefully defined circumstances and to strictly defined persons—in fact, only to someone fit to receive such confidences: each other. Yet they did not rebel against the idea of communication between one another. Mrs. Crowborough also explained that the usual place for such confidences was the bed; and the usual time, the small hours of the night. Privacy in place, in time, and in person was necessary to them, and organized by them. The relatively new pattern that stresses the need to "talk" indiscriminately, and continuously to articulate feelings, seems to deny the strength of the feeling itself.[21] In this pattern, Mr. and Mrs. Crowborough reflect their own generation's preference, as well as that of the faithful generally, for discretion and for keeping all discussion of intimate matters to intimates. On the other hand, that same generation (those who married before 1960) barely discussed anything with anybody.[22]

Again, it is not that communication is unimportant, only that it has taken on the status of a general panacea. Where once the advice might have been, "Have a good cry dear," it is now, "Talk it over and all will be well." No less on the factory floor, where poor communication between workers and management is as likely to be blamed as low pay or disagreeable working conditions, as between married couples or in the schoolroom.[23] Instead of analyzing the power imbalances within those relationships, the daily struggle, and the poor rewards that gnaw away at self-esteem and *lead* to the therapist or counselor, the solution offered is better communication. Indeed, Mr. Crowborough complained that with his wife's new ability and readiness to say "I" and "me" more often and in her new "knowingness"—all examples of his loss of control over her—the "communication had taken another knock." As Phyllis Rose explains, love (or good communication) is often used to cover imbalances in power.[24]

Perhaps this belief in the efficacy of talk and the Myth of Me itself is peculiar to the middle class. Perhaps, also, the pursuit of selfhood is a luxury affordable only once people are warm and sheltered, there is bread and meat on the table, and anxieties center on the rate of pay, not on whether any money is coming in at all. (It is a particular disaster when people, facing concrete problems of poverty or legal tangles, are urged to "talk things through"; such problems, of course, require articulation, and one may find relief in talking about them, but talk will not solve them.) But such considerations do not make unimportant either talk or the Myth of Me. The middle class are the media managers and opinion makers.[25] Furthermore, popular culture has rapidly picked up both the myth and the related themes—self-expression in both talk and sexual relations. The advice columns of women's magazines in particular encourage the exploration of the self, even if this is "self-ish," and constantly advise their readers to bring problems out in the open and to talk things through.[26] The Myth of Me is pervasive in the American context and easily spotted; in the United Kingdom, the roots of the advice given are simply less open and less clear.

Recent plays, too, have begun to place working-class families in dilemmas that focus on the woman's right to self-fulfillment, and to encourage her resolution of problems through communication. In England, recently, a television play showed two friends who were truck drivers, each unwittingly trying to have an affair with the other's wife. In this world, the women do not know their husband's mates nor, of course, one another.[27] The husbands need no permission to go out, to go away, or, indeed, to have other women. These two women take matters into their own hands; and each, in her husband's absence, gets dressed up and goes out because she feels *entitled* to do so. Each says to her would-be lover, when he discovers she is married: "Well, you're married too, aren't you?"

Several films have also illustrated the myth, some commenting through a sardonic smile, on its possible toxicity, such as *Bob and Carole, Ted and Alice*, first shown in 1969, where a couple go for a weekend to "The Institute" (Esalen) and learn to express their true *feelings* all the time about everybody and everything. Doing this, they understand, leads to growth. It also leads to "affairs" ("Well, perhaps affair isn't the right word—just sex—purely a physical thing," one of them says, which must be "confessed") and to joy in the "gift of sharing" rather than to misery because of the despair of jealousy. It leads Alice, the unfaithful wife, to encourage her faithful husband, Bob, to experience fully every moment of his "six-second" existence on earth by having his own sexual escapade. It also leads the four of them to attempt an incestuous (because they are intimate, loving friends) "orgy" (their word) in Las Vegas. Carole, the only one not to get high on pot and *not* to have "purely physical" sex, goes into psychotherapy: that is, she it is who becomes the sick one of the four, the one who now needs to deal with her problems in growing, through talk.

Other (later) films, like *Kramer v. Kramer*, make an attempt to understand the mythology, perhaps even suggesting that people should pursue it.

On radio "phone-ins" and the like, and transported across the Atlantic Ocean to England, the message still seems to be that all problems can be and should be resolved through talking to, or, in line with the "good communication" principle, talking *with*, others. Furthermore, no subject, it seems, is unsuitable for airing in public. Anyone may telephone and ask for help with the most intimate problem, even giving their first names and where they live. Anonymity is preserved, it seems, by the withholding of the last name and the full address. People seem to believe they cannot be recognized by their voices: a person, to be known, needs to be *seen*. In these circumstances, "Ann from London" telephoned a popular, weekly program dealing with personal relationships, broadcast at six-thirty in the evening, to ask what she should do about the fact that, every time she became excited in intercourse with her boyfriend, she wet the bed. The problem was explored in the minutest detail—from changing the sheets to techniques of love making and feelings about the normal and the abnormal. The boundaries between what is suitable for the public arena and what for the private are elastic in the extreme.

That people will seek help in this way indicates a profound unmet need within their own circles, something that the Crowboroughs clearly did not feel: but this practice also could flourish only in a society that places the rights of the individual over the needs of the collective, for at least at one level, it disregards the audience. It is as if two people only are speaking when four million are listening and, in that way, participating. It is this climate and this strong emphasis on separateness of selves that has enabled the Myth of Me to flourish.

The idea of personhood, of separate individuals, has often been liberating. It is in its extreme version (as in the abortion case when the fetus may be identified as a separate subject of the state, suitable for court deliberation and action) that the idea becomes doctrine; and doctrine, dogma. A separation of selves together with a proliferation of rights accruing to individuals rests in turn on a certain mode of thinking, one that perceives separateness as prior and connectedness as occurring through the meetings of separate bodies, and one requiring increased specification, factorization, and reductionism. Although this is the mode of science, it is by no means limited to the world of science but is reflected in all our institutions and workplaces. It encourages each individual to perceive himself or herself as *entitled* to something, though it is by no means always clear to what. Thus, the self is *entitled* to development separately from any other individual, and regardless of that other individual's parallel need for self-development. The concept of the self that arises in this search ignores the fact that the self or the whole person is unimaginable without understanding that it is *created* through interaction, through the playing of different and complex social roles, through taking on responsibilities, engaging in commitments and changing these as life progresses.

A strange image of what a "self" may be comes to mind: each self is a spinning top occasionally bumping up against another, sometimes knocked off course, sometimes momentarily slowed, occasionally spinning in unison with another, but usually spinning off again, the course altered but not fundamentally affected by the bump. Then sometimes the tops crash, or one top stops. Yet the Myth of Me appeals to people as if they really could dance or spin through life in such a way, achieving the pinnacle of self-actualization by bumping up against others without being fundamentally diverted from the upward climb. It appeals to women who have been unable to spin at all, kept in check by duty and by the power of others to control them. It appeals to men as it releases them from obligations to institutions and organizations unresponsive to their needs and feelings and from the sense that they owe support to the wives who care for them and their children.

Women as mothers and as wives have, to date, always been prepared to sacrifice this self-interest in favor of the needy and dependent infant or child and in devotion to husbands and other relations. Thus when they now search for a sense of self no longer rooted in the daily business of nurturing family members, where *connectedness* is the keynote, but in worlds of work where different relations operate and where it may be of critical importance to retain a firm sense of separateness, their actions are perceived by others, and experienced by the women themselves, as more *selfish* than are those of men.[28] Not, of course, that these actions are more selfish, or even selfish at all; only they appear so and feel so. This evaluation makes a decision to "do something for *me*" fraught with greater conflict for women. Hence, perhaps, the particular salience of the Myth of Me for women in this study.

If both partners to a marriage are contributing to it financially—even though the pattern of women's employment is discontinuous,[29] inequality becomes more difficult to maintain. However, there has been, as I have pointed out (see pages 85–87), only slight movement in the sharing of traditional women's roles within the home. That is, while women are doing men's jobs, men are not doing women's. Women simply take on more.

Still, the fact that more women now work for more of their lives than women did in the recent past and that they do this by combining paid work and domestic work has meant that expectations about women's roles have changed.[30] Expectations about women's roles do not result in changes in practice unless there is a concomitant change in expectations about men's roles. We do not know at present what it is to be a "proper woman" or a "proper man," and hence cannot know what it is to be a "proper wife" or "proper husband." Rather, women moving in men's worlds must be like men although there seem few parallel changes for men. The woman in management, politics, or the professions tends to dress in gray, black, or navy two-piece suits, worn with shirts; and she often has, if not a tie, a bow at her neck, since, in taking her place in the world of men, she must minimize the fact she is a woman. A scientist working in a large corporation told me that she has two complete wardrobes. The clothes she wears for work (dark and undistinguished) she hopes disguise the fact she has any sexual identity at all. Her out-of-work clothes permit her "true self"—that is, her sexual self—to emerge and make claims on her companions.

It is to such other values, other ways of thinking and behaving, that Mr. Crowborough and Mr. Inkerman fear they will lose their wives. And, indeed, the wives of other men have gone out into worlds beyond home.

The World Beyond Home

"She's not the woman I married." "He's changed. I don't love the man he's become. I loved him as he was." These common cries are particularly well illustrated by Audrey and Ian, who were married when she was twenty-five and he was thirty-five. As a bachelor, Ian had always had at least one girl-friend and now suddenly, the week before his wedding, and despite the strong love he felt for his bride-to-be, he became passionately and sexually involved with her sister, who had come to stay with them before the wedding.[31] On their honeymoon, when questioned by his wife, Ian told her of this affair. "Being straight and honest," was, he believed, essential to any marriage. Audrey now, some fifteen years later, said she was profoundly shocked, feeling the affair must have meant he did not really love her. Yet she did not at the time react strongly. Now she says that was because she was so afraid of losing him.

> I mean, this is my picture of the marriage. At the beginning I was totally wrapped up in Ian and the marriage and I had to hang onto it. . . . Faced, right at the beginning, with the possibility that it might just blow up straight away, because of his relationship with my sister, [I thought], 'I have got to hold onto this. I can't have this marriage busted up right away and be separated from Ian.' . . . It was Ian I was looking after—and me, our relationship, and I was doing everything in my power to keep it together.

Ian said:

> I thought her cool reaction meant she didn't really care. I thought it
> showed she didn't really care about me and that it left me free to go on
> having sex with other women. She never seemed that interested in "that
> side" of our relationship anyway. I mean, I felt very sure that I would not
> be totally sexually faithful, and we discussed that before we got married.
> I think I just assumed Audrey would be, because of the way she was.

As Audrey came through the stage of having and then caring for two little
girls and running their apartment and then their family house in an area of
London that was becoming increasingly gentrified—and as she approached
her fortieth birthday—she began to feel she was missing out on life. She
felt entitled to "grow":

> I packed a whole lot of things into the year I was coming up to forty. I
> flew for the first time. I did a lot of things for the first time. I had a hair
> perm for the first time. But this was right at the beginning of the year
> that I set off the situation for committing adultery for the first time after
> thirteen years of marriage.

She fell in love, like a teenager, from afar, with a television "personality."
He appeared on the screen; she adored. But then she met him and he prop-
ositioned her. She went home to her husband and told him what had happened. He told her to go ahead. After all, he had had many affairs; she was
entitled to hers. It would do her good. Might wake her up sexually. Might
be good for them together.

As it turned out, when she had the affair, Ian was profoundly jealous. He
felt destroyed by this act of his wife's. Even worse, he could not really express his anger because, after all, he had encouraged her, and his own behavior scarcely entitled him to such feelings. He was completely confused
by the changes in her:

> I don't recognize her. There is a sort of central core of a person that
> is the person I know and this person isn't. She is really fundamentally
> unpredictable. There are things outside of that that *can* change. New in-
> terests can develop, opinions can change and all sorts of things but the
> central core of that person is there. I don't see how you can live with
> someone in the world of things unless you can go on the assumption that
> you have got a central core of certainty.

Unlike Mrs. Crowborough but somewhat like Mrs. Inkerman, Audrey—
although she did not much enjoy her relationship with the television perfor-
mer—was delighted with the changes in herself and was unprepared to halt:
"I do not know what I am going to think or feel tomorrow, next week or in

two months time, because I am changing all the time and I do not intend to stop."

As Ian and Audrey experienced it, their marriage (which both saw as having always suffered from problems, particularly problems of "communication") had not changed; their ground rules were the same. Ian had thought he could be daring and generous with his wife's life, but now found his security fundamentally shattered. He seemed terrified by the actual loss (of his sense of knowing he had a firm base from which to conduct his life) and by the potential loss of Audrey's moving further and further away, perhaps even leaving the marriage altogether. He suffered from a gross sense of betrayal and unmanageable uncertainty. Audrey's pursuit of her own development and her awareness of her potential and capacity for new experiences, new thoughts, and new relationships *outside* the boundaries of the marriage, together with real changes in her personality, led to confusion for her but also joy.

Ian, we might say, was not entitled to be free with his wife's life; it was not in his gift. His intellect was not in sympathy with his feelings; jealousy raged even as he saw no reason for it. He did not *think* he should control his wife, but felt that he had done so, that now he no longer did, and that he did not even know her. She barely knew herself but she knew she was feeling better than she had done for a long time, perhaps forever. What she had done was to say, "Enough. It's my turn to fly."

Where Ian and Audrey exemplify the contradictory and painful operation of the Myth of Me in both partners to a marriage, the story of Fanny (whose words first appeared as an epigraph on page 21) most clearly exemplifies it for an individual. In the early days of their marriage Fanny had worked with her husband, Dick, but could not once her children were born and needed more of her time. She had recently returned to work and had taken a job as an office manager. She had left school with "ordinary" but not "advanced" scholastic achievement, while her husband was less well educated than she.

Then she had awakened one day, looked at herself in the mirror, and said:

My God, look at me. I'm thirty-five. I remember consciously thinking, "I am thirty-five—that's halfway to threescore years and ten. What have you done with your life? I've got teenage kids. I've been married seventeen years. There must be more to life than this." I wasn't thinking particularly in terms of I wanted to get involved with another man. It was more "What have I done so far? What have I achieved?" I think I was very much aware of being my parents' daughter, my husband's wife, my children's mother, but who was I? There must be more in it, I felt, for *me*.

Fanny went off to her local sports club and fell in love with the best player, a married man, escaping from another affair in another town. There followed distress and considerable turmoil for everyone in the family.

But change, as we have already seen with Mrs. Crowborough and Mrs. Inkerman, is not always followed by an affair. Mrs. Waterford, thirty-nine, also married very young and has four adopted children; she became bored with playing the "little wife-and-mother." Her husband was a professional man with a university degree, but she left school when she was seventeen and trained as a nursery nurse. She was firmly committed to the Myth of Romantic Marriage, (indeed, her words provide the epigraph for the section "Love and Marriage," page 66) having, as she said, "promised herself" to her husband at the age of fourteen, and was "honestly in love with him— really adored him" when they married: "I really wanted God's blessing in the romantic way you do. . . . The whole idea was to marry and have lots of children. We both loved children and it was all going to be so lovely, wasn't it?"

Mrs. Waterford, a virgin when they married, came to wish she had had more boyfriends:

I bitterly regret really that he was really my only boyfriend. He's a very jealous man, and the only arguments we really had and still really have is because he says I flirt. Hmm . . . I think I naturally like people. I'm interested in people, and I honestly think that's as far as it is. I have no wish to leap into bed with the next guy down the road or something. . . . at the end of my life I'll think, "Well, what a shallow life it's been" [having only the one boyfriend].

However she might play with the idea of having another sexual relationship, she was not quite prepared to do so—partly because her husband was so jealous,[32] and partly because she and her husband had a good sexual relationship.

Mrs. Waterford described how efficient and competent she had become. When they married, she said she lacked any self-confidence. She described herself then as being dependent on her husband in a clinging and tearfully incompetent way: a " 'yes dear, no dear' housewife." Now she no longer needed to be so dependent. Indeed she felt she had "grown up" and away from her husband. Instead of a relationship between superior and subordinate, she wanted a relationship between equals—not because she no longer loved him or he, her, but because she had changed and wanted to go on changing. She was determined to take a job. He was trying as hard as he could to stop her from doing so. Their conflict was not resolved but was regulated through the avoidance of the topic. This couple is, indeed, a good example of "regulated conflict," as described by John Scanzoni.[33]

She wanted a more egalitarian relationship to develop; she has become what I think is well described as a *home-grown executive*, talented at administration and certain of her own capacity. When she married, she believed only in her capacity to care for small children. Hence her work as a nursery nurse. She found she was infertile. The damage to her idea of herself as a woman was profound. But the adoptions worked well, and now she knows her own value. She does not need a sexual relationship to gain a new sense of "being fully a woman"—something Fanny missed—but does need less security and greater freedom.

Janet Askham writes of the continual conflict as the spouses within a marriage seek constant reassurance of their sense of identity in their relationship with one another and attempt to combine this need with that for stability within the marriage.[34] She based her work on an idea first set out by Peter Berger and Hansfried Kellner, who argued that a sense of identity is nurtured by constant recognition from significant others—particularly within a marriage.[35] Askham sees that identity is not a static and unchanging, but a developing quality; hence, others outside the marriage are also required to relate in such significant and intimate ways. Both Fanny and Mrs. Waterford have a new sense of their own identities derived in part from their relationships to their children, and some awareness of their effectiveness as home-grown executives, but they need affirmation which is not, it seems, available to them from their husbands; and that, in any event, they might still require from others. They seek to discover this beyond the boundaries of the marriage; Fanny, through her sports club and, hence, through her lover; and Mrs. Waterford, through work.

The feeling that growth did not occur simultaneously or in the same direction was voiced by men, too, but men's sense of their own effectiveness has nothing to do with home-growth. Rather, they have "grown up" independently of running a household. Francis said:

> I now think that when I married I was looking for someone to look after me—mother me, if you like. At the same time, maybe I wanted her to be dependent on me—my little sister perhaps. Now I absolutely don't need any of that. I've grown up. I want a wife and lover but I think she still wants us to be as we were.

Francis began by having sex with someone when he was on a brief holiday coupled with a business trip. In the years that followed, he had two serious affairs during which he left his wife. (See also the story of Jack in chapter 5, pages 155–57.)

Each of these people responded to change in themselves, and between themselves and their spouses, with ambivalence and difficulty. None was prepared to give up personal development, although each did feel that various routes were possible. Each marriage had its good and its bad aspects from the point of view of each speaker. While it might, therefore, be fair to say that the first liaison arises from fertile ground, that does not imply that the ground is a great bog of misery and wretchedness. Rather, individuals do not stop developing at the wedding ceremony and women as a group seem both to change more and to desire more change than do men. Nor is it simply that they lack work outside the home, for some kept working all along while others did not. Rather, as home-grown executives, women are becoming increasingly aware of their abilities and of their undervalued potentials simultaneously, it seems, as the scales fall from their eyes; and the men who both protected them and kept them in, appear less admirable. At the same time, women continue to desire men who are strong and capable but also prepared to show vulnerability.

Only by taking account of this desire can we understand a woman willingly giving up on her own deeply felt needs and on her strengths, to please her husband, for it is hard to tolerate Mr. Crowborough's attitude when it seems that women need to begin to say 'I' and 'me' a great deal *more* often, to attend courses and not give them up on their husbands' say-so.

Indeed, this was the cry of both faithful and unfaithful wives. Here is Mrs. Long, a beautiful woman from Scotland, who desired "dominant," strong men but recognized that "unfortunately . . . I have become more dominant" while her husband "has become less so":

> I would love him to take charge, I really would. I mean I think that when I married him when I was sixteen I can see now that to me he was a dominant character—he was successful in business. He was his own man, sort of thing and I like successful men; I like clever men who are used to getting their own way. . . . It was not that he slipped down at all, but he had no further to go probably in his development, whereas I wasn't to know that I had. . . .
>
> I hate, I really detest that terrible phrase "your pride of possession" yet I know there is this pride of possession sort of thing when he takes me out and men flock round and ask me to dance and I would love it if he were to turn round and say, "Don't you dare!" I don't want to be a possession but I would think that perhaps if he really cared—he does care for me, but I mean sexually as well—he wouldn't particularly want me to have to say to them, "would you mind unhanding me, sir." I was blazing because my husband had walked away [at a dance where various men overzealously pursued her] and left me to cope with the situation.

Mrs. Long did eventually have an affair with a man who could "do anything," and was everything she desired as a lover, and was planning to leave her husband, though not *for* her lover, who was "safely" married. The lack of equilibrium she felt within herself was not buttressed by a powerfully sexually satisfying marriage. Rather, she was held in her marriage by her fear of losing her children whom she was convinced her husband would not let her keep, her anxiety about doing something "which is basically wrong," and economic uncertainty. She re-created with her lover the relationship she felt she needed—one with a potent and successful man. In other words, because Mrs. Long did not share with her husband any longer the idea of how their marriage should be, she set out to live her "story"—the one she had in her mind—with her lover. (See Mrs. Long's further story in chapter 6, pages 170–72.)

Sophie, too, whose full story is told in the next chapter, had for some time experienced her husband as weak, an unequal partner in their marriage, as well as failing to meet her sexual needs. These women all illustrate a powerfully compelling line to the gender script for women—to be vulnerable and needy and to prefer a man who can be dominant. Dominant, but not domineering or autocratic: hence Mrs. Inkerman's distress as her husband's lack of growth makes him now seem bigoted and authoritarian where once he was a "tower of strength." Working or not, these women are competent: they have raised children and run houses. Their executive skills are undervalued as is much else about them. They undervalue themselves. The Myth of Me is like a lifeline for them, and they clearly often survive to breathe more freely and with much excitement and pleasure. Its unexpected toxicity for the marital relationship is, however, apparent.

There is, then, both a yawning gap between the faithful and the adulterous (within the traditional marriage) and, at the same time, no difference of much significance. A good sexual relationship is a cement, it seems, sweetening and making tolerable what appears intolerable to those without it. For men, passion in the marital bed may keep them from feeling they need or are entitled to dally elsewhere, even when they are successful and accomplished and might, given the historical pattern of parallel adultery for such men, pursue a variety of liaisons. For women, such passion may lead to further education rather than adultery. For both, even when much else is less than satisfying, and even when the call to the self to explore new pastures is strong, a good sexual relationship—coupled with the feeling that they still share a joint project together, that they can imagine a future together which is not too disparate—is likely to lead to contented continuity. Being a successful woman, whether measured by achievement in the outside world (as in Sophie's case in the next chapter) or, as in the cases of Mrs. Inkerman, Mrs. Waterford, and Mrs. Long, by an acknowledgment that they are home-grown executives, does not lessen the pull of the successful man, but it does shift the emphasis. It is a great deal more exciting to be desired by such a man than by one who is threatened by a women's own achievements and her capacity to be independent. These women seek to be able to be dependent *and* independent, to relate as equals, but to be "taken charge of," especially sexually—to be able to "Relax," as expressed by the pop group Frankie Goes to Hollywood.

BOOK II

THE LIAISON

The Debate

But as any young woman engaging in her first infidelity knows, being willing is not quite the same as being able.
—David Matza, 1969

I don't think sex has much to do with morals. It's more a compulsion—like murder.
—Alice Thomas Ellis, 1983

Women Debate

Sophie's Choice

Sophie knew the precise moment when she had decided to embark on her first liaison. Her husband was away. Her children were at school. The telephone rang, and the man who was to become her lover asked her out to lunch. Sophie had known Philip since she was small; she had kissed him when she was six, and had remained friends with him over the years. As she said, "I don't know if I would have done it if it hadn't been that particular person."

Sophie had been a powerful and independent young woman. When she first met her husband (whom she married in 1969), he had been the gentler, quieter, steadier person, earning an adequate but not very startling salary at his adequate but not very startling job as a manager in a medium-sized business. Sophie, at that time, "traveled all over the world" as a travel agent and had already held other senior positions. But when her children came along (in 1974 and 1976), she spent several years fitting in little bits and pieces of part-time work, using her artistic and organizational skills. Although Sophie said she had "never felt guilty—never," she had worried about the deceit involved and had certainly conducted a debate (albeit a rapid one) with herself as this man offered her the concrete opportunity for what she called her "adulterous relation . . . liaison." She saw this decision as critical in her life and described the relationship that followed as "this first, critical affair." This is how she spoke of this moment:

> The telephone rang and he asked me out to lunch. I pretended someone was at the door and for that minute and a half that you can keep someone hanging on the phone, that it must have taken me to work things out, I argued with myself. If our relationship—mine and Damien's [her husband]—had been good, then I don't suppose I would have gone ahead. But it wasn't. We went through a very good period when he was in therapy during and after his breakdown in 1977. We were in family therapy and we were talking about things, and we had the best period of our marriage in the first six months after he came out of hospital, but then it just tailed off as he was less involved in therapy and less able to put things into context, and a year after he had his breakdown I had to recognize that he hadn't really changed at all—that essentially he was just a bit better at covering it up.
>
> When I walked away from the telephone that day, I had a quick sort of negative and positive check list, and one of the positive things was that if I went ahead with this relationship, and if it turned out the way which I was sure that it would, it would bring something exciting into my life. It would offer potential emotional support, partly because I had known this person so long and it would possibly compensate for this very dependent relationship. I mean Damien was dependent on me, that dependent relationship that I had at home. It would give *me* someone to lean on. Because what was really getting to me about my marriage was the constant . . . I mean I felt like I was holding up this crumbling brick wall all the time.

Sophie explained that she needed for her first affair a man who was a powerful and successful lover. That first night, in bed at the hotel, he reminded her of the "assertive, dynamic, imaginative" (his words) person she had been "up to about two or three years after" her marriage. She went into this first affair, she said,

> as a housewife and mother. All right, I was doing some freelance art work so I wasn't totally immersed but I had a very low image at that time, you know. Here I was, trapped—kids, nappies, nursery schools, husband who wasn't what I wanted a husband to be, and I was sunk, you know, I was lumbered with it.

As a direct result of the reassurance she felt in bed and from listening to her lover's view of her, Sophie then did things. Like going off and taking "A" levels, and going off to college and, you know, training. I picked a career that would fit in with my commitments and went all out for it and got involved in political movements and, you know, life has really taken off since that point in all sorts of planes. That was such a fundamental conversation.

The imagery is clear. For Sophie, this liaison moved her from the heaviness of being "trapped," "sunk," and "lumbered"—under the control of others and firmly placed in two roles—wife and mother—to another world where she could be released. She would be "going off," and indeed she has "taken off," to a place where "commitments" were recognized but where she herself was "involved" in the real world—men's world of educational opportunity and politics.

At the time she went into this first liaison, she was not consciously using it as a means for transferring out of the marriage, but this new lover seems to have served unconsciously for her as a person who, like a bridge, enables the steps, faltering as they may be, away from total dependent security, to the risky external world which offers great opportunities but also dangers. D. W. Winnicott coined the term *transitional object* to describe the cuddly blanket, cloth, or teddy bear, the object to which the baby clings as security enabling him or her to begin to separate from the person to whom the baby is most closely bound—in Winnicott's imagery, the mother.[1] The transition between dependence and independence that is being negotiated by the toddler benefits from the use of these objects. John Fader, an English counselor, has employed this same idea to describe the changes in one marital partner who seeks to develop the self and cannot within the constraints of even a loving marital relationship where one spouse is dependent and unchanging and the other is growing.[2] In these conditions, the lover is the *transitional person* as Philip was for Sophie.

This critical, first affair seems to have enabled Sophie to separate herself from the institutional arrangement lacking emotional meaning which she felt her marriage had become. It did permit her to find a new independence at the same time as, paradoxically, it permitted her dependence. This did not occur by accident but by her choice. She chose a particular partner who permitted that particular long-term outcome. Now (four years and another four liaisons later) she was in the process of divorcing her husband—the last step that had to be negotiated to sever herself from what she experienced as empty and constraining. Yet she said that another part of her rapid deliberations when the telephone rang that day had included the anxious thought that she might be found out. That anxiety arose because the discovery of an affair would "jeopardize" her marriage. We had the following exchange:

SOPHIE: The first thought was that I would be found out—that was the immediate reaction and, "Can I get involved in this without being found out?" But it was centered around knowing that if I was found out (my husband was away at that time) that it would jeopardize the relationship at home and what would the effect on the children be if I jeopardized the relationship at home? . . . I went through all that and I decided that, no, I wouldn't be found out. I was cleverer than that and the relationship at home was so impoverished for it not to matter whether it came to an end. I would survive and the children would survive because children are amazingly resilient if they are handled in the right way, openly, and it was just too good a chance to miss. So I said, 'Yes' and went to lunch.

INTERVIEWER: So it was important for the children to be handled, as you say, openly, but equally important for your husband to be handled secretly—for him not to know?

SOPHIE: I wasn't financially independent at that time. Had I been financially independent, I think it would have taken me less time to make up my mind.

INTERVIEWER: So what you were risking was security?

SOPHIE: It was the roof over my head, yes. And the trauma of divorce. I mean it is twice as traumatic as I ever thought it was, you know.

Several things are going on here. First, Sophie's anxiety about "being found out" is not connected to any fear that she will lose her husband's trust or love, because that is no longer important to her. But her anxiety is connected to her need for a secure home in which her children are safe—both materially and emotionally. She appreciates that even if she no longer loves her husband, he might still love her or simply feel devastated for other reasons; and hence his reaction to her infidelity might well lead to divorce. She does not experience this liaison as "infidelity" on her part because the quality of her marriage is so "impoverished" (her word) that she does not feel she has anything to be faithful to. Sophie's words indicate her unconscious understanding that her unfaithfulness would conclude her relationship with her husband; her apparent continuing fidelity would permit the marriage to continue for her children.

Sophie was, however, committed to her small children. Because of her feelings for them, she had to stop and think about the possible involvement this lunch date offered her, but her commitment to them was to be dealt with, first, by her "cleverness" and, if that failed, by their "resilience" and her good "management." In other words, even the children were not seen as a *joint* project, something she and her husband shared still within the marriage.

It was characteristic of this study that people in interview rarely mentioned their children as playing any part in their deliberations or in their feelings about having or not having affairs. I learned that I had to raise the topic. When I did so, then I would hear about the distress of a possible separation: fathers worried about the potential loss of their children, recognizing that children usually stay with their mothers; mothers worried about financial security and about emotional loss for their children. But these were realistic and well-grounded[3] fears about a possible (but normally both unexpected and unwanted) breakup of the marriage. This they foresaw *might* happen if they became more deeply involved with the new partner than they intended, or, as in Sophie's case, if the reaction of the spouse on discovery of a liaison would require a break even if the emotions of the straying spouse were *not* deeply involved—a kind of formal recognition of breach of contract. These were rarely anxieties about the possible difficulties the children might experience simply because one of their parents was involved in a relationship with someone outside the family circle. Again, if (as was usually intended) this liaison remained emotionally superficial, this would seem a realistic attitude. Perhaps, as increasing numbers of married women work, at least part of the time, in paid employment away from home (as did over half the women in this sample at the time of interview), it seems more feasible to conduct such liaisons (just as it has always been for men) with less impact on the children.

In the questionnaire, people had to confront the issue by answering questions in three places about children. The first invited respondents both to cast their minds back to the time when they had contemplated their first liaison or had been tempted, and to consider the extent to which they would have agreed with the statement: "I would worry about hurting my children." Those who agreed were then asked whether this had been of importance in their decision whether to go ahead or not.[4] Just a little over one quarter (28 percent) agreed that they would have worried (or did worry as they contemplated a first liaison) about hurting their children at the time; but of these, only about one quarter of the men said that it had been important for them in their decision whether to go ahead (that is, 8 percent of the total sample of men). The women showed greater concern: of those who did agree that they worried about the children, about two thirds also said it had been an important consideration in their decision (that is still only 16 percent of the total sample of women).[5] Children were much more commonly mentioned as a worry and as having played an important part in the decision by those (both men and women) who did *not* go ahead: that is, worrying appears to have diverted them. Although the numbers are small, those young women who married in the 1970s were less worried about their children than were their predecessors who married before 1960 or during the 1960s (a mere 15 percent of the youngest—compared with nearly 40 percent—of the oldest women).[6] By contrast, the young men marrying in these years were worrying *more* about their children than did the men who married earlier and than women who married in the same period.

I do not think these findings indicate any less feeling for children among those women who married most recently. Rather, they may indicate that the capacity men have always had (and still demonstrate, the change for them over time being a trend rather than a significant difference) to "compartmentalize" their lives is now becoming something women can also do. That is, men have been able to separate the domestic from the public sphere and yet within the public to conduct another private life—to say quite comfortably, "But it has nothing to do with my children. This is my private life outside, away from home." Psychologically, women may have begun to internalize changing values that no longer decry (at least not so regularly and with such strength) women's efforts to lead both a life in work outside the home and to continue their responsibilities within it.[7] Not that there is no conflict in this situation—for the testimony of millions of women tells us the contrary; but those most accustomed to several images of themselves as "proper women," and not just to that which says "mother," are more capable of making decisions about an important and intimate area of their lives that is not *governed* by their roles as mothers. These are the youngest and most recently married who have been brought up under the umbrella of the women's movement and at a time of profound social changes in the place of women in society.

Sophie belongs in this group in that she did have several clear images of herself as a woman. Mother is one and, at the moment of decision, was the most important image of herself that might hold her back from the liaison. It did not, however, *govern* her decision. Other images—such as that of herself as "dynamic, assertive, and imaginative" and hence capable of becoming again a "proper worker"—pulled her out of the marriage and into the liaison.

The more liaisons people reported, the less the part played by their children in the decision and, if the children were considered to have played some role, the less important it felt to them (see appendix A, question 26). But it is not, of course, merely the *number* of liaisons that affected these attitudes. The more serious the relationship with the other man or woman, the greater the likelihood that children played an increasing role in the thinking of the involved parent. Again, however, it was mothers who became most concerned about their children as a liaison deepened in emotional significance: six to seven out of every ten women felt their children played a role of at least some importance, compared with only one to three of every ten men, varying according to the type of liaison.[8] Those who had "committed adultery" and had an "extramarital relationship" differed even more than those who had had a "serious affair" or a "relationship." In the latter two types of liaison, where the emotional involvement is deepest, therefore, children play the most important role.[9]

Sophie foresaw possible serious effects on her children, but went ahead believing in her own power to control the outcome and, if she failed and was "discovered," then in her power to manage her children's problems. In other words, she would not stop being their mother even if she had an affair that led to the breakup of her marriage. She, unlike some other women, could imagine successfully being *both* mother and breadwinner, lover and divorcée. None of this would become necessary, however, unless the control she believed she could exercise over the affair failed.

This is another feature of Sophie's story. She had a considerable sense of herself as an effective and efficient manager, a sense she was prepared to act on despite the fact that, simultaneously, she lacked belief in herself as the "dynamic and assertive" person she once had been. Unlike Mrs. Long or Mrs. Waterford, who never had much faith in their own capacities and became, as I suggested in the last chapter, home-grown executives searching for outlets for their talents and for ways of expressing new aspects of themselves which have developed over time, Sophie needed to *rediscover* what she knew was there before. She felt in control and believed she could control what happened at the same time as she yearned for a powerful man to take control of her (at least sexually). In this sense, Sophie did not feel her world was as it should be. She believed strongly in the possibility of a sexually and intellectually satisfying relationship—one that was loving and warm but also stimulating; while, in her sexual relationship with her husband, she felt exploited and was revolted.

Sophie's husband had barely shown her affection but expected sex as a service:

> One of the things that went wrong with my marriage was to do with what we [the group] were discussing—the concept about the body as property. My husband has not for many years made any overt demonstration of affection towards me. Held my hand or patted me on the shoulder or any of those things, and it is one of the things I have great problems in coping with. I mean it is one of the reasons why I went into an extramarital affair, and yet he wanted sex very regularly, and I eventually got to the stage where I had got out of bed in the middle of the night, . . . and said, "I cannot allow you to have sex with me if you are not prepared to show that you care about me because my body is the one thing that I own and I will not use it for any purpose that I don't want to use it for and I don't want to have sex unless it is part of a wider relationship.

This was a painful subject for Sophie, as she showed in her description of what had earlier been an "adulterous relation . . . liaison" and "this critical, first affair" and had now become an "extramarital affair," thus distancing herself with a scientific, cool expression, remote from the passion she experienced in the relationship itself.

Understanding this aspect of Sophie's marriage helps clarify the strength of her feeling that she needed to be "open" with her children; while her problem in relation to her husband, in debating whether to accept the lunch date, was merely technical. That is, secrecy was to be maintained in order only to avoid separation and divorce until she felt able to cope materially. Thus, she was unconcerned about her husband's possible adultery. She said she rather wished he *would* have other partners, permitting him experiences he seemed to lack and perhaps filling needs she was not meeting. She would feel no jealousy because she no longer loved or desired him; the only threat, again, would be the technical one of her security and that of the children.[10]

Sophie's marriage had two elements: her relationship with her husband, which was weak; and that with her children, which was strong. She was prepared to believe that the latter was only *perhaps* jeopardized if a liaison of hers were discovered. The former she no longer cared about. Her marriage was not her joy, but it was her bread and butter.

And, at the same time, Sophie's mother died. It was, she acknowledged, part of her misery. At the time, said Sophie, she had not tied the two things together (her misery in her marriage—particularly the sexual servicing—and her mother's death); but with her mother's death, Sophie had no one to talk to about her unhappiness, no one on whom she could lean. Hence the urgent need not to be, as she felt, an inadequate, if strong, brick or cement to her husband's crumbling wall. Her own foundations had gone; her inner sense of herself crumbled.

Because Sophie had known Philip since she was six, she was rediscovering her past, perhaps helping to lessen the loss of her mother who also knew him. In this way, she reached her mother and gained, as she said, someone who could do for her what her mother did—provide a leaning tower, or even the foundations to her own brick wall. Since the relationship was already a loving one, it lacked the immorality of letting her body be used solely for sexual service or, indeed, solely for sexual pleasure, which might reduce it to a "one-night stand." Although Sophie sought a satisfying and exciting sexual relationship, she also needed friendship, the mental and emotional stimulation of a good friend, someone who would talk about important things and not only when particularly vulnerable—the only time her husband had been able to articulate feelings and ideas. Women in this study as a whole particularly sought and welcomed "friendship."[11] Indeed, some wanted only friendship (the "mind") and so felt it difficult to say no to sex. As Lucy said: "The chap with the mind was only my second experience, and I had really got carried away with the conversation, and I really, I couldn't. . . . I didn't know how to say, 'Oh, I'm sorry, it's your mind I am interested in.' I just couldn't figure it out!"

Such a relationship is possible but it is also rare in the one-night stand and certainly not long-lasting! Yet, with this first night of love making and one conversation, Philip does make Sophie's life move on. And he promised more; he "brought something exciting into my life." She "did things" after that. He brought her life *to* life, gave it a new story. She became able to say, "And then . . . and then . . . this happened and I did that . . . and so on."

This first liaison is thus a story which Sophie has actively created, one in which she plays the leading role, through which she has lived, which she enjoys telling, and which, in a sense, she *needs* to tell. It is one part of her autobiography and forms part of her *being*; whereas, before, she was existing. Marilyn Yalom, in a work examining why certain literary women went mad and linking the threat of death in maternity to their potential loss of mind and the need to write—to tell their stories—cites the modern French writer Marie Cardinal whose emotional disturbance was masked by a physical symptom—constant menstruation (she bled for three years). In analysis, Cardinal was forced to speak, to tell, to find the words (her book was called *Les Mots pour le dire*, "the words to say it") to unwrap what was secret even from herself. Yalom suggests: "The attempt to convey one's particular life story in the fullness of one's feelings, flaws, feats and aspirations is propelled by the hope, however dim, that one's life is *worth the telling* [author's italics] and that someone out there is listening"; and quotes the Chinese-American writer Maxine Hong Kingston: "You have to be able to tell your story . . . or you go mad.'"[12] In other words, by telling one's story, in Meadian terms,[13] the "me" of the self reflecting from the outside world and internally toward the core "I" is, perhaps, being created in this way. If so, then the self (which consists of these two aspects) would be served; it would be moved on by this story-telling.[14] Sophie's story had the effect of "renarrativizing" her life, giving her self-esteem and permitting her to move on and engage in new dramatic twists and turns. Sophie, then, lived this story and related it to us, but she no longer shares a story of her life with her husband. They have no joint project.

Sophie was already strongly committed to the Myth of Me when she married but, at the same time, also believed that both love and sexual fidelity were important in marriage. At the point of marriage, she was already as fully developed at work as she hoped or expected to be; and in marriage, she foresaw the fulfillment of her sexual and maternal capacities. She had willingly retracted her work to part-time free-lance jobs while her children were small; but the lack of a satisfying job meant there was no counterbalance for the absence of joy in her marital relationship, with its paralyzing sexual servicing and the lack of real talk and communication.

Sophie's closure toward Damien paved the way for her to say yes to Philip. This step in emotional management—or in what Arlie Hochschild has called "feeling work"[15]—was essential for the preservation of her sense of self, for her whole concept of herself was endangered: hence, her sense of being trapped. It is precisely when a person's sense of self is threatened—or, in less extreme instances and when a person is basically secure, challenged—that self-awareness is at its height, and that people make choices involving their past selves with their present and become "open" to a new transformation.[16] Sophie fits the idea of a basically secure person, particularly because her feelings about her mother lead us to imagine she was strongly attached to her in infancy, and that her mother had provided for her a "facilitating environment."[17] She also worked hard to integrate her past, present, and future selves, to move on from compartmentalization in life, and to feel alive. It is these features in the striving of human beings that, (according to existential thinking) lead to the resolution of conflicts in values and emotions and between emotions. (Sophie's progress is mapped in figure 5.1.)

FIGURE 5.1
SOPHIE'S CHOICE
(Sophie was born in 1943)

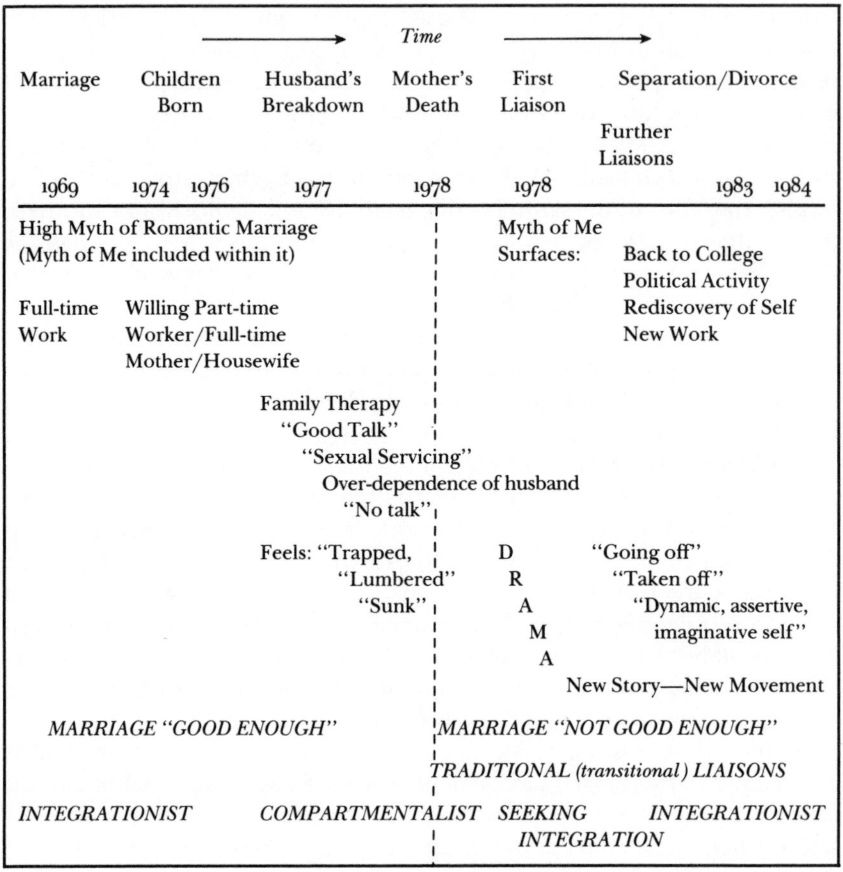

			Time				
Marriage	Children Born	Husband's Breakdown	Mother's Death	First Liaison		Separation/Divorce	
						Further Liaisons	
1969	1974 1976	1977	1978	1978		1983	1984

High Myth of Romantic Marriage | Myth of Me
(Myth of Me included within it) | Surfaces: Back to College
                                             Political Activity
Full-time Willing Part-time   Rediscovery of Self
Work   Worker/Full-time   New Work
           Mother/Housewife

                    Family Therapy
                      "Good Talk"
                    "Sexual Servicing"
                Over-dependence of husband
                      "No talk"

        Feels: "Trapped,   D   "Going off"
               "Lumbered"   R   "Taken off"
                  "Sunk"   A   "Dynamic, assertive,
                               M   imaginative self"
                               A
                                     New Story—New Movement

    MARRIAGE "GOOD ENOUGH"   MARRIAGE "NOT GOOD ENOUGH"

                                  TRADITIONAL (transitional) LIAISONS

INTEGRATIONIST   COMPARTMENTALIST SEEKING   INTEGRATIONIST
                                       INTEGRATION

   The most difficulty is aroused in dealing with the profound emotions of
intimacy, sex, and love. These areas are often the most effectively repressed;
and in them, social values *held by the individual*—the very stuff of their sense
of who they are and what place they occupy in the world—often conflict
with desires and wishes.[18] People need to feel rooted in the past yet moving
forward. Others may not accomplish a successful *integration* as Sophie eventually did, but need to split themselves into warring factions, perhaps breaking down in the process, or, in less extreme form, divide themselves into

careful compartments (*this* belongs here, and *that*, there), becoming, as had also for a time been necessary for Sophie, *compartmentalists*. This may be a most effective if not an ideal way of coping with such conflicts.

Mary and Others

Mary, a thirty-eight-year-old American woman living in Italy with her American husband and their adolescent children, managed her life in precisely this way. Her husband belonged in Italy with the children and animals—the whole panoply of marriage; while her lover stayed securely in London. She literally carved out two geographically and emotionally separate worlds. She was absolutely clear that this was what she was doing. Another and even more careful deliberator than Sophie, Mary managed her guilt by encapsulating her conflicts so that they did not erupt to spoil each segment:

> MARY: I think perhaps we don't feel guilt if we carry on . . . I think if one honestly feels guilty one stops . . . and that either you work it out and you justify it, however you figure that out, in order to continue (because I don't think anybody can live with constant guilt). So either you justify it and do it, or you do decide there's something to be guilty about, and you stop.
> INTERVIEWER: What is true for you?
> MARY: I don't feel guilt. I have very little truck with guilt—I think it is a useless emotion, and so I (with somewhat of an effort of will) if you will, just resolve that as fast as I can. Figure it out. Work it out. And be done with it.

In slipping from the pronoun *we*, to *one*, and then to *you*, unable to employ the first person *I* until prompted to do so, Mary indicated the distancing she had accomplished. Others in the group were a great deal less certain that guilt could be avoided by simply willing it to go away. Yet it is perhaps this sense that David Matza had in mind when he described a young woman facing her first infidelity who may be willing but is not able because she has not yet prepared herself for the actual task of breaking the rules (see the chapter epigraph).[19] Mary, on the other hand, had done the necessary emotion management, noticed that she was *supposed* to feel guilty, determined what she felt and why she need not, and then failed to feel guilt through what she calls her act of will. Yet for her, continuous debate (or emotion management) remained necessary:

> For me, the debate is constantly a conflict between responsibilities to my husband or my children and more for my children than my husband just because they are younger and more dependent. . . . I think the debate

has got to be almost axiomatically continuous unless you just blot out a responsibility that exists. . . . You say, "All right, I will not do what I'd like to do. Responsibility to the children comes first," and you just cease to have that affair, so you just blot out what you may be needing yourself—not only what makes you happy but what may be really good for you.

Unlike Sophie, Mary has not given up on her husband; like Sophie, she sees the major part of her marriage as the moving staircase on which her children are supported, and herself as vital to that. In some sense, her marriage remains a project involving both herself and her husband with the children and all that goes with them. She finds that she must keep that part of her life in one area in order to keep it moving forward; but, without her affair, she is not sure she would herself move forward. Her affair is not only what makes her happy, but is "good" for her.

In Mary's firm separation of her worlds and her articulate sense of oppositions, the opposition of the two myths is clear. What was good for her, what made her happy was not found within her marriage any longer, despite the fact that she still considered herself to have responsibilities to her husband. The structure of her marriage which contained her children was weighty (although her children were much older than Sophie's), and not merely negatively so but had a place which seemed rather one of obligation than of rights, of serious work and responsibility than of play and reciprocal enjoyment.

Sophie's deliberations did not directly oppose the Myth of Romantic Marriage to the Myth of Me because the former was dying or already dead in her perception of her marriage, while the latter was just resurfacing. And Sophie desired integration in her life. She was prepared to compartmentalize lover and husband—to keep the former secret from the latter; but this is like a fraud, something to be endured only temporarily, while she prepared for the overt and public ending of what was, at the stage of her debate about this first affair, already privately over. Rather than having to maintain her (very young) children's movement and their world *with* their father and *inside* the marriage, they belonged with her and would leave, too. It was because she had *not* given up on her idea of romantic love (though she now sought it in adultery and not within her marriage) that she took this particular path. Indeed, she sought a way of rediscovering all of the elements of the two myths in one. In Sophie's story, we can see the old myth of romantic adulterous love resurfacing and separating from its modern marital boundaries, for it is marriage that, for Sophie, was in the way of love; she was convinced that her self-interest and passionate love could be simultaneously pursued. It was because she wished to be in love and passionately involved as well as a nurturing "mother," because she wished to be not only a wife but also a "proper worker," that her answer to her would-be lover on the telephone was yes. Finally, a passionate love affair with a man who did fulfill her image of a *real* man provided her with the explicit encouragement to seek out her own *real self*. We can picture the two myths as circles almost completely overlapping in Sophie's imagery, but now the Myth of Me has slipped to one side, and is separated from, and only partially overlaps with, the Myth of Romantic Marriage. She seeks to have them overlapping completely again.

Both Sophie and Mary had "traditional" adulterous relationships, since both were illicit. Mary's, however, ran in parallel with her marriage: she conducted it for her deep pleasure alongside her marriage which remained "good enough"—the term Winnicott coined to describe the "good enough" care given by "ordinary" mothers to their babies. Indeed, her adultery was *supportive* of her marriage. Sophie's was *dangerous*, organized so that she was unlikely to be found out, but a great deal more likely than Mary was. As already seen in figure 5.1, Sophie's marriage was no longer "good enough": without intimacy or passion, commitment is destroyed.[20]

In contrast to Sophie, Janey, a slightly younger woman with similar problems, decided to say no to adultery:

What happened was that I realized that in my marriage half of me was not functioning. I didn't do anything about it because it would have been totally foolish. I had four young children. It would have been ridiculous. What happened after that—some time after that—was I had a very serious car accident in which I nearly died and, in order to recover from that car accident, the other half of me *had* to come up and function—that's what kept me going. It was after that that I realized there is no going back because once you have allowed something in yourself to come out—do you know what I mean?—there was change, and that is maturity. As you grow, you are adding a little bit to yourself or you are enlarging yourself. Nobody actually changes. They just become more of themselves.

Janey, like Sophie, acknowledged the economic and political weight of marriage but strained within it because she was only "half" functioning. She seems, though—through another equally dramatic story and one where she directly faced the terror of death, which merely lurks, carefully repressed, for most of us most of the time—to have become whole again. Faced with the existential reality of death and final isolation, she resolved the dilemma of freedom and responsibility. She was able to draw on all her inner reserves, on the *whole* of herself, and "grow."

These stories of women deliberating show that the decision is not simply a matter of weighing two competing myths in their lives, although their actual working out does include balancing the values they had placed in marriage against a discovery of aspects of themselves. This is because marriage is much more than a set of ideals, however central and important those ideals are to those who are involved. Marriage is bread and butter, shelter and commitment, children's lives and whole networks of family members.

It is practical investment of time, energy, and money. The discovery of the self with another person who is *not* one's husband, risks all that, still. Often these aspects are not clearly separated from the *feelings* a person holds about the marital partner or the marriage. Rather, they see the problems only in terms of the quality of the relationship (a further example of the power of the Myth of Romantic Marriage), but both Sophie and Janey clearly also saw the economic reality of their lives, which entered into their deliberations with some force.

The sense of yearning conveyed by these stories is supported by the rank order of the most common responses women gave about the feelings they had as they first contemplated a liaison:

1. I felt compelled by my emotions to have an affair.
2. My spouse and I had grown apart.
3. I had sexual needs which were not being met at the time.
4. Life felt very empty.
5. Life was for living.

The men in the sample listed their feelings slightly differently:

1. With care, the affair would not harm my marriage.
2. I was curious to know what sex would be like with someone else.
3. Life was for living.
4. I had sexual needs which were not being met at the time.
5. I felt compelled by my emotions to have an affair.

Some statements in the men's top five are the same as those in the women's list; but there is a greater sense of calculation for men, of care and thought, but less feeling.[21] And this interpretation is lent further support when those other aspects are listed that weighed with the men, even though, in making the decision, great importance was not ascribed to them. Thus, around 40 percent of the men said that "I was sure my spouse had never had an affair," "I would not want to put my marriage at risk"; and that they would "worry about the deceit involved"—all fairly deliberate ideas. The women's list is similar, except that they did not calculate the risk to their marriage as highly, saying instead that "my spouse and I did not discuss difficulties in our relationship." It is not that women and men are worlds apart in their concerns; rather it is that women emphasize feeling and men, rationality.[22] Seeing marriage as the place where women invest most of themselves, while men's investment lies in the commitment they have (or traditionally have had)[23] to supporting their wives and families within it,[24] clarifies this difference and the fact that there is nothing inevitable about it.

Men Debate

Men, unlike women, do not normally experience the collective values of the family as "at odds" with their own individualistic needs for self-fulfillment, for they have never been expected to subordinate their own interests to those of the family—that is, to their wives and children.[25] In this sense, adultery for men is less "a problem." Less breach of the marital boundaries is implied; less debate perhaps even necessary. Indeed, a man can effectively utilize the outside world (like a business) to serve his own interests and those of the family.

For example, John, aged twenty-nine, assistant manager in a small business:

> To be honest, on the few occasions when I have had affairs outside marriage, I realized that I could cope. And I looked at the situation at a slightly different angle and my wife from a slightly different angle. I know this sounds very cold and callous, but I learned a great deal, and I think that half of going into affairs, I would like the person, and I would say that I used them because I thought something could be learned which could be put to keep my marriage going and make that better. Of course, I learned to become more self-sufficient.

And Antony, a naval officer of thirty-five whose chance arose in the officers' mess:

> You could have an adulterous liaison without interrupting your long-term goals with your partner and your family and your children. I think it's a question you have to ask yourself before you enter or go into an . . . [he did not name it] particularly if it's a rather greater commitment than a one-night stand. "Why am I doing this? What will I get out of it? How does this affect the status quo?" And that's one of the reasons I was interested in your article because I wasn't quite sure what effect my planning was going to have on my short-term goals and the commitment to my family. And you know it is still in the very early stages—six weeks now.

He spoke of his possible liaison as if it were a campaign requiring careful strategic planning, and as if the woman had nothing to do with it. Like many others, he described his purpose in contributing to the study as a means to help him understand more about himself and his (potential) liaison, but his words were task-oriented, lacking feeling. He set the agenda for this liaison, "permitting" his partner participation, just as other married men speak proudly of having "allowed" their wives to work:

> The "other person" involved knows fully the situation, and we have talked long about it on the occasions when we have met, and we are both

in agreement that if it looks as if it is going to take over (and that might be naïve because it may become something before you realize that it is taking you over), then we will say, "Thank you very much. Let's remain friends."

Antony must remain in tight control of the ship, but he did appreciate that a storm of emotion could beach him despite his intentions.

Will, a Scotsman and junior lecturer in a technical college, first obtained his wife's agreement that he might have "other relationships":

We never really talked about it until it was actually upon us, but it always seemed the least difficult way to go about it. . . . I knew all right [about his wife's own proposed liaison] and I actually encouraged her. Because I felt she would enjoy the experience and also, I guess, as well, I felt . . . well, I wanted, I suppose, to distance myself from her to some degree.

He followed the considered approach of those who agreed that, "with care, the affair would not harm my marriage"; and that, "I would not want to put my (or my partner's) marriage at risk" (two separate statements on the questionnaire), and then had to debate the issue with his potential partner and persuade her of the goodness—and hence the rightness—of a love affair. The goodness would, in part, be determined by telling both spouses. That is, if both were in the know, then it would not count as adultery. Neither would be deceitful, and neither need feel guilty:

Well, my basic argument was—she [his lover] had her doubts—and my arguments were that it would be a good thing for both of us. . . . As far as my wife was concerned, it wouldn't worry her. Now it was quite different as far as her own husband was concerned. . . . I think it must have become quite clear to me that somehow she wasn't all that committed to observing what her husband really wanted.

Unlike Antony, who was still debating his decision at the time he participated in the study, Will had made appropriate arrangements, successfully persuaded his partner, and did have the liaison. But Will did not anticipate what Antony had feared, and was completely swept up in emotion: "In any case, it turned out to be the most intense experience of my life and quite emotional. An enormous emotional upheaval."

None of these three men were, it seemed, on a voyage of self-discovery, but they were seeking experiences that they might manage within the context of marriage, that would have consequences beneficial (or at least not damaging) to their marriages, and that would permit them a certain freedom to have other sexual relationships. Sophie, too, had been clear that there were risks and benefits to her liaison; and she, too, had weighed them.

But her reasons for weighing the costs were to do with her disillusion with her marriage and her need for self-discovery. These men, however, did not seem to experience their marriages as at fault, something much more important for women. Indeed, while some men certainly felt needy in their marriages and also explained that this was their reason for the liaison, it was more common for men to justify or explain—as Steven did—their choice of partner on the basis that *her* marriage was unhappy:

> Beth effectively made it obvious that there was a relationship there if I wanted to take it up. And, eventually, it did become an affair about six months or so after that. After having fought my conscience for six months on end. Because I thought that I loved my wife, and thought we had a happy marriage. I didn't have any qualms about Beth's marriage, because I knew it wasn't happy anyway. She told me about her previous affairs, and I think I realized then that her marriage wasn't really a very good marriage. It couldn't have been, otherwise those affairs wouldn't have taken place, and I wasn't really breaking up anything that was terribly valuable.

This position is, of course, quite illogical. If a woman has affairs only if her marriage is unhappy, how could his own marriage be happy if *he* was considering having an affair? There would seem a remnant of the double standard showing its edge here, although women, too, were conscious of the illogicality of their attitudes when, as often happened, they made commonplace judgments about *other people's* marriages as necessarily being faulty if one spouse had liaisons, yet could not evaluate their own that way when they, themselves broke their marital vows. Mrs. Long expressed this quandary well, for she had said that "there must be something wrong" with a person's marriage if they had affairs, and yet was not happy with that motivation to explain her own feelings. She fell "head over heels" and said, "Let's face it—physical pleasure—the minute we see one another, we're in bed." She used the double standard not to express a different (higher) standard to be achieved by wives over husbands on the sexual-fidelity rule, but to describe the discrepancy in her judgments:

> It is amazing how you have——I don't know——is it double standards for yourselves or——? . . . I have always thought if someone had an affair, there's feelings involved and there are always reasons, you know. I always feel if a marriage is truly solid, it won't happen because the two people involved won't see anyone outside anyway.

Beth, who became Steven's second wife, placed more emphasis on the dangers that might follow the loss of her marriage than he had. She valued it more than he had appreciated: "I was really unhappy because I realized that I was hurting my first husband, and that divorce would cause pain to my children, and might possibly have harmful long-term effects on them. For the first time I despised myself for being selfish and weak.''

In our culture women are permitted and expected to express themselves in terms of their feelings and to act on emotion. Indeed, this "fact" about women is often used derogatorily: "mere woman's intuition"; or, when someone sounds illogical, "that's just like a woman." Boys learn early not to cry, not to show their feelings, and to reason carefully about action. Because of the stress on rationality in our modern, scientific culture, and because of the greater power held by men, they come to be seen as normally "right," the corollary being that women more often can be seen as "wrong" and, hence, as blameworthy. It may be that women really do not have liaisons unless they feel there is "something wrong." It may also be that women need to reconstruct in their minds their marriages as poor or missing essential ingredients *in order to* feel at all comfortable about their breach of the marital boundaries.

Thus, for women, it is said, there has to be "something more. A relationship. Not just the sexual thing." As Jessica said:

> I felt very much that sex was something very special for a very special person. But my husband's attitude was—well—the sexual side of a relationship is just another facet of a relationship and I think that that has obviously affected me over the years, but I still don't think I would say that it is just simply one side of the relationship because I think it is so involved with the emotional part of the relationship that it is a very powerful aspect of it. I tend to feel that that's a difference in approach between men and women generally in relationships . . . but . . . maybe not.

These cultural beliefs about what women may feel and what men may think and about *how* each must think and feel play such a central part in the construction of the consciousness of each that any attempt to unravel what is surface appearance or "justification" from what is more "real" or "true" is bound to fail.[26] However, the fact that emotion does rise up to strike people in ways they have not expected indicates that something is happening outside the bounds of that which is expressed and recognized. And also leads us to recognize the similarities in motivation as well the differences. For some people, the debate focused on the risks entailed.

The Doctor's Dilemma

One doctor risked everything—his partnership, his marriage, his relationship with his children—for the woman who became his second wife and yet felt he could manage it all with "no risk." Like Will, the Scot, his actions and his emotions completely overwhelmed him, but his calculations had included a concept of himself that seemed extraordinarily potent, a concept it is hard to imagine any woman possessing and few men.

If the debate were dependent on an assessment of real risk indeed, then Dr. Reynolds' would have been interminable. This man was, at the time of his first liaison, in conflict with his partners in their group practice. It was, he said, touch and go whether he would have to leave the partnership. His wife, he said, did not understand these partnership problems. At this time, her own sister died, and Dr. Reynolds came to feel he did not offer her the help she needed. Neither, according to his account, was supportive of the other. At the same time, he was leaving his wife and children alone a good deal, spending—after a full working week when he would have been on duty for night calls at least once—many weekends traveling fast through the night to the most remote shore or mountain he could find. He would sleep out alone and try to climb the most perpendicular rock faces or swim the most dangerous currents.

He admitted that some of these trials of strength, endurance, and skill he was setting himself were near suicidal. He was also aware that he might well be wishing to die, his successful life—"with a dependable and delightful if not very stimulating wife and two children whom I adore"—boring him and leaving him feeling already dead. He told me his lover was a patient, and that he used to have sex with her *in her own house*, while her husband, who was also his patient, watched television next door with their children, who were *also* his patients. When I asked whether his affair with a patient was another calculated risk, providing physical pleasure like swimming and rock climbing, he replied:

Oh no! Well, yeah, but all this pleasure—I thought I could manage it without it being a risk at all—until when I got to the stage when I knew I'd have to jump. One way or the other. The present I was walking along was a fence and I could have jumped either way. There was no question of blackmail or the General Medical Council, or anything like that, but——

As it happened, she did not tell on him nor blackmail him, and they were not found out. Had they been, he risked being struck off the Medical Register, for becoming sexually involved with a patient is an offense which, in Great Britain, is quite as likely—perhaps more so—as medical error to lead to dismissal from professional practice. (Since doctors are entitled to hear secrets and to view and touch the naked bodies of patients, this rule requires serious sanction.) His disagreements with his partners were resolved, and he and his lady announced to their respective spouses their wish to be divorced and to marry one another. But the absurd contradiction that this was somehow to be accomplished "with no risk" compared with his terrifying weekend exploits was not because he was unable logically to calculate and to weigh benefits and dangers, but because he longed for success in this, the most dramatic of tales—the seduction of another man's wife. In his castle and in her home. To prove through such trials his worth and then to win, overcoming all the dangers, was a great benefit worth all the anguish. Indeed, he seemed to me to be courting various kinds of death. His death as a doctor, the death of his wife and of his role as father, and the destruction of "home"—something he said he so much missed in his new marriage.

Dr. Reynolds also was at some pains to convince me that this lady of his dreams was exceptionally beautiful and desired not only by him but by all other men. He could not, he said, leave her "even for an instant": if he did, "two or three others would be ringing her up and saying, 'What about it?' meaning anything from lunch out, to their making love." Having married her, he needed to ensure she *might* still belong to another man; it was less exciting if she did not. He also—or so it seemed—needed to continue to live in this heightened, risky way, for not to do so would mean giving up on what he had found. His discovery was that "true love" and passionate sexual love could be combined in one relationship, giving him an immense feeling of vitality and strength far removed from the suicidal feelings he had had before; and that this romance could be encapsulated in marriage. As in the ancient legends of adulterous love, however, his winning of another man's wife was not at all what he had hoped. He was racked by the danger of perhaps losing this woman to others (after all, if she had betrayed her husband, why should she not treat him in the same way?). He missed the calm and mundane life of his first marriage "when shirts were washed and there was food on the table—ordinary things which I took for granted and cannot any more, because she was a practical girl and she cooked well"—these things having been exchanged for "someone very intelligent, very feeling, immensely feeling," who provided him with tempestuous and passionate love making—"something I never knew with my first wife. I mean, we made love, but it was never like it is with Katherine, but if I had never known it, maybe I wouldn't have missed it, would I?"

And he despaired of the loss of his children. Although he saw them regularly and "had them for two weeks every summer," he knew very well that not seeing them every day meant he was not really in touch with their growing and changing. He was missing their childhood. The emotion that had driven him, Dr. Reynolds said, was "lust." And so serious did he feel his actions had been that he described them as murderous. He had "murdered" his first wife for "lust" of his second. He used the word *murder* three times in the course of his interview, supporting the novelist Alice Ellis's idea, quoted in the chapter epigraph, that adultery has little to do with morals and is more akin to murder.[27] Despite acknowledging that he had been driven by lust ("I was compelled by my emotions to have an affair"), clearly Dr. Reynolds did a great deal of thinking and working out of each step. Indeed, he pointed out to me how easily, practically speaking, he had been able to conduct his liaison because a doctor has to do regular surgeries and write up case notes and reports and contact hospitals. The doctor also has to go on visits to home patients, and this is precisely what Dr. Reynolds did and what made it "easy." That, too, is what he meant by thinking he could conduct the whole relationship without risk. Because he was entitled to be in a patient's bedroom. She had a chronic condition which required regular attendance. On Dr. Reynolds's description, she was an extremely powerful woman whose husband would have been foolish, perhaps, to intervene in her private arrangements with her doctor. For example, she "made" Dr. Reynolds "dismember" his marriage by setting new targets regularly for him about the extent to which he was to continue to have contact with his wife:

> At first, you know, I wasn't to touch her [first wife]. Then they [Katherine and her husband] came to dinner as a couple. She didn't like me touching my wife. And then she didn't like me to make love to her. And then more and more and more—that I was to tell her . . . that I was to tell her that I would never make love to her again. I cannot think now how—but she . . . as I say, she's a powerful girl and she has——

He was very near to tears. His sense of shame was profound:

> I feel I am partly cold bread pudding and I think to have treated her like that is almost cold-blooded murder. . . . In church, we vowed.

Although he felt so controlled by his second wife, he nevertheless had conducted the affair itself with careful planning and delight in his success. It was only after the anguish of divorce and (so it appeared) the mixed joy of remarriage, that Dr. Reynolds reflected, with the advantage of distance, on what it had cost him to gain this fascinating woman and her children who detested him:

> No punishment is too great really. I think I should be put in the stocks for what I did. I feel very strongly indeed that what I did is really without any mitigation. Totally wrong. Because, honestly it wasn't a bad marriage. It's just that Katherine was so exceptional in so many ways. It leaves me with an immense conviction really that the case against adultery is immensely strong. My marriage wasn't intolerable, and I really have no grounds on any score.

But he did have grounds—that his wife "didn't understand" him or his problems; whereas Katherine was interested and thoughtful, listening with care to all the difficulties he was experiencing in his partnership:

> And I found I could talk to her. . . . And she understood, she understands. And then, of course it grew from friendship into a pretty time-consuming and thoroughgoing affair and into marriage. My wife was a virgin when I married her and rather naïve sexually. Katherine is very highly sexed.

Dr. Reynolds attempted to avoid finding fault in his first marriage but did note two areas that were really uppermost in Sophie's story: a lack of good and passionate sex; and friendship—the talking about important things which lends vitality to the daily relationship.

Indeed, his whole account is a constant balancing of his first wife against his "mistress" [his word], his first house and home against his second, his own children against his second wife's, his first marriage against his second. He has created a story, a most dramatic one, but for him, it has more tragedy and less comedy than he desired. His Myth of Romantic Marriage has suffered severely in his pursuit of adulterous love. He has gained something for himself—the knowledge of what passionate sexual love is like—but has also learned that it seems to mix poorly with marriage. Passion had played no part in the "monolithic institution" that marriage had been; but with it, in his second marriage, he feels the marriage can never be that same kind of institution which now, paradoxically, he longs for. He said, however, that if he had met this second wife when they were both twenty-five and had married then, he thought everything would have been different. In particular, they would have had children together, and it is children who form an essential part of this monolith and whose loss is so painful. He knows that the division of new property will not benefit his own children. Thus his sense of continuity—looking to the future of subsequent generations—has also been lost to him in this second marriage. Like Sophie, his dreams and his mythology are only to be understood when the economic and political aspects of marriage are incorporated. Thus, his experience, even now, has not destroyed his belief in the Myth of Romantic Marriage.

In his recent work on the nature of the self, Jack Douglas argues that it is when there is a *threat* to the self that a person feels a crisis of identity (as, indeed, we saw operated in Sophie's case). In other words, if something recognized as socially valuable occurs that transforms a person—say, into becoming married, or president of a corporation—the person may reflect and ask, "Is this really *me*?" but does not experience such a change as full of conflict, as a crisis of identity which must be resolved. But when something threatening happens—in Dr. Reynolds's case, a loss of control over his emotions and his life—then a crisis of what Douglas calls "self-insecurity or ontological uncertainty," occurs.[28] Now, having pursued "lust" and "murdered" his first wife, Dr. Reynolds is no longer certain who he is at all. He does not know what he stands for; he knows only what he is against. His is the ancient and destructive form of adultery which, having been consummated and even hallowed, turns ugly and sour. It is the adultery that can be accomplished only as long as the adulterer stays within the marriage from which he began his adventure. In leaving his wife, Dr. Reynolds lost everything. The shape of this form must remain triangular. Figure 5.2 maps his course.

FIGURE 5.2
Doctor's Dilemma
(Dr. Reynolds was born in 1940)

Marriage	Children Born	Partnership Problems Wife's sister dies	Risk Taking	Liaison	Separation/ Divorce	Marries Partner
→			*Time*	→		
1967	1969 1971	1972–74	1973	1974– 76 →	1978–80	1981

High Romantic Myth of Marriage ⁞ Romantic Myth of Marriage Maintained

⁞ Myth of Me Surfaces:

Enjoys "monolithic institution"
Wife good "housewife/mother" but no sexual passion "Mundane" life ⁞ Partner is:
    Wife not "curious" "Immensely feeling"
      No good intelligent "talk" "Intelligent"
        Cannot help him or children with intellectual
          needs/problems
            Wife "does not understand" Partner "understands"

D
R Discovers "talk"
A Discovers sexual
M passion
A Loses control of Own
  life to partner
  Marriage DESTROYED
  Loss of Self
  Loss of Children

  Fails to re-build "monolith" in
  Second Marriage
  Longs for success
  Blames Self

FIRST MARRIAGE: *NOT "GOOD ENOUGH"* *SECOND MARRIAGE:*
"GOOD ENOUGH" *NOT "GOOD ENOUGH"*

TRADITIONAL (dangerous) ADULTERY

INTEGRATIONIST → *COMPARTMENTALIST* → *ATTEMPTING BUT FAILING INTEGRATION*

Jack's Story

If Dr. Reynolds's experience indicates a fundamentally flawed calculation of risk—which women, being customarily (but not, of course, always) more aware of the power of emotion, are less likely to make—some men also enter affairs in ways similar to Sophie's. Jack's story, indeed, almost mirrors hers and turns traditional roles around. Having had a traditional job as a businessman, marrying young and inexperienced to a woman of similar background, Jack, as he approached forty, "felt there was a side of me that wasn't in touch, or I was going through my male menopause or whatever it was. But it was a very fundamental time of change." Identifying with a woman going through the menopause, Jack makes the reversal of roles specific—his debating is done, as it were, from a wife's perspective. With his wife's support, Jack gave up his business life and returned to college. He was given a place at a university some seventy miles from his home and began his training in social work. Soon he met a young woman who tempted him to "cross the bridge" (the boundary around his marriage which he would have to breach). He chose someone much younger ("I was almost old enough to be her father") and foreign, rich and definitely committed to her own career and to not breaking at any time into his marriage. She refused, for example, to let him pay for any of their joint expenses, because that would involve him spending money that she saw as properly belonging to his wife and children. They met only away from home and in a place— the university—where the normal and conventional rules of social life are not only questionable, but imperatively (for the task of students is to learn to think critically) *to be questioned*. Indeed, he linked his university course, which was making him reassess all his values, including his religious values, and his liaison:

> [It was] a time of very much religious doubt . . . what I am talking about are actual fundamental changes in thinking and the recognition that I ought to take on board my responsibilities for my own actions and that the notion that somehow . . . that one can, that somebody else will make it right, or, if you pray, that it will all come right, it will come right in the end, is actually something to do with parroting the "Our Father" bit. And, actually, I ought to take on board this thing myself. The decision would have to be mine.

> Gradually it dawned on me that there was a potential. It was possible she would become my lover. We would make love and I agonized over this for a long time.

> I wondered what it would be like to make love to somebody who was beautiful. What would she look like without any clothes on? What was she like?

He described vividly—everything invested with symbolic meaning—his moment of decision, standing a little away from the building where she was, tempted by the warm glow of light from her room, daring himself to move, to get there, to go in. Yet, according to his own account, there had been a long period of preparation; he even understood a vasectomy now as leading to this moment: "In retrospect, I am absolutely convinced that part of the reason I had a vasectomy was the potential of being able to sleep with somebody else and not make them pregnant." Again, his narrative account and his preparation includes a traditionally female anxiety—pregnancy.

This first liaison and a later one are also both conducted more like those of the traditional wife, with Jack's own wife remaining completely ignorant (as he believes), although he is equally sure that his nearly adult children are aware of them. His sexual needs were strong, and the pleasure he found in sensuous expression with these two women has certainly led to an enrichment of his life. He has taken the route that Mary chose in keeping his family life separate from his liaisons; they are a part of his development as a social worker (his second lover was met through this new work and shared his values) and seem to be partitioned into that "other side" which has been permitted to emerge but not (as yet) *merge* with what he had before. As he gets older and is more secure in all aspects of himself and his investment in his family diminishes, this balance may shift, and Jack might well leave home. Indeed, he hinted in interview that had the second lover been more "compatible," he might have left his wife then. On the other hand, given his new awareness that, as he said, the "gaps" he sought to fill in his marriage were not gaps at all—for his wife could, he now thinks, have met his needs—what he has discovered in his love affairs might, just might, alter what exists between himself and his wife.

In his debate, Jack shares much with Sophie in his awareness of his own need to grow and change, to fill the gaps and seek passion and intimacy; but his life stage was very different, as were his circumstances. After all, his wife supported him in his use of their savings and continued to run their business as well as caring for the family while he was "going off." Mardi Gras and May festivals continue only in a few special places—when the world is turned topsy-turvy and a woman may (literally) be "on top";[29] but Jack's story reversed many things. It is a reversal for the man, the traditional breadwinner, to give up this role and go to college; and it is a reversal that the mistress keeps her lover. Furthermore, Jack was taking a course in social work—a traditionally female occupation—not one, for example, in business studies or economics—traditionally male spheres.

Women Who Debate Like Men

If men can debate in similar form to women, so women, too, can be cool and calculating—determining to take something they want without too much anguish or remorse, and clear that the matter is within their control.

Just as Jack was beginning a career normally and traditionally associated with women, so these more cooly calculating women were more often in careers traditionally reserved for men. A recent American study of women working in the financial world in New York and San Francisco found them taking a fairly cool approach to problems more typical of men, and this approach was followed through in their extramarital lives as well.[30] For example, a senior hospital administrator from our sample said, "I kept it completely from my husband. Did it quite deliberately. Planned it for some time. . . . Just picked out some half-decent guy." And a businesswoman: "I very consciously decided, you know. 'Sod everything past. I am going to have a wonderful time and you [husband] are going to feel sorry and all the rest of it.' And I did a bit of bed-hopping for several months." These two women sound much like these two businessmen:

> I am sure I could always talk somebody into falling in love with me. I think I could anyway. I don't think there is any great art in it. I think you have just got to be kind to somebody and it automatically follows. [Note "some*body*," not "some*one*."]

> Several girls fancied me and I quite fancied them but they were young. They wanted much more than a casual sleeping together thing, and I find it hard—I know it's playing God, but saying, "Well, O.K., I can handle this all right," but I'm not sure they can. They want something more out of it.

It seems he could reject as well as initiate with ease.

Thus, both women and men commonly do debate at some length, especially internally, with themselves, the pros and cons of the first liaison. Women seem generally more intent on the discovery of the emotional resources, aspects of themselves they have come to feel are lacking within their marriages. There is, usually, a strong sense of yearning in their stories, and the creation and living of the adulterous tale instills a new sense of being, a new sense of who they are, of being alive, ready to move on, whether within or outside their marriage. Men take a more pragmatic and calculated risk; and for them, the risk itself may be central to the adulterous tale. But there are men whose experience is similar to that of women and women whose tales are similar to those of most men. In each case discussed here, the men who sound like women are entering traditionally female-dominated occupations, and the women who sound like men are in occupations more commonly associated with men. Employment itself seems to be altering the importance women have traditionally placed on maintaining a marriage for the sake of the children or of worrying about the effects on children as they, the women, move out from hearth and home into the marketplaces of the world. The men beginning to sound more like women are particularly those younger men, married most recently, those most affected

(at least insofar as they express themselves differently from older generations of men, if not yet altering their actions) by the women's movement
and by ideas about the equality of women and men at home as well as at
work.

Surely, however, there were people who did not debate at all, who "did
not stop to think," acting on impulse?

Acting on Impulse

Those who had the strongest allegiance to the Myth of Romantic Marriage
had the most difficulty and suffered the most acute distress in taking the
plunge into a sexual relationship with someone other than their husband
or wife. They were also the most inclined to deliberate carefully over the
decision, weighing the pros and cons as Sophie did; but there were those
among them who used the strength of their feelings as a justification for
their actions. Thus, "I didn't stop to think" and "I felt compelled by my
emotions to have an affair" became explanations for what happened *despite*
their strong allegiance to the Myth of Romantic Marriage. In other words,
they "acted on impulse."

Given all I have said about the acceptance of emotion in women and its
relative unacceptability in men, it is not surprising that women claimed
more often than men to have been driven by their emotions (51 percent of
women compared with 39 percent of men), but exactly equal proportions
(13 percent) of women and men said they "did not stop to think." In other
words, the vast majority of both men and women in this sample, whether
"compelled by their emotions" or not, still felt they had thought things
through, recognizing an element of choice, however sudden or rapid the
decision.

David Matza describes people in a state of "drift" when they may be willing, but not necessarily able, to act in a deviant way. This, he argues, is
because their decision to act arises out of their experience in actual situations and not in the abstract, and because they have to have the *will* to
behave in a deviant way. Matza uses the example of delinquent boys in
America who, he says, share a desire for "kicks" with all members of their
age group whatever their skin color or social class, and obtain these kicks
from lawbreaking. When they break the law, they gain a sense of "human-
ism"; whereas, before, they were in a mood of desperation and "fatalism"
because they lacked the power to make anything happen. It is in making
things happen (what I have referred to as creating a story, gaining the capacity to move on in life, to become, to feel alive) that they can feel, according
to Matza, human at all. It is not, however, easy to break the law. Although

they belong to a subculture of delinquency which provides support and an environment in which they can acquire the skills to do deviant acts, they do have an allegiance to the moral bind of the wider (and more powerful) social order. This they have to "neutralize."[31]

These boys have available to them certain techniques to neutralize this moral bind, including denial of responsibility ("I didn't mean it"), blaming or denying the existence of the victim ("He had it coming to him," or, "No one got hurt"), and denial of worthiness of others to judge ("Who does he think he is to tell *me* what's right or wrong?"). Accepting for the time being that adultery is a deviant act (and we have seen that some people change the rules so that it is not), then the need to "neutralize" the moral bind of the Myth of Romantic Marriage seems generally necessary. Indeed, the kinds of argument Matza describes are familiar by now. Thus, people blamed their marriages or—as a result of themselves evaluating a spouse's behavior as worse than their own—felt entitled to an affair, perhaps taking revenge (see chapter 6). If the spouse did not know, there would be no "victim"; and if he or she had already had a liaison, who were they to judge? The people who use these "techniques of neutralization" do not pretend they were unwilling partners, nor that their own choices had nothing to do with what happened. Yet, at first appearance, the people who say they were driven by their emotions, or did not stop to think, seem not to have willed anything to happen, but to have had something happen to them. They were out of control. Impulsivity can, however, be understood as one form of deliberation, a form that permits one to escape a sense of personal responsibility for one's actions.[32] Indeed, even the most impulsive and sudden of acts is preceded by a whole series of tiny events, small moments, which have prepared those who act with such spontaneity.

Jack Douglas gives an example of a beautiful woman who describes her infidelities as arising out of situations where she was quite out of control— seduced by her lovers to the extent that she would still be protesting as they undressed her. As if she had had nothing to do with being in that situation at all. But, of course, she had made many tiny decisions (not perhaps at the level of consciousness) which led her where

> [she] was quite conscious that she avoided guilt by "allowing" her sexual desire to grow until it "swept her off her feet." She knew she "went along with" actions and situations which allowed her desire to grow until she could no longer resist it, or, as seemed more common, until she could resist it only verbally while her clothes were being taken off by her "seducer."

This self-preparation is a necessary part of the largely unconscious work that is conducted between the socially oriented "Me" and the inner-directed "I"—the reflecting mirrors of the self described by the philosopher-psychologist George Herbert Mead. Jack Douglas explains: "If the conflicting emotion is still great enough to threaten the sense of self, this inner self, which is dominated by the repressed emotion, may secretly (predominantly out of consciousness) override the outer, socially oriented self by leading the person" to put himself or herself in situations where "desire will be permitted" in such a way that he or she will be absolved of responsibility.[33]

Thus, such a woman has spent time making sure she is alluring, that she is dressed and perfumed in particular ways, that she will not feel ashamed of her body as her clothes are removed to her protests; she has accepted an invitation to dinner or to the place where she can be seduced, or has herself invited the lover there. She has probably ensured that her husband is away or otherwise occupied and her children protected. She may, even consciously, have thought a little about the moral arguments and "excused" herself (using some of Matza's techniques of neutralization) so that, in the moment when desire overwhelms her, she can permit her seduction and *not* experience it as rape.[34] Mrs. Inkerman, after all, refused the advances of her "dishy sociology tutor" as a result of similar small, thinking moments before she had lunch with him (see page 112).

Sophie, in telling her story, detailed many moments over the years where her readiness to engage at the moment the telephone rang was being prepared. In this light, the final moment when she could say yes or no was the culmination of these "many small moments." Thus, both the deliberator and the impulsive person function according to similar rules. The way they feel about themselves and their explanations are quite different.

Not every impulsive person is conscious that this is the way they avoid guilt. Hence, such people may be as shocked by the result of their impulsivity as were some of the deliberators by their careful reflection. But there are aspects they share. The impulsive person is saying, "I didn't mean it," "It just happened to me," "I was drunk or stoned at the time, or just didn't know what I was doing"; but the mood that has led them to this action is often not so far removed from that of Matza's delinquent boys, or from Sophie's trapped sense, Dr. Reynolds's need for risk, or Jack's feeling that he was out of touch with his "other half." The mood may be desperate, fatalistic, bored, sexually frustrated, lacking friendship, a sense of value, a sense of growth and movement in life, powerless (or so it seems) to "make things happen"—something which will set death a bit further away, put off the aches and pains of daily living and of aging, help them know that they are alive and, better still, why they are alive. Sometimes, too (and much less serious and ponderous, and perhaps more common), life feels just too serious. What is missing is fun, play, and joy. Marriage is presented as something you have to "work at." Even the pleasures of eating meals and sharing conversation become mere routine.

A woman in a job she had had for twelve years which was stimulating but leading nowhere, married but without any sexual life and sharing little with her husband except the occasional trip abroad, said: "I was dying to meet

this guy and I didn't fix anything. I mean, I really didn't. It just happened."
She really believed this and yet also described seeing this man's application
for a job and "knowing" (she did not say "deciding") that "something
would happen. I saw the writing on the application and thought, 'Wow! This
man is something. I really want to meet him.' " She was a party to his getting
the job and becoming her colleague. So she *felt* her role as unimportant yet,
clearly, it was far from irrelevant in producing the "small moments" that
would lead it "just to happen."

So, too, did it "just happen" for this thirty-five-year-old academic who
was giving a paper at a conference and noticed, in the audience, "this beautiful blonde" sitting in the front row. Afterward they went for a drink and
ended up in bed together: "I didn't stop to think at all. She was beautiful
and we met in the bar later. We had a drink and went to bed that same
night."

Here was a classic situation: powerful man of high status, older, earning
more, clever, standing "above" the woman—on a stage at a lectern; while
she is alluring, young, possibly foolish, and certainly less powerful. According to many stories, they are "made for each other." One problem: he, but
not she, is married. In one sense, this man does not *need* to think because
he is in a privileged position, permitting him at this time in this place to
"take advantage" of the opportunity presented. Nor, being committed still
to his marriage (and to the romantic myth) can he *afford* to think: if he does
he will have to deal with the danger and the possible conflicts such thinking
will arouse. Hence the fact that, of the men and women who did say they
"didn't stop to think," well over half of both groups said this had been of
importance in their decision: in other words, they do lose responsibility
through claiming impulsivity:

> It got completely out of hand. I was crazy about her. She was my beautiful
> dream girl. I was ready to give up everything for her. Maybe if I had
> realized that it might lead to my leaving my wife and kids, I would never
> have begun it . . . but I didn't.

It was not until he spoke of his strong emotion—his love for her (and even
that was tempered with the irresponsible "crazy," the mad person being, by
definition, not in their right mind)—that he used the personal pronoun *I*.
Rather, "*it* got completely out of hand"—all by itself. He took his "dream
girl" away on holiday, bought a flat in an expensive area of the big city near
where she worked, and very nearly did leave his family:

> I couldn't do it. It was the kids, I think. They were so desperate about my
> going. But I still love her. If she walked into this room, I might well just
> walk right out after her. I can't afford, even now [some years later] to
> think too much about her.

He was able only at the beginning to permit his inner to override his rational or socially oriented self (the *I* and the *me* to which I have already referred), and to do so partly because he was in a situation that, as I have already pointed out, gives temporary "permission" to the liaison—that is, in a conference, away from home, with a "strange" person. Hence he need not hold himself responsible for his actions, in this way perhaps also avoiding some of the guilt which his socially oriented self would, and later did, feel.

In other words, such people do not feel they have made any choice. Their emotions "compelled" them. They do not experience moral dilemma because they did not feel free agents at the time. The academic barely recognized that there could be a conflict. And given a man's long entitlement to his "bits on the side," "flings," and other kinds of "playing around"—recreational therapy to make up for the work of marriage—perhaps less conflict and less debate *is* necessary. The moments leading to this choice can, indeed, be small ones.

Thinking about these kinds of liaison as *recreational*, while accepting that the participants may be in a state of "drift," free but not compelled, to have such a liaison, allows a modification of the deliberator/impulsive divide. Indeed, this is (as we saw in chapter 3) part of the modification made by those who change the rules, making private contracts removing sexual exclusivity from the center of their marriages. Sexual encounters become, for them, part of leisure, part of personal development and fulfillment, something as much for relaxation, fun and pleasure as to fill emptiness or loneliness. Sexual relations and sexual relationships are supportive of the marriage, keeping the romantic myth alive rather than escaping it or trying to re-establish it in another monogamous relationship.

Such a modification takes account of the context: Who is impulsive? Where were they? What was their mood? In particular, the person of greater power (and both the woman who had been influential in her lover's success in getting his job [see pages 161–62] and this academic were in positions vis à vis their partners, of relative power) can afford to play at adultery more than the less powerful can. This is true however power is measured (see chapter 9). It may be a question of status or of economic power in the social world, but it may also be a question of emotional dependency and independence. The person who is the more dependent emotionally in a marriage is the one who stands to lose most and is hence the one with least power. Sophie and Dr. Reynolds, for example, were the most powerful in each of their marriages.

That power plays this role is also true of certain whole social groups: thus, the élite and the aristocracy have been most able to play at adultery, to deliberate least and act on impulse most; and, within each social class, it has been men as opposed to women who have had this power. Paradoxically, it may also be that the least socially secure—for example, working-class people or black men—similarly act on impulse most, playing at adultery both as a way of avoiding responsibility—which is a daily grind—and as a form of legitimate recreation. Usually their wives have this advantage only in certain circumstances and in particular couples.[35]

Recreational adultery, it appears, together with the liaison that is under-taken "impulsively," do not require the same degree of emotional work and careful neutralization as other forms because, in these contexts, the moral bind is less strong. However, as in the case of the overwhelmed academic, this depends on an ability to keep it a game and to control the outcome.

The *When,* the *Where,* the *How,* and the *Who*

Life must be understood backwards
But . . . it must be lived forwards.

—Sören Kierkegaard

Miriam, a fifty-seven-year-old, elegant magistrate, married to a successful and much-traveled businessman, explained that if he had affairs on his business trips, she would find that acceptable—"normal":

> I suppose in every year he was away for at least three months. Three to four months. I think I was intelligent enough to realize that a nice-looking young man who goes away would possibly have affairs that were fleeting, and it didn't bother me that he might take up with somebody whilst he was away because I didn't think he would ever indulge in anything that would be lasting. I thought it is only natural and if he did it would be normal—he would only be a normal man; as long as it wasn't a lasting friendship, and my particular marriage wasn't in jeopardy.

Miriam sets certain boundaries around her husband's activities: he should have nothing "lasting"—indicating the care he would have to take in making his choice of person as well, and when and where he might choose, thus controlling possible damage to the marriage.

For a long time, despite these feelings, she was faithful herself ("It never occurred to me *I* might do the same") until, during one of his absences, she was "seduced" by her glamorous tennis coach. This was certainly not "lasting," though she learned her husband "was not the lover I thought he was—not at all!" Hence, she did not construe her own transgression as destructive of her marriage either.

Another woman, when asked how she tolerated her husband's six-month absence in Hong Kong, replied, "I couldn't if it were not for my lover." Thus, location and separation—where a person is and where the spouse is—customarily confer freedoms to *play* not permitted on other occasions and in other places. This theme is well understood by novelists who "permit" their heroes and heroines license or condemn them with this distinction. In Erich Segal's novel *Man, Woman and Child*, the hero, a Harvard professor, has only once, during a long and apparently happy marriage, strayed from the path of fidelity.[1] To allow him this freedom, Segal places him several thousand miles away from Boston, in France, the notorious nursery of seductive women, sets the year as 1968, a year of social unrest and upheaval, and has him at a conference which he is attending not for pleasure but for science. In other words, geographical and social barriers which normally circumvent him, are down; and new conventions—those of the conference—provide the opportunity for an *otherwise* illicit encounter.

David Lodge, another novelist, uses the same convention to allow his academics to jet-set from one seminar and one shared bed to another.[2] In these geographically and socially different settings where the timespan of involvement is (apparently) strictly limited, a certain, perhaps spurious, security is offered for the adulterous meeting. The suggestion is that the conference will end in a few days and so will any adulterous liaison—ships that pass in the night. The problem in Segal's novel is that his hero's brief and passionate encounter has resulted, without his knowledge, in a son. The mother has now, some nine years later, died, the hero is confronted with the extremely physical presence of his child—and the few days are no longer safely encapsulated but explode into his life, suggesting just how critical clear-cut boundaries are if dangerous adultery is not to cause havoc in ordered lives.

There is nothing new about these altered boundaries for travel has always offered opportunities for otherwise forbidden sex as it would have done for those, usually the wives, who stayed at home—hence the chastity belt for the ladies of crusading knights. The pilgrims seeking the salvation of their souls, who walked across Europe through France and Spain to St. Jean de Campostelle in the months between sowing and reaping sought and found many women as they went.[3] And Chaucer's ribald fourteenth-century tales, related among pilgrims *en route* for Canterbury—in which the husbands were frequently depicted as cuckolded figures of fun and the wives as lecherous and lewd mistresses, prepared to sell their favors even to monks and priests, as in, for example, the Shipman's Tale—perhaps reflected much of the pilgrim's own experience.[4] In modern times, a joke is made of the freedom the traveling man has in the film *A Touch of Class*. George Segal plays a married American insurance executive living in London who, quarreling over a taxi as the rain pours down, meets a divorced Englishwoman (Glenda Jackson) who is working "in the rag trade." At his first date with her (tea at the Churchill Hotel), he tells her: "I've been married eleven years and all that time I've never been unfaithful to my wife . . . in the same city. She's out of town just now."

In China at the present time, husbands and wives are often separated for the major part of every year since they may have been assigned jobs in different places and cannot move to live together. This may be helpful when there is a policy of tight population control, but it has led to an increase in adultery which is a serious matter of public and private concern. Indeed, the recent increase in divorce and separation is blamed on a corresponding increase in adultery, something considered "contrary to the social good," and hence liable to criminal prosecution.[5] Adulterous women are sometimes jailed for causing this breach of the social good.

In other societies with very different economic and political systems, travel has similarly affected the rules about acceptable and forbidden sexual encounters. Westermarck describes the Kakoodja, on the South Alligator river in the Northern Territory of Australia:

> If a man goes away for some time, he hands over his wife to some other man of his own class, who, during his absence, is entitled to have sexual intercourse with her. In case she were left alone she would probably be seized by somebody else, or she might herself invite somebody to have connection with her.[6]

Here, too, the separation does not permit the wife unlimited license: rather, she may have as a lover only someone *suitable*, of the same social status, thus ensuring any child of the union is of the right class. The wife must not bring shame on her husband for preferring a lover of lower social status, nor can she be permitted the autonomy of free choice. Alternatively, since she is often assumed to possess extraordinary powers over life and death which are linked to her sexuality, wives have been controlled by being required to engage in elaborate rituals; and, if they failed to follow them or were in fact unfaithful, men in many societies have believed their own lives were at stake. Thus, the Sea Dyaks of Banting in Sarawak thought they would be killed fighting in enemy territory,[7] and elephant hunters in East Africa believed they would not be successful in the hunt in these circumstances.[8] Worse, a woman might even be thought to have caused her *own* death by her infidelity: among the Lele,[9] a woman dying in childbirth was assumed to have been "guilty of adultery and her lover was liable for blood payment. . . . Blood debts were paid in women."[10]

But the geography of place has other meanings, too. Tristan and Isolde, we can recall, drank the potion on board a ship, moving on a shifting sea from her place in Ireland to his and his uncle's at Tintagel, in Cornwall. These places represent the ordered society that must live by known rules; and when, later, they spend some months together, they must be outside the city (or *polis*, the political society) in nature—the forest. Hence, when

Segal and Lodge place their adulterous heros—or would-be lovers, in the case of Lodge—in "conventions" far from home, they employ an ancient metaphor. When Anna Karenina tries to visit her son on his ninth birthday, she trembles with anxiety as she is admitted to what was once her own house because it represents all that she has rebelled against, all that would destroy her, yet it contains a very part of her Self. She it is who is now in the *wrong* place—inside where she should be outside.[11]

An architect (Martin), dreamed he had gone to visit his girlfriend (who was the wife of a friend of his) and was overwhelmed with the sense of invasion of his friend's house. He dreamed he wandered round the rooms which were both familiar and strange. He knew, he said, that he did not belong there. Clearly, he was invading another man's territory in both senses—the house and the woman's body, stealing from his friend. So powerful was this dream that Martin became incapable of making love with his friend's wife unless he took her to "neutral" territory. He was in no doubt that it was his profession that made *where* he was so critically important but, again, novelists and literary critics are aware of the same symbolic meanings:

> It is a truism to note that the house is like a human body. More importantly in this novel [Goethe's *Kindred by Choice*] the house becomes a generative model of relationships, every consciously arranged separation suggesting new combinations by another route. Spaces and the connections between them become entirely problematic and if more than two people are introduced into the house, all relationships become potentially volatile as people put themselves into different rooms or different chairs or, indeed, different beds.[12]

Martin muddled not only houses and territories but friendship and family by choosing his friend's wife, again reminding us of Tristan's double betrayal in choosing Isolde.

People in the study sample often commented on the particular (and poor) choices made by their spouse: they feared the destruction or wounding of their own image, reflected by this poor choice—he or she evidently prefering someone of so little merit. Stendhal long ago explained that adultery involves a greater loss of *amour propre* than of *amour*, and modern people like the Countess of Arcira remain profoundly disturbed by the "idiotic strumpets" or modern "wimps" chosen by their husbands and wives. They were required to look at themselves and renegotiate the marital relationship in the light of this choice. A man said: "I wouldn't mind so much, but he seemed so dull and stupid. Why did she have to choose *him*, for God's sake?" And a woman felt equally affronted: "She really was such a tart. I mean she wore a ton of make-up like you've never seen." In addition to the personal attack poor choice represents, it also is a further undermining of the proper way of the world.

But some choices are more acceptable, because group, clan, or family solidarity is maintained as well as social status: for example, the Banyoro or

Bakitara (in Uganda) permitted sexual intercourse between a man and the wives of those whom he called "clan brothers."[3] If his own wife wanted to have sex with such men, he "might use his influence with [her] to make her refrain from such action," but he could not accuse her of adultery. And among the Nayar on the Indian subcontinent—where men were away a great deal as warriors, and a girl went through a marriage ceremony on entering puberty with a man who "would never be in the everyday sense her husband'"[4]—the "wife" could have as many lovers as she chose so long as they were not of lower social status than her brothers.[5]

Clearly, *who* a woman chooses has mattered in line with the wishes of the men who control her. In modern times, both husband and wife are concerned by the choices their spouses make, though in my sample it was sometimes sexual orientation as much as social status that concerned them. A woman whose husband, after sixteen years of marriage and two children, had declared his homosexuality and taken a male lover, said:

> My first reaction was I felt sick. You know, physically sick. I could have understood it if he had gone for another woman. But then, in a way, I've got to feel easier about it. Because, I mean, well, it can't mean I haven't got what she's got, can it? I *can't* give him what he needs. It's not my fault. I don't have to compare him [the lover] with me.

In other words, there can be comfort as well as pain in the choices made.

In this chapter, I examine each of these issues: When did people have a first liaison? Where did they meet, and whom did they choose? In their thinking, *how* this came about (including the role of opportunity) loomed large: it clarified for many why they had begun an affair. In each case, there are two ways to think about the problem: a person's liaison might be triggered by a specific crisis or reason, but that person may also be one of a group who are all having liaisons sooner or later in a marriage. Similarly, a couple apart, one at a conference and one at home, might have affairs and, at the same time, may be typical of a group beginning, more than in past times, to have affairs at work or with people met through work. Furthermore, *where* they conduct the liaison is subject, as I have suggested, to important and highly charged constraints.

Grace and Ed were in their second marriage, having begun their relationship as sexual partners during their respective previous marriages. Grace was clear that a crisis had precipitated her into many liaisons in her first marriage. The last one had been with Ed, now her husband. She wrote that the ending of her university course, when she and her first husband faced eviction from their home and neither of them knew what to do with their lives, had been critical for her:

> I had a mini-nervous breakdown. This was 1972 when I was twenty-two, and we had been married three years. I had my first three adulterous

liaisons that summer, and another five that winter before we moved to a remote area which is when I should have left him.

Triggering events like these form the central dramatic episode in many accounts of a liaison (though, since as many "faithful" as "unfaithful" re-corded them, they cannot have *caused* the affair).[16] Rather these events help the narrator *make sense* of her or his action: nor is the "moment when" readily or usually separated from where the narrator was—both physically and metaphorically—in space and time. Thus people have an imagined project for their lives, running somewhat according to a social-personal clock,[17] that a crisis event might interrupt but could also usefully move for-ward. A liaison takes on particular meaning in the context of such a precipi-tating crisis or event—even one that is not serious—as Andrea observed:

> In my "affair" the time was right: (a) We were both restless; (b) I was attracted to a man I met at a party; (c) He asked me out—I was tempted but said "no"; (d) My spouse annoyed me by announcing he was going to a football final and coming home about 1 A.M.; (e) I accepted the invite and got involved at that point; (f) THERE WERE NO CHILDREN.

Andrea's life project apparently was set at the "right" time with both her husband and herself "restless" (but without children) and he provided her with a triggering event that also gave her a motive—revenge: since her hus-band annoyed her, or did not give her the time and attention she needed at a period when the flesh was weak and the will even more so, she felt more or less entitled to go ahead. But not with anything more than "a quick one night ego trip" because "one's emotions get so churned up"—a particular reason why, she said, she would never consider any "extramarital involve-ment" if she had young children. Furthermore she *did*, she insisted, "stop to think. [I] went to a party determined to fuck someone." The timing was connected with the fact a particular person was in her mind and a particular place—the party—where she could feel free of restraint. She also was very young—married in the late 1970s and accustomed to sexual pleasure orga-nized and taken at her will and under her control—in this she follows her age and marriage cohort.

Mrs. Long, by contrast, was in her thirties and not at all accustomed to sexual pleasure—from her husband or anyone else. She was firmly bound by convention and determined not to breach the norms and values of her community—that is, no one could know about her affair. Her story echoes much of the ancient adulterous myth—dangerous and exciting, bound to end, both partners married and hence, forbidden. Timing, place, and per-son are all critical. Much more serious than Andrea's "one-night stand," Mrs. Long's passionate and long-lasting affair nonetheless was also trig-gered by a particular set of events at a particular time in her life, when she was in a certain place and the "right" man sought her out and won her.

Mrs. Long had also just been through a particularly trying and, at the same time, exhilarating and sexually tantalizing time when she met her first lover. She had married when she was sixteen. Her groom was five years older—a thoroughly suitable Jewish businessman, part of her own community. She fell in love with his drive, ambition, and competence. She has two sons whom she says "are his sons. He would never give them up. There'd be no forgiveness." This home-grown executive longed for someone to "take charge." She found that her husband no longer met her needs and, despite her wide interests and the fact she had become a magistrate, was not fully "stretched." The summer of her first affair, her widowed mother had remarried and was intensely and marvelously happy. Mrs. Long was delighted by her mother's great joy and went to spend a week's holiday with her and her new husband. All week she was with two people profoundly in love. On the train, on the way home, Mrs. Long met a man who, in fairy-tale tradition, "carried her off":

> I am not at my best in the morning, and I looked a mess, and I didn't have any makeup on. . . . Maybe my resistance was low, but this very charming, dashing young man said to me, "Let me carry your case for you," and I said, "All right." And he took my case, and, "We'll find you a seat," he informed me, and then he got me and put my case down and said, "Come and have a cup of coffee with me." And that was it. Hook, line and sinker.

This man was not Jewish, was university educated and "in big business on the financial side—on the contract side and he dashes all over the world." Mrs. Long had barely finished school. She was "down south"—always sensed as warmer and freer than the chilly north—on a journey; neither here nor there on no one's territory, although she was headed home. Indeed, she wished she had not to return there to her predictable life where everyone knew everyone. It could have been "ships that pass in the night," but this man had everything Mrs. Long needed at that time. She rejoiced in his potency, in bed and out:

> He is the most capable, got-together person that I have ever met in my whole life. . . . It's quite incredible.

> Once I met him and his car wouldn't start. It's automatic and I was always told that if it won't start, really, I mean you might just as well call in the A.A. No. No, no. Out he got, went to his boot [the car trunk], got a screwdriver, opened the lid of the bonnet [the hood], juggles around with the screwdriver, and he'd fixed the damn thing.

> At first it was purely physical. He is the first person I have ever met who physically really does——I mean, let's face it, the minute I see him, we are already in bed, and that's it. Quite incredible.

Her lover was different from anyone else she knew, and married, making him "safer" for he was not, apparently, unhappy and had no intention of leaving his wife and children. The affair lasted a long time and was kept entirely separate from both their homes. They met always in London, staying in her friend's flat (the one confidante she permitted herself) or in hotels paid for by her lover. Like others marrying in the 1960s, Mrs. Long was faithful for quite a long time before this affair. The circumstances, the place, the opportunity, and the choice of person fitted perfectly with the adulterous myth and helped her make her fantasy come true.

The Timing of the First Liaison

The leading characters of chapter 5 chose to have their first liaisons at varying times in their life dramas. Jack, at forty—after some fifteen years of marriage with a capable if cool wife, his children teenagers, and his business well established—made a fantasy come true, propelled to do so by what he called his "male menopause." Sophie—married less time and at an earlier life stage altogether, her children much younger, and her marriage much less satisfying—sought comfort and a renewed sense of herself, the crisis of her husband's mental breakdown past, but her mother's death a fresh wound. Dr. Reynolds was not so long married or at such an early life stage but between the two as he played security and comfort against passion and danger. In earlier chapters, one man, after a mere three weeks of marriage, went off with a "whore"; while another had sex with his wife's sister in the week before his marriage; and Bud and Lee or Maisie and Harry continued liaisons without interruption or began new ones as they became married couples.

What, I wonder, happened to various commonsense theories current in our culture about the timing of affairs such as the somewhat lighthearted attitude to the "seven-year itch," suggesting the time in a traditional marriage when a desire for variety or perhaps disillusion with the ideal might surface? (This was a phrase used more than once as an "explanation" for a readiness to "look around for opportunities.") What about theories about the jealous or frustrated father when the first baby is born, and "that dangerous age"? Indeed, there are some general patterns in timing that do play a part in the individual decisions each person makes. In particular, as the examples of Grace and Ed and of Andrea—who went to the party and "fucked someone" when she had been married four years—indicate, people are having their first liaison *sooner* after marriage than they used to—a tendency particularly marked for the generation married in the 1970s, and women especially have shortened the "waiting time" or what we might call

TABLE 6.1
*Duration of (First) Marriage before First
Liaison (Women and Men Who Have
Had at Least One Liaison)*

	Mean (Years)	
	Women	Men
All Marriages	8.9	8.2
Those Married before 1960	14.6	11.3
1960–69	8.2	7.9
1970 or later:	4.2	5.3

their "fidelity span." However, the 1970s turn out to be a time of change for everyone: whatever was happening in each individual private marriage and in each person's emotional life, the decade—1968 to 1978—is a time of shifting marital boundaries. Indeed, one in three of all first liaisons had taken place by 1972 and half by 1977.[18]

The average length of time waited before the first liaison was around eight, and the midpoint for waiting was around seven years.[19] It seems the seven year itch does not remain unscratched. But this "fidelity span" was much longer among older people married before 1960 and much less for those who have married in the 1970s or later as table 6.1 indicates.

Whereas women married before 1960 waited on average fourteen and a half years for a first liaison, those married in the 1970s waited just over four years, overtaking men who used to wait about eleven and now a little over five years. In other words, only one in four of those persons who married before 1960 had a first liaison within the first five years of their wedding; but by 1970, this was true of *two out of every three* of the women marrying at that time or later and of *nearly half* the men. Thus, younger women have overtaken younger men in the rapidity with which they have affairs, and have caught up with men in the number they have.

One problem: it is difficult to be certain about this change because, of course, those married most recently have had the least "opportunity" to have a liaison. That is, someone married twenty years has been "exposed to the risk of an affair and of having more than one" (as the doctors might say about a disease) twice as long as someone married only ten years. On the other hand, if the person in a longer marriage had spent most of that time in prison, the risk (at least of heterosexual relationships) would be much less than that of the ten-year married person who is freely mixing with others. In order to take account of the shorter duration of the most recent marriages, therefore, I have calculated for everyone the proportion *remaining faithful* after two, four and six years, up to thirty years of marriage.[20]

As many as one quarter of people marrying in or after 1970 had their first

affair within two years of their wedding date. Even after eight years, between about two thirds and three quarters of those married before 1970
were still "faithful," but this was true of only just over half of the 1970s
marriages. Furthermore, there was little difference between the wives and
the husbands in the timing of this first liaison for those married before
1970. But women married in the 1970s had their first liaison sooner than the
husbands. In this marriage cohort, only just over half the wives had *not* had
at least one liaison by the time they had been married eight years, while 60
percent of the men were still faithful.

Given these "waiting times," it is apparent that regardless of when people
had married, the late 1960s and the 1970s were the time when most had their
first liaisons. In this sense, then, the young people marrying in the 1970s
were not behaving very differently from their older sisters, brothers, uncles,
aunts, and parents. Premarital sex became commonplace; and extramarital
sex, if not commonplace, certainly more common, not just for those marrying at that time but for everyone. In particular, this seems to be true for
women. The women in this sample have moved from waiting on average
four years *longer* than their husbands for a first liaison to waiting one year
less. It is both the oldest and the youngest women and men who are the most
faithful—though, given more time, the youngest may surpass their older
brothers and sisters. It is not so much age, however, that is important here,
but gender. That is, although it matters that you are fifty or thirty, the major
influence on whether you remain faithful, and on the number of affairs you
have, is (according to a statistical analysis using regression) whether you are
a woman or a man. Unlike Jack who regretted that he had so often failed to
say yes to life's opportunities (in a sense before his conversion to the Myth
of Me), the youngest and most recently married women do not seem to have
said no. Indeed, they were willing to create opportunities themselves. How
can these patterns be explained?

Unhappiness and Timing

Common sense would suggest that people have affairs because "there is
something wrong." As faithful Vicky said:

> I would say there would always be something lacking in it to make them
> need to go outside. There must be. They're perhaps getting on very well
> in certain ways, but there must be something that is lacking. Don't know
> what it is because that's obviously such a personal thing—what people
> need from each other and life in general.

And the newly married Susan: "I would immediately try and find out what
had gone wrong to make him do it at this particular time."

Certainly Sophie and many like her would explain their liaisons as arising
out of troubled marriages. But these explanations refer to the need for an

affair whenever it occurs, rather than giving a reason why some people would wait longer or less time than others. Unhappiness might explain why 1960s marriages had the most liaisons, but then how can it also explain the speed with which 1970s people, especially the young women married then, had their first affair?

What mattered most, it seems, was what people believed about marriage and about the freedom they had to pursue their own goals—in other words, their adherence to one or the other of the two myths. And the relative salience of the two myths had altered by the late 1960s. Thus, people who were unhappy and disappointed in the marital relationship but married before 1960, and who believed strongly in the traditional rules of marriage, were unlikely to have a liaison. If they did, they waited a long time, until general beliefs and attitudes changed in the society. In this way, people's feelings are supported by the culture of the time even as they as individuals contribute to that culture. Even people happy in marriage but married in the 1970s and feeling entitled to explore the self, including the sexual self, were highly likely to have a liaison.[21]

When people have their first liaison is also related very strongly indeed to the number of affairs they eventually will have. Those who have only one wait longer for this experience than those who have two to four, and those who have more than this have their first a great deal sooner after marriage than everyone else. In fact, those who had many were likely to have had the first *within* the first five years of the wedding day; while those who had only one waited for it, on average, over ten years. Someone with a strong commitment to the Myth of Romantic Marriage sees this as "promiscuity," "cheating," "fooling," or "playing" around. It becomes a habit, something "outside" the marriage and well compartmentalized from it. For strong adherents of the Myth of Me and to the open marriage, no equivalent protection by means of derogatory labeling is necessary. The liaisons are for pleasure and fun, without being seen as a betrayal of trust or threat to the marriage; and their timing is thus irrelevant.

Timing is, however, related to whether a couple stay together. That is, those who would separate had their first liaison earlier than those who stayed together (at least they had done until 1982–83 when the data were collected). Furthermore, this was true of the permissive as well as of the more traditional marriages. These figures fit well with the reduced duration of marriages before divorce and indicate a continuing strong link between adultery and the end of a marriage. In England in 1961, 11 percent of marriages ended within five years. In 1981, 20 percent ended within that period.[22] Even if AIDS had not appeared to give everyone second thoughts about multiple sexual partners, these two trends indicate that adultery is unlikely to increase; people will not stay married long enough.

Not surprisingly, especially given the need people have to make sense of their actions, those who were most unhappy, or reported the most conflict in their marital relationship at the time of their first liaison, had their first affairs much faster than those who reported less conflict.

Unhappiness is a subjective state, of course, and depends on a person's expectations. During the last two or three decades, the expectations people have of the quality of the marital relationship have probably increased, while their chances of getting out of one that does not meet those expectations have certainly improved through better economic conditions and easier divorce.[23] At the same time, it is women who invest so much more of themselves in their emotional lives than do men, and women who are less willing to sacrifice the chance of happiness in a satisfying long-term relationship by staying in one that appears to have failed. It is also women who now believe they can manage without marriage, even without a man (witness the increase in women choosing to have babies without living with or, on occasion, acknowledging the child's father). Even if the liaison does not lead to a divorce and remarriage (and few do) the hope is often that it will provide emotional rewards previously sought in the Myth of Romantic Marriage.

I am suggesting, then, that it may be those whose disappointment is greatest (which is not the same as experiencing the most conflict, as crudely measured) who have the most liaisons and have them soonest after marriage. Women, especially since the women's movement and other material changes already discussed, can expect and hope for more than ever before. The reality of both love and work is, however, often far from the hope.

Taking Revenge

Frieda, who married during the 1960s and had her first liaison in the 1970s, is a woman whose disappointment was considerable. She and her husband had no children. He blamed her for this, and Frieda herself, being a Catholic, saw her lack of children as a mortal sin. She was made periodically miserable by a husband who expected her to look after him and to run his house according to his standards but never telling her just what these standards were. Thus, often for "no reason"—or, if there was one, she was ignorant of it—he would "put her in coventry"—refusing to talk or sleep with her. Sophie would not have understood nor would she have approved Frieda's need or her actions: "Oh, yes. Many's the time I've been down on my knees, begging him for sex. Oh yes."

But Frieda had tried to deal with these problems early in her marriage (in only three years they faced sexual estrangement and, as she felt, a lack of understanding on his part about their difficulties in conception). "Raging and furious inside," Frieda then took her revenge. In the discussion group, she described the events that led to her first liaison:

> I think it started off with the first affair when I did say to him, "You know, if we don't do something about this problem" (because I like to talk things

through, straight to the end) "something will happen sometime." But the attitude of my husband is that I must never rock the boat. I must never want to discuss things. I must never ask for anything. I must not want a social life because if I rock the boat to this extent which disturbs what is a nice, deadly dull, bloody life sitting around doing nothing, you know, if I complain, then sex is over, conversation is over. . . . He doesn't discuss anything, because he won't. And I struggled with myself and eventually opportunity presented itself. Somebody cared.

Somebody cared at a moment also when—having promised he would— her husband had refused to sign papers that would have given her a stronger share of the marital property, *and* she was in coventry again.

Frieda's delight was almost tangible as she related her adventure, bring- ing a lover home under a rug in the back of the car and driving right into the garage:

This way it meant even the neighbors don't see. I used to take this guy into my place on the back seat of the car with a blanket over him. It was quite funny really because I used to leave the garage gates open, we have a big fence at the side. I used to drive right into the garage, shut the garage gate behind me, have a little shifty round, open the garage gate into the patio which went into the kitchen, take a look around and say, "Right, in you go." It was hilarious. He found it terribly funny. We used to be screaming laughing, tears streaming down our faces, you know. Have a quick drink when we got in. Fine and . . . up to the actual nitty gritty in the bedroom and no one could see a thing or had any idea what I was up to.

And when I thought about it, the first time I did it I lay in bed that night giggling. I could see it all happening. You know what I mean? Like a picture and I thought, "God, what are you doing?" Then I thought, "Well, it's a practical way of dealing with the situation so let's do it."

I changed the sheets and everything, and then that night—oh, it was amazing really because he wouldn't speak to me. I'm in coventry at the moment you see, and I could lie there just thinking, "Oh, you don't know, you don't know the half of it!" Cuckolded he was and in his own bed.

Her husband exerted considerable power over her. Her adultery was her way to deny him success in keeping her down and to do something solely for herself, thus exercising her own power. Her chosen moment seemed an "opportunity" that "presented itself," but she was clearly ready. As she said, she had both threatened him with "something will happen . . ." and offered him a way to reduce that possibility. She said, too, she had already "struggled with herself." Having fleshly communion with her lover who "cared," she denied herself the comfort of communion in Church. In other words, she chose her "moment" because she felt miserable in her marriage.

(This is a case where there was certainly no problem of overkill on "talk and communication"; there was none.) She shifted position from the Myth of Romantic Marriage to the Myth of Me. She told the others in her group, several of whom were, by chance, also believing Christians: "I couldn't say 'God joined us together and marriage vows are sacred and that's it.' I . . . put myself ahead of that, put *my* needs which were very strong *at the time*."

Changing belief was used both as part of the motivation for an affair (as in Frieda's case, to do something for *me* and to get back at her repressive husband who coerced her into fulfilling, not a romantic but a powerless, traditional role in her marriage) and as a response to a triggering event (Frieda's husband's refusal to sign the property papers)—that is, as justification. When a senior administrator in the civil service first discovered his wife's affair, he felt "shattered"; but as they talked and discussed it, he and his wife came to a new agreement about what should and should not be permissible. Hence, both were freed—she to continue her affair; he to begin one of his own. Her actions are now justified and he is provided with a new motive. Those, like this man, who have become more permissive since marriage, had their first liaisons longer after their wedding day than did those who did not alter their beliefs—whether permissive or not. Like him, these people made their actions consistent with their changing beliefs.[24]

Birth, Death, and Illness

The figures overall give little support to the idea that men are particularly vulnerable in the period around the birth of a first child. Indeed, only about 15 percent of new fathers or mothers had a first affair in the year preceding, the year itself, or the year following the birth of the first child. Furthermore, over half the women waited until after the birth of the *youngest* child before they embarked on a first liaison. The *timing*, thus, does not seem to have been affected much by the first baby's arrival, but events surrounding the birth, including the death or illness of a baby, were mentioned as disturbing events altering the relationship between spouses (women accusing husbands most commonly of lacking understanding of such an event's meaning for them), and both being liable to seek comfort in another person's arms.

This, indeed, was the reason the civil servant who reached a new agreement with his wife, gave for his wife's affair. One of his children, he explained, had been very ill at birth and his wife had felt he had lacked understanding of what this meant to her; he now thinks his wife's affair (which triggered his own) was partly due to the loneliness she felt at that time. Again, we are drawn to the drama that is being described and to the immense weight placed in the modern marriage on the *quality* of the relationship—on the intimacy achieved. This man is acknowledging his wife's need and justifies her affair with his own emotional absence. Thus, it is not the fact of the baby's birth, nor its illness, but the impact on their marital relationship that must be integrated into the story of their liaisons.

In age, women averaged thirty-one years, and men nearly thirty-three, when they had their first liaison. Thus, parental death was not a common experience; yet in contrast to the birth of a child, it was powerfully placed (as by Sophie) in the narrative of the first liaison, particularly by women.

Early in the study, various women spoke of the deaths of parents—specifically, of their husbands losing their mothers. When Miriam's mother-in-law died, her husband was away on a business trip. Miriam told me that her husband "did not come near" her for a whole year—and even then, only when she insisted that they begin to pick up the threads of their marriage again. Twenty-nine-year-old Suki, who, as she said, surprised herself by returning from a holiday in Italy "having fought the good fight and won" by *not* having sex with a man whom she felt was extremely desirable and about which she felt cross rather than pleased, also said her husband had "turned against her when his mother died." Yet, by contrast, sun-tanned Helen, a faithful woman in her mid-thirties and a marriage counselor, who lived in the depths of a small country village, explained that the death of her husband's mother had "made a man of him" and not just sexually (though that was important) but also at work and in his dealings with the children. Miriam (then forty-three) learned only later that her husband was, during this period, deeply involved with a much younger woman (she was twenty-eight) as if his mother's death had released him for such a relationship but turned him away from his own hearth and home, his mother's forcefulness possibly having kept him in at least a semblance of his "proper place." Helen's husband was instead released in a much more general sense to become more fully adult. In a later interview, Mrs. Inkerman talked of *her* husband's response to his mother's death as permitting them a rare closeness. She could offer and he could accept, at that time, comfort, which brought them together.

Each of these responses varied but it would be strange if parental death did not have important effects on adult children, and on their own parental and sexual lives. So, too, does the fact of one's own eventual mortality, particularly as a *parent*, have profound effects that must be integrated into the ongoing narrative of one's life. Marilyn Yalom, in her recent *Maternity, Mortality and the Literature of Madness*,[25] has analyzed—through the writings and the lives of certain literary women (among them, Sylvia Plath, Margaret Atwood, Maxine Hong Kingston, and Marie Cardinal) who "went mad" and/or wrote about women struggling with madness—the meaning of childbirth, as with each birth the delivering mother faces the fact of her own mortality and, sometimes, as her body takes control, a terrifying alienation from it and hence, from herself. The very fact of maternity, her own and her mother's in giving birth to her and in the mothering that follows, requires a reconciliation with the real or imagined mother, for the daughter's identification with her mother is the most important psychological dynamic in her development.[26] In the case of Lucy, a sophisticated Londoner of thirty-eight, this loss had also been closely tied to her sense of her body as belonging to her, something over which she, and no man, should have sole control:

> I feel that my body is mine and what I choose to do with it is my responsibility, but it has taken me a long time to get here. . . . In the midst, after her [mother's] death, definitely, in the midst of all the sadness and all the rest of it, there was a relief, not that she was gone, but that I am now free to decide what I must do with myself. . . . Took a while to articulate it.

In other words, death of a parent may have an optimistic face—a potential for maturation and freedom (and for making decisions about having an affair) which is hidden by the continuing presence of the parent.

While only 8 percent of men thought illness or an accident had played some part in their marital or extramarital lives, over one quarter of women thought such events had affected them—a further explanation of a continuing greater need for women to explain their adultery.

It was housewives (according to their own description) who were the most likely to explain their actions by the crisis of illness. Indeed, if women were employed in any capacity—full- or part-time or self-employed—they were less likely than full-time housewives to feel that illness or an accident had affected them. Some were perhaps at home *because* of such crises. Thus a woman with multiple sclerosis who participated in another study[27] explained she did not know how long she would have a body that anyone found desirable: she was "going to make the most of it" while she could. It seems likely, however, that sickness at home, whether one's own or someone else's, looms larger without both the emotional and material support that may be available from working.

Illness in a spouse is also an event used to *justify* or excuse an affair. An elderly man whose wife became disabled now lives with his "mistress"; he supports his wife in a nursing home, visits her, and tries to feel that he is doing all for the best. He knows, however, that his wife, although condoning his "parallel" arrangement, is not happy about it.

The Mid-Life Crisis and Choice of Person

Even the "mid-life" crisis—a ready reason for many upheavals—is more commonly described by women than by men, but this was an experience that substantial numbers of men also described as having impinged on them. Thus, of those who answered this section of the questionnaire, over one in four of men and more than one in three of women said they had been affected by some such crisis in their lives. But men outnumbered women in believing they, rather than their spouses, had been affected. And wives agreed that their husbands were most affected.

We can think of Jack's "male menopause" perhaps, and the longing of the man as he passes some specific age, perhaps thirty-five, perhaps later,[28] for certainty that he is still potent, still capable of "conquering" the hero-ines of his youthful days. It is the notion of "that dangerous age" that we see here, the same, perhaps, as when the hero Peter Nichols portrayed in *Passion Play* is seduced by a younger siren-lady dressed in black underwear and heavily perfumed.[29] It is very much part of the adulterous tale.

This male mid-life crisis also affects *who* is chosen as the adulterous part-ner: Not, of course, always—but frequently enough for the idea to have entered into our jokes and comic strips—these are the men who choose single and younger women. The men in this sample who described them-selves as having been through a mid-life crisis were much more likely to choose single (younger) women as their first partners than were men who did not go through such a crisis. Less than one quarter of these men chose a married woman, but half of the men who did not experience a mid-life crisis did so. In this way, their choices complete the drama they are enacting.

The mid-life crisis was not, of course, experienced only by men. Women, too, repeatedly commented on the overwhelming feeling they had that life at thirty-five or forty was slipping away too fast.

This was the time when Fanny, looking in her mirror on her thirty-fifth birthday, thought, "There must be something more to life than this." While Sara, talking in similar vein, said, "I was coming up to forty and I remember consciously thinking, 'Forty, that's horrible. It's getting too late.' I'm not sure I was looking for another man, but I did feel: 'What had I done so far? What had I achieved? What about *my* life?' " But this did not lead them into choosing single or younger men. Women generally "preferred" married men and did not change in this preference according to whether they had had a mid-life crisis. It is difficult for women in our culture to find younger lovers—though the picture is changing;[30] while older men have always been desirable partners for younger women. This is one of the factors that makes fewer single men available to women than there are single women available to men. In addition, whereas men's response to a mid-life crisis seems to be to re-enact the Tristan role, women more often sought someone *safe* as well as someone strong and dominant (as we saw with Mrs. Long). Whereas Jack's choice of a young, foreign, wealthy girl had permitted him to consum-mate his love and yet, because she made it so clear that she would not disrupt his family, was also safe, Fanny's choice of a married man who was currently escaping from a previous affair with another married woman and wanted very much to "go straight," was much safer. Indeed, remember, she "never slept with him." Sara's response to her crisis was to have an affair and she chose someone whom she thought would meet all her needs for intimacy and safety, but he proved no more satisfying in this respect (though he was a "great lover") than her husband.

Women married in the 1960s particularly described "other crises" as hav-ing been important to them. Perhaps the crisis (mid-life for men and "other" for women) affecting this generation was the crisis of 1968, with turbulent civil disturbance in the United States and Europe, and the years immediately following; but for many, it was the discovery of a spouse's affair or perhaps some general malaise, difficult to pinpoint.

A Spouse's Affair

Although the civil servant felt his wife's affair had triggered his own, women more frequently described this situation: they felt betrayed and abandoned and very angry. Sharon, a "housewife with small children," said she was "badly affected" by her husband's extramarital affair in the spring of 1977 when he left home for three months. Feeling unattractive and undesirable, she was spurred into an affair herself; Sharon was twenty-eight years old and had been married eight years. Another woman, feeling "great restlessness" and that "life was passing by" (although she was only just thirty) explained she "returned to college, lost a lot of weight and opened my mind to other relationships. . . . Committing adultery," she felt, caused her husband in his turn to start a relationship with someone in 1981. In a similar way, Leila's husband's affair led to her own. She had a dream about her husband being unfaithful. When she asked him about this, he did not deny it, and Leila said "I even got her name right!" Later she tackled him about his secretary, and "he couldn't deny this either." She said, "I felt devastated and let down." Eventually she came to terms with it, discussed things with her husband, and, like the civil servant and his wife, they changed their agreement about other relationships. She encouraged him to continue his affair with his secretary and "began to have one myself." Now, she says, "we both make opportunities for each other." Leila had, like Sharon, been married eight years, and was thirty-two years old in 1981 when she had this first "relationship." Over the next two years, while the first continued, she had another six, of which the last had been going on for nearly a year— both the patterned stories typify their age and gender: an entitlement to be more equal, to grasp the same opportunities as are available to men.

Opportunity: The Role of Work and Education

Everyone who completed a questionnaire was asked what part "opportunity" played in their actions (see appendix A, question 22). Most thought it very important. Opportunity had been either "important or crucial" for 30 percent of women and 35 percent of men and 'not relevant at all' for a mere 6 percent of women and 10 percent of men. A fifty-two-year-old aeronautical engineer, who had two liaisons during his first marriage and is now happily (and faithfully) married to the latter of these partners, wrote:

I think there is a lot of truth in [the idea that adultery is 90 percent opportunity]. Opportunities played a large part in my two adulterous liaisons. Being rather "slow-witted" I have recognized since that there were a number of other opportunities that were offered that I missed!

And a forty-two-year-old Scotsman (a lecturer), who said his mid-life crisis consisted of a general feeling of being fed up, observed:

This is complex. Given that I had no objection in principle to extramarital relationships and a positive wish to pursue them, I would have been pleased to have had greater opportunities than in fact I did. However, I also imagine that my temperament and social conditioning inhibited me from taking advantage of opportunities which did in fact exist.

Two people, both married and living with their respective spouses, replied together as an adulterous couple. They felt they had made no actual *decision* to have an affair, since there had been "an inevitability about the relationship"; yet, in fact, they had mulled over the possibility of consummating it for more than a year, keeping it during this time to a nonsexual bond (an affair of the heart, without sex). Both said they loved their spouses and had good marriages. Each discussed their feelings with others: he with his mother; she with her brother and four female friends. They felt all of these confidants had encouraged them to continue their relationship, and it had now become a fully sexual one. About their opportunities, the man, an architect, aged forty-five, wrote: "If I had not been self-employed, I would not have been able to have a daytime 'affair,' nor would I have met my partner, who was a client." And the woman, a housewife trained as a teacher, and aged thirty-eight, said:

We both took one step each to create opportunities for our relationship to flourish. He invited me onto a committee. I, a year later, invited him to come and talk as I wanted to thank him for the good he had done me. This tipped us into expressing openly our feelings for each other. From then on, we were able to make use of our comparative freedom to meet— he, self-employed; I, a housewife (although with a baby)!

Around 13 percent of both women and men believed they had created their own opportunities, many simply writing, as this man did: "One can always create the opportunity." Yet for some it was easier than for others, as Miriam recognized:

If there is an opportunity there and there is the right "chemistry," then it is easier for a "liaison" to take place. My husband had opportunities all the time as he spent weeks away abroad on business in hotels when I was tied at home bringing up the children.

Perhaps the right "chemistry" can be enhanced by other kinds of chemicals. One man used "booze," writing that he had happily enjoyed "fifty, one hundred, maybe more" liaisons, and that his wife had had "fifteen":

> I had probably created opportunity through booze parties with, say twenty plus, married couples . . . in the early 1960s in Kenya. The experience enabled my wife and I to cope with adulterous relationships from then on, whenever the opportunity arose.

He and his wife were clearly emotionally open to the "right chemistry" and the right practical opportunity. They expressed the idea voiced by many others over many centuries that there is freedom to experiment and freedom to break rules or to create new ones in new places. Being away from home is a push-and-pull situation: at home, the rules are well known and better "policed," and the chances of being caught and punished greater; traveling offers new experiences and the chance to experiment, and there is a relaxation of customary practices. Furthermore, white people in Kenya in the early 1960s were a special class with their own boundaries, loosened toward one another, in order perhaps to ensure the meshing of people into one another's lives in many ways and at many levels, while at the same time boundaries were tightened against the black people beyond. This couple was saying that such conditions, especially if remaining inhibitions are loosed by "booze," enable the necessary openness.

This openness has to be motivated, and that motivation is widely varied. As we have seen, those in open marriages already have set the scene for opportunity. They are motivated to ignore "conventional morality," to enjoy what comes, and to help find and create opportunities for themselves and for each other. Yet Maisie wrote that "neither of us feels it necessary to search for other lovers." The freedom to be open resulted for her not in celibacy but in a lack of incentive to have multiple lovers. In contrast, Frieda became open to an opportunity through her twin needs for revenge and for comfort; while Suki longed for her husband to "do something horrible" so she could feel "open" to take up her Italian suitor's offer. Similarly, Dennis, desperately climbing the stairs every Wednesday to his young mistress's apartment, afraid each may be his last time, said of his wife's possible involvement with another man, "It's better if she's having one, too." You need, these people were saying, a "reason" to have an extramarital affair. It remains something bad; something about which you will feel guilty and, perhaps ashamed (even if it is also delightful, even essential to your well-being). Hence if he does "something horrible" or she "has one, too," you can feel relieved of the responsibility for behaving "properly," and entitled to your own misdemeanors or to taking retribution into your own hands. Thus, the moment *when*, for those who sense a continuing ban, has to be placed in the context of events in a person's life that enable the "neutralization" of his or her doubts (see pages 160–61).

Lynn Atwater found that the forty American women in her study could be divided into those who, like Andrea (see page 170), having first refused an invitation, reflect and think it perhaps not such a bad idea, and those who do not quite know how to say no. In all cases, they have to perceive themselves as *open to an opportunity*: "the first tentative step toward involvement begins with personal awareness of opportunity for [extramarital sex]."[31]

But some are better at creating their own opportunities than others. Gender scripts are changing, especially for women; and the youngest generation have a wider range of possible scripts to pursue than their older sisters. But, of course, these women change in relation to men with certain dramatic effects. Thus, Keith, the twenty-nine-year-old delivery man who was invited by "bored housewives" to "go upstairs," was actually "frightened" by this unusual (because a reversal of expected patterns) event:

The frightening thing is that there's more women asked *me* than I asked. There's none of this groping sort of thing and, you know, hand on knee sort of thing. None of that. It's just straight out with it, "Would you like to go to bed?" "Wow, yea!" Or I would say, "Do you fancy going to bed?" dead casual like, and expecting to put my coat on and head for the door, you know, and when they said, "Yeah, let's go," you know, wow! It's really difficult to explain how one feels about it. You just take it as a matter of . . . as a matter of fact.

Well, it's a great example of the opportunity presenting itself and me being a good heterosexual, well, obliged. I mean, there are times when it didn't always work because you were frightened to death.

So far as Keith was concerned, there was no particular moral dilemma (nothing exactly sensed as "bad"), but he was concerned and anxious. Normal roles were reversed; his own gender and sexual script questioned, sometimes causing him to be unable to function because he was frightened. Indeed, this was a fright "to death," perhaps also because if the husband came back, murder might follow. The old tales of adultery and death are not far distant from Keith's conscious reasoning.

For Keith, the choice of both *who* his adulterous partners were and *where* they might meet and cement each "brief encounter" was made through his particular opportunity. His macho image of himself provided the psychological openness; his work, the practical potential.

Place and Person

Work and Education

Keith was not alone in finding his partners through his work. (And his favored place for making love was almost his workplace! It was certainly his lovers' homes.) Let me explore where and in what circumstances liaisons arose and then where they were conducted. One in three of lovers were people met at work: that is, those who actually worked in the same place as the respondents. Another fifth arose in work-related meetings. Indeed, this probably still underestimates meetings that were "work related" since those lovers who were "friends already" (13 percent of those saying "other") and those who met through a friend (15 percent), have not been included here, though they were acquaintances that had often been made through work or work-related meetings. For example, lovers were colleagues or work-mates of husbands and wives, while teachers and professionals reported that their first lover was a pupil or client or that they had met another teacher or a colleague who worked in the same profession. Similarly the partner was often someone in the same company but not in the same building. Some examples were: "business acquaintance"; "contact met through work—lunch"; "worked in same occupation"; "wife of works' colleague"; "a client"; "customer"; "sister of an employee"; "professional colleague working in a different place"; "husband of boss"; "traveling to work."

Clearly, if women are not at work, they cannot meet lovers in this way; but the increasing number of women who do work outside their homes does not account for the facts that *more* women than men find their first lovers there now, and that although similar proportions of women married before 1960 and in 1970 or later were in paid employment at the time of the survey (actually rather fewer of the younger than of the older women), 44 percent of the younger women had met their lovers through work compared with about one quarter of the older women. We need to find other reasons for this pattern. They lie in the excitement of the workplace which holds in our culture the key to value and esteem (even when the work may be mundane and unexciting); in the nature of the work done by women and by men; and in the strain experienced by women as they make the psychological shift required in moving from hearth and home, where a female ethic is predominant, to work environments which have been largely mapped to suit the demands of a male-ordered world controlled by a male ethic.[32] By female ethic, I mean those beliefs and practices that set personal relations, connectedness, and continuity—perhaps caring—as paramount. By the male ethic, I mean those values that stress justice, logic, and rationality. Both are valuable, both necessary; and women can operate according to the male ethic, men according to the female. The structures and demands of work settings, the potential to exercise power and control and to gain tangible material rewards, tend toward the male ethic; hearth and home, to the female.

Paid work and a return to education as an adult both may offer new people, new environments, changing horizons and practical opportunities for a love affair or even a brief encounter. People also *felt* that work was important in rather more symbolic ways. Nearly a third felt their own success at work had influenced them toward a liaison—an attitude more true of women than men. Being successful outside the home seems to mean the opening of other kinds of success—perhaps a modern form of conquest. Similarly, of the one fifth to one quarter who felt their jobs had "changed their outlook on life," 70 percent were women. Again, of men, only 8 percent, but of women 20 percent, thought returning to work or changing a job had been of profound importance in influencing them toward a liaison. These people—mainly women—gain a new kind of independence at work as well as practical opportunities.

But, as with the "mid-life" or other crises, returning to work or re-entry to education does not lead necessarily to a first liaison. Mrs. Inkerman's educational course, for example, was offering new ideas, prospective lovers, and practical opportunities although she continued to live at home; but for the time being, it was the ideas that mattered, not sex. Where Plato enthralled her, another women said she "was turned on by walking into a room full of Freud's books." Perhaps this had to do with their content, but I think she meant that the intellectual excitement of discovering great ideas was fulfilling enough without an actual "other," without another body. On the other hand, for Jack, being in a university both opened his mind to new ways of thinking and offered him a young partner, freedom from home, and practical opportunity which he used.

Generally speaking, women were more affected by education (around a quarter compared with around a fifth of men), and it is those women who married in the 1960s for whom it was most important. These are the women whose education was less than their abilities and who grasped the opportunity to take up Open University courses or other retraining schemes. The husbands agreed that their wives had been so affected, and Mr. Inkerman's fears of his wife's extramural (if not extramarital) course were well founded. He was losing her, perhaps not to another man in the flesh, but certainly and surely to Plato and Aristotle and to all those much more recent philosophers and, as she said, sociologists whose ideas "were terribly exciting." To say he had every reason to fear is not, of course, to say he was right. It is to say that his attitude was thoroughly comprehensible in terms of his own self-interest, just as hers was comprehensible in terms of hers.

Education has the power to change people in fundamental ways; if the partner will not follow or cannot follow where education beckons the adventurer, a gap that might not previously have been there is opened. We have already seen (in chapter 2) that wives who are better educated than husbands are likely to have not only one liaison but more than other women, while husbands in these marriages have fewer liaisons than average. A woman begins in this respect to "look like" a man, and he to "look like" a woman. Even when, at the outset of marriage, the educational differences were in the expected direction—that is, the husband's equal to or higher than the wife's—women like Mrs. Inkerman, Mrs. Long, and Mrs. Waterford learned their own strength as home-grown executives; and, in each case, their husbands, as we saw in chapter 4, were frightened to let these newly powerful wives go. And *power* is the clue. People with traditional backgrounds feel it unnatural that wives should be more independent, more capable, more educated than their husbands. It reverses long-accepted understandings of the proper place for each to occupy. This reversal becomes confusing and threatening. Returning to higher education may not mean that a wife or a husband actually has an affair (though many did, particularly at weekend or summer courses involving several days spent with tutors and fellow students away from home), but it sets the mood (the yearning I noted in chapter 5) for a new intimate relationship.

Independence is another key word. When Mr. Crowborough asked his wife to give up her course, he expressed his dislike in terms of her increasing independence of him, not materially but in her *thinking*. In thinking she was saying "I" a good deal too often, Mr. Crowborough had put his finger on something important. For the capacity to think and act independently is a necessary precursor to taking any opportunity. If the primary idea one has of the self is as half of a couple, then it is not *I* but *we* taking decisions and moving through life. Indeed, the use of the personal pronoun in everyday speech tells much about the way individuals think of themselves, and such use is altered as they contemplate an affair. *We* may be employed consciously to make it clear to the listener that there is "another half," perhaps to warn, perhaps to play the honesty game ("Well, you knew I was married"). Equally, *I* can be used to hide the facts and to begin an engagement. In a new educational setting, *we* would be inappropriate. It is not the couple who must achieve that diploma or those typing speeds; not both husband and wife who will sit the exams or hand in the essay. The man who wrote, "My wife had affairs with her tutor and a fellow student and we have both had liaisons at work," spoke for the nervous spouses and illustrates a common pattern.

At work, a person is even more "single." The job is done not by the couple but by the individual. The pay check comes not to the couple but to the employee. Troubles and even work may be taken home, but the responsibility for dealing with the trouble and returning the work completed belongs not to the spouse but to the worker. The "couple society" does not exist at work.[33]

The workplace was considered by more than half the men and nearly as many women to have played some important part in their extramarital lives. In particular, meeting new people there was very important to both.[34] There was a trend for those who were the most committed to self-exploration and least to the Myth of Romantic Marriage *now* to have found their most recent adulterous partners through their work (one third) and for the most traditional to find this most recent partner through their neighborhood (one fifth). Certainly, the more traditional person is more aware of and concerned with the maintenance of boundaries—perhaps also of the boundaries around the work group. Ruth knew she had to keep each liaison with a colleague strictly secret precisely because it was so dangerous to breach those boundaries. It was also what gave such liaisons their extra *frisson:* "I remember being in a meeting. I looked around and thought, 'Little do they know!' I had slept with each and every one of them! I hugged myself with pleasure. It was wonderful."

Whatever one's beliefs, work is the place where one can legitimately spend time in close contact with others and without a wife or a husband. At work, people may spend long periods of time sharing a problem or task, getting to know others well, eating meals with them, sometimes traveling with them, sharing jokes, seeing them look well and less well, sharing delight in their children's achievements, perhaps also in the achievements of spouses, often in settings that encourage intimacy. Rosabeth Kanter quotes a psychiatrist:

> As people who have interesting careers have always known, work is very sexy, and the people with whom one is working are people who excite. A day spent launching a project or writing a paper or running a seminar is more likely to stimulate—intellectually and sexually—than an evening spent sharing T.V. or discussing the lawn problems or going over the kids' report cards.[35]

Intimacy is supposed to be found at home, the place where people can still be less "on guard" than anywhere else and where the support, encouragement, and services (food, warmth, shelter) do not depend on the adequate performance of tasks to a set standard—though standards may be set and, if too often breached, lead to the breakup of the family.[36] Work relations should be "instrumental" or task-oriented, carried out in a contractual arrangement for material gain. But especially as people live increasingly alone, as divorce shakes couples, intimacy—valued and needed by virtually everyone—must develop elsewhere. And the main *elsewhere* for most people, occupying at least one third of their time every weekday, is work.

Lisa Kraymer argues the major tie between the home and the outside world is the workplace. Perhaps once it was church, school, college or club, movie theater or sports ground. Now the workplace becomes the major social environment for alternative encounters and intimate relationships outside the family. As she says, "it can provide a stable environment for the development of intimacy and pair-bonding."[37]

Of course, work does not necessarily provide situations that might lead to intimacy; these depend in large measure on the nature of the work task, and on what we might call the "culture of work organizations." For women in particular there are dangers in becoming involved in a sexual relationship with someone at work: when the relationship ends, the one who is most likely to find it difficult and even to feel it necessary to leave or move, is the woman. Thus Karen (see page 57) explained that she would not even consider having an affair with a colleague. She was the only woman in her department and needed her job. She knew that she was the most vulnerable to any office politics if only because of the prevailing assumption that a woman (even a divorced one who is responsible for her house and children) does not really need the work. Indeed a woman is twice as likely to lose her job in this situation.[38] Karen classified all the men at work as taboo in this way—so successfully, she claimed, they did not even enter her fantasies as potential lovers.

Patricia McBroom's recent study of professional women in financial institutions in America highlights this problem. The women in her sample recognized this "widespread taboo on sexual relations in the office," but half still went ahead and had at least one such liaison. According to one female executive who reviewed "the cases of women she'd known who found lovers and mates in the working environment": "The women were probably viewed less favorably in the environment where they met. I think I know that for sure. They experienced a loss of prestige."[39]

Two other facts about work—the sexual division of labor, whereby both women and men often work just with others of their own sex, and the hierarchical organization of most workplaces—have conflicting effects on the development of intimate cross-sex relationships. For example, if most female employees work in the typing pool and most male employees in the sales force, both sexes have less opportunity for heterosexual affairs at work than they would if work were better integrated. On the other hand, the secretaries may go to lunch together, but the service they offer their boss, and the knowledge they have of him (if he is male) and his family and of his particular problems and achievements at work, bring them into a relationship that can become intimate—in these latter respects, reflecting that of a wife. Indeed, as Kanter explains, the metaphor of "office wife" is apt, one woman describing her change in job as a "divorce." Kanter quoted a manager who said to his secretary's husband, "You have her body, I have her head."[40] Perhaps a reversal or capture of the whole is not far off.

Secretaries work to make the physical environment of an office more "like home," adding color and personal touches. "Patrimony" typifies this relationship where elsewhere within the vast rationalized bureaucracy it may have been eradicated. That is, bosses choose secretaries to enhance their own status; they expect personal service with limits negotiated privately; they exact loyalty and make the secretary part of their private retinue—she goes with them. Secretaries get rewarded for their loyalty and devotion to their bosses—symbolic rewards. Not career advancement—they take on the emotional tasks of the relationship.[41]

Again, Kraymer has pointed out that a society organized by powerful males has kept women in the largely low-status and gender-segregated jobs, but this has not impeded work-based sexual relations—usually between high-status men and lower-status women, such as boss-secretary, professor-student, doctor-nurse. Until recently, she suggests, there were real benefits to the men in such relationships and few disadvantages; men have always gained status through power and sexual success. The workplace offers both at once.

Women, too, gained, especially when such liaisons led to marriage; and Kraymer believes the workplace now offers chances for mutually satisfying relationships as women gain higher positions, perhaps more than ever. The irony is that whereas hierarchical organization has not hindered men from benefiting from such liaisons, it may now prevent women from doing so. Organizations are developing policies suggesting that "women avoid sexual relationships with people in their work group, particularly mentors. . . . Women seeking advancement" may, with some wisdom, *"refrain* from any intimacy in the office, fearing their relegation to a sex object."[42] In other words, a new double standard may be emerging. It was manageable, so it seems, to have higher-status men with lower-status women, but not vice versa and not when both are of equal status.

If the partners work closely together or even just in the same place, the emotional intensity and electric charge of their relationship is disturbing to others in the work group. People can feel jealous of the individuals in-volved, especially if they have themselves "been there before" or envy their pleasure. Customary patterns of confidentiality break down: "Well he's not going to keep what I tell him secret from *her,* is he?" If one of the lovers is promoted, the envy that this normally generates (especially when it is a woman) is fueled by thoughts of the injustice with which it "must have been" accomplished.

It may not even be something as concrete as promotion that others find disturbing, but just what appears to be preferment or informal advantages. McBroom's work has several examples of this feeling and the disappoint-ment of those female lovers whose opportunities were *not* improved—in fact, sometimes made worse—because of their office affair.[43] When a deeply felt affair ends, not only may promises not be kept but the reward may be replaced by "punishment," a real injustice that can seldom be corrected, short of taking the company or the lover to court.

The highly placed female corporate executive or law partner is much less likely to find a clerk or a secretary desirable as a lover if only because most women seek a dominant (but not domineering) man as a lover. Indeed, many women's affairs at work are with an immediate superior.[44] While the clerical worker might have such a personality, the barriers to her discover-ing it are considerable, and on the surface he holds few charms for her. Whereas power in a woman may not excite but make men fearful, power in a man is deeply appealing to many women.

At work, these emotional needs and experiences can destroy the solidarity of the group. In one study, only around 10 percent of cases were characterized by any positive effects, such as better co-ordination or lowered tensions, while a third produced serious negative effects—"complaints, hostility, and distorted communications."[45] Top management is fearful that, in each division, on each floor, and in each company, such strains are damaging to the effective functioning of the whole. Hence, some companies have policies requiring those who engage in office affairs to leave.[46]

Men, of course, as well as women are constrained by their roles at work and by the expectations and structures they must fit into. By and large, these organizational demands function in such a way as to keep relationships between men and women to the traditional male-superior, female-subordinate, and service role. There are still too few instances of how a more egalitarian relationship would work, particularly within the work setting. Thus, Kanter found many examples of women doing "men's work": for example, saleswomen, who would be evaluated by their male colleagues according to their looks. This is in direct contrast with the evaluations made by the same colleagues of the men doing the selling jobs. The fact that managers must still behave like managers who must behave like men, and secretaries still behave like secretaries who must be like women, may explain the changes that appear to take place when occupational roles are filled by the "unexpected" sex.

The fact that men have more and women fewer liaisons is well established. In chapter 2, I pointed out that the total number of liaisons people had was powerfully affected by the kind of work they did. When women enter typically male occupations, they increase the number of their affairs, perhaps because of greater opportunities; but men entering typically female occupations, where they, too, have greater opportunities, *decrease* the number of their liaisons. The pattern of their affairs begins, in both instances, to resemble that more typical of the opposite sex (see pages 80–83). I suggested an explanation that would be adequate for both would need to take into account the ethos and working patterns of these occupations.

A male accountant, in describing his own experience, gives us a view of the ethos of his occupation: he said he had had "perhaps one hundred" liaisons and was saddened by the "morality" that prevented the lovers in the film *Brief Encounter* from expressing what they really felt. He pointed out that, as treasurer for a large, international company, he had endless opportunities for sexual encounters and enjoyed them. He met only some of these partners through his work, but enough to make the proportions typical of others in the sample with less experience. (Indeed, those who had the most liaisons also were the most likely to meet their lovers through their work.) The accountant spoke not of any pressures but of the enabling features of his work so far as his adulterous liaisons are concerned. Nonetheless, there are pressures. The person in this accountant's position must thrust and compete with others. Such people have power in the real world and material advantages. Their relative wealth and freedom makes them exciting. Women in this world are having to cope with this status and with these attributes, for which they have been wholly unprepared. One alternative is to play the game and become "like a man." It is certainly very difficult to take the family, let alone the husband, along on this emotional journey. But a colleague can understand and share and has things to gain and to lose from an office affair. Women have traditionally used their bodies to gain material advantage. It may be that these women seek rather emotional advantage—or, at least, emotional equality. They may also gain an ally or allies and lessen the loneliness in being one of not many others like themselves.

Just as a woman accountant must learn what it is to be a "good" accountant, a man who is a social worker has to learn what it is to be a "good" social worker. When those jobs have traditionally been done by one sex rather than by another, their shape, the way they must be done, and the expectations of others about them will best fit a model that allows a "proper" man or a "proper" woman to do it well.

In 1982, in England and Wales, 9 women but 940 men general surgeons held consultant positions.[47] One of the women asked for two sessions (half-days) free a week to be with her two-year-old. She was refused. Once she was in the job, she asked for the same two sessions in order to take a private clinic elsewhere. No problem. Surgeons are men. Men do not look after toddlers. Surgeons do not look after toddlers because they are men. Good surgeons do take on clinics even if that means time away from their main job. It is appropriate and good experience to work extra clinics. The experience that would have come from handling or caring for the young child is not thought valuable to the surgeon. In this way, occupations themselves create ideas about gender—that is, about what it means to be a proper man or a proper woman; they do not merely reflect those ideas. Indeed, the demands of jobs also alter the very internal dynamics of the marriage, as Rosanna Hertz has recently argued in a study of dual-career marriages.[48]

The Choice of Place

A further display of the power that may come with high-status jobs is provided by the top-ranking civil servant who said he used to lock his office door and have sex there with his mistress, a writer. The possibility someone might find out, especially someone from the press, was an additional thrill, although he admitted the place was not very comfortable and often, since the heating went off early, rather cold! Jack, too, described one of his partners coming up to his office "at Christmas time and just letting me know she was there if I wanted it. So we made love right then and there, in my office." But the office was not a popular place with most people. Although it transgresses the idea that intimacy belongs at home (or at least in beds), most offices are simply not either exciting enough or comfortable enough. Nor, in this sample, did many spend money on hotels except as a special treat or when on a holiday. Some knew about "short-time" places—hotels that let rooms for half a day, for example—again, when at least one of the partners was relatively sophisticated. There is, after all, a certain learning process to be gone through in the conduct of an affair, just as in all other sexual adventures.

Most women are still pursued rather than pursuing and, hence, more at the mercy of "what comes along." Indeed, one woman said, "You make it sound as though we all had free choice. No one has ever asked me!" But women were often invited or able to invite people from within the relative security of their own homes. This was particularly true when the man who comes along, like Keith, works in an occupation that is not merely segregated within the organization—which does, in fact, employ the opposite sex as well—but quite isolated from the opposite sex. While a bus conductor collects tickets from strangers with minimal contact with the driver, she or he goes to lunch or on a tea break with others: hence, "she was a conductor when I was driving the buses. Met in the canteen." Both these jobs and the highly segregated ones, however, involve being away from home, and people in those jobs are moving in worlds that do not include the "other half."

Men in jobs where all their mates were men were the first lovers for these women in the study: "he was working on some houses near where I lived"; "builder's joiner working on new housing estate we moved to"; "central heating engineer working on my new house"; "builder working on my house." In every case, the women were the (albeit temporary) "mistresses" of these men: even if the money that would pay the man came from her husband's pocket, the woman held a position of relative power.

Only one of these women said "we" to include her husband in the move to a new house. Rather, a woman felt the house was hers: it provided in some sense a secure base, for if a woman's place is in the home, she is entitled to the feeling that she is in charge there. This despite the fact that "a man's home is his castle"—a fact Catherine MacKinnon, the feminist legal scholar, has recently argued is supported by laws against pornography that *exclude* the home (viz—a man's home), thus making a woman's right to control private space secondary or irrelevant.[49] These women reversed their roles with their adultery. The idea that the woman owns and has charge of her home is reflected in the choice of place to make love: the most popular choice of place for women was their own home and usually their own—that is, the matrimonial—bed. *Nearly one third of women had taken their lovers home* or invited them in. The men in the sample agreed: only one in five had taken his partner back to his own home, but well over a third went to "her place." Only those who had just one liaison hesitated to take their partners to their own home or to hers. These people preferred, by and large, to go to a hotel or some other "neutral" place, but everyone who had more than one affair followed the pattern.[50]

Whereas Frieda laughed herself silly over the experience of making love in her home and in the matrimonial bed, she admitted that her lover had not been so comfortable once they got upstairs. Louise, too, told us that she felt "quite comfortable in my own home. He didn't though, because his sister lived next door, and once he nearly bumped into her. We had been in his house while his wife was away, and I felt extremely nervous in his home but he didn't."

It seems men are prepared and perhaps (despite the anxiety) enjoy the added risk of being caught; the added excitement, too, of challenging another man—the one who owns the woman—by trespassing on his territory. Louise's lover was bothered about being caught (by his sister); *she* was bothered about invading another woman's home. Clearly, if the fear is overwhelming, another place must be found. While Martin's fear about being in his partner's home made him impotent in that situation, another architect took his fantasy of changing buildings to suit his needs as far as a blueprint (see page 252). Yet Dr. Reynolds flirted with murder, it seemed, as he had sex with his lover while her husband watched television in the next room.

Some people found a special thrill in other places. Jack, for example, particularly delighted in the outside including a chase across fields described in chapter 7 (see pages 200–201). And Mrs. Long enjoyed the luxury of beautiful hotels with fresh sheets and no worries about leaving telltale signs. In fact, she never met her lover in her hometown, nor did they go near his neighborhood. For her, the liaison was a great adventure, and she wanted to do new things, go to new places, experience worlds as different from home as possible. She was not using the liaison as a transition out of her marriage and carefully shielded each from the other. Few people, indeed, did so deliberately, though, as I suggested in considering Sophie's choice, it may become such a stepping-stone. It is hard not to see in these choices links with the ancient tales of adulterous love. What makes them thrilling are the transgressions of the known and customary territory—of physical place, bodies, and personal space.

The Choice of Lover

Yet the preference for the first if not for later liaisons, when men especially, as I have suggested, sought more dangerous lovers, seems to be for someone relatively safe. One way of finding this relatively nonthreatening first lover is to chose a neighbor or a long-standing friend. Similar proportions of women and men chose a neighbor or a friend as a first lover, although there was a trend for women to choose neighbors or friends *of their husbands*, who would be fully aware of their marital situation and would be reluctant to break into the marriage of a friend "for real." It is one thing to "screw" your friend's wife; another to have her divorce him and for you to marry her, especially when you are married yourself. In fact, the foursome—or wife swapping—was one solution to the fear of breaking up a marriage.

Bernard, who asked me if I would like to know how many women he had "known" (see epigraph on page 59), and who described himself as having had "a squint eye and a foreign father and so was exceptionally inhibited by everything," believed that "we are here to have a lovely time. There is no purpose in life." He and his wife had their first extramarital experience when a couple came to dinner and at coffee time passed mildly pornographic photographs around. He ended up making love to the wife on a bed upstairs, and she had the husband on the sofa downstairs. The rules for safety were clear: Not only in full knowledge but in full company. Neighborly friends and in one's own house, and after having broken bread together. In fact, Bernard still remembers with some anxiety his wife's distress that he had had sex with his partner while lying on a patchwork quilt given to his wife and himself by his mother. This insensitivity appeared, because of its potent symbolic meaning for them as a married couple, to mar the care with which the whole event had been conducted so that no such breach would occur.

The informal rules for any such foursomes and any future meetings were well understood. Bernard explained that any breach of these informal rules—for example, seeing one of the four without the others—was absolutely forbidden. He, wanting and enjoying the risk, met the woman alone and took photographs of her naked. These were nearly discovered; and even now, many years later, in relating the story of the photographs and their near discovery, he became excited, speaking in heightened tone and fast.

Despite his original inhibition, Bernard seems to have managed quite well, but such inhibition was for many a real factor in the search for someone relatively unthreatening for a first encounter. As Mrs. Inkerman worried about "how you take your all-in-one off in front of a stranger," Jack hesitated long before daring to "go in." He said he had never felt really attractive to a woman; he did not know that his body was appealing. Someone you see every day, who lives in the same kind of house as you do, who is perhaps not too dissimilar in class and life style yet illicit and forbidden as a lover, gives the necessary sense of adventure without requiring Everest to be climbed on the first outing. This is why (as in Jack's case) the person well known through education or work appears less threatening.

If security was not to be found through choosing someone known, someone not too different, someone who would not merely be a casual contact (at work, for instance, contact is continuous), security of a different kind was, paradoxically, to be found in the one-night stand, perhaps with a stranger. Women were less comfortable with this kind of liaison unless they were fairly strong adherents of the Myth of Me; at least this was true for older women who waited some time before a first liaison and less true of younger women who have married most recently. But it would be a mistake to think such meetings were meaningless for some were described in glowing terms. One woman met an Australian man at a party when her husband was away, and took him back to her own house for the night. She had sex with him just that once and she can no longer remember his name: "He was a wonderful lover. I felt completely safe with him and was abandoned with him in a way I have never been able to repeat and had never experienced before."

Ruth, the professional woman who wanted to experience "certain sexual things" and was quite aware of the importance of her own "mid-life crisis," had her first liaison with someone who was a friend of both her husband and herself. She had known his wife for a long time and had been responsible for introducing them as a couple to her husband. Always taboo, Mark had been seen as attractive, intelligent, and delightful. It had been a real pleasure for her that the four of them got along so well. Often, she said, when people marry, their old friends drop away because it is hard for four people all to get along well. When Mark confided in her that his wife was having an affair and that he had also had various lovers, she felt the taboo had been lifted. She saw him as someone accessible and "safe" to have an affair with herself. She was someone who carefully deliberated the pros and cons of going ahead:

> When I realized Mark might actually be my lover, I was thrilled because it seemed really a practical possibility—not just some ridiculous fantasy. I knew him. I knew what he was like. I could take so much for granted. And you know, I usually think of myself as not particularly attractive— too fat, too tall, too something! But I knew Mark's wife and knew what she looked like and knew that she wasn't some amazing Twiggy figure or anything, so that seemed . . . well, I suppose I felt I could be desirable to him.
>
> The other thing that was important was that I didn't need to feel guilty about his family because I wasn't the first and his wife was having an affair herself. I didn't feel I would be breaking up anything or breaking into anything. I didn't feel either their marriage or ours would be put at risk.

Ruth made love to her lovers in her own house, but drew the line at the matrimonial bed:

> I do talk about the bedroom as "mine," it's true. But I just feel the bed is "ours." I'm not sure why, but I think it would just make me feel too guilty. Silly really because what's the difference having sex in another room? Actually I like it best away in a hotel or somewhere, though I still feel odd about being Mrs. Smith or whatever.

If the chosen place and chosen person could be used to reverse traditional roles, the pattern of who pays (that is, if anyone does, for 16 percent claimed their liaisons cost nothing) seems to repeat traditional roles rather than reverse them. Men are still the ones who most commonly pay; they say their

partners pay on very few occasions. However, this is the pattern typical
of those most committed to the Myth of Romantic Marriage. The more
permissive men, those who adhered more strongly to the Myth of Me, "let"
their partners share expenses. Women, however, claim that they pay a great
deal more often than their partners give them credit for, and that they share
the expenses more frequently. Still, the majority of women agree that the
men pay for them. Here the changes that might come from greater equality,
or perhaps in a reversal of normal roles in the illicit relationship, are
scarcely in evidence.

About 40 percent of the money goes on food and drink, and another 6
percent on accommodation and travel: the big treat is going away together.
Only about 5 percent admitted to buying each other presents. Indeed, the
signs of having had an affair are often just a bill or a menu card, things that
take on great significance in later years. The American sociologist Laurel
Richardson tells of interviewing "other women" who have had affairs with
married men, and of being taken by a woman, on tiptoe and with hushed
voice, into the sanctum (often her bedroom) where these symbols were kept,
perhaps in an album or carefully mounted around the mirror or on a board,
daily reminders of what once was.[51] For validation cannot come from the
outside world in the adulterous encounter. Instead the sense of self-esteem
and worth, the knowledge that the relationship is good, has to be found
from within it or perhaps with the help of one or two confidantes. This is
one of the pains as well as one of the pleasures of the adulterous encounter.

Pleasures and Pains

People feel both extraordinary joy and misery as a result of a liaison, as members of this sample—women and men ranging in age from thirty-two to sixty-three—made clear:

A WOMAN: I cannot convey to you how marvelous I felt . . . I felt I had been made whole. That I had been made complete in some way.

JACK: I felt ten foot tall. I came out of there and knew I was alive. A man. I felt as if, suddenly, I was dealt a new set of cards as far as life was concerned.

A MAN: I felt sick—really sick. I mean I had to stop the car and get out to vomit. I felt so awful.

FANNY (describing her husband): Jealousy ate away at him. He lost a lot of weight.

A WOMAN: The whole affair made me—well, I mean, ill. I just couldn't cope. All the lies and everything. Horrible.

A WOMAN: When my last liaison ended, I went into a deep depression even though my husband and I had talked things through and decided we were free to have other relationships. Now I am not so sure my marriage will survive.

AMELIA: For years I could hardly bear to exist after he told me. It is impossible to describe the mental and physical pain.

Particular feelings arose out of an individual's position in the triangle: whether principal actor and initiator; courted, wooed, and won participant; betrayed spouse or victim. The nature of the liaison itself, its course, its

resolution (even a "one-night stand" can be important) and its consequences for a marriage—all enter into the experience, how it is perceived,
how constructed and reconstructed in the mind. Moreover, a person's experience during the first liaison plays a major part in whether there will be
others and, if so, whether they bring joy or misery.

However, pleasure and pain are not exclusive; the common experience
is a fair dose of both—just desserts, perhaps. And there are also differences
in the pleasure-pain balance of the older and the younger groups, of women
and of men, and in whether they were describing a liaison of the earlier or
the later years covered by the study. Finally, whether the experience described was the first, perhaps only liaison, one of many, recent and continuing, whether over long ago or recently ended, and its intensity and duration—all play a part in the "benefits" and "sufferings." First, I explore the
feelings of the adulterers.

Richard, an advertising strategist, thought he had been influenced by the
"sixties feeling" that there was an entitlement to enjoyment, but indicated
the mixed blessings:

> I think my first and most important liaison was tremendously helpful and
> instructive to me as a person, as well as exciting and stimulating. I can't
> even now reconcile this with the awful hurt and stress it caused my wife—
> she still curses this woman's name. The delight and cruelty have the same
> source. It's as if one were (it's going to sound very Freudian) growing and
> shrinking as a human being at the same time. By everything I'd been
> taught and knew, it was wrong. But I would have understood less about
> life as well as love without it.

Over all, around 80 percent of people found "a lot or some" happiness
in their liaisons (even more in the later ones), but over half also experienced
"a lot or some" *un*happiness. People were adding up the benefits of a sense
of sexual fulfillment and the gaining of self-esteem which was such a common and welcome effect of the liaison, at the same time as they also summed
the conflict, especially any deceit experienced in the conduct of the liaison,
and their loss of self-esteem when it ended. In fact, being so happy reflects
the "sense of being alive," so peculiarly characteristic of these sexual encounters, enabling people to regain a sense of drama in their lives and to
move on. Jack's experience is typical. First the joy:

> She [his first lover] was everything that one's fantasy as a mistress could
> have. Used to wear that perfume, too, and she covered her[self] every-
> where with it, and that's terribly exciting . . . And, of course, one of the
> myths that got knocked on the head is that if you have a fantasy and work
> it out, it won't be as good. . . . For the first time I felt sexually wanted.

> I can remember her [his second lover] running across the field with
> high grass with a blanket and taking her clothes off, you know, "My God,

someone will see us." She is tall, very attractive (I don't know why I have ended up with such attractive girls), this tall girl, taking, shedding all her clothes and encouraging me to take mine off, too. Here we are in this field, off some road somewhere—you know, walking across fields and making love so that we will come as the train goes over the embankment type thing. All impossible but . . . I can remember it, but I can't experience—re-experience the completeness of it.

She would make me do things I had never done before. I went and visited cathedrals. My life was enriched and has been enriched vastly as a result.

And the fun—and I yearn for it.

Jack's affair had all the ingredients of the old story. It was dangerous, secret; his lover, wild and free, unafraid of the outside world, breaking every boundary, making him live out his fantasy and finding him entirely desirable even when he felt unworthy. Sexual symbolism pervades his story: there are bridges, lights, a warm building where his beloved waits, "going in" and cathedrals, too, with their soaring heights and passionate music, the ecstasy of the love of God (Jack stopped "parroting the Our Father bit," thus giving up religious faith for human adulterous love) indicating the centrality of those ancient feelings in his liaison.

The pain for Jack had little to do with his wife and family, although he wrote: "I had a row with my wife and we never row. I think it arose because, after talking to you, I realized that all the things which I had found in Hannah and Amy were there—there all the time in my wife, and I had failed to draw them out." Rather, he felt bereft because his two liaisons were over:

Making love . . . after making love, I felt as if you had a picture in sand that you tried to hold and it trickled out—through—and it's one of those experiences that somehow has to be reaffirmed. I can't hold it. . . . Somehow the feeling of affirmation or reaffirmation of me and my sexuality has gone or goes. Fades away. And I ache desperately for it, to tell the truth.

It is clear that even in the first liaison most people felt very happy. By the time they were reporting the consequences of the most recent liaison—of which many, of course, were still continuing—everyone described even greater happiness (see table 7.1).[1]

But, for women, *unhappiness* increased, while for men it decreased in the most recent liaison, about twice as many women as men feeling quite unhappy in this liaison (63 percent to 32 percent, respectively). Meanwhile, the more liaisons a person had, the greater happiness and the less unhappiness

TABLE 7.1
Amount of Happiness

	First Liaison	Most Recent Liaison
A Lot/Some	75%	85%
A Little/None	25%	15%
TOTAL (N = 100%)	399	256
	p < .01	

Amount of Unhappiness

	First Liaison		Most Recent Liaison	
	Women	Men	Women	Men
A Lot/Some	59%	48%	63%	32%
A Little/None	41%	52%	37%	68%
TOTAL (N = 100%)	239	157	143	113
	n.s.		p < .001	

they experience. Nine out of ten of those who had *more than three* affairs reported a great deal of pleasure, while "only" 40 percent of this group reported much unhappiness in any liaison, compared with 60 percent of those who had one, two, or three liaisons. For women, of course, the most recent was generally the second, third, or fourth; while for men, it was the fourth, fifth, or sixth—a difference that does not explain the greater distress for women.

Richard and Jack effectively summarize the sense that people had of "being alive" again on the one hand and of profound loss when the affair was over—Richard simultaneously "growing and shrinking." These feelings seemed to express more than the words *jealousy, sexual fulfillment* or, say, *intellectual excitement*—all choices listed for sample members to check and rank (see appendix A, question 32).[2] Indeed, a separate subsample analysis of one hundred questionnaires showed "being alive" was the most important pleasure for two thirds of women and one half of men, while the "ending" of the affair brought the greatest pain to 40 percent of people.

The Pleasures of a Liaison

"Sexual fulfillment" was the most commonly mentioned benefit for everyone, although—while men always placed it not only first but considerably higher than the next most important feeling—women placed it equally with "being loved" and "friendship."

In interviews and in the group discussions, there was a surprising absence of talk about sex. Surprising because what the adulterous act, of course, does, *par excellence*, is breach the sexual exclusivity of marriage. Face to face, however, people talked about the quality of their marital and extramarital relationships and worried about breaking trust and dealing with dependence and independence. Dennis, from a working-class background, insisted on talking about sex, much to the embarrassment of the polite middle-class group of three women and two other men who attended that evening with him. Dennis's voice was deliberate and cockney-accented:

I assume that at this meeting, seated around this table, whether we are married or not, that we have all had a physical relationship with another married person?

There was much shuffling of feet and bodies moving to present shoulders to him.

Now, I don't know what you all think, but my first wife, well, she was, well she was *carnal*. There's nothing she didn't like about the sex act, nothing she wouldn't do. For me to have had another physical relationship and be married to her would have been a physical impossibility.

In California, there was this black woman. . . . She was *beautiful*, really luxurious and sensuous. She had me on the floor, anywhere, I mean— really laid me out. Talk about fantasy coming true.

The discomfort grew acute. Coffee cups were picked up and put down, making a noise, but he was undeterred.

Now I've got this girl. She's lovely, and I visit her every Wednesday in her flat. Every week I climb the stairs to where she lives and my heart is racing and I'm scared one day I won't be able to do it—one day I'll wake up and —— We watch pornographic films together and eat and fuck, and it's marvelous. And no one knows. No one.

Then Mary grasped a point of entry: "You mean you *think* no one knows." There was tangible relief, and the discussion shifted to knowledge and secrecy and guilt. At first I shared the discomfort of others in the group and worried that the meeting would disintegrate, but Dennis taught me to notice what was *not* being said by everyone else. I learned in subsequent groups to raise the topic of sex.

Although most people (unlike Dennis) did not easily express their desire for sex, and their joy when they experienced it in the adulterous affair, the commonest reason they gave on the questionnaire for a liaison was that they "had sexual needs which were not being met"; and the high ranking of sexual fulfillment as a pleasure of the liaison also demonstrates its real importance for adultery, indicating a further reason why so many felt "alive." Indeed, since adultery is, as so many also felt, "basically wrong," there must be some excellent reasons for participating in it!

Many in the sample seemed, as they told their stories, to be struggling with the existential conflict between, as the psychoanalyst Marianne Eckardt put it, being dead or alive and bored or dead.[3] While men and women are faced with these conflicts at different times and in different contexts and have varying resources for dealing with the conflicts, both often expressed (like Jack) the sense they were only half alive, half functioning, or practically dead. For Dennis, the terror that he would one day—perhaps soon—be unable to experience orgiastic sex both acted as a spur to continue his love affair and loomed over him—his personal incubus.

One strand of psychological theorizing understands orgasm as performing the "function of affirming the reality of the individual's existence in terms of emotional conviction. The orgasm . . . serves the 'ego function' of establishing the incontrovertible truth of the reality of personal existence."[4]

Orgasm on its own is, of course, not a sufficient explanation for the self-affirmation so often reported, for masturbation could (presumably) achieve the same effect. Rather, this adulterous liaison permits the person (even as she or he breaches social norms) to experience orgasm according to a conventional social script—the heterosexual love story—and, further, in accordance with the ancient romance untrammeled by marital boundaries. It is this that enables Dennis's reaffirmation, Mrs. Long to tell us "it is the loveliest experience" she has ever known, and Jack to feel "ten feet tall—a man."

This is an experience shared by women and men, but there remain differences. The main and obvious difference between the men and women is that men were much more specific about their pleasures: by far the greatest proportion of men (over 70 percent) said "sexual fulfillment" had given them pleasure; and, at the same time, only one quarter had gained a sense of freedom and independence.[5] The women did not separate out their pleasures in this way. Sex was not a much greater pleasure than being loved or than friendship—each of these delights enjoyed by around 60 percent of the women. "Loving," "having fun," and "being needed" were important, to around half the women, and the remainder of the pleasures listed (being understood, intellectual stimulation, enjoyable risk, and freedom/independence) to around a third to 40 percent. But sex stood out for men. There was then a drop, only around half saying that friendship and being loved mattered to them; they also, to much the same extent, enjoyed the great sense of fun of the first liaison. Whereas women valued having fun *in the same proportions* as did men, men did not value loving or being needed nearly as highly as women did. Women and men placed little difference on intellectual stimulation and taking an enjoyable risk; but only just over a quarter of the men, compared with about 40 percent of the women, felt understood in this liaison. One third of women compared with one quarter of men had gained a sense of freedom and independence.

We are seeing not only differences in *pattern* but also absolute differences as well as similarities in what men and women actually gained from a liaison. To summarize: women's emotional feelings cluster around sex; they separate this less from emotion than men do. The general importance to women of emotional pleasure in a liaison is supported by a major survey carried out by *New Woman*, an American magazine to which more than 34,000 women, aged sixteen to sixty, responded in the summer of 1986. This survey found that, although sex was extremely important, "women get a real *emotional* workout from their affairs."[6] Women, it seems, do not seek in isolation the affirmation of the sex *act*, but couple it with affirmation of their desirability.

Both the women and the men frequently mentioned sex and friendship, almost bracketed together as "sex'n'friendship." There is a striking parallel, it seems to me, in the words of the !Kung woman Nisa, interviewed by the anthropologist Marjorie Shostak, who wrote her story.[7] The !Kung are gathering-hunting people who now live in Botswana on the edges of the Kalahari Desert. They used to be known as bushmen. Women there have a good deal of autonomy and are relatively equal, contributing about 80 percent of the gathered food, which is, in turn, the mainstay of the people's diet. Sex is extremely important to them. In a system of "imperfect monogamy,"[8] Nisa described the two major axes of sexual life: having your "heart going out to a man"; and being able, as a woman, to "give him life," to offer him "food," to "finish the work" (your own as well as his), and to "feel full" (all ways of describing having sex, making love or experiencing orgasm). Her idea that a woman can "give life" through sex is strikingly like the idea of coming alive in the successful liaison, although she has a sense of her power rare in my sample of women. This experience is not restricted in her life to sex with just one other man, nor to her five husbands. She told Shostak she had "had many lovers, as many as I have fingers and toes"; and that a woman does not sit alone with the man of her hut (who is nonetheless the most important man in her life) but takes lovers. They will give her many different things. She asked: "Does one man have enough thoughts for you?"[9] With these words, Nisa also expressed the delight of that third of people for whom intellectual stimulation was important.

According to the actual ratings of importance for each pleasure made by sample members themselves (as compared with the order produced by summing total responses) in their most recent liaison, women ranked "intellectual stimulation" third and men, fourth (rising from ninth and sixth place, respectively). It seems that, once one has successfully "managed" the first breach of the rules and found it worthwhile to continue along this path, guilt and suffering are reduced, and the qualities that go with new friendship become relatively important. For women whose education and working lives have been limited, the chance to expand their intellectual life and their delight in a lover who is *interesting* and *interested* in them has partic- ular importance—as Mrs. Long found (see pages 128–29).

According to people's *own* ratings, again "sexual fulfillment" stays at or near the top for both men and women; but among women who have had not more than three liaisons, friendship was first. Men ranked "being needed" first if they had had just a few liaisons, but when (as was more common) they had had at least four, then a "great sense of fun" ranked first. Indeed, one man stressed this recreational purpose when he said "I go outside marriage for *living*." In general, the fewer the liaisons anyone had, the greater the stress placed on the emotional content of the affair. In fact, those who had only one affair differed from others significantly in the emphasis they placed on being loved, needed, and understood, on friend- ship, and also on their own experience of loving their partner. Paradoxi- cally, this was, it seems, enough to *prevent* some from continuing along this path. Strong emotion leads to a desire to alter or leave the marriage and to strong reaction from others.

This was Dan's experience who felt his life had been made miserable by social workers, doctors, friends, and relations, who "seemed to descend from nowhere" to keep him in his family. His wife had been ill and had seemed to be condoning his relationship, a deeply felt love affair. He had felt desperately irresponsible and anxious about his two young children but had nonetheless been preparing to leave his family to live with his partner. Such feelings were typical of those who have only one affair; it was this group who felt the most fearful of being found out and the most guilty. Dan gave up his relationship, moved away from his hometown, and changed his work to start again. He was, he felt, most unlikely to have another affair.

Marriage emerges here as the place of emotional *work*; and the liaison, as the place for sexual and emotional fun and *play*. Everyone knows, even if they experience a kind of shock as they actually take on the marital choice, that marriage is "hard." On marriage, things previously enjoyed are supposed to be given up—things, for men, like "going out with the boys" on Friday night and, for women, meeting women friends in the evening. The costs of marriage, setting up a home, and having children restrict the evenings out together even just for a drink, and eating out, going to a film, play, or taking holidays cannot be undertaken lightly. The liaison is letting go, a way perhaps to *avoid* "working out" a particular problem—by playing. By playing it out. Indeed, it is the experiencing of a lived fantasy and of finding it possible to "fill the gaps," as Jack said and Dennis made clear, that is so enjoyable.

This sense of the liaison as the relationship of play is expressed by the way "having fun" was rated (again, using sample members' own rankings) third or fourth with sex, being loved, and friendship by both women and men. Commitment to either the Myth of Romantic Marriage or the Myth of Me did not seem to alter this score, but one's belief system did influence other answers. "Enjoyable risk" thrilled the more traditionally committed as they breached a rule that was less important or not important at all to the more permissive. Not surprisingly, those most committed to the Myth of Me were also the people for whom a sense of independence and freedom was most important. Thus what made people happy and permitted them to play varied with their stance on marriage and self-fulfillment, but this quality of fun—of being able to make up the rules of the game, even when what you sought was perhaps more of what you had once had, or more of what you had hoped to find in marriage—gave everyone much pleasure. The "one-night stand" was particularly liberating in this respect.

In fact, the social purposelessness of the liaison heightened its *recreational* side: it could remain a drama, a romance, its rules forged by the two people in it but at the same time kept clearly demarcated from society. A woman in Laurel Richardson's sample captures this untrammeled quality:

> We didn't have any expectations of each other, and we didn't have to exploit each other. The relationship didn't have to have a goal. . . . I don't think it was done consciously, but we did stop the clock—freeze the relationship when it was particularly romantic. It didn't have to deteriorate because of having to be in day-to-day situations where demands are made on each other that are unpleasant or mundane. It was encapsulated.[10]

This woman speaks in egalitarian terms—everything done, it seems, without conflict, as "we," without "demands . . . on each other"; yet even within an "encapsulated" relationship, the fact that one is male, the other female, one married and (perhaps) the other single—always the case in Richardson's sample—one older, the other younger, one a more powerful personality, and both (usually) employed in different status occupations, means such equality is difficult to maintain, customary scripts for such group and class differences likely to surface. (Indeed, that is what Richardson found.)

Men have traditionally complained about being "caught" by women in marriage, being "trapped," and "having to give up their freedom," whereas women have wanted marriage more intensely, often seeing it as their primary goal. It has seemed to be the place where they can be mistress of their own lives, offering security as well as love and the chance to have children. But about a third of women in this sample stressed the sense of freedom and independence that they found in a liaison. Both Sophie and Mrs. Inkerman spoke of the dependence of others on them, Mrs. Inkerman writing of how, at forty-one, she "had discovered autonomy"; and Sophie explained her own capacity to engage and rejoice in an affair in terms of her emotional *independence* from her husband: "My mother used always to say that there was in every couple one who was more dependent. One kissed, and the other turned the cheek to receive it. The one who turned the cheek was the less dependent." There was no question but that Sophie turned the cheek.

By comparison with the women, men did not expect or find much independence or freedom in any adulterous relationship. Men normally begin, of course, from a higher level of independence in the material sense though, like Sophie's husband, they may be very dependent emotionally; it may be more difficult for men to admit that they sought freedom or independence in an adulterous liaison for this reason. The women in this sample who take pleasure in freedom and independence may be reflecting what Laurel Richardson also noticed: her sample of unmarried women often began with a sense of control over their affair with a married man and hence a feeling of autonomy. The woman usually, however, became the more dependent partner, ending by being the one to sit by the telephone waiting for the lover to call just as she thought she had left all that well behind her.[11] Even if one is married, though, a liaison is a bid for independence, and the liaison a new place to work out an intimate relationship. Richardson also argues that in the liaison marital status is as important as gender in, for example, determining how long it will last.[12] The married person has greater strength because marriage is privileged over single status; it is, for instance, generally important only for the married, not the single person, that the relationship be kept secret. The fact that most married men choose single women, and most women, married men as their adulterous partners suggests the continuing difficulty women, compared with men, have—even in a liaison—to maintain independence.

Maintain it or no, the married women in this study often achieved a sense of autonomy in the course of a liaison; hence their emphasis on freedom and independence, simultaneously reinforcing their commitment to the Myth of Me. This gender difference, like the speed with which people enter a liaison after marriage, is narrowing: whereas a mere 4 percent or 5 percent of men married before 1970 ranked freedom and independence first, as many as 21 percent (or one in five) of those married in or later than 1970 did so. Similarly, nearly twice the proportion of the youngest women compared with their older sisters ranked freedom/independence first. Again, we notice a convergence in the attitudes of women and men. And we see women valuing and seeking things that have been held as within the man's rather than the woman's domain.

So far as sexual pleasure is concerned, the changes are notable for both women and men, with older people experiencing liaisons in different decades in ways that appear to reflect the permissive revolution. Men in every age group rated "sexual fulfillment" more highly than women did; but 43 percent of the youngest, 31 percent of those married in the 1960s and 27 percent of the oldest group of men ranked it *first* in importance during the first liaison. And the youngest women ranked sexual fulfillment first (about 25 percent compared with around 18 percent for older women). However, in the *most recent liaison*, the oldest men and women ranked sex first or second (those married before 1960). In other words, the youngest and most recently married men *and* women ranked sex during the first liaison most highly; but in the most recent liaison, taking place on average *in* the 1970s or later, the gap has narrowed so that there are no statistically significant differences between the different age groups, and a greater stress is placed on sexual fulfillment by the oldest people compared with their younger brothers and sisters. It is as if the period itself changes the experience. People who married for the first time in the 1970s could not have had a liaison before that decade, but their experience in their first liaison was closer to that of their older brothers and sisters who were reporting their most recent liaison during this time.

The *date* of the liaison itself, then, is critical. Just as for the timing of the liaison, the historical and cultural time through which people are living and to which they are contributing is central; even sexual pleasure is itself experienced and evaluated differently in different periods. With the hindsight of the 1980s, it is possible to construct a picture of these changing patterns in sexual behavior which distinguishes the different *meaning* "sexual fulfillment" and "pleasure" might have for women and men; but this makes better sense if first we explore the pains of the liaison.

The Pains of a Liaison

Guilt (the experience of well over half the women and 46 percent of men during their first liaison) may surface whether or not anyone other than the two people involved has any knowledge of their actions. Shame depends on the knowledge and repudiation of others:

> I was guilty as hell. I think I suffered quite a lot of guilt. It was nothing in particular; it all fizzled out. My husband came home and—well, it could have been like one of those bedroom farces. I felt ridiculous. Ashamed. Dreadfully ashamed.

As a result, the liaison ended. As Miriam said, it "fizzled out" like a damp firework. Then as an afterthought and perhaps for comfort, she added, "He [her lover] used to ring me up occasionally."

Miriam's story illustrates the continuing social taboo that some manage to turn to their own advantage. One engineer said his wife had been "so distressed" when he told her of his affair. Now, however, that she has agreed to sexual freedom for both of them, he claims that "the sex, the adventure, and the sense that my wife and I are doing something secret that society would openly condemn but covertly rather envy, makes both of us happy."

This man brings the adultery back to the society, back to the difficulty the whole relationship engenders. And, in the first liaison, it is the guilt, the deceit, and the fear of being found out that are disturbing, especially to women. Indeed, whereas men varied more on pleasures, women experienced a greater range of pains, indicating the continuing greater conflict for the married woman compared with her husband in adultery. Hence, we might expect those who felt they had "committed adultery," whether male or female, to feel more guilt.

Guilt was, indeed, much more common among those who had described themselves as having "committed adultery" than among their fellow respondents who, although they had had at least one liaison, did not describe themselves this way.[13] Because, too, these liaisons represented serious breaches of the rules, those who had "committed adultery" had to conduct them with maximum secrecy.[14] This deception caused immense distress, involving a double betrayal: first the sexual infidelity and then the deception. They were constantly afraid, too, of discovery—of being "found out" and hence of bearing public shame as well as private misery. In 1988, a young, married California woman pleaded guilty to the murder of her lover and explained she had not informed the police before *because* she "didn't want the children ever to know I was an adulteress." She was afraid they would think her "a bad person."[15]

In this sense, "adultery" is that which is done by people who maintain fairly traditional roles within their marriages. Indeed, the people in the study who were the most traditional in their outlook were also those most inclined to feel guilty about their extramarital relationships of whatever duration and however they termed them. Thus, the more committed a person was to the Myth of Romantic Marriage, the more likely it was that he or she (but especially she) would feel guilty. Such feeling went along with the terminology people employed: as we have seen, the most traditional men spoke more than did other less traditional men of having "casual affairs" because, I suggested, this can accompany the traditional marriage; but the most traditional women exceeded others only in their preference for describing themselves with the use of the sinful "committing adultery."[16] These, then, were men whose relationships were kept secret from their wives, but almost expected as of right; and which were something possible to engage in casually without necessarily feeling guilty. For the women with similar attitudes, there was no sense that any such relationships were permitted them. They felt bad about their actions.

Again, the notion of parallel and traditional adultery comes into play: for the men, adultery may be a game to be played alongside marriage; but for women, adultery requires an effort to place themselves outside marriage and alone, free to engage with another.

Yet emotions are not necessarily rationally based, and guilt often knows no rhyme or reason. Those who were by no means traditional in their attitudes or behavior—thinking they had "come to terms with" a new way of leading their lives, permitting one another freedom in their sexual relationships—were frequently "bowled over" by their emotions; and those who "had no reason" to feel guilt because they were only doing something they felt entitled to do—those committed to the Myth of Me, following their own self-fulfillment, rather than to any Myth of Romantic Marriage—were similarly sometimes afflicted with guilt, if not toward their spouse, then to their children, or to their lovers' or mistresses' families. Worse, the guilty feeling was free-floating and destructive. Winnicott, describing a mother's reaction to the evacuation in wartime of her children, may hold the key to this conundrum:

> So powerful is the latent sense of guilt about the possession of children (or anything of value for that matter) that . . . one can almost hear her saying, "Yes, of course, take them away, I was never worthy of them. . . . it is my own self that fails to provide them with the home they ought to have." It will be understood that she does not consciously feel this; she only feels confused or stunned.[17]

It is no accident that Winnicott writes of mothers feeling so unworthy for—although both can feel, as she or he turns inward and finds fault within, "What did I do that was wrong?" "What is wrong with me, or, perhaps, with us?" "How have I failed?" "I did not deserve to be happy and to have a successful marriage"—this reaction is more typical of women who are acculturated to believing men must be right, so they must be wrong. (Hunt found the same expression of opinion among Americans.)[18] These assumptions of fault are clearly widely accepted in our culture, so that people take for granted there must have been "something wrong"; if not with the betrayed spouse, or the straying one, then with the relationship between them. Among study participants, Peter assured us he had been "immature," "not at all grown up," "unable to feel"; and Kate explained that if her husband had an affair, she would at once "try to find out what was wrong. Because there must be something wrong, musn't there?"

With adultery defined both as a measure of the failure of the marriage and as a failure of personality or of the relationship (rather than, for example, as the pursuit of legitimate pleasure like having a good meal, playing a favorite sport, or becoming absorbed in a book), then feeling "unaccountably" guilty begins to be explicable even at the conscious level. Hence, those who described their actions as "having an affair" or as an "extramarital relationship," but not as "committing adultery," were not exempt from such feelings. In the "serious affair," the emotional content of the new relationship is so important, however, that any guilt felt *toward the spouse* is diminished. The reasoning seems to be:

> What I am doing is wrong but it is so good, it can't be bad. If it is not bad, it can't be all wrong. If it is not wrong, I have done no wrong. So I don't feel guilty.

Guilt was not avoided altogether in the "serious affair," however, because it was often the precursor to the breakup of the marriage. Hence, even had they managed to reduce their guilty feelings toward their spouse, people in these relationships felt more guilty (than those in other kinds of liaison) about their *children.*

Guilt was not, of course, the only painful emotion. As we have seen, men were made less unhappy than women overall: women also suffered more from the deceit they practiced than men, but each equally feared being found out by their spouses. Men were sad that their marriages had been hurt more often than were women; but men felt a good deal less guilty about their children, were only half as jealous as women were, and suffered about equally when someone else was jealous—usually the spouse or the lover's spouse.[19] Occasionally a lover was jealous about the marital relationship or about not being able to spend time together or about a lack of fidelity in the *adulterous partnership* itself. As one distressed woman said, "Maybe I was cheating on my husband but he [her lover] was just *using* me, using me. He had other women all along and I never knew. I felt horrible—horrible." And a woman of forty-seven, a teacher and an artist in an open marriage, described how she felt:

> My husband and I never have lovely, fulfilling sex. For years I loved him enough to try not to mind. My present lover is wonderful in bed, and I with him. My husband says he will never want me like that, though he does with his girlfriend. My first affair made me sad and dissatisfied. My last makes me hopeless because I want to marry him and can't.

This younger woman (born in 1951), in a traditional, secret affair which she began when she was twenty-nine years old with a "much older, successful academic," feels "guilty regarding my spouse and my lover. The deceit and lies, the stress and mental and physical illness it causes. [I like] the fantasy side when we are apart, the short times together and the sex." She explained that she loved her husband very much, but that

> Rarely a day goes by when I do not think about my lover. I think I did fall in love with him (silly me!), but I think the hope that he may have given *us* a child [she and her husband have been unable to conceive] was paramount in my subconscious. Horror of horrors, I now realize my lover looks a lot like my husband! Maybe my plan was to choose a man as close to one's own image as possible!

The pleasure lay in the relationship itself; the pain, in the difficulty of balancing the two relationships. Ben listed the pains of his affair:

1. Being unable to be with her for more of the time.
2. Seeing her unhappy and being unable to help her.
3. Rows after my wife found out.
4. Seeing the affair die.

As long as the person involved remains in a marriage, there is a struggle to maintain a balance in the triangle. One younger man (thirty-five at the time) described the importance of the *shape* of his affair. He made a triangle with his hands and showed how the apex shifted its position in relation to the base line. If the third party (at the point) pulls the married lover too far over to one side enlarging the angle ever nearer to 180 degrees, where it disappears, neither the affair nor the marriage can maintain integrity: the triangle is destroyed. The picture is complicated if the lover is also married for she (or he) has her (or his) own triangular baseline as well. This is further complicated by pacts of freedom intended to strengthen the marital relationship. Such a balancing is described by a man, born in 1932, who had obtained his wife's agreement to have other relationships. He also reminds us of the dangers of work liaisons:

> Slight anxiety that my partner, a fellow employee, might become indiscreet to my colleagues or boss or that she might become too fond of me and suffer pain. I felt guilty that I wanted only a physical relationship (because emotional involvement disturbs the balance) while she wanted more, and anxiety that my wife would become unhappy and ask me to stop.

His wife did ask him to stop: "[she] feels she would rather I had no more affairs now because she feels less able to attract lovers than I am, and feels insecure though rationally she knows that my affairs don't endanger her."

Jack also worked hard to balance his marital and adulterous relationships, at the same time playing out the old story. During his first affair, he spent most time away from his home, physically, emotionally, and intellectually. He was in transition, a student, at a university where no one is in a family and people make their own rules. But there was, as at a conference, even a time limit in sight, whereas his marriage had no such limit.

His girlfriend was going back to her own country, and he knew she would be "wrong" for him. Yet his own background was of mixed British and European parentage, and much of his childhood had been spent abroad. His first "falling in love," never consummated, had been with another "foreign" girl. He *successfully* surmounted difficulties (like the knight of old), forging links between his past and his present that would permit him to move on and to "get in touch with the other side" of himself. His pleasure in his girlfriend was not marred by his awareness that she needed him as a "father figure." Rather, it made him more confident that he could manage an ending when the time came. He did so. His "trials"—his moral debate and his terror that he might be rejected after all—simply added to his enormous sense of himself as a powerful man when he succeeded. The toxic possibilities were kept at bay; he was not going to die—not just yet. He could even abandon his need (as he saw it) for God to take responsibility for him. He thus made a virtue out of an otherwise sinful act and order out of what might otherwise have been experienced as chaos. Jack—staying within the triangular shape, conducting a traditional liaison, which could become dangerous but was, as he experienced it, supportive of his marriage because he found balancing the triangle so rewarding—permitted the Myth of Me to flourish and maintain the Myth of Romantic Marriage, too, albeit a little tarnished. He and his wife are still moving on, their joint project as yet not concluded.

As people become more "expert"—that is, as they "manage" their extra-marital lives either by forging or insisting on new agreements or making peace with themselves in their compartmentalization of their lives—the pains associated with maintaining a balance lessen. In the most recent liaison, the men indicate why few felt only a little or not at all unhappy. Only just over one third said they had suffered because they were afraid of being found out and because they felt guilty, and only around one quarter worried because the marriage had been hurt and they had been deceitful. Just under one in five felt guilty about his own children and was upset because someone else had felt jealous. A mere 9 percent suffered because of their own jealousy. Women, having "managed" a first liaison and continued at least to a second, suffered also from fewer of the listed problems relating to the marriage rather than to the content of the liaison itself, but reported much more overall unhappiness because of the pain involved in the adulterous relationship. In this last liaison, it is jealousy that distinguishes the two: women suffer because of their *own* jealousy as well as that of others; men, because of the jealousy others only.

Charlotte, a residential case worker, was born in 1928. Describing her affair and the reaction of her lover's wife, she invites us to pay attention through her eyes to several sides of the story. A convert to Roman Catholicism, she said religion played a "very important part" in her life. Yet she was divorced. She wrote that she waited a long time for her divorce because "it could have led to the ruin of my partner's career," and despite the fact that "my adultery was so total an experience that sex with my husband was horrific." Perhaps she was thus able to experience her marriage as annulled and even as amounting to an infidelity to her adulterous relationship. This began after many years of "athletic sex and empty marriage, . . . when he [her lover] put his hand on my leg at a party and I realized with a shock that I was in love with him." They became "engaged" and entered the next month

> what we considered a marriage. We symbolically ate bread and salt in the Russian way, and for several months after that he said he felt he was committing adultery when he slept with his wife. From then on the pain of separation increasingly took its toll [on me], and the risk of professional exposure and ruin did of him so that, between bouts of ecstasy and happiness (I was flax and he was flames of fire), we slid down the long slope which led to his total rejection of me and my collapse.

Charlotte loathed the difficulty of conducting the affair: they had "no base. And having to hide under a rug in the back of his car was disgusting." She had also taken three other lovers—only, she felt, "to lift his guilt, to relieve my sexual jealousy and, I suppose, hoping to make him jealous." Others tried the same thing, sometimes in relation to a husband who was already himself "carrying on." Louise felt it might make her "desirable again. After all, someone else wanted me." It had worked in neither case.

Charlotte's account was permeated with the imagery of the woman with whom and for whom love is almost a mystical and religious experience. It has to be toxic and sad: "He pervades my being all the time. I want only for us to look once again at each other in our deep friendship before I die, and I plan how I could just bribe the undertaker to let me see him for the last time if he dies before me." Her tale was full of conflict and turbulence, and she idealized her "darling," who apparently had tried to murder her, "having driven his car straight at me seven years ago." She lives still in her love story—long over for her lover. Over because they, the proper married couple, together and excluding her, "confessed." Her lover's wife clearly set stringent limits to his roaming; and he, too, after this wicked encounter, appeared stricken with the need to be "saved" and "redeemed."

Charlotte, without the one relationship that gave her life meaning, that enabled her to feel valuable and powerful, "collapsed" into depression and tried to kill herself. Others also became ill, like the man (quoted at the start of the chapter) who "had to stop the car and get out to vomit"—not because he had been abandoned like Charlotte, but because he felt so guilty. He was not a Catholic but he was a believing Jew. His girlfriend was a very young gentile. She was expecting his baby and refused an abortion. He felt "dirty" and literally "sick to his stomach"—both sickened and sickening. It was one thing to mess with a girl for fun; another to have a miscegenous (as he felt) child. He was frightened of the responsibility and of the likely reaction of his wife and wider social circle. He had not only breached boundaries but polluted relationships both inside and outside.

The reactions of Charlotte, of her married lover, and of this man are not untypical. Rather, pain, bewilderment, shock, and anger are common responses to the discovery of adultery, and even a spouse who has known or suspected may be overwhelmed by unexpected and profound feelings when forced to "face up to it." While the sense of grief and loss is expressed most commonly with tears, anger is unleashed in words, perhaps exchanged within the hearing of the most intimate of relations, including children and friends but not much outside those relationships.

Indeed, *passion* is a word used to express not only sexual love but also fury, and the passions roused by the discovery of an adulterous spouse do sometimes lead to revenge or punishment beyond the intimate circle of the family. Every year, murders are committed in the aftermath of a discovered "affair"—sometimes by a betrayed lover, not a spouse, especially when there has been a long relationship modeled on a marriage; he or she sets out to destroy the partner when the love they shared has already, as they experience it, been destroyed. In New England, in 1983, Jean Harris, middle-aged headmistress of a girl's private school, murdered Dr. Herman Tarnower, the author of the Scarsdale diet; he had been her lover for many years but betrayed her with another (younger) woman. While many more stop short of murder, they still seek retribution or revenge, perhaps as fierce and intense as that of the Lele, for jealousy is not an emotion that is easily contained. Pat Lamb, in *Touchstones: Letters Between Two Women 1953–1964*, describes receiving a telephone call in the early hours of the morning from her friend Joyce.[20] Hysterical, Joyce sobbed that her husband, Hans, now separated from her, had broken into their house and sawn the matrimonial bed in half, his revenge for a destroyed marriage of which part was his wife's new relationship. Pat could only inanely ask, "Horizontally or vertically?" to which her friend screamed, "Diagonally."

Although Morton Hunt thought the less the emotional involvement and commitment in time, the greater the pleasure,[21] in this sample the effects of different liaisons (as named by people themselves) is not so clear-cut. What best distinguishes an affair is not whether it was "casual" or more "serious" but how effectively a balance was maintained between liaison and marriage (even discussion having different effects depending on the pact or agreement the married couple had about sexual fidelity). Indeed, it is not happiness but *unhappiness*, pain, and suffering that distinguish the different kinds of liaison, just as unhappy marriages are different, each in its own way, while the happy ones are all happy in the same way.[22] Suffering is also a more powerful measure of difference in women's experience compared with men's, although, of course, there is extensive overlap. The positive experience of having successful sex mixed with good feeling does, however, distinguish between the great love affair and the mundane liaison. This potent mixture gives people a "high," literally "turning them on." Without it, they lack "kicks" and do not feel they are living or even that life is worth living. Jack said his feeling of joy and the "fun" had gone, and he "yearned" for it; while a Scotsman agreed:

SCOTSMAN: The feelings I had are gone and have been gone for two years and haven't come back; whether they do come back or not I really don't know.
INTERVIEWER: Do you sleep together [with his wife]?
SCOTSMAN: Uh, hmm, yeah.
INTERVIEWER: But it's without meaning for you?
SCOTSMAN: It's hard to explain: I used to wake up in the morning feeling full of life you know, and, you know, "It's a wonderful day!" I was happy, content with things and I've lost that. It's that I've got to find again. Somewhere or somehow.

The Masculinization of Sex

Several differences but also many similarities are apparent in the experience of modern women and men in adultery, the sense of yearning described by Jack and the Scotsman being much more typical of the way women spoke of their affairs. As I noted in discussing how people took the decision to enter a first liaison (see chapter 5), the rhetoric employed indicates a greater calculation for men. In describing their liaisons, this clear-cut matter-of-factness remains while women were more expansive: they seem still to indicate greater conflict.[23] For example, men on the questionnaire listed their delights:[24] "Sex; friendship"; "Novel and uncomplicated sex" (Harry); "Change of sexual partner; sexual satisfaction without emotional ties"; "Sexual release and good company"; "Physical excitement; pleasure in conquest—for example, a boost to be thought attractive by younger woman."

Very few women wrote about their experience in this way. Similar ingredients were weightier: "Emotional height and longing; sexual passion and total ease of being together"; "Feeling someone cared and enjoying being with him. Feeling loved and giving love to someone who needed me" (school resources technician); "Sexual fulfillment. I have learned to live without fierce sexual passion though I'm glad I had that brief experience to see what it was like" (student and part-time secretary); "Feeling attractive and wanted. Feeling excited. Romance. Sexual reawakening" (midwife); "Temporary release from tension of home situation and of undeclared sexual attraction between us. An element of excitement"; "I realized I was desirable to other men and that it was my husband that was at fault."

Thus, it appears that women's feelings are more "important." Yet when men describe their feelings in detail and speak of the quality of particular relationships, the difference between them and women disappears (since work plays an important part in people's liaisons, the speaker's occupation, when known, is given):

INVESTMENT MANAGER (MAN): Being with someone who thinks and acts and just *is* like I am and with whom I can be utterly myself. . . . Extreme depths of up and down feelings never before experienced.

CHARLOTTE: Unbelievable union of hearts, minds, and bodies. I had so much happiness from the fact that I was loved, confided in, and that, at last, I was a complete person.

COLLEGE LECTURER (MAN): It turned out to be the most intense experience of my life and quite emotional. An enormous, emotional upheaval.

SECRETARY IN A GOVERNMENT OFFICE (WOMAN): *First liaison*: Reassured to find I was sexually "normal" and that sex could be very good. *Last liaison*: Discovered at last the joy of an intense, deep love (mutual), coupled with an exciting physical relationship.

BEN (TEACHER), who listed his pains (page 212), also listed his delights:
1. Being loved by someone I loved.
2. Making love *with* her not *to* her.
3. Talking to her and watching her listen.
4. Being with a beautiful and younger woman when I was middle-aged and fairly repulsive.

Again, there is a coming together of women and men at the same time as certain differences remain. These questions of style are reflected in the changes in the fact that *men* are beginning (those married in 1970 or later) to *reduce* the number of their casual affairs, while contemporary *women* are *increasing* the number they report. These men write more like women, and more women—especially those in nontraditional occupations and younger—expressed themselves less ponderously. Thus, a thirty-one-year-old computer shift leader delighted in "the thrill of doing something that seemed very daring and wicked at the time." She was typical of her generation of women who have begun to report more "casual" affairs just as the contemporary men have reduced theirs. This is particularly marked among the men most committed to the Myth of Romantic Marriage: the "casual" affair has dropped from the repertoire of these (most traditional) men without entering the repertoire of the equally committed (traditional) woman. Whereas only about 30 percent of these recreational affairs were accounted for by women married before 1970, over half are accounted for by women married since 1970. It may be that because past values made it acceptable for men to "have a bit on the side," the traditional man, committed as he was to lifelong, monogamous marriage, could nonetheless feel comfortable with a "casual" relationship, while it would take a very permissive woman to describe her affair in this way. (This idea certainly fits with the fact that 83 percent of these oldest men checked sex as a major benefit of their liaison.) Now, men are less sure that this is an acceptable relationship while women have begun to feel it may be. Rather than the casual affair losing stigma for women over time, it appears to have gained more stigma for men so that traditional men are reluctant to engage in such relationships or to use the term. It remains the most permissive people who report casual affairs: instead, the Myth of Me must now, it seems, play a stronger part in either a man's or a woman's thinking before either can accept a "casual affair."

Despite its rhetoric of equal freedom for both sexes, the sexual liberation of the late 1960s and the 1970s took little account of women's own desires for the expression of sexual intimacy in a loving relationship, but concentrated on encouraging women to please men by liberally dispensing their bodies to all comers. An analysis of the pages of *Forum*—especially its advice columns, mainly directed to the painfully expressed problems of women— makes it clear that whatever men wished to do *to* as much as *with* women was acceptable, and that women's task was to satisfy them.[25] Only in this way would she, it was suggested, be happy, her own insatiable orgasmic self as satisfied as possible. Rosalind Brunt[25] found similar advice in popular sex manuals of the 1970s, like Alex Comfort's *Joy of Sex* and *More Joy of Sex*, David Reuben's *Everything You Always Wanted to Know About Sex* and *Any Woman Can!*, and various other publications, especially *Nice Girls Do: Vanity Fair's Guide to the New Sexual Etiquette*, serialized in a magazine called *Honey* and including a chapter entitled "A Philosophy of Considerate Adultery."[26] Every woman had a right to male-defined heterosexual pleasure, this alone being the modern liberating force for women, while female sexuality was infused with a high degree of consumerism, being transformed into a narcissistic commodity. The "sexually marooned woman" was viewed as a creature of pity, almost a pathological specimen.

Dr. Ruth, the diminutive, Jewish sexual-marital counselor who has a popular phone-in television program in America, also, seems to advise women to play along with "whatever" her husband (or lover) wants, even when the caller says how much she dislikes his sexual "games" (which often include, if not actual pain, humiliation).[27] She stresses the idea that "anything goes between consenting couples in private": there is no "right or wrong" to any sexual act. The advice is tempered only by the suggestion that the woman has the right to persuade her husband sometimes to "do it her way," thus "allowing" the woman her fantasy, too. In other words, what is good for him is good for her—rather than what is good for her is good for him. The norm is set by the man's desires, because the woman will "get nothing" if he cannot maintain an erection. Thus are women made the servants of the penis, still.

This is not to say that *all* women want only to relate to others closely in every sexual encounter or at every stage of their lives. Lee, as we saw, did not (see page 95). Nor did the young woman who just decided to go to a party "and fuck someone." But, given the high ranking of friendship, love, and being needed, and the yearning for intimacy reported, it is clear that women *as a group* do seek for more than the "zipless fuck" that the novelist Erica Jong envisaged in *Fear of Flying* (1973)[28]—something more welcome to men, *as a group*. Nick, a media man, both assumed such a male desire and believed that women of his generation, those under thirty-five, had changed:

Girls around today think *as men do*. . . . They have the ability to make their own minds up. I don't think they look for long-term commitments. . . . That's a generation that's in their mid-thirties now and grew up in the formative years in the middle sixties that have this *more realistic outlook*. [My italics]

But the women who had tried acting like men (or as they thought men acted) were not quite so sure:

FRIEDA: Well, Erica Jong [with her "zipless fuck"] got it wrong for me.
SUKI: Well, if I could get away with just that, then I think I probably would but I don't think I can. I think, like her [Frieda], it doesn't exist for me.
LUCY: I tried that and it didn't work for me.
INTERVIEWER: Was that the one where you felt 'a bit like a whore'?
LUCY: Yes, a bit, yes. Because I find that I don't have to fall in love with someone—I'm not that unrealistic—but I have to *like* them. I mean, I have met a lot of guys; I meet them in work and in the things I do in my spare time and all this, and I meet a lot of people—that one is attracted to physically, I mean, but one doesn't necessarily like them very much. . . . And I have tried and through trial and error found that it is no good for me. . . . However good the sex was. And it *was* good. Inside I felt dreadful because I didn't really like the person and it turned into active *dislike* and I think this was as much my fault as his because he didn't behave as I would have liked him to behave. But he did behave totally in character with any indications I'd had before but I pushed that aside because I wanted to go to bed with him.
   I wanted to behave with him like I imagined men behaved with casual pickups. . . . It might work for other women but [it was] almost as if you are left with a nasty taste in your mouth. If that isn't mixing up my metaphors or whatever! [My italics]

Feminist scholars have recently struggled with the problem of grasping what female sexual pleasure, defined in women's and not men's terms, might be.[29] Dale Spender shows that heterosexual behavior is customarily defined from the "imperious" male viewpoint. Men act sexually—that is, they engage in *the* sexual act, implying something done, a goal achieved. Women have (as my sample shows) sexual relationships—states of being, fluid, not tied to any particular physical action, time, or place. She also points out that the term *penetration* describes whether full intercourse has occurred—not, for example, *enclosure*.[30]

Certainly, if men need (and in adultery find—indeed seek) obstacles to create desire and sustain an erection, women's pleasure cannot be separated from danger.[31] Always men can use the obvious form of attack on women—rape; but as Carole Vance points out, "sexuality activates a host of intra-psychic anxieties" as well as raising "the fear of competition, as we recognize our own wishes to compete for attention and for loved objects," the competition being other women. Furthermore, to the extent that women's experience of desire signals the giving up of vigilance and control—the responsibility of a proper woman—it causes profound unease about violating the bounds of traditional femininity. Transgressing gender raises the specter of separation from other women—both the mother and literal and metaphorical sister—leaving one isolated and vulnerable to attack.[32]

Certainly women in this sample repeatedly expressed a desire for autonomy and control, to be free to be vulnerable and surrender to a strong (even dominant) man and not be annihilated. In their greater unhappiness and guilt, in their nonseparation of sex from friendship, in their many attempts to embrace sexual freedom—often at the behest of loved men—and their distress when such freedom fails to provide a much needed security especially when it conflicts with a desire for children, women indicate their ambivalence as they struggle to recognize their own needs and meet them,[33] for their behavior—in particular of the youngest and most recently married, challenging the male order—has, to the extent their behavior is male-like, often appropriated it without necessarily finding what it was they sought.

Despite the delight women express in accepting and controlling their own bodies and in having breached and been released from conventional boundaries that circumvented them, I think that these trends, together with those already identified before marriage, reflect not, as Ehrenreich and her colleagues felt, a *feminization*, but a *masculinization of sex*.

The Victims

At least those women who had affairs had some rewards. The uninvolved, betrayed spouse often does not. In the accounts of "victims," it is less the pain of jealousy that is evident and more the sense of profound loss.[34] It is the destruction of an imagined past, of the capacity to believe any more that their marriage, their relationship, and their very selves were as they had thought. They must construct a new truth about the past just when the sense of who one is and who the other is, of what each shared with the other, itself has to be reconstructed. This is necessary in the light of new knowledge, new information withheld from them quite deliberately. These spouses say, "It was the deceit I couldn't bear—that he had been carrying on with her for *years* and I never knew"—a value very much shared by the adulterous spouses, who say it is the deceit they necessarily practice in the traditional adulterous liaison that causes them so much distress. Indeed, they often choose to tell precisely because they cannot stand the guilt associated with the continuing deceit—a point I return to in chapter 8.

Even when "guilty" oneself, the excluded spouse in the more traditional and secret adultery suffers because he or she either discovers and is racked with jealousy and anger, or feels the "victim" of unscrupulous behavior. The spouse has been betrayed and deceived, and is unloved and unlovable. The common response is to blame first oneself for having brought it all about and then the thief who stole the straying spouse. Suddenly the spouse is desirable because desired; she or he cannot be hated.

Amelia, now a chartered librarian of sixty-three, married at twenty-two a highly intelligent and well-educated man of twenty-four. (At the time, Amelia had no qualifications.) She had sex only with him before they married. Her husband was in the army at this time; and, at first, because of the Second World War, they were separated a good deal but both believed in sexual fidelity. She thought he might well have had "one or two brief affairs" but never thought much about it. When, however, she learned of a much more serious affair, she went through "hell":

> During the past ten years I have gone through mental and physical hell. . . . I am still unable to come to terms with the fact that for eighteen years of our then thirty years' marriage, my husband lived a lie to me, that is, a fifteen-year affair, then about three years before he told me.

She was particularly distressed that his partner was a mutual friend. She well understood the tensions and intimacy of his workplace, perhaps the site of secret work on nuclear weapons:

> A large government research establishment where there were literally hundreds of highly intelligent and ambitious men in their thirties or forties with young families—in close living proximity to colleagues and wives. It was a highly competitive set up.
>
> The woman with whom my husband had an affair was the wife of a colleague of his. She was also a "friend of mine" if, in retrospect, you can call it that.

Amelia believed her husband may have turned to this woman (whose husband had an illness at the time the affair began) "when he had any sort of row with me [because] he is incapable of calming anger by showing or accepting physical affection."

Amelia's husband told her about his liaison "because there might have been a child." She says she loved both him and their own children "passionately": "For years I could hardly bear to exist after he told me. It is impossible to describe the mental and physical pain. But because of my husband's job and my children, it was necessary to show no outward sign of this." And she added, "If he dies before me, he will have died twice."

Since her husband is already dead, perhaps she does not need to try to kill him. Nor has she tried to kill his mistress in any mortal way, but Amelia "was determined to wipe her [his lover] out of his mind" and "eliminate her sexually." Hence, immediately after her husband told her of his affair, sex was "fantastic" but now she can no longer enjoy sex or even disguise her antipathy to her husband satisfactorily, although she would like to be able to do so: "I wish it were not so." She has tried to die herself and has talked to her family doctor, a psychiatrist, and an emergency "hot-line" counselor.

The psychiatric advice (as she heard it) was to leave her husband to save herself—that is, to regain her self-esteem and remake her life, not easy at sixty-three. She has been told that she allows her husband to "put her down," but he tells her she "dominates him." All she knows is he has had a lover whom she thought was her own friend. She finds herself in a world whose rules and nature she does not recognize; she is extremely frightened. Indeed, she says she has searched books (as a librarian) for answers and finds them *supporting* "extramarital relationships. . . . I do not know if that is right for people today. It is not right for me personally."

Far from either the other woman or her husband being "punished," it is the "virtuous" wife (she has never had a sexually consummated liaison, though she did say she had a relationship "of the heart" after her husband told her of his affair) in this tale who is punished—to a life of mourning for the love and the life that has been destroyed. There can be only one real and true love. Her husband's relationship with a second woman destroyed her belief in his love for her;[35] his living a lie is translated into a requirement that *she* now live a lie because she cannot show any outward sign of what has happened.

Amelia cannot bring herself to argue that she would rather never have known. The pages of books reveal only facts and truths she does not accept for herself. She is tied through her marriage to a man of "honor"—in the army—and, given his sensitive work, to one to whom secrets are the commodity of everyday life. Perhaps they are for us all.

This Telling Business

I made him swear he'd always tell me nothing but the truth.
I promised him I never would resent it.
No matter how unbearable, how harsh, how cruel.
How come
He thought I meant it?

—Judith Viorst, 1976

For us, it is in the confession that truth and sex are joined, through the obligatory and exhaustive expression of an individual secret.

—Michel Foucault, 1980

Ferne's Confession

Ferne, raised in a convent and overwhelmed with feelings of guilt because her husband did not know about her long-standing (ten year) affair with a married colleague, felt she should "confess" not to a priest but to her husband:

I was shaking like a leaf. I thought, "Yes, I must do this, you know, because, you know, it might improve things." Yeah? And then I realized that, by confessing it, it was just causing havoc and he couldn't cope with it. I said, "Well of course, this is all in the past. It isn't in the present. Not now. Not any more." And that was the only way he could deal with it. So, having discovered myself that he couldn't cope with it, I just pretended that it was over.

Ferne tells her husband even though, like Judith Viorst's speaker in her poem "Nothing But the Truth,'" he does not want to hear what she has to say. In Foucault's terms, Ferne seems to feel it is "obligatory" (she "must do this") to confess her sexual life (she feels no need to tell her husband the details of her long staff meetings with the same man) and, in so doing, to discover truth and to *be* true—no longer "false" either to her husband or in her own estimation. It is as if the telling might remove the problem not only of secrecy but also of having a lover. All three—Ferne, Viorst, and Foucault—illustrate the deep conflict faced by people in this sample about telling or keeping secret their affairs. Openness, honesty, talk and telling—good communication—are valued goals at the same time as keeping certain information to one's self, not telling secrets, and being discreet are the signs of the reliable, honored, and mature person. Self-revelation and a capacity to merge and share are at the heart of the intimate relationship[2] at the same time as autonomy—the ability to think, feel, and act on one's own behalf and in one's own interest—requires a separation and maintenance of clear boundaries.[3] Indeed, the value of the adulterous relationship may lie in the way a person has been able to create a private space for an erotic, exciting, and *unknown* adventure that will, in the very act of telling, be destroyed even if the response is not to require its ending. Certainly, the adulterous liaison is, *par excellence*, the illicit and secret liaison, as Lee, the wife in an open marriage, confirmed when she confessed to me that in not telling her husband, Bud, about her affair, she had "now committed the *real* adultery." Hence, perhaps, the feeling that both the fact of having a lover and the deceit are resolved simultaneously in the confession. The confessor has the power to punish, and thus the sin is expiated.

In modern times, adultery as sinful is scarcely a pervasive idea; it seems quite outmoded, however guilty or bad individuals may feel. Nor do great numbers of people go to confession. But huge numbers do speak of deep feelings and thoughts in other professional settings and sometimes within families. Foucault argues that the demand of the Church (at times extracted with torture—hence, one unconscious reason for Ferne the convent girl's terror as she speaks) for its penitents to confess was transformed as it entered into the general relations between "children and parents, students and educators, patients and psychiatrists, delinquents and experts." In particular, it has been "solidified" by "medicine, psychiatry and pedagogy."[4] I should add, "and by the media." For television and radio are the modern confessors of the masses. Clearly, it is no longer only the believing Christian who is required or will feel a need to confess.

Each of Foucault's pairs stands in clearly unequal relation to one another. In particular, there is no reciprocity of confession. Parents need confess nothing to their children; the television personality does not speak of a personal life; while the psychiatrist works through a specific and directed *absence* of personal communication. In psychoanalysis, the transference permits the exploration of all a patient's emotional responses and reveals unconscious motivation only when nothing of any material substance is known about the analyst. "Real facts," it is thought—that is, knowledge at the conscious level—inhibits the patient's capacity to transfer thoughts and feelings onto the therapist and, hence, also inhibits the work of the analysis. This idea is true of all professional encounters. Social workers do not reveal much or anything of themselves to clients, nor do lawyers nor doctors of any kind. Indeed, this is part and parcel of what *makes* someone "the professional"—discreet, self-occlusive, centrally concerned with the needs of the client. Although this ethic provides the rationale for their actions, and their actions do, at least some of the time, meet the needs of those searching for solutions to problems, professionals have considerable powers, too.

In Foucault's analysis, these and any listener—those to whom the sexual secrets must be confessed—hold power to "judge, punish, forgive, console and reconcile,"[5] while the *effects* of these actions are felt within the speaker who may be exonerated, redeemed, and purified. The confession "unburdens . . . wrongs," "liberates," and "promises salvation."[6]

Thus Ferne's dilemma rests on the fact that, while she may unburden herself of the wrong she feels she has done her husband and be liberated, he has the power also to punish her. In telling him her sexual secret, she grants him—not the capacity to act against her, for he has that already—but the specific reason to do so.

Two recent television programs, both enormously popular in the United States, serve to illustrate the paradox of a society that demands that sexual secrets be spoken and, at the same time, suggests they be kept secret. The Phil Donahue show[7] broadcast from Chicago on 26 February 1987 had "infidelity" as its theme. Peggy Vaughan, a woman married for over thirty years and described as an "infidelity survivor," had discovered her husband's "numerous" infidelities and had survived them through "talk." Through "talk, talk, talk," she explained. Now she runs a newsletter to support other people in the same position.[8] The audience, when not attacking the youngest woman on the panel (who had a pact that she and her lover could have other sexual encounters), also supported strongly the idea that it was communication that mattered. Then a woman telephoned:

> I feel terrible because I have had an affair recently while my husband was away, and I haven't told him about it. It really weighs on me. Do you think I should tell him?

Everyone roared:

> NO!

Similarly, and during the same week, Dr. Ruth told a young woman with the same problem who called her, that not only should she *not* tell her husband about this lover but that, when she made love to her husband, she should fantasize about her lover. One or two people in the audience asked whether the woman should not be questioning her relationship with her husband. Should she not be thinking of leaving him? For them, the fact of the extramarital sexual relationship itself meant there was less than perfect love in the marriage; that would be grounds enough to end the marriage. But Dr. Ruth was clear that this woman loved her husband (though the grounds for her certainty were quite unclear), and fantasy about any other figure, if it helped toward good sex, was fine. "I am not supporting cheating," she said, "but honesty is not always the best policy."

Melissa, a twenty-five-year-old student participating in the study, had in the same way been advised by a friend not to tell her husband about her affair and, although she very much wanted to, did not do so

> for two reasons. Partly because I was terrified he would say, "That's it, the relationship is finished," and partly because a good friend of mine said the reason I wanted to tell him was because I just wanted to unload all the guilt and give it to him. I do the act [sexual] and I do a second, even worse act, in telling. My friend said I should be responsible and cope with it myself. That was a doddle!

The friend recognized the pain Melissa could cause—and perhaps the fact that telling her husband would be, in this way, a hostile act, not one of reconciliation. In suggesting that Melissa should act responsibly by not confessing—Melissa's "doddle," or the easy route—the friend expressed the idea that in this confession Melissa would be granting her husband authority over her to determine right and wrong. It was as if Melissa would become the innocent (albeit straying) child again and her husband play the powerful father. This idea was exactly captured by a woman dental secretary who had had just one "affair of the heart" because to have "let it develop would have meant my sons coming from a broken home if it had been discovered." She wrote: "An adulterous liaison should be a private relationship between two people, and one's spouse should have no right to approve and disapprove."

Melissa and the callers in these two shows must have felt very much like Ferne as she contemplated telling her husband about her love affair. Let us look more closely at Ferne's feelings. She needed to confess; she felt frightened (she was "shaking like a leaf"); and she hoped to "make things better," including achieving "better verbal communication with him," as she wrote on her questionnaire. She never had any intention of giving up her lover. Her intention was only to stop "living a lie," to bring things out in the open. Her actions were to tell her husband, to notice his distress,[9] to respond to it with another lie in a cover-up, and to keep her lover. Indeed, she says, "I am now really worried my husband might find out *who* my lover is, so I have to lie even more." She returns to the earlier state of deceiving but now she is also protecting her husband from burdens too great for him to bear; she is nurturing him with the secret, herself with her love affair.

Where do these feelings come from, and why these actions and not others? Ferne was raised in a convent, and Catholic values worked their way under her skin although she rejects Catholicism. The values of the convent would certainly have included the idea that adultery is sinful, and that a way to salvation can be found through confession to a priest with the power, should she complete the penance required, to grant absolution. This, for example, is what Tessa, "raised in a Catholic home," said about her own desire to confess her adultery: "I *missed* communion. I watched everybody else trotting down the aisle to take communion, and I used to feel, 'I am missing something.'" After four or more attempts, which failed as she struggled to find the courage, Tessa finally managed to go to confession:

> The confession is known and it is unknown. The priest behind the barrier is not supposed to know who you are, but still you know who he is and he sometimes knows you.[10] This particular priest was understanding. . . . I think he was one of our up-to-date priests. If it had happened in my hometown [Liverpool] thirty years ago, I think I might have been read the riot act and given every penance possible.

Tessa needed to belong to all those people "trotting down the aisle." Confession is a way to "communion" in more senses than one.

Ferne also hopes her confession will lead to better communion between herself and her husband, but she does not have the safety net of the "unknown" part—the part Tessa describes. Ferne and her husband know one another in the Biblical sense; she is about to inform him of a part of her self—also carnal—currently unknown to him.[11] She is a teacher of the humanities—a young woman who, after obtaining her degree, has worked all her adult life. She has one child, a teenager, and her husband is a businessman who travels a good deal. They have a comfortable but not wealthy life, living in a flat in London. She acknowledges that she did feel somewhat guilty about the love affair but not overwhelmingly so, especially since she thought that she and her husband could arrive at a pact permitting each of them to have other relationships. Certainly, he had been told by her that, since he traveled so much, he was free to sleep with women while he was away: "My husband has always done what he wanted to do anyway, . . . and we have this agreement. . . . I have always said to him, you know, 'Whatever you want to do when you are abroad, you know—fine by me.'"

What she did feel bad about was not telling her husband what was going on in her life. She found "it hard to cope with deceit and did not like a situation where I had to lie to him." She wrote: "*I* would love us to be open, I really would, but it seems my husband can't deal with that. We've got to where he can tell me about this great air hostess or whatever he's made it with in Addis Ababa, yeah? But he can't stand to hear about me."

What Ferne is straining to accomplish is in line with the cultural imperatives with which she, especially given her involvement in counseling at her work, is surrounded. These imperatives demand openness, the ability to speak frankly about intimate things, especially sexual things, an absence of secrets—good communication; and trust between the marital pair. These qualities make for the *security* and *integrity* of a marriage. We have already seen that what makes for trust in any particular marriage varies with the beliefs each holds about the rules of the marriage (see chapter 4, especially page 101). Equality is also demanded. Equality to engage with others, to have equal strength to hear about the other's life and share the other's joys as well as their miseries. Marriage is now supposed to be a relationship between equal partners. Clearly, since Ferne's husband has "always done what he wanted anyway," her granting him "permission" to do what he pleases has a very different meaning from any permission he might grant her. Similarly, the fact he can tell her about his "air hostess or whatever," but cannot "stand to hear" about her, demonstrates his greater, and her lesser, freedom. The sense that she is his is stronger than the sense that he is hers. They are not equal.

These ideas fit, too, with the way she sees her marriage and her love affair, the one failing to provide the kind of reciprocity she finds in the other. She likes her husband but, as she said, he "has never turned me on. Never. I mean, it's just no good with him, yeah? But with my lover, it's quite different. And it's not just sexual, it's intellectual, too. I mean we just get on marvelously, in every way."

Ferne's love affair is, thus, an important relationship—one that meets her ideas of the Myth of Romantic *Love* rather better than does her marital relationship. One to which she also feels committed. In speaking of her love affair, she, therefore, betrays her lover just as she has already betrayed her husband. Ferne's desire to confess, then (she scathingly referred to herself as "starting my confession bit"), included the thought that confession might make things better, partly because a better marriage would be one that was accepting of these things and open to discussion about them: one in which she and her husband would meet as communicating equals; one where intimacy was established or restored. One in which the myth was restored as the Myth of Romantic *Marriage*. She does not *consciously* think her husband has authority over her or that her telling him will make him more powerful. Quite the reverse. She believes their partnership will be more equal.

What, then, frightened her so much? Ferne is not confessing to a priest who might actually grant her absolution and hence make things better that way, nor is she confessing to a friend who might be supportive and encouraging and who, in this way, might similarly make things better for her. No. Ferne's need is to confess to her *husband* who appears to her to have a *right* to hear what she has to say; but, in her fearful feelings, she acknowledges his power to do her harm and her own to make things not better, but worse. It is frightening, too, to reveal (literally, to bring out into the light) such a vital part of her secret self—kept hidden, out of sight, in the deep dark. You do not confess just anything, but sins. Damning secrets. Sissela Bok has argued that the ability to control both revelation and secrecy is actually essential for individual health and illness.[12] This control is necessary for four purposes—identity, plans, actions, and property:

Some capacity for keeping secrets and for choosing when to reveal them, and some access to the underlying experience of secrecy and depth, are indispensable for an enduring sense of identity, for the ability to plan and act, and for essential belongings. With no control over secrecy and openness, human beings could not remain either sane or free.[13]

Ferne does have the power to reveal or keep secret her affair but does not control the consequences of her revelation. She does not risk her sanity, but her freedom is, perhaps, at stake.

What harm might her husband do her? He might, at the extremes of anger, kill her. Violent reaction is not far from the surface; and, while a mistress or a wife has been known to kill her husband or her husband's wife or mistress (see Verity's story in chapter 9, pages 278–83), the violence of men is commoner and even excused.[14] He might, quite simply, be very angry, and she would have to listen to his abuse and deal with what he might say or require. He might demand that she give up her lover. He might end the marriage. Each of these would mean some loss of freedom. In other words, revealing her secret is to risk losing her lover or her husband, either her love affair or her marriage.

Ferne's fears acknowledge her husband's greater physical strength, his capacity to wound her emotionally (because she still cares for him, and his view of her still has the power to affect her own self-image), and the material advantages he offers in the continuing marriage. She has said that they were comfortable. They can afford to go on holidays, provide well for their daughter, and give her the things she wants. The marriage is a continuing joint project. Without it, on her own but with a child and a poorly paid profession (she had just been made redundant from her job), her life would be very different. Her love affair was her own personal and private delight which made everything worthwhile; she is not prepared to give that up. If we think of the shape of her particular triangle at that time, the base line of her marriage is short and the angle pulling her toward her lover at the apex, wide. She said, "You have to weigh up the benefits of various relationships and make the judgment accordingly. And I'm not willing to give up the other relationship."

In fact, none of these worst fears was realized, but her husband became "incredibly distressed. . . . He went to pieces." This is the harm Ferne did her husband. She knows she was responsible for making him so distressed; she feels she was "causing havoc." The havoc is partly within her own psyche, for opening her inner world to her husband's vision (as if he had said, "Oh, I see!", meaning, "I now know. I understand. It is revealed") clearly breached a boundary that has now to be re-established with higher and more impermeable walls. Ferne's bid for a more equal and more open relationship with her husband thus ends, as a result of his misery, in less equality and more closure, both because her own private world is damaged by the rejected knowledge she proffered and because she does not want to hurt him. She shifts out of the ethic that made it feel important to her to be open and into an ethic requiring the avoidance of doing harm—an ethic of care. She feels at fault since the "havoc" arose not, as she sees it, from her husband's reaction to the information she offers, but from her own need to confess. Now she tolerates and hears about his sexual exploits while remaining silent, protecting him from her own love affair. She has gained some emotional power (while still blaming herself) but, having hoped her marriage would last and having intended it to last for ever, she is beginning to consider not so much *whether* but *when* she might leave.

Telling and Keeping the Secret

How common was Ferne's effort to tell? How typical was she in her motivation to tell? How many spouses did discover the liaisons of their wives and husbands? What were the consequences of discovery? Was there a difference if they had been told by their spouses or discovered in some other way? Is there a difference between men and women and over time in this telling business?

There has been an increase in recent times of discussion, particularly about sexual secrets.[15] According to the men and women in the study,[16] around 60 percent to 66 percent (including 7 percent of "don't knows") of their wives and husbands knew at some point about their liaisons or, at least, about the first. There is no difference between them on this. This is despite the fact that, excluding those couples who had prior discussion about sexual relationships and agreements that they could be free, over half of spouses (rather more husbands—60 percent compared with 53 percent of wives) never even suspected anything.[17] These figures are very similar to those reported by Blumstein and Schwartz about American married couples in 1983 and quite different from those found by Kinsey for the women in his sample in 1953. Around 65 percent of Blumstein and Schwartz's sample said their spouses knew, but only 40 percent of Kinsey's women thought their husbands had known about their extramarital liaisons.[18] In my sample, this increase in knowledge is indicated, first, by the numbers saying they ever discussed their affairs; and, second, in the way wives have come to learn of their husbands', but not in the way husbands have come to learn about their wives', liaisons.

How Did They Know?

Neither Blumstein and Schwartz nor Kinsey asked *how* the spouse had found out. In the adultery study, two thirds were told by their own husbands or wives, a mere 7 percent learning from "someone else." About a quarter were told after having discovered some kind of evidence, while 10 percent were told without ever suspecting. (Of the total sample, one third discovered evidence of the affair.) These overall figures mask considerable differ-

TABLE 8.1

Men and Women Who Told Their Spouse Themselves*
by Year of First Liaison

	Before 1965	1965–74	1975 or later
Men who told wives (N = 62)	47%	59%	78%
Women who told husbands (N = 99)	71%	64%	67%

* Proportions of those whose spouse knew at some time about a first liaison: for example, given
that their wives knew at some time about it, less than half of men whose first liaison occurred
before 1965 told their wives themselves about it, while nearly 80 percent of those whose first
liaison occurred in the second half of the 1970s or early 1980s did so. For men, the increase is
significant (p < .01); for women, there is no significant change.

ences between women and men over the time covered by the study. Men in
each successive marriage cohort and in later rather than earlier liaisons have
markedly increased the frequency with which they tell their wives themselves, while women have changed less.[19]

Table 8.1 shows this trend for the *date of the first liaison* (until now I have
given the date of first marriage). It is clear that men used to speak much
less about their affairs to their wives than now they do; and whereas they
used to speak about them less than women did to their husbands, they now
speak about them more than women do. These differences have increased
steadily over the time studied. Whereas women used to learn about a husband's affair from noticing things and finding "evidence" or by being told
by someone else, she now learns from him directly, partly because, when
she finds the evidence, she challenges him. Just as most liaisons appear to
have occurred in the decade 1968 to 1978, so it now appears that the change
in this telling business for men can most accurately be set in the 1970s, since
less than half of men whose first liaison was *before 1965* (47 percent) told their
wives themselves, about 60 percent did so when this affair had occurred
between 1965 and 1974, and *over three quarters* (78 percent) did so when it
had occurred *after this date*. Again, it seems the changes in the culture had
consequences for the most intimate of relationships.

To Tell or Not to Tell: Pacts and Consequences

Few explained why they had told their spouses. Of those that did, the
commonest reason involved a feeling that it was important to be open, that
such things should not be kept from one another, that spouses were entitled
to know, and that they had a responsibility to tell. And the numbers giving
this explanation rose considerably over this period. Both women and men
who thought they were permitted sexual freedom normally told one another, but women did so slightly less than men. (Even "open marriage" Lee
described a "real adultery" when she did not tell her husband, Bud, about

it.) The desire to be open motivated only 14 percent of men married before the 1960s but well over half of those married in the 1970s or later.[20] Women also think being open is important (as Ferne did), but although there is an increase in the numbers thinking so over this period, the change is much less marked than among the men. Men in this sample have embraced the ideology of openness (what Gary Hart once called "reform marriage"), perhaps in a way that these women have not. However, men who understood they were meant to be faithful, and yet did have an affair, were more inclined to tell their wives than if they thought they had no particular pact; while the reverse is true for women. By the 1970s, this trend is striking.[21]

The reason may be because those men who have agreements to be faithful feel more guilty about their breach of the marital rules and a greater need to confess. Yet it was women who suffered more acutely from deceit when they thought they were meant to be faithful (and they did not tell their husbands) than when they felt they had no pact or were in open marriages. Furthermore, in general, the more guilty people felt, the *less* they spoke at all. Indeed, those whose fear of being found out was most pronounced and those for whom deceit was most oppressive were also those who normally did not voluntarily tell. These were the people who were most strongly committed to the Myth of Romantic Marriage. They also tended to have fewer liaisons than others because the penalties were heavy. They suffered from "cognitive dissonance"—that is from conflicting ideas and emotions.[22] "I am not a dreadful person, doing wrong, yet I am breaking my marriage vows, breaking faith with my spouse, breaking one of the ten commandments and a fundamental social rule. I love my spouse and I am cheating on my spouse. I seek intimacy with my spouse yet I keep secrets from my spouse. I love my lover but I should love only my spouse. I have found intimacy with my lover but I betray marital secrets to my lover. I believe in being honest but I am lying." And so on. Unable to continue secret affairs, these people's solution was either to give them up rather than to tell the spouse and try to have a new arrangement, or to get divorced, hoping to recreate the Myth of Romantic Marriage in another pairing. Having already prepared the way by undertaking the necessary emotional labor (as Ferne did), those people who did voluntarily tell, even when the spouse was not suspicious, attempt a different solution to similar conflict. Men—coming from a very different historical position and, over this period (formerly valuing discussion and intimacy less than women), having now taken on, at least to some extent, an ideal that openness about these things is desirable—feel it is necessary, especially if they know they are meant to be faithful, to confess an affair. They expect to be forgiven; and, in so far as they experience telling as largely inconsequential for their marriages, they are right.

By contrast, it seems that women, whether they acknowledge it or not, know they are meant to be faithful. To tell a husband about an affair, if there is a clear agreement that she should be faithful, is really to court the end of the marriage or at least, as Ferne discovered, to risk his considerable distress. Indeed, although there is no difference in the low proportions of women and men thinking the consequences of telling for their marriages were positive (about one in five women, including those in "open" marriages), much more than men, experience the consequences of telling as damaging, even though they more commonly told only when they said they had no particular pact or agreement about sexual fidelity. In addition, those whose affairs had remained secret were also those (especially women) who felt their marriages had benefited from the affair.

Thus, as many as 40 percent of women, compared with only around 30 percent of the men, were clear that telling had had *adverse* consequences for their marriages: they had "worsened or ended." By contrast, *more than one quarter* of the men but only one tenth of the women believed these conversations had had *no* effect on the marriage—a significant difference. This is one clear reason why telling appears less fraught with risk for the men: it simply does not appear to them to make much difference, perhaps, as we will see, because men still stress the sexual betrayal of their wives over the betrayal involved in keeping the liaison a secret. Women suffered from deceit itself more than did men, and this despite the fact they were better, if anything, at keeping their affairs secret than were men.[23] Once challenged, however, women seemed to feel a greater need to confess. This is consistent with a continuing feeling that a woman's adultery is a greater sin, so that she has less sense of any entitlement to "play around." Indeed, the fact that between twice and three times as many men as women believed that they could be sexually free in their marriages (depending on their experience and the date of their marriage)[24] makes it clear that women continue, by and large, to feel less entitled to their own liaisons than do men. Thus, the conflict remains greater for her than for him. She is restrained in her desire to tell by the greater risks still inherent in her telling than in his. Since he is less likely to condone her adultery than she is to condone his, she knows she risks her marriage by revealing her infidelity even more than he does in the same position. We have already seen that divorce has more impoverishing effects for women than for men. But it is not only the material risks that concern women; they also appear more sensitive to the impact such information will have on the marital relationship.[25]

In summary, both wives and husbands are behaving with due awareness of the likely consequences of their telling: men whose wives do discover their liaison at some time are responsible for telling them more than in the past, believing such information has no or little effect on their marriages; but women have changed little over this period, appreciating that such information does have damaging effects on their marriages. The special contribution of the pact, then, is to ease the conflict experienced as people had affairs *and* broke their own explicit or implied marital rules. A clear goal in telling, just as it was for Ferne, is thus to clarify the agreement and taken-for-granted understandings so that what may be relied on—what trusted—is better known; and to arrive at new pacts.

New Pacts

Every affair, even the one-night stand, is a relationship of some sort. Thus far, I have considered the consequences of telling only from the perspective of the marriage; but telling has consequences for the liaison as well, as Ferne was well aware. Indeed, the likely consequences for her affair had been uppermost in her mind as she confessed: she was not going to give it up. Thus, there is, for both women and men, as for Ferne, an eye to the future of *the liaison*. The consequences of bringing a liaison out into the open might be beneficial both for the current affair and for future ones. They hope, in this way, to gain permission to continue this or other liaisons[26] and forgiveness for the past. In fact, women reported positive benefits for their current and future liaisons more than did men. More than one in four of the women and one in six of the men said they were helped by these conversations to feel less anxious or guilty, and a mere 10 percent of the total thought the consequences, in this sense, had been bad. Thus, it appears that women still feel a greater need for their husband's permission than men do for their wives'. In particular, if there is no pact, men do not feel they need such permission: they remain more in the mode of earlier generations of men—keeping the secret.

Any positive feelings arose, then, from having confessed, from no longer having to live a lie and, in this sense, to "cheat," and because the freedom to engage with another was, perhaps, also offered. The consequences of the sexual permissiveness of the 1970s is reflected in the fact that, of the people who felt they had been encouraged to have other sexual relationships, over half had had a first affair in or after 1975, but only 19 percent of these men and a mere 6 percent of these women had had their first liaison before 1966. Over all, more men believed they had been encouraged by their wives to go ahead.[27]

This feeling—that one's spouse has encouraged one's affair (albeit not explicitly); or that, having discovered one, the spouse "permits" it to continue; or that new agreements have been reached—arises in different ways, sometimes without too much freedom of maneuver by just one of the marital partners—overwhelmingly, the wife. Leila, while her husband was in France, dreamed that he had slept with a woman, even "guessing her name correctly." Challenged, Humphrey admitted it. He was astonished because he had only met his partner there, in France, and slept with her just during that week: "You're not going to believe this. I couldn't at first. . . . There was no way she could have known except by telepathy or something like that." He had been conducting another affair for a year, though. In secret.

In England. He felt it was now necessary to confess that one, too. Despite the "dramatically bad" initial effects of her knowing: "Once she found out, she realized that to try and stop it might have broken up our marriage and therefore, she did the opposite: that is, encouraged it and started her own liaison. Now we both encourage each other."

Barbara, a cook married to a builder's laborer, felt their agreement had little to do with her views: "*He* did the agreeing. Not me. It was in bed!" Barbara (now divorced) thought both she and her husband should always have been faithful, and has not changed her mind. She had five children, was married fourteen years, and then discovered her husband had "got three women pregnant in a year among messing about with hundreds of other girls and women (thirteen years to thirty years). I got my divorce on unreasonable behavior and adultery."

She did not know for a long time and was particularly disturbed because she thought she and her husband had

> a very good sex life. I think I'm still uptight [after a second brief marriage to someone who drank and threatened her with physical violence] because of my first husband's infidelity. It hurt me dreadfully—especially when I found out and realized my neighbors had known, my kids knew, my best friend knew. Not that I would have believed it had anyone told me.

Barbara also did not understand why her husband had chosen to tell her except that "he had a fit of pique when he found out his then girlfriend [Barbara's best friend] was going out with other men." She said: "I couldn't stand him telling me about all these women."

The problem for Barbara lay, it seems, in having a husband who had a profoundly different plan for his marriage from the one she held, and in his decision to tell her what he had been up to. She chose a lover (just one) to "get her own back," but he merely "used" her, fitting her in

> between his work, his wife, his ex-mistress, his illegitimate child, his car, his garden, et cetera. I didn't mind being second fiddle, but I wasn't even in the bloody band! I used to have to wait for him to pick me up in his car in a bleak and cold place, and I felt cheap and stupid and USED—he was often late.

Although her pride was restored through a divorce, her financial position was precarious, and her life became even more stormy and miserable.

To say that people entered new pacts, therefore, disguises the fact that some did so less from a considered approach to what a marriage should or should not be about, what the quality of the relationship was like and so forth, and more from a sense of desperation or of inevitability, especially when, as in Humphrey and Leila's case, the most likely alternative appeared to be the end of the marriage. It seems as if Leila shrugged her shoulders and thought, "Ah well, if that's how he's going to play it, I might as well join him." Her choice was limited by her husband rather than by her own desires.

Discovery

Perhaps for a similar reason, men reported their wives as suffering more from discovering their husbands' affair before being told than if the husband proffered the information first. Thus, the consequences were reported as negative *three times* as frequently by men whose wives discovered their affairs before being told as by those who volunteered the information.[28] Yet, for husbands, how they learned was, by comparison, relatively unimportant.

Richard's wife was one shattered by finding evidence of his affair (see page 200); she confronted him with it. He admitted it and wrote: "It destroyed my wife's trust in me. It made me more deceitful though not better at deceiving!" It destroyed his wife's trust because she no longer *knew* him; she could not be sure of anything about their relationship. He had broken trust—deceived her both by having another sexual relationship and by keeping that information; both (she felt) reflected profoundly on their love. Still, like Ferne, Richard would not be without either this or other love affairs. He was an advertising strategist who had been married twelve years and had two children when, at the age of thirty-seven in 1967, he had his "first and most important liaison." "Even today," he added, "my wife, when under stress, curses the name of my first adulterous partner." Richard's wife, instead of blaming him for the "cruelty" which he does, himself, recognize as coming from the "same source" as the "delight"—that is, that the pleasure of the affair lies partly in his betrayal of his wife—blames his adulterous partner, the "other woman," and "curses" her. She excuses him (somewhat in the same way that Ferne found herself responsible for the "havoc," rather than her husband responsible for his reaction to her information), condoning his cruelty to her, because she cannot afford to find him at fault. To do so would be to accuse herself of staying with a man who wounds her, a deceiving liar who, perhaps, does not love her as she believes, wishes, and hopes. Rather, she must see him as the misled child. Thus the two women fight over the man, competing for him.

In a similar way, Miriam was unable to blame her husband when he voluntarily, but in an extraordinarily cruel way, told her of a lasting relationship. This was the elegant lady who thought it "perfectly normal" for her traveling husband to have affairs so long as nothing was "lasting," and who had herself eventually had various "physical" relationships (none, by her design, at all "lasting") which had proved to her that her husband was "a lousy lover and hadn't taught me well at all"—in fact, that he was "useless in that way" (see page 165). For her, too, it was somehow the fault of the "beautiful, blonde, American, twenty-eight-year-old" (when Miriam was forty) and also somehow her own fault. She had been "too busy with children and running the house. . . . Maybe I had neglected him in some way—I didn't know." Perhaps Miriam's husband, like Richard, also experienced the delight and the cruelty as coming from the same source. Miriam said:

> He had been to New York. He always used to travel back on the weekend. He used to travel over Friday night so that he could be at the airport on Saturday morning and spend Saturday and Sunday with us—myself and the children—and be back in time for the office on Monday morning having got over his jet lag, you know, getting his mealtimes straight and everything. . . . We used to have a family Sunday lunch, and I can clearly remember going into the sun lounge, bringing in the coffee. And I sat down—my daughter was twenty, my son seventeen—and we sat in the sun lounge and I looked at him and said, "Well, what did you do in New York last week?" And he said, "Monday I did so-and-so, Tuesday I saw my girlfriend, Wednesday I did so-and-so, Thursday I saw my girlfriend, and Friday I came home." "And I said, 'Pardon?' "
>
> It was a little bit like . . . the sort of thing you see on television: our two children on one side of the table and he and I on the other—four sitting in a square. . . . I think my son at the time thought it was fantastic that, you know, Daddy was away with a younger girl. I think he thought that was great . . . a sort of admiration for his father in middle age—sort of a conquest of a younger person. My daughter was shattered. I don't think she has ever actually got over it. They were working then in London and it was Sunday and I can recall going upstairs and taking all my things out of my room. . . . I stayed in my daughter's room for a week.

Miriam refused to speak to her husband that day. She told him he had had months to make up his mind what he would say and how he would say it; she needed time to think. In the morning, she let the family go off to work in London without coming out of the room and then went straight to her solicitor. He pointed out to her she had "nothing": no money of her own, a "pittance of an allowance"; no skill (although she knew she was "quite clever" from having brought up her children and run her house so well for so long); no job. She felt, not that she *had* nothing, but that she *was* nothing:

> After twenty-two years, I was nothing. And, you know, it's funny. I never thought I was nothing until I was told I was nothing.
>
> I was nothing. I was a good little wife in the kitchen. I was the good little wife to look after the children. When problems occurred, I was always there, but in fact I hadn't even got my foot on the first rung of the ladder. I was nothing.

Miriam told her husband—when, weeping, he called her at midday from the office saying he had not realized she would be "so hurt" and asking if she would take him back—that he was to make her a director of the family company, that he was to pay a certain sum into her bank account, and, finally, that this whole affair was to be kept absolutely secret. No one was to know beyond the family "square" already broken open. (Miriam was particularly shocked to learn that her husband had introduced his girlfriend on a brief visit to London, to their daughter, although he had not told his daughter who she was). This way, Miriam said, she would be able to try and make things better between them inside the marriage, present a solid face to the world, and would herself "at least have what you call 'running-away money.'" There was to be a rebuilding of the secure block facing the outside world, apparently the same as before, but with internal change. Miriam went into social work and became a juvenile court magistrate. Meanwhile, her husband became impotent with her. They sought help; and in one interview, the psychiatrist asked, "Have you ever been with anyone else?" She knew she "had to tell the truth" about her own sexual affairs, so she did: "And he then asked, 'How was it?' and I said, 'It was great.' [My husband] did not bat an eyelid, never asked or showed any curiosity." She insists she "loves him very much." They are still together.

There was no question in Miriam's mind but that the discovery of this affair had been devastating, especially because her husband had broken the square of the family and turned her into "nothing." The disclosure, both of her husband's relationship to her and of hers to him did not subsequently prevent him from leaving her when she was desperately ill, or help him respond to her efforts to rejuvenate the marriage with romantic holidays and communicate her deepest feelings by writing letters to him. He never replied; nor would he discuss them. It is as if he has successfully turned her into his mother and his children into siblings in front of whom he can boast about his sexual conquests. He is not interested in her sexually, but sees her only as someone who keeps his life running smoothly and helps him recover from jet lag. She, staying with him and loving him, perhaps has to deny what a cruel and unpleasant person he is; otherwise what kind of person is she to love him? Thus, she cannot blame him: she must be contributing something to their problems. Besides, all those specialists who required her to confess and speak the truth about her sexual secrets thought it took two to have an impotent husband. Her aim, she said, in participating in the study, was to have her experience used for others. "It's too late for me," she said. Her life, she felt, had required her to divide too sharply the physical from the emotional. The man she loved, she could not have satisfying sex with; those with whom she had "great" erotic relationships, she did not love. And devoting her life to husband and family had left her, after twenty-two years, feeling empty. Yet, at the same time, her husband's disclosure had helped her move on in life, in a sense to be "empowered." She has built herself a life that helps her to feel she both has, and is, something.

Why Tell?

Miriam believed her husband's "girlfriend had issued him with an ultimatum." The liaison was stuck: it had to move forward or perish. In this case, the confession led to the ending of the affair. Could Miriam's husband really have believed that she would not be "so hurt"? Did he hope, like Ferne, that he would gain permission to run the relationship in parallel? Did he intend to leave his family? Whatever he intended, his confession was experienced as hostile.

As we have seen, the commonest reason for telling was a desire to stop the deceit and to be open. Very few admitted to hostile goals (although some therapists think all telling of an affair is hostile)—only 6 percent of women and even fewer men (3 percent). These goals included wishing to hurt the spouse, to exact revenge, or to inflict a loss of face in some way— like Frieda, with her desire for revenge, and Lucy, hoping to make her husband jealous: "My mistake was telling my husband—I suppose I hoped he'd be jealous . . . find me desirable again. I was wrong." To admit to hostile goals is a considerable responsibility to shoulder, especially if one is already feeling bad about the "act," as Melissa said. Usually such overt hostility was set in the context of the spouse's unreasonable behavior. They had done this, so I did that.[29] Thus, Anne: "I told my husband about the affair to make him realize what his apparent lack of concern and affection had done to me." However, Anne blamed her husband in this way only because she was hoping to persuade him to change so that their marriage could be restored: "I ended our love affair because I realized one day that I should be putting my energies into my marriage, not away from it."

Then she told her husband. The pronouns show how external to the relationship with her husband she felt and how close to her lover (*our* love affair but *my* marriage). At seventeen, Anne had married a man who was only eighteen. They had three children in the first four years. She thought they were "very happy for the first ten years." Her husband (a roof tiler and self-employed builder) then fell in love with a woman who was a friend of Anne's and started "popping round" to see her. Anne "found a love letter from her to him and ended the relationship": that is, she asked her husband to give the girl up, but Anne also lost her friend. She then "fell in love with my next-door neighbour . . . who showed me more affection than my husband had for a long time." It was this relationship that she ended and then told her husband about. She and her husband had another "three years which were happy but the 'sparkle' had gone from our love lives." One day, in 1981, she came home from work as a school resources technician "to find he had taken his clothes and left us and that was the end of eighteen years of marriage. I have not seen him from that day." He had gone to someone else to whom he is now married.

Clearly Anne's husband had been having affairs kept secret from his wife. Perhaps he wanted to avoid confrontation; his final departure certainly suggests he was not able to face her with the truth. It was only from his sister via "a little note" that Anne even learned what he was doing. Departing in this way is certainly quite as hostile an act as any confrontation by telling would have been.[30] If Miriam's husband turned his wife into a mother who might be told anything and remain nurturant and forgiving, perhaps the flight of Anne's husband lends further support to the idea that for men to tell wives is to attempt to achieve a lost intimacy and closeness they may once have experienced with their mothers (or another woman caregiver); the man who no longer seeks such intimacy with his wife, or has found it elsewhere, does not need to confess. Because he is, it seems, no longer interested in gaining or restoring intimacy with his wife, he simply leaves her. Perhaps, if he did seek a new intimacy, he had found it with his partner. Keeping the secret (not telling) does not avoid hurt in all cases.

Telling is, of course, not the only way to allow a spouse to learn of one's liaison. That as many as one quarter had discovered the affair through some kind of evidence, and about another one tenth had become suspicious in this way, indicates there are less overtly hostile routes to "managing" discovery.[31] What are we to make of the woman who chooses to make love with her lover in her husband's study during his working hours? She may have many reasons for wishing to be discovered, and she "manages" to ensure she is. The "tell-tale" lipstick on his shirt or the lingering perfume are well-known ways that a husband may "permit" his wife to know where he has been. Of course, it is difficult to avoid discovery, and we should not assume that "evidence" is always planted, even unconsciously, in order for the spouse to know. There has to be a sufficient interest in knowing and a sufficient awareness of the other for discovery to occur. And *not* noticing may so incense the adulterous spouses as to confirm them in the rightness of their actions. Feelings that a marriage is basically over may also be confirmed in this way, for a partner who is so inattentive to looks, moods, and gestures, may no longer care. Thus, Sophie had despised her husband, Damien, for not becoming suspicious: "He accepted the lamest excuses without question. I mean, I was *really* coming home from a meeting at two thirty in the morning? If it had been him, I would have known right away."

Here is a woman who managed both to prevent, and—when she was ready—to permit, her husband's discovery. She was very unhappily married. Her husband thought "sex was a necessary evil to be got over as quickly as possible," and never, she felt, really loved or needed her, marrying her only, she thought, to give him a way to leave his career in one of the military services. She believed marriage was "for life" and "felt trapped":

My first three adulterous liaisons were unimportant really, and none lasted long. But each taught me something and were good for me at the time. My husband never suspected any of them, I am quite sure. At that stage I did not want him to know as I did not want to hurt him. My fourth relationship was more important, and this one my husband suspected. I never found out how he knew—he said he knew because I had "become happy."

Although her stated reason for not telling was the avoidance of hurt, she was also beginning to plan to leave her husband, and knew she "would never again be able to live without a warm and loving sexual relationship"; and so, despite an ultimatum from her husband, she "stood firm." He left. She *managed* her husband's discovery of her liaison. It is as if he was "allowed" to discover this one because she was ready to deal with his "hurt" or unmentioned alternative reactions. Perhaps she did not try to hide her happiness—whereas, in another frame of mind and less determined to "stand firm," she would not have let go of her emotions in the same way.[32] A need to compartmentalize has given way to a capacity for integration. Confident of her capacity now to love and be loved, and determined she can manage to support her children if necessary, she leans toward the Myth of Me, including within it the desire not to deceive at any level but to go her own way.

When the adulterous person is not ready to deal with the consequences of the discovery, they deny it. Tarquin's wife repeatedly denied her affair, only confessing after six months of suspicion. (And Ferne, of course, ended up denying her affair, too.) With the strength of her new confidence, though, and after a year's separation, this unhappily married woman took her husband back with a clear pact "not to be physically unfaithful to him while he was living with me." When she fell in love "with a colleague," she did not wait for her husband to notice her happiness but rapidly warned him he would have to go. They are now divorced. She has not given up on the romantic dream:

> I regret nothing except perhaps my initial choice of the wrong husband, yet even that wasn't all bad—I have three beautiful daughters. I am happier now than ever I was with my husband, and have decided I would rather live the rest of my life alone than trapped in a loveless, sham marriage. However, what I really hope for is a permanent relationship (not necessarily marriage), as intense as the last but without the guilt between us and so "good adultery" would be unnecessary. A dream? . . . perhaps, but I'll keep hoping.

The Need for Intimacy: Confidantes and Friends

It seems this woman found a relationship, albeit temporarily, that combined the things she needed—sex and a talking intimacy. In this study, it was not that the people whose spouses did not know had *no* need to talk and to combine, as it were, talk and sex. Rather, they talked to others than their spouse. In particular, they talked both before the affair and during it to partners in the affair[33] as if this were to be the ideal relationship—marrying sex and love. In the affair of the heart, it was the intimacy of the talking relationship that gave people what they sought—a dear friend, love without sex. And the spouse's jealousy recognized the betrayal of that, too. Hence, the demand of Tarquin's wife that he give up his talking relationship with another woman. On the other hand, when one desired a more complete love affair, this need to talk could be experienced as obsessive, even pathological. This woman, for example, gave up her lover when distance led to the whole thing being conducted by telephone and letter:

> Talking wasn't enough for me. He [her lover] seemed to get a great deal of pleasure from it, and eventually I began to think this was strangely perverted somehow. I think that, for him, the *idea* of having a "mistress" was as exciting as actually having a physical relationship with me.

It was as if her lover sought a confidante rather than a lover. And men, as well as women, talk in this way—about intimate things, about shared intellectual passions, and about problems in their lives—to other women.[34]

The role of the confidante was more important to women than to men but both commonly reported having at least one such person, usually another woman, in whom they could confide. Again it is men who, in this area of their lives, have changed more than women. Mirra Komarovsky, in her study of working-class American marriages, and Daniel Levinson in his of upper-middle-class men, found having a close confidante a rare experience for men compared with women.[35] Yet, in my sample, men now more commonly had such confidantes and regarded them as more important than they used to.[36] When asked whether others confided in them, men not only report this as happening more frequently now than in the past but also think this happens less often in order to boast and "show off" and more often for moral support, sympathetic understanding, and advice.

The confidante is—like the influential books read and television programs, films, or plays seen—an important way in which people can hear another's views and test out their own changing values and desires. Edwin Sutherland, the criminologist, argued first in 1924 that the way people could commit criminal acts was through being exposed to "an excess of definitions favourable to rule-breaking over those unfavourable."[37] That is, if the majority of beliefs people hear are favorable to extramarital sexual relationships, the necessary groundwork is set for them to feel it might be appropriate for them to follow suit. They have still to learn how to commit the "crime," and they need support networks to sustain them. Sutherland's theory is supported in this study by the fact that the more liaisons people had, the more they said their friends were also adulterous. And the confidante was regarded with the greatest importance by those launching into their first, rather than any subsequent, liaison. Indeed, the faithful overwhelmingly believe they mix only with other faithful people.[38] Similarly, people sometimes deliberately mixed only with those they felt were like-minded. This was what Jay and Sacha had done to protect themselves from "bourgeois" values, saying their friends all thought as they did (see chapter 3).

Even a confidante who simply listens, refusing to advise either way, plays an extremely important part in protecting the person from anxiety and distress once they become involved in an affair as well as beforehand. Fanny, for example, turned very much to her "friend in the country, who was marvelous, just marvelous. She was always there and didn't mind how much of her time I took talking. It was to her I went at first when I left home." To have such friends is important even at such a fundamental level as one's mental health,[39] especially as the outside world stresses the centrality of talk. One reflection of it lies in the increasing numbers of *men* in each marriage cohort who turned to women to talk to in this way.

If talking to one's adulterous partner or a woman friend was helpful, it remains the case that *comparatively* few women or men actually experienced any beneficial effects of discussing their liaisons with their spouses. These were typical responses:

> PETER: She always wanted to know the truth about things. Her mother had a thing about people telling lies. . . . I mean it was natural to tell her. I think in retrospect I shouldn't have told her until things sorted themselves out because, I mean, she wouldn't have known otherwise. Unless someone else had told her of course.
> INTERVIEWER: But you would have told her later anyway, yourself?
> PETER: I would have told her, but in retrospect I don't think I should have because I have given her a rough time in the past year. . . . I mean she appreciates the fact that I was honest with her, but, I mean, I'm not offering her any answers or anything at the moment.

Jenny's husband had a liaison with someone she thought "stupid and silly." He told her all about it—to be open and aboveboard. After a while, the girl's husband turned to Jenny; and they, too, had an affair. When Jenny and her partner told her husband and his wife, they were horrified. What had been sauce for them was certainly not sauce for their spouses. Jenny felt everything was a terrible muddle:

> It seemed to me there was so much talking going on, and I thought all this talking is not getting anybody anywhere, so I even stopped talking to [my girl friends] and had nobody. If you don't want to break up your marriage, then it's best to keep the secret. I think I would be far more capable of keeping the whole thing quiet now. I would be very, very good at not saying anything. You see, he [her husband] couldn't do that, and neither could she [her husband's partner]. At the time when [the affairs

were] still carrying on, I felt very vulnerable because I had nobody to turn to.

I'm sad that it happened because I think it has made me unsure of myself, and I still feel quite inadequate . . . still feel sexually inadequate. Because he went into such details about things I found quite difficult. I don't like him talking in such detail about sexual things, and I suppose that always comes into my mind. I must admit I always think—it always crosses my mind in-between, "Is this what it was like [with her]? or is this so different? or why was it so different?" So I am never totally relaxed, I suppose.

Jenny made clear that telling-talk without adequate attention to what is being said, and to a listener's needs and desires, is no panacea.

People, disliking the deceit, may wish to speak but—like Peter, Jenny, Richard, and Ferne—find that doing so, at least with respect to their marriages, is damaging.

The Feminization of Love

Since men have increased their discussion rates so much, and since it is the youngest group who are talking most, and since some liaisons are not spoken about for many years until after they have ended, most women married in the 1970s will learn about their husband's affair and do so from him.[40] But the quality of an adulterous relationship affects whether a husband will learn about it. Time—that is, the duration of a liaison—is not the only measure of the quality of a relationship, of course; but it is the one most readily quantified.

The affair that men were most likely to discuss was the one lasting between about six months and two years,[41] and these affairs were also the most often discovered by telltale evidence. The one men were least likely to discuss until it was over was the "casual" affair or the one lasting less than six months. The most important one—the one lasting ten years or more—they either told their wives about themselves, or she was told by someone else. These "ordinary" medium-length affairs perhaps are of the kind that we might call traditional adultery—the kind that is not condoned and run in parallel but the kind that *may* be condoned, is of some emotional importance, and could threaten the marriage. For men, it is these that they now need to discuss. They still, it seems, try to keep the long-term parallel relationship without talking much about it, while the short liaison is not considered worthy of discussion. As Donald, who did not tell his wife about his visit to a "whore" nor about two other relatively "unimportant affairs," explained: "I didn't think it impinged in any way on my marriage." Eventually he had to tell his wife, Pat, because he had contracted a venereal disease which he had passed on to her, making her suffer a great deal of pain and requiring an operation. Pat was, not surprisingly, extremely distressed by it all and felt, above all, bad that he had not told her. For his part, he was distressed by his wife's liaison which involved "so much talk," because that broke into the "communication" which was the basis of the loyalty you should have to one another. He said he did not mind whom his wife slept with "provided I am the number one and dominant . . . well, principal, male, and the partnership isn't threatened" (in this instance apparently expressing a desire that would meet that of many women in the sample if not of his wife). Donald and his wife used the same words to describe what was important—*communication* and *loyalty*—but they meant entirely different things.

It seems that the meaning of talk and telling about these sexual secrets varies depending on whether the speaker is a man or a woman. On the surface, both want to achieve a new equality, new levels of honesty and freedom, to improve the marital relationship and, perhaps, more freedom to engage with others. But if, as I have suggested, the woman who tells her husband grants him an authority he traditionally has had[42] making herself into a child and him into her father, and the man who tells his wife attempts to recapture the nurturant and accepting mother with whom he can find intimacy and forgiveness, then feelings about this telling business are not the same, although the behavior looks similar and follows a broad cultural trend.

Men, traditionally, have greater problems with self-disclosure and the expression of feeling.[43] If intimacy, achieved through better communication in talk, is a primary, valued goal for *both* husband and wife, then it is reasonable to say there has been a "feminization of culture,"[44] especially a "feminization of love."[45] Women (being already "feminine" in this sense) began with higher levels of talk and telling, always believing the discussion of feeling particularly important, and therefore had less far to go. Men have, in fact, overtaken women, because the emotional benefits are great for men, while the adverse material consequences of telling are still greater for women than for men.

Men, it seems, are reporting behavior more typically associated with women: a *feminization of love* accompanying the *masculinization of sex* described in chapter 7. Each is behaving like the opposite sex—similar facts masking quite different experience. The discomfort, particularly among women in the current situation, is an expression perhaps of the fact that neither trend meets the needs of women that, as I have pointed out in chapter 7, are ill understood, and may not meet those of men either. That is, relatively easy sex modeled on male desire may not satisfy female desire or, indeed, whatever it is the participants seek; and a mere increase in talk and discussion, telling and openness fails to take account of what it is people really need to speak about, hear, and respond to. A cartoon expresses this well: A woman and a man are seated in comfortable chairs opposite one another, and each bears a placard. Hers says, "No sex without love." His, "No love without sex."

But there are important reasons why people are driven to tell—some with a long past, others of more recent origin.

Why Not Tell? Reputation, Feeling, and Pragmatism

To avoid hurting the spouse particularly, so far as wives were concerned, to save the husband's face, was the commonest reason for *not* telling. This was how women expressed their anxiety about their husband's loss of face:

> LOUISE: I don't feel guilt. Now that might possibly be because my husband doesn't know about it. . . . The morality I have is that I know my husband's pride would be so damaged if his friends or our neighbors knew that I was having an affair with someone or I had had a sexual relationship with someone. I don't think he would be bothered about the fact that I had slept with someone. He would be bothered about the fact that somebody *knew* I had slept with someone.
>
> MRS. LONG: I really don't want to hurt my husband and it would be a terrible blow to his self esteem. Because I would have preferred someone else to him, because I would have let him down, because it would have been a lack of loyalty and because it really was rather crude and rude and "one doesn't do that sort of thing." You see? At least nice people don't!

Men never expressed any concern for a wife's reputation; they clearly did not see their extramarital affairs as reflecting on their wives in the same way as wives understood theirs to reflect on their husbands. This concern for the reputation of the husband has a long history: it is *the* important fact of cuckoldery. Indeed, in the past, throughout the eighteenth century in England, Wales, and Ireland, and until the 1857 act permitting divorce in the Civil Courts was passed, thousands of suits of *criminal conversation*[46] were brought by (generally wealthy and high-born) husbands against their wives' lovers.[47] There were two purposes; first to gain an adultery payment from the lover for damages to the husband's *reputation*;[48] and, second, to prove in the civil courts that "*crim.con.*" had occurred, a necessary prerequisite to the gaining of a divorce in the ecclesiastical courts.

Sometimes these cases were clearly organized as a collusion between the married man and the wife's lover or even as between the couple with a third party so that they could get a legal divorce; but, more often, it appears that the husband brought them to restore his image as a man who would not tolerate such behavior from his wife or her lover, and to gain financially through an "adultery" payment or fine from the lover. As Alan Horstman points out in *Victorian Divorce*: "[In the eighteenth century] no man wished to look the fool and that wish was the father to many a divorce petition." Gossip, he says, governed appearances: "Wives and lovers maintained appearances as adultery could become a desperate game, not a joyful or loving tryst," because it might result in a duel and death.[49]

Of course, the reason it might result in a duel and death was because the husband could not permit his reputation to go undefended. His wife was his property. He was clearly incapable of giving her what she needed, of keeping her within proper constraints and exercising his authority effectively. He was not a proper man. Nor might his children be his own.

At the same time, in France, prior to the Revolution, the whole game of seduction and cuckoldery rested, it seems, fundamentally upon what would be *said* in society about these deadly games. In *Les Liaisons Dangereuses*, Pierre de Laclos's contemporary novel about sexual adventurers among the eighteenth-century aristocracy (recently rewritten as a play by Christopher Hampton for the London stage and later transferred to New York), the adventures are clearly about power—the battle for conquest and pleasure, the manipulation of people according to their *reputations*.[50] Although the life of both (male) lover and husband are at stake, what matters is less what someone has or has not done and more how such acts will be reported and discussed within aristocratic "society." The major difficulty then, as now, is that, during such games, the emotions, even of the great lover, may be aroused; love may alter in fundamental ways the original plans. The irony was that for the man to love in this merry-go-round was to damage his reputation as a great lover. In the eighteenth century, in this class, what men wanted from women was less intimacy and talk and more sexual conquests and gossip.

Thus, the husband needed to feel that *his* wife (and his child) was no one else's, that he was a strong man capable of keeping her and his household under control, perhaps also capable of satisfying her sexually. The lover needed as many notches on his stick as possible and the sexual skill to have women ready to be added to it, while he cocked a snoot at the powerful men to whom the women he had possessed, in fact, belonged. Different reputations but central to the successful conduct of each life. These men, relative to the wives and mistresses, were powerful. In law, in England, at this time (and even until this century), married women had no standing. They were "one" with their husbands, and he was it. The wife was not a legal subject separately from her husband. She could not be called in *crim.con.* cases as witness nor to defend her own reputation, which was, in any event, immaterial. Since she had no *public* persona, she had no reputation. The most powerful men of all, such as the king, could not be slandered.

Not until comparatively recently—since President Kennedy in America in the early 1960s and similarly in Europe—have politicians been so subject to detailed investigation of their sexual and family lives. Gossip known to insiders was not published or spread by newspapers or radio, and television was less widespread. Now, however, this private knowledge is considered what everyone should know. An informed electorate in an equal democracy: increased knowledge/information with increasing democratization.[51] It is not mere salaciousness, however. Reputation has come to mean something rather different. The reputation of those running for public office is now closely bound to what is felt, known, and understood about their sexual life and the way they relate in intimate settings quite as much as to their political knowledge and expertise in governing. Public figures are not different (because we are all equal); hence, what is known about them must be as close as possible to what is known about you and me. If they arrive in my living room regularly on my television screen, I want to know whether I would like them as a friend.[52] "Sexuality [is] the key to our personalities," suggests Rosalind Coward, or, as used to be said, to our "characters":[53]

> We are enjoined to confess our innermost feelings and thoughts about sexuality because they seem to be, in this society, the key to our personalities.
>
> These are the secrets that must be told. There has been an increase in the ways in which sexuality is talked about, medically, sociologically, statistically and legally. And with this increase in discussion there's also been an elevation of the significance of sexuality.[54]

Now, of course, death is not usually the price paid for a poor reputation, although loss of public office may be; but women remain aware of the hurt to the husband's sense of his own masculinity. Hence, their awareness of their power to hurt with telling. Men no longer legitimately have authority over their wives' actions; each person is an individual freely determining her, as well as his, future. But he is supposed to meet her sexual and emotional needs. Hence, the continuing loss of face. Yet men did not blame themselves for a wife's liaison ("What needs was I not meeting for her?") as often or as readily as women blamed themselves for their husband's infidelity. Where women said, "There must be something lacking if he wants to go elsewhere, and that is up to me," men said, "There must be something wrong." Period.

Men were more pragmatic. You just don't set out deliberately to inflict pain on your wife. Not if you value her and the marriage still. But the hurt was not tied to her reputation. She might well feel hurt because he had preferred someone else: "What is wrong with me?" might be her feeling, but she does not suffer shame, a public loss of face, as he might. This recognizes the sympathy extended to the wife who is betrayed (at the same time as the "other woman" is blamed). Thus, still, the cuckolded husband is a figure of fun, and there is still no such person as a cuckolded wife. This does not mean that a woman cares nothing for her reputation—that is, what others might think of her, creditable or discreditable; nor does a woman care to "look a fool" through having remained ignorant of a husband's affair.

Indeed, the more women come to occupy public positions of power and influence, the more important their personal-sexual reputations will become. Perhaps women, just as powerful men have womanized, will "manize" as they become powerful politicians—something the columnist Ellen Goodman discussed following the Gary Hart affair[55]—and I have already suggested that women do begin to increase the number of their affairs as they enter previously male worlds. Yet, in the minds of individuals, women's repute remains without the central importance that men's reputations have. In summary, her actions destroy *both* her own reputation as the faithful, loving, and *good* wife (for she is now a loose woman), *and* his. By contrast, his actions destroy or make only his *own* reputation.

Jeremy had not told his wife about his affair. He did not want to hurt her, or risk his marriage or that of his partner. These are the risks that concerned him rather than the reputation either of his wife or of his partner. He was devoted in many ways to his wife. Neither he nor the woman in his affair were prepared to continue their liaison when it seemed the consequences might be grave for both of them "if it got out." His partner was a married woman of about his own age—a colleague from the office. The affair had given him very much pleasure. They had been extremely discreet because "I considered that if she [his wife] even got a hint about it, she would be very much upset and I don't want to upset her."

Jeremy's group debated with him his entitlement to keep silent. Lucy had tried to reach, with her husband and "with a group of friends, a different way of managing our relationships where these things were spoken about." By "these things," she meant the dreadful consequences of liaisons. Her husband's had left her "desperately . . . just devastated. It was completely overwhelming—the amount of actual sexual jealousy, when I was trying very hard to be civilized and reasonable. I just . . . I had no idea I had so much emotion in me. Absolutely none."

Louise thought it not right that Jeremy should decide for his wife what she should or should not hear. He was determining even whether she should be permitted to be hurt, to feel sad. On the other hand, although Lucy was still pursuing the goal of open discussion and knowledge, she told Jeremy: "That said, I would do exactly what you are doing."

By contrast, Cara did think that whether people were likely to be hurt was material in the decision to tell or keep silent. It was wrong to inflict pain unnecessarily. Besides, since the "affair was delightful and fine and part of the fun of it was the deception anyway," telling was likely to ruin the liaison! She was sure that three of her friends were "having perfectly satisfactory adulterous relationships where no one was getting hurt": "My mistake was telling my husband." Cara admitted that she had told her husband to get even, to try to make him find her desirable again, to improve a rocky relationship. None of these goals was achieved. For these reasons, she thought that for Jeremy to have told his wife would "just be stupid, plain stupid."

Jeremy did not disagree with what she said. He did not feel proud of the fact he had had an affair. Equally, however, he had no regrets and no guilt. There was "no point" in telling his wife. Hence, perhaps, the absence of any need or desire to confess. The relationship had in fact been ended by the "other woman" because of her fears of discovery. Jeremy thought her fears were rational for, because she lived halfway between office and home, their meetings tended to be "more in her neighborhood than mine." She was running a greater risk of discovery. But the risk was less one of her reputation as, say, a "loose woman," and more one of losing her marriage. For Jeremy, there was a balance to be achieved—opportunities taken and developed, risks spread, and a policy of minimal disturbance to the peace pursued. Yet he did think he and his wife were more equal within their marriage than they had been: "Things have changed, changed a lot over the years."

Jeremy thought he had begun his marriage in the strongly dominant role, but decision making and many other things had shifted so that his wife made as many of the decisions and there were fewer assumptions about who did what. The affair was nothing to do with that: telling or keeping it secret was a separate issue. Still, Jeremy's original reason—not hurting his wife—is only one of the factors that led to Jeremy's wife not being told and to the end of the affair. For Jeremy, the liaison was in a private space outside the marriage, but his lover did not experience it in the same way. In practice, she controlled the liaison, setting limits to it, while he managed his marriage. She ended the affair; he kept his marriage.

Women could be coolly pragmatic, too. When I asked one woman whether it was important that she keep her relationships secret from her husband, she said, "To me, yes. Yes. Though I am not happily married. But for various reasons, I intend to stay in the house where I am with my children." Clearly, she, like Jeremy, has an eye to the future. If the person in a marriage without a license "to be free" is still invested (for whatever reason) in that marriage, then keeping liaisons secret is necessary—here, in Bok's sense, in order to be able to plan.

The Pull of the Liaison

If the liaison is, by contrast with the marriage, relatively unimportant, a "casual affair," or a "one-night stand," to tell would be to risk too much. (Although some expressed the opposite view: that it was possible to tell about such unimportant events because they did *not* threaten the marriage.)

As we have seen, when judged by the length it lasted, the type of liaison does affect the decision to tell. So do the intentions to continue it or to end it. It is the more serious affair that is spoken about: the traditional adulterous relationship, one that has emotional importance.

There is another sense in which the love affair affects the decision to tell. It has its own dynamic and demands its own loyalties. Unless the lover is pressing that the spouse be informed, either because he or she wants the whole thing to be "open," or because a divorce and another marriage is planned, the involved spouse, in speaking of her or his affair, betrays and, in a sense, exploits the lover, just as the two of them have already betrayed the wife or husband. The boundaries around both the marriage and the love affair are breached in the telling.

Chris, an architect, was clear about the importance of all kinds of boundaries and wished he could invent ones that would better encompass or create new ways of meeting the needs of different people in new kinds of relationships. Especially geographically constructed ones—indeed, he even had a blueprint of a housing arrangement he thought would suit his circumstances which permitted him access through narrow staircases and entrances both to his partner and his child! But also psychological ones, based on who knows what about whom—he also understood. Chris, divorced, with a nine-year-old son, was in a committed relationship with a liberated young woman who believed in sexual fidelity but not in marriage. He "landed up" in a cottage in the countryside "more or less by accident" alone with Sal, the wife of a friend. They became close that week "through sharing ideas and emotions." It was an idyllic, passionate, and "talking" relationship. Sal told her husband, and when I asked Chris why, he replied:

> That's what I asked her. Because she is less concerned about boundaries than I am? Or has less experience about trying to worry about them. . . .
> There are all these questions. Why did she tell him and then, having told him, what is that conniving to do with our relationship? I mean her telling him. The stronger thing to me seems her telling him threatens *our* relationship rather than theirs.

Chris's feeling that he—the outsider—was betrayed, and that there is a "conniving" of the spouses when the lover tells, indicates both that the boundary round the love affair was breached, and that he was exploited without his being able to exercise any control over that. The love affair was brought into the marriage; the marriage, into the love affair. Understood as wholes, each was wounded. Chris went on, when challenged by his girlfriend, to admit the affair to her. He made a slip of the tongue: "I don't know why *we* told her" (my italics). In this tiny way, he showed his sense of the love affair as essentially a relationship *both* of himself *and* of Sal. If he spoke about it, both seemed to do so. He seemed to wish he had lied. Ferne, in telling her husband, similarly betrayed her lover and, in some sense,

brought him into the marriage, as a homosexual lover to the husband perhaps, as well as competitor for her. She offered her husband an intimacy
through knowledge that this man had her body; she had already offered her
lover, in her intimate relationship with him—*in carnal knowledge*—a share
in much that her husband had thought was his personal and private domain.
All of this was being accomplished with *talk*. It is not that the husband, the
wife, and others invite the unknowing to come to bed with them, or to watch
them in bed, or to share in their delight in each other's company.[56] No.
They are *informed*. Told. Spoken to about it. It is discussed. The commodity
exchanged is knowledge. Not bodies.

Chris wanted to distinguish talk, telling, privacy, and secrecy:

Talking is something I like doing, . . . and we talked about all sorts of
things, and it encouraged a particular kind of intimacy, but it was nothing
to do with revealing other intimate relationships so that may be more
what you mean by "telling."

Clearly Sal does not have a talking relationship with her husband. They
can talk urbanely about the weather or art or whatever but not about
themselves, which is very different from the relationship I have with my
girl friend which is continually plowing over us, maybe too much, maybe
too much, I don't know. I see a relationship *with virtually no boundaries*
between us, which doesn't allow any space for the individual which is not
either threatening or threatened by the other individual; which doesn't
allow space for privacy and any privacy becomes secrecy. . . . I think privacy is allowing your partner to have a place which is his or her own and
which you *don't* pry into.

It's—I think it's knowing if you ask a question, you will get an honest
answer, and knowing when not to ask questions or what questions to ask.

Chris wanted independence and dependence and intimacy and distance—personal space and place; he sounds typical of a particular "bourgeois late 1960s and early 1970s" person (according to one research assistant). But bourgeois or not, he was clear that you can talk about important
feelings, and that is good communication; you tell about other sexual inti-
macies, and that can be "traumatic," "not nice, a using of lovers to connive
in *their* (married) relationship." Not everyone, however, finds it so easy to
distinguish between the kind of talk that amounts to good communication
and the kind that damages rather than enhances intimacy. For telling secrets
is part of talk.

Although Jenny, who described "all this talk" (pages 244–45) as leading her even to despair of discussing matters with her girlfriends, did not
say so, it seems her husband fulfilled a fantasy of possessing and controlling
two women at the same time. He accomplished this by insisting on telling
Jenny all about his adulterous relationship and by trying to get her to make
a friend of his girlfriend, Katie. He perhaps would have liked "his" two

women in bed together at the same time, his desire and his girlfriend's to include a reluctant Jenny in the details of their sexual and emotional life being an attempt to dissolve the boundaries between them in an incestuous and homosexual as well as heterosexual relationship. They manipulated Jenny and controlled her through their insistence that she be included in this way through their talking. Jenny did not distinguish between telling and talking. She recognized that this kind of talk is not acceptable and not at all helpful. The secret would be better.[57]

When the adulterous relationship is, in fact, homosexual, whether to tell causes even more distress—partly because the world outside the marital pair will have more to say about this particular adulterous liaison, and partly because the spouse's own sexual identity is threatened even more than when the liaison is heterosexual. The boundaries feel even more uncertain. As one woman whose husband had a homosexual liaison said: "My parents seem to think I must be 'odd'—homosexual, too, for having chosen him. And you do wonder, don't you?" Another woman had a lesbian affair:

> One thing you have carefully got to gauge is, "Should I tell my partner [husband]? Should I tell my partner and can they take what I am going to tell them?" Because it has got this special nuance and slant, you know, which they probably won't understand and won't like and all the other things.

She had discovered what she needed but remained constrained by her lack of freedom with "all the other things"—pressures, stigma, and hurt—there are to deal with. And for the spouse who is told, there then follows the question of who she or he can, in turn, tell for support:

> It's the loneliness when you know, the blow does sort of hit your marriage. If your husband had an affair with another woman, I think you could probably go and knock on your neighbor's door. You could talk to friends. But it was the total loneliness. I just didn't know who to . . . to turn to. I couldn't go to my mother—she's the last person I could go to because there is a social stigma attached to homosexuality. . . . So, you have really got to pick and choose who you are going to tell.

In fact, Chris's idea that there is an appropriate way to be—"knowing when not to ask"—is beautifully depicted by Kingsley Amis, in his recent novel, *The Old Devils*. As one of the women says about her husband's endless philandering in answer to her daughter's affectionate "Don't you mind about, well, any of it?": "What are you talking about, of course, I bloody well mind. But that's all I do, I stop myself doing any more than that. Like brooding or going back or joining things up, no point in it. As long as I don't *know*. And this isn't knowing."[58] It is "not knowing" because her husband does *not* actually tell her, does not confront her, speak the words and make her hear and respond. "Living a lie" is what makes their marriage possible and even good. "Living a lie" compartmentalizes life, ignoring the appalling conflicts that would arise if the truth intruded and a real attempt were made to integrate beliefs and actions, desires and moral imperatives.

Ursula, the marriage guidance and sex counselor who was in the same discussion group as Ferne, suggested that, just as Ferne had felt a need to confess, so Ferne's husband had needs and might very well "know . . . and presumably take care . . . make sure he never does find out. I mean, in your position . . . the damage that would be done to him then perhaps and to your relationship might be so enormous that it would be irreparable, possibly." Ursula suggested the husband should be treated as an adult who is permitted his own preferred route. Just as Judith Viorst (see chapter epigraph) expects a husband who really loves his wife to protect her from such pain, Ursula saw people struggling to protect themselves from hurt rather than seeking to integrate ideals and practices. For Ursula, this, too, is a kind of equality; the husband can be relied upon to look after his own interests if he is permitted to do so—by not being forced to confront what he knows but does not wish to be told. Ferne could not see things this way. She managed, in fact, "by compartmentalizing my life into about ten compartments, yeah?" but not because she felt she had achieved equality, or from any recognition of any "rightness" in her husband's not knowing.

The Exclusive, Secret Liaison and the Desire to Merge

There is, often, not only pleasure for the spouse in not being forced to "know," but in the one who is having the affair, also a *desire* to keep this matter secret, in a private and personal space, away from the spouse. As Lee, married to Bud in an open marriage explained when she had her "real adultery," keeping it secret from him: "[This is the] first time I've not told my husband. Decided I preferred to have my own private secret. Enjoyed having it—but feel guilty because THAT is being unfaithful in our books. But, repeat, selfish enjoyment of my own guilty secret."

This was essentially *not* something to be shared, perhaps, as she explained, because her partner was a man she had been in love with before she ever knew Bud, and belonged to her and in her life, separately.[59] Secrecy for people like Lee, and for those in traditional marriages, was part of the pleasure in the relationship with the lover. They were also clear that speaking about it—especially to "someone who would not understand," who might be hurt or made jealous or disturbed by the comparison being drawn or imagined—would involve a betrayal of the relationship with the lover. Having breached the rules—either the sexual exclusivity rule of the marriage or the telling rule (perhaps both)—this relationship was going to be maintained as exclusive to the person. Indeed, exclusivity through secrecy was a central idea for the adulterous liaison, as it is in a public and acknowledged sense in the marital relationship. This, in a word, was something for Me, not Us. Hence, the salience, in so many accounts, of the Myth of Me as both motivation and justification for the liaison.

Chris is one who longs for privacy that *includes*, but knows it must *exclude*. Another paradox opens up, however, from *within* the adulterous relationship. The lover longs to breach the boundaries of the other's marriage; the way to it is through information gained from the lover's talk. But this may be refused, clear rules being created for their talk, as Mrs. Long said:

> We talk about his children, we talk about my children. We don't talk about my husband, we don't talk about his wife. And I am not prepared to be the first to say . . . although I am *consumed to know* what his wife looks like . . . I would be fascinated; or what she was like. . . . I can't bring myself to ask.

The lover, if talking about the spouses and their relationship is permitted, is admitted as a third into an invisible area made up of shared information, shared secrets, shared experience. Ferne's opening to her lover marital secrets, making him the interloping third in the relationship between herself and her husband, was part of the wound her husband experienced at the center of the liaison if not at its very heart.

Mrs. Long strains to know what the marriage is like because she is jealous of her lover's wife, and to get inside that part of his relationship would open it up to her, letting her into something from which she is currently excluded, making it in this way nearer to being more completely hers, because she would then both know what his wife knows, and still know all about her own relationship. As long as her lover keeps both women ignorant in some way of the other and of the details of his relationship with each, he is setting the boundaries around his marriage and his love affair and maintaining both. He holds the cards; the power lies with him while the women compete. But it is a tightrope he walks, and "giving himself away" (as Simmel says)—that is, losing control—threatened at each side—the fascinating "abyss":

> The secret contains a tension that is dissolved in the moment of its revelation. It is surrounded by the possibility and temptation of betrayal; and the external danger of being discovered is interwoven with the internal danger, which is like the fascination of an abyss, of giving oneself away.[60]

For some, this tension is particularly thrilling and leads not to keeping things clearly demarcated but risking discovery. Some invite their lover to their own houses, perhaps to make love (see chapter 6, pages 177, 194–95), but at other times, openly, to dinner with the spouse present. The secret is hugged; the game of flirtation, dangerously enacted. We might call this *domestication*—a need to bring the lover right into the marriage, into the family circle, into the geographical and psychological space of the marriage. This is what Dr. Reynolds did when he invited his mistress (the woman who later became his second wife) to dinner with her husband. Dr. Reynolds also had sex with her in her own house while her husband was in the next room. Ruth often had her colleagues (including those who had become her lovers) home for dinner or to a party. Susan deliberately had her partner to dinner, too: "That was my lover and that was my husband and I sat and entertained in my own home. That was my lover and that was my husband. I'm as rude as that."

It is not easy to understand what she meant by "rude," but she made clear her actions were a deliberate slight to her husband, and that there is something dirty about the trick she was playing: "He said he wanted to come home and see my home and he—— Obviously one thing led to another, and I was very happy, actually, in my own surroundings. I felt I was playing a role. He was doing what I was hoping we'd end up—being married."

When her husband discovered her affair: "The first thing my husband said to me, 'I hope you never made love in our bed?' And I had to say to him, 'No, we never did it here.'"

Like Ferne, Susan was trapped into another lie by the fact she had brought her lover into the marital circle. She, it seems, exercised some sense of her own power and her entitlement to "use" *her* home (she spoke all the time of "my own home") as she pleased. Dr. Reynolds really did seem to be courting punishment, even death; while Ruth's motives included the desires to bring her lovers into her domestic life, to merge the public and private which seemed to her too much divided, enjoying and hugging her secret (just as Sophie had done outside the primary school gate until she learned so many others had lovers, too!), and, paradoxically, to avoid possible discovery. What legitimate or plausible reason would there be for inviting this colleague and not that one?

In this way we see the continuing power of the adulterous story and, at the same time, the continuing material and emotional importance of the modern marriage. He wants to conquer, risking real danger, another man's woman; she nurtures her secret delight but has a clear eye to the risks of breaking up her marriage. Both know they may lose, as well as gain, love.

However, keeping everything strictly demarcated was the choice of many. Mrs. Long's lover had told his wife nothing about the affair because he planned never to leave her; to do so might threaten his own long-term plans and hurt her. Nor had Mrs. Long told her husband because, although she planned one day to leave him, she knew that if she did, she would not be able to keep the children: "His sons are his sons. There'd be no forgiveness." Therefore she would wait until the children were old enough to manage.

Mrs. Long shared Ferne's fear of the consequences of her telling, saying what is important is that "nobody knows and nobody gets hurt." In fact, she went to great lengths to ensure that no one in her home town in Scotland would ever find out: by meeting her lover only in London; by telling only her best friend there, whose flat they borrowed; and by telling her that, since she was the *only* other person to know about the affair, if anyone else ever found out, she (Mrs. Long) would know who had told: "I told her on pain of death and I told her no one else knew so, therefore, if anyone found out, it could only come from her. Aren't I rotten?"

There is a straining, on the one hand, to keep both relationships as separate as possible; on the other, to merge them. The important thing is that these are what we might call "monopolistic relationships." There is a longing to keep it to oneself. Exclusively. And an awareness that one is not entitled to it. That it belongs elsewhere, to another. And, at best, must be shared. Although it and one's feelings about it can be kept secret.

Deceit—A "Mere Mask"?

An American man had found his wife and her much younger lover in bed. "People," he said, "who say that all that matters is whether she has *told* you or not are kidding themselves—they're lying." He felt "as if something was being dragged from my guts."

Violence was very near, though he did not permit it to surface. In other words, the stress on the deceit and on the secret nature of the liaison is a *mere mask*, according to this man, for what is really important—the sexual contact: the "taking" of his wife's body and her betrayal in "giving" herself to another man. It is this that is at the center of his marriage; this that represents, symbolizes everything else of value in it. Despite this feeling, he did not differ from others in recognizing that marriages are much more than sex: "Marriages are about thirty shared years. About kids and mortgages and the house and cars." He put the gut feeling back not only in the context of his private and personal relationship with his wife but into the gestalt of the marriage and of its whole weighty structure. He said he and his wife had talked about it. It was, he thought, her fears of aging that had made her do it: "Not exactly an affair. She was drunk. After a party."

Even so, some five years later, he does not know if they will stay together. Something has gone, been lost. He does not exactly know what. He has talked to no one else at all. No one knew about it. What had been her secret shared only with her lover takes pride of place now as the *marital* secret. But the fact cannot be avoided: that the lover (a mutual friend, "which made it worse," he said) still shares this knowledge. At least in this case, the lover no longer shares the woman's body, and her husband does not speak to him. The loss of the bodily integrity of the marital pair stands for this man's whole complex of feelings about his marriage. This loss *is* the loss of love— monopolistic love. Just as an older child cannot blame the baby for being born, for (or so it appears) the parents chose to replace the child in this way, so this man cannot blame his wife's lover. She chose to "have" him. The analogy with sibling rivalry is apt: When a toddler puts on a fixed smile as she propels her tense little body toward the new baby intent on doing him serious damage,[61] she lies—her smile a "mere mask" for her murderous thoughts. She longs to restore the monopolistic love she recently enjoyed but must now share with the baby. To share that place and space and divide that affection is intolerable and yet must be tolerated and without murder. But the child, I think, is not asking that her secret be told or that it be kept; she suffers because there is a new beloved someone in her place. She has no power (she is impotent) to *do* anything about it. To *wish* the baby dead *is* within her power if not her control. However, the child has been taught, or will rapidly learn, that to hurt anyone else is bad. If she feels like hurting the baby, *she* must be bad. Her thoughts and her feelings thus become discreditable. They fuse into a secret that has dynamic and form—something that she can, but would unwisely, reveal or keep to herself,[62] but that may take the place of and become more important in itself than the original despair and pain: the deceiving becomes the focus of pain.

In a culture that emphasizes so strongly openness, communication, and honesty, the secret is doubly bad: it masks the underlying pain, the bad (murderous) self, but is also bad in and of itself—hence, the adulterous spouse "cheats," is "false," and "messes around," as she or he hides both act and thoughts—longing to recapture a monopolistic love. But, as this American man demonstrates, the underlying pain also still surfaces. This man's feelings are like Lucy's, who experienced such "devastating sexual jealousy" about her husband's affair despite the openness with which it was undertaken and the fact they were, with a group of friends, actively attempting to work out in discussion new ways to relate which would not demand sexual exclusivity. And like Ian's, who had encouraged Audrey to sleep with her TV man, and then could not bear it (see page 125). Audrey wondered out loud why she "didn't go on and just not say anything and keep it secret and deal with it." But "that would have been—it's not to do with feeling guilty—that would have been giving up on my relationship with Ian." Indeed, this couple made another agreement, according to Audrey:

> I had an expectation which I expressed that at some time in the future he would have an affair . . . Since then I have agreed (1) not to see someone I had a brief affair with [the TV man], (2) not to become involved with another man emotionally or sexually for a year or so, (3) to tell my husband of anything significant happening between me and another man.

This is a fidelity pact (for her, though not, it seems, for him) guarded by the requirement that she disclose "anything significant" between her and another man.

The need to confess, the feelings about deceit and the desire to achieve good communication, are not, it seems, *merely* masks for the deep—and, perhaps, deeper—wound of the sexual act which breaches the bodily integrity of the marriage. The telling comes to be the very center of the relationship.

Knowledge—The Commodity of Exchange in the Intimate Relationship

In any long-term, intimate relationship, there has also to be a deep knowledge of the other and a profound trust that what one knows is reliable. Furthermore, in the long and developing marriage of, as the distressed American man said, mortgages, kids, and cars and many years of shared *experience*, sex may be relatively unimportant: "It's not about sex," one woman said. "My husband is . . . is, he's my family, I can't think how to tell you. Even if one is carried quite away by the passion and the whole newness . . . the erotic and marvelous thing [of the affair], I would cut off my arm rather than be without him." And another woman said: "My husband has taken on all the aspects of my most important relationships. He has been father, brother, and son to me as well as husband." Indeed for this thirty-four-year-old teacher of the deaf, a woman who had not had an adulterous relationship, to have an affair of the heart would be even worse than to have a one-night stand, for example:

> I think I would feel much more guilty and inflict more hurt if I were to choose to confide in another man about matters I would normally only talk to my husband about, or talk to him intimately about. It is that aspect of adultery rather than actual sexual affairs that hurts the worst.

She noted, however, "One doesn't feel this way if one discusses it with a person of the same sex, so it has to be with a potential sexual partner." She recognized that intimacy links, in the mind, both sex and talk. Thus, the desirability of talking, of not lying, and of being honest have been internalized as central to the committed intimate relationship, at the same time as sexual activity can almost lack intimacy. Indeed, sex cannot be the focus, for with sexual freedom of *both* sexes came the absurdity (if not the impossibility) of continuing to value virginity (especially of the woman) and to gain, in marriage, the body of the other (especially hers). In the 1960s, after the relatively free availability of the contraceptive pill, women became able to control their own fertility and their own sexuality.[63] Men could not possess women's bodies as once they had done. There was greatly increased sexual activity for both women and men. This was not only heterosexual, for there was also a rapid growth in homosexual relationships, both gay male and lesbian.[64] Before marriage, not merely did the numbers of remaining virgins decrease but the number and variety of sexual partners increased. At the same time, there were more divorces; and among these people, between marriages, and among those currently unattached, there was also no reason for remaining chaste. Knowing the sexual history and current activity of the Other became impossible. It had never been easy to know about men; but now, women, too, could not be "known." (Indeed, this is one reason why AIDS presents such a potent threat.)

What then was to be special about marriage (or, now, in the long-term and committed relationship of either heterosexual or homosexual couples)? A commitment to monogamy, as an indicator of the special quality and long-term plan for the relationship, was still made, but, because sexual fidelity—the possession of the body—could not have the same meaning as once it had, fidelity in the relationship was to be counted on through a willingness to depend on the other, to be told about failures in the relationship, to achieve high levels of communication, to avoid secrets. On the Other's *word*. Thus was a notion of intimacy constructed that included sexual fidelity but shifted it off center, emphasizing, instead, close communication through talk. Hence the concentration (if only at the level of discourse—of public declaration) on deceit as the greater sin.

Yet the ability to rely on one's long-term partner has always been central to a marriage—indeed, to any relationship. What is new is the greater *salience* of the idea of openness and honesty and the stress on the achievement of intimacy through talk, especially through self-disclosure and the confession of sexual secrets.[65]

At the same time, this was the period when some gave up on monogamy altogether. Open marriages boomed during the 1970s. This was the time when people set out with nonmonogamy pacts (rather than arriving at such arrangements). This was the period of films like *Easy Rider*, when the "earth mother" was an "old lady liberated" into an object for male pleasure, to be passed around between all the "hip cats." It was the same period when couples could "swing" and wives could be "swapped" in the same house and under the control of the husband. Thus, the idea of the exchange[66] of women's bodies (they were not "husband-swapping parties") shifted to the exchange of information as the crucial element in marriage. Love was more about talking since, at the same time, the pleasure of the body could be divorced from love and any talking. Honesty displaced honor—even that honor between thieves (an appropriate code when women's bodies were possessed and hence, stolen) that protected the secrets of the group, as does still, for example, the rule of *omerta* or silence among the Mafia to cover all crime, including theft and murder.

Knowledge and information have, in the currency of members of this sample—and, I think, well beyond—replaced the woman as the commodity of exchange. Men's fury at another man's possession of "their" woman's body is now equally felt by both women and men as a fury about a breach of contract—spoken words—the theft of information, of shared secrets, shared knowledge. Telling becomes a business transaction or a gift. If I tell you this (offer you this piece of information), "it will make things better." Hence I write of *this telling business*. I used the pronoun *she* in the example of the small girl desperate when her place in her parent's lives (or, more usually, her mother's life) is displaced by a new baby because I had in mind a specific little girl and her baby brother, but for other reasons I think this secret (though not the pain of the experience) may be more important for girls than it is for boys.[67]

Physical hurting—aggression—remains less tolerated among girls than among boys. "Roughhousing" or "ragging" is more acceptable play for boys than for girls. Baby boys, more often than baby girls, are physically bounced, thrown in the air, tickled, and sometimes encouraged to play "fisticuffs" with or even to "beat up on" their mothers. No parent will allow a child, whether boy or girl, to murder the younger baby; yet perhaps the intensity of feeling and the degree to which the boy's thoughts must not be revealed is mitigated by a generalized "permission" to make a lot of noise, to pummel his toys, knock down his bricks, and kick the ball. Furthermore, the world beyond babyhood is one of greater acceptance and admiration for him, offering him opportunities to be grasped that are still more slippery to the reach of the girl. Nor is it material whether the child has siblings. Every child faces the problem of possessive longing for an all embracing and accepting love from and for the parent—a love that has to be given up, shared, and divided among competitors, in particular with the same-sex parent.[68]

For, if Nancy Chodorow, Dorothy Dinnerstein, Jean Baker Miller, Carol Gilligan,[69] and others are correct, the girl's capacity to identify with the mother, and to remain close to her because she is *like* and not unlike her, explains why women stress continuity in relationships and their tendency to see themselves-in-relation to others. The girl experiences this primary authority figure (who is more than nine times out of ten a woman even if not the mother) as a nurturing and caring person—and as like herself. The boy's task is to recognize that he is *unlike* this beloved figure, to separate from her and make a different way in the world, stressing his autonomous being and achievement. Thus, he is, perhaps, more "entitled" to keep his secrets, to share less, and to dance in and out of relationships. In changing times, however, the signs, as we have seen, are that such a difference in entitlement between men and women is breaking down.

Liaisons may, in fact, permit such a dance to continue,[70] but they are also sometimes a search for a new, wholly absorbing, exclusive, sexual, and loving relationship; they certainly exclude (except among the swinging and occasionally among the open couples) the spouse. A one-to-one absorption is often created between the adulterous couple, although there are structurally three.[71] Especially is this true of the serious and "successful liaison." In fact, the pain of the excluded spouse in such situations is, it seems to me, very much like that of the child whose place is usurped by a new sibling. Energy is diverted from both child and spouse to another. And the energy that is sensed in the "gaze" (in the Foucauldian sense of seeing with a new capacity to know and understand—new power)[72] of the lover renews a feeling long lost of being primary and powerful. The involved person knows that; and the spouse who is told, or who discovers it, knows, too. The tension between keeping and revealing these intimate secrets, which wound loyalty to the spouse at the same time as that monopolistic and potent feeling has, perhaps, at last been restored to the adulterous person, is stressful for both women and men; they seek to escape it.

When Ferne's need for openness in her marriage failed, she turned to the only other member of her family—her thirteen-year-old daughter. Ten, she had felt was "too young." But now her lover has suggested she leave her husband (beloved by his daughter) and move in with him and his wife! Ferne discussed the problem with her daughter, arguing that since her decision would fundamentally affect her daughter (anyway Ferne thought she "knows something, if not everything"), she should be included in it, but swore her to secrecy: the child must not tell her father. All three family members must now "live a lie"—precisely as described by another adolescent told a similar family secret:

> I felt strangled to death, like I can't get air, and like every time I turn around, I hear clocks starting and stopping and starting. Talk about the people you live with being strangers. I don't know who they are, what they are. The big secret is the big charade. The all-night, all day drama playing over at Willow Road.[73]

Ferne's daughter has to keep a secret without any real control over revelation and not for her own sake, but for her mother. In the very act of keeping her mother's secret, Ferne's daughter betrays her father, her loyalty to both parents split. So, exactly, is the loyalty between lover and spouse split with the secret of the adulterous liaison.

The weight of this secret may then come to control life, shut down activity, and impose unbearable limits to living comfortably.

Power and Control

I felt my control over life had gone.
    —A woman, teacher of the deaf, aged thirty (before a liaison)

It was only by "chance" that a relationship started; and once it had, it seemed completely out of our control.
             —An adulterous couple

"Power" is almost a dirty word—in somewhat the same way as "sex" has been.
             —Jean Baker Miller, 1986

The Liaison: A Playground Within One's Control

At the outset, a liaison seems to be a relationship within one's control. From the security of a marriage, to have a little adventure, a "bit on the side," a "fling," or even something more serious is a fantasy that, like all other fantasies, is subject to the direction of the dreamer.

Fantasies are not boundless; rather, they are dreams whose boundaries are set not by outsiders, not by anyone more powerful than the dreamer, but by the dreamer, herself or himself.' If the marriage is crumbling and a way out is sought, if what the dreamer desires is a transitional affair—then the fantasy can include a great romance, an erotic and emotionally liberating relationship which might (if that is what is really wanted) lead to another pairing. Retribution for past wrongs can be as central a part as finding a personal better future. If, on the other hand, what the dreamer wishes is, like a picnic, a tasty, hazy, out-of-doors, and out-of-the-ordinary experience at the end of which one returns to the reality of three meals a day in houses with strong foundations, carefully preserved and with mortgages, electricity bills, or rents attached, then that is what the liaison offers. In other words, a liaison offers the chance to play—the chance to escape from marriage as the emotional and everyday workplace.

In fact, most people in this sample, as they began a first liaison, did not intend their marriages to suffer. Even those who were unhappy did not usually use a liaison right from its beginning as a steppingstone to leave the marriage; rather, they viewed it as light relief. Those in open arrangements believed a liaison would do nothing but good to the marriage; those in more traditional arrangements believed they could control the conduct of the liaison, that they were capable of ensuring it did not "get out of hand." The difficulty lies in the fact that while a fantasy *is* within the control of the dreamer, emotions are another matter. When these are aroused, the liaison becomes a relationship with its own demanding momentum.

Nor is the partner in this relationship under the control of the dreamer. In fantasy, the partner does whatever the dreamer wishes that person to do and is whatever the dreamer wishes him or her to be. In fact, partners have their own dreams with scripts that may be quite at variance. Then, what was to be a once-in-a-blue-moon picnic may turn into a series of delicious meals that make everyday breakfast, lunch, and dinner tasteless, and the indoor reality into something with peeling paint and cracking walls. This is what happened to the adulterous couple quoted in the chapter epigraph. The man was an architect who worked on the woman's house. Both were married. At the time they met, she was not employed, and his self-employment enabled them to spend time together "in a way that would otherwise have been impossible" (see chapter 6, page 183). For about a year, they kept the relationship an affair of the heart, but it developed and finally took them over: they became "completely out of control."

Lenore, a woman of fifty-three who fell in love with the twenty-six-year-old ex-boyfriend of her daughter, wrote: "When I felt the first stirrings of interest in someone else, I had no idea that it was possible to feel these giant emotions. I have never felt such happiness but now also understand the 'depths of despair.' " She had been married twenty-six years, quite happily. She was a kindergarten teacher married to a media man. She had three children, the oldest being twenty-four when this, as she felt, *happened to* her. In other words, she had no power over the events: they simply happened to her. Her assumption was that things would remain within control because she had "no idea" what emotions she might feel. Once immersed, however, she was taken over by her feelings. In these circumstances, she failed to put up the barriers around herself to protect the new relationship from discovery and possible destruction. With this failure, she lost both her marriage and her affair. Because she "looked very good and was obviously very happy" and her "excuses for disappearing were so weak," her husband suspected the affair, and she told him about it. He refused to participate in any "soul searching" and "departed, very hurt, with a great deal left unsaid." Now, Lenore says, he tells her he "feels very little toward" her and is mainly distressed "at the way" she "did it—right under his nose."

In Lenore's case, the assumption of an ordered world where emotions do not run away with you led her to fail to exercise care, or to realize the power she had to control outcomes, not even perceiving her secret as a powerful pleasure. She played her part well, however, since the old adulterous tale insists that the woman is wooed and conquered, overcome by love so that she can break out of the conventions with which she is surrounded—an act of rebellion which must be punished but is comprehensible because impossible to resist. She *cannot* control anything, says the subtext, because she has succumbed to the desire of the man who has aroused her own hidden desire: "I had no idea"; she did not imagine . . . nor did she imagine that the young lover, playing his part, too, wanted to possess her partly *because* she belonged to another, and more powerful, man. Free, she became a terrifying fact of his daily existence. This was not what he wanted. Nor, in the event, what she wanted. Lenore wrote: "I think it is worth stressing the (probably) obvious factor of the *complete* loss of control. I have felt like a spectator for the last eighteen months." Now that both her marriage and the affair are over, she says: "I long to regain some control of my life."

The irony, then, is that the successful liaison—the "good adultery," as it was called by the woman who, having found the "right" lover, "stood firm" and told her husband to go—the affair that fulfills the romantic dream, is precisely the one that threatens the marriage most and, at the same time, may leave the major participant feeling quite out of control. "Bad adultery"—the affair that lacks the great romance of the ancient story, or that does not fit the fantasy—perhaps leaves the individual in pain but not without a sense of control and harms the marriage less.

In this chapter, I explore several kinds of power and control. This—the kind of control that individuals believe they have over the liaison itself—is the first. When thought out, and not experienced as having "simply happened," it enables a would-be partner to say to the other, "No strings, right?" or, "I'm not ready for any involvement. Just a bit of fun. It would be fun, don't you agree?" Or even, "Let's go ahead but on the understanding we are both going to stay married."

The idea is the ancient one of parallel adultery. One can find sexual pleasure—even a relationship—*alongside* marriage in another and *private* sphere. The difference with the old (normally male, privileged pattern) is that people, as we saw in chapter 8, often want their spouses openly to know and approve. They want to translate it into the modern "relationship"—no longer sinful, guilt-inducing, or adulterous because it is known and consent is given.

Patrick told his wife about his "unimportant, purely sexual affair":

The problem was that this gave her license to do the same thing and her relationship started affecting ours through *my* attitudes.

I feel, with my relationship with this other person that I didn't stop loving my wife. It was done for purely sexual reasons, and it didn't affect our relationship.

You see, if I thought that it would risk our marriage and break up our marriage, then I wouldn't have gone into it at all; and it didn't really affect our marriage as such.

"As such." The problem was that for his wife to run a parallel relationship in *her* private sphere did affect the marriage—albeit, as Patrick admits, because of *his* attitudes. She had begun an affair that was of some importance emotionally to her although she, too, assured Patrick it did not threaten their marriage. Nonetheless, her partner was pressing her to divorce Patrick and marry him. Patrick felt that his wife loved her partner in a way that he did not love his. He thinks (much as he resisted the idea because it offended his desire to see women as equally capable with men of handling "purely sexual" liaisons) that it might, after all, be true that women cannot have "other sexual" relationships without them meaning too much. In other words, he feels the affair is out of control. The reality is that his wife's affair is out of *his* control.

Fanny's husband, Dick, expressed the same idea when he explained how "worried" he was "about her getting used by somebody because our physical relationship, up to two or three years ago, really wasn't very good." If his wife had better sex with someone else, the affair would pull her out from under the marriage where he had at least some control. He knew that good sex can lead to love. That idea is very painful, so rather than seeing Fanny as a person making choices, he understood her as just a weak woman, who would be "used" by someone who made her happy sexually.

These two men, Patrick and Dick, were frightened. Unable, as they felt, to please their wives, to satisfy and contain them, they worried about the potency of other men who might fulfill their wives' deep desires. They were in competition with these unknown lovers, and their wives' sexuality was untrammeled, uncontrollable by them. Fanny, it will be recalled, never actually had sex with her lover but she certainly fell deeply in love with him, and the relationship was profoundly threatening to Dick and to the marriage.

Dick's sense of his power to control the outcome of Fanny's liaison was directly related to the extent of his knowledge about her lover:

He was an unknown quantity really. . . . He was somebody I didn't know anything about, that was the threat. Later on I would know how to deal with this guy because I knew him a bit better. I had worked him out or summed him up or whatever you want to say about it.

He even insisted that his wife talk to him more than she wanted to; in other words, he brought her own private life back within the marital boundaries:

And you [to Fanny] used to get uptight and say, "Oh, I don't want to talk about it," but I think by just pushing and pushing and talking and talking, that's how we have sorted it out. This is why we talk a lot more between us than we used to do.

Every night we talked about it, coming home in cars, going places. Fanny would be sitting there in the car and the record would come on and she would suddenly burst into tears. I knew what it was about, and I would say, "What's the matter?" and she would say, "Nothing." I would say, "Come on, what's the matter? What are you thinking about? Are you thinking about Charles?" And I would always bring the subject up, and from there on we would just talk and talk about it and I think that's how we worked it out.

The anonymous author of the nineteenth-century sexual autobiography *My Secret Life*[2] also "pushed and pushed and talked and talked" in order to conquer reluctant women: he made them talk as *he* desired. Only if it happened to please him did he give *his* women pleasure, while they almost always pleasured him. It is as if Dick had a symbolic sexual liaison with his own wife: he did not actually make love to her as she desired; and, in her adulterous affair, Fanny, in not "actually" sleeping with her lover, did not even allow this bodily pleasure for herself.

Dick repossessed not only his wife's body (she had left home for a while) but also her soul. He even appropriated her liaison.

There is an echo here of the Foucauldian "joining" of truth and sex through speech that we saw in chapter 8. It was Dick's way of exercising power because to leave Fanny to explore her own liaison in her own thoughts would be to give way to the profound fear, perhaps a universal fear, men have of women's sexuality (see chapter 1, pages 50–51). Let loose, it threatens to engulf and has no limits. A woman can be multiply orgasmic—a monster of sexual pleasure and desire that, surely, no man can satisfy. But perhaps this lover can?

For Fanny, the liaison was a place to play, to discover her own self, to escape from the workaday marriage, a relationship that you have to "work" at in order to keep it going. Although her lover had not remained within her control—his script diverged from her own—she had managed it for a while, and it had been very much her own delight.

It was not, however, only that husbands feared that their wives might love the men with whom they found sexual pleasure, or that women felt overwhelmed by their own emotions in such liaisons; men, too, sometimes recognized the risk for themselves. Peter, having had three marriages—the last two both with people he had liaisons with during the previous marriage—now doubts he can "risk" sexual involvement for himself: "For me, having my history of being tempted—that is, my sexual antennae are very quick and strong, if I sense that there is a sexual relationship about, if my marriage was a good one, I wouldn't want to put it to the test."

The power of the Myth of Romantic *Love* pulls the adulterous spouse toward the affair. But the wish remains to find it within marriage. As Lenore, her divorce pending, said, "I still love my lover *and* I love my husband. I *need*, ideally, a husband who is also a lover. I think that says it all."

The Marriage: Working Things Out

Desiring the liaison to remain controllable, people simultaneously fear that it is not. Worse, adultery may be an exercise in controlling the marriage, an attempt to maintain or gain control over the spouse. It certainly is—as Peter, Dick, and Lenore indicate—understood as occurring always *in relation to* the marriage. For the relatively powerless person in the marriage, the liaison offers a certain counterbalance vital to his or her position. We have already seen in chapter 8 that secrecy and telling are themselves the currency of this game. Much that happens works at an even less conscious level, however.

Psychologists sometimes understand nonmarital relationships wholly in terms of the marital relationship and perceived unmet needs—often too deep to be consciously recognizable to the participants.[3] The liaison becomes a way of playing with the marital relationship. Often, following Freud's dictum that there are at least four people in the marital bed—the wife, the husband, and their respective opposite-sex parents—this becomes also a way of "acting out" parental relationships, desired or avoided. (In addition, relationships with the same-sex parent and perhaps with sisters and brothers can be played out, too.) These two spheres—the liaison and the marriage—where the attempt to maintain or exercise control is made, are related because the liaison is, of course, both fantasized and played out from within the context of the marriage. The power that can thus be exercised in relation to a spouse springs from the current dynamic and past history in marital and familial relationships. Members of the sample who were psychologists or in social work, or who had been in therapy, often explained themselves in this way; that is, they were able thus to make sense of the liaison, especially when it was experienced as "quite out of character," as an attempt to "make him notice me," as Lucy said, or to "deal with problems in my relationship with my mother" as one husband, currently having psychotherapy, put it.

Peter, on the other hand, felt he was "playing out the pattern of my father, I suspect. I did not know what to do. I think it must have been something to do with insecurity." He went on:

> Marriage was beautiful. A lot of happiness, a lot of closeness and then because the unconscious, all the unexpressed life. . . . I went and had an affair with a girl who lives just around the corner from here who still remains, what I would call now a sister. I went to live with this girl. It was traumatic. It became clear in two or three days to me that I was acting out angry feelings against my second wife. I went back to her. We didn't even talk about it . . . just settled back into our childhood bliss.

Peter, also having had psychotherapy and studying psychology, talked in psychodynamic terms to explain himself, referring all his actions to familial

relationships. He clearly took on board the power exercise, too. This is how
he explained the way he made his first wife take a lover, the husband of his
own adulterous partner. (His first extramarital liaison was "with a prostitute," which he explained as the result of sexual frustration following the
birth of his first child.) He refers here to a later relationship:

> I had manipulated my wife into that, so I could enjoy Jo-Anne without
> any guilt. I think it was the boredom—I bought sports cars and that type
> of thing—and then I fell in love with this beautiful blonde and that led
> to my wife—this lovely English Rose—being told this, and I *led her*
> *through*—perhaps the force of my personality—into accepting that I was
> doing this and that she should have an affair with him—a foursome. [My
> italics]

Thus, finding the marriage a place of boredom, dealing with the daily grind
of young children, little money or leisure (at that time, Peter was teaching
in a boarding school), and no excitement, he played with Jo-Anne. He and
his wife, he says, "were children, really." But his wife must join in the game,
dancing to the tune he played.

Jack, a social worker, it will be recalled, similarly felt much could be explained by what was going on (or was absent) in his relationship with his
wife. He was "filling gaps." These gaps were filled originally in fantasy only,
but then lived out in his two dramatic and passionate affairs which he continued to describe as "fantasies." In this way, Jack, too, indicated that his
affairs were plays, real-life dramas perhaps, but nonetheless, not part of the
drama of the mundane world. He gained, as he said, a marvelous, magical,
sense of his own potency ("I felt ten foot tall. . . . A man") and he did manage his liaisons effectively. But he also used them in another drama of power
with his family.

In the attic of the marital home, Jack stored the memories (letters from
his lover) in a box ("a Pandora's box") with which he tempts his wife and
fate. His liaisons turn, in this way, into weights on a scale on which he and
his wife are precariously balanced. He has the power to tip her right off
with disclosure. During one affair, there was, he admits, a "phone call" that
he knows his wife overheard when, he feels, she made a choice to avoid the
information available to her: "I didn't even try to hide it because I
couldn't." Jack is sure his wife suspects nothing while "knowing" that his
(grown-up) children do. Thus, he teases his wife and also plays a little with
his children. He spoke of a childhood without siblings and of being sent to
a famous Scottish boarding school that emphasized cold showers, exercise,
and the companionship of his own sex. In this way, he suggested, as he
recounted his story and accounted for his affairs, that they were deeply
related to needs he has in his present and past familial history.

After an afternoon spent talking to me, Jack wrote saying that he and his wife had had a terrible row that night, "and we never row." It was, he thought, because the interview had brought home to him the fact that all these "gaps" could have been met by his wife. He had been blind and incapable of eliciting those aspects of her that he so desired in his partners. He felt guilty and ashamed, perhaps because he appreciated the extent to which he was continuing to exercise a dangerous power over his wife—his affairs being like Damocles' sword. Indeed, he had said that if he and his second partner had been more "compatible," he "would have left his wife for her."

Jack, unlike Peter, also realized that the particular women with whom he had each liaison, his age and theirs, their needs as well as his, the particular jobs and settings in which they had met (university and work), were also central facts of the whole experience. That is, he understood his affairs in terms not *only* of his marriage, family, or childhood but also of his own and their current situations. The liaisons were certainly rooted in his marriage and in his own earlier history, but changes in his family life were understood as side effects and consequences of conducting these particular affairs as much as they were the results of conflicts unresolved or a continuing desire to control his wife's life or that of his children.

A much older woman, Mrs. MacGregor, suffered from the totally subservient position she held in her marriage. Not only was she older and, she assured me, much less special and glamorous than her politician husband, he "could not bear me fat" [when she was pregnant] and "went off all sex with me." He also

> much preferred me when I was down, being low and depressed, and being the underdog and saying, "Please, we must sort things out." He didn't like me being flippant, which on occasions I could be. He didn't like that. I think at one time I said he was behaving like an adolescent teenager [because there were adoring female party workers pursuing him] or something, and he didn't like that.
>
> I was never allowed to do anything without his acquiescing and he got so angry and he kept shouting and shouting and I just used to weep. Yes, that's what I always did when we had rows. I could never argue back. I just used to cry and cry and cry and then hate him behind his back.

What Mrs. MacGregor knows is that she is grossly unequal in her marriage. In addition to the psychological games they play during which he administers all the blows and she "cries and cries," falling into the typically female response expected of her and to which she has been trained, she is economically totally without resources. Although both she and her husband came from poor working-class backgrounds in Scotland, her husband now has fame and money; she has pregnancy and children. She is undesirable in his eyes and in her own. For Mrs. MacGregor, a liaison, preached by glossy magazines aimed at middle-class women, appears to offer an empowering experience and also a *possible* one (since the chosen man would "take care" of her). She, unlike Lenore, however, is fully aware that it is hard to retain control of the new relationship. Mrs. MacGregor doubts her power there, too:

> Because of Roger's neglect of me, I nearly ran away with a young man in 1963. . . . I also thought magazines like *Nova* and *Cosmopolitan* were making statements that—it seemed to be the done thing to be having affairs and I suppose with my husband neglecting me so much, I thought it would be quite safe to have a kind of affair, but you never think that you are going to get terribly . . . unable to do without the person and have to make a decision to go away with them or stay with your husband.

In fact, Mrs. MacGregor's liaisons (eventually she became "quite promiscuous," she said) did return to her a knowledge that she is physically desirable and even lovable. But they gave her no satisfying revenge or control over her own life or that of her husband. First, he refused to have sex with her any more. Then he divorced her. At the time, it was still necessary for someone to be at fault, but honorable men usually provided the evidence. This man made Mrs. MacGregor "prove" adultery (despite his own well-known and numerous affairs and her admission of guilt) by entertaining a paid "correspondent," thus ensuring her public humiliation (her mother would not speak to her afterward) and his security. Mrs. MacGregor also sickened herself because, "although I didn't *have* to—they just needed photographs and that sort of evidence—I did actually have sex with the man," thus demonstrating to herself anew her powerlessness.

Frieda, however, did gain a sense of her own value and felt proud of the revenge she enacted on her bullying husband with his constant silences. Her delight in the successful accomplishment of the secret liaison, her partner smuggled in under a blanket in the back of the car and under the nulliparous nose, gave her the strength to mind a little less when he refused to "sign the papers—mortgage papers" he had long promised to sign, and when he repeatedly sent her "to coventry."

Suki provides a contrast with these two older women (both the same generation as Jack and Peter) in her conscious understanding that "marriage is all about power," as she said. She is by no means a free spirit either, but she is articulate about the problem. She is a young woman, married in the early 1970s with two young children, who appreciates the possible toxicity of adultery and, at the same time, is also engaged within her marriage in "a sort of power struggle." For Suki, however, the liaison promised even further loss of control. Yet she wished she could make it. She avoided adultery because: "I know certainly in the beginning if I did go into an adulterous relationship it would be completely out of control. I would be either up in the air or down on the ground or——" and linked this frightening desire to her marriage:

There is a sort of power struggle going on all the time with us which never used to be there. I started off, I mean this wasn't all that long ago, I have been married nine years nearly, and I started off with a very sort of idealistic view of marriage and of him. I idolized him at the time. Absolutely. And he had a huge influence on me. Everything was sort of referred to him. I wouldn't go out and buy a pair of tights without asking him first if it was O.K. . . . To do him justice, he never abused that—he never played the lord and master because he could, at all. But now, now I am independent of him in thought and so on, he is still trying to wield the big stick so we get into fights over that although we don't actually row. It is all very much under the surface.

INTERVIEWER: What do you mean when you say you are independent of him in thought?

SUKI: Well, as I say, I used to do everything, you know—like politics. For instance, we vote the same way because I assumed he knew best, you know. . . . Early on in our marriage, I found a job which was wonderful and I really enjoyed doing it. But it took up a lot of my time, and he said to me, "You have got to stop it because you are not here to cook the dinner when I get home." And I did. I actually did. Looking back, [I feel,] "What is the matter with you, you cretin?" But at the time [I said], "Oh, all right!" And I did it. Everything. All those things I just sort of did as I was told without even realizing I was being told half the time.

INTERVIEWER: So what do you think has made you now think that you were, then, a "cretin"? What has changed?

SUKI: I changed. I have grown up.

Suki thinks it was being at home and in charge of small children that "gave" her "time to think": "None of it really requires any thought, so sort of peeling potatoes and washing up, I was thinking, thinking about the things he had been getting away with."

She does not resent her husband's past daily control over every aspect of her life and thoughts because, she says, it "was right at the time." Now, however, she has recognized that he is, for example, making decisions about their money without consulting her. He "went out and spent six hundred pounds on some equipment" for his photographic hobby despite her feeling that "he did not really need it," whereas the family did. Looking after children and a house does not merely allow time for thought, but also demonstrates to the person doing those tasks that she (or he) is an effective manager. Like Mrs. Inkerman, Mrs. Waterford, and Mrs. Long, Suki also discovered her own capacities in this way and now does resent that such important decisions are being taken as if she were incapable of making them and not worthy of consideration in them. She, too, is something of a home-grown executive:

Now I have got to change it [the relationship], and it's like walking up a hill against a force-nine gale because he doesn't want anything to change. He is trying to assert authority now because I am sort of going against it. Whereas before he never needed to. You know, it was a sort of automatic process.

Suki seems to understand the very possibility of an affair as a rebellious act against her husband but accepts her relatively powerless position in relation not just to her husband but to all men: "I am not confident at all with men. No. I am hopeless, I'm . . . a kid. I am just like a kid. I either turn them into father figures or eunuchs in my mind."

In Italy, she was offered the opportunity of a passionate affair, but described "fighting the good fight" (refusing to sleep with this man) because of "fear." He was "very virile." Scared of his overwhelming sexuality, Suki needed to turn him into a eunuch and could not.

At the same time, she holds another image of her husband as not at all someone she needs to idolize as once she did, but as most vulnerable. Because she recognizes this aspect of him, particularly in relation to her, she has a further reason to "fight the good fight":

I don't want to cause him that kind of pain. He is a very vulnerable man in many ways. He said the other night: "I've only got one area of vulnerability and that's you," and that's true. . . . There isn't anything else he cares about sufficiently that would hurt him, and I can't hold myself responsible for bringing that kind of pain down on his head.

As men lose their status as "lord and master," as Suki said, so their vulnerability emerges. If you cannot rely on status and authority to secure your position, then the quality of the relationship must be enhanced. Intimacy needs to be achieved and a degree of mutuality constantly reinforced, not just by wives but by husbands, too.

This argument was brought out by David Clark, director of the Scottish Marriage Guidance Council in a recent article.[4] He argued for a reconsideration of men's emotional dependency on their wives as compared with women's economic dependency on their husbands. Men, given their higher rates of illness when not married and their difficulties in being and remaining effective workers without women to smooth the daily path, *need* their wives in a way that women do not appear to need their husbands. If the couple is to achieve new levels of equality within a long-term relationship, room has to be made for men to feel and express such vulnerability and for it not to be seen as "weakness." Confusion arises for women, however, who respond to vulnerability (as Suki does) and yet desire men who are strong and dominant. Ferne, for example, compared her husband and lover as follows:

I respect and care for my husband, who is a gentle and caring man of above average intelligence, and who respects my need to live my own life.

> I am aware, however, of my ability to dominate him, and this is unsatisfactory for both of us. My lover, on the other hand, is exceptionally intelligent, very highly sexed, totally unneurotic, and has the ability to dominate me in a very subtle way, which I can accept, even though I stick closely to my feminist principles.

Ending as she did with a reminder of her feminism, Ferne drew attention to the fact that what she desires is less an absence of vulnerability and a presence of domination, and more a strength that can be relied on, that makes her feel safe and cared for. Her lover is no bully, not domineering, but someone she loves for his leadership and talents, which she implies are not only greater than her husband's but also (because he "dominates her," albeit in a "very subtle way") greater than her own.

This need for a dominant man—expressed, as we saw, also very clearly by Sophie and Mrs. Long—helps us understand what young, intelligent (she had graduated *magna cum laude*), and beautiful Donna Rice found in Gary Hart as well as what he found in her. She was lifted from "part-time" work as an actress or model to the world of politics where decisions of the utmost importance are being made for the lives of everyone. She might have become a president's mistress, joining the ranks of many other women who have found considerable status and wealth along this path (while others have been left holding the baby, as Cleveland's mistress was). Perhaps, even, she might have become first lady. He, on the other hand, could avoid the emotionally vulnerable person he may be in relation to his wife, and play at the more macho, conquistatorial being he seems to prefer. These are ancient patterns, yet even now they realistically reflect the less powerful woman's need for a man who can effectively care for her in a world still lacking opportunities for her equivalent to those for him, particularly if she has children and leaves or reduces her work, albeit temporarily, at that time. Simultaneously, the more powerful man knows he can provide just what the woman needs, and that is immensely satisfying to him, too. Meanwhile, if he is married, his wife provides the security and stability he also needs.

Rosalind Coward argues that for men, "the sexual encounter represents access to power, a series of encounters and experiences which build up a sense of the individual's power in having control over women's bodies."[5] Coward also says the female desire for a strong, dominant man is the desire for the father, to be cared for, to be enabled to be safely dependent again. In winning him, the woman takes the place of her rival, the mother. But this is not necessarily the *particular* father. Rather, the powerful man stands for the power and dominance of all men in the social world.

Coward continues, talking of "women's novels," that women's sexual experience "represents access to knowledge, rather than power. Sexual experience becomes the way in which a woman finds out about herself." So much is a psychic struggle, and women's fantasies are so complex that women actually want to "get away from the stories in their heads into the safely circumscribed world of the novel or film." Clearly, they also want to get away into the less safely circumscribed world of the real affair, which, as we have seen, is the story *par excellence*, providing all the drama anyone needs, and permitting the woman to play the lead part, rare in fact. Furthermore, although it is clear that "becoming [learning about] my own person or woman is in the grain of the sexual—it is how a woman deals with her sexuality"[6]—knowledge of the self is gained not only for its own sake but because the experience is, itself, empowering. Indeed, even as she feels "overwhelmed" by her lover, she also knows it is because "he finds me so beautiful that he cannot resist me."[7]

It is perhaps in this way that Ferne's affair restored her sense of what the ideal ordering of the relations between women and men should be. It is as if marriage has turned out to be rather less orderly than it should—a place full of particular expectations not only about love and the unfolding of reasonable hopes for work, houses, children, cars, and foreign holidays (as Clark says)[8] but also about renegotiating the proper gender relations within it. The feeling that life within marriage is chaotic and disordered was well expressed in the epigraph to this chapter by the teacher of the deaf, who said she felt her "control over life had gone"—even though hers was not an unhappy marriage and she had not—yet—had a liaison.

The Liaison as a Way to Reorder the World

Yet it is adultery, not marriage, that is readily—and has traditionally been—understood as a form of deviance and is, as I described, still a crime in many parts of the world.[9] Adultery, not marriage, breaks out of a carefully ordered world with clearly demarcated lines around the principal actors—in particular around the wife. At the same time, it breaks into the wholeness of the family. In this frame, adultery is itself something chaotic and disordered, and it produces chaos and disorder. For the person in the liaison, the feeling becomes, as it did for Lenore (understanding the world as normally calm and lacking tempests), one of *loss of control*, a feeling that may even be welcome. Like those who act on impulse, such people do not feel responsible for what is happening. However, far from *always* being something chaotic, experienced as a loss of control over one's own life, adultery is often a way in which the world is actually *reordered* according to strongly held beliefs about the proper relationship between women and men. The marriage comes to be seen as where the chaos is; the alternative relationship one where sense and meaning are rediscovered or perhaps discovered for the first time. This, for example, is what those who "unwrap" their preference for their own sex (10 percent of the sample had at least one lover of their own sex) seemed to feel—as if their marriages had been traps requiring them to follow paths and rules that wound in disordered ways around a much straighter path lacking such confusion.[10]

A man who had always felt bisexual, but had tried to repress his desire for men during ten years of marriage, said:

> Now I really don't know why I did that [waited so long]. Of course it was dreadful when I first came out with it and told Juliet the truth. The worst thing was her feeling about the kids. She seemed to think they would be ruined and couldn't cope. And it was tough—I mean grandparents and all of that. But I just feel *so* much better—my life is on target. I know where I'm going. At last.

And this woman:

> Discovering I was a lesbian was like becoming a new person. Things I had never been able to understand fell into place, . . . though I can't pretend it was easy. Also I think my husband still believes he can "save" me— from myself I suppose.

Thus, the adulterous spouse may experience the liaison itself as reassuring about the stability and "rightness" of the world during a particularly stressful period. It is a way, as Lenore said, "to grope towards some sort of meaning." Indeed, she had been motivated to contribute to the study through her "need to be in touch with current feelings about this."

It was men who more readily spoke of the fantasy being played out in their liaisons. It was women who spoke more often of the shifting balance of power within their marriages, though they rarely spoke precisely of power, since especially for women, as Jean Baker Miller has pointed out (see chapter epigraph), it is something of a "dirty" word now. It is a dirty word because it normally is used to describe a capacity to act *for* oneself *over* others, to exploit them, and to take little account of the other's desires or needs: "[Power] has rested almost solely in the hands of people who have lived with a constant need to maintain an irrational dominance; and in their hands it has acquired overtones of tyranny."[11]

Not having or exercising power, however, means to be a perpetual "victim," unable to exert long-term effects on the world and using psychological mechanisms such as cunning, thus inducing guilt, to attempt to obtain what is desired. Baker Miller suggests instead that, for women, power should mean a "capacity to implement." To achieve this, she thinks women will have to face the issues of power, to "struggle," and, especially, to gain "the power to advance their own development." Her ideas underpin much that is expressed with the Myth of Me, but she adds that the power to limit the development of others should be avoided.[12] We have already seen, however, that this is a rosy picture of an unreal world where women, by seeking such paths for themselves, are certainly perceived as restricting those of others. The reality, as Ferne, Suki, and others expressed, is of struggling to make such a personal space and of upsetting the family applecart as they do so.

Although Suki was clear that she was engaged in a *power* struggle, others spoke, as Sophie did, of dependency and of being able to "turn the cheek to receive the kiss" or of feeling that their bodies belonged to them, of needing to discover "who am I?" In particular, as we have seen, the sense of being without autonomy or a sense of self outside their family roles plays a central part in women's attempts to gain control over their own lives and, hence, to redress the imbalance of power between themselves and their husbands sometimes through further education or work which may in time lead to a liaison. Establishing a better order in the liaison itself, or rediscovering what the relationship between women and men should be, was of importance for everyone. Each form of the exercise of power and control has elements of the other two. A fantasy of what might be precedes the attempt to redress the balance of power within the marital relationship, offering a new sense that one may take control of one's own life and a chance to reorder what appears disordered.

Verity's Revenge

Verity, a black woman of forty-three from Barbados, worked in a local mental hospital as a nursing auxiliary. She lived in an area of southwest London which has a high proportion of Indian and Pakistani people but also many West Indians. Verity had been married some years to a man from the same island who rarely had regular work. Together they had saved for and bought a small house which Verity had furnished and lovingly decorated, making curtains for it, and in which she delighted.

For Verity, a legal marriage was not important to her understanding of male-female relationships. She spoke often, not of husbands and wives, but of one's "man" or "woman." As a fact of material consequence, however, marriage was of the utmost importance to her. This was Verity's account of the three years before they married:

> We lived three years before we got married. You see, we got married in '64. . . . Most of the time I was hungry—those were poverty years but I was happy because he was always there. And from the moment I move into the house (and we have got a telephone and we have got a car), that's when my troubles started. I never feel like wife. I never feel like my husband loves [me] . . .
>
> I was left to pay all the bills. You know what I mean when I says *all* the bills—eighty pounds a month, *all* the bills—and my husband would never provide. . . . I asked for a part-time job to buy clothes to put on my hus-

band's back. . . . I didn't mind you see, I thought I was doing it for us, you see. I thought I was doing it for us. . . .

He has never taken me to a show. If I want to go to the pictures, I have to pay for two—my husband and myself—and when we go to a restaurant I have to pass my purse on.

Verity was clear: her husband had a duty to provide for her. He did not. As long as he "was always there," loving her, she could tolerate poverty and would take a job (an additional one) to put clothes on him, never mind herself. She also described what her general principles were about the proper relationship of a committed couple, using the example of the affair to spell it out:

A man you love—he has an affair and when the wife find out, they will back down and tell a little lie. When they start that way, don't poke into their private life, because at least the home is not short of the bread and you are happy. Give them that freedom; that is how I look at life. If my husband is having an affair outside and I am happy and I get what I want— not in the way of a millionaire, in the way a poor man can afford, and he has got a woman on the other side—I am not going to pester him.

In other words, there is the world of *inside*—the marital home—belonging to the wife's sphere; she is in command there; she manages it and helps create it. Then there is *outside*, where the man can even have his "private life" which he will keep discreetly hidden and "tell a little lie" about. *On the condition that* he is a good provider, Verity will not pester him.

Muriel, also present as Verity described this, asked her if she had ever experienced violence from her husband (Muriel had). "Once," she said, puzzling us by adding he had "touched" her "for another woman." She, in her turn, had "threatened" him that if he did that again, she would "kill" him and, "I mean it!" When I asked her what she meant, Verity replied, "Because I found out."

Verity had found out her husband had been having an affair with a very young girl, someone he had met through his sister. He had left airline tickets on the kitchen dresser for his girlfriend to come from Canada to London and then for them both to go to the West Indies for a holiday—an expenditure of hundreds. Not surprisingly, since she was a houseproud person (as her husband, of course, knew), Verity found them. Only once had she and her husband been able to afford to go away together, and then she had paid the fares "*and* the spending was on me." She was profoundly offended by the fact he was spending *their* money, which had, in fact, been earned by her, for her husband rarely had a job. She assumed he could have raised so much money only with a bank loan. She put on her coat and went down the high road to the bank. Telling this story in the small group, Verity got up and acted it for us:

First I tackle the bank manager who lend my husband money to go abroad. . . . I make an appointment and I walk in and I say, "Good morning." "Morning, Mrs. Curran." I says, "My husband has borrowed loan from the bank and I would like to know what my husband does with the loan." He says, "Mrs. Curran, whenever a customer comes and borrows a loan, it is personal and private."

I was mad when he told me that, because I had a joint account, and I was mad, and I looked up to him and I says, "White man, do you know what a black woman have to go through under a black man?" I says, "Do you know we have got a joint account here and I ain't leaving until you tell me what my husband do with the loan and how much it is." So I took a seat and I say, "I'm waiting." He says to me, "Mrs. Curran, I never know that you and your husband has got a joint account," and I says, "Look before you leap. You look into the account and see when money gets paid into the bank—when *I* get paid at the end of the month." I says, "My husband does not give me money to pay the bills. All I get is money to buy food."

Eventually, the bank manager admitted that her husband had told him the money was needed for redecorating the house. That stung Verity where it hurt most. She told the bank manager to come and see the house, "a poor woman lives in." Nothing was needed. The bank manager asked Verity to tell her husband he would like to see him. Verity told him, "Do your dirty work yourself."

She went to the counter, withdrew £200 of the remaining £250 ("I left him enough to get himself to Birmingham"—an industrial town where he had relatives and might get work), went down the road to another bank, and opened a new account in her own name. Next, Verity took the tickets to the airport and got "her" money back on them by pleading—"with the tears running down my face . . . because I was hurt bad, real bad"—that her husband was in hospital, too sick to travel.

Having got her financial affairs under her own control, she then sought the advice of other women in her community who "know." She was clear that she did not want to divorce her husband, because, if she did, the judge might "give away" to her husband the property she considers belongs solely, or at least more than half, to her: "If that house has to stick up for sale and split, I deserve more than half because I put in more than twelve years of it. . . . [It is] my house, yes, because everything in that house is mine."

Verity mentioned by name one of the women who advised her and told us she was renowned for her wisdom. This woman told Verity:

The mortgage you take, so I hold the mortgage ever since we been in the house—it is mine to pay so it is steady then. You take the telephone bill, because when I sick or want a doctor or need the ambulance, I must be phoning. And to take all the insurance for the house, the building and the contents, and for the rest—I say, "Damn the rest." The light bill, they can cut it off—I will go and buy fish and chips down the street. The gas—they can cut it off. The water, they can cut it off. The rates—*he* will go to prison, so I leave all those.

She also consulted a solicitor who told her *how* to pay:

Whenever you pay any bill, you always pay with a check. He told me because I used to pay the mortgage cash. He says, "Who pays the mortgage?" and I say, "I always do." He says, "How do you pay the mortgage?" And I says, "Cash." He says, "When you take your husband to court, you tell the judge you paid the mortgage, is he going to believe you?" And I says, "Yes, because I signed the paper." He said no. "Your husband could give you the cash to pay, and you sign your name." He says, "Everything you pay, you pay with check. Everything you buy, buy with check. Do everything with check."

From this time on, Verity quietly paid those bills with checks and left the others for her husband.

Next, she took revenge on the girl. By talking to neighbors and "those who know," Verity learned that, the previous summer, while she had been away, her husband had had his girlfriend to sleep in her house, in her bed. Not only had he grossly failed to perform his side of her imagined marital bargain by adequately providing for her, he had invaded her territory with his woman. Evidently even her husband's friend had begged him: "It is better you have your fun and let the girl go, but never let her sleep in your wife's bed." But Verity's husband had said, "It's all right. This one stays with me until my wife come back."

Verity braved her husband the day after his sister's wedding when she came by with a piece of her wedding cake for them. Verity addressed her remarks to her sister-in-law, but her husband was present:

"I would like to have a word with you about your brother (which is my husband). He's messing about with Rita, and I am going to trim her down to size." My husband, he look at me and he says, "You touch that girl and I beat you." In front of his sister's face, he said that. So I challenge him.

Verity went to North London—a long and difficult journey by bus and underground transport—to an area she had never visited before. She found the house and sat on the stairs, refusing to move until the girl appeared. Then, in front of her husband's brother-in-law, she "just grabbed her, and I just take her near the cooker and near the pot"—threatening her with boiling water.

When she got home, her husband was waiting for her. His brother-in-law

had telephoned him to tell him what had happened. Verity wished she had
had the sense to tear out the telephone. Her husband beat her up. He was
furious not only that he had been found out, but also that Verity had dishonored him by going for his girl in front of his sister's husband, "an *African*,"
which, according to Verity, made it all much worse because he was not "one
of us." Her whole story thus far was to explain what she had meant about
her husband's violence toward her "for his woman," and her own, "If you
touch me for another woman, I kill you and I mean it."

There was one more step to take in Verity's effort to put the world to
rights. She likes men. She needs love. She took a lover.

> Some years before, I was working for London Transport as a catering
> assistant and we met but we weren't friends. Just on an ordinary basis.
> He asked me out but I refused. I said I was living with a man, and I was
> quite happy with him. I asked him, "Would you be happy if you had me
> to know I am having an affair?" I told him then, "I don't play games."
>
> When my husband started playing games, I said, "Well, I am getting
> on a bit—might as well do my thing." So, out of the blue one day, I
> rang him up. I says, "Oh, I'm sorry, I was checking through the diary for
> someone's number and automatically see yours and since you are on the
> phone, we might as well talk."
>
> Nobody knows. We never meet in [the place they both live].

Verity's lover has a car. They make love in the car but always well "outside"
the area where they might be "known," avoiding kin and neighbors. She
tells her husband she has been shopping and goes shopping, endlessly, to a
major chain store—Marks & Spencer, where she buys "panties, forty-six
panties I have in the drawer that I haven't worn."

Verity had reached a point of fundamental change. Not in her values.
There, nothing was new. Men provide, and they give affection. Under these
conditions, they are free to have their affairs "outside," but they must "tell
a little lie"—keep them secret. They lie for the sake of the face they turn to
one another in the marital pair and, more important, to the world—especially of the family and wider kin. A man must never beat up a woman—
certainly not "for his woman"—so long as she does her bit. (She had earlier
described what a woman must do to fulfill her "bit," telling her husband he
had "the right to beat the hell out of me . . . if you walk in this house and
the house is untidy and the food is not cooked and you see me sitting here
yapping with a woman and your clothes is not clean.") Thus, far, Verity had
estimated what was just and unjust given the damage she had suffered and
the contribution she had made to the material well-being of the marriage,
had taken advice from the appropriate people—both someone of her own
cultural group—the wise woman—and a white professional man, and acted
to put her life back on course—acting, indeed, like an effective executive.
She was empowered.

How could Verity square her own position now with the fact her lover was a married man?

> I meet his wife on the street, and I don't talk to her because we are not friends, and I don't want to be close to my lover's wife. I don't think that is right. That is where it hurts if she finds out. If I have to go out with my lover, I turn to him and I says to him, "Don't forget one thing—I always call her the queen—don't forget your queen comes before me." I say, "And if I have to go with you tonight and she wants to go, I expect you to tell me that you are taking your wife out, and I am quite happy that way."

Unlike all those who would have their wives and lovers be friends (I did not hear from any woman that she desired this of her husband and her lover), Verity thinks it is "not right" for her and her lover's "queen" to be close. She insists, even in her love affair, on the boundaries of proper relationships. And it is in her love affair that she re-establishes the order between a man and a woman that she so desires: "So we are two of a kind, you see. He gives and he takes. I don't go with him because I need or want gifts or presents, but he gives them anyway."

Her lover makes her feel "like a lady." Like others in the sample, she, too, follows echoes of the Myth of Me ("I am getting on a bit—might as well do my own thing") and is rewarded for doing so. With her lover she gets "respect and love," and her self-esteem is restored. Also, it seems, her faith in the possibility of ordered relationships. Here, the one that breaches convention, when it is carried on according to clearly delineated rules, sets the world back as it should be.

Verity—through her take over of the family finances, in her silent declaration to her husband of independence demonstrated in the setting up of her own bank account and in the division of bills from now on, in the cutting down to size of the intruding young woman, and in her own secret adultery—accomplished a degree of control over her husband and in the conduct of the marriage, took control of her own life, managed her affair, and reordered the world according to the values in which she believed.

Verity is not concerned about theoretical equality. Her ideal world is strictly divided according to gender roles, and even includes some wife beating—not a desirable dream; but there is a sense in which her ideal is equitable and balanced, each obtaining rewards for giving, and she gains support from others in her community. The world is a tidier place again.

BOOK III

THE END OF
ADULTERY

The End of the Affair

You'd think with feminism and all that, they'd be different—
more realistic—but they're not. It's all moonlight and roses still,
perhaps more than ever.
—A woman talking about the aspirations of young people

Divorce and Separation

Verity, as we just saw, staying married, went through a kind of divorce. She
scarcely is left with an intimate marital relationship, and she makes her own
accommodation to the possible in a world where many doors are closed to
her. Fanny and Dick "talked and talked," made a new agreement that each
was free, had "other relationships," this time sexually consummated, and
divorced. Lenore's husband left her; Sophie left her husband. Although
Jack stayed with his wife and yearns for the magic of another affair, in fact
separation is often the outcome of an affair; divorce is very much more
likely for the adulterous, even among men and women in open arrangements, than for the faithful.[1]

While over 70 percent of the faithful remained married to their original
spouse, this was true of just over half of the adulterous; and the more liaisons a person had, the more likely it was that they would not remain married
to the first spouse.[2] If they did divorce, only about 10 percent, like Dr. Reynolds, married their lovers; one did so twice; and another, four times. Given
the number of liaisons in total, these forty-seven serious affairs represent
barely 2 percent of all liaisons. They are the ones that do not remain outside
the boundaries of the marriage as parallel, traditional, or recreational adulteries. They successfully challenge the marriage, perhaps serving as transitional affairs, helping the partner out at the same time as he or she begins

the marital story all over again. Others remarried someone else, and some (more women than men) never remarried after divorce.[3] Altogether, around 40 percent of the sample divorced or separated at some time from their first husbands or wives; and at the time of the study, one quarter were separated or divorced. About 15 percent—that is, eighty-three people—remarried at least once, fifteen of them three or more times; and a small number lived in a long-term relationship but did not legally marry.

The chances of divorce as well as remarriage also differed for women and men: whereas the number of affairs men had, or when they began them following marriage, made no difference to their chances of becoming divorced, if a woman had even one liaison, she was more likely to separate: only the "serious affair" led to a man's divorce, but if women had more than three "extramarital relationships," her chances of separating were very high indeed.

The historical entitlement of men to "play around" or to have someone "on the side," to have a mistress or sexual liaisons while traveling does not seem to have died out. Parallel or traditional but not dangerous forms of adultery, where the liaisons do not disturb the "fact" of the marriage, remain relatively acceptable for men, it appears.

What patterns are there in these various endings? What hopes and fears, what beliefs do people bring to the new marriages?

First, any changes have to be set in the context of rapidly changing beliefs about marriage and fidelity and about an entitlement to pursue the development of the self. As the stories of just a few of the 2,550 or so liaisons described by members of this sample have unfolded, these changes have become quite evident. People who began their first marriages (as they recall) already committed to the Myth of Me have stayed that way, while those who began with a strong commitment to the Myth of Romantic Marriage have somewhat abandoned those beliefs, replacing them or substantially increasing the extent to which they now believe in the Myth of Me. This swing is especially marked among women. Women are not mealy-mouthed about their feelings in this as in other areas; they do not cluster around the middle position. To be female is to be traditional—strongly committed to the Myth of Romantic Marriage both *then* and *now and* to be strongly permissive *now*. To be male is associated only with having been strongly permissive when first married. The trends for women and men are similar; and, since women have changed more than men, the net result now is that women and men differ not at all. There has been a convergence in thought and feeling between the two sexes that cannot be explained simply by suggesting women have learned to express themselves in similar ways to men since women vary, as we will see, depending on their marital careers; men do not. Yet there remain striking differences because for women the experience of adultery and divorce is different and much more serious than for men.

For example, women who have stayed married to a first spouse, but have also had at least one adulterous liaison themselves, no longer think sexual fidelity is important (a mere quarter still expecting to be faithful—see chapter 2, pages 71–74 and note 37). But, by overwhelming contrast, over 90 percent of women who have had an affair, then divorced, and married their lovers think sexual fidelity is important, and even more (96 percent) believe their husbands should be faithful to them—more even than thought this first time around. Men now stress sexual fidelity less than they did at first marriage, whatever their marital experience.

Men are perhaps afraid that the loss of freedom entailed, and also of what they understand to be truly and differently masculine, would be too great.[4] A man, at the top of his career, middle-aged, asked whether he intended to remain faithful in his recent remarriage to his adulterous partner, herself also having been married before, thoughtfully stared out of the window and then said: "Well, I don't know. I really can't be sure. I suppose so. My wife would be devastated I think if I were not because our sexual life is very important to her—to us both—but it's a long habit. Perhaps she would never know."

This man is right: his wife would be devastated. She enters her new marriage with quite different feelings, hopes, and fears from him as well as holding values that are different from those of her adulterous sisters who have stayed in a first marriage. She is like those women who have remained faithful and who continue to adhere to the Myth of Romantic Marriage and to stress sexual exclusivity. Yet both women and men stress the *quality* of their intimate relationships. Both seek good sex in a satisfying relationship that will permit an exploration of the self. This intimacy is what is desired in any marriage. When, in the conventional marriage this experience is lacking or disappointing, adultery offers the hope of re-creating or discovering it anew. In the open marriage, the belief from the outset is that intimacy is best achieved by not overplaying the primary relationship and by avoiding monogamy. It may be that in fact what is avoided in this arrangement is intimacy itself, and that it is the recognition of this by one of the pair that leads to the breakdown of the open arrangement. But those in both conventional and open marriages and those who alter their pacts generally seek "sex 'n' friendship" in both marriage and adultery. Thus, it may be that the "devastation" that this man knows his wife will suffer if he were to be unfaithful and she were to discover this, reflects his awareness that he avoids, in this way, the intimacy based on profound love that she expects from him and hurts her because of that. With the massive reduction in any stigma associated either with long-term living-together arrangements or with illegitimacy, and the capacity for some women to support themselves without depending so heavily on a male partner, there is less reason now to marry, however, than ever.[5]

At the same time, according to the woman quoted in this chapter epigraph describing young people with whom she works, and similarly noticed by several parents who worried about the "starry-eyed" attitude of their young adult children, the very freedom to engage with others outside marriage seems to be putting a heavier burden on marriage itself. If you do not need to marry in order to live with someone you love, then the actual step of marriage becomes invested with special meaning: it must be more vital, more perfect, more romantic, more satisfying sexually and emotionally, than ever.

This is the desire that is powerfully reflected in the attitudes particularly, but not only, of women who have divorced a first spouse and remarried. Far from being readier to tolerate further adultery and flexible marriage boundaries, they draw them more tightly. Especially fierce are the feelings of women who divorced their first husbands and married an adulterous partner. At the time of the first marriage, these women were three times more likely than other women to agree that it was "O.K." to have affairs outside of marriage "so long as the spouse did not find out." Now they are half as likely to think this as other women. Similarly, twice as many of the women who later married an adulterous partner had thought it was "O.K. to have an adulterous liaison if the spouse was not hurt," while now, one third of them but 43 percent of other women think this. These remarried women also believe more strongly than other women that "people ought to put up with problems in a marriage."

Men who have married an adulterous partner vary much less or not at all compared with other men, although, like the women, they have reversed their position on whether it is "O.K. to have an adulterous liaison if the spouse will not find out." But half as many *now* think they should put up with problems in a marriage as did so in a previous marriage, and this is many fewer than other men and than similar women.

Indeed, the remarried man who is uncertain about his fidelity to his new wife may just be realistic, for, even in second and later marriages, while many more had remained faithful up to the time of the study, the *pattern* that men have more affairs than women continues. Furthermore, if they do have affairs, the remarried have more than they did before (about seven liaisons each, although they have, in general, been married for less time than those married once only). Some begin this new marriage as open couples, but the difference between the genders is marked here, too. Ten men but only one woman claimed this was true of their new marriages; this represents 7.5 percent of all remarried people but one third of remarried men and less than 2 percent of remarried women! It seems men are much more likely than women not only to believe both they and their wives need not maintain the sexual exclusivity of their new relationship, but also to think their wives agree with them.

In summary, it appears that those men who have divorced at least once, and have subsequently married someone with whom they had an affair, continue less than similar women to pursue the Myth of Romantic Marriage. They stress sexual fidelity less than women, less than other remarried men, and less than all other men, whether married once only or never remarried following divorce. Despite having once been through divorce and remarriage, they do not think it worthwhile to persist with problems in a marriage. It seems marriage no longer includes a stress on fidelity or permanence. Indeed, adultery is seen as a legitimate, albeit temporary relief from a difficult marriage. Women, by contrast, seem strongly *re*committed to all the beliefs they previously held and, in some instances, more committed than they were first time around.

Why do these differences remain between women and men even when their experience—marriage, liaison(s), divorce, remarriage to an adulterous partner or someone new—is similar, and they belong to similar generations and have lived through similar social upheavals? First, it is evident that, while objectively they have lived through similar events, subjectively they have experienced these events in very different ways. And they do so for solid material reasons as well as emotional ones—more difficult to pinpoint.

Marriage itself, as I argued in chapter 2, is not one estate but two—his and hers. Still, the women in this sample had overwhelmingly taken care of the children while husbands worked; they did so even when they also worked. At home, they grew, matured, and changed, learned they were efficient and effective administrators and managers, capable of maintaining a complex organization, budgets, and the welfare of members in reasonable equilibrium but often feeling constrained and sometimes (like Frieda) humiliated. These are not Betty Friedan's 1950s housebound women suffering from the malaise they could not name (the "feminine mystique"), for most were aware of new standards and hopes for a differently organized relationship between the sexes within as well as outside families, even though such hopes were not equally strongly held or articulated by everyone (as Verity's story illustrates). Rather, the pace of social change in the workplace, in attitudes and beliefs, but especially in behavior among men as well as among women has been slower than the women's movement desired and than the contribution of women to the economy of the Western world deserves. And this slow change is reflected in the continuing weightiness of marriage for women as compared with men.

One small indicator of this remains in the fact that, despite what I have called the "masculinization of sex," of which one indicator is the readiness of the youngest women to have affairs sooner following marriage, nonetheless these women still have fewer liaisons than men and, as we have seen, experience their adultery as more serious, as trying to pursue the Myth of Romantic *Love*—even into another marriage—with more intensity than men. But nowhere does this show more clearly than in divorce.

There is now overwhelming evidence for a "feminization" of poverty of which one major cause is single parenting—largely the responsibility of women. Overwhelmingly, women care for their children after divorce, and they do so with much lower chances of remarriage and with inadequate incomes both from their own jobs and from the fathers of their children. Nor do I think women would welcome a change so that, following divorce, the fathers would more often take care of the children, for, quite apart from the emotional loss, that usually means he pays another woman to do the work—work that the mothers would prefer to do, especially if they had the resources to do it better, themselves. He can obtain tax allowances and, in England, social security benefits to help him pay for this. A woman in the same situation is not entitled to such benefits because she is expected to care for children, and an assumption remains deeply embedded that some man is caring for her. In the face of compelling evidence that this is not so, men have not worked out that someone has to pay for this, or, if they have, are not willing to be the ones who foot the bill.

Not only do divorced women care for their children with irregular (if any) support from the fathers of those children, but fathers far too often lose all contact with their children. Even among those who maintain contact and pay child support, there is a recent and disturbing pattern recurring in studies of youngsters and their fathers: legally, a father need offer no further support—material or emotional—to his child once the child becomes eighteen—the age of majority in Britain and in many states in the United States of America. According both to Judy Wallerstein and her colleague Shauna Corbin and to Leonore Weitzman, who have different theoretical perspectives and have conducted studies using different samples and different methods, fathers in California (one of the states where the majority age is eighteen) are increasingly failing to support their children through college—indeed, denying their children help with college education.[6] "You're eighteen and none of my responsibility," they seem willing to say. Perhaps they attempt to snap the tie to their first wife and all that "belongs" to her. Perhaps what they really say is, "*You* are none of mine. If I am not *pater*— the emotional-social father, nor will I be *genitor*, the one who biologically is tied to you." Even as the biological tie is employed in argument to support a father's entitlement to his child in maternal-surrogacy cases, fathers themselves appear to be shedding it at the first (legal) opportunity. In a society where it is intellectual wealth and earning power (education) that is passed on from parent to child rather than land or money, this disinheriting has concrete and serious consequences as well as profoundly distressing emotional ones for the children so disinherited. Of course, not all fathers act like this; some states (for example, Washington) require, even beyond the age of majority, support from an able parent for education; and some children do not like to ask fathers for financial help even though the fathers might be willing to give it—they feel "home" is with their mothers, and she is the appropriate resource even if she cannot afford to help them.[7]

A woman does not have to experience personally any of this, or even to believe that her husband would ever fail to look after their children in this way, to be affected by such social changes in her personal decision making, quite apart from the fact that her own material circumstances are so weakened by divorce—factors that have emerged in earlier chapters. Especially she is unable generally to earn equivalent amounts to the husband she has divorced, for she works in a system that offers women less pay for the same jobs and less well paid work in jobs demanding skill. Furthermore, she has usually still pursued a discontinuous career, taking time off when her children were small, and has often worked part-time and so lacks minimal benefits of insurance, health, and unemployment as well as entitlement to holidays and sick leave.

The difficulties of divorce first time around are magnified for the woman in a second marriage. Mainstream heterosexual "couple" society is much more difficult for the divorced woman still than for the divorced man to negotiate, her material problems extended by her increasing age in a society that values youth in women far more than it does in men (especially since she is less likely than he to have developed her education and skills to the levels of which she is capable or to which an equivalent man would have reached). Men are accepted—even particularly desired—for the elegant graying hair that women attempt to hide, and their potent self-assurance. They are very likely to remarry. There are some signs that this disadvantage is changing; articles in popular magazines are beginning to appear about older women successfully married to or in happy "living together" arrangements with younger men;[8] and Sophia Loren and Jackie Collins both celebrated their fiftieth birthdays recently with erotic images and clear messages that they remain fully sexual and desirable, even though the emphasis was not on "how lovely she is at fifty" but on "how lovely she *remains* even though she is old. Good, considering. . . ." One "other woman," as she ruminated about her role in sustaining the marriages of her lovers while her own chances of permanent happiness and children eked away with each birthday, put it succinctly: "Even the Joan Collinses and so on—they're not admired for looking their age—they're admired for looking so much younger."

Such chinks here and there do not change the fact that women still have less control over their lives than men do. The younger man is still likely to control the extent of his involvement with the free older woman (although the *married* older woman with whom the younger man has an affair has the advantage both of marital status and of her experience in controlling the relationship. French women have known this for centuries, as Laclos's novel *Les Liaisons dangereuses* makes clear.) In general, the other man is not younger than the woman, and *his* circumstances still set the agenda for them both—his job, his family, his desires.[9] The female erstwhile lovers in this sample who, as remarried women, seek *his* fidelity with great persistence express some of this anguish. They need him to be faithful and committed in a way that he does not need to be himself, nor even need his wife to be. Not that they articulate their need this way. Rather they have not given up on the romantic myth. For women, there remains some truth in the idea that love is central to their existence in a way that it is not for most men.

A woman, then, is constrained by these external forces more than a man. Indeed, women seek contentment in their relationships when what they are really discontented about is their disadvantage in other respects. Even if women are successful in making "transparent" their relationship—something Rosalind Coward has pointed out is the responsibility of women—this does nothing about the structures that still maintain their dependency and subordination. Thus Coward asks: "Can conflict and distress, which may well be caused by the structural inequalities between men and women, really be solved within the interior of that relationship?"[10]

Structural inequality reaches very far: I do not speak here only of unequal pay for the same work, or of lower pay for work of comparable worth, or the shift downward in the status of occupations once women make appreciable inroads into them, or about the closure of ranks against the promotion of women at work, or about the fact that many women are ignorant of the amount their husbands actually earn and that they have no say about how he spends "his" money, whereas he may decide not only how much she shall have but also what it is appropriate for her to buy. No, I speak here of her unequal emotional contract, too. The wife who becomes involved in an adulterous affair attempts to redress the emotional imbalance as well (often) as seeking sexual delight. She needs emotional sustenance that she gives but does not receive, or rather, receives in unequal quantity and, perhaps, quality, from her husband.

Thus women search in the wrong place to satisfy their yearning:

> Female desire is courted with the promise of future perfection, by the lure of achieving ideals—ideal legs, ideal hair, ideal homes, ideal sponge cakes, ideal relationships. . . . Female dissatisfaction is constantly recast as desire, as desire for something more, as the perfect reworking of what has already gone before—dissatisfaction displaced into desire for the ideal. . . . [T]he pleasure/desire axis appears to be everything women want but it may involve loss—loss of opportunity, loss of freedom, perhaps even loss of happiness.[11]

Particularly poignant are the efforts of those young girls and women who seek to achieve the perfect body—concentration-camp thin—that will make everything happen when all that happens is loss of health and, even, loss of life.

Second time around, especially when the new husband was the past lover, women, knowing the person they married is capable of cheating once and might do so again, attempt to guard against those painful losses, in particular against the loss of the beloved person, against the loss of newly found self-esteem and sexual joy—loss that in the old adulterous tale led to death and remains intensely toxic for women still. The terror of loss is perhaps the key to the more elusive second aspect to which I pointed earlier, in the different feelings women and men express as they enter second marriages, especially to erstwhile adulterous lovers. Men have more often had, as partners in their adulterous affairs, single, divorced, separated, or widowed women. Thus, cheating themselves, they did not so often marry someone who had herself been cheating (although, in competition with his wife, they were, perhaps, cheating another woman). When men did marry such women, they were often as concerned as women. Dr. Reynolds, for example, was terrified that his second wife, having made a cuckold of her husband as she seduced Dr. Reynolds under her husband's nose and in his house, might be unfaithful to him especially since, as she was so desirable and beautiful, any man would want her.

While loss certainly particularly confronts women, perhaps because they wish strongly to remain connected to those they have loved and especially to those they currently love, the fact that men in the same position as women feel similarly threatened suggests that what is important here is the *role*, rather than whether it is occupied by a male or a female, particularly whether the person is in the more powerful and independent position, something I earlier suggested applied to relationships at work and within any particular marriage. Steven and Beth, for example, having begun as adulterous partners, seemed equally devoted to one another, and reckoned they had "a little paradise" in their second marriage, satisfying the dream of many that their affair would end in marriage. As one woman said when her lover took her to his home while his wife was away and they made love in his matrimonial bed: "I felt quite comfortable there because I could imagine us as I wished we would one day be—married and always together."

Divorce, is, however, but one ending of the affair, certainly not the commonest; and marriage to one's lover, much more rare.

Other Resolutions

What, then, were some other endings to the affair? How many continue to reach for the Myth of Romantic Marriage, unsatisfied with the adulterous tale of love and/or sex? If, at least for women as Coward suggests, "becoming my own person is in the very grain of the sexual,"[12] does adultery serve women especially well? If the social institution of marriage is changing, adultery, as its underside—as another but hidden institution, deviant, like the Mafia, the rules of which are secret—must also change. Does the particular triangular shape of adultery limit its nature and its capacity for renewal and difference? Have the principal actors in the drama been written out, or have their roles become star parts? How is the script altering, the story changing? One way of dealing with the fact that once a person has an affair, it is "there"—as one character in the popular ABC series "thirtysomething" complained—is to turn and face the marriage, seeing it as the place of emotional work. Indeed, this couple in "thirtysomething" decided to work at it through counseling.

Working at It—Facing the Marriage

Lucy and her little group of friends decided they had "all been married very young and with unrealistic expectations." They decided—given that "two of our friends had had exactly the same thing happen, that the husband had had an affair"—"to try to sort things out":

> There was all this feeling going on amongst all of us, and the honesty part was absolutely central that it had to be conducted openly, and it was to be for the good of the marriage. . . . It was done seriously with an idea that it was for solving some problems.

They needed to face what had happened and asked: "How are we going to look at it? Can we go back to the marriage as it was? It obviously didn't work that way."

These various affairs were resolved by altering expectations about marriage, trying to be more "realistic," permitting more other relationships, and especially by being open and honest. There is a clear understanding, however, that something had happened to the marriages. There was no going back to how it was. The stress is, indeed, on "making transparent" the relationship and on discussing everything—in order to achieve a new and more mature intimacy. And the effort came from the women involved, all of whose *husbands* had strayed, although Lucy had thought, if either, it would be she who would have an affair, and this was one reason she was so shocked by her husband's first liaison.

Miriam also returned to her marriage as the place of emotional work—writing a long letter to her husband:

> I wrote that if we were going to live together to be a great age . . . possibly I was very much at fault in certain things . . . but I was very determined our marriage was going to work. Our marriage was more important to me than all these little stray [adventures].

Miriam, attempting to deal with her husband's impotence, insisted on romantic but quite unsuccessful holidays and also, as we saw, took him off to doctors. Other couples also turned to professional helpers for counseling or therapy, especially when they felt there was a real risk to their marriages; and, as in Miriam's case, this was sometimes the occasion for confession, not that it appeared to have any impact on her husband.

Despite her relative lack of success, Miriam also denied herself continuing sexual pleasure: "I decided that this [having lovers] was not my style at all and [told myself] . . . 'Pull yourself together.' . . . I didn't need it. It was a risk. I was taking a risk. I wasn't prepared to take that risk."

There is, it seems, to be no more fun. It is, as another woman said: "Hard going—marriage. Marriage is hard work. Anything worthwhile in life is hard work." Such attitudes fit with a strong commitment to the Myth of Romantic Marriage, representing here the view especially that women must be prepared to sacrifice their own interests to an ideal—marriage—that supports others, especially their husbands and children. Of course, not *all* their own interests are sacrificed; Miriam, for example, has achieved a new security with her husband, and she has him under control—he has given up his young American woman. But it is hard for her to be sure he has no other "strays" while her own delight and her own pleasure are severely curtailed.

In this kind of ending, if death was not the solution (as it was for Emma Bovary), adventure and growth seem stifled and resignation is the order of the day.[13] Some struggled to retain the benefits of their adultery—its opportunity for role reversal and advancement in a *ménage à trois*.

The Ménage à Trois

Flaubert's Emma Bovary longed for a lover who would have every brave and free masculine quality and be all that only men were permitted to be in her world; instead she, herself, takes on all those characteristics and more, dressing like a man, going at night in dangerous ways to dangerous places, initiating and active, dominating and heroic. Leon, her lover, by contrast diminishes in stature, unable even to play the adulterous game with panache. "He never disputed any of her ideas; he went along with all her tastes, he was becoming her mistress, more than she was his."[14] At the same time her weak husband, Charles, is taken over by Emma who comes to make all the decisions and effectively to run their lives. Trying to transform herself, Emma challenges the whole order of her society; she is bound always to be disappointed because her dream—essentially of becoming a man because women had no life worth living—can never be lived. She takes poison and dies. Emma's freedom, then, to choose, was strictly limited by her sex and her social position in the society of her time. She also ignored or had not appreciated that the very shape of her triangular relationship, even as it freed, also constrained her. She could play as a married woman who was afforded certain practical freedom from company and custodians of her virtue; she could turn the traditional tables and control not only her affair but also her marriage; she could become powerful in relation to these two men; but her reputation was always at stake and her marital baseline always heavy, heavy enough to cause her to choose poison and death over life.[15] Even in modern times, freedom to choose such challenging roles is heavily restricted, especially to a woman.

A woman divorced from her first, harsh husband, without a home and needing to earn her living, had answered an advertisement for a residential "mother's help." The couple seeking such help lived in an old vicarage next door to a ravishing Norman church in a tiny hamlet in the West Country. The master of the house served on the parish council. Arriving there to interview this "mother's help," I felt displaced in time; there was nothing modern about the ironic situation or about the place, set deep in a valley, with barely a twentieth-century building. It turned out that Jennifer's duties were not restricted to housekeeping and looking after the couple's two children while the man and his wife were in London each week. The schedule was arranged so that when they returned on Fridays, Jennifer spent the night in her master's bed. She "had" him that night and Saturday nights; her "mistress" had him on Sunday and for the rest of the week in town. Jennifer, it appears, was expected to help not only as mother but also as wife. Nor was she a mere pawn in this; she collaborated fully and clearly held a very different position in the household (albeit a very familiar one of past times) as a result. In a sense, she, like Emma Bovary, also turned tables—from servant to mistress. Her most distasteful task, she said, was changing her employers' sheets on Monday mornings. But Jennifer claimed to care for this man while disliking his wife who was, in her turn, jealous of Jennifer. Any difficulties, said the master, were to be sorted out between the two women; it was not his problem if they could not get along: he could be happy with either, even were "t'other fair charmer" not away. The wife eventually turned her "helper" out. Jennifer lost lover, home, a relationship with children of whom she had grown fond despite their fury about the *ménage* and their refusal to accept her authority, friends in the area, job, and income—everything except her life.

The wife had thought her husband would be happier, and that she would at least know with whom he was dallying, when and where. She could, in this way, exercise some control over her husband. She had formed a coalition to support Jennifer's struggles with the rebellious children; but, in the end, she could not tolerate her own exclusion from her husband's apparently satisfying relationship with Jennifer, which he, of course, claimed "had nothing to do with his primary tie to her and that did not threaten her in any way." For his wife, this was a mere mask for a veritable rival who was operating in terrifying proximity.

The husband (who had admitted that he could not remain monogamous) had thought he had behaved fairly, maintaining each woman roughly equidistant from himself—in this way, avoiding real intimacy with either—and, given their different roles, balanced. One—his wife—was deserving of special privilege; while the other was vulnerable and needy. Others before had managed such arrangements successfully. Why not he?

Blessed, or so it would appear, with the freedom to choose where she went and with whom she would stay, Jennifer was deeply restricted by her lack of money, by her lack of education, by her lack of skills to engage in a well-paid job in a world that is not exactly rushing to employ a middle-aged divorced woman without training or experience. The couple in the marriage had lost nothing. He had had two women—anyway for a time; his wife regained her exclusive rights and remained protected. Indeed, it was the husband who became the *tertius gaudens*—the "enjoying third," the one who gains from the quarrel of the other two in Simmel's triadic relationship of three people or three elements.[16] In this triangle, the husband was also the wanted third when the two women had conclusively rejected one another. While they remained in some kind of coalition, placing the interests of the group—both those of their own triangular group and the wider family—ahead of the individual interest each had in the husband, the latter was less powerful.[17] Giving up on their "dyad," to continue Simmel's language (or that of his translators), could not but benefit the third member whether he chose to be benefited or not. It is as I have suggested—when the lover at the apex of the triangle—in this case an "other woman"—reaches too extreme an angle to the baseline of the marriage, either the adulterous relationship must collapse or the marriage fail. The tenuous coalitions forged between husband and mistress, husband and wife, and even between wife and mistress, that kept the triangle in shape even if the angles altered, broke down as the wife made new demands that her husband felt unable to resist. Jennifer's freedom to choose, like Emma Bovary's many years before, given her unequal position, was in practice severely restricted.

For it is by forming coalitions that greater power may be exerted, but who will form those coalitions, who act as mediator, who as oppressor, who as nonpartisan, is also determined by who is the more powerful in the first instance—who, in a word, is the better politician.

The *ménage à trois* forces us to see more clearly what in fact occurs in all the triangles: the couple consists of two people each of whom feels "confronted only by the other, not by a collectivity above,"[18] but the third party introduces that collectivity—the outside world, the watcher and knower who can play each of these parts. Conflict is endemic and even necessary to the structure of the society (in Simmel as in Hegel, for the synthesis that comes from the dialectic), but this particular triangle is, as we have seen, particularly destructive.

In this story, the weight of the classic triangle exerted pressures that the hopeful, modern, married, "open" couple failed to acknowledge. It was clear at the outset to Jennifer that she held little power in the *ménage*, although she had been able to negotiate certain additional benefits and gain a comfortable home, but it was always fundamentally insecure.

Yet the *ménage à trois* can remain stable over long periods; it can work—especially when roles are more clearly demarcated and when sex and love are separated. A much younger woman (in her late twenties) had fallen out of love with her husband. As the Scot who could remember just sitting over coffee, and suddenly realizing that he no longer loved his wife, felt "empty," Jacquie no longer loved her husband. She moved into a spare bedroom, and they stopped making love. When her husband brought his girlfriend home and she moved in, Jacquie maintained she was quite happy to carry on living in the same house. Her husband, who was well off, continued to provide the basic necessities for them all, although both young women also worked and made their own contributions. Jacquie said:

I know him so well; it's really comfortable (if unconventional) living this
way. Without the sexual bit we have a really good relationship and I really
like his girlfriend—they have a much better relationship than we ever
did. It works—well, anyway for now.

Yet Jacquie does not take her own lovers home. She meets them elsewhere.
It is as if, another woman having moved into the matrimonial bed, she cannot feel her home is her own. While Jennifer's master and mistress were
experimenting together on expanding their own parameters, financially secure and with no intention of "allowing" anything to break up their marriage, like those whose sense of trust depends on sex being seen very much
as playful so that adultery is a game and played by the rules of the game,
Jacquie—independent, competent, and single, seeking a much more integrated relationship where sex and love would not be separable—had quietly
and unofficially divorced herself from her husband in preparation for what
appeared an inevitable recoupling and legal divorce.

   An unmarried lover looking clearly at her or his own particular triangle,
is faced with a similar problem. Penelope described the strain of seeing her
friends getting married and having children while she was, as she felt, at the
beck and call of her married lovers. One always had required her involvement in his married life, showing her pictures of his wife and children, needing, when out with Penelope, to make phone calls to his wife

   in the middle of Leicester Square or something having to find a phone
   and me standing around hearing him telling her everything's fine and
   hearing all her news. I hated that. He was just full of guilt all the time.
   Arthur's completely different. He doesn't involve me in his family at all,
   thank goodness, except to show me pictures of his kids sometimes. But
   I'm beginning to feel there's not enough in it for me—just propping up
   other people's marriages. I've got to think of my future and I would like
   a child of my own.

Penelope clearly is moving away. She no longer wants the coalition with her
lover against the wife; her position at the apex is no longer comfortable.
She now feels she has been "far too undemanding," pretending, for example, when her lover canceled a planned vacation, that she did not really want
to go abroad.

   There is one other sense in which the triangle must be maintained or both
relationships collapse, and that is when the relationship *depends* on its being
impossible and also secret. The obstacle is necessary to it. Beautifully expressed in Milan Kundera's *The Unbearable Lightness of Being*—seen recently
as a film (1988)—when her married lover leaves his wife for her, the perpetual mistress Sabina makes desperate passionate love to him knowing that it
will be the last time. Her passion and cries he interprets as desire for him
and as her promise to marry him now he is free. The next day she has gone,

back on her path of betrayal, flying from him out of the country and to another city, leaving him without warning or any hope of pursuit, for she "felt as though Franz had pried open the door of their privacy. . . . Now she would willy-nilly become the rival of a woman who did not interest her in the least."[9] Ferne similarly endangered her affair (and her marriage). Only by reconstituting the triangle and replacing the parts back into their separate angled boxes, could either her marriage or her affair continue. In this respect, adultery has changed not at all.

Continuity and Change

The nature of adultery, I am suggesting, has changed—if not dead, it is perhaps dying—and yet it remains unchanged. It has changed because women's roles, both as wives and in the world of paid work, have changed; because beliefs and attitudes about what marriage is or should be, about sexual freedom and restraint have all altered. This man, a writer who had had two marriages, his second wife being an adulterous partner from his first marriage, and four affairs, wrote:

> I am now sixty-seven, and have led a pretty active life. In my opinion the reason for the greater freedom and increase in the number of "affairs" or liaisons, call them what you will, has come from the ladies—and the reason, without doubt—THE PILL! For better or worse, I don't know.

This man is explaining the rate of adultery, rather than its nature; but he, too, stresses women's role in the change. In this sense, it is appropriate that we rarely now speak of "adultery," for adultery is a feminist issue where the affair, sometimes, is not. Yet the shape of adultery does *not* change, and it is this that gives it its permanence and a certain fascination. Characters in the drama, such as the "kept woman" or "mistress," have converted to "lover" as women seek to avoid being identified as sexually or materially subordinate. This is not to say the roles are so very different, however. Penelope gained material benefits from her married lovers, and a male "philanderer" was happy to admit his delight in the company of many women who "treated" him, and he them. The confidante, as we saw, is quite as important as ever she was (and she remains overwhelmingly female), and men are experiencing the comfort and pleasure of her company more. Friends, too, continue to provide accommodation and alibis, to take in letters or transfer messages. Often, these facilitators were adulterers, themselves.

The Public and the Private

There are certain other features that remain in place but changing. First, public knowledge and reputation. I have pointed out that a man's reputation has always been of great importance in the adulterous tale. This has worked in opposite directions; he both is desirous of being known as the great lover, gaining kudos and admiration especially from his peers, and appalled at being made a cuckold. He must protect his masculinity in the public eye. Hence, the legal actions of *criminal conversation* and, simultaneously, the gossip of royal courts, political corridors, the office and the pub. In recent times, the mass media have extended the corridors of gossip to the sitting rooms of everyone who possesses a television set or buys a newspaper. In this sense, the private and public spheres have been effectively merged. Hence, the fall of Gary Hart and hence the failure of Mrs. Thatcher's appeal that Cecil Parkinson's affair with Sara Keays was entirely a "private matter" and of no concern to anyone else.

I have also suggested that a woman, not being a *public persona*, has not had a reputation either to protect or display in the same way. Yet her reputation was never completely *un*important. It is mistaken to make too sharp a divide between the public and the private spheres, placing women as properly dominant in the home or private sphere and men in the everywhere else, or public, sphere. This does not hold up under scrutiny for, even when the middle- and upper-class woman has been prevented from working in paid employment outside the home, she has always been active in neighborhoods, the local community, the church, tending the sick in hospitals, and elsewhere.[20] In these spheres, her reputation did matter. It could destroy her freedom to engage with others within the local community, as Nathaniel Hawthorne's heroine, Hester Prynne, wearing her embroidered scarlet letter *A* first in shame and then with pride, so vividly demonstrates.[21] Equally, a courtesan, mistress to the rich and powerful, such as Violetta in *Traviata*, before she falls in love with Alfredo, depends somewhat on her reputation to amuse and satisfy her patrons. Access to the means to protect or enhance either reputation has been severely limited to women, however. This, now, is changing. And it is changing in line with the need to tell or keep secret from the spouse the adulterous affair itself—that is, with the general stress on deceit and honesty, on lying or speaking truth, rather than on the immorality or acceptability of actions.

In our times, few areas of our lives are not closely controlled and bounded by others rather than by ourselves. The poorer you are, the more true this becomes because the less power you can wield. All of us have the frustrating experience of trying to deal with some bureaucratic organization—an insurance company, a mortgage institution, a law firm, or a business, perhaps a bank (indeed, in England, the Midland calls itself the "listening bank" to impress on us how *un*like the bureaucracies we all detest and know they are). Or, on a less grand but still difficult scale, a school, a college, a social service department. A shop or large store. Men, when they get promoted become, according to a recent survey, sexually active. Their potency is literally ignited. It lasts little time before the tightness of their empire grips them, and the fact that this seemingly greater field of power is not so grand hits home. But *at* home, in the "privacy" of the marriage and the family, people feel they are in control. They can, indeed, close the door, draw the curtains, fight or make love, eat or watch television, play with a child or hit one for quite some time before the outside world may intrude, and determine whether the hitting was within "normal" limits or not.

This is so whichever opposing view is taken of the role of the state in family matters. One view sees the family as a bulwark against the state; the other, as requiring much more intervention in its affairs, especially as women and children are less powerful within the family than men and their powerlessness has surfaced in recent times in the tragedies of incest (nearly always perpetrated by adult males against girl children), wife battering, and child abuse—domestic violence erupting behind the closed doors of this haven in a heartless world—the very place meant to be safe for all its members.[22] It remains, nonetheless, this tight circle of family—often smaller now than ever before—that offers the best possibility of control. In particular, it seems that the value of our relationships within the family consists not only in having them for themselves but also, as I argued in chapter 8, in sharing knowledge about them which we hide from and reveal as and when we choose (or so we feel) to others. If we lose control over revelation or secrecy, we struggle to recapture it, to re-establish our reputations and re-draw the boundaries. We try to protect family and personal secrets.

Some groups even exist as a secret in themselves—secret societies, much beloved of children but in adult life often ominous. Ominous because of their very inaccessibility and the tightness of the boundaries they set against intruders, permitting perhaps dangerous or unlawful activities. Similarly, and also on occasion ominously, the family's secrets provide the boundary around what may be a physically and psychologically fluid relationship. Indeed, sharing the information kept within those boundaries marks status and delineates hierarchies, determining even who is to count as family. "We won't tell Aunt Bee about that—she doesn't need to know—but let's discuss it with Jane when she comes" may protect Aunt Bee from something she would rather not know—after all, "what the eye doesn't see, the heart can't grieve over"; but it also sets her outside the magic circle of "knowing ones" in which Jane, who may not be a blood relation, is to be included, granting her status within the family and leaving Aunt Bee relatively powerless. It is the mark of the intimate relationship that the family secrets are shared; thus, the difficulty of including a newly chosen adult partner of a family member lies partly in trusting her or him with the family secrets. What will happen (are they to be trusted?) when they know that Uncle Tom was an alcoholic, or that Susie is not really Jack's daughter but Jim's, and that Bill is gay?

Yet much is already public knowledge about the marriage and the family: when it occurred, where, how many children have been born and when, whether there have been any previous marriages, and what the reconstituted families consist of. A good deal about the quality of life is judged by where they live and in what kind of dwelling, the car(s) possessed, the holidays taken, and perhaps whether one or both of the couple has or has had a lover. Each person has a public reputation, too, both separately and in the marriage itself. "They seem very good together"; "They're always fighting"; "He drinks, you know. Poor woman"; "She'll help. Ask her, she's always game"; "He's a great lawyer. Gives good advice. Strange he's married to that flighty woman." Knowing or being told, and telling or permitting discovery, about a liaison affects the person's sense of herself or himself not only vis-à-vis the spouse and the lover but also vis-à-vis the world beyond the family. Those included in the secret often want to share their success and pleasure—to gain affection, status and support. Those not included feel fools in the face of worldly knowingness. The boundaries invaded are the sense of the personal and the private. Hence, as we saw, the sensitivity both of Penelope to her lover's telltale behavior and of the wronged spouse to the secrets that the lover now knows about the family. "Is nothing sacred?"

When such matters become public, revealed not by the participants but by journalists, control is lost; both family and person are invaded and feel profaned. Two women, one British and one American, one a mistress, and one a betrayed spouse, have recently felt both capable of telling, and that it was necessary to tell their stories publicly, in this way re-establishing a certain control over their reputations and over the events. In this attempt to put the record straight, individuals behave just as the American administration under both Nixon and Reagan did—compelled to analyze and publish the truth of its scandals.

Sara Keays says that what she was most concerned to do was to defend her reputation by telling her story—the story not only of her twelve-year affair with Cecil Parkinson, who lost his cabinet position only later to regain it, but also of the way she was hounded and mistreated by the powerful institutions of the media and of the Conservative party itself.[23] She had been drawn as promiscuous, as a woman who had "trapped" Parkinson into making her pregnant, as mercenary, vengeful—*merely* a woman scorned. At the center of the story is a woman, single and never married whose lover is a married man of considerable authority and public position. At the center, in other words, a pair in traditional and unequal relationship.[24] Nora Ephron, the writer, also felt she needed to recount, as a novel, the story of her husband's affair with the wife of the British ambassador to Washington, later made into the film, *Heartburn*.[25] Ephron's family was split by divorce; but in the telling, she redrew the boundaries still more sharply. Of course, other, less honorable motives may also play a part—a desire to shame the lover and the husband, respectively; and they may, as I suggested earlier, *need* to speak, to tell their story in order to avoid going mad. Clearly, the need to speak and the contrary need to remain silent and keep the secret (but, in so doing, perhaps to tell lies) are opposing forces of some consequence. Both can best be understood as ways to recast or maintain reputations and to challenge or alter the balance of power between individuals even when the actual structural arrangements of the marriage and the adulterous relationship have been destroyed or are being altered.

I think it important that these two women have told their stories, but I do not want to exaggerate the ease with which recasting boundaries and reestablishing reputations can be done, especially by women. Keays felt unable to entrust her manuscript to any publisher but published it herself, and Ephron told her story in fictional form. By contrast, Parkinson is back in government and Gary Hart (albeit not for long) re-entered the public race for the presidential candidacy. For these men, a boundary is rebuilt between their public and private lives that is still less clear-cut for women. They seem identified more with governments that are paranoid about secrets and about whether there has been a lie or deceit rather than whether, for example, arms have been sold to Iran for hostages and the profits transferred to supporting arms for the *contras*. Thus it becomes appropriate, whatever the morality or immorality of their actions, for them to defend their right to privacy and secrets. Americans may be able to force their nominated justices to the Supreme Court to speak about their pot smoking[26] and to investigate wrongdoing by their governments and presidents; while the British have no such access to secrets and their government engages in disgraceful and ludicrous power plays against clerical officers like Sara Tisdall, who leaked a memo about cruise missiles being moved from one place to another (not even particularly secret), and against ex-spies, such as Peter Wright, the former assistant director of M15, attempting to right personal and public injustices by speaking them out loud;[27] yet both societies guard their secrets with passion. They say it is necessary for their *security*, just as the family, too, feels secure by guarding its secrets. The struggle weaves a net around knowledge, relying no longer on the physical coercion of men or the seduction and cunning of women.

Shoshana Zuboff has given us a clue to why these games of state have assumed such importance and why, too, they are being played out in the intimate relationship. *In the Age of the Smart Machine*—the title of Zuboff's book—our modern age, when the computer has begun to manufacture objects, file information, draw plans, and graph ideas, when the work that people used to do and to know how to do through their bodies—hands on—is now increasingly done by watching a screen and touching only the keys that will (it is hoped but not known—not for sure) make something or inform somebody of something, the skill lies less in *doing* but in *knowing*. The computer, says Zuboff, automates but does more—it informs or, as she says, *informates*.[28] Just as the body has been moved, as it were, to one side and knowledge/information has taken center stage in the intimate relationship, so the body has been moved off center in work and knowledge/information has become the central component of the new technological society. Learning from all the new information has the capacity for positive change in the workplace, but it is also used to reinforce the structures of domination, to maintain the divisions of manager and managed, and to keep authority authoritarian.

States seek to retain control over their populations at the present time less by controlling their bodies and more, much more, by controlling access to information. Even as greater and greater amounts of information are daily published and accessible (if one knew what there was and where to look), so tighter controls are placed on who is to know what, when, and where. The capacity to keep secrets, to create them and to destroy them, to reveal them as and when necessary, maintains order but may, as well as covering the path of destruction, also lead to death. The playwright and author John Mortimer built the Tisdall scandal into an episode of his famous *Rumpole of the Bailey* series on English television, shown on public television in the United States.[29] In this, the man who was leaking *real* secrets while framing the Tisdall character, kills himself, and Rumpole says, as part of his tirade against the paranoia of the British government, "Secrets lead to death. They lead to death." This is the aspect of the modern affair that remains so toxic: the secret, or its revelation, can be deadly. Because it remains illicit, and still, as Chris said, "must hide its face," adultery is particularly relevant to these games of states. Adultery, in a word, is the private, couple-centered place for the playing out of paranoia about secrets from which whole states currently suffer.

One area of knowledge/information in particular has enabled sex to be enthroned again as a metaphor (if it was in truth ever dethroned, as John Gagnon and William Simon, the authors of gender scripts writing in 1973, believed), and that is AIDS. "The sexual act," these authors write, "used to be linked to experiences larger than the self. . . . Sex as power, as transgression, as reinforcing the natural masculine and feminine roles, as the apocalypse," was replaced, following the sexual revolution, by sex as play when it became unimportant, or no more important than a game, losing these symbolic meanings.[30] The participants in this study and the outpouring of literature, film, and plays argue rather that illicit sex, even as it became less illicit, lost little of these and other, older, symbolic meanings: legitimacy and transgression, pleasure and danger, commitment and autonomy, conservation and excess, health and illness. Indeed, adultery, even as it suffered something of a demise and was translated into the affair or the extramarital relationship, never lost its metaphorical place. AIDS (despite the remote chances of many heterosexual people getting it[31]) restores to all sex the metaphors, especially of health and illness and legitimacy and transgression and excess. And this secret hidden in the body leads to death.

We have not been told how many are surviving. Yet, as with other "plagues" sent to punish evildoers—except where the social group has organized to act in concert and to help one another, as, for example, gay men in San Francisco have done—resistance to change is high. Among heterosexual people, there is little sign of change in sexual behavior, especially among the married.[32]

If this is so, there will be no less adultery in the near future. But it will also not decrease because people will not stay married long enough.

A New Story?

A woman wants the self-same sovereignty
Over her husband as her lover,
And master him; he must not be above her.
— Chaucer, "The Wife of Bath's Tale," *Canterbury Tales*

And what of the future of adultery? Will there, as I have suggested in chapter 10, be no more adultery than at present even though the trends that go to make up the masculinization of sex might suggest an increase? And what of the story? Now and in the future? Can we now see Isolde's tale more clearly; and does she, as women and men become more alike, even as they continue to differ, seek to conquer as Tristan did?

There will, I say, be less rather than more adultery not only because the AIDS crisis may give people pause for thought, but also because, unless divorce becomes less accessible or less sought following adultery, people will not stay married long enough to see it increase. There is, after all, increased stress on fidelity in marriage among the newly wed and those who remarry— especially among women; there continues to be a high value placed on marriage as the long-term committed relationship; and although the youngest women have overtaken men in the speed with which they have affairs, this age group were also no less faithful over all than the older sample members. If spouses were unfaithful, they generally separated, because, like Harry and Maisie, they heavily stress *feeling*—the quality of the relationship. If either felt a desire to spend more time with someone else, then, sadly, their marriage would end. If this were acted upon on every occasion, there would, of course, be much less adultery; people would, instead, constantly split and recouple— even more serial monogamy than we already have.

Yet, there are many cultural and structural changes that make adultery more likely, including expectations that things can be different and always better than they were before. Women, as we have seen, have begun to feel entitled to their own bodies; they have been freed to some extent to play with sex, to *be* as men have always been, free to explore their own sexuality and pursue their desires, if not during marriage certainly prior to it. This freedom has delighted men (even though they have sometimes found the ground rules so changed that their fears of women have surfaced, and some have shrunk from women altogether). But the cultural and structural changes in women's position as wives and mothers and at work have not permitted such liberation as there has been to go unpunished.

Indeed, writing about *Fatal Attraction*, a film released at the end of 1987, Marsha Kinder, professor of film at the University of Southern California, says it is not sexual repression but sexual liberation that causes the psychosis in the film—the career-other-woman becoming a vampire who threatens to destroy the entire family, man, wife, and child, symbol of the normative if not the normal, eventually turning the nice, companionable husband and wife into murderers.[1] The women have both negative and positive power in this film; the vampire woman-man, "Alex," has power over nice married Dan (who, unlike his Biblical namesake, is helpless in this den of lionesses); while Beth, whose very name conjures the good "Little Woman," can defeat Alex when Dan cannot. Maternal, nurturant love can defeat erotic, sensuous love.

The liberated—whether female, black, or homosexual—threaten the status quo because they have become empowered. In practice, they often still have little power relative to the male, white, or heterosexual community, but even the *idea* that there could be movement in the power structures is threatening. And power, as this film so clearly demonstrates, can be employed to destroy as well as to create, to constrain as well as to enable. In both marriage and adultery, the problem of power is by no means resolved. I have argued that women generally have less power than men. Yet women do exercise power, especially in familial and intimate relationships. The strong mother of matriarchal families—particularly Jewish, black, or working class—is not a figment of the adoring son's imagination, nor merely a remnant of a time when he, like his sister, experienced his mother as omnipotent. But it remains true that men still hold the reins in most instances. Thus, adultery is still the place where women can turn the tables or re-create a relationship of dependency that also paradoxically permits autonomy. Men, in their encounters, also feel powerful even as they are able to show their vulnerability and dependency. They can become "Baby" even as, literally or metaphorically, they pay for the privilege. Furthermore, they can do this in an environment that is, as Donald said,

> the opposite of security and feeling safe. I am sure sexual adventures are a return to excitement. We work so hard at creating incredibly dull lives, you know. Unemployment may be stopping it now, but the period, say, 1945 to 1975 must have been in Western society the most stable period in history—very few diseases, stability of employment, of food, shelter, the

welfare state, and so on. . . . The converse of that is the rise of the betting shop. People don't bet to win money, they bet for excitement. They actually want this little nervousness.

Thus marriage is the safe place, adultery the dangerous one, still. Adultery is the place where reversals of all kinds *may* occur.

Adultery, because it is secret, permits people endless variation. In adultery, each partner can make the lover represent anyone or anything—mother, father, sibling, superordinates or subordinates, angel or devil—with very little risk because, unlike marriage, adultery does not, at the outset, include permanence. Truth need never be revealed; the inadequacies or the reality of the self need never be demonstrated to the other. So long as the adultery is brief, the fantasy can endure. In this sense, adultery is far from dangerous; it is safe. Partners can switch gender roles, play with sex and fantasy, satisfy particular desires, *be* all the things for which marriage has no room. Mrs. Long said about herself and her lover, both of whom were justices of the peace: "Here we are, these two pillars of society, having so much fun and breaking all the rules." At her most feminine and sexual, she is also most brave and "masculine," because she is so active and positive, planning escapades and meetings with great skill, the strategies complex and dangerous.

Thus, both genders can escape into the other's world. Men's adultery may be a potent declaration of independence and conquest, but their desire is also for connection, bonding, and intimacy. Emma Bovary, as we saw, sought to reverse her gender role but also remained loving: she sought not conquest, power, or freedom alone. Similarly, the adulterous relationship at work personalizes the work setting, bringing erotic and home life into the bureaucracy; while having a passionate affair with a neighbor risks public scandal—politicizing the marriage, bringing the outside world home. Despite the question "Who else do you fall in love with if you work eighteen hours a day?" posed by someone in the film *Broadcast News*, office affairs are not mere opportunity.

I have also emphasized differences between women and men in this study, although it is quite clear that there is considerable overlap. At the extremes, women *are* more nurturant and caring, men more self-interested and matter-of-fact in their personal relationships; but this does not mean that each does not have qualities of the other or that many are not quite similar. In *Fatal Attraction*, the women are presented as opposites, one possessing the "masculine" qualities of drive, ambition, and cool-headedness (even though she is, of course, also extremely sexual); the other, "feminine." This oppositional perspective also occurs when there is a public scandal. Thus Mrs. Hart is seen only as strong, intelligent, nurturant, and caring, while Donna Rice is sensual, flighty, with a body rather than a brain. As if the two can never be combined in one woman. There does, indeed, remain a tension between erotic and passionate love and nurturant, committed love, between autonomy and dependence, vulnerability and strength, connection and individuation. Men are not permitted the freedom they need to be vulnerable and dependent, women to be strong and free. In other words, the gender scripts, especially within marriage, constrain both women and men. Indeed, so deep in our unconscious minds does the image of the proper male and female reach still that, in *Broadcast News*, the gentle, funny, caring, intelligent but somewhat shy and clumsy man becomes the "wimp" with whom the pretty, clever, competent, and hard-working career girl cannot fall in love, while the attractive, somewhat stupid but charismatic young man will not tolerate her, an "iron lady"; one is unsuitable as a lover, the other unsuitable as a wife, however delightful their company. Yet the fact is that the "feminine" qualities of nurturance, caring, and kindness are the qualities of *both* wife and husband most likely to make for the happiest marriages. Indeed, it seems "happiness is a feminine marriage partner"![2] Thus, the "new man" heralded in a recent survey—an "80s man [who] is family and fidelity oriented and no longer afraid to discuss his feelings" (or *tell* them?); a "sensitive, balanced man" who thinks fathers "as vital as mothers" in the tasks of child rearing, even though about one quarter confessed to anxiety about their sexual prowess—perhaps *is* this "feminine" marriage (or committed) partner.[3] The women in this study had not, by and large, alas, discovered him.

The idea that marriage is the place where all strong and good erotic and loving feelings should be expressed helps explain why public opinion polls continue to show sharp disapproval of adultery. If you want to be free sexually, then do not marry, and leave other people's marriages alone.

How, then, has the ancient adulterous tale changed? If, as seems clear, men still desire the unobtainable, the secret, the challenge to another man, even as they also, like women, hope for long-term intimate relationships, it is much less clear—as, indeed, it always has been—what it is that women most desire—the question to which Freud sought an answer, one posed long before by Chaucer in his story of the Wife of Bath. The answer (if, indeed, there is only one) would enable a modern story—the myth not of Tristan and Isolde but of Isolde and Tristan. Let me briefly remind you of the Wife of Bath's tale.

The Wife of Bath

She begins her entertainment for her fellow pilgrims *en route* for Canterbury with a rather long prologue in which she tells them about her five marriages, three to rich old men and two to beautiful young men. She ruled the roost and gained the wealth of her old husbands; had some trouble with the fourth who had a "paramour" so that to get the better of him she "fried him in his own grease," by "seeming rather gay" to other men; and loved the fifth to distraction. He, however, treated her badly, once—when she tore the pages of his book about "wicked wives"—hitting her so hard that it made her deaf in one ear. She gave as good as she got, however, and—after a "mort of trouble and heavy weather"—succeeded in making him gentle. She *mastered* him: "He gave the bridle over to my hand," she says.[4] Then she tells her tale.

A knight, by very force, has taken a young woman's maidenhead: he raped her. The king—Arthur—condemns him to die, but Queen Guinevere begs her husband to be allowed to determine the knight's fate, for this is a matter of love and should be decided by women as in the courts of love in France. Guinevere tells the knight he has a year and a day to answer the question "What is the one thing women most desire?" The knight travels the world and cannot answer the question, but as he nears the court again at the end of his time, he meets an old hag in the forest who tells him the answer. On the morrow he goes to the court and says:

> A woman wants the self-same sovereignty
> Over her husband as her lover,
> And master him; he must not be above her.[5]

Yes, says the court, and sets him free. Now the hag has her turn and demands that, in return for his life, the knight should marry her. It is also her turn to ask him a question or offer him a choice. She tells him to choose between having her as she is, old and ugly but faithful since such traits are "good wardens of chastity," or young and fair but, like as not, unfaithful. Offered the power of choice, the knight hands it back to the hag, insisting that she is best placed to choose wisely for both of them: you make the choice yourself; whatever pleases you suffices me. Have I won the mastery? she asks. Do I then have mastery? And because, of course, she does, the knight wins all: she metamorphoses into a beautiful, young, desiring, and sensuous woman; yet she will be faithful, too.

Women then, want mastery over husbands—something they already have, it appears, over their lovers; and, indeed, although Isolde followed Tristan where he took her, her beauty and his desire of her gave her a certain sovereignty, too. Yet, in this tale, whenever women held power, they handed it back or offered something even better in return. The moral seems (at least according to the man who created the woman who told the tale) to be that men who grant women "mastery" (in marriage as in love) will obtain their deepest desires for beauty and fidelity, and there is no questioning of the man's privileged position to *grant* a woman power.

In the stories of all those home-grown executives and women simultaneously seeking dominant men yet wanting independence and autonomy, I think this paradox is still being played out. Played out because such men are desirable still. In a world where one message calls for equality even as women remain the "other," and another message makes plain that powerful men hold the aces; where the symbolic father is, as Lacan would have it, culture and language itself; and flesh-and-blood fathers, whether present in our lives or absent, hold imaginative sway, it is difficult, but perhaps not impossible, to imagine desire differently constructed for women. This is particularly so in a world where romantic love between husband and wife is a primary axis of human relationships—love playing a part at least as powerful, although infinitely more widespread in the society, as it did in the brilliance of the days of courtly love in medieval Europe.[6] A modern Isolde, in these circumstances, loving men of power and influence and perhaps seeking a father figure far from home, would, I think, still marry King Marc of Cornwall, but I suspect she would manage her affair better than her mythical prototype.

Isolde would desire Tristan still. He is young, talented, beautiful, and in love with her. He is extraordinarily gifted—the kind of man who, if he were a chimpanzee, ethologists would call an "Alpha" male, the one who gets the best and most females. Yet, evidently, the Alpha male chimpanzee gets the female, not because he chooses her but because she chooses him. Like chimps, one of the powers women have is seduction. If a woman does not give a man the "right" signals, he will choose someone less attractive to him to court who does.[7] The difficulty, of course, may be that the signals are wrongly read.

It is not only men who read signals wrongly, and the occasions when they must try to read women's signals correctly are rather more limited for them than for women because they enter women's worlds less often and control more spheres where they have invented the games. Thus, as I pointed out in my prologue, as women enter increasingly into men's worlds, they have to try harder to learn the games and to send and read the signals correctly. Even when the game does not please women and is not their choice. Referring to work carried out in a Mayan village, Nina Eliasoph suggests that deference in women's speech cannot be explained, however, merely because they are relatively powerless. In the village, women use, for example, the questioning ending, "isn't it? am I right? wouldn't you?"—strategies of politeness—not only to men but in many situations when they are among equals. She suggests rather that they are playing different games and that, even when there is a power imbalance, power will mean different things to women and men. She writes: "I am suggesting that women came to the playground with different ideas of what games to play, so that they adjusted the rules not only because power forced them to but because the male game did not please them."[8]

These basically different choices in the games to play and how to play them relate to the psychic differences that are formed through the infant's fundamentally different tasks in separation and identification with the same- and opposite-sex parent. Because the boy must learn he is different from mother and identify with father, he will, as a man, be generally more likely to act as if independent of constraint or "field free," as the language theorists put it. Women, identifying with the same-sex person who also nurtured them, are generally more comfortable enmeshed within the particular context. An increase in parenting by men, as Dorothy Dinnerstein suggests,[9] should (but may not) lead to less distinction, but it could not obliterate difference: first, because some difference is inevitable since, after all, we *are* both bodily and thinking creatures and our biology underpins, though it does not determine, our development; and second, because early experience in the formation of psychic and behavioral difference is but one ingredient in the molding of a culture that encourages and demands difference. Some difference is, I believe, with the French and Betty Friedan, also desirable.[10] Alas, our culture does not merely demand difference—each as valued as the other—but demarcates the superior and inferior, the superordinate and subordinate, the prior and secondary. Usually, the male holds the former, the female, the latter position in the social structure.

Given such powerful basic elements in the psychology and structure of society, it is not surprising that women still yearn for the "dominant" male to whom they will return any power "granted" them even as they also seek passionately for autonomy and control over their own lives, and men still seek to remain separate and powerful even as they desire total dependence and the expression of vulnerability.[11]

Isolde and Tristan

Playing on the same stage but with the new scenery of modern times, the modern Isolde is busy learning more about herbs—not content with what she learned watching at her mother's knee. She has started an Institute for Herbal Skills. The Queen of Ireland is patron, for Isolde does not sever her relationship with her mother when she marries but retains her connection with her. Even though she is faraway, she writes or telephones. She has wondered many times whether to tell Marc about Tristan, for he suspects, just as he always has, that she and Tristan are lovers, but she does not want to hurt him. She begs Tristan—who, although he is married and has children (for in the modern version, he does consummate his marriage), urges her to leave Marc and come away with him—to be patient because Marc is really quite old now. She provides the court with health-giving treatments and marvelous scents. Marc benefits, too, and shows much of his youthful spark—a side Isolde has not seen before. She runs her institute well, gathering a group of colleagues—mainly women—who have become good friends, and sending all over the world for the latest discoveries. Experts call on her for advice; seminars are held. Isolde has her own dominion. Sometimes she travels herself and, on those occasions, invites Tristan to join her. At those times, both she and Tristan feel alive and even understand why they are alive.

Tristan's wife always knows he is with Isolde because he made it a condition of marriage to continue his affair. His wife is also "free," but since the early days, when she had several lovers who pleased her less than Tristan, has not desired anyone else and, besides, what with her job and small children, she has not had the time. She is looking forward to returning to college, however—something she plans for the next year or two.

One day Tristan decides he cannot continue to deceive Marc and, without consulting Isolde, tells him about the affair. Marc, forced to face his deep fear, is shattered by the deceit and betrayal of both Isolde and Tristan. He considers suicide. He tells Isolde she is free to go or stay as she pleases, but he cannot love her as once he did. Tristan will no longer inherit his kingdom. Isolde is appalled by Marc's distress and, as she experiences it, Tristan's betrayal of her—of their relationship. For many days, she remains cloistered in her room thinking, emerging to tell Marc she has decided to stay with him. Then she meets Tristan and tells him he must leave—go far away, not write or telephone. Tristan reluctantly agrees, but not before giving Isolde an emerald ring, telling her if she sends the ring, he will understand she is free and wishes to marry him. He does not care where he is, he will come to her then.

In only two years Marc dies, some say of a broken heart.

Isolde, some days later, takes Tristan's beautiful ring and walks to the cliff's edge at Tintagel. For many hours she sits, watching the sea pounding the rocks below, the ring cupped in her hands. She has never seen his children or met Isolde of the White Hands. Longing for him, why can she not conjure his face and his presence but only see his shadow surrounded by these three faces—ones she does not even recognize? At last his beloved face swims into view, but it is older than . . . Isolde catches her breath . . . Is it Tristan or Marc she has in her mind's eye? As gently as it came, the image disappears, leaving Isolde engulfed in a deep sadness that has repeatedly swept over her these past few days; and empty.

Tristan, of course, has already heard of Marc's death; he does not need the ring to know she is free, only to know she wants him. Perhaps he has divorced his wife already? No, she knows that is not so. (It never occurs to her that Isolde of the White Hands might divorce Tristan, though she had heard rumors—something about a tutor and a fellow student at her college.)

Isolde shivers. It is getting late, and she has not even glanced at today's mail. She wonders if that rare plant from the Himalayas has arrived—the one that she has heard has to be administered in just the right dosage, for its powers to enchant or poison are strong. She will have to do a great deal of research on that. It will take all her energy, skill, and concentration. Rising, she slips Tristan's ring on her finger—the fourth of her left hand, just to keep it from falling into the sea or dropping off as she runs back to the palace.

Or perhaps the modern myth ends otherwise.

Allowing an appropriate period for mourning, Isolde sends Tristan the ring. Tristan and his wife are divorced, and the new marriage begins.

Who knows how it ends?

APPENDIX A

The Questionnaire

Introduction

In answering this questionnaire please comment freely in the places provided AND, if you wish, on additional sheets of paper on any aspects of the questions. You will find the questionnaire concentrates on FIRST AND LAST marriages and on first and most recent "adulterous liaisons." This may mean that something important is not being asked about. You may also dislike the words chosen and so on. If this is so:

DO PLEASE SAY SO AND EXPLAIN THE DIFFICULTIES, if necessary on the blank sheet at the end of the questionnaire.

Precisely because much is changing in sexual morals and manners, it has been extremely difficult to choose appropriate words for the questionnaire. Here is your:

Glossary

1. *Marriage*
   i. If you are still married to your first spouse the word "marriage" covers the period from your legal marriage ceremony (wedding) until the present. Otherwise it covers the period from your wedding until either the death of your spouse or until a divorce is finalised (decree nisi). But see
   ii. If you have been DIVORCED, you may have been living apart (whether legally separated or not) before the divorce. If it seems appropriate to YOU, please consider the marriage as having ended when you began living apart. If you decide to do this please circle the appropriate number at Q.11(g).
   iii. Sometimes, married couples SEPARATE but never get divorced. If it seems appropriate to YOU, please consider the marriage as having ended when you began living apart. If you decide to do so please, again, circle the appropriate number at Q.11(g).
   iv. If you have been married more than once, the same rules apply to the length of marriage. Usually our questions apply to your first and (if you have been married more than once) your current or most recent marriage.

2. *Spouse*
   Spouse means your wife or husband in a marriage.

3. *"Living Together in a Long-Term Relationship"*
   You are given the opportunity in this questionnaire to "treat" the period before a marriage as the beginning of that marriage (Q.14d). However,

APPENDIX A

those who have NEVER been through a legal marriage ceremony, although they may live or have been living with a partner in a stable relationship, are asked to return this questionnaire after Q.18(b). Please do let me know about these relationships and any "adulterous liaisons" you consider occurred at the end or on another sheet of paper.

4. *Long-Term Relationships Whether or Not You Lived Together*
Other long-term relationships including those which began as "adulterous liaisons" may not be the subject of questions in this questionnaire. This may be because they were neither "first nor last adulterous liaisons." Please let me know about them at the end or on an additional sheet of paper and about any other long-term relationship you have had.

5. *"Adulterous Liaisons"*
   i. This term because it is NOT common has been chosen to cover any sexual relationship with anyone other than your spouse during a marriage. It can be the single most important and long-lasting affair/relationship outside your marriage or it might be a brief encounter with someone you met at a party. And, of course, there are many other kinds of "adulterous liaisons."

   ii. Please consider only YOUR OWN marital status when deciding if a relationship is "adulterous." For the purpose of this questionnaire, it is immaterial whether your sexual partner in the "liaison" was married or not. What matters is whether you were. (But see numbers 1 and 3 above.)

6. *Partner*
Partner means your sexual partner in an "adulterous liaison."

Confidential

No: _____

1.   FULL NAME: (You may leave this out if you wish)

_____

2.   SEX:
(Circle the number for your answer)   MALE   0
                                        FEMALE   1

3.   YOUR DATE OF BIRTH: _____

4(a)   Place you live in now   (your home):
        TOWN/VILLAGE (Name): _____ COUNTY (Name): _____
4(b)   Place you lived in for the longest period as a child:
        TOWN/VILLAGE (Name): _____ COUNTY (Name): _____

5(a)   Please circle one number in each column to indicate the religion (if any), or other belief system: (i)   you were brought up in
                                   and   (ii)   you believe in now.

	(i) Religion etc. you were brought up in (if any)	(ii) Religion etc. you now believe in (if any)
CHURCH OF ENGLAND	0	0
ROMAN CATHOLIC	1	1
CHRISTIAN/NON-CONFORMIST (e.g. BAPTIST, EVANGELICAL) ..	2	2
JEWISH	3	3
┌ OTHER	4	4
└► Please write in: _____		
NONE	5	5

6.   How important a part (if any) does religion or other belief system play in your life?
(Circle one number)   NO PART AT ALL   0
                              AN UNIMPORTANT PART   1
                              A FAIRLY UNIMPORTANT PART   2
                              A FAIRLY IMPORTANT PART   3
                              AN IMPORTANT PART   4

The next questions are about your education, qualifications and work. . . .

7(a) Your education: Please circle the number representing the highest level achieved.

NONE	CSE'S	O'LEVELS/ SCHOOL CERT (or equiv.)	A'LEVELS/ HIGHER SCHOOL CERT (or equiv.)	FIRST DEGREE	HIGHER DEGREE
0	1	2	3	4	5

7(b) If you have gained any of the following qualifications, please specify what they are:
COMMERCIAL (e.g. TYPING, SHORTHAND) ⎯⎯⎯⎯⎯⎯⎯⎯⎯
CITY AND GUILDS CERTIFICATE(S) ⎯⎯⎯⎯⎯⎯⎯⎯⎯⎯⎯
O.N.D., O.N.C., H.N.D., H.N.C.* ⎯⎯⎯⎯⎯⎯⎯⎯⎯⎯⎯⎯
PROFESSIONAL (e.g. M.D., TEACHERS CERT., B.ed. ⎯⎯⎯⎯⎯

OTHER VOCATIONAL (e.g. APPRENTICESHIPS) ⎯⎯⎯⎯⎯⎯⎯
OTHER . . . please specify: ⎯⎯⎯⎯⎯⎯⎯⎯⎯⎯⎯⎯⎯⎯

8(a) Are you in paid employment at present?
(Please circle one number)

No	Retired	Employee Full-time	Employee Part-time	Self-employed
0	1	2	3	4

8(b) What is the name or title of your main, current (or most recent) job or occupation? (e.g. marketing manager, self-employed builder, lecturer at a technical college, medical secretary, housewife):

8(c) Please briefly describe your main tasks at work, even if you think they are obvious from your job title: (Retired persons—please give information for main previous occupation.)

* Various technical-professional British diplomas and certificates—Ordinary National and Higher National.

9.   Your present Marital Status:
       (Please circle one number only)
                        SINGLE, NEVER HAVING BEEN MARRIED 0
                        MARRIED AND LIVING WITH SPOUSE 1
                        DIVORCED 2
                        LEGALLY SEPARATED 3
                        SEPARATED 4
                        WIDOWED 5
       OTHER . . . please explain: _____ 6

Now some questions about children. . . .

10(a)   Have you had any children?
                        ┌─ NO 0
                        └─► Skip to Q.11.
        ┌───────────────── YES 1
10(b)   (If yes) In the table below, for each of your children write in his/her first
        name and date of birth. Please also indicate the child's sex and whether he/
        she is living with you by circling the appropriate numbers.

	NAME# (omit if preferred)	SEX male female	DATE OF BIRTH	LIVING WITH YOU? ONLY IN SCHOOL			
				YES	NO	HOLIDAYS	OTHER*
First-born	_____	0 1	_____	0	1	2	3
Second-born	_____	0 1	_____	0	1	2	3
Third-born	_____	0 1	_____	0	1	2	3
Fourth-born	_____	0 1	_____	0	1	2	3

* Please specify: _____

\# If any have died, please note this and the date of death against the child's name.

10(c)   If you have more than four children, or have not listed any adopted, foster
        or stepchildren in 10b above, please give the same details about them:

11.   IF YOU ARE SINGLE, NEVER MARRIED → Skip to Q.15.
     ┌——— IF EVER MARRIED
11(a)   How many times have you been married?
           (Please circle one number only)
               ┌─ ONCE, STILL MARRIED AND LIVING WITH SPOUSE 1
               └► Skip to Q.11(h)
               ┌─ ONCE, STILL MARRIED BUT SEPARATED FROM SPOUSE .. 1
               └► Skip to Q.11(g)
                  ONCE, BUT NO LONGER MARRIED 1
                  TWICE 2
               ┌─ THREE TIMES OR MORE 3
               └► Write in number: _____

11(b)   How did your first marriage end? Were you:
          (Circle one number)   DIVORCED 0
                                   WIDOWED 1
          OTHER . . . Please explain: ——————————————————— 2
       ┌─ IF YOU HAVE NEVER BEEN SEPARATED OR DIVORCED
       └► Skip to Q.11(g)
     ┌——— IF YOU HAVE EVER BEEN SEPARATED OR DIVORCED
11(c)   Was adultery by you or your spouse used as a ground or as a "fact" in obtain-
          ing (any of) your divorce(s) in court?
                              ┌─ NO 0
                              └► Skip to Q.11(e)
     ┌────────────────────────YES 1
11(d)   Please give details, including whether adultery was cited by yourself or by
          your spouse, and, if applicable, which divorce you are referring to:
          _____

11(e)   Whether or not adultery was cited do you think it played a part in (any of)
          your divorce(s), or if you are separated, did adultery play a part in your sepa-
          ration?
                              ┌─ NO 0
                              └► Skip to Q.11(g).
                              ┌─ YES 1
                              └► Go to Q.11(f) over the page.

11(f)   Please explain your answer to Q.11(e), including noting whose adultery:

11(g)   For each marriage when you were separated before the divorce (including your current marriage, if applicable) do you consider the marriage ended when you began living apart?

	Your first marriage	Any subsequent marriage	Which marriage? (e.g. 2nd, 3rd)
NO	0	0	
YES	1	1	

For the remainder of the questionnaire please consider your marriage as having ended from the time you began to live apart. Therefore for a relationship to be "adulterous" it must have begun or have occurred prior to this date.

11(h)   Please give: (i) Your own age
         and   (ii) Your spouse's age when each of these events occurred
         and   (iii) the place where you married—i.e. church, register office, other (specify).

	AT YOUR FIRST (PERHAPS ONLY) MARRIAGE	(If applies) AT SEPARATION	(If applies) WHEN DIVORCED/ WIDOWED	(If applies) AT SUBSEQUENT (MOST RECENT) MARRIAGE
(i) YOUR AGE				
(ii) SPOUSE'S AGE				
(iii) PLACE (Specify)				

11(i)   If your second marriage has ended, please give details (ages when divorce, separation etc. occurred) and similar details about any subsequent marriages:

12(a)   Please circle the number representing the highest qualification(s) gained by your first (perhaps only) spouse and, if you have been married more than once, i.e. if different, your present (most recent) spouse: Please list any other qualifications in the last column (See Q.7(b) for guidance):

	NONE	CSE'S	O' LEVELS	A' LEVELS	FIRST DEGREE	HIGHER DEGREE	OTHER QUAL.
FIRST (PERHAPS ONLY) SPOUSE	0	1	2	3	4		
(If different) PRESENT (MOST RECENT) SPOUSE	0	1	2	3	4		

12(b)   Please give full title of job done by your spouse(s) for longest time during your marriage. Feel free to write "housewife," "retired," etc. if these are most appropriate.
First (perhaps only) spouse: _____
(If different) Present/most recent spouse: _____

13(a)   Many of the following questions will use the term "sexual relationships." Does this term seem at all ambiguous to you?

       ┌─NO .... o
       └►Skip to Q.13(c).
             ─────────────────YES 1

13(b)   Please explain the difficulty:
_____

13(c)   Please state how you will be interpreting the term "sexual relationships" for the remainder of the questionnaire:
_____

14(a)   Prior to your FIRST marriage, with whom, if anyone, had you had sexual relationships?
(Circle as many numbers as are appropriate)

No one	Future spouse	Other single person(s)	Married person(s)	Person(s) of same sex as yourself
0	1	1	1	1

14(b)   Before you married did you live with (either of) your spouse(s)?

	First (perhaps only) spouse	(If different) Current/ most recent spouse
NO	0	0
YES	1	1

⌐ IF YOU DID NOT LIVE WITH YOUR FIRST OR (IF DIFFERENT) YOUR CUR-
└ RENT/MOST RECENT SPOUSE PRIOR TO THE MARRIAGE
→ Skip to Q.15.

⌐ IF YOU DID LIVE WITH (EITHER) SPOUSE PRIOR TO THE MARRIAGE
→ 14(c)   At the time did YOU consider that period as:
(Circle one number only in column (i), and, if you have been married more than once (i.e. if different) in column (ii) as well)

	(i) First (perhaps only) marriage	(ii) (If different) Current/most recent marriage
SIMPLY LIVING TOGETHER	0	0
A TRIAL MARRIAGE	1	1
NO DIFFERENT TO SUBSEQUENT MARRIAGE	2	2
⌐ NONE OF THESE └ Please describe . . . (Which spouse?)	3	3

14(d)   Do you regard (either of) your marriage(s) as dating from this period when you lived together?

	First (perhaps only) marriage	(If different) Current/ most recent marriage
NO	0	0
YES	⌐1	⌐1
NOT APPLICABLE	↓9	↓9

(If yes to Q.14(d) for either marriage)
For the remainder of the questionnaire, please consider THIS marriage as starting from the time you first lived together.

15. IF YOU ARE SINGLE, NEVER MARRIED → Go to Q.15(b).
┌── IF YOU ARE NOW OR HAVE EVER BEEN MARRIED

15(a) After reading each statement below, please circle the number which most closely indicates the strength of your agreement or disagreement with the statements AT THE TIME OF YOUR (FIRST) MARRIAGE.
[Ignore the last column for the time being]
Feel free to comment on the content of any of the statements at the end.
(Please circle one number only for each statement)

Your opinion at the time of your FIRST marriage:	Strongly agree	Agree	Neither agree nor disagree	Disagree	Strongly disagree	Your opinion NOW: 0, 1, 2, 3 or 4
WHEN YOU ARE MARRIED, SEXUAL RELATIONSHIPS OUTSIDE OF MARRIAGE ARE ALWAYS WRONG	0	1	2	3	4	
IT IS ESSENTIAL TO BE TRUE TO ONESELF EVEN IF THE MARRIAGE SUFFERS	0	1	2	3	4	
TRUE LOVE IS THE ONLY GOOD REASON FOR GETTING MARRIED	0	1	2	3	4	
IN CERTAIN CIRCUMSTANCES A MARRIED WOMAN IS NOT DOING WRONG IN HAVING AN "ADULTEROUS LIAISON"	0	1	2	3	4	
MOST PROBLEMS IN A MARRIAGE CAN BE SOLVED IF BOTH PARTNERS WORK AT IT	0	1	2	3	4	
IT IS O.K. TO HAVE AN "ADULTEROUS LIAISON" IF ONE'S SPOUSE WILL NOT BE HURT	0	1	2	3	4	
MARRIAGE SHOULD LAST UNTIL "DEATH US DO PART"	0	1	2	3	4	
IT IS NOT WRONG TO SEEK SEXUAL FULFILMENT OUTSIDE MARRIAGE	0	1	2	3	4	
PEOPLE OUGHT TO PUT UP WITH PROBLEMS IN THEIR MARRIAGE	0	1	2	3	4	

	0	1	2	3	4	
IN CERTAIN CIRCUMSTANCES A MARRIED MAN IS NOT DOING WRONG IN HAVING AN "ADULTEROUS LIAISON"	0	1	2	3	4	
HONESTY BETWEEN SPOUSES IS THE CORNERSTONE OF A GOOD MARRIAGE	0	1	2	3	4	
IT IS ALL RIGHT TO HAVE AN "ADULTEROUS LIAISON" IF YOU CAN BE SURE YOUR SPOUSE WON'T FIND OUT	0	1	2	3	4	
IN A GOOD MARRIAGE ALL OF A PERSON'S NEEDS WILL BE MET WITHIN THE MARRIAGE	0	1	2	3	4	
IT IS IMPORTANT TO CHANGE AND DEVELOP AS AN ADULT EVEN IF THE MARRIAGE SUFFERS	0	1	2	3	4	
IF ONE SPOUSE HAS AN "ADULTEROUS LIAISON" THE OTHER IS NOT DOING WRONG IN HAVING ONE TOO	0	1	2	3	4	
IT IS ALL RIGHT TO HAVE AN "ADULTEROUS LIAISON" IF ONE'S SPOUSE APPROVES OF IT	0	1	2	3	4	
FEW PEOPLE REMAIN IN LOVE WITH THEIR SPOUSES FOR MORE THAN A FEW YEARS	0	1	2	3	4	
IF ONE SPOUSE HAS AN "ADULTEROUS LIAISON" THE MARRIAGE IS OVER	0	1	2	3	4	

Comments on any of the statements:

15(b)   Please now return to the beginning of Q.15(a). After reading each statement in the question write in the last column the number which most closely indicates the strength of your agreement or disagreement with the statements NOW.

⌈IF YOU ARE CURRENTLY MARRIED AND LIVING WITH YOUR
⌊SPOUSE
↳Skip to Q.17.

⌈IF YOU ARE MARRIED BUT NOT CURRENTLY LIVING WITH
┤SPOUSE
⌊IF YOU ARE CURRENTLY NOT MARRIED

16(a)   Are you *currently*:
         (Circle one number)   LIVING WITH A PARTNER .... o
                                NOT LIVING WITH A PARTNER 1
⌐OTHER 2
↳Please explain: _____

16(b)   Please circle the appropriate number to indicate the nature of your most
         important relationship *at the moment*:
                                A LONG-TERM RELATIONSHIP..................... o
                                A RELATIONSHIP WHICH IS (PROBABLY) NOT
                                LONG-TERM 1
                                ⌐NOT CURRENTLY HAVING A RELATIONSHIP 2
                                ↳Skip to Q.17.
                                OTHER . . . please explain: _____
16(c)   Is your partner currently:
         (Circle one number)   MARRIED, LIVING WITH SPOUSE .... o
                                MARRIED, BUT SEPARATED FROM SPOUSE   1
                                DIVORCED 2
                                WIDOWED 3
                                SINGLE, NEVER MARRIED 4
⌐OTHER 5
│
↳Please explain: _____

16(d)   Please briefly explain what this relationship means to you:
         IF YOU ARE SINGLE, NEVER MARRIED → Skip to Q.18(a).

IF YOU ARE OR EVER HAVE BEEN MARRIED

17. Please now think . . .
     (i) about the time of your first (perhaps only) marriage
     and (ii) (if you have been married more than once) about the time of your
     present (most recent) marriage.

17(a) When you married did you feel that you were in love with your spouse?
(Circle one number in the first column. If appropriate, then circle one number in the second column)

	(i) Your first (perhaps only) marriage	(ii) (If different) Your present/most recent marriage
NO	0	0
YES	1	1

17(b) When you married, did you think that:
(Circle one number in the appropriate column(s))

	(i) Your first (perhaps only) marriage	(ii) (If different) Your present/most recent marriage
I WOULD NEVER WANT A SEXUAL RELATIONSHIP WITH ANYONE EXCEPT MY SPOUSE	0	0
I MIGHT WANT A SEXUAL RELATIONSHIP WITH SOMEONE ELSE AT SOME TIME	1	1
I DID NOT KNOW WHETHER I WOULD WANT A SEXUAL RELATIONSHIP WITH ANYONE ELSE AT SOME TIME	2	2

17(c) When you married, did you and your spouse discuss your feelings about extra-marital relationships?

	(i) Your first (perhaps only) marriage	(ii) (If different) Your present/most recent marriage
NO	0	0
YES	1	1
I DO NOT REMEMBER	2	2

17(d)   When you married did you feel you had any agreement, explicit or implicit, with your spouse(s) about whether to have or not to have sexual relationships with others?

	Your first (perhaps only) marriage	(If different) Your present/most recent marriage
NO	0	0
YES	1	1

17(e)   (If applicable) Please briefly describe:
What was agreement?   Explicit (formal,
_____ informal) or implicit? _____
Any change during marriage?
_____

Why was agreement(s) made?
_____

17(f)   If you have ever made an agreement with any partner or spouse about whether sexual relationships with others was permissible or not, please give these details:

Who with? (e.g. 2nd spouse, person lived with at age 22)	What agreement?	Why made?
Was it formal/informal?		

17(g)   Please cast your mind back to the period just before:
   (i)   Your first (perhaps only) marriage
   (ii) (If different) Your present (most recent) marriage and then:
   (iii) Think about your attitude now.
Please circle ONE of the numbers from A or B AND ONE number from C or D to represent YOUR attitude —

at the following times:	A That you should be sexually faithful	B That you should NOT be sexually faithful	C That your spouse should be sexually faithful	D That your spouse should NOT be sexually faithful
(i) At first (perhaps only) marriage	1	2	1	2
(ii) (If applies) At present (most recent) marriage	1	2	1	2
(iii) Your attitude now	1	2	1	2

17(h) Do you think that your spouse felt very differently about any of the statements in Q.17(g)?

NO .... o
↳skip to Q.18(a).

YES 1

Which statement(s)   What did spouse feel?

18(a) Although it is now over a year since you wrote to me, please cast your mind back and, if you can, briefly write down your reason(s) for replying to the article describing my work in the "Sunday Times," OR if a NEW respondent, please give your reasons for helping:

18(b) Were/are you responding mainly as:
(Circle one   A " RULE BREAKER" (OF THE MARRIAGE VOW
  number only)   PROMISING SEXUAL FIDELITY) .... o
                     A CONFORMIST (TO MARRIAGE VOWS) 1
                     SOMEONE "TEMPTED" BUT NOT (THEN) HAVING
                        SUCCUMBED 2
                     SOMEONE WHO DENIES THE RELEVANCE OF THE
                        MARRIAGE VOW OF SEXUAL FIDELITY IN THEIR
                        OWN LIFE 3
                     A VICTIM OF YOUR PARTNER'S RULE BREAKING ... 4
         OTHER ... Please write in _____ 5

ALL EVER MARRIED → Go to Q.19.

ALL SINGLE PEOPLE WHO HAVE NEVER MARRIED

> Please do use the blank sheet to give any further information which YOU consider important. Then, please return this questionnaire in the s.a.e. provided.
> THANK YOU VERY MUCH FOR GIVING YOUR TIME AND THOUGHT IN COMPLETING THIS QUESTIONNAIRE.

Now some questions about any "adulterous liaisons" you may have had . . .
PLEASE READ YOUR GLOSSARY FIRST.

19(a)   Have you ever had any "adulterous liaisons"?
        (Circle one number) ┌NO .... o
                             └▸Skip to Q.20(a).
        ↓─────────────────────────────── YES 1
19(b)   With (approximately) how many people have you had an "adulterous liai-
        son":
        During first (perhaps only) marriage   ____ (Approximate) Number
        (If different) During your
           present (most recent) marriage   ____ (Approximate) Number

        ┌────── IF YOU HAVE BEEN MARRIED ONCE ONLY
        │ ┌─── IF YOU HAVE BEEN MARRIED MORE THAN ONCE
        │ 19(c)   Did you subsequently marry anyone included in Q.19(b)?
        │   NO .... o
        │   ┌─────────────── YES 1
        │   └▸Please give the number of your marriages for which this is true:
        │   ____ Number
        └▸19(d) Please give the number (if any) of these "liaisons" mentioned in 19(b) which
                 were with people of the same sex as yourself:
                                 ____ Number

19(e)   At the time these "liaisons" started, how many (if any) of the people included
        in Q.19(b) were:

                                                                        (Approx)
                                                                        Number
              MARRIED, LIVING WITH SPOUSE ....   ____
            ┌ MARRIED, BUT SEPARATED FROM SPOUSE ....   ____
            │ DIVORCED, NOT REMARRIED ....   ____
        ┌───┤ WIDOWED, NOT REMARRIED ....   ____
        ↓   └ SINGLE, NEVER MARRIED ....   ____

19(f)   Were any of these living with someone else at the time?
                                 NO .... o
                             ┌ YES 1
                             └▸How many?   ____   Number

20(a) To the best of your knowledge, has your spouse ever had an "adulterous liaison" WHILST MARRIED TO YOU?

	First (perhaps only) spouse	(If different) Present/ most recent spouse
NO	o	o
YES	1	1
	(Approx) how many: _____	(Approx) how many: _____

⌐IF YOU HAVE EVER HAD AN "ADULTEROUS LIAISON"

Please answer Q.21 by thinking back to the time when you were making up your mind about having your FIRST (perhaps only) "adulterous liaison."

⌐IF YOU HAVE NEVER HAD AN "ADULTEROUS LIAISON"

Please answer Q.21 by thinking back to the FIRST time you seriously considered having an "adulterous liaison" (or the first time you were tempted).

21. Please go through all the following statements, circling the ① only where you consider:
(in column i) that you would have agreed with that statement AT THE TIME.
(in column ii) that it played an important part in your decision to have or not to have a "liaison."
Column (iii) is for your comments, particularly if your attitude has changed.

Your opinion at the time:	At first "liaison" or temptation		Any comments?
	Agreed (i)	Yes, important for decision (ii)	Attitude NOW Inappropriate words etc. (iii)
MY SPOUSE AND I HAD GROWN APART	1	1	
IT WOULD BE WRONG OF ME TO HAVE SEXUAL RELATIONSHIPS OUTSIDE OF MARRIAGE	1	1	
LIFE FELT VERY EMPTY	1	1	
I WAS WORRIED ABOUT THE DECEIT INVOLVED	1	1	
LIFE WAS FOR LIVING	1	1	

I WAS SURE MY SPOUSE HAD NEVER HAD AN AFFAIR	1	1	
I WAS CURIOUS TO KNOW WHAT SEX WITH SOMEONE ELSE WOULD BE LIKE	1	1	
I WOULD NOT WANT TO PUT MY MARRIAGE AT RISK	1	1	
I WOULD NOT WANT TO PUT ANYONE ELSE'S MARRIAGE AT RISK	1	1	
MY SPOUSE AND I HAD AGREED WE COULD BOTH HAVE AFFAIRS	1	1	
IT WOULD BE EASY TO KEEP AFFAIR SECRET	1	1	
I WOULD WORRY ABOUT HURTING MY CHILDREN	1	1	
I HAD SEXUAL NEEDS WHICH WERE NOT BEING MET AT THE TIME	1	1	
I WOULD FEEL GUILTY ABOUT MY LOVER'S FAMILY	1	1	
IT WOULD HELP RECAPTURE A LOST YOUTH	1	1	
MY SPOUSE AND I DID NOT DISCUSS DIFFICULTIES IN OUR RELATIONSHIP	1	1	
WITH CARE, THE AFFAIR WOULDN'T HARM MY MARRIAGE	1	1	
I FELT COMPELLED BY MY EMOTIONS TO HAVE AFFAIR	1	1	

I FELT I HAD THE RIGHT TO HAVE AN AFFAIR	1	1	
I WANTED TO HAVE AN AFFAIR BECAUSE MY SPOUSE WAS HAVING ONE	1	1	
I DIDN'T STOP TO THINK	1	1	

22. Some people claim that "adultery is 90% opportunity"....
If you consider the presence or absence of opportunities, your "openness" to them, your ability to make opportunities and so on has been of importance for you or your spouse, please give the details below:

_____

23. Certain events are frequently selected as important for marital relations and for the decision to have or not to have an affair. These include:
(a) A "mid-life crisis," other crisis or major life-event
(b) Ill health or accident suffered by self, spouse or close relative
(c) The death of a close relative or friend (particularly parents of self or spouse)
If any such event(s) has influenced you or your spouse, please give details below:

What crisis or event?	Date	Who affected?	What happened?
1)			
2)			
3)			

People also claim that work is of importance in their marital and extra-marital lives . . .

24(a) Please circle the number against those statements which you consider made
it more likely:

in column (i)   that YOU would have an "adulterous liaison," whether or not
you actually had one.

in column (ii) that YOUR SPOUSE would have an "adulterous liaison"
whether or not he/she actually had one.

Then, if you have been married more than once, please note in column (iii)
to which marriage this refers:

	Influence on:		
	YOU	SPOUSE(S)	Which
	Towards	Towards	marriage?
Statement:	(i)	(ii)	(e.g. 1st/2nd)
A WORK INTRODUCED ME TO NEW PEOPLE	1 ...	2	_____
B WORK INTRODUCED MY SPOUSE TO NEW PEOPLE	1 ...	2	_____
C MY SUCCESS AT WORK AFFECTED MY RELATIONSHIP WITH MY SPOUSE	1 ...	2	_____
D MY SPOUSE'S SUCCESS AT WORK AFFECTED OUR RELATIONSHIP	1 ...	2	_____
E MY JOB CHANGED MY OUTLOOK ON LIFE	1 ...	2	_____
F MY SPOUSE'S JOB CHANGED HIS/ HER OUTLOOK ON LIFE	1 ...	2	_____
G I WAS WITHOUT WORK FOR SOME TIME	1 ...	2	_____
H MY SPOUSE WAS WITHOUT WORK FOR SOME TIME	1 ...	2	_____
J I RETURNED TO WORK/ CHANGED MY JOB	1 ...	2	_____
K MY SPOUSE RETURNED TO WORK/CHANGED HIS/HER JOB	1 ...	2	_____
L OTHER ... Please specify: _____	1 ...	2	_____

24(b) If you have responded to one or more of the statements in question 24(a) I
would be grateful if you could briefly give the details and explain what happened, noting to which statement(s), (A, B, C etc.), you are referring:

IF NEITHER YOU NOR YOUR SPOUSE HAS EVER BEEN A MATURE STUDENT → Skip to Q.26.
┌────── IF EITHER OF YOU HAS BEEN A MATURE STUDENT
Similarly, being a mature student is often said to be of importance in a person's marital and extra-marital life. . .

25(a) Please circle the relevant number against any statement which is true, whether or not you/your spouse had an "adulterous liaison" as a result:
        in column (i) for yourself
        in column (ii) for your spouse.
Then please note in column (iii) to which marriage this refers.

	(i) Yourself	(ii) Your spouse	(iii) Which marriage (e.g. 2nd)
EDUCATION GAVE ME/MY SPOUSE NEW HORIZONS	1 ...	2	_____
EDUCATION INTRODUCED ME/MY SPOUSE TO NEW PEOPLE	1 ...	2	_____
EDUCATION GAVE ME/MY SPOUSE PRACTICAL OPPORTUNITIES TO HAVE AFFAIRS	1 ...	2	_____
OTHER . . . please describe: _____	1 ...	2	_____

25(b) If you have responded to one or more of the above statements, please briefly explain and note whether the event(s) led to an "adulterous liaison":

_____

26. IF YOU HAVE HAD NO CHILDREN → Skip to Q.27(a).
┌─IF YOU HAVE HAD CHILDREN
└→Some people have said that the presence of children of certain ages makes it wrong to engage in extra-marital relationships/"adulterous liaisons." Others say that it only makes them rather impractical!

26(a) What part, if any, do (did) your children play in your decisions about whether to have such relationships?
(Circle one number)┌─NONE 0
               └→Skip to Q.27(a).
             ┌ A SMALL PART 1
─────────────────────┤ A FAIRLY IMPORTANT PART 2
             └ A VERY IMPORTANT PART 3
26(b) Please briefly describe what part the children played:

27(a)   Since your (first) marriage have you ever had what you feel was an affair or extra-marital relationship with someone even though the two of you NEVER made love?

           ┌─NO 0
           └▶ Skip to Q.28.
                             ─YES 1

27(b)   (If yes) Please give brief details, including noting the terms you use to describe the relationship, and why you consider this was an affair or extra-marital relationship:

_____

IF THIS IS THE ONLY KIND OF EXTRA-MARITAL RELATIONSHIP YOU HAVE HAD → Please, wherever possible, answer the following questions thinking back to the first (perhaps only) such relationship.

28.   IF YOU HAVE HAD AT LEAST ONE "ADULTEROUS LIAISON" → Please answer Q.28(a) thinking only of your first "liaison."
IF YOU HAVE NEVER HAD AN "ADULTEROUS LIAISON" → Please respond ONLY to columns (i) and (iii) in Q.28(a).

28(a)   Who (if anyone) did you discuss having any "adulterous liaison" (affair) with? Did they tend to encourage you TOWARDS OR AGAINST having the/an "adulterous liaison."

Please circle ONLY the appropriate number(s).

	(i) EVERYONE SHOULD ANSWER	(ii) ANSWER ONLY IF YOU HAVE HAD "LIAISON"	(iii) EVERYONE SHOULD ANSWER	
	Discussed before affair	Discussed during affair	Person(s) encouraged	
Whom discussed with:	YES	YES	TOWARDS	AGAINST
SPOUSE	1	1	2	3
OTHER RELATIONS Who were they?	1	1	2	3
SAME SEX FRIENDS NOT WORKING WITH YOU	1	1	2	3
OPPOSITE SEX FRIENDS NOT WORKING WITH YOU	1	1	2	3
SAME SEX WORK COLLEAGUES	1	1	2	3
OPPOSITE SEX WORK COLLEAGUES	1	1	2	3
(POTENTIAL) PARTNER	1	1	2	3
PAST LOVER	1	1	2	3
PROFESSIONAL HELPERS e.g. GENERAL PRACTITIONER, SOCIAL WORKER, MARRIAGE COUNSELLORS Who were they:	1	1	2	3
RELIGIOUS ADVISOR (e.g. VICAR, GURU) Who were they:	1	1	2	3

28(b)   If you discussed having affairs with any OTHER people, please give similar details about them:

IF YOU HAVE NEVER DISCUSSED HAVING AFFAIRS → Skip to Q.29(a).

IF YOU HAVE DISCUSSED HAVING AFFAIRS WITH AT LEAST ONE PERSON

28(c)   Would you describe any of the people you have indicated in question 28(a) as "confidantes"?

NO, NONE	YES, ONE PERSON ONLY	YES, SEVERAL PEOPLE
—— 0 Skip to Q.29(a)	1	2

28(d)   Please list which people have counted as "confidantes" (e.g. same-sex work colleague, past lover, etc.):

IF YOU HAVE NEVER HAD AN "ADULTEROUS LIAISON" → Skip to Q.29(a).

IF YOU HAVE EVER HAD AN "ADULTEROUS LIAISON"

28(e)   (If applicable) Would you say that one or more of these confidantes played an important role in:

Your first "adulterous liaison"
NO ... 0
—————YES ... 1
28(f) Please explain their importance:

Any "adulterous liaison(s)"
NO ... 0
—————YES ... 1
28(g) Please explain their importance:

29(a) To the best of your knowledge, approximately what proportion of: (i) your male married friends, and (ii) your female married friends have had or are having an "adulterous liaison."
(Circle one number in each column)

	(i) Male married friends	(ii) Female married friends
ALMOST ALL OF THEM	o	1
MOST OF THEM	o	1
ABOUT HALF OF THEM	o	1
ABOUT A QUARTER OF THEM	o	1
ONLY A FEW OF THEM	o	1
NONE OF THEM	o	1
DON'T KNOW	o	1

29(b) Has anyone ever confided in you about their "adulterous liaison"?
————————————NO .... o
————————————YES 1
(Approximately) how many people: _____

29(c) Please note who confided in you on the most recent occasion (e.g. "boss," female friend etc.), and the reason:

_____

29(d) Have you ever supported someone's "adulterous liaison" in practical ways? (e.g. lending accommodation or money, acting as an alibi, etc.).
————————————NO .... o
————————————YES 1
29(e) Please give details:

_____

29(f) Thinking of the most recent occasion you learnt of a friend's "adulterous liaison," who was the first person to tell you?
HAVE NEVER LEARNT OF A FRIEND'S "ADULTEROUS
LIAISON" .... o
MY FRIEND 1
HIS/HER SPOUSE 2
OTHER ... Who was this: _____ 4

IF YOU HAVE NEVER HAD AN "ADULTEROUS LIAISON" → Skip to Q.35.
IF YOU HAVE HAD ONE OR MORE "ADULTEROUS LIAISONS" → Please
answer the following questions about phrases and words . . .

30(a)   Please go through the following words and phrases, circling the appropriate
        numbers to indicate:
        (i)   Each phrase that you feel *applies* or *has ever applied to you* in any "adulter-
               ous liaison."
        (ii)   Each phrase ever *spoken by you* in describing yourself.
        (iii) Each phrase that you feel *applies,* or *has applied to your partner/lover* in
               any "adulterous liaison."

	(i) You feel phrase *applies* (has applied) *to you* YES	(ii) Phrase ever *spoken by* *you* in describing yourself YES	(iii) You feel phrase *applies/* (has applied) *to a partner/* *lover of yours* YES
BEING UNFAITHFUL	1	1	1
LOVER	1	1	1
HAVING INFIDELITIES	1	1	1
BEING PROMISCUOUS	1	1	1
MISTRESS	1	1	1
CHEATING ON SPOUSE	1	1	1
COMMITTING ADULTERY	1	1	1
CONFIDANTE	1	1	1
HAVING AN AFFAIR	1	1	1
VICTIM	1	1	1
ADULTERER/ADULTERESS	1	1	1
PLAYING AROUND	1	1	1
PARTNER	1	1	1
OTHER WOMAN	1	1	1
CARRYING ON	1	1	1
OTHER . . . please write in: _____	_____	_____	

30(b) For each term below, please indicate the (approximate) number of your liaisons which you feel are best described by each of the terms.

(Approximate) number of "liaisons"
for which term applies

EXTRA-MARITAL RELATIONSHIPS .... ——
CASUAL AFFAIRS .... ——
ONE-NIGHT STANDS .... ——
RELATIONSHIPS .... ——
BRIEF ENCOUNTERS .... ——
SERIOUS AFFAIRS .... ——
OTHER ... Please describe: ————————————— ——

————————————————————————— ——

31. Please answer the following questions about your first (perhaps only) "adulterous liaison" and, if you have had more than one (i.e. if different) your present/most recent "liaison."

	Your first (perhaps only) "adulterous liaison"	(If different) Your current most recent "adulterous liaison"
(a) PARTNER'S MARITAL STATUS: (see Q.9. for examples)		
(b) YOUR AGE WHEN "LIAISON" BEGAN/HAPPENED:		
(c) HOW MANY YEARS HAD YOU THEN BEEN MARRIED (TO THAT SPOUSE):		
(d) IS "LIAISON" STILL GOING ON?		
(e) HOW LONG DID IT GO ON FOR/HAS IT BEEN GOING ON FOR:		

32(a) Overall, would you say that the "liaison(s)" has given you:
(Please circle one number in the appropriate column(s).

	Your first (perhaps only) "adulterous liaison"	(If different) Your current (most recent) "adulterous liaison"
A LOT OF HAPPINESS	0	0
SOME HAPPINESS	1	1
ONLY A LITTLE HAPPINESS	2	2
NO HAPPINESS AT ALL	3	3

32(b)   (If applicable) Please describe what aspects of the "adulterous liaison(s)" gave (gives) you the most happiness:

Your first (perhaps only) "adulterous liaison"	(If different) Your current (most recent) "adulterous liaison"

32(c)   And have the "adulterous liaison(s)" caused you:

	Your first (perhaps only) "adulterous liaison"	(If different) Your current (most recent) "adulterous liaison"
A LOT OF UNHAPPINESS	0	0
SOME UNHAPPINESS	1	1
ONLY A LITTLE UNHAPPINESS	2	2
NO UNHAPPINESS AT ALL	3	3

32(d)   (If applicable) Please briefly describe what aspects of the "adulterous liaison(s)" cause(d) you most unhappiness:

Your first (perhaps only) "adulterous liaison"	(If different) Your current (most recent) "adulterous liaison"

32(e)   (If applicable) Overall, would you say that each "adulterous liaison" is (was) worth this degree of unhappiness?

	Your first (perhaps only) "adulterous liaison"	(If different) Your current (most recent) "adulterous liaison"
DEFINITELY WORTH IT	0	0
PROBABLY WORTH IT	1	1
PROBABLY NOT WORTH IT	2	2
DEFINITELY NOT WORTH IT	3	3
I AM NOT SURE	4	4

32(f)   And taking everything into account, do you think that the "adulterous liaison(s)":

	Your first (perhaps only) "adulterous liaison"	(If different) Your current (most recent) "adulterous liaison"
DEFINITELY IMPROVED YOUR MARRIAGE	o	o
PROBABLY IMPROVED YOUR MARRIAGE	1	1
NEITHER IMPROVED NOR DAMAGED MARRIAGE	2	2
PROBABLY DAMAGED YOUR MARRIAGE	3	3
DEFINITELY DAMAGED YOUR MARRIAGE	4	4

32(g)   Please note the reasons for your answers in Q.32(f) above:

Your first (perhaps only) "adulterous liaison"	(If different) Your current (most recent) "adulterous liaison"

32(h)   Which of the following do (did) you benefit from in your "adulterous liaison(s)":
Where appropriate, please circle the "yes" response under column (i) and, if applicable, under column (ii) as well.
(Please ignore the boxes for the time being)

	Your first (perhaps only) "adulterous liaison" YES	(If different) Your current (most recent) "adulterous liaison" YES
INTELLECTUAL STIMULATION	1 ☐	1 ☐
BEING LOVED	1 ☐	1 ☐
ENJOYABLE RISK	1 ☐	1 ☐
SEXUAL FULFILMENT	1 ☐	1 ☐
BEING NEEDED	1 ☐	1 ☐
FRIENDSHIP	1 ☐	1 ☐
BEING UNDERSTOOD	1 ☐	1 ☐
LOVING	1 ☐	1 ☐
FREEDOM/INDEPENDENCE	1 ☐	1 ☐
GREAT SENSE OF FUN	1 ☐	1 ☐
OTHER . . . Write in: _____	☐	_____ ☐

Instructions for completing the boxes are given.

Now please look back to those items in Q.32(h) which you have indicated as giving you benefit in the "liaison(s)." Please choose just the three which you consider the most important and rank them by placing the number 1, 2 or 3 in the box beside each of these items.

If, for example, "being needed" was the most important of these benefits for you in your first "liaison" put a "1" in the first box by this item. If "great sense of fun" was the second most important, you should put a "2" in the box by this, and if "friendship" was third, a "3" in that box.

32(i)   Which (if any) of the following do (did) you suffer from in the "adulterous liaison(s)"?
(Circle as many numbers as are appropriate)

	Your first (perhaps only) "adulterous liaison" YES	(If different) Your current (most recent) "adulterous liaison" YES
FEAR OF BEING FOUND OUT BY SPOUSE	1 ☐	1 ☐
GUILT TOWARDS YOUR SPOUSE	1 ☐	1 ☐
GUILT TOWARDS YOUR CHILDREN	1 ☐	1 ☐
YOUR JEALOUS FEELINGS	1 ☐	1 ☐
OTHER PEOPLE'S JEALOUS FEELINGS	1 ☐	1 ☐
DECEIT	1 ☐	1 ☐
MARRIAGE HURT BY AFFAIR	1 ☐	1 ☐
OTHER . . . specify: _____	☐ _____	☐

32(j)   Looking back to the items in Q.32(i) which you have indicated as causing you suffering in the "liaison(s)," choose just the three which you consider cause(d) you the most suffering, and rank them by placing the number 1, 2, or 3 in the box beside each of these items.

32(k)   If the "liaison(s)" had other important effects not mentioned above please give brief details:
(For example, you may have made new agreements about your marriage, your spouse may have chosen to have an "adulterous liaison" because of yours)

Your first (perhaps only) "adulterous liaison"	(If different) Your current (most recent) "adulterous liaison"

33(a) Thinking now just of your first (perhaps only) "adulterous liaison," when did your spouse first come to:

	Suspect you were having an "adulterous liaison"	Know you were having an "adulterous liaison"
EVEN BEFORE "LIAISON" TOOK PLACE	0	(Not applicable)
WHILST "LIAISON" WAS TAKING PLACE	1	1
(Approx) how long had it been going on for at the time:	_____	_____
AFTER "LIAISON" STOPPED	2	2
AT NO TIME	3	3
DON'T KNOW	4	4

33(b) Still thinking of your first (perhaps only) "adulterous liaison," *how* did your spouse first come to:

Know you were having an "adulterous liaison"

I TOLD HIM/HER 0

SOMEONE ELSE TOLD HIM/HER 1

Who was this: _____

HE/SHE FOUND EVIDENCE OF "LIAISON" 2

OTHER 3

Please write in: _____

I DO NOT KNOW 4

33(c) If you know, please describe why this person (people) told your spouse of this "liaison" (their reasons, motives etc.):

_____

_____

33(d) (If applicable) *How* did your spouse come to SUSPECT you were having an "adulterous liaison"?

33(e)   Did your spouse ever talk to you about his/her knowledge or suspicion that you were having an "adulterous liaison"?

Your first (perhaps only) "adulterous liaison"

NO, NEVER 0
YES, WHILST "LIAISON" WAS GOING ON 1
YES, BUT NOT UNTIL AFTER "LIAISON" HAD FINISHED .. 2

33(f)   What effect (if any) did these conversations have:
          (i) on your marriage
      and (ii) on this or future "adulterous liaisons"?

(i)

(ii)

33(g)   (If applicable) Why do you think your spouse chose not to talk to you about his/her suspicion or knowledge (for some time):

33(h)   Some people have told me that their spouse consciously or unconsciously encouraged them to have an "adulterous liaison."
       Do you think that (any of) your spouse(s) at any time:

(Please circle one number on each line)   NO   YES
ENCOURAGED YOU TO START AN "ADULTEROUS
   LIAISON" .... 0 ... 1
ENCOURAGED YOU TO CONTINUE AN "ADULTEROUS
   LIAISON" .... 0 ... 1

33(i)   (If yes to either) Please give brief details of the circumstances and the result (e.g. which marriage—if applicable—what spouse did, why you feel he/she behaved in this way, and what your response was):
First occasion:

(If different) Most recent occasion:

34(a) Thinking now of your first and, if you have had more than one (i.e. if different), your current (most recent) extra-marital partner:
(Circle one number on each line in the appropriate column(s))

	Your first (perhaps only) extra-marital partner		(If different) Your current (most recent) extra-marital partner	
When you first met were they:	NO	YES	NO	YES
WORKING IN THE SAME PLACE AS YOU	0	1	0	1
A FRIEND OF YOUR SPOUSE	0	1	0	1
A NEIGHBOUR OF YOURS	0	1	0	1
⌐OTHER └▸Please write in: _____	0	1	0	1

34(b) Where do (did) you usually make love (e.g. hotel, own bedroom, partner's office etc.)

Your first (perhaps only) "adulterous liaison"	(If different) Your current (most recent) "adulterous liaison"

34(c) Thinking now of your current (most recent) "adulterous liaison" ONLY, please note the major things that you and/or your extra-marital partner spend money on, (e.g. meals, presents, theatre, hotel rooms etc.):
Most money spent on: _____
Other important items of expenditure:

34(d) Who usually pays for the things you have listed above?
(Circle one number)   I DO 0
                      MY PARTNER 1
                      WE SHARE THE COST OF MOST THINGS ... 2
                      THERE IS NO EXPENDITURE 3
      OTHER (e.g. your Company) specify: _____ 4

35.   To finish, I would be grateful if you would answer some general questions
        exploring how your attitudes to sexual fidelity may have been influenced . . .

35(a)   If you have read any fiction or non-fiction books which have influenced your
        views about sexual relationships outside of marriage please note which are
        the books and explain briefly in what way they influenced you:

35(b)   Please give the same information about any films or plays seen on television,
        at cinemas or theatres:

35(c)   If you recall hearing or taking part in any particular discussion or conversa-
        tion which influenced your own views and/or actions, please give the details
        and effects:

35(d)   Sometimes people's opinions and behavior have been influenced by their
        experience of the "adultery" of others (e.g. of father, of friend or colleague).
        Please give details below if this is true for you:

36(a) Since writing in response to my article in the "Sunday Times" would you say
that your marriage has:

NOT CHANGED .... o
DEFINITELY IMPROVED 1
PROBABLY IMPROVED 2
PROBABLY WORSENED 3
DEFINITELY WORSENED 4
HAS ENDED 5
OTHER 6

Please explain:

36(b) (If appropriate) Was this change the result of an "adulterous liaison"?

NO .... o
Skip to Q.37.

YES 1

36(c) (If yes) Whose "adulterous liaison"?

Your own	Your spouse's	Both	Other (Please specify)
0	1	2	

36(d) Please give brief details for your answer to Q.36(c):

37. If you feel that I have not asked questions on important aspects of "adulterous liaisons" I would appreciate it if you could write below and/or overleaf
what these are and explain how they are important:

If you have NOT had an "adulterous liaison" but your present (or previous) spouse
has had one or more whilst married to you would you be willing to fill in a short
questionnaire about them? If so please tick this box: ..... ☐

Give details here if you wish this questionnaire to be sent to a different address:

THANK YOU VERY MUCH INDEED FOR GIVING YOUR TIME AND
THOUGHT IN ANSWERING THIS QUESTIONNAIRE.

APPENDIX B

Sample and Methods

Most research is presented as if it had been carefully planned and organized from the outset—indeed, as if the work had actually been done before it had been started—and as if none of the problems that plague us all ever touched the researchers. This project, by contrast, took shape very much by chance and bit by bit. Like Topsy, it just grew, but it also suffered many a setback, filled many a wastepaper basket, and provided too many despairing moments to record.

Still, although my ideas were far from clear at the outset, I did approach my chosen topic with certain values and certain imperatives that I have pursued.

I have explained (in my prologue) that I wanted both figures and stories. Both depend on language, however: Language has to be translated into numbers for computer analysis, whereas stories can reach the page sifted (of course) through me but in the same form that I first heard them. For numbers, however, language has to be used in much stricter ways, categories imposed, interpretations limited in the interests of comparability and reliability, always in the hope that validity—truth—is minimally sacrificed. Indeed, the survey method is based on this systematic and careful standardization of question and answer, with categories for coding developed ahead of the answers. This, it has long been argued, best obtains and protects truth. In practice what it best achieves is *reliability* (that is, agreement among independent interviewers, coders, and observers on the interpretation of the answers) rather than *validity* (that the question is the right one and the answer accurately reflects a respondent's thought, feelings, or behavior). Thus, a reliability check that I carried out using two coders for a 5-percent random sample of questionnaires demonstrated very high agreement (96 percent) overall, but this masked very low agreement on "open-ended" questions where the categories could not be worked out in advance. Reaching a sample of people who would tell me their stories and complete questionnaires that could be translated into numbers, then, was but one of the problems, and, at the outset, not the most pressing, for *how* to ask the people questions, once selected, was more deeply problematic.

This problem is not specific to work on a taboo subject, but it is magnified there. Jessie Bernard, the doyen of American sociological and feminist scholarship on marriage, pointed out some time ago that researchers engaged in work on a taboo subject such as adultery necessarily also do some "de-tabooing"—even when, or perhaps especially because, we avoid those terms (like *adultery*) that carry connotations of sin and crime and hence are moral evaluations—and speak instead of the "extramarital" or even the "co-marital" relationship. Seeking objectivity, we may even valorize rather than condemn with our language choices.[1]

I wanted to speak of adultery for two reasons: first, I wanted not to avoid but to point to its long history as sin and crime and, further, to dramatize the greater sin, the greater punishment inflicted on the married woman—that is, on the adulteress as opposed to the adulterer. In this sense, "adultery" is a feminist issue where the "affair" or the "extramarital relationship" might not be. Second, the way words are used in everyday language indicates both the psychological and the sociological space the concept occupies. When someone says she (or he) has "committed adultery," they send a message about what it meant to them and, when substantial others like them use the same term, they suggest modern times might have changed less than first we thought. In any event, I wanted study participants to forge categories for me before I imposed my own on them. The early days of the study were therefore spent traveling around England and Scotland interviewing people in unstructured ways—seeking to listen to the stories they had to tell in their own words before a more formal questionnaire could be developed that would provide the frame for answers that could be translated into numbers.

But I had also to think about my own motivation and about how I might be perceived, about the way I spoke, for how I couched even the most open of questions would elicit certain and not other responses. Since, too, adultery is illicit, and hence usually secret, the narration of these stories would often have a special place in the lives of the storytellers—something difficult yet important to grasp. Was I engaged in vicarious adulteries as I listened to these tales—indeed, as I became the confidante and, for couples, the third party to their adventure in telling? Were there things I especially wanted to hear, things that would fulfill my own but not necessarily their needs and hence—albeit unwittingly—lead them to consider issues not central to their concerns? Like the psychoanalyst, it seemed important to me that I be as fully aware of these things as the analyst must be before listening to the secrets of the analysand. I cannot be certain how successfully I accomplished this, but people raised issues that I had not thought important, and, within a range of ideas, seemed readily prepared to reject as well as proffer interpretations. I certainly learned much about adultery that I had not even suspected. Much that was said resonated strongly with me; I could identify readily with the speaker, but generally I felt not desire but, worse, I sometimes had to struggle to follow where the speaker led, to empathize with his (and it was more difficult for me to get inside the heads, never mind the hearts, of the men who contributed to this study) or her experience.

For the contributors, I think the telling did, on occasion, perform a vital role in their whole adventure. Some gave excuses in order to attend a small-group discussion in the evening in just the same terms as if they had been meeting a lover: "I told him I was going to a meeting about my job. Well, 'e knows we've got troubles down there." "I often have to work late and I'm on the road, so being late back tonight won't cause any raised eyebrows." I have suggested in the book that telling plays a central role in the lived adulterous experience, and that adultery itself can be understood as "renarrativizing" lives that have become interminably dull, merely "good enough" (or worse, not good enough), and lacking moral goals. To speak of their experience was to make it come true but also to end the adventure, to encapsulate it and, as it were, to put it to bed.

I cannot tell in what role I was cast by some storytellers—but if I was mistress, wife, sibling or parent, lover or husband, child or friend, or, perhaps counselor, so long as I was also researcher, so be it.

Before turning to an analysis of the sample, let me return briefly to the chronology of the study, for I had initially thought the best way to proceed might be to interview a relatively small number of middle-class people over some time and in depth—people who, because they were like me, might be prepared to speak and whom I would have little difficulty in understanding, though how to reach them, since some, at least, would have to be adulterous, was unclear. By chance, I was offered the opportunity through a friend, who was also a free-lance journalist, to appeal for volunteers through a newspaper article describing my ideas. Appearing first, early in 1981, in the London *Sunday Times*, a paper with a readership of over four million, I some months later was afforded similar openings in the *Guardian* and the *Sunday*

Mirror—the latter reaching an even bigger and more working-class population.[2] It was the response to the first article that dictated the subsequent shape of the study, for I decided that more than six hundred replies should not be wasted and to pursue both quantity and quality—to develop a postal questionnaire and to conduct in-depth tape-recorded interviews and hold small group discussions where themes could emerge as participants addressed one another as much as responding to questions from me.

About two thirds of the replies to the first article were from women; of the remaining third, most came from men; and the rest from people writing in as couples—usually married, sometimes adulterous. Letters and cards varied from a few cryptic remarks handwritten on a scrap of paper: "Kindly send six questionnaires," to ten double-sided, single-spaced pages of autobiography. Three cases seemed not seriously intended. Apart from these, even the one open proposition was, nonetheless, serious about being interviewed: he had, after all, experiences to relate relevant to the "problem."

Given this distribution, I decided to sample all the men and couples and one in three of the women. I used the *Guardian* to attempt to reach more men, more "victims," and people in business and the media as I had begun to develop my ideas about the institutionalized settings for adultery and about the institutionalized practices that might be "part of the job." For example, a study participant had reported her ex-TV director husband as having been profoundly offended by her serious affair and yet as seeing no incompatibility in that attitude and one entirely accepting of the mundane, repetitive "affairs" of his colleagues on the set and after.

During this time (1981–82), I developed the questionnaire in response to the way people spoke in interview, permitting still as much freedom to the respondent to comment on my choice of words, questions, and layout as was compatible with this method of data collection, but requiring them to answer as if they were replaying their entry into adultery, concentrating on the first and the most recent liaison and choosing the term *adulterous liaison* to cover the long affair, the one-night stand or visit to a prostitute, or the affair of the heart only—a term not in common use and, hence, more inclusive.

In interviews I had discovered that people wanted a framework—preferably a chronology within which to locate their story. They could not respond when I asked, "Why not tell me why you wrote? What was it you wanted to tell me?" but wanted me to "ask questions." Some made their need for a clear biographical beginning explicit: "Well, I was born in 19——, the third of three children," and so forth. In our psychological and medical age, what was once moral deviance has become psychopathology, so people feel comfortable with an interpretation that begins with childhood. The questionnaire similarly locates people within their families and moves to feelings, beliefs, and attitudes about marriage and adultery.

In the small group, however—a technique common in market research but not in sociology—I thought it might be less necessary to set a biographical framework; that people would talk as much to one another as to me. It seemed to offer an economic and elegant way both to pursue certain themes and also, through the very use of the method itself, to test the idea that people did still engage in a moral debate about the issue and, if they did, to know more clearly what form the debate took and what content it had. It might be argued that such a group is nothing like a model of any real-life situation where such debates as surround adultery do actually take place; and, therefore, the group did not and could not perform this function. Certainly, the context in which debates or actions occur profoundly influences the outcome; it would be absurd to suggest otherwise. And the group is not in any sense set up as a natural model of, say, discussion with a spouse, with a potential lover, or with friends. Nor, obviously, as a model for internal debates. But enough is known from the conduct of therapeutic groups to know that patterns of response—"nor-

mal" for a particular person—are displayed; that, given leadership in certain directions, the interactions are typical of those occurring in other settings. In the therapeutic group, however, individuals often feel threatened because their self-esteem
may be attacked through the analysis of what they say or how they say it. I felt one
of my primary tasks had to be to prevent anyone becoming the scapegoat of any
group; to prevent interpretation of motive at a level that someone might experience
as threatening; to insist on the research nature of the group. If I was successful in
that, then the focusing on the topic; the motivation of those who came to participate;
the fact that, without exception, everyone shared with me a wish to "understand"
themselves and the topic, led me to believe that we would hear in these varied groups
(varied in membership, by size and by the sex of those present, as well as by the
source from which people had come, by their stance to adultery, by the presence of
different graduate students, by time of day), whether debates occurred and, if they
did, then the content, accurately portrayed.[3]

In the event, certain themes did recur: the moral dilemma, the fear of aging and
death, the importance of honesty, and yet the need for secrecy, privacy and personal
space, for autonomy and the desire for intimacy. Certain themes were also
avoided—in particular, sex. From Dennis, a man who disturbed a whole group with
his opening remarks about his "carnal" first wife, his amazing exploits in California,
and his regular Wednesday dash up the stairs to his mistress's room where they
watched pornographic films and made love as if it was the last time—his deep fear—
I learned what was not being said and to ask about it (see pages 184 and
203–4).

The questionnaire breaks all the rules of postal questionnaires. It is absurdly long
and demanding to answer. However, my self-selected sample was highly motivated—
though no one was paid for participating—and highly educated. The length and
difficulty, therefore, perhaps held fewer terrors for them than it would have done
with a differently constituted sample. However, I think it important not to simplify
this topic. Adultery is not simple: it touches on people's deepest emotions and on
areas of their lives that some will not share with anyone, others with only a few
people within certain well-defined roles. Of course, some have no such inhibitions
but they are in the minority. Recently feminists have questioned the applicability
of traditional (and hence partriarchal) social research techniques to women; and
particularly to women when the subject matter is of the kind in this study—pertain-
ing to private and personal areas of social life that are intimately concerned with the
development and expression of female sexuality.[4] Laurel Richardson, for example,
called her method a "communal research model," aiming to avoid non-interactive
"expert" cuts at knowledge that predetermine the relevance of *parts* of experience,
and to achieve a more equal power balance between researcher and researched. She
reports that two thirds of the women in her sample experienced her interview as
"therapeutic."[5] Similarly, some of the participants in this study experienced relief
even in just filling out the questionnaire. Perhaps this goes some way to explaining
the high response rate—66 percent.

The Sample

Comparison with National Population

The people in the sample are distributed by sex, social class, and level of education, quite differently from the ways we would expect if they had been randomly
drawn from the population. I have a ratio of 59:41 women to men, rather than 51

percent women to 49 percent of men—this despite the sampling procedures aimed at increasing the numbers of men. There are good sociological reasons why more women than men would come forward for a study of this kind since adultery has always been more problematic for women than men. It remains more central to women's concerns, more salient as a matter affecting the family and their role in it as moral guardians as well as their own deepest feelings and needs. More pragmatically, the first newspaper article appeared, as did the second, on the "women's" pages of the newspapers—thus, in a way, excluding men although many read those sections. Men have greater difficulty in talking about these areas of their lives, too, and may have been particularly reluctant to come forward because I was a woman. In addition, the sample is overwhelmingly middle-class as measured by the kinds of occupation in which people are engaged (82 percent of my respondents are in nonmanual occupations, as compared with 48 percent in a sample of the national population).[6] My sample is also, compared with their brothers and sisters in the general population, highly educated. Only 11 percent of my sample have left school with *no* educational qualifications, and 31 percent had a first degree. No less than 13 percent attained higher degrees. As would be expected, this was differently distributed between the men and women, the men being better educated than the women. Thus, while 9 percent of the men had left school without any formal academic qualifications, 13 percent of the women had none; while 22.5 percent of the men had achieved a higher degree and another 35 percent had a first degree, only 7 percent of women had a higher degree, although 23 percent had achieved at least a first degree. In the age groups, twenty-five to sixty-nine years covered in the national sample used for comparison, we could expect 15 percent of men and only 10 percent of women to have achieved a first degree; yet in my sample in these age groups, no less than 54 percent of the men and 36 percent of the women have reached this level. Thus, nearly four times as many people in the adultery study as in the general population have a degree.

Again, there are both good sociological and more pragmatic reasons why few working class people came forward—even in response to the *Sunday Mirror* articles. These articles were placed near pictures of a nude woman and had a much less serious tone than the earlier two. Still, the whole newspaper is written much as were these two articles. Working-class people may feel they have less to contribute to a middle-aged, middle-class academic in a university, and there is a more customary silence about such personal-sexual areas of their lives. Thus, even the ordinary "facts of life" passed on as a matter of course by middle-class mothers to daughters may, according to some recent oral histories of the experience of working-class women, be less often passed on to them.[7] Although researchers have found the numbers engaging in adultery to vary according to social class—working-class men, for example, beginning sooner after marriage, and middle-class men later—the overall incidence may not be different. Given the pervasive influence of the Myth of Romantic Marriage and the customary distress suffered in all classes when infidelity is discovered and still to be witnessed every week in the pages of newspapers and advice columns addressed especially to women, I think class differentiates adulterous experience less than do gender and age.

The age range of the study population is wide—from twenty-two to eighty-three years old at interview; but respondents are not distributed across this age range as they would be had they been selected to represent the general population from which they were drawn: there are fewer in the age groups to thirty-five and more in those years until about fifty-five. Because *Guardian* respondents were slightly younger than *Sunday Times* respondents, there are two modal ages: that is, the most common age for *Guardian* readers was thirty-four and for Sunday *Times* readers, forty-two years. Adultery, depending on when people marry and how soon following

FIGURE 1
Urban/Rural Distributions over Time

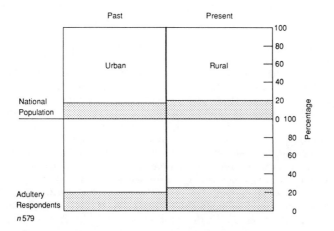

marriage they are prepared to have affairs, tends to be a problem for those aged thirty to fifty-five; in this respect, the sample is well suited to the purpose.[8]

Study members are distributed throughout England, Scotland, and Wales, with only slight differences from those expected. Although there is an excess of people responding from the Greater London area, the southwest, the southeast, and East Anglia—and less than might be expected, given the distribution in the population as a whole, from northern areas and from Scotland and Wales—each area is well represented, the average difference from expected distributions being around 2 percent. Furthermore, the people in the study are drawn from rural and from urban areas almost exactly as we would expect (see figure 1). Historians who have studied particular villages or towns in great detail would, I think, expect there to be variation at least as between town dwellers and country dwellers in adulterous behavior and attitudes.[9] People gave the name of the town, village, or other place where they were brought up for the greatest length of time (Q4 (b)), and where they now live (Q4 (a)). This provides a measure of "past" and "present" rural and urban dwelling. In the population as a whole, in 1961, just under 20 percent were country and just over 80 percent town dwellers. In 1981, country dwellers had risen to 23 percent. There has been a rather general shift out of the towns, though there are considerable variations in different parts of the country and from and to towns of different sizes and character. My sample reflects this change.[10]

1961 does not provide a direct comparison, since my study includes people who were children before the First World War as well as those born only twenty-five years ago; but, in the "past," 21 percent of study members were rural dwellers, while *now* (1982–83), 26 percent live in rural areas. Since the study members are almost entirely middle-class (Registrar General's social classes I and II)* where an excess of country

---

* The Registrar General classifies individuals in the United Kingdom into classes: I (professional)–V (unskilled manual workers), subdivided at III into nonmanual and manual occupations.

dwellers is likely to be found, the small excess in the study over total population figures is probably correct for their social class.

Having looked at the rural-urban distribution, it remains to be said that there is no difference in the number of adulterous liaisons reported by people according to the region in which they used to live (for most of their lives) or in which they now live.

The critical question to be asked about any sample is not whether they do or do not represent the general population from which they are drawn, but whether the characteristics on which they vary *matter*, given the focus and purposes of the study. The way such a question has to be answered is dependent on the theory or theories held about the topic under study, and upon the kinds of statement it is intended to make as a result of the study. Social class, age, sex, and other critical demographic measures are normally included in sociological work because they repeatedly discriminate among groups. That is, people from different social classes of different ages, and depending on whether they are men or women, behave in very different ways. This is so, whether what is being studied is health, housing, attitudes to work and play, voting patterns, child rearing, or, perhaps, adultery.

Furthermore, if it is intended that general statements about the incidence and prevalence of "adultery in Britain today" are to be made, then a sample would need to be drawn that represented the distribution of people "in Britain today." However, when a study is being undertaken in a new area, when it refers to an illicit behavior surrounded by much secrecy, when it is intended not to make such grand statements but rather to look in depth and in detail at adultery, then this sample has certain advantages. Looking in depth and in detail means to explore the way adultery is being defined, to examine how people enter into adulterous relationships, to try to describe the place it has in their lives and how it relates to their marriage, to delineate its natural history, noticing the words used to describe the various adulterous relationships, and the explanations people proffer for their actions and the stories told of the joys and tribulations experienced, and then to try to relate all that to the world in which these people live, then a relatively homogeneous group has considerable advantages.

A well-educated group does not, of course, have any monopoly of feeling, nor of capacity to express themselves, but given my own background, there are considerable advantages in being able to take for granted certain meanings, certain ways of using words. In a study of this kind, there are advantages in the sharing of experience, as discussed by Jennifer Platt, between researcher and researched.[11] I would find less difficulty in understanding and interpreting what was said—and they would, similarly, take more for granted about my knowledge of their lives—than if our shared experience were more dissimilar. The problem of shared language and of shared meaning is much debated by anthropologists; sociologists have, until recently, been more assured about their work, given that they normally work only in their own society and hence in their own language; but the problem of providing accounts that differ from those provided by the actors themselves has become of central concern to sociology and of particular concern to ethnomethodologists.[12]

Throughout the study I have been consistently interested in feelings and attitudes; and, although I am suggesting there are advantages in my sharing understanding with the respondents, I have not relied only on my own interpretations and judgments. Eight different people have helped with the study, four employed as research assistants, three men and two women, and three from different age groups from myself. Although, by definition, they are all now well educated, they come from a wide range of social backgrounds; they also vary by marital status and by whether or not they have children. They have worked at different stages, for different lengths of time, on different tasks. Some have helped to derive measures and to assess the content of group discussions and interviews. Clearly, such researchers are not wholly independent of me; yet there has been a high level of agreement about the nature of the stories being told, about the "right" and "wrong" or "possible" and "not possible" interpretations to put on things.

Given my hypothesis about the role of values in people's decisions—that individuals creatively employ the Myth of Romantic Marriage in competition with the Myth of Me as both motivation and justification—we might expect those from different religious backgrounds, those with different current faiths, and those for whom religion is more important to vary in their adulterous liaisons (see pages 106–7). Questions were asked that provide that breakdown (appendix A, question 5(a)–6). The study sample follows neatly the general "secularization" of modern society with 58 percent having been brought up in the Church of England, 11 percent as Roman Catholics, and another 16 percent in "other Christian faiths," but only 26 percent, 6 percent, and 9 percent, respectively, now answering that they still believe in those faiths. David Martin in 1967 quoted a similar distribution for the "population of Great Britain identifying itself as . . ." but the adultery study has about 4 percent altogether reporting they were brought up as Jews, while his figure is 1 percent.)[13] Whereas 6 percent considered they had been brought up as agnostics, humanists, or as atheists (none), as many as 51 percent classified themselves in those ways now.[14] In answer to the question "How important a part, if any, does religion or other belief system play in your life?"—and the scale against which the answer could be given ranging from "no part at all" to "an important part"—more than twice as many said "no part" as "an important part" (32 percent to 14 percent).[15]

Finally, this is a study of adultery. Adultery occurs only in relation to marriage. (Its meaning is varied and for many it includes all and any infidelity, including that of the heart. Nevertheless, given its history, its general meaning clearly is consequential on marriage.) The sample must, therefore, cover the range of marriage patterns, including people who have been divorced and whose family sizes and household composition is representative at least of age group and social class. In each of these respects, the sample is adequate.

Furthermore, since one hypothesis expects the increasing participation of women in the marketplace to be important for their sexual patterns and to have consequences for the feelings of both men and women about themselves and about each other, the sample must include reasonable proportions of women in various modes of employment. My sample turns out to have fewer than expected in part-time employment but very similar proportions indeed of women "economically active"— that is paid, excluding the retired, students, and full-time housewives but including the unemployed—in the labor force to those that would be expected. Thus, nationally, in 1981 in England and Wales, 62 percent of the currently married (regardless of the number of previous marriages) were "economically active," as were 72 percent of "non-married women" aged sixteen to fifty-nine (that is, single, divorced, and widowed in 1979–80). The comparable figures for the adultery sample are 64 percent and 74 percent (taking the current date as 1982–83).[16]

So far as family size and household composition is concerned, the numbers of children born to respondents needed calculation by year of marriage (to provide a "marriage cohort" for which there were comparable figures), by the numbers of women of "fertile" (that is, child-bearing) age, and by current age. The calculations were complex but, insofar as I have been able to find comparable material and to compute these figures for the women (there are no such national figures for fathers), the numbers of children in these families is much as expected.[17] I also analyzed the numbers of "grown-up" children and asked specifically about where the children generally live. These figures are used to examine the effects on adultery of having children of different ages at home. See chapter 5, pages 136–38.

In a study of adultery, it is not surprising that those who have been divorced and separated are overrepresented compared with the general population. But it is important to be able to draw inferences about the part adultery plays in separation and divorce; and, for this, the "excess" in this sample is an advantage.[18] The law relating to divorce changed in England in 1971. Of men and women divorcing for the first time, 24 percent and 20 percent, respectively, were divorced before 1971. Of those divorced at any time, 54 percent said adultery was cited in court. Nationally, men more commonly give adultery as the "fact" that demonstrates their marriage has irretrievably broken down.[19] In the adultery study, 92 percent of men and 72 percent of women, divorcing for the first time before 1971, said adultery had been cited. After 1971 the proportions dropped to 61 percent of men and 43 percent of women. Finally, a sample that did not include the "faithful" in marriage when exploring the "unfaithful" would be deficient. They act as "controls" for each other. The number of adulterous liaisons, regardless of meaning, turns out to be an excellent measure, correlating highly with many of the dimensions in which I am interested. But it would not be enough to have only those with, say, one to three liaisons and those with four or more for comparison. We need those with none; in the sample, about 27 percent had no liaison; 42 percent, one to three; and 31 percent, four or more.

Any conclusions about work, or about the effects of the "mid-life crisis" on adultery, without a comparison of the effects (if there are any) on the non-adulterous, could easily be spurious. For the same reason, those who have experienced the adultery of a spouse and may feel themselves to be "victims" of adultery are a necessary ingredient in telling the tale. Eighteen percent describe themselves as having responded as "victims" of another's adultery. This was given as a first reason by 15 percent and by another 24 percent as a second reason. Not all, however, had been faithful themselves. Of these people who described themselves as victims, 52 percent had also had at least one adulterous liaison.

In sum, the sample is different in its educational and social-class composition from that expected in the general population. (However, working-class people are not unrepresented: there are forty-five. Simply, they are underrepresented in order to be able to make sensible generalizations about them.) The composition of the sample by where people live (rural/urban areas), by religious affiliation, by age (the most important ages for adultery are well represented), by marital experience, including the separated, divorced, and remarried but with few widows (largely because the population is younger than in the general population), by working patterns, and by the proportion of non-adulterous as well as adulterous people, is—given the topic and the intentions about the kind and generality of statement to be made—appropriate.

However, given adultery's special place, even in modern life, as breaching important social norms, the sample was further tested for the probable reliability of the accounts given by those who were self-selected compared with a "snowball sample" reached via the volunteers.

The Snowball Sample

We can never know for certain to what extent those who chose not to come forward and participate in this study are like or unlike those in the study. Of course, in all samples (except in covert observational studies), at the point of cooperation everyone is self-selected. No one can be coerced into a study if they do not wish to be, although the kinds of pressure that can be brought to bear are substantial. A patient in a hospital bed has numerous reasons for agreeing to participate in research, not least anxiety about the possible ill effects if she or he refuses to do so. It sometimes takes very little for the words "uncooperative patient" to be written on a report. And such words carry consequences for the way people react and deal

TABLE 1
Number of Adulterous Liaisons

	None %	One to Three %	Four or More %
Snowball	26	47	28
Sunday Times (A)	15	47	38
Sunday Mirror (B)	42	39	19
Guardian (C)	36	26	28
Total of A + B + C	27	32	42

subsequently with that patient.[20] A person accosted on the threshold of her or his house by a market researcher may be flattered that their opinions are valued, and likely to think, when assured it will only take a few minutes, that it is easier to answer the questions than refuse. However, when the topic is as delicate as this is, when the whole area is surrounded by secrecy and the practice itself is illicit, when people have very good reasons for not wanting their "affairs" to be known, then the problems about just who is responding, and who not, become more acute. Furthermore, we should distinguish between a refusal to cooperate (a *de*selection of oneself) and not volunteering (*non*selection of oneself).

I decided to use one well-known technique, the "snowball" sample, for reaching people who had not responded to any direct appeal from me, either via a newspaper article or the radio. In the main survey of *Sunday Times* readers, which went out in October 1982—later than a pilot survey—I enclosed an additional questionnaire, a stamped, addressed envelope, and a letter in which I asked the recipient to try to find someone, preferably not a *Sunday Times* reader and preferably male, who would complete the form and return it to us, anonymously if desired. In the event, this produced another forty-five completed questionnaires which are different in certain respects from those not gathered in this way. However, the figures all fall within the very large ranges observed within the rest of the sample. For example, 26 percent of the snowball were non-adulterers, compared with 15 percent of the *Sunday Times* group as a whole. But then, 36 percent of the *Guardian* and 42 percent of *Sunday Mirror* respondents were also non-adulterers. Since my letter requesting *Sunday Times* readers to pass a questionnaire on specifically requested a search for "victims," it is not surprising that there should have been an increased number of non-adulterous people in the snowball. Table 1 sets out the comparison between the snowball and the rest of the sample (that is, non-self-selected and self-selected) according to the number of "adulterous" liaisons they reported.

Since the snowball contains proportionately more men than the *Sunday Times* group does (the proportions are 51:49, as would be expected in a sample drawn randomly from the population), the pattern of the proportions reporting low and high numbers of adulterous liaisons is not explained by gender. This pattern (most falling into the one-to-three ["low"] group) is typical of women in the sample as a whole; while men, if they were adulterous, were more commonly "high" adulterers (four or more adulterous liaisons).

The social-class distribution of the snowball group is similar to the rest of the study group,[21] but their stated reasons for responding are not. Since I had made a special request for "victims," the snowball contains a higher proportion of people giving this as their first reason for responding to the study (24 percent) than in the rest of the survey (14 percent). The exception is provided by the *Sunday Mirror* readers who are very similar in this respect (35 percent), as they are in other ways. First, they contain higher proportions of people who have been married twice (14 percent), compared with the *Sunday Times* and *Guardian* groups; and their first spouses were much less well educated, only about 13 percent achieving a first degree, whereas 31 percent of the spouses of *Sunday Times* respondents had a first degree. Furthermore, their first spouses also fell heavily into those who left school with a certificate of secondary education at around "Ordinary" level, with none gaining "Advanced" level examinations as their highest educational achievement, compared with 2 percent of the spouses of *Sunday Times* respondents reaching this level. Thus, while the snowball differed from their contact people (*Sunday Times* respondents), they were similar, in these respects, to another self-selected group—the *Sunday Mirror* respondents.

The snowball group also has a disproportionately high number of respondents brought up as Roman Catholics (23 percent) as compared with the average for *all* self-selected groups (10 percent). However, the *Sunday Mirror* group had 19 percent reporting that they, too, were brought up as Roman Catholics. This difference disappears when "religion now" is considered, the snowball group following all others (apart from the *Sunday Mirror* respondents, who rarely categorized themselves as having "no" religion now). The average over all source groups who reported that religion played no part in their lives now (on a scale ranging from "a very important part" to "none") was 30 percent, but 46 percent of the snowball said it played no part in their lives.

Further, only 35 percent of the snowball were still married and living with their first spouse when they took part in the study, compared with an average of about 60 percent. The corollary follows that there were also considerably more snowball people who were divorced or separated—over half, as compared with only one quarter of *Sunday Times*, one fifth of *Guardian*, and one third of the *Sunday Mirror* groups. It is this "naturally" selected group that varies most in terms of marital status from the general population, and *not* the self-selected groups. In this sense, it is the snowball, and not the self-selected, sample that is "biased."[22] This fits well with the fact that one quarter of the snowball group were responding as "victims" of another's adultery, were people who had had rather less sexual experience before marriage,[23] and, as we have seen, were less adulterous than some of the other groups. However, we should also note that, despite their claim to having primarily responded as "victims" of another's adultery, *fewer* than in other groups thought the term *victim* applied to them or had used it in speech about themselves.

As might be expected, given their status as victims and as people who were separated or divorced from their spouses, they scored lower on permissiveness (adherence to the Myth of Me) and higher on adherence to traditional values (adherence to the Myth of Romantic Marriage) than either the rest of the *Sunday Times* population or than the average, but were less traditional in the past and more permissive now than were the *Sunday Mirror* group. Nevertheless, with only four exceptions, their scores were all within the ranges of other source groups.[24] Furthermore, the differences between the non-adulterous snowball and non-adulterous other sample groups, and between those who were in the "low" and "high" adulterous groups according to whether they came via the snowball or from other sources, are slight.

There is, however, one important variable that distinguishes the snowball people from others. They were people who rarely, if ever, discussed their feelings and attitudes about the possibility or the actuality of adulterous liaisons with others. Ninety percent said they had not discussed with their spouse the possibility of an affair before having one; and, of the thirty-two people for whom there is this information, only three discussed with their spouse an affair in which they were then engaged. Fewer went to professional helpers or talked to work colleagues, although similar proportions (slightly more) to those responding from other sources did talk to same-sex friends.[25] Thirty-one percent regarded no one as a confidante (compared with 21 percent of *Sunday Times*, 17 percent of *Guardian*, and 24 percent of *Sunday Mirror* respondents). Perhaps, however, they were, if not talkers, then listeners, since about 76 percent had at least one person who confided in them! In this respect, they hardly differed from the *Sunday Times* readers who had enlisted their cooperation, were slightly better listeners than *Guardian* readers, and very much more commonly confided in about an affair than were *Sunday Mirror* respondents. I draw some support from these figures in my assertion that those who did not respond to the study differ from those who do in one important way: they did not choose to respond, perhaps because they do not like to discuss these matters, particularly not with professionals. Because the snowball people differed significantly only in this respect, they have been included in the total of 579 for analysis.

Premarital Sexual Experience

There are also particular demographic features of the sample members that, on theoretical grounds, are important to compare with the population from which they are drawn. The most directly relevant facts are those about *premarital* sexual activity. If this sample reported very different experience from others of the same age and class, we might, for two reasons, expect their postmarital behavior also to be atypical. First, reporting sexual activity itself may, because these are private matters and sometimes heavily sanctioned, be particularly unreliable; and hence, if the people in this study give very different accounts from others in their age and class groups about their premarital sexual activity, they are more likely to be unreliable about their extramarital sexual activity. Secondly, existing studies show a strong relationship between premarital sexual behavior and extramarital sexual behavior. Thus, Lynn Atwater, in her *Extra-Marital Connection*, summarizes the position: "The impact of premarital sexual experience stands out as the first factor in the path to extramarital involvement."[26]

The sample members reported the number and variety of their sexual partners before their (first) marriage. This information was compared with the expected rates derived from earlier national and representative samples studied by Geoffrey Gorer and Michael Schofield (see table 2).

The average age at marriage has varied very little over these years, but Schofield's sample were all "young people"—that is, people in their twenties who married during the 1960s; and Gorer interviewed only those whose age was less than forty-five at the time of his study. The percentage difference between the most nearly comparable groups—that is, Gorer's sample married before 1969 (although he includes single people in his calculation) and my sample married before 1970—is only one percentage point, and between Schofield's sample of young people and my sample marrying at similar ages (but including some slightly older) during the 1960s is two percentage points. Since my sample was slightly older, we might expect them to be minimally more experienced. These figures are so close that *we can assume that my sample members are reliable in describing their sexual experience; and that they are typical of others of their age and marriage cohort, at least up to the time of marriage, in their sexual behavior.*

In fact, the relationship between premarital and postmarital sexual behavior is strongest in this study when the *number* and *variety* of premarital lovers is considered. Thus, the most adulterous were rarely "virgins" at (first) marriage (23 percent, compared with 35 percent of those who had no liaison during this marriage), and they also had experienced the most variety in the marital status and sex of their lovers at that time (61 percent, compared with 55 percent of those who later had between one and three liaisons, and 40 percent of those who stayed faithful). In particular, none

TABLE 2

Percentage of Women and Men Reporting "Virginity"
(or "No Intercourse") at First Marriage
over Time in Three British Studies

Gorer	Lawson		Schofield
	Year of First Marriage		
Before 1969	Pre-1960	1960–1969	1960s
(Aged up to 45)	40%		("Young People")
34%		33%	
		27%	29%
N (100%) = 1986*	169	207	267
All marrying before 1970: 376†			

* Gorer calculates all his percentages from this total, which includes all respondents—that is, the married and those still single at the time of his study.
† No sample including both women and men was available for comparison with those in my sample married *in the 1970s*, of whom only 11 percent were still "virgins" at marriage. However, Karen Dunnell (1979) reports that 26 percent of women marrying in the early 1970s had not had sex with their husbands before marriage (though they might have had other premarital partners) at that time which compares well with my figure of 28 percent marrying as virgins between 1960 and 1969 and does not yet reflect the drop to a mere 9 percent of women marrying as virgins throughout the 1970s and into the 1980s (to 1982).
Sources: Geoffrey Gorer, *Sex and Marriage in England Today* (London: Nelson, 1971), p. 273, table 20; Michael Schofield, *The Sexual Behaviour of Young Adults* (London: Allen Lane, 1973), p. 161; Karen Dunnell, *Family Formation* (London: Her Majesty's Stationery Office, 1979), p. 7.

of those reporting any premarital sexual relationship with someone of their own sex (about 4 percent) remained faithful after marriage, as can be seen in table 3.

Yet the striking increase in premarital experience is not directly reflected in adulterous behavior. Only 9 percent of women and 14 percent of men marrying in 1970 or later were virgins at that time, compared with 42 percent of women and 36 percent of men marrying before 1960; yet those marrying in the 1970s or later have reported fewer liaisons overall (perhaps because their marriages are of shorter duration). The detailed picture shows that those men marrying before 1960 who were virgins remained the most faithful, and that those who were most experienced before marriage were the most adulterous subsequently. The same trend continues but to much less marked degree for the men married in the 1960s. Among the men who married in the 1970s, however, there is no clear relationship between premarital and postmarital behaviour. The picture for the women is reversed: the older women (those marrying earlier) do not show a clear relationship between premarital experience and the number of subsequent liaisons until the 1970s, when the most experienced had the most liaisons.

This suggests that, during the period covered by the study, in this, as in other respects, men are beginning (statistically speaking) to "look like" women and vice versa—and indicates that future researchers need to reconsider the relationship

TABLE 3
Premarital Sexual Experience and Number of Liaisons

	Number of Liaisons						
	None		One to Three		Four or More		Total
	N	%	N	%	N	%	N
Virgins:	51	35	57	25	40	23	148
Future spouse only:	36	25	46	20	28	16	110
A variety of lovers:*	57	40	124	55	107	61	288
Total	144	100	227	100	175	100	546

* Sexual relations reported with future spouse *and* combination of at least two of the following categories: other single persons, married people, divorced or widowed, and same sex (less than 10 percent).

$X^2 = 15.59$ with 4 degrees of freedom. p < .005

between sexual behavior before and during marriage or in and out of committed relationships.

There is also a more sensitive measure of representativeness. Blumstein and Schwartz, who, in America, interviewed both spouses in a marriage, give information on the extent to which they knew about one another's extramarital liaisons.[27] The similarity with that data from my sample is striking (see table 4).

Of course, my study participants could have been lying or not revealing things because they were not asked about them or because they seemed irrelevant. They might have come forward for bravado or for other reasons more complex or unconscious leading them to stress some and not other feelings, attitudes, beliefs, and actions. Acknowledging this possibility does not invalidate the findings, for all social

TABLE 4
Spouses' Knowledge of Extramarital Liaisons

	Blumstein and Schwartz		Lawson	
	Wives %	Husbands %	Wives %	Husbands %
Spouse knew	65	64	61	61
Spouse did not know	28	27	33	33
Spouse suspected/not sure if spouse knew	7	9	6	6
N = 100%	716	914	154	122

Source: Blumstein and Schwartz 1983, p. 273.

communications are organized in this way. Stressing anonymity helps the shy or ashamed person to reveal what otherwise might be kept hidden, and lessens the opportunity for gain from boasting; but everyone must (because there is no other choice) respond from within an available repertoire of cultural beliefs. Sociologically speaking, I believe that these accounts are accurate representations of what people have done and of what they feel about those actions.

Notes

Prologue

1. Donald Winnicott used this expression to describe the ordinary mother's capacity to care for her baby and to provide what he termed a "facilitating environment." She might not be perfect; she would be "good enough." (See Winnicott 1965.)

2. Walter Kiechel (1984, p. 91) makes a similar point.

3. As defined between "economically active and inactive" in the OPCS (Office for Population Censuses and Surveys) Labour Force Survey and excluding those over retirement age (*Social Trends* 1984, p. 57, chart 4.1).

4. *Social Trends* 1984, p. 58, table 4.3. Figures include all women over school-leaving age.

5. For example, Finch 1983; Fonda and Moss 1975; Martin and Roberts 1984; Swidler 1980, pp. 120–47.

6. Hunt 1969; Linda Wolfe 1975; Neubeck 1969; Lake and Hills 1979; Yablonsky 1979; Atwater 1982.

7. Further reasons are given in appendix B, pages 355–60; see also table 2, page 364, for the figures on premarital sex.

8. A racecourse near Windsor. At the beginning of June, a week of racing is attended by members of the royal family who stay at Windsor Castle. Those with tickets to the Royal Enclosure have to follow a dress code: men wear morning dress (tail coats); and women, exotic hats.

9. In 1857, in England, the first act permitting divorce in the civil, as compared with the ecclesiastical courts, was passed. This did permit women to divorce their husbands but not on the grounds of adultery alone; and for practical purposes, divorce continued for some time to be something attainable for husbands, not wives.

10. In Jewish law, although followed rarely, a man may still "put away" his wife after ten years if she remains barren.

11. In England in 1987, the government had a pamphlet about AIDS delivered to every household. The surgeon general of the United States has announced a similar plan.

12. De Rougemont 1983, p. 25. Denis de Rougemont first published *L'Amour et l'occident* in 1939. It has been translated twice, first as *Passion in Society*, but is commonly known by its later title, *Love in the Western World*. This change in title aptly captures the conflict: de Rougemont emphasizes that passion—the *eros* of love—is deadly, while the *agape* of love, altruistic or nurturant loving, is creative.

Introduction

1. De Rougemont (1983 [1939]) argues throughout that passion is inseparable from suffering and death. Further, desire is kept aflame by not having conquered; it must meet successive obstacles or invent its own. There is a debate in the literature about whether the great epic pair, Tristan and Isolde, ever consummated their love, particularly since, after finding them sleeping in the forest, King Marc—Tristan's uncle, foster father, and liege lord—replaces Tristan's with his own weapon. The symbolism is scarcely veiled. In addition to de Rougemont, see, for example, C. S. Lewis 1959; Lerner 1979.

2. De Rougemont 1983, p. 18.

3. Bedier 1965. See also accounts by de Rougemont (1983, pp. 26–30) and Robert A. Johnson (1983, pp. 9–15 and passim).

4. To borrow Tony Tanner's term (1979, p. 377).

5. Bedier 1965, p. 33.

6. That Isolde is "only" betrothed on the journey means her sin lacks full-blown condemnation, but the marriage is not clearly separated (if at all) from the betrothal: Isolde belongs to King Marc. Lucy Mair points out that adultery is considered to occur before marriage where virginity is prized: "This is the case in Africa as well as in the stricter societies; his [the husband's] right to compensation for an adultery begins from the time of betrothal" (1971, p. 173).

Similarly, among the Pisticcesi in southern Italy, studied by John Davies (1969), a man's honor was something for which he was entitled to fight from the moment of betrothal. Adultery was still a crime in Italy in 1970, and the notion of honor served to control women so as to secure the lineage—that is, to avoid her adultery and hence the birth of illegitimate children "passing" as her husband's. The same code stresses chastity as a virtue, particularly for women.

In China, however, it was thought better to accept the fact the wife might have been dishonored *before* marriage if this was only discovered later, after the marriage had occurred, because to send her away would bring worse loss of face.

7. Barbara Walker 1983, p. 862.

8. De Rougemont 1983, pp. 115–21.

9. For example, it is suggested that Lancelot may have failed to find the Holy Grail because he consummated his love for Guinevere. The Grail displayed the same supernatural powers as the female body, while the Quest "bore all the characteristics of an initiation into Femininity not to be seized by the carnal senses" (René Nelli, *Lumière du Graal* [1951], cited in de Rougemont 1983, p. 126).

10. *The Saga of Tristram and Isonde* (early thirteenth-century version), translated by Paul Schach (1973).

11.

> *Tristan Tantris Tristan*
> *Je suis Yseult, il est Tristan*
> *Tu me répousses, tu me dédaignes*
> *Tu préferès l'amour d'un pere*
> *A l'amour de la femme."*
> [Verse omitted]
> *Sur toi, Tristan, je lance un Geis*
> *Que Tristan aime Yseult*
> *Un Geis*
> *Qu'il l'aime éperdument*
> *Un Geis*
> *Qu'il l'aime*
> *Et qu'il en vive.*
>
> Tristan Tantris Tristan
> I am Iseult, he is Tristan
> You reject me, you disdain me
> You prefer a father's love
> To the love of a woman
>
> . . . .
>
> On you, Tristan, I cast a Spell:
> That Tristan should love Iseult
> A Curse
> To love her hopelessly
> A Curse
> That he love her
> And be damned.

Verlet 1977, p. 41; my translation.

12. De Rougemont 1983, p. 52.

13. Tanner 1979, p. 13.

14. See Shirley Eskapa 1984; her very title is *Woman versus Woman*.

15. "Pleasure in marriage does not bring full satisfaction. . . . It can easily be shown that the psychical value of erotic needs is reduced as soon as their satisfaction becomes easy. An obstacle is required in order to heighten libido; and where natural resistances to satisfaction have not been sufficient men have at all times erected conventional ones so as to be able to enjoy love (Freud 1977 [1912], vol. 7, p. 256; also see p. 233).

16. Firestone 1970, p. 130.

17. Nichols 1981; Stoppard 1982; Pinter 1978.

18. Reported in the Sunday *New York Times*, 14 February 1988, pp. 19, 24.

19. *Jackie*, 7 March 1983.

20. See Armstrong 1976; Tanner 1979.

21. Schorer 1946, p. 27.

22. De Rougemont 1983, p. 18.

23. Joseph Campbell 1979, p. 3.

24. De Rougemont 1983, p. 18.

25. Rose 1984, p. 6.

26. Rose 1984, pp. 126–40.

27. De Rougemont 1983, p. 51.

28. Perhaps because, although they were not aware of challenging death, it nonetheless was challenged and overcome.

29. Rose 1984, p. 6.

30. Brookner 1984, p. 85.

31. Gramsci 1973.

32. Barthes 1976, p. 121.

33. For example, while in Madrid the former and in San Francisco the latter myth might be emphasized, people in both cities are exposed to both mythologies.

34. We should perhaps recall that the medieval courts of love (of which one of the best known is that of Eleanor of Aquitaine) were *women's* courts: women set them up, women held them, women were the judges.

35. C. S. Lewis 1959 [1936], p. 13.

36. Ferrier 1984 [1818], pp. 1–2.

37. Stone 1965, p. 670; 1977, pp. 270–71.

38. Lerner 1979, p. 67.

39. Macfarlane 1978.

40. Macfarlane 1986.

41. Ellen Rothman 1984, p. 31.

42. De Rougemont 1983, p. 292.

43. Lasch 1977.

44. Kenneth Walker 1957, p. 113.

45. Macfarlane 1986, p. 173.

46. Ann Swidler elaborates this idea in Smelser and Erikson 1980, pp. 120–47.

47. Sternberg 1986.

48. Shorter 1975; Trumbach 1978; Willmott and Young 1973. See also Jeffrey Weeks 1985, p. 27; and Barrie Thorne and Marilyn Yalom, eds., 1982, p. 13.

49. Freud thought a marriage was made between at least four people: the couple and their respective opposite sex parents. This can be readily extended to include other family relations; many unconscious expectations are brought to the marriage. See Scarf 1986; and Skynner and Cleese 1984, for a more light-hearted look at family patterns in this vein.

50. Voysey 1975.

51. Although, in England, up to the present time, a married woman's investment income is taxed together with her husband's, and certain social security benefits are paid to single but not to married parents.

52. Maslow 1968.
53. Cancian 1987.
54. Degler 1980.
55. Right up until the 1920s, one parent often died before the youngest child left home, thus marriages ended frequently because of death and remarriage was not uncommon. The meaning of a marriage broken by death rather than divorce is different, however, as are some of the consequences. See J. W. B. Douglas 1964 and J. W. B. Douglas, W. Simpson, and Jean Ross 1968, for a comparison of these effects on British, and E. Maris Hetherington 1972 on American, children.
56. Marilyn French, in her recent *Beyond Power* (1986), wishes the paramount value placed on power to be replaced with pleasure.
57. Barbara Ehrenreich, Elizabeth Hess, and Gloria Jacobs (1986) use similar data to argue for a *feminization* of sex. But this term implies a movement toward previously accepted feminine or female patterns rather than an appropriation by and for women of masculine and male patterns.
58. Francesca Cancian (1986, 1987) suggests this has occurred through a powerful, cultural stress on communication for intimacy, and argues for the incorporation of the more masculine, instrumental ideals of caring in love.
59. Ann Oakley in her autobiography, *Taking It like a Woman* (1984), describes telling her daughter of her affair in order to foster openness in her relationship with her daughter. It seems that the openness she seeks is centered on the telling of sexual secrets.
60. Richardson 1986, especially chap. 7.
61. Tanner 1979, p. 13.

Chapter 1.   What Is Adultery?

1. Denise Franklin, "How Far Is Too Far? Even 'Experts' Disagree," *Santa Cruz Sentinel*, 30 June 1987, p. D1.
2. *Shorter Oxford English Dictionary*. Ariès (1985, p. 36) thinks the word *adulteratio* indicates "debasement rather than the sexual act."
3. Howard 1983, p. 14. The dictionary definition of adultery in *Webster's Third New International Dictionary* (1981) reads: (1) voluntary sexual intercourse between a married man and someone other than his wife or between a married woman and someone other than her husband ["if a man commits adultery with the wife of his neighbor, both the adulterer and the adulteress shall be put to death"—Leviticus 20:10 (RSV)]—compare *fornication* (2) *a*: unchastity of thought or act ["everyone who looks at a woman lustfully has already committed adultery with her in his heart"—Matthew 5:28] *b*: religious infidelity; especially idolatry ["she (Israel) polluted the land, committing adultery with stone and tree"—Jeremiah 3:9 (RSV)]
4. Dr. Anthony Lodge of Aberdeen University, private communication, 1982.
5. The showing in the United Kingdom of the television film *Death of a Princess*, in which the princess and her lover were executed by stoning in an open space used as a parking lot, caused a diplomatic incident with Saudi Arabia in 1980.
6. Cassian's *Conferences*, cited by Foucault in Ariès and Béjin 1985, p. 14.
7. Twenty-three women and fourteen men (1 percent of the sample) had only this kind of liaison—"an affair of the heart." It was an experience of 31 percent and 26 percent of faithful women and men, respectively. Respondents to the study were also asked to explain any ambiguities they felt about the meaning of "sexual relations." Although only about 10 percent thought there was any ambiguity, 14.5 percent thought it might include a relationship "without intercourse"; this did not vary with the class of respondents.

8. Augustine said the only reason for being parted was "fornication," and later added "whosoever does this" (putting away a wife who is barren) is guilty of "adultery by the law of the gospel, though not by this world's rule" (*On Marriage and Concupiscence*, in *Works*, trans. Marcus Dods, vol. 2, book 1, chap. 11 [x], p. 109. Originally written A.D. *c.* 419–20.

9. Voltaire, ed. Woolf, 1924, pp. 9–14.

10. Four scores were obtained for each study participant: one for traditionalism (or adherence to the Myth of Romantic Marriage, and one for permissiveness (or adherence to the Myth of Me) both at the time of a first marriage (using the respondent's recall of feelings and attitudes as well as some behavioral measures) and "now"—that is, at the time they completed the questionnaire, using current attitudes, feelings, and behavior. Thus, throughout the book I refer to adherence to these two myths and to various other beliefs and attitudes *then* and *now* although information was collected only once. (Attitudes about sexual fidelity were also collected for the time of any second marriage—or most recent marriage in the case of more than two). Clearly, we are dealing with *remembered* feelings. However, problems of recall cannot explain differences *among* sample members—for example, between women and men *then* and *now* or between different age groups. Thus, people under thirty-five with relatively short periods to recall were more permissive (believing more often in sexual freedom) than their older counterparts at the time of their first marriages yet they were more likely to believe in sexual fidelity in a second, or later, marriage than any of the older groups (except the eight people over sixty).

11. Hunt 1969, p. 9. Hunt's overall view is that circumstances alter cases. Hunt makes extensive use of Fletcher's 1966 work on situation ethics. A. P. Thompson, in Australia, similarly found that men have more extramarital relationships than women, and particularly more "sexual only" affairs; but when liaisons that were "emotional only" were included in the count, the difference between women and men was diminished (1984, pp. 34–42).

12. Janet's attitude fits well with that of other young people described by Bernard in Bohannan 1971: "Still there is evidence that fidelity is prized among young people at least for the duration of a relationship" (p. 20).

13. Writers on the topic tend to use, as sample members did, the terms *faithful* and *unfaithful* without considering the pacts that individuals may have entered. If, for example, a couple have agreed that extramarital sex is permitted, to what are they being unfaithful when they have another partner?

14. Freeman, in Ismond Rosen 1979, p. 393.

15. Ibid., pp. 392–93.

16. I am aware that this may be read as the generic *man* to include "woman." Given the history of adultery and Hebraic law on the matter, I think it more appropriate to read this as meaning "male." In modern times, I think it inaccurate and inappropriate to use the generic *man* or *he*. I, thus, for inclusive meaning, use "human beings," "humanity," or "people." When using the singular collective noun, I also occasionally follow it with the plural (*they, their,* or *them*) that is regularly and comfortably used in everyday speech, rather than the sometimes clumsy *he* or *she, his* or *her.*

17. For Catholics and Lutherans, this is the sixth commandment. The decalogue is found both in Exodus 20:1–17 and in Deuteronomy 5:6–21.

18. Should either wife or lover escape into the street, however, he was powerless to kill either.

19. Code Justinian, I. IX, tit. XI, cited in Cabrol 1907, tom 1, pt 1, p. 550.

20. *Digest*, 48, 5:14.

21. Justinian *Novellae*, cited in Westermarck 1939, p. 347.

22. Articles 324 and 336–39. When this law was changed (in 1975), there was a fierce debate whether the best thing to do was to give wives similar rights or to

abolish it altogether. Now, in French law, adultery of the wife is no plea in mitigation of murder.

23. Groslière 1976, sections 105 and 305.

24. French Institute of Public Opinion (1960). A later opinion poll (see Moynahan 1987) found French men twice as unfaithful as women but women's infidelity had tripled over the last ten years.

25. Mueller 1980, appendix, p. 35.

26. In Hawaii, however, where there is a pre-colonial history of powerful women, the penalty is *less* for the offending woman than for the man. Peggy Reeves Sanday has recently suggested that male dominance may fall into two categories: *mythical* and *real*. The former exists "where females have political and economic power but men act as if males were the dominant sex" (1981, p. 8). Hawaii may have been such a society, for the queen clearly wielded power although there was a king with whom at any rate the colonial rulers and missionaries dealt. Certainly Sanday's work shows sexual relations are generally less constrained for women where there is mythical rather than real male dominance. In addition, she says there "is a third category, in which the balance of power between the sexes is not obscured by the myth that males rule" (ibid.).

27. Cases include Kraus v. Village of Barrington Hills, 571 F. Supp. 538 (1982), when the U.S. District Court upheld the principle that the "State may make adultery a criminal act without violating constitutional rights of adulterers." In Massachusetts, in 1983, the defendant argued, unsuccessfully, that the adultery statute violated the right of privacy guaranteed by the Constitution: the police had spied on the unlucky pair in the back of a van! (Commonwealth v. Stowell, 449 NE 2d 357 [1983]).

28. Allen v. State, 316 SE 2d 500.

29. See, for example, Stewart 1887 (no page numbers), in a work on the law relating to husbands and wives, published in San Francisco, who says damages could be "penal" for the loss of a wife's "society" and the only defense against the "injury" to the honor, reputation and happiness" of the husband was the plaintiff's consent to his wife's adultery.

30. Remnants are found in the continuing requirement, for example, that a woman's marital status be declared in swearing an affidavit: "I, Jane Smith, *married woman/spinster*, of such and such an address"—but: "I, John Smith, *occupation*, of such and such an address."

31. See Hoggett and Pearl 1983, especially chap. 2, "The Legal Structure of Marriage," for a clear exposition.

32. Shakespeare, *The Taming of the Shrew* III, ii, 232–35.

33. Blackstone, *Commentaries*, vol. III, pp. 655–56.

34. "A Countess of Arcira" is probably a figment of Voltaire's imagination.

35. Freeman 1979, p. 395, citing Crozier in 1935.

36. The Lord Chancellor at the Second Reading of the Divorce and Matrimonial Causes Bill, 19 May 1857 (Hansard, vol. 145) said that between 1715 and 1775 there had been 60 private acts of Parliament for the adultery of a wife, but from then until 1857 two or three *annually*—that is, about 260 in the period described. Stone (1977, p. 38, and graph 1, p. 39) found only 131 divorces between 1650 and 1799, of which a mere 17 were granted before 1750. Bromley (1971, p. 204, and 1981, p. 187 n.3) suggests there were about 200 divorces for men in the century preceding the 1857 act; while Joseph Jackson (1969, p. 39 and n.3) found 229 "successfully promoted," although there may have been as many as 317 according to other authorities he cites.

37. Discussion, Divorce and Matrimonial Causes Bill (Hansard 1857, 3, s., vol 145, col. 813).

38. Adultery of the husband had to be coupled with incest, bigamy, cruelty, or two-year's desertion, or alternatively, rape, or an unnatural offense (Matrimonial Causes Act 1857). Not until 1923 with Herbert's Act in England and Wales was equal-

ity of the sexes conceded and a husband's adultery alone sufficient grounds for a wife to obtain a divorce.

39. Sir Morris Finer and Professor O. R. McGregor (Finer Report on One-Parent Families, 1974, appendix 5, "A History of the Obligation to Maintain"), explaining the relationship between values and the institutional structures which supported them and which they served to support in Victorian England, wrote:

> Differing provisions for the inheritance of family property were an important factor, too. The sexual waywardness of the territorial aristocracy did not endanger the integrity or succession of estates which were regulated by primogeniture or entail. Countless children of the mist played happily in Whig and Tory nurseries where they presented no threat to property or interests of heirs. But middle class families handled their accumulating industrial wealth with a system of partible inheritance which demanded a more severe morality imposing higher standards upon women than upon men. An adulterous wife might be the means of planting a fraudulent claimant upon its property in the heart of her family; to avoid this ultimate catastrophe, middle class women were required to observe an inviable rule of chastity. Just as the new poor law of 1834 represented a political triumph for philosophic radicalism by establishing an effective means of policing poverty, so it imposed middle class morality upon pauper women by seeking to police their sexual virtue.

40. Thomas 1959, p. 19. Stone 1977 (p. 530) employs the same example (though he thinks women were also very free at court at this time) and, further, points out that precisely because it was so common, the word *adultery* was dropped: "This age gives it the soft and gentle French names of gallantry and divertisement in apology for it"—something a century later Hannah More decided was "one of the most dangerous abuses of language" (More 1788, p. 64).

41. Duby's 1978 account is drawn from a cleric called Lambert who served in a household related to the Guines and whose writings date from 1201 to 1206.

42. Duby 1978, p. 93.

43. Stone 1965, p. 664.

44. Ibid., p. 671.

45. Ibid., p. 664.

46. Lowie 1933, p. 150.

47. McGregor 1957, p. 69, citing David Cecil's biography of Melbourne, the Victorian British statesman (1939), first published in 1930.

48. Elliot Liebow (1965) and Jerry White (1986) supply oral documentation of the experience of male adultery in marginalized working-class American and British communities, respectively.

49. Westermarck 1934a, p. 136.

50. Kinsey et al. 1953, p. 143.

51. Robert Whitehurst (in Neubeck 1969, p. 139) found that men explain their *own* adulterous behavior using the biological explanation of the male "sex drive," but that of *other men* was explained as "either opportunity to indulge in sex undetected, or dissatisfaction with sex from one's wife."

52. Every social and cultural anthropological study includes description of sexual behavior and gender roles. Peggy Reeves Sanday's 1981 analysis, using the Human Relations Area Files (in which data from the 186 societies analyzed by George Murdock and Douglas White in 1969 [5th ed.: New Haven: Human Relations Area File Press, 1975] are stored) as well as detailed studies of particular societies, takes an unusual and careful line that emphasizes the way sex roles and behaviors are linked

to myth and particular environmental exigencies (see particularly part I, "Plans for Sex-role Behavior," pp. 13–54).

53. See the excellent review of primate studies by Jane B. Lancaster (1985) in Alice Rossi's edited volume *Gender and the Life Course*, in which she argues that earlier work was "male-oriented" (p. 3). She shows that the best explanations currently offered by animal behaviorists of the factors underlying sexual dimorphism, as well as sexual differences in behavior among primates, include the level of parental investment in rearing offspring. Thus, for example, when the demand for paternal investment is high, males are less aggressive, there are more monogamous mating patterns, and fewer differences between females and males in body size and aggression, territoriality, nurturance of the young, sexuality, and bond formation (p. 4, citing Trivers 1972).

This does not mean I think there are *no* biological differences between women and men or that animal behavior is irrelevant to understanding human beings. Clearly, there are biological differences and animal behavior may be relevant, but I do deny claims that because certain biological differences are observed—for example, that male animals and birds tend to be the aggressors and hunters of females, or that "bonding" pairs behave in ways understood by their human observers to be typically male and female patterns—these patterns *explain* human behavior. Lancaster is among many other scientists who have recently re-evaluated biological findings, among them: Ann Fausto-Sterling 1986; Hirst and Woolley 1982, especially the first section, "Biology and Culture"; Brown and Jordanova, in Whitelegg 1982; Lane and Hubbard 1979; Steven Rose, Kamin, and Lewontin 1984; Weeks 1981, especially chap. 7, and 1985, especially chap. 5.

54. Fox, in Ariès and Béjin 1985, pp. 1–13.

55. Safilios-Rothschild, in Neubeck 1969, pp. 78–79. See also the Greek new family law—Law 1329 GG25.

56. Lucy Mair (1971) explains polygyny, not as a means for providing "lots of sex" for a man but as a way to provide material advantage. A Gisu chief in Uganda, although a Christian, told her he could hardly do his job as a monogamist. Rather, "he should marry several wives, then he has friends and can rule the people" (p. 152).

57. Thomas 1959.

58. Details in this section are taken from Barbara Walker's *Encyclopedia* (1983, pp. 1034–37), entry: *Vagina Dentata*. See also Becker 1973, citing Karen Horney and the poets Heine and in *Lorelei* and Schiller in *The Diver*, as well as Ulysses, who fear the lure of woman, the enchantress, who will overwhelm them (pp. 134–35).

59. Freud 1959 [1927], vol. 5, p. 199.

60. Miró's paintings were exhibited in New York at the Guggenheim Museum's Miró retrospective, summer 1987. See Guggenheim Museum 1987, pp. 153–54. The picture I refer to is in the collection of Mrs. E. A. Bergman, Chicago.

61. See Ernest Becker's *Denial of Death* (1973) for a clear and profound exposition of the relationship between sex and death.

62. Shostak 1985, p. 28.

63. Barbara Walker 1983, p. 1035, citing Wedeck 1975.

64. Chagnon 1968, p. 1.

65. Harris 1974, p. 101.

66. Reeves Sanday 1981, p. 46.

67. See Reeves Sanday 1981, pp. 45–50.

68. Barbara Walker 1985, p. 1034, citing Neumann 1963, p. 174.

69. See Kate Caffrey 1976, who also says Ernest Keppel (Mrs. Keppel's husband) "did not mind" his wife's affair with "Kingy" (p. 45).

70. Reported in *Life*, "Sex and the Presidency," August 1987, p. 75. Eleanor Roosevelt did not condone F.D.R.'s long-standing affair with his social secretary, Lucy Mercer, but did accept, and "perhaps was even relieved" about, his intimate relationship with his secretary, Missy LeHand (Youngs 1985, p. 143).

71. Salaman 1984, p. 53.
72. Ibid., p. 21.
73. Bernard 1972.
74. Of course, these are broad group differences; in any given marriage, she may be better off than he.
75. Koehler 1980, p. 151.
76. See Eskapa 1985 for an account of the battle between wives and mistresses.
77. Havelock Ellis 1921, pp. 10–12. He thought play was "health-giving, developmental and balancing on the whole organism of the player" as well as "utilizing superfluous energies left unemployed in the practical work of life" (ibid.). Although "always used with a touch of irony," *playing around* was the preferred term Linda Wolfe's women used to describe their sidestepping (1975, p. 4).
78. Nichols (1981) has his hero, James/Jim, becoming thoroughly excited at the prospect of having his lover, the siren-woman Kate, and his wife in bed together.
79. Westermark 1934, p. 59, citing E. S. Haynes writing in 1915.
80. Laslett, "foreword," in Ariès and Béjin 1985, p. ix.
81. In particular in endless sermons: "Pre-Reformation and Puritan writers alike condemned adultery," and, "mediaeval sermons frequently condemned adultery and fornication," according to K. Davies, in Outhwaite 1981, p. 72.
82. Philo, *The Decalogue*, in *Works*, vol. 7, pp. 69–73 (of which I have made a précis here).
83. Goody 1956, pp. 286–305.
84. Ibid., p. 295.
85. Ibid., p. 95.
86. A brief summary is given of changes in family structure in the United Kingdom in a report of the Study Commission on the Family, *Happy Families* (1980); a more extensive account is in Leslie Rimmer's *Families in Focus* (1982) published by the same organization, now the Family Policies Study Group.
87. Libby 1973, p. 8.
88. Ash, London *Sunday Times*, 10 May 1981.
89. Armstrong 1976, p. 12.
90. Although, of those who had ever been divorced or separated (40 percent of the women and 37 percent of the men), most said that they felt either their own or their spouse's adultery had played an important part (whether actually cited or not) in their divorce or separation (that is, three quarters of the women and two thirds of the men).
91. Rivière 1971, pp. 62, 70.
92. Evans-Pritchard 1969 [1951].
93. Rivière 1971, p. 70.
94. Work currently being conducted on the expectations of marriage, both in the United States by Philip and Carolyn Cowan and in Britain by Penny Mansfield, shows prospective husbands and wives with highly egalitarian expectations. They believe they will be able to act differently from their own parents, and are shocked when their own marriages do not work out as they intended. It is also the case that these expectations are not fulfilled. (Presentations, University of California, Berkeley, 1986; and Marriage Research Centre, Middlesex Hospital, London, 1985.)
95. Armstrong 1976, p. 12.
96. Some would argue that a spouse always "knows" as I discuss in chapter 2. Nevertheless, in real situations, there certainly are people who say they had no idea at all about a spouse's adultery, and there are, by contrast, those who not only know but who may actively participate in it. Participation can range from connivance or silent misery to sharing the bed.
97. See Augustine, translated by Kavanagh, 1951, vol. 11, p. 71 (50).
98. I have paraphrased the story and added that the man in jail was to die, a fact omitted by Lyndhurst (Hansard 1857 3.s, vol. 144 Lords col: 1687).
99. Augustine, "The City of God," in *Works*, quoting Paul to the Galations, 5: 19–

21, vol. 2, book 14, chap. II, p. 27, in Everyman edition, edited by R. V. G. Tasker, 1950. Written about A.D. 420.

In the 1907 edition of the *Catholic Encyclopaedia*, the following is found: "certain casuists, early in the C17 [seventeenth century], declared that intercourse with a married woman, when her husband gave his consent, constituted not the sin of adultery, but of fornication"—requiring a lesser sanction (p. 164).

100. Augustine, referring to Romans 7: 23, in "The Retractations," in *Fathers of the Church*, v. 60, translated by Sister Mary Inez Bogan, 1938, chap. 33, p. 135, and chap. 79, p. 236.

Anger was similarly condemned but less strongly because it was, at least in principle, controllable through the exercise of will and reason: "Anger may be allowed for the enforcement of a just authority and lust for the duty of propagating offspring." Anger is not hidden because it is moved by will, but "the organs of generation are so subjected to the rule of lust that they have no motion but what it communicates. It is this we are ashamed of" (Augustine, *Works*, edited by Marcus Dods, 1871, vol. 2, book 14, section 19, p. 35, and chap. 19, pp. 49–50, chap. 24, p. 55, in Everyman edition, edited by R. V. G. Tasker, 1950).

101. Tanner 1979: "Christ disperses the social stare that petrifies the wrongdoer, just as he uncongeals the legal language that seeks to imprison her in a category" (pp. 20–22).

Chapter 2.   Marriage Lines

1. Falk 1984, p. 4.
2. Simmel, "The Isolated Individual and the Dyad: 7. Monogamous Marriage," 1950, p. 129.
3. Weber 1946, p. 334, essay XIII.
4. Ibid.
5. Falk 1984, p. 5.
6. De Rougemont 1983, p. 292.
7. See Gagnon and Simon 1973; Laws and Schwartz 1977; Weeks 1986, p. 57; Brake 1982, pp. 197–222.
8. Cancian 1987.
9. Ibid., pp. 71, 76.
10. Lillian Rubin 1983, p. 90.
11. I am thinking here of Turner's (1970) classification of love:

   1. *Physical Bonds*: sexual, erotic—characterized by desire and impulsive gratification.
   2. *Psychological Bonds*: of affection and empathy—characterized by interpersonal communication and individual development.
   3. *Social Bonds*: legal and economic—characterized by rights and duties and continuous domestic responsibility.

12. Zetterburg, quoted in Moskin 1969, pp. 50, 53.
13. Rich 1983 [1980].
14. Gagnon and Simon 1973. An extract describing the pattern of these scripts over the life cycle and the differences for women and men is given in Brake 1982, pp. 197–222.
15. Lees 1986, p. 30. See also the television researcher Marie Dobson's account of her effort to behave with equal sexual freedom to her boyfriend, in Chappell 1984, p. 83.
16. Bellah et al. 1985, p. 90, citing Yankelovich 1981, pp. 252, 98.
17. Brinkgreve 1982, p. 56 n. 2; see also Lawson 1983.
18. See Sarsby 1983, especially her chapter "Who Needs Love?"
19. Goode 1984, pp. 64, 82 n. 22.
20. London *Sunday Times*, 2 May 1982.

21. Swidler, in Smelser and Erikson 1980.
22. Bellah et al. 1985.
23. Sarsby 1983, p. 170, table 1, and p. 120.
24. Simmel, "Faithfulness and Gratitude" (1950, pp. 379–95).
25. Social and Community Planning Research (SCPR) 1984, p. 138.
26. The study was conducted by Market and Opinion Research International (MORI), London *Sunday Times*, 2 May 1982, p. 34.
27. SCPR 1984.
28. See Laslett 1977, and the Cambridge Group for the History of Population and Social Structure.
29. Anne Robinson, *Daily Mirror*, 7 November 1984.
30. In Sweden, the *Royal Commission* (only available in Swedish) conducted by Hans Zetterburg found over 98 percent of both men and women had had sex at least with their future spouses; and this increase in sexual experience was measurable as between the married women aged over and under thirty at the time of the survey (1969).
31. Gebhard 1980, pp. 46–47; Packard 1968.
32. Only 9 percent of women and 14 percent of men marrying in 1970 or later were virgins at that time, compared with 42 percent of women and 36 percent of men who married before 1960; some comparative figures are given in table 2 in appendix B, page 364.
33. See, for example, Yalom, Estler, and Brewster 1982, pp. 141–54; Bell and Buerkle, in Shiloh, ed., 1970, pp. 130–34.
34. *Psychology Today*, 1970; *Playboy*, 1974; *Redbook*, 1975—all cited in Gebhard 1980. See also Tavris 1977.
35. Gebhard 1980, p. 47.
36. See Ira Reiss, for example, on premarital sex as deviant behavior in 1960, in social context in 1967, but on extramarital sex in 1980.
37. When they remarried, around two thirds of these men believed in fidelity both for themselves and their wives. There was little sign of a continuing "double standard" in beliefs about the adultery of husbands as compared with wives as this table indicates. But for detailed figures, please see Lawson and Samson 1988.

Belief in Sexual Fidelity: Self and Spouse According to Marital Career

| | Fidelity "Yes" | | | |
| | FOR SELF | | FOR SPOUSE | |
	Women %*	Men %*	Women %*	Men %*
THEN				
At first marriage	94	84	91	88
At marriage two +	88	69	94	67
NOW				
Married once only; still together				
(now)	52	54	55	57
Remarried living with spouse (now)	88	57	94	71
Others (i.e., those not living with a				
spouse now)	79	73	77	70
All—Now	65	59	64	60
(N†) =	(190)	(115)	(180)	(116)

* Proportions are of those saying that fidelity was necessary, compared with those saying that it was not or that sexual freedom was desirable.
† Including five single (never married).

Differences between wives and husbands *then*, in the *top* part of the table (i.e., at first and most recent marriage) are statistically significant at p < .05 (i.e., the likelihood that these differences occur by chance is less than 5 percent) for all attitudes except that for the spouse at the time of the first marriage. Looking at the *bottom* portion of the table, differences between women of different marital statuses *now* are statistically significant at the p < .01 level (or less than 1 percent), while those for men are not.

38. These are the detailed figures. The likelihood that these differences occur by chance is less than 1 in 5,000.

Belief in Fidelity NOW Among the Unfaithful:
Those Reporting At Least One Liaison

	Women %	Men %
Married once only; still together	27	40
Remarried living with spouse	87	48
Others (i.e., those not living with a spouse)	79	62

Percentages are of the total answering "yes" (shown here) and "no" to the question whether they should be sexually faithful during marriage.

39. Weitzman 1985; McLean and Eekelaar 1986.

40. Gorer 1971, p. 309; Hite 1978, p. 142, 1987, p. 856.

41. Nass, Libby, and Fisher (1981, p. 128) suggest that this proportion of married men and from 45 percent to 55 percent of married women will become extramaritally involved by the age of forty.

42. Blumstein and Schwartz 1983, pp. 273–74.

43. Bell and Peltz 1973, p. 18.

44. Kinsey, Pomeroy, and Martin 1948, p. 348; Kinsey, Pomeroy, Martin, and Gebhard 1953, p. 416.

45. Grosskopf 1984; Hite 1978, 1987.

46. Grosskopf 1984.

47. Hite 1987, p. 856, and see chap. 10, pp. 395–430.

48. *Woman*, September 1983; *Woman's World*, October 1985.

49. Gorer 1971, tables 42 and 43, pp. 308–9.

50. Wolstenholme and Fitzsimmons, eds., Ciba Foundation Symposium 1973.

51. Atwater 1982, p. 31.

52. This difference is statistically highly significant: that is, the likelihood is less than 5 in 1,000 that it would occur by chance (see table 2, page 364, in appendix B).

53. Gebhard 1980, p. 416.

54. The adultery sample and Blumstein and Schwartz's sample (1983, fig. 47, p. 273) show similar patterns (as did Kinsey for women [1953, p. 425]) when divided into groups reporting one, two to five, and six or more liaisons.

55. It may be that men overestimate the number of liaisons they have had (on the "macho means more sex" principle) and women underestimate (on the basis that they might be thought "promiscuous" or "whorelike"). It is difficult to sustain this possibility, however, for, in order to make statistical sense of the distribution found, we would have to imagine that the difference in being "counted" macho fell between four and five liaisons for men and, in being counted "promiscuous," between three and four for women. Also, Swedish, American, and British samples all have similar findings, suggesting the reports are reliable. Finally, there are no differences in the

number of liaisons reported by women and by men according to the year when they married; that is, women in different marriage cohorts report fewer liaisons in each cohort; and men, more. Yet women do not deny that they are having their first liaison much sooner than they used to and sooner than men in the youngest cohort.

I have settled for most analyses on this grouping since these "cutoff" points appear to distinguish best between the women and the men. When there are differences, for example, between those with only one and those with two or more, then I have looked at those people separately.

56. Those men with higher degrees married to women with a first degree only are the exception: they have fewer liaisons than might be expected on this hypothesis.

57. I see maturation and development as continuing; it does not stop at five with the resolution of the Oedipus complex, nor at seven with the Jesuits, nor at adolescence, nor at twenty-one, nor at marriage—nor, indeed, at any age.

58. At the same time there have been massive changes in the social visibility and acceptability of homosexuality, as represented by changes in the law permitting "homosexual acts" between consenting adult males—over twenty-one—in private and making illegal discrimination according to sex, as well as race and religion. There has never been any legislation dealing with female lesbian relations: that is, it was never criminal and has not needed to be decriminalized. These changes affect the climate of sexual morality quite generally and make for tolerance to diversity.

59. Arlie Hochschild (1981) has developed the idea that women do emotional labor, and Shere Hite (1987, for example, pp. 410, 664) considers the emotional contract implied between wives and husbands to be unequal.

60. Jack Goody illustrates this point: "The Tallensi allow sexual intercourse with distant clansmen where they do not allow marriage. The reason is clear. Marriage affects the alignment between groups . . . [unlike] sexual intercourse . . . [which] . . . when carried on in semi-secrecy requires no realignments of social groups" (1956, p. 302). And see Leach 1961: "There are two kinds of marriage. The first results from the whims of two persons acting as private individuals; the second is a systematically organised affair which forms part of a series of contractual obligations between two social groups."

61. Mansfield 1982, p. 7.

62. London *Sunday Times*, 9 December 1984.

63. There have been advances in the entry of women into male professions and occupations and into higher positions within occupations, but detailed analysis of published figures regularly reveals little positive change for women vis à vis men, either in status or in pay. Furthermore, as occupations become occupied by more women than men (certain fields in medicine, for example), those occupations become devalued and resources restricted (Reskin 1988).

64. Bernard 1972.

65. See Gavron 1966; Lawson and Ingleby 1973; Oakley 1976; Ruddick 1982.

66. Pleck 1986. Pleck does not consider class variables, yet earlier work suggests that the professional and working class families had least involved fathers (in child care) while those in the middle ranges of occupations were more involved. Furthermore, the nature of the occupation is likely to be important—shift workers, for example, sharing more of the tasks than others (Harriet Presser 1986, and personal communication, 1987). Other studies that have analyzed time sharing include: Berk and Berk 1979; S. F. Berk, ed., 1980; Blood and Wolfe 1960; Huber and Spitze 1983; Nye and Hoffman, eds., 1963; J. P. Robinson 1977; O'Kelly and Carney 1986. In England, Myrdal and Klein 1956; Newson and Newson 1966; J. W. B. Douglas et al. 1968. Henwood, Rimmer, and Wicks have recently (1987) reviewed changes in task sharing and found little for the United Kingdom, citing studies by Jowell and Witherspoon 1985; Piachaud 1984; Lewis and O'Brien 1987; Brannen and Moss 1987; Martin and Roberts 1984. And for Europe, Szalai, ed., 1972. Theoretical arguments include feminist critiques from Morgan 1970 and Glazer 1976, as well as from Pleck.

67. "Born and Bred," *Women Direct*, BBC4, 22 January 1985.

Notes to pages 90–101

Chapter 3.   Changing the Contract

1. See Hochschild 1979, 1981, 1983.

2. Many of those who never had a liaison failed to complete the section about their attitudes when "tempted," declaring they never had been, or if they had, that it was not serious. However, they do differ from those who did have at least one liaison in that more of the faithful thought the deceit involved was important for their decision.

3. Psychology has not only affected the substance of motives and arguments used (the Myth of Me) but also proffers a *scientific* explanation: thus, the assumption that people have known needs, sexual and emotional, is used, as here, to support certain moral decisions.

4. Michael Schofield, an expert on British sexual attitudes and behavior, expressed a similar opinion:

> We are apt to take our sexual behaviour a little too seriously. Sexual intercourse, as often as not, is no more than an incident—very enjoyable but soon forgotten. People worry about trivialising sex, but this is because they are comparing it with love and marriage, which should be taken very seriously indeed. Love and marriage often includes strong sexual attraction, but it is the deep involvement, of one person with another, that is paramount. . . . Sex by itself is a different matter. It is basically playful—the innocent enjoyment of the body. (pp. 216–17)

5. *Alternative Lifestyles* 4 (1981). Others have also explored alternatives to traditional marriage: Lenore Weitzman (1981) has analyzed new forms of contract being worked out by couples in the United States. Albert Ellis, the "rationalist therapist" of sexual relations and author of the *Encyclopaedia of Sexual Behaviour* and numerous works on special aspects of sexual behavior (nymphomania and homosexuality), has written, together with Robert Harper, two books that also aim to suggest alternative forms of marriage: *Creative Marriage* (1961) and *A New Guide to Rational Living* (1975). Ronald Mazur, one of the major writers encouraging new forms of sexual relationship and of ways of staying married (he claims the "open-ended marriage is certainly monogamous—a primary commitment based on mutual commitment and intended to last a lifetime" [1973, p. 16]), nonetheless cites the president of the Motion Picture Association of America in 1971 as justifying *Ryan's Daughter* as follows: "Everyone who takes part in adultery comes to a horrible end. It was a beautiful picture" (p. 16).

6. In England, the well-known open-marriage journalist Anne Hooper—whose partner is Phillip Hodson, a regular broadcaster-therapist for emotional problems—wrote, in accordance with her principles, to the *Guardian* in 1987, seeking discussion to ease her jealous pain. A little later, she wrote saing it was too "sensitive" and that they had "sorted out" their relationship. See Ayala Pines and Elliot Aronson (1983) for a good review of the literature; Clanton and Smith's (1977) edited volume, *Jealousy*; and, more recently, Peter van Sommers (1987), who covers biosocial, anthropological, and psychological theories of jealousy.

7. Henriques 1970.

8. Mair 1971; see also note 56 in this book, page 374. E. Burch (1971), studying the Eskimo or Inuit people, believes both man and wife chose *which* guests would be offered the wife. Rules of kinship and reciprocal benefit were followed, rather than the wife's being made available against her will to any male visitor.

9. Evans-Pritchard 1969, pp. 120–22.

10. Mair 1971, p. 198.

11. Mazur (1973), in his first chapter called "Open-Ended Marriage versus Adultery," writes: "What a new model of open-ended marriage seeks to promote is risk-

taking in *trust* [my stress]; the warmth of loving without anxiety; the extension of affection; the excitement and pleasure of knowing sensuously a variety of other persons; the enrichment which personalities can contribute to each other; the joy of being fully alive in every encounter" (p. 17).

12. These proportions were completely reversed in subsequent marriages when over 60 percent of both men and women had discussed their feelings about extramarital sex, and nearly as many felt they had specific agreements about it. A slightly curious feature of these agreements, however, is that, while the faithful were similar to the adulterous in their lack of discussion at the time of first marriage, and in the frequency of their discussions in any subsequent marriage (fewer divorced and remarried), they did *not* have agreements with later spouses, although they had done so with their first husbands and wives.

13. Of the 243 men and women who thought their agreement entailed keeping to sexual exclusivity, a little over one third had no liaisons, about a quarter had over four, and the rest one to three. But of the 38 people who began their marriages believing they were entitled to sexual freedom, nearly two thirds had four or more liaisons, and very few had none. Those who had no agreement or who did not answer this question hit a middle path, about 20 percent having none; and the proportions having one to three or four or more, about 45 percent and 35 percent, respectively.

14. Generally there was less than a 1 in 10,000 likelihood of these differences occurring by chance (p < .0001).

15. Bengis 1976, pp. 62–63.

16. The O'Neills' book (1972) clearly reached a wide audience, but more academic papers are also frequently cited in the exploration of variations in the rules of sexual behavior between married couples. Among the most frequent are: Smith and Smith 1974; Ramey 1972, 1976; Francoeur and Francoeur 1974. The Francoeurs' description of "Hot and Cool Sex—Closed and Open Marriage" in Libby and Whitehurst 1973 has a lovely description of the hot-sex culture as "reducing marital fidelity to what I did not do in Dubuque. Marital fidelity is synonymous with genital exclusivity." On the other hand, "Cool sex requires a degree of self-identity. . . . In [the leading psychologist Abraham] Maslow's language, they must be self-actualizing. . . . The ability to stand alone is essential to the Cool-Sex mentality" (pp. 34–35). They also understand about the place of myth: "Threads arise out of the past, emerging sometimes gently, sometimes with a twisted violence, but they inevitably combine their web to catch up their unwitting weavers in the final fabric" (p. 30).

These American books (like the O'Neills') were frequently written by married couples who, instead of following common practice in giving precedence in authorship according to alphabetical order, have all, without exception, listed the wife's name first. Another English book (which does not follow this example) by Tony Lake and Ann Hills (1979) aimed not only to describe extramarital or co-marital relationships (the preferred term for these sexual encounters when they occur by agreement) but also to help those who would, to follow this route with a "how to" section.

17. French 1977.

18. Havelock Ellis, e.g. 1940; Albert Ellis 1961, 1975.

19. Kahlil Gibran, cited in McBride 1964, p. 15.

20. These figures are extremely significant, achieving a probability level of <.0001, or less than 1 in 10,000 chance finding.

Chapter 4.   Keeping Faith

1. Slightly more of the faithful had been brought up in and lived now in the country than in urban and suburban areas.

2. The irony is pointed up if we consider two men and one woman in the same situation: the idea that two men would not be able to swim, or that they might not save one another, or that they would depend on a *woman* to determine their fate, is wholly absurd! Thanks to Colin Haycraft for this riddle.

3. Phyllis Rose 1984, p. 17.

4. Horney 1967 [1928], p. 91.

5. Winnicott 1965.

6. Over one quarter agreed, and just under 60 percent of the faithful disagreed, that a marriage is over if one spouse has an adulterous liaison—an opinion held by only 13 percent and three quarters, respectively, of the most adulterous.

7. Furthermore, the faithful began marriage significantly more often expecting not even to *want* any other sexual partners, compared with the adulterous, who began their marriages with (as it turned out) realistic doubts. Thus nearly 100 percent of the faithful required sexual fidelity in their marriages and nearly 90 percent still do so. The adulterous said they never began with such pronounced ideals or such certainty; and many more of them have given up on fidelity, with 58 percent of those who have had four or more liaisons saying that "now" they should *not* be sexually faithful in marriage. However, of the adulterous, only 6 percent said they were not in love if they married on a second or subsequent occasion, perhaps because this group contains the greatest numbers who had begun an affair during a first marriage and had subsequently married their adulterous partners.

8. For example, another woman described working and not getting home until 7:30 P.M. and then having to start dinner. She could not get it on the table in time for her husband's return (in fact, he was often home before her but never cooked the dinner). He disliked being kept waiting. And she gave up her job.

9. See Sennett 1977. People constantly seek "to find validation in a reality which in truth admits of no coherent limits to the self" (p. 332). And Ralph Turner has proposed "that people variously recognize their real selves either in feelings and actions of an institutional and volitional nature, such as ambition, morality and altruism, or in the experience of impulse, such as undisciplined desire and the wish to make intimate revelations to other people" (1976, p. 989). He sees a shift toward the impulse pole.

10. Maslow 1968.

11. Some were attracted to the Eastern mysticisms with their emphasis on life forces that also, sometimes, encourage asceticism but were interpreted here as celebrating sexuality and the flow of energy from the yin and yang. This dream seemed also to offer the hope that there could be a union, a union of the male and female elements but also of the self with the rest of the world. It appealed to those who sensed with Thoreau in *Walden* that "the mass of men lead lives of quiet desperation."

12. Max Weber described this link in his famous *The Protestant Ethic and the Spirit of Capitalism* (1958).

13. French 1977 and 1985, respectively.

14. Ehrenreich 1984.

15. See, for example, Pleck and Sawyer 1974.

16. Ehrenreich 1984, pp. 90–91.

17. Fromm 1956; Erikson 1980; Hartmann 1980 [1937].

18. Wallach and Wallach 1983, p. 272.

19. Cancian 1987, pp. 105–21.

20. R. D. Rosen 1978.

21. David Riesman's preface to Michel Crozier's (1985) *The Trouble with America* recognizes the paradox that ready "talk" and easy friendship are common as a superficial first step; it is very hard to achieve the real letting down of barriers required for greater knowledge of both Self and Other.

22. There has been a highly significant shift in the amount of talk quite gener-

ally—that is, to anyone; but this is also true of talk with and between spouses. This, it seems, is the side of the coin that has led people to complain of the lack of real communication, the emptiness of the marital relationship, and its boredom. The youngest cohort not only begins marriage more aware of and feeling entitled to sexual and bodily pleasures but also much more open to discussion of these and other matters with their spouses. Taking just one subject of talk—sexual relations outside marriage—those marrying in the 1960s spoke to one another more about it than did the oldest people in the sample, and those marrying in or after 1970 spoke about it the most. The change is significant for both women and men (p < .001); viz:

Discussion of Extramarital Sex with Spouse
Percentage of Those in Each Cohort Saying Yes

Year of First Marriage	Women		Men	
	N	%	N	%
Before 1960	99	18	71	13
1960–1969	130	26	78	26
1970 or later	85	48	64	47

23. Janet Askham (1976, 1984) has taken the amount spouses talk to one another about themselves as one measure of identity affirmation, but did not question whether talk—or talk about the self—is the way that all spouses gain such identity affirmation.

24. Rose 1984, pp. 7–8.

25. Gouldner (1981) agrees that professional and middle-class people are the mainspring of the new morality. The response, for example, of middle-class males (the New Class) to the emancipation of women has greatly contributed to the spread of changes in emotional and relational management, though their relinquishing of certain claims to continuing power and domination is a "trade-off . . . in return for alliances with women and for a mantle of legitimacy" (p. 417). See also Bellah et al. 1985, preface.

26. There is even a magazine called *Self* aimed at women in which such values recur.

27. "Dogfood Dan and the Camarthen Cowboy," ITV London, 11:30 P.M., 29 January 1985.

28. Carol Gilligan (1982) described two ethics: the female, directed to moral judgment based on connectedness, caring, and continuity of relationships; the male, on logic and rationality. Both can, of course be employed by women and men, and neither is better than the other. Nell Noddings (1984) makes a similar argument.

29. That is, while most women, even most married women, now work in paid employment outside the home, they tend not to do this all their married lives but in patches and not always in full-time employment. Also, despite an increasing participation overall in the labor force of all women but particularly of married women, the figures for women in full-time employment and in the better-paid or top positions of even the traditional "women's jobs" such as teaching and nursing have recently worsened in the United Kingdom, the rest of Europe, and the United States. See several publications from the Equal Opportunities Commission, especially (1981) *Women and Underachievement at Work*; Organization for European Cooperation and Development (1980) *Women and Employment: Policies for Equal Opportunities*; also, Alan Franks "Why Aren't More Women Fellows?" *The Times*, 14 January 1985. The role of women in employment and the pattern of women's work is well described

by Huber and Spitze 1983; and Department of the Environment and the Office of Population Censuses and Surveys 1984.

Some research indicates there has been greater movement toward egalitarianism among middle class than among working-class families; for example, Sarsby (1983, p. 121) noticed egalitarian ideas were most prevalent among the private school boys and girls perhaps because the power men exercise in the outside world is greatest for the best-educated middle classes. Hence, possibly, the need to display power in the domestic circle of the family is reduced. See Comer 1982, pp. 178–89.

30. Department of the Environment and OPCS 1984, p. 191.

31. Ian was not the only person in this sample to report having a sexual relationship with a sister-in-law. Marriages where sexual access to brothers or sisters of the husband or wife is accepted or even required are not uncommon in other societies—a marital arrangement called "sororal" (sisters-in-law) or "levirate" (brothers-in-law); see Mair 1971 or Murdock 1949. Furthermore, most marital therapists believe that, unconsciously, every marriage incorporates the family relationships of those experienced by each of the partners; for a simple and amusing introduction to this theory, see Skynner and Cleese 1984.

32. Perhaps he was even "morbidly" jealous. "Morbid jealousy," a condition recognized by psychiatrists, is difficult to diagnose precisely because the cultural rules about the entitlement of husbands to possess their wives varies in time and with social class and other cultural differences. It is a serious problem because both the "normally" jealous man or woman and the mentally ill one—differentiated according to how real appear one's doubts about the fidelity of the spouse—leads to great misery and may lead to murder (see Shepherd 1961).

33. Scanzoni 1978.

34. Askham 1984.

35. Berger and Kellner 1974.

Chapter 5.   The Debate

1. The transitional object was described by Winnicott 1958, pp. 229–42.

2. Fader 1982, pp. 75–80.

3. The sociologist Lenore Weitzman (1985) calculates that, on divorce, the average income of American women of all social classes decreases by 73 percent while that of their ex-husbands increases by 42 percent—despite the widespread introduction in the United States of "no fault" divorce and "equal" distribution of marital property between the pair. But the calculation of total property ignores persistent inequalities in the earning powers of women and of their contribution to their husbands' earning capacity, fringe benefits, medical insurance, pension rights, and the need for continuity, particularly for children, within the matrimonial home and neighborhood; and it also ignores the fact that income, while the husband lives with the wife and children, is available to all of them. On divorce, he lives (usually) alone on his "equal" share, and she lives with the children on hers (including any child support). For England, see McLean and Eekelaar 1986.

Parental fears about the emotional losses for children are well founded, too. Although the consequences for children of divorce are complex and vary according to their age, social class, and gender and subsequent arrangements made for them, studies continue to show they tend to experience more difficulties at school and in their emotional lives than do those of nondivorced parents (see, for example, Wallerstein and Kelly 1980 and E. Mavis Hetherington 1972). This situation may change, however, as divorce becomes increasingly part of "normal" experience, is less and less stigmatized, and, if legal and social conditions change, has less devastating material and social consequences.

4. The format of the questionnaire was designed to encourage everyone to attempt answers to these statements (see appendix A, question 21). Only twenty-seven

people (that is, about 18 percent of the "faithful") were certain they had *never* thought of an affair at any time.

5. Only 13 percent of women and 15 percent of men were without children in this sample; while it is true that those who had the most liaisons were slightly more frequently childless, and those who were faithful were slightly less often childless than would be expected, these are not significant differences. When those without children are excluded, it seems that people who have two or three children feel they play a more important role in these decisions than do those with one child or with four or more.

6. Since it was true of both women and men that those who had only one child were less concerned about the effects of a liaison on that one than people were who had two or three children, these women had not yet completed their families and may, if they follow recent trends, end up with fewer children than their older sisters.

7. I am grateful to Sharon Jenkins of the Institute of Human Development at the University of California, Berkeley, for this suggestion. Some support is lent by the fact that those women who had children and were in paid work outside the home appear to worry less in each marriage cohort about their children than do those not so employed (44 percent of those married before 1960, but 27 percent of those married in the 1970s or later).

8. The difference here occurs partly because men less often than women had children living with them: of the women in the sample, 70 percent had their youngest child living with them all the time and only 6 percent did not have this child at any time; while of the men, 53 percent had their youngest child all the time and 14 percent did not have a child at any time. Since more men had four or more liaisons, it is also not surprising that this group least often had children living with them. These facts do not, however, explain the substantial differences in the proportions of women and men saying that the role their children played (if any) was *important*: nor the differences according to the *type* of liaison.

9. This analysis is based only on those people who had at least one child and just one liaison, when we can be certain the name they gave this liaison applies to this particular one and to no other.

10. Sociobiologists would agree that the mother's efforts are directed to ensuring her own children's survival to maturity and hence their chances to reproduce her own genes. This notion of "inclusive fitness" is premised on a "Selfish Gene," as, for example, described by Richard Dawkins in his book of this title (1976). The gene is elevated to a guiding force more fundamental than other more accessible motives, intended to explain much of the behavior of human beings as mere "survival machines." For the use of this argument in this matter, see Essock-Vitale and McGuire 1985, and chapter 1 in this book, pp. 48–49.

11. Although these were all women who had been married at least once, and Laurel Richardson (1986) focused on single and divorced women, she also found the "new other woman" seeking friendship in her sexual relationships. Indeed, they most commonly arose through a relationship, particularly at work, that already was warm and, to these women, intimate. The sexual boundary comes to seem increasingly absurd as intimacy deepens in such situations.

12. Yalom 1985, p. 111. Talk does *not*, however, always have these positive effects: the motivation of the speaker, the content of what is said, the perception of the listener may all lead not to an escape from madness but to a way to it—as in the film version of Ken Kesey's *One Flew over the Cuckoo's Nest*, when Nurse Ratched holds her "therapeutic groups." Similarly, the conversations in Marge Piercy's *Woman on the Edge of Time* in the mental hospital are a sure recipe for madness.

13. George Herbert Mead's ideas of the Self and its reflective capacity takes greater account of the social in the actual creation of a sense of self than does Freud's archeology. The socially oriented "me" reflects, in interaction, from and to the external world and then internally toward and from the inner "I." The whole

works always toward integration of conflicting emotion in the creative activity of forming and changing identity. See Jack Douglas's chapter "The Emergence, Security and Sense of Self," in Kotarba and Fontana (1984, especially p. 71) for a modern use of Meadian theory.

14. In a lecture (Jing Lyman Series, summer 1986, the Center for Research on Women, Stanford University), Laila Said described writing her autobiography, *A Bridge through Time*, as a process of *becoming*. Once written, the self was then "frozen" on the page, taking on a reality not felt or experienced beforehand. She also said this is not the end, nor the ultimate experience of becoming, but provided another place from which to move on.

15. Arlie Hochschild (1983) writes of the rules for feelings which have to be managed when the actual emotion experienced is out of step (deviant) with what a person is *supposed* to feel. "We can experience it as a private mumbling to ourselves, the voice of a watchful chorus standing to the side of the main stage on which we act and feel" (pp. 57–58). Sophie, having prepared for the moment of the telephone call, did not "feel guilty, never": she had accomplished this debate, or "feeling work."

16. Jack Douglas 1984, especially pp. 77–79.

17. Winnicott 1965.

18. Freud posited that such repression is a necessary precondition for social life; see especially *Civilization and Its Discontents* (1961 [1930]). Another more profoundly sociological way of understanding the relationship between values held in the culture and those internalized and re-created by each individual is well expressed by David Pole 1961, pp. 19, 21, cited by Mary Douglas 1966: "The public code that makes and moulds the private conscience is remade and moulded by it in turn. . . . In the real reciprocity of the process, public code and private conscience flow together: each springs from and contributes to the other, channels it and is channelled. Both alike are redirected and enlarged" (p. 129).

19. Matza 1969, p. 12.

20. Sternberg 1986.

21. A slightly different rank ordering is produced when the proportions thinking this was of importance *of those who agree* with the statements, rather than the proportion of the total number of women and men, is calculated (see question 21, appendix A). Thus:

At First Liaison

	(A) Agree	(B) Important for Decision	Percentage (B) of (A)
Women			%
1. "Life was for living"	101	80	79
2. "My spouse and I had grown apart"	140	99	71
3. "Life felt very empty"	122	84	69
4. ". . . Sexual needs not being met . . ."	145	94	65
5. "I felt compelled by my emotions"	167	104	63
Men			
1. "Life was for living"	82	53	65
2. "I felt compelled by my emotions"	83	49	59
3. "I was curious about sex with someone else"	92	53	58
4. "With care, affair wouldn't harm marriage"	106	60	57
5. ". . . Sexual needs not being met . . ."	92	51	55

That life was for living now emerges as of the most importance for both those women and men who agreed with this statement; but, over all, the men still appear as slightly more careful in their deliberations and the women show a greater sense of yearning.

22. Carol Gilligan (1982) has illustrated the importance to women of continuity and connectedness as underpinning their moral choices compared with the importance of rationality and logic as underpinning those for men.

23. Ehrenreich 1983; and see chapter 4 in this book.

24. Joseph Pleck has explored the breadwinning role and consequent emotional commitment, as summarized in Pleck 1979.

25. Degler 1980.

26. Virginia O'Leary (1985, 1986) describes the emotions as "social constructs and individual innovations." People have to make cognitive decisions about the meaning of what they feel. Anger, for example, has to be understood in terms both of *intentionality* and of *wrong-doing*; otherwise the feeling is experienced or interpreted not as anger but as something else. This has to be learned. Children play not only at roles (being mothers and fathers, say) but also at emotions (being "in love" or "jealous" or "angry"). *What* you learn, O'Leary argues, depends fundamentally on whether you are a male or a female.

27. Alice Ellis 1983, p. 55 (Penguin ed.).

28. Jack Douglas 1984, p. 77.

29. Natalie Davis (1975 [1965]) describes festive occasions in France, for example, when the world was turned topsy-turvy, permitting roles to be reversed both sexually and politically, the women taking superior stances in all ways.

30. McBroom 1986. See also Laurel Richardson's (1985) discussion of the way professional women expect to be able to maintain control and to conduct a liaison with a married man by reversing the normal power relationships. While she found some women able to accomplish this, it was more typical for women to fall in love with their lovers and to be back where they have always been, waiting for him to ring, for his pleasure to satisfy theirs, and not the other way around. See also Lynn Atwater 1982.

31. Matza (1964) found that—contrary to contemporary opinion asserting that different values are held by different subcultural groups, and that this leads to less troubling moral dilemmas for delinquents—working-class boys, whether white or black, while they certainly do belong to a delinquent subculture, also conform to a wider set of ideals. That is, they are "morally bound" to the wider culture whether white and powerfully dominated or not. Therefore, to lessen guilt and, indeed, to commit criminal actions, this bond has to be neutralized. They have to debate. Thus, conflict rather than consensus typifies the social world, particularly in cultures with a florid pluralism, like America or Britain.

This florid pluralism, at least for certain age groups and perhaps for certain class and ethnic groups, means that conflict in cultural values is endemic. Yet certain overall values, such as those of the Myth of Romantic Marriage and, to a lesser extent, of the Myth of Me, are recognized by the vast majority. Indeed, Jack Douglas, too, speaking of the society now, supports the more widespread concern with the individual in such pluralism: "As internal social complexity, change and conflict grow, openness and identification erode and concern with the individual grows" (1984, p. 73). Thus, would-be adulterers must change the rules or debate them.

32. Thus, Matza: "The delinquent's . . . neutralization proceed[s] along the lines of negotiation of responsibility, the sense of injustice, the assertion of tort, and the primacy of custom" (1964, p. 61).

33. Jack Douglas 1984, pp. 79–80; see also p. 71 for an explicit use of Meadian theory.

34. A similar argument is often made as a *defense* for those who commit rape: that they were driven by their emotions and overwhelmed, not responsible for their

actions. Indeed, this may be reified as a new diagnostic category of the American Psychiatric Association (DSM-III-R) as a mental disorder called "Paraphilic Coercive Disorder AKA Rapism." At the same time, the men making this argument blame the woman whom they raped by insisting that she led them on, enticed them—again, as if they had no control over what subsequently occurred because of *her* actions. Using the example, not of rape, but of "kleptomania" or "compulsive theft," Donald Cressey (1962, pp. 451–52) explained that even such acts are motivated by the idea, by the "linguistic construct" the actor uses in explaining the action. There are only differences in *degree*, not in kind, in the extent to which actions are controlled by these words (or ideas) that have been learned from the social group. In a macho-dominated society, the rapist learns to use such arguments, just as in the idea of the woman who may be "overwhelmed and seduced," Douglas's beautiful girl finds her explanation. Because *he* has greater power than *her*, however, if she changes her mind (and this argument presumes a subject who *wills* outcomes), rape may be the dangerous result.

I am uncomfortable with Cressey's formulation in that he seems to avoid the *affect*, or feeling, that accompanies the idea, but it is possible to build emotion into the theory since feeling and thought have a reciprocal relationship.

35. During the Great Depression, working-class women were said to have sex with those who still had jobs while their husbands waited on the street corners or stood in queues for the dole. It was a means to recuperation and re-affirmation, taking a little joy for themselves (and perhaps some gifts—money, food, or clothing) as they kept the home together and "took charge." Their husbands, without work, lost everything that made them masculine. Whether similar reactions are occurring in the current crisis of unemployment in Britain is not known.

Chapter 6.   The *When*, the *Where*, the *How*, and the *Who*

1. Segal 1980.

2. Lodge 1984.

3. See a modern account of this pilgrimage which draws on contemporary texts by Pierre Barret and Jean-Noël Gurgans (1978).

4. For a marvelously illustrated account of life at the time of Chaucer, see Brewer 1978.

5. Reported in the London *Guardian*, 9 March 1985, from the Chinese official press as represented by *Women in China*.

6. Westermarck 1936, p. 274.

7. Frazer 1936 [1922], pp. 127–28, citing Florence Hewitt 1908.

8. Ibid., pp. 123–24.

9. The Lele illustrate the importance of place and person, too: there was also the custom of the "village-wife." These were women who were the "group-wives" to the men of a younger generation who could not yet acquire sufficient wives of their own to go around. The wives were still available to the old men, however, so long as they took them *in the bush*. Their children were treated as the children of the village. See Mary Douglas 1963 and Mair 1971, pp. 75, 151. And Luc de Heusch (1977 [1971]) shows that the social and generational groups were visible according to the way they were housed around the four sides of a square in the village; he notes that the old men

own both the women and the wealth, but they "give" one woman to the younger men as a "village wife" who then becomes available to the elders only if they take her "*in the forest*" (p. 85).

10. Mair 1971, p. 75, citing Mary Douglas 1963. The reasons for who is ashamed are complex, varying with the structure as well as the culture of each society.

11. Tolstoy 1964 [1878], pp. 560–66.

12. Tanner 1979, p. 187.

13. Westermarck 1934a, p. 284, citing Roscoe 1923.

14. Mair 1971, p. 147.

15. Mair (1971) reports that the children called all males visiting the house "lord," suggesting their status also as "paters." Should this fail, the wife's brothers or her husband could provide her children with "paters," a term defined by Bronislaw Malinowski (1929 [1962]) as the social father who gives his status, probably psychological meaning, and other benefits, such as inheritance, to the child; *genitor* he used to describe the man who biologically fathers the child. Obviously, in our own, and in many other cultures, these two aspects are found often or normally in one and the same person.

16. These crises (see appendix A, questions 23 and 24), known as "life events" by researchers in mental illness, occur with greater frequency in the lives of poorer people but can happen to anyone, are difficult to deal with, and may cause breakdown. Some are chronic difficulties such as long-term unemployment, bad housing, ill health. Others occur suddenly and may be resolved, such as losing a job but finding another, leaving a marriage for a lover, or, as in Grace's case, being evicted; but some are painful events that simply have to be "got over," such as the death of a beloved person. The best example of carefully conducted life-event research examining the effects of such events on depression in women is the work of G. W. Brown and Tirril Harris (1978) and their colleagues at the Bedford College Medical Research Unit. An excellent review of the literature is available in Thoits 1984.

Prospective studies that follow groups of people over time can differentiate those events that occurred before and those that result from an illness or, as here, before or from a liaison. Thus, a person saying he or she felt very tense at the time might be describing an effect rather than a precipitating event.

17. Helson, Mitchell, and Moane 1984.

18. See chapter 7 of this book, pages 208–9, for further support; and Annette Lawson and Colin Samson (1988) for the detailed argument for this case. In addition to the figures given here relating to the timing of the first liaison, changes in belief are also extensively explored.

19. The mean or average number of years waited by those who reported at least one liaison is 8.3 years; and the median or midpoint, at which equal numbers of people are found on either side—that is waiting less and more time—is 7.4 years.

20. The figures in the following table take account of the duration of the marriage by eliminating people from the calculation as they separated or divorced or as the number of years passed the maximum they could have been married given the date of marriage. Since some people "fool around" only as their marriage is disintegrating, and the two processes are deeply enmeshed, we asked respondents to define for themselves when they felt their marriage had ended. If they felt it had ended at the time of the separation rather than at the time of the divorce, they were then asked to account only for liaisons pre-dating the separation. In employing the respondents' self-definitions of the duration of their marriages, this calculation is thus a conservative measure of fidelity.

Proportion of Women and Men without a Liaison

Proportion remaining "faithful":	Year of First Marriage					
	Before 1960		1960s		1970 and later	
	Women %	Men %	Women %	Men %	Women %	Men %
After two years	95	93	89	85	72	81
After four years	87	83	83	80	61	75
After eight years	78	69	63	68	51	60
After ten years	75	70	53	57	46	48
After twelve years	74	64	43	49	58	55
After fourteen years	68	63	43	43	—	—
After twenty years	53	46	41	29	—	—
After twenty-two years	48	38	29	36	—	—
After twenty-five years	49	39	—	—	—	—
After thirty years	53	50	—	—	—	—

21. Marital conflict was estimated crudely by summing the answers to several questions. Each agreement with any of the following received a score of 1: "My spouse and I had grown apart"; "Life felt very empty"; "I had sexual needs not being met at the time"; and "My spouse and I did not discuss problems in our marriage." In addition, if the spouse disagreed with the respondent's own views on sexual fidelity in the marriage, they received another score of 1. Thus maximal conflict would be 5; no conflict, 0. Few received scores of 4 and 5; hence these two were combined to produce the following distribution for women and men:

Marital Happiness Score
for Women and Men

	Women %	Men %	
	%	%	
No conflict (0)	22	29	
Minimal conflict (1)	20	30	
Some conflict (2)	23	20	
Medium conflict (3)	19	13	
Maximum conflict (4 + 5)	16	8	
TOTAL N = 100%	253	162	(415)

Women reported more misery than men—a finding in keeping with the greater attention paid by women to their feelings and greater concern with this aspect of their lives. This score "makes more sense" of their extramarital lives than it does for men: women with higher conflict scores separate more than men with equivalent scores, remain less faithful over all, and have a first liaison with greater rapidity than similar men. These findings are compatible with the different roles of both marriage and adultery in the lives of women and men.

22. The main change occurred after the Divorce Reform Act of 1969 became effective in 1971 (*Social Trends* 1983).

23. There are no longer class differences in divorce rates because material diffi-

culties no longer prevent people from getting a divorce; this does not affect the economic *consequences* of divorce.

24. The difference in the timing of the first liaison according to *past* belief is highly significant. That is, those who recalled themselves at the time of their first marriages as most traditional and least permissive waited longest, while the least traditional waited the shortest time for the first liaison to take place. Over the period covered by the study (shorter for the youngest marriage cohorts and longest for the oldest group) about 30% of the respondents believed they had shifted direction, normally toward greater permissiveness or toward a stronger belief in the Myth of Me and a weaker one in the Myth of Romantic Marriage. This shift in attitude is another reason there is also an association between current attitudes and past behavior.

25. Yalom 1985; this argument is found in her concluding chapter.

26. See Nancy Chodorow's (1978) exposition of this theory.

27. Lawson, Robinson, and Bakes 1985.

28. Elliot Jacques (1965) gives a psychoanalytic understanding of the feelings both women and men may have around the thirty-fifth birthday.

29. Nichols 1981.

30. See the article by Richard Cordless in *Time* magazine, 16 November 1987, p. 9.

31. Atwater 1979, p. 41. Atwater's study of American women also found they did not believe in the possibility of an affair as they entered marriage.

32. Rosabeth Kanter has shown (1977; particularly in chap. 4 on secretaries) how the exigencies of the corporation and its reward systems actually encourage women in those jobs to be "just like women"—emotional, self-deprecating, and so forth; while the managers and executive jobs require quite different forms of behavior known as masculine.

33. Kanter (1977) found that the managers' wives were largely excluded except as decorative and supporting agents, particularly as entertainers of business acquaintances.

34. The women who were in full-time employment had their first liaison more quickly after marriage than other women (though this was not a significant difference), while men who were self-employed were the fastest with the first affair. Perhaps these men have a spirit of entrepreneurship, but it may also be that they are the Keiths of this world who travel and meet people through their work without being hedged about by the restricting knowledge and informal rules of the workplace.

35. Kanter 1977, p. 107.

36. Arlene Skolnick called her book about families and marriage *The Intimate Environment* (1983), choosing the feature that perhaps best defines families, not work.

37. Lisa Kraymer (1979, p. 17) says this is because a considerable strain is placed on the conjugal unit by higher expectations and because there is no need to go outside the home even for entertainment.

38. Quinn 1977, p. 44.

39. McBroom 1986, p. 231; see chap. 14, pp. 218–34. McBroom finds an interesting difference between her New York and her San Francisco sample: the former were more aware of the politics of such office affairs, while the San Franciscans spoke of personal damage—which she calls "ego-crucifying" (p. 233).

40. Kanter 1977, pp. 70–74, 80–84, 90–91, in chap. 4 on secretaries.

41. Kanter (1979, p. 91) argues that perhaps no other job category in the large corporation displays so vividly the constraints that give rise to characteristic behaviors, attitudes, and styles on the part of the workers. Secretaries were assumed to display the properties of "women as a group." But what they really displayed were the orientations of people whose strategies for achieving recognition and control were constrained by the social organization of their job.

42. Kraymer 1979, p. 29.
43. McBroom 1986.
44. Quinn 1977, p. 44.
45. Ibid., p. 42.
46. *Wall Street Journal*, 1986.
47. *Health Trends* 14 (2 [May 1982]): 29, table 1.
48. Hertz 1986. Melvyn Kohn and C. Schooler (1983) also argue that certain job conditions (though through the experience of self-directedness) *affect* personality— work can be constraining or enabling (p. 2).
49. MacKinnon 1988.
50. The figures are as follows:

Preferred Place for Sex with First Partner

	Women	Men
	%	%
PLACE		
Own home	31	19
Partner's home	22	41
Hotel	8	8
Other*	39	32
TOTAL N = 100%	174	128

* This category is large because it contains all those who gave more than one answer and various combinations of favorite places for making love.
These differences are highly significant ($p < .005$).

51. Richardson 1988, pp. 215–16.

Chapter 7.   Pleasures and Pains

1. The difference between the first and most recent liaison is statistically significant, but there is no difference in happiness between the women and men.
2. Being asked to think about the first and last sometimes meant that people felt they were writing only about relatively insignificant relationships. Occasionally people chose to write about the "one that changed my whole life"; thus, there may be a slight excess of serious or dramatic accounts. The questionnaire also had space for people to write about the overall happiness and unhappiness, to assess whether it had been, after all, "worth it," and to describe what, if any, had been the consequences for their marriages—questions 32(a) through (k).
3. Eckardt 1977, cited by Giele in Smelser and Erikson 1980.
4. Helen Lewis 1976, p. 170, citing Lichtenstein 1970. This argument is Reichian; see Wilhelm Reich 1945 and 1973 [1942].
5. These figures are based on the order produced according to the *total* numbers of women and men who said that they experienced each item during their first liaison. They could say that an item had brought pleasure *and* could rank it first, second, or third in importance. Thus, two lists were produced. This list includes anyone who

said "yes" and/or who ranked it but is a simple count; the order produced here does not take account of the respondents' own rankings:

The Pleasures of the First Liaison

	Women (N = 244) %	Order of Importance		Men (N = 165) %
Being loved	62	1	3=	50
Friendship	61	2	2	54
Sexual fulfillment	60	3	1	71
Loving	52	4=	5	39
Fun	52	4=	3=	51
Being needed	49	6	6	37
Being understood	39	7	9	27
Intellectual stimulation	38	8=	8	32
Enjoyable risk	38	8=	7	35
Freedom/independence	36	10	10	25

6. *New Woman*, October and November, 1986. Pat Miller, the magazine editor and publisher also said that "men like to exercise their sexual equipment" although no men were included in this sample, which is not representative of all American women. These quotes are from Louise Woo, "Women Set New Standards for Sexuality," in the *Oakland Tribune*, 6 October 1986, pp. C1, 3.

7. Shostak 1983.

8. Shostak, in a presentation, Institute for Research on Women and Gender, Stanford University, December 1986.

9. Shostak 1983, chap. 12, and pp. 381 n. 3, 288, 271.

10. Richardson 1986, pp. 58–59.

11. Ibid., especially chap. 9, p. 145 and passim.

12. Richardson 1988.

13. A correlation matrix for all those reporting at least one liaison against the benefits and sufferings listed in the first and (if appropriate) the most recent liaison shows guilt either toward the spouse or the children of the marriage as a persistent feature of those who thought they had "committed adultery." Guilt toward spouse < .001; guilt toward children < .001; deceit < .002; fear of being found out < .01.

14. The "adulterers" (men and women with the difference achieving significance at the p = < .04 level for women) discussed affairs less with their spouses *before* any liaison had occurred; and, even during the first affair, fewer of the men "adulterers" discussed it with their wives. More of these people (as compared with those in the sample who did not use the phrase "committed adultery" to describe themselves) also report that their wives and husbands *never* discovered this affair.

15. Christine Beverett reported by Raymon Coronado, *Oakland Tribune*, 19 and 21 August 1987.

16. The diagram sets out the differences between women and men who had had at least one affair, in the descriptions of their liaisons according to their adherence to the Myth of Romantic Marriage and/or to the Myth of Me, as indicated by their scores on traditional and permissive scales. These scores have been combined by grouping high traditional and low permissive and high permissive and low traditional scorers and the medium scorers of both groups:

	Women	Men
High Myth of Me [permissive]	one-night stand relationship casual affair brief encounter	one-night-stand relationship
Medium	extramarital relationships serious affair	brief encounter
High Myth of Romantic Marriage [traditional]	committing adultery	casual affair serious affair committing adultery extramarital relationships

Certain words are consistently used much more frequently by women than by men, and vice versa, and according to the extent to which people are traditional or permissive in their attitudes. Thus (at least in the past, because these measures relate to the point of first marriage), "casual affairs" are what highly traditional men but highly permissive women used to have.

17. Winnicott 1984, edited by Clare Winnicott et al., p. 32.

18. Hunt 1969. Arthur Miller, the playwright, notes that men blame themselves in America for unemployment (interviewed by Studs Terkel on National Public Radio, San Francisco, 9 April 1988, about his autobiography, *Timebends: A Life*). The same is probably true of men everywhere whose sense of identity is bound to their work.

19. These figures are derived in the same way as those for pleasures in note 5.

Pains of the First Liaison

	Women (N = 237) %	Order of Importance		Men (N = 158) %
Guilt to spouse	57	1	1	46
Deceit	52	2	3	39
Fear of being found out	45	3	2	44
Marriage hurt	31	4	4	37
Guilt to children	28	5	5	18
Own jealous feelings	20	6	7	10
Other's jealousy	16	7	6	14

20. Lamb and Hohlwein 1983, pp. 326–27.

21. Hunt 1969.

22. After, and with apologies to, Tolstoy, *Anna Karenina*.

23. We cannot distinguish between rhetoric and experience, but the way women and men use language has repeatedly been found to vary, especially with their status as superordinate and subordinate. Indeed, language use may reflect this *role* relation rather than gender, men in subordinate relation to other men using speech patterns that are more typically female. See, for example, Crosby and Nyquist 1977; and Thorne, Kramarae, and Henley 1983.

24. A randomly selected sample of questionnaires (100 of the women and 100 of the men) were examined; and the comments to question 32(b), inviting people to describe the aspects of the liaison that had made them happy and unhappy, analyzed.

25. Coveney, Kay, and Mahoney 1984.

26. Brunt 1982, pp. 143–70.

27. I am not suggesting Dr. Ruth encourages sadomasochism or activities that the woman cannot tolerate or that would seriously harm her. Dr. Ruth Westheimer, a national figure in the United States, speaks frankly about all sexual matters on radio and television, giving detailed advice about lovemaking techniques. On one show she said, "You know we talk about sex, here, right?"

28. Jong 1973.

29. See, for example, "The Sexuality Debates" in *Signs: Journal of Women in Culture and Society* 10 (11 [August 1984]): 142–58, introduced by Estelle B. Freedman and Barrie Thorne; Sue Cartledge and Joanna Ryan's edited 1983 volume; Ferguson, Philipson, Diamond, and Quinby, and Vance and Snitow, 1984; Gayle Rubin 1975, 1984; Tiefer 1987; and Valverde 1987.

30. Spender 1985, citing Ruth Herschberger 1970 and Susan Brownmiller 1985, pp. 178–82.

31. Indeed, Carole Vance called her book—a collection of papers, poems, and images originating at the Scholar and the Feminist IX Conference, "Towards a Politics of Sexuality," held at Barnard College on 27 April 1982—*Pleasure and Danger*.

32. Vance 1984, p. 79.

33. See the collection *Powers of Desire: The Politics of Sexuality*, edited by Snitow, Stansell, and Thompson (1983), especially Trimberger (p. 149), who shows that these are the same contradictions as were faced by left intellectuals in early twentieth century Greenwich Village, and they have yet to be resolved.

34. Peter van Sommers (1987) has recently shown that jealousy is a stigmatized emotion. In a period when possession of another human being is unacceptable, jealousy comes to represent a weakness or failure in the personality: the person who feels it is blamed for the feeling.

35. According to Simmel:
In regard to marriage forms, the decisive difference is between monogamy and bigamy, whereas the third or twentieth wife is relatively unimportant . . . for it is precisely the duality of wives that can give rise to the sharpest conflicts and deepest disturbances in the husband's life. . . . The reason is that a larger number entails a de-classing and de-individualizing of the wives, a decisive reduction of the relationship to its sensuous basis (since a more intellectual relationship also is always more individualised) (1950, "The Isolated Individual and the Dyad, 9: The Expansion of the Dyad," p. 139).

Chapter 8.   This Telling Business

1. Viorst 1976, pp. 38–39.

2. Michel Foucault argues (1980, vol. I) that self-disclosure, confession, and the knowledge of the other are the prerequisites of the modern love relationship. This requirement was stressed in (if not new to) the nineteenth century, which also saw the development of massive forms of public surveillance, as in the collection of information about populations (statistics was a nineteenth-century science) and the gathering together of people in institutions—hospitals, prisons—as well as in cities. The "discourse" about sex becomes a new form of control—setting the boundaries of the normal and directing desire through knowledge and speech: Foucault's power relation.

3. Some have argued that *required* self-revelation can be psychologically harmful (see Lieberman, Yalom, and Miles 1973). This supports Sissela Bok's assertion (see notes 12 and 13 in this chapter) that control over revelation and secrecy is necessary for sanity and freedom.

4. Foucault 1980, p. 63. In writing this book, I, too, form part of Foucault's description of the *Scientia Sexualis* which demands to be told: not just the fact of the

sexual act but the details, "thoughts that recapitulated it, the obsessions that accompanied it, the images, desires, modulations, and quality of the pleasure that animated it" (ibid.), so I certainly hope my work will not be employed in a worsening repressive "normalization" of the population.

5. Foucault 1980, pp. 61–62.

6. Ibid., p. 62. I think Foucault sees such positive effects because his imaginary dyads (or collectivities) consist of men or male-dominated institutions: they are seen through the imperious male eye with the collective "man" as actor. It does not matter that he writes of sexuality; he has nothing to say about women, about their will to knowledge (if it was present), or about their pleasures. The Church is the church of the priest with the penitent seeking to save *his* soul. Most penitents were, in fact, women, bidden to bear another baby or abstain from sex.

7. Phil Donahue is a television journalist who takes a theme usually based on someone's new book and discusses that theme with a studio audience on ABC. Since his program takes place during the day, normally the audience (and often the panel) consists overwhelmingly of women, as is the viewing public. This was true of the infidelity show. Hence the discussion was largely about husband's infidelity to wives.

8. Peggy Vaughan's infidelity support group is by no means the only one: they are dotted around the United States and hold meetings as well as run newsletters.

9. Work in other fields indicates that those in subordinate positions are more attentive to the needs, desires, and feelings of the superordinate. Faye Crosby and Linda Nyquist (1977) found that those in subordinate roles (citizen of either sex approaching a police officer, women approaching men, employee approaching employer) use pleading, unassertive linguistic strategies: for example, using the interrogative ending, as in "I think we should do it this way, shouldn't we?" The important fact is not gender but the *role* relationship. (Thorne, Kramarae, and Henley 1983.)

10. Tessa added that it was because she did *not* know me that she had felt comfortable contributing to the study. It was a form of confession without risk of punishment. Perhaps sociologists are the new confessors.

11. Ferne and her husband have many kinds of knowledge about one another, including *carnal knowledge*. The information she offers her husband tells of such knowledge that she now has of another man, and that this man has of her.

12. Bok 1982. Bok distinguishes between personal and private as well as between private and secret: for example, the private garden is not necessarily a secret garden; and while a marriage is personal, a great deal of it is not private but recorded in public offices (p. 11).

13. Bok 1982, p. 24. The holding of a secret that presses to be told is one of the reasons that people feel sick, lose weight, and vomit. It becomes a considerable burden to their sense of well being. But keeping a secret also gives people (such as Frieda or Sophie) considerable pleasure—a sense in the former of justifiable retribution for her husband's silence; and in the latter, of autonomy. In this case, it is unclear whether it is as much the keeping of the secret—an exercise of power—or the love affair itself that makes them "feel alive" and extraordinarily well.

14. For example, in parts of Central and South America and around the Mediterranean, a man who kills his wife (or her lover) is not pursued or, if pursued, is treated leniently. In France, until recently, the law distinguished between the murder by a man of his wife's lover and other kinds of murder. A woman who killed her husband's mistress did not have similar rights (see chapter 1, pages 42–49). Texas also, until 1973, had a special category of murder in such situations. And in many societies, "voluntary murder" committed upon "sudden quarrel or heat of passion" is a special category (Joan Robinson 1978).

15. See Blumstein and Schwartz 1983, pp. 268–72; and Kinsey et al. 1953, pp. 433–35. Kinsey did not obtain this information from the men in his study of male sexuality reported in 1948. Perhaps in the 1940s, male adultery was more clearly not the busi-

ness of wives that it has now become. In 1969, Morton Hunt found about one third knew and another third were suspicious (pp. 146, 121).

16. Since respondents were asked about their own liaisons, the figures all reflect the reactions of wives and husbands as reported by the adulterous spouse (see appendix A, questions 28(a) through (e) and 33(a) through (h). Additional information about the reaction of "victims" and of people who had had affairs themselves, but also recounted how they had felt on learning of a spouse's liaison, are derived from interviews, group discussions, and comments written on the questionnaires.

17. Of *all* those with at least one liaison, about 40 percent of the spouses never suspected.

18. Blumstein and Schwartz 1983, p. 270; Kinsey et al. 1953, p. 434.

19. There is also a significant decrease in the numbers of men who say their wives *never knew* about their liaisons: the proportions of men who believe their wives never knew drops from 44 percent of pre-1960s marriages to only 25 percent of those married in the 1970s.

20. Fourteen percent of pre-1960s, 27 percent of 1960s, and 55 percent of 1970s marriages.

21. Among those married in the 1970s, men who had a pact *to be faithful* were more likely to have wives who knew about their liaison than equivalent women in the sample (63 percent vs. 42 percent). But women with *no pact* were more likely to have husbands who knew than were equivalent men (69 percent vs. 33 percent).

22. Festinger's (1957) theory states that one cannot simultaneously maintain profoundly conflicting ideas and values without seeking resolution.

23. This despite the fact men believed that "with care it would be easy to keep the affair secret," and that "it is O.K. to have an affair if your spouse won't find out" significantly more often than did women (p < .05). Nonetheless, two thirds of men and three quarters of women disagreed with such statements, stressing the importance of honesty. In a representative poll carried out in California by a local radio station on the day Gary Hart withdrew from the Democratic nomination race for President on the first occasion, women ranked "to be honest" as the "best advice" their mothers ever gave them while men ranked it second.

24. At first marriage, nearly three times as many men as women believed they should be sexually free (16%:6%) and more than twice as many men as women believe in infidelity *now* (30%:12%). Those (especially women) who have had at least one liaison themselves and have stayed married to the same spouse believe *least* in fidelity either for themselves or for their spouses. People marrying in the 1970s for the first time believed most strongly in freedom at that time—18 percent compared with 2 percent of pre-1960s marriages. These are very substantial changes, especially for women. The following table shows the attitudes people held *at the time* of first marriage:

Marital Pacts by Year of First Marriage

| | Year of first marriage | | | | | |
| | Before 1960 | | 1960–69 | | 1970 or later | |
Pacts	Women %	Men %	Women %	Men %	Women %	Men %
To be faithful	48	37	49	45	43	44
To be free	2	1	2	8	18	17
None/other	50	62	49	47	39	39
TOTAL (N)	(100)	(71)	(129)	(77)	(86)	(64)

p < .001 for women across time and p < .01 for men across time.

25. Pepper Schwartz, interviewed for the *New York Times* by Trish Hall (1 June 1987), reported finding "a higher correlation with breakup if [women] told their husbands." Similarly, Lynn Atwater, in the same article reported the women in her study as "disturbed most by their deception." These findings from American samples clearly are precisely in line with those in this British sample.

26. Fifty-six people made new agreements to be sexually free, only six of whom did not have at least one liaison. Nine people also changed but toward monogamy. Nor did they all agree to tell. Thus, sexual freedom could be limited by a "no telling" pact. In practice, if a new pact was made, three quarters said their spouses knew about the liaison. This was especially marked for the men, of whom 85 percent said their wives knew compared with 60 percent of the women. Perhaps this is the "Ferne syndrome": women can hear about husbands' liaisons, but men cannot so readily reciprocate.

27. Looking at the figures another way, of those who discussed their liaisons, equal proportions of women and men (15 percent) said they were encouraged by their spouse both to start and to continue a liaison, but more men said they had been asked not to continue even after having been given permission to go ahead, and more women said they were told to continue but not to start an affair.

28. That is, 56 percent to 18 percent (p < .01). Women reported a similar, but much less marked, distinction for their husbands: 52 percent to 32 percent (n.s.).

29. Because people may hurt the spouse—an immoral act—they must engage in the same kind of reasoning as before breaching the marital boundary in the first place. It is, again, "emotional labor." Hence, the few people prepared to admit to telling because of "unkind" motives. To find a reason for being hostile oneself is to use a technique of neutralization; of justice ("she or he deserved this")—as it is to argue that the end justifies the means.

30. "Talking" as a desirable path to intimacy may well be class related: that is, especially for working-class men *as a group*, the ability and need to "communicate" feelings and to confess sexual secrets may be less than for middle-class men. It is, nonetheless, clear that Anne was distressed by her husband's departure and by the fact he did not tell her, himself, what was happening but left it to his sister to rescue him. Thus, women in each class are expected to deal with emotional troubles and to keep the family wheels turning.

31. Ian Robinson (1983, pp. 9–12) has described the way patients may be permitted to discover their diagnosis by a relative when they have been kept ignorant of it— sometimes on doctor's orders—as "managed discovery": a letter is left open, a telephone conversation is carelessly revealing, medical notes are made available. Indeed, nurses and doctors may employ similar strategies to manage the painful truth.

32. Lynn Atwater is reported by Trish Hall (*New York Times*, 1 June 1987) as saying that women had to "deliberately tone down their happiness" to avoid discovery and the likely consequence of breaking up.

33. Both women and men who accepted they were meant to be faithful, discussed the ins and outs of their possible liaison more with the future partner than did those without pacts and more than those with open marriages. The latter had no need of such discussion, but the faithful had a greater amount of "emotional work" to accomplish before they could "commit adultery." Only those with open arrangements discussed a possible liaison beforehand with a spouse; this figure is significant for men (p < .01) but even more so for women, half of whom in open marriages did so; but 80 percent of all other women did not.

34. Before a first liaison, both women and men who had pacts to be free talked to women other than their wives and potential partners more than did people without pacts or with fidelity pacts (p < .001 for men and p < .01 for women). It seems that those who are in open arrangements in their marriages are also quite open in other ways.

35. Komarovsky (1964, p. 135) had 64 percent of men and 24 percent of women with no confidante. Levinson (1978, p. 335) said having such a close relationship was "rarely experienced" by his men.

36. Thus, of men marrying before 1960, one third reported they had *no* confidante; but of those married most recently, only 16 percent had no one they described this way. Around half of *both* women and men now have more than one such person. It remains the case that women talk to their sisters and mothers more than men talk to any relative (21% to 8%). Whether one is unfaithful also makes a difference to the number and importance of the confidante, the faithful more frequently having no one (other than their spouse), and less often having many such people. They, perhaps, confide more in their spouses, as Mrs. Crowborough did.

37. Sutherland and Cressey 1974 [1924], p. 75.

38. For example, only 5 percent of faithful men and women believed "all or most" (the strongest statement) of their male friends, and only 2 percent believed all or most of their female friends, had ever had an affair. This compares with 10 percent of the people having one to three liaisons and about 28 percent of those having four or more believing this about their male friends, and 5 percent of those having one to three and 14 percent of those having four or more, thinking this was true of their female friends. These differences according to the number of liaisons are highly significant both for men and for women (p < .001).

39. Having a confiding relationship with a husband or partner was considered in one study to act as one of four factors that could, in the face of severe life difficulty, protect the person (the study was of working-class women in London) from depression (Brown and Harris 1978). Perhaps when a liaison prevents discussion in this way with the spouse, a confiding relationship with another woman provides the same kind of buffer, a way to deal with conflicting emotions.

40. Unless, of course, these trends shift back from talk and telling. AIDS might lead to a reduction in the number of sexual partners in liaisons, but it is uncertain what the effect will be on talk and telling. It will be important to be open about one's sexual partners, and there will continue to be a premium on truthfulness, but there will also be fear.

41. Women rarely spoke about affairs lasting less than three years.

42. Because men *as a group* hold greater power than do women, the husband does, in a sense, still have such authority. But not in the way that once he did in law; nor in the sense the father does over the child; nor, necessarily, in any given, particular relationship—for example, that between Sophie and her husband.

43. See *Self-Disclosure* by Gordon J. Chelune and associates (1979) and Cozby (1973) for a review of findings.

44. Ann Douglas, in 1977, depicted a changing American culture as having become "feminized." However, this "feminization" is a kind of sentimentality rather than a gaining of the finest of what might be included in the rubric *feminine*: "Feminization . . . guaranteed, not simply the loss of the finest values contained in Calvinism, but the continuation of male hegemony in different guises" (1977, p. 13).

45. Thanks to the members of Sociologists for Women in Society (1 May 1987) in Berkeley who suggested this. Francesca Cancian has used this phrase (derived from Douglas 1977) to argue for an "androgynous" love, one that would support not only the relational, talking, and self-disclosure (or expressive) aspects but what she terms the more "masculine" (or instrumental) aspects of love, the helping, active, and supportive tasks (1986, 1987).

46. *Criminal conversation* meant sexual intercourse, rather than a discussion of criminal matters. There is a nice irony in the phrase, given the subject matter of this chapter.

47. An unknown author railed against these cases in his book published about 1887; as did lords Lyndhurst and Brougham, and the Marquis of Lansdowne in the

House of Lords before the passage of the Matrimonial Proceedings Act of 1857, who thought it scandalous, especially since the married woman was not a party to them and could not defend herself or her reputation (see introduction and chap. 1). (*Crim. Con. Actions and Trials and Other Legal Proceedings relating to Marriage before the Passing of the Divorce Act*).

48. The matter of reputation was important at all levels of the "deeply hierarchical and misogynist society": G. R. Quaife, (1979), describes village life in Somerset between 1601 and 1660. Cuckolded peasant husbands would take the seducer of their wives to the local court, but the seducers would sometimes try to "prevent this fame," protecting "themselves by claiming they were defamed and taking the husband and wife to court" ("Attitudes to Adultery," chap. 5, p. 142).

49. Horstman 1985, pp. 9–10.

50. In this world, a woman's reputation, though not her life, was also at stake. The Marquise who plots with the Vicomte for the downfall of the virgin and the seduction of another man's pious wife, argues passionately that, as women are unequal, they require much greater skill to manage games of seduction: "Promises reciprocally given and received can be made and broken at will by you [men] alone" (Laclos 1985 [1781], p. 179). The woman's reputation (losing her virginity, becoming an adulteress) depends on her ownership by men. In both cases, they are to be conquered, the former virtually by rape.

51. Whether there has, in fact, been increased democratization is contentious. With high unemployment and an increased "feminization of poverty," the gap between rich and poor may be widening, while power to influence the political process may be narrowing into (for example) the hands of extremely rich and powerful lobbies and of the media. The *idea* of democratization is, however, without question, powerful.

52. On radio KGO in San Francisco (21 May 1987), the Gary Mora phone-in concentrated on evaluating Gary Hart—following accusations that he had "committed adultery" during his presidential nomination campaign—as a *friend*.

53. *Character* may include the idea of moral fibre. It was the word much more often used in the discussion about Gary Hart (see note 52, above). In radio phone-ins and the like at this time, it was clear that people were asking themselves and being asked, "Well, is he the kind of character you'd want as a friend?" His "womanizing" was his master status: that is, it defined his very essence (or *character*) more than any other attribute. This was the way to judge the next president.

54. Coward 1985, p. 138.

55. Goodman 1987.

56. Sometimes group sex does follow telling, or a *ménage à trois*. For the one such household in this study, everything (eating arrangements, bathrooms, household expenditure) was shared *except* sex. Rather, the man was shared between the two women—one his wife; the other, a paid "mother's help" of the same social background but in impoverished circumstances. Everyone, including the children, *knew* everything, but the sexual encounters were "behind closed doors" in either the wife's or the helper's bedroom. He flitted from bed to bed (see chapter 10, pages 297–99).

57. Talking about sex is often the precursor to sexual activity. I do not suggest that all telling represents an invitation to expand the boundaries of heterosexual to homosexual relationships, but I think it sometimes does. Similarly, discussing love affairs with a same-sex confidante may be a way to express repressed sexual feelings. See Rebecca Goldstein's novel, *The Mind-Body Problem* (1983, chap. 6). The married heroine spends an evening discussing her heterosexual love affair with her close woman friend and knows "if I had thrown out my arms and embraced her [. . .] she would have taken me" (p. 220). And in *My Secret Life*, the Victorian "gent" loved talking dirty as a precursor to or during his various sexual exploits.

58. Amis 1986, pp. 149–50.

59. At the time Lee had this liaison, she was in some conflict with Bud because she no longer *wanted* to have other sexual partners, and those she did want—casual "quick fucks"—he couldn't bear her to have. He wanted her to have sex with loving, good friends. Lee wanted to "settle down" and have a family. Having this relationship—which was, indeed, a loving one (see chapter 3, pages 91–92, 95–97)—with a very good friend—was to fit in with Bud's wishes; not to tell him was to exercise some power, some freedom of maneuver for herself.

60. Simmel 1950, "Secrecy, 3: The Fascination of Betrayal," p. 333.

61. I am grateful to Katrin Stroh for suggesting this. Hunt (1969) wrote: "Lovers yearn to confess" their affairs like a child's wish to have a "loving parent forgive his naughty deeds" (pp. 146–47). Lily Pincus and Christopher Dare have written about other family secrets (1976). The strong link between the secret and power relations is readily discernible in the family secret stressed most recently—incest or childhood rape, committed mainly by fathers and stepfathers or by the male lovers of adult women on their daughters. Diana Russell describes this in *The Secret Trauma* (1986).

62. Paul Ekman distinguishes between these as falsification and concealment lies, but both are lies if they are part of one person's deliberate intent to mislead another "without prior notification of this purpose, and without having been explicitly asked to do so by the target" (1985, p. 28).

63. Women certainly have not always done so, however. For some, access to such contraception remains difficult or too expensive; some have taken serious note of possible detrimental health effects. For others there are more complex reasons for becoming pregnant. These decisions have been made in the context of powerful attempts (for example by the Catholic Church) to prevent a takeover by women of the control of their own bodies and a separation of sexual pleasure from reproduction.

64. At least, these became, with decreasing legal and social stigmatization, much more visible.

65. One sign of this change is the fact that, under English law until divorce reform law came into effect in 1971, there had to be physical proof of adultery: photographs taken, testimony from chambermaids of beds slept in, stained sheets, and so forth. Now, "facts"—such as adultery—to demonstrate the irretrievable breakdown of the marriage are simply sworn to.

66. In the sense that anthropologists (Meyer Fortes 1962, Edward Evans-Pritchard 1965, Claude Lévi-Strauss 1969, 1976) use the term *exchange*: the father "gives his daughter to her husband; the woman brings her reproductive and productive labor to the marriage. Claude Meillassoux: "The social role of women begins at puberty with their potential reproductive capacities." "Through their marriage, women are taken out of circulation, consumed and used until their reproductive capacity is exhausted" (1981, pp. 76, 68). Such analyses miss all the other fundamental economic and political roles women have, but make the point. See critiques by Elizabeth Fisher (1979) who argues, "Aboriginal Australians had a reciprocal relationship" (p. 8); and Francis Korn 1973.

67. The same theory has been employed by Jennifer Pierce (1987) to explain the greater prevalence of depression among women than among men. For women, she suggests, pain is experienced from a *loss* of intimacy which threatens her whole gender identification. Intimacy, on the other hand, is threatening to the boy's gender identity because he achieves masculinity through separation and individuation; girls, through identification. If the changes noted in this study are widespread, and if both girls and boys are more often experiencing nurturant *fathers*, these differences might also diminish.

68. The oedipal phase, as Freud developed it, has been subject to much revision particularly so far as little girl's development is concerned, and it would look differ-

ent if parents were of the same sex. Nonetheless, the child cannot maintain the monopoly of devoted and powerful attachments and attention experienced and/or fantasized in early infancy.

69. Chodorow 1978; Miller 1986; Gilligan 1982; Dinnerstein 1976.

70. Goldstine 1977.

71. There may be four if both adulterous partners are married; but from the vantage point of the married adulterous partner, there are psychologically three.

72. Foucault (1973) used *le regard*, usually translated as "the gaze," to describe a new capacity to see, observe, and notice the human body in medicine. It seems peculiarly appropriate to me to describe the controlling and absorbed gaze of lovers seeking deep knowledge of one another; it calls to mind the old song "Drink to Me Only with Thine Eyes."

73. As cited in Bok 1982, pp. 38–39. Willie Fryer, at the age of fifteen, was told by his mother that she intended to leave his father, and that he (Willie) was to keep this secret from both him and his sisters. Later, both parents told him they intended to divorce, and *this* was the new family secret: "The greatest family project the Fryers ever undertook was the keeping of that secret." It caused him immense pain, his inability to control revelation and the requirement of secrecy splitting loyalties at the very base of his existence (Cottle 1980).

Chapter 9.   Power and Control

1. In practice, even fantasies are social. They take place within imaginable settings, on the basis of ideas gleaned from real life, from history, film, or drama, from books read, from accounts of other cultures, exotic images, stories heard, and so forth. Hence, the fact that hallucinations and delusions are culture-specific: that is, they vary not only with the personal history of individuals but according to the social world they inhabit. Hence, perhaps, the reputed frequency of fantasies among men of overcoming women's resistance to their advances and among women, of being overcome.

2. *My Secret Life*, 1966. The whole eleven volumes detail the anonymous author's use of power to take his pleasure.

3. For example, Maggie Scarf (1987) uses the mid-life crisis and psychodynamic explanation to understand all marital infidelity. She says there is an "inevitable biological and psychological push towards separation and individuation." This is true for children and "explains just why it is that marriages—paradoxically, it seems—become stronger and more intimate to the degree that the overall rules of the interactional system permit the partners to be separate and different people." "Projective identification," when an internalized part of the self is split off and projected onto the other at the same time as one identifies with the other because one has attributed qualities or imagined qualities of one's own to them, is the Kleinian concept Scarf thinks "most useful" (extract, *Atlantic Monthly*, November, p. 51). In this explanation, we can see aspects of the Myth of Me made explicable in psychological, scientific terms.

4. Clark 1987, p. 15.

5. Coward 1985, p. 184.

6. Ibid.

7. Ibid., pp. 199–204. This is the sense in which women frequently fantasize about what Coward describes as "nearly rape"; but it is not rape because in fantasy, the man who overcomes her resistance is *chosen* by the "victim"; also the experience is

pleasurable to the woman—regardless of whether it is also pleasurable for him. The woman *controls* absolutely the outcome of her own fantasy. In real-life rape, of course, she is (unless trained otherwise) wholly powerless, and her very life is at risk.

8. Clark 1987, p. 14.

9. See chapter 1 for modern law. The five states within America that do *not* have adultery as a crime still on their statute books, also continue to have acts against *crim. con.* and the theft or "alienation of a wife's affections." Although cases are rare, they are still being brought. In Utah—the conservative, Mormon state—as recently as 1984, a husband, who was acknowledged to be a drunkard and violent, won an award of $84,600 because of his wife's adulterous relationship with another man; the grounds were alienation of his wife's affections. The Utah Supreme Court upheld the cause of action but reversed the trial court's decision on procedural grounds (Steffensen 1984, p. 893). In August 1986, in New York, a married woman was arrested and charged with adultery under the 1909 state law. The charges were dropped but not until she and her lover had pleaded guilty to harassment, a lesser charge. It was the husband who found his wife and her lover in bed in his house and, as we might expect, who brought suit. He took photographs which his wife and her lover tried to recover by physically attacking him (report from Corning, New York).

10. This represents about 3 percent of all liaisons. The thirty-nine people reporting own-sex liaisons had about ninety-five such affairs, or between two and three per person.

If, as a result of a homosexual liaison, the marriage is abandoned, then, of course, the problems faced by all the participants are severe. This is so when the new partner is of the opposite sex, too; but there are additional problems of social acceptability and, for the children, of understanding what special meaning the homosexual relationship might have for them. Grandparents are often even more distressed and uncomprehending than they are in the "normal" divorce, and legal guardianship and custody are more likely to be fought over. But the children's experience in any divorce is often chaotic as they deal with splitting parents, new homes, and new adults—perhaps new siblings, too.

11. Jean Baker Miller 1986, p. 115; see also chaps. 10 and 11, pp. 115–42.

12. Ibid., pp. 116–17.

Chapter 10.   The End of the Affair

1. Those who separate are not *more* concentrated among the most permissive than they are among the most traditional. Indeed, 82 percent of permissive men and 65 percent of permissive women remained married to their first spouses. Faithful people of both sexes in traditional marriages (around 75 percent) also stayed married. Rather, it is those who change position (*relative* to others) who have the most separation, divorce, and remarriage. These are people for whom pursuing the good life in search of self did not work or who, having found someone different, feel it will not continue to work. Similarly, it is those people whose marriages failed to fit a traditional model, or who could not live by it, who changed position. The conflict internally and externally with a forbidding society, as Dan and Ross Ash described (see chapter 1), can be overwhelming.

2. The table shows the relationship between the number of liaisons and the likelihood of divorce:

Number of Liaisons	Married to First Spouse at Time of Study	Divorced, Separated from First Spouse*	
	(N)	(N)	
None	71% (103)	29% (42)	
One to three	56% (129)	44% (100)	
Four or more	51% (89)	49% (84)	
All	59% (321)	41% (226)	100% (N = 547)
		$p < .01$	

* Remarried not separately shown.

3. A recent study (see Norton and Moorman 1987) has found remarriage rates for American women falling still further.

4. There are some signs that masculinity has wider definitions in recent years (see Franklin 1984).

5. In Sweden, recent reports suggest a society where marriage is disappearing but intimate and long-term relationships remain highly valued (see David Popenoe 1987).

6. Wallerstein and Corbin 1986; Weitzman 1981, pp. 278–81.

7. Weitzman 1981, p. 280. Wallerstein also says many of the fathers in her sample continued to see their children regularly even while continuing to refuse to help them. They take on the attitudes of some who feel children *should* pay their own way but often have not prepared for the expense ahead: no "thinking time" or psychological preparation has been put to the problem that probably would have been extended to it in the intact family (personal communication, April 1988).

8. See, for example, Toufexis 1987, p. 75.

9. See Richardson 1985, 1988.

10. Coward 1985, p. 141.

11. Ibid., pp. 13–14.

12. Ibid., p. 184.

13. Sometimes this was recognized by professional helpers: Tarquin, in his misery at his wife's breach of contract; Amelia, with her deep distress about her husband's affair with a friend of hers; and Ian and Audrey, facing her profound changes—all were being advised to consider separation. Still, separation was, as I have already suggested, no panacea.

14. See Vargas Llosa (1986, p. 143), who cites this passage and discusses this role reversal.

15. In Tolstoy's *Anna Karenina*, only one chapter is titled, and that one is "Death."

16. Simmel, "The Triad," pp. 145–69, in Wolff 1950, pp. 154–62.

17. See Caplow 1959 and Caplow 1968, pp. 19–20.

18. Simmel, "The Dyad," pp. 122–26, in Wolff 1950, p. 123.

19. Kundera 1984, p. 115.

20. See Hansen 1987.

21. Hawthorne, *The Scarlet Letter*, first published 1850.

22. See Lasch 1977 for America and Mount 1980 for England, representing the view that the family needs protection from state intervention; and Barrett and Mac-Intosh 1982, representing the opposing position. A third, Foucaultian approach is presented by the French writer Jacques Donzelot in his *Policing of Families* (1979). Most recently, the whole concept of the private-public dichotomy is under question; see, for example, the debate between Mensch and Freeman and Paul Starr in the columns of *Tikkun*, March/April 1988.

23. Keays 1985.

24. Conor Cruise O'Brien noted that Sara Keays was, unlike many predecessors,

"a woman of some importance," daughter of an army officer, but her struggle was bound to fail all the same (*The Observer*, 16 October 1983).

25. Ephron 1983.

26. Justice Allen Ginsberg was forced to retire from the nomination because it became known he had "abused" marihuana. Note the drug had not been "smoked" but "used" or "abused": thus was the act constructed as incriminating.

27. Tisdall was prosecuted, on 10 January 1984, found guilty, and sent to prison for six months, and the newspaper (the *Guardian*) to which she leaked her story forced to reveal its sources. Wright was prevented, by the British government's pursuit of him in the courts, from publishing *Spycatcher* in Australia, and it may not be sold in Britain or serialized in newspapers or its contents divulged in broadcasts, although it has been published in America (1987) and is freely available on coffee tables throughout Britain—that is, among those who can afford to travel or know people who do.

28. Zuboff 1988.

29. San Francisco and Bay Area, April 1988.

30. Gagnon and Simon 1973, p. 304, and their last chapter, pp. 303–7.

31. With a condom and a negative AIDS test, the risk was calculated at one in five *billion* (Hearst and Hulley 1988, reported in the *New York Times*, Friday, 22 April, pp. A1 and 6, Philip Boffey, "Researchers List Odds of getting AIDS in Heterosexual Intercourse").

32. More research has been published about attitudinal than behavioral change, but Professor Tony Coxon at University College in Cardiff and Ray Fitzpatrick at Nuffield College in Oxford find few signs of behavioral changes. See *Psychological Bulletin*, Spring 1988, for the evidence that *group* organization is most effective. (See especially Abrams and Abrams 1988, p. 47, citing C. Bradbeer 1987, "HIV and Sexual Lifestyle," *British Medical Journal* 294: 5–6; and p. 48, where Lorraine Sherr reports that knowledge did not, but perceived personal risk did correlate with change to condom use.) See also Temoshok, Sweet, and Zich 1987.

Chapter 11. A New Story?

1. Cited in *Time* magazine, 16 November 1987, p. 9, by Richard Cordless.

2. Ickeys 1985, pp. 187–208. He calls the statement "Happiness is a feminine marriage partner," the femininity hypothesis. He takes this from J. K. Antill 1983.

3. Survey conducted for *GQ*, reported by Karen Peterson, *USA Today*, 24 March 1988, p. 1.

4. Chaucer, *Canterbury Tales*, the "Wife of Bath" prologue, 1973 ed., pp. 288, 289, 294, 298.

5. Ibid., p. 304.

6. The anthropologist Francis Hsu (1972 [1961]) divided the world according to different axes of love: the Western world was dominated by husband-wife love; much of Africa, by that between brothers; India, by mother-son love; and so forth. Marion Levy, in the same volume (pp. 33–41), points out that the parent-child category (not one of Hsu's categories) is another major, if not dominant, axis in the West. See also Hsu 1971, p. 29.

7. Moore and Butler, forthcoming, "Predictive Aspects of Non-verbal Aspects of Courtship Behavior in Women," *Semiotica*.

8. Eliasoph 1987, p. 85.

9. Dinnerstein 1976. Also part of the logic of Nancy Chodorow's (1978) work.

10. "*Vive la différence*," they say. Friedan in 1985 suggested the women's movement should "celebrate difference" (*New York Sunday Times Magazine*, 3 November 1985, p. 26).

11. Elaine Hatfield argues that both women and men seek to achieve a separate identity *simultaneously* with deep intimacy; for men, the former and for women, the latter goal is easier (1983, pp. 106–34).

Appendix B

1. Bernard in Bohannan 1971, p. 21. Lonny Myers (1976) felt it timely to stress the positive aspects of extramarital sex if only for the "relatively sophisticated, middle-class and upper middle-class, urban marriage partners"; while many of the chapters in Smith and Smith's *Beyond Monogamy* (1974) appear to attempt a similar program, these authors preferring the term *comarital relationship*. Other researchers—such as Hunt 1969, Yablonsky 1979, and McGinnis 1981—have regarded the term *extramarital relationship* as "ambiguous."

2. *Sunday Times* (London), 8 March 1981, p. 38; *Guardian*, 22 November 1982, p. 10; *Sunday Mirror*, 19 December 1982, p. 11, and 2 January 1983, p. 19.

3. Tom Douglas (1983) makes the point that groups are essentially similar rather than dissimilar: "There are no absolute differences between apparently widely disparate groups" (p. 1). There are differences largely of scale. All groups, for example, must have time, whether the immensely long time of membership of a family or much shorter time on a committee; and all exhibit leadership, by individuals or groups within the groups. Douglas's purpose, he says, is "to try to divert some . . . attention to a recognition of existing group situations where the same skills that are essential to the 'created' group can be used for less obvious but equally useful and productive group work" (p. 4). Alas, he, like most others, fails to address the research as a "created" group, writing, in the main, of the processes noticed in therapeutic settings; but among others who have are: Banks 1957; Chandler 1954; and Hoinville and Jowell 1978.

4. See, for example, Stanley and Wise 1983; and Gamarnikow, Morgan, Purvis, and Taylorson 1983.

5. Richardson 1985, pp. 235–39.

6. *Social Trends* no. 12 (1983), table 6.2. See Lawson and Samson 1988, note 7, p. 435, for a further description of the sample.

7. Elizabeth Roberts 1984, p. 80.; Chamberlain 1983, chap. 4. See also Seabrook 1982, especially chaps. 12 and 13.

8. The median age is forty-one years. The table below shows a comparison of the age distribution of the study respondents with the United Kingdom population, excluding those aged under twenty years.

Age Group	Adultery Respondents		United Kingdom Population %
	Sunday Times %	Guardian %	
20–34	18	29	31
35–44	36	38	17
45–54	27	21	15
55–59	7	6	8
60–64	5	4	7
65–69	3	1	7
Over 69	4	0	14
	100%	100%	100%
N =	255	215	37,459,835

Source: United Kingdom population figures derived from General Household Survey 1981, no 11, p. 6, table IE.

9. Le Roy Ladurie 1978; Laslett 1977.

10. Census 1981, Preliminary Report for Towns; England and Wales.

11. Platt 1981.

12. Much modern sociology has become concerned with the analysis of accounts only, arguing that the relationship between accounts and the actions they describe can never be known, or that the knowledge is corrigible. Peter Halfpenny (1984), in a review of Nigel Gilbert and Peter Abell's (1983) collection, however, points out that such an approach suffers from a loss of inferential nerve and: "In the course of their empirical studies, they [many of the contributers to the volume] encountered the difficulties of making inferences from accounts to actions and of the corrigibility of both accounts and descriptions of actions, but *for the success of their work* [my italics] they still made inferences" (p. 134). For the success of this work, I make numerous inferences, providing, I hope, sufficient evidence for the reader to conclude similarly or to be enabled to contradict those inferences. To do this, I appreciate that we (author and reader) will draw, each of us, on a stock of (probably) shared methods and practices that themselves normally go largely unarticulated. We will use the "members" methods of reasoning, including perhaps, the "proto-science" employed both by the Cro-Magnon and next year's journals (according to Michael Moerman 1974); it is a rationalist critique which has to be employed in facing ethnomethodology. The other argument is more pragmatic: this says that the accountist position, despite its critical edge which has been influential and useful to sociology, is uninteresting—anyway for me, because, inter alia, it does not permit me to pose the questions I wish to pose, and "it involves no predictions about social conduct and confines itself to naturalistic, retrospective descriptions of the procedures which members use in the construction of social order" (Rojek 1983, p. 129).

13. David Martin 1967, p. 36. This figure does not appear to have altered much, although approximately 4.5 percent of people who attend places of worship are Jews (*Europa Year Book*, 1987, pp. 2866–68).

14. The following figure shows the religious affiliations and beliefs of respondents:

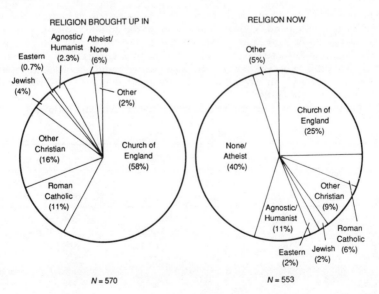

RELIGION BROUGHT UP IN

Eastern (0.7%)
Agnostic/ Humanist (2.3%)
Atheist/ None (6%)
Jewish (4%)
Other (2%)
Other Christian (16%)
Church of England (58%)
Roman Catholic (11%)

N = 570

RELIGION NOW

Other (5%)
Church of England (25%)
None/ Atheist (40%)
Other Christian (9%)
Agnostic/ Humanist (11%)
Roman Catholic (6%)
Eastern (2%)
Jewish (2%)

N = 553

15. The importance of religion or a belief system in the life of respondents is shown in the following figure:

Not Important at All (32%)	Unim-portant (13%)	Fairly Unimportant (20%)	Fairly Important (21%)	Important (14%)

0%   100%

N = 567

16. *Social Trends*, no. 11 (1981), p. 93, table 5.1.

17. The number of children ever born to the women married for the first time in the years 1965 to 1969 inclusive:

Number of Children	National Population (Data collected 1980)	Adultery Study (Data collected 1982–83)
0	7%	9%
1	13%	10%
2	51%	54%
3	20%	18%
4 or more	9%	9%
	—	N = 68

SOURCE: Personal Communication, Office of Population, Censuses and Surveys, 1982.

The figures are close but the adultery sample has slightly fewer children. The age of the national sample is not known. The women in the adultery sample married between 1965 and 1969 ranged in age from thirty-two to forty-eight years and are, as we know, of a higher social class than a national sample. These two facts are sufficient to explain any differences. Alternatively, perhaps larger numbers of children reduce the "risk of adultery": one respondent said hers acted as "effective chaperones." Another said she had no time!

18. Marital status (excludes those under twenty-five years and widowers):

	Men			Women	
	Adultery Respondents	National Population		Adultery Respondents	National Population
Single	4%	13%	Single	2%	11%
Married and separated	85%	83%	Married and separated	79%	84%
Divorced	11%	4%	Divorced	19%	5%
	100%	100%		100%	100%
N = 228			N = 327		

SOURCE: *Social Trends*, vol. 13 (1983), p. 13, table 1.3.

The figures show that the adultery sample contains an excess of married, separated, and divorced over single (that is, never married) people.

19. In 1980, 71 percent of divorce petitions were filed by wives. Adultery was still the "preferred" fact for husbands to cite in divorcing their wives, followed by a two-year separation with consent. For wives, the "preferred" fact was the unreasonable behavior of their husbands, followed much less commonly by adultery, and then by a two-year separation with consent. (Office of Population, Censuses and Surveys, "Marriage and Divorce Statistics" (1980), Series FM2 no. 7, table 4.7 (p. 93).

20. See, for example, McIntosh 1977 and Davis 1963.

21. The snowball group contains a greater proportion of respondents who fall within social classes II and III (nonmanual) than other source groups. However, over all social classes I, II, and III (nonmanual), this discrepancy is evened out.

22. Marital status—a comparison between self-selected, non-self-selected sources, and the national population:

	Snowball	All Self-Selected	National Population
Single	0%	2%	12%
Married and separated	68%	84%	83%
Divorced	32%	14%	5%
N =	42	513	—

23. Fifty-eight percent of the snowball group reported either that they had had no sexual relations before marriage, or that they had had sexual relations only with their future spouse. This was so for only 46 percent of *Sunday Times* respondents, and 43 percent of *Guardian* respondents.

24. The following is a summary of the percentages from each source group according to low, medium, and high scores on each traditional/permissive scale—that is, to the Myth of Romantic Marriage and the Myth of Me:

	Adherence to Traditional Values (Myth of Romantic Marriage) Then			Adherence to Permissive Values (Myth of Me) Then			Adherence to Traditional Values (Myth of Romantic Marriage) Now			Adherence to Permissive Values (Myth of Me) Now		
	Low %	Medium %	High %	Low %	Medium %	High %	Low %	Medium %	High %	Low %	Medium %	High %
Sunday Times	37	36	27	34	30	36	32	39	29	24	40	37
Snowball	21	35	44	40	37	23	19	42	40	37	37	26
Guardian	33	33	33	33	31	36	36	28	36	35	30	36
Sunday Mirror	21	28	51	37	33	30	19	35	46	53	28	19
All sources	33	34	33	34	31	34	31	35	34	32	35	34

25. Discussion of adulterous liaisons with others—a comparison between sources (each figure represents the percentage of respondents who *did* discuss an adulterous liaison):

Discussion before affair [N = 530]	*Sunday Times* %	Snowball %	*Guardian* %	*Sunday Mirror* %
with:				
Spouse	21	10	28	16
Same-sex friends	23	18	23	30
Opposite-sex friends	6	8	9	5
Same-sex work colleagues	11	5	9	14
Opposite-sex work colleagues	3	8	3	3
Potential lover	37	26	34	23
Professional helpers	6	0	5	5
Religious advisors	2	0	2	2
Discussion during affair [N = 410]				
with:				
Spouse	24	9	33	17
Same-sex friends	37	41	34	25
Opposite-sex friends	14	12	15	6
Same-sex work colleagues	20	12	16	19
Opposite-sex work colleagues	6	9	10	8
Potential lover	40	44	38	19
Professional helpers	12	6	15	14
Religious advisors	7	0	3	3

26. Atwater 1982, p. 31.

27. Blumstein and Schwartz 1983, p. 273. Given that they interviewed married *couples*, but that equal numbers of husbands and wives did not respond to this question, some must have refused to reply.

Bibliography

Abell, Peter. 1983. "Accounts and Action: Surrey Conferences on Sociological Theory and Method I." *British Journal of Sociology* 18 (1): 134.

Abrams, Dominic; and Abraham, Charles. 1988. "Social Psychology and the Spread of AIDS." *The Psychologist* 1 (2 [February]): 47.

Allgeier, Elizabeth Rice; and McCormick, Naomi B. 1983. *Changing Boundaries: Gender Roles and Sexual Behavior*. Palo Alto, Calif.: Mayfield.

Amis, Kingsley. 1986. *The Old Devils*. London: Hutchinson.

Antill, J. K. 1983. "Sex Role Complementarity versus Similarity in Married Couples." *Journal of Personality and Social Psychology* 45: 145–55.

Araji, Sharon. 1977. "Husbands' and Wives' Attitude-Behaviour Congruence on Family Roles." *Journal of Marriage and the Family* 39: 309–20.

Ariès, Philippe; and Béjin, André, eds. 1985. *Western Sexuality: Practice and Precept in Past and Present Times*. Translated by Anthony Forster. Oxford: Basil Blackwell.

Armstrong, Judith. 1976. *The Novel of Adultery*. London: Macmillan.

Armytage, W.; Chester, Robert; and Peel, J., eds. 1980. *Changing Patterns in Sexual Relations*. London and New York: Academic Press.

Ash, R. 1981. "How Not to Break Up Two Marriages." London *Sunday Times*, 10 May.

Askham, Janet. 1976. "Identity and Stability in the Marriage Relationship." *Journal of Marriage and the Family* (August): 535–47.

———. 1984. *Identity and Stability in Marriage*. London: Tavistock.

Atwater, Lynn. 1979. "Getting Involved: Women's Transition to Extramarital Sex." *Alternative Lifestyles* 2 (1 [February]): 33–68.

———. 1982. *The Extramarital Connection: Sex, Intimacy and Identity*. New York: Irvington.

Augustine. *Commentary on the Sermon on the Mount*. Translated by Denis J. Kavanagh, 1951. Fathers of the Church, vol. 11. New York: Catholic University of America.

———. *The Retractations*. Translated by Mary Inez Bogan, 1968. Fathers of the Church, vol. 60. Washington, D.C.: Catholic University of America.

———. *Works*. Edited and translated by Marcus Dods, 1871. Edinburgh: T. & T. Clark.

———. *Works, The City of God*. Edited by R. V. G. Tasker, 1950. Everyman Edition. London: Dent; New York: E. P. Dutton.

Banks, Joseph Ambrose. 1957. "The Group Discussion as an Interview Technique." *Sociological Review* 5 (1): 75–84.

Banks, Olive. 1986. *The Face of Feminism*. Oxford: Basil Blackwell.

Barker, Diana Leonard. 1980. "Sex and Generation." In Diana Leonard Barker and Sheila Allen, *Dependence and Exploitation in Marriage*. London: Tavistock.

Barker, Diana Leonard; and Allen, Sheila. 1980. *Dependence and Exploitation in Marriage*. London: Tavistock.

Barret, Pierre; and Gurgans, Jean-Noël. 1978. *Priez pour nous à Compostelle*. Paris: Hachette.

Barrett, Michele; and MacIntosh, Mary. 1982. *The Anti-Social Family*. London: New Left Books.

Barthes, Roland. 1972 [1957]. *Mythologies*. Translated by Annette Lavers. London: Jonathan Cape.

———. 1977. *Roland Barthes*. Translated by Richard Howard. New York: Hill & Wang.

Becker, Ernest. 1973. *Denial of Death*. New York: Free Press.

Bedier, Joseph. 1965. *Tristan and Isolde*. Translated by Hilaire Belloc and Paul Rosenfeld. New York: Vintage Books.

Belenky, Mary Field; et al. 1986. *Women's Ways of Knowing: The Development of Self, Voice, and Mind*. New York: Basic Books.

Bell, Robert; and Buerkle, Jack V. 1970. "Mother and Daughter Attitudes to Premarital Sexual Behaviour." In Ailon Shiloh, ed., *Studies in Human Sexual Behavior: The American Scene*, pp. 130–34. Springfield, Ill.: Charles C. Thomas.

Bell, Robert; and Peltz, Dorthyann. 1973. "Extramarital Sex among Women." *Medical Aspects of Human Sexuality* 8 (3 [March]): 10–40.

Bellah, Robert N; Madsen, Richard; Sullivan, William; Swidler, Ann; and Tipton, Steven. 1985. *Habits of the Heart*. Berkeley: University of California Press.

Bengis, Ingrid. 1976. "Love." In James Leslie McCary and Donna R. Copeland, eds., *Modern Views of Human Sexual Behaviour*. Chicago: Science Research Associates.

Benson, Douglas; and Hughes, John A. 1983. *The Perspective of Ethnomethodology*. London: Longman.

Berger, Peter; and Kellner, Hansfried. 1970. "Marriage and the Construction of Reality." *Recent Sociology* 2: 49–72. New York: Macmillan.

Bergmann, Barbara. 1986. *The Economic Emergence of Women*. New York: Basic Books.

Berk, Richard; and Berk, Sarah Fenstermacher. 1979. *Labor and Leisure at Home: Consent and Organization of the Household Day*. Beverly Hills, Calif.: Sage.

Berk, Sarah Fenstermacher, ed. 1980. *Women and Household Labor*. Beverly Hills, Calif.: Sage.

Bernard, Jessie. 1971. "No News but New Ideas" Introduction to Paul Bohannan, ed., *Divorce and After*. Garden City, N.Y.: Doubleday Anchor.

———. 1972. *The Future of Marriage*. New Haven: Yale University Press.

Blackstone, Sir William. 1976 [1915]. [1765–69]. *Commentaries*. Edited by William C. Jones. Baton Rouge, La.: Claitor Publishing.

Bleek, W. 1977. "Young Parents and Children in a Kwahu Lineage." Legon Family Research Papers, no. 4, Family Welfare and Planning, I.A.S. Legon Accra.

Blood, Robert O.; and Wolfe, Donald M. 1960. *Husbands and Wives*, Glencoe, Ill.: Free Press.

Blumstein, Philip; and Schwartz, Pepper. 1983. *American Couples*. New York: William Morrow.

Blythe, Ronald. 1978. *The View in Winter*. New York: Harcourt Brace Jovanovich.

Bock, Kenneth. 1980. *Human Nature and History: A Response to Sociobiology*. New York: Columbia University Press.

Boffey, Philip. 1988. "Researchers List Odds of Getting AIDS in Heterosexual Intercourse." *New York Times*, 22 April, pp. A1, A6.

Bohannan, Paul, ed. 1971. *Divorce and After*. Garden City, N.Y.: Doubleday Anchor.

Bok, Sissela. 1978. *Lying: Moral Choice in Public and Private Life*. New York: Pantheon Books.

———. 1982. *Secrets: On the Ethics of Concealment and Revelation*. New York: Pantheon Books.

Bradbeer, C. 1987. "HIV and Sexual Lifestyle." *British Medical Journal* 294: 5–6.

Brake, Mike. 1982. *Human Sexual Relations: Towards a Redefinition of Sexual Politics*. Harmondsworth, England: Penguin.

Brannen, Julia; and Moss, Peter. 1987. "Fathers and Employment." In Charlie Lewis and Margaret O'Brien, eds., *Reassessing Fatherhood*. London: Sage.

Brewer, Derek. 1978. *Chaucer and His World*. London: Eyre Methuen.

Brinkgreve, Christien. 1982. "On Modern Relationships: The Commandments of the New Freedom." *The Netherlands Journal of Sociology* 18: 47–56.

Bromley, Peter Mann. 1971. *Family Law*, 4th ed. London: Butterworths.

———. 1981. *Family Law*, 5th ed. London: Butterworths.

Brookner, Anita. 1984. *Hotel du Lac*. London: Jonathan Cape.

Brown, George W.; and Harris, Tirril. 1978. *The Social Origins of Depression*. London: Tavistock.

Brown, P.; and Jordanova, L. 1982. "Oppressive Dichotomies: The Nature/Culture Debate." In Elizabeth Whitelegg et al., eds., *The Changing Experience of Women*, pp. 389–400. Oxford: Martin Robertson, in association with the Open University.

Brownmiller, Susan. 1985 [1984]. *Femininity*. New York: Linden Press, Simon & Schuster.

Brunt, Rosalind. 1982. "An Immense Verbosity: Permissive Sexual Advice in the 1970's." In Rosalind Brunt and Caroline Rowan, eds., *Feminism, Culture and Politics*, pp. 143–70. London: Lawrence & Wishart.

Burch, E. 1971 [1970]. "Marriage and Divorce among the North Alaskan Eskimos." In Paul Bohannan, ed., *Divorce and After*. Garden City, N.Y.: Doubleday Anchor.

Burgoyne, Jacqueline. 1982. "Contemporary Expectations of Marriage and Partnership." In *Change in Marriage*. London: National Marriage Guidance Council.

Cabrol, Ferdnand; and Leclerq, Henri. 1907. *Dictionnaire d'archéologie chrétienne et de liturgie*, tom. 1, part 1. Paris: Letouzey et Ane.

Caffrey, Kate. 1976. *The Edwardian Lady*. London: Gordon & Cremonesi.

Campbell, B. H., ed. 1972. *Sexual Selection and the Descent of Man*. Chicago: Aldine.

Campbell, Joseph. 1979. *The Hero with a Thousand Faces*. New York: Pantheon.

Cancian, Francesca M. 1986. "The Feminization of Love." *Signs: Journal of Women in Culture and Society* 2 (4): 692–709.

———. 1987. *Love in America: Gender and Self-Development*. Cambridge and New York: Cambridge University Press.

Caplow, Theodore. 1959. "Further Development of a Theory of Coalitions in the Triad." *American Journal of Sociology* 44 (March 1959): 488.

———. 1968. *Two Against One: Coalitions in Triads*. Englewood Cliffs, N.J.: Prentice Hall.

Cartledge, Sue; and Joanna Ryan, eds. 1983. *Sex and Love: New Thoughts on Old Contradictions*. London: Women's Press.

Catholic Encyclopaedia. 1907. Vol. I. New York: John Melody.

Cecil, David. 1939 [1930]. *The Young Melbourne, and the Story of His Marriage with Caroline Lamb*. New York: Bobbs Merrill.

Chagnon, Napoleon. 1968. *Yanomamo: The Fierce People*. New York: Holt, Rinehart & Winston.

Chamberlain, Mary. 1983. *Fenwomen*. London: Routledge & Kegan Paul.

Chandler, M. 1954. "An Evaluation of the Group Interview." *Human Organisation* 13 (2): 26–28.

Chappell, Helen. 1984. "The New Fidelity." *The Mail on Sunday*, 29 April, pp. 80–85.

Chaucer, Geoffrey. 1973. *The Canterbury Tales*. Edited by Nevill Coghill. Harmondsworth, England: Penguin. Originally written *c*. 1386.

Chelune, Gordon J., ed. 1979. *Self-Disclosure*. San Francisco: Jossey-Bass.

Chodorow, Nancy. 1978. *The Reproduction of Mothering*. Berkeley: University of California Press.

Clanton, Gordon; and Smith, Lynn G., eds. 1977. *Jealousy*. Englewood Cliffs, N.J.: Prentice-Hall.

Clark, David. 1987. "Wedlocked Britain." *New Society*, 13 March, pp. 12–15.

Comer, Lee. 1982. "Monogamy, Marriage and Economic Dependence." In *The Changing Experience of Women*. Elizabeth Whitelegg et al., eds., Oxford: Open University Set Books.

Cook, Mark; and Wilson, Glen. 1979. *Love and Attraction*. Oxford and New York: Pergamon.

Cordless, Richard. 1987. "Fatal Attraction." *Time*, 16 November.

Coronado, Raymon. 1987. " 'Other Woman' Admits Killing Wealthy Lover" and "Beverett Tells of Fear Children Would Learn about Affair, Slaying." Oakland (Calif.) *Tribune*, 19 August, pp. A1–2, and 21 August, M.

Cottle, Thomas J. 1980. *Children's Secrets*. Garden City, N.Y.: Anchor Books.

Coveney, Lal; Leslie, Kay; and Mahoney, Pat. 1984. "Theory into Practice: Sexual Liberation or Social Control (*Forum* magazine, 1968–81)?" In L. Coveney, M. Jackson, S. Jeffreys, L. Kaye, and P. Mahoney, eds., *The Sexuality Papers: Male Sexuality and the Social Control of Women*, chap. 4. Explorations in Feminism. Dover, N.H.: Hutchinson.

Coward, Rosalind. 1985. *Female Desires*. New York: Grove Press.

————. 1983. *Patriarchal Precedents: Sexuality and Social Relations*. London: Routledge & Kegan Paul.

Cozby, Paul C. 1973. "Self-Disclosure: A Literature Review." *Psychological Bulletin* 79 (2 [February]): 73–91.

Cressey, Donald. 1962. "Role Theory, Differential Association and Compulsive Crimes." In Arnold Rose, ed. *Human Behaviour and Social Processes*. London: Routledge & Kegan Paul.

Crim. Con. Actions and Trials and Other Legal Proceedings Relating to Marriage before the Passing of the Present Divorce Act (anonymous). 1887. London.

Cromwell, Ronald E.; and Olson, David H. 1975. *Power in Families*. Beverly Hills, Calif.: Sage.

Crosby, Faye; and Nyquist, Linda. 1977. "The Female Register: An Empirical Study of Lakoff's Hypotheses." *Language in Society* 6: 313–22.

Crozier, Michel. 1985. *The Trouble with America*. Berkeley: University of California Press.

Cuber, John Frank. 1969. "Adultery; Stereotype *versus* Reality." In G. Neubeck, ed. *Extramarital Relations*. Englewood Cliffs, N.J.: Prentice-Hall.

Cuber, John Frank; and Haroff, Peggy B. 1965. *The Significant Americans*. New York: Appleton-Century-Crofts.

Davies, John. 1969. "Honour and Politics in Pisticci." Proceedings of the Royal Anthropological Institute. London.

Davies, Kathleen. 1981. "Continuity and Change in Literary Advice on Marriage." In R. B. Outhwaite, ed., *Marriage and Society*, pp. 58–80. London: Europa.

Davis, Fred. 1963. *Passage through Crisis: Polio Victims and Their Families*. Indianapolis: Bobbs-Merrill.

Davis, Natalie Ann Zemon. 1975 [1965]. *Society and Culture in Early Modern France*. London: Duckworths.

Dawkins, Richard. 1976. *The Selfish Gene*. New York: Oxford University Press.

DeCrow, Karen. 1988. "The Significance of Becoming 50." *New York Times*, 7 January, p. A27.

Degler, Carl. 1980. *At Odds: Women in the Family in America from the Revolution to Present*. New York: Oxford University Press.

de Heusch, Luc. 1978 [1971]. *Why Marry Her?* Translated by Janet Lloyd. Cambridge and New York: Cambridge Studies in Anthropology, Cambridge University Press.

de Rougement, Denis. 1983 [1939]. *Love in the Western World*. Princeton, N.J.: Princeton University Press.

Dicks, H. V. 1967. *Marital Tensions*. London: Routledge & Kegan Paul.

Dinnerstein, Dorothy. 1976. *The Mermaid and the Minotaur: Sexual Arrangements and Human Malaise*. New York: Harper & Row.

Donzelot, Jacques. 1979. *The Policing of Families*. Translated by Robert Hurley. New York: Pantheon.

Douglas, Ann. 1977. *The Feminization of American Culture.* New York: Alfred A. Knopf.

Douglas, J. W. B. 1964. *The Home and the School.* London: Eyre Methuen.

Douglas, J. W. B.; Simpson, W.; and Ross, Jean. 1968. *All Our Future.* London: P. Davies.

Douglas, J. W. B.; Lawson, Annette; Cooper, T. E.; and Cooper, Elizabeth. 1968. "Family Interaction and the Activities of Children." *Journal of Child Psychology and Psychiatry* 9: 157–71.

Douglas, Jack. 1984. "The Emergence, Security, and Growth of the Sense of Self." In Joseph Kotarba and Andrea Fontana, eds., *The Existential Self and Society,* pp. 69–100. Chicago: University of Chicago Press.

Douglas, Mary. 1963. *The Lele of the Kasai.* Oxford: International African Institute.

———. 1966. *Purity and Danger.* London: Routledge & Kegan Paul.

Douglas, Tom. 1983. *Groups: Understanding People Gathered Together.* London: Tavistock.

Duby, Georges. 1978. *Mediaeval Marriage: Two Models From Twelfth Century France.* Translated by Elborg Forster. Baltimore: Johns Hopkins University Press.

———. 1984. *The Knight, the Lady and the Priest: The Making of Modern Marriage in Mediaeval France.* London: Allen Lane.

Duncan, Otis Dudley; Schuman, Howard; and Duncan, Beverly. 1974. *Social Change in a Metropolitan Community.* New York: Russell Sage Foundation.

Dunnell, Karen. 1979. *Family Formation.* London: Her Majesty's Stationery Office.

Dworkin, Andrea. 1987. *Intercourse.* New York: Free Press.

Eckardt, Marianne. 1977. "New Challenges to Adulthood in Our Times." Paper presented at American Academy Conference on Love and Work and Adulthood. Palo Alto, Calif.

Eekelaar, John H. 1978. *Family Law and Social Policy.* London: Weidenfeld & Nicolson.

Ehrenreich, Barbara. 1983. *The Hearts of Men: American Dreams and The Flight from Commitment.* London: Pluto.

Ehrenreich, Barbara; Hess, Elizabeth; and Jacobs, Gloria. 1986. *Re-making Love: The Feminization of Sex.* Garden City, N.Y.: Anchor/Doubleday.

Ekman, Paul. 1985. *Telling Lies.* New York: W. W. Norton.

Elder, Glen. 1987. "Families and Lives: Some Developments in Life-Course Studies." *Journal of Family History* 12 (1–3): 179–99.

Ellis, Albert. 1975. *A New Guide to Rational Living.* North Hollywood, Calif.: Wilshire Books.

Ellis, Albert (with Robert Harper). 1961. *Creative Marriage.* New York: Lyle Stuart.

Ellis, Albert; and Abarbanel, Albert, eds. 1973. *The Encyclopedia of Sexual Behavior,* 2nd ed. New York: Jason Aronson.

Ellis, Alice Thomas. 1983. *The Other Side of the Fire.* London: Duckworths.

Ellis, Havelock. 1921. "The Play-Function of Sex." London: British Society of the Study of Sex Psychology, no. 9.

———. 1940. *Studies in the Psychology of Sex.* New York: Random House.

Elshtain, Jean Bethke. 1988. "What's the Matter with Sex Today?" *Tikkun, A Bimonthly Jewish Critique of Politics, Culture and Society* 3 (2): 41–43.

Ephron, Nora. 1983. *Heartburn.* New York: Alfred A. Knopf.

Equal Opportunities Commission. 1980. *Women and Employment: Policies for Equal Opportunities.* London.

———. 1981. *Women and Underachievement at Work.* London.

Erikson, Erik. 1980. *Identity and the Life Cycle.* New York: W. W. Norton.

Eskapa, Shirley. 1984. *Woman versus Woman.* London: Heinemann.

Essock-Vitale, Susan; and McGuire, Michael. 1985. "Women's Lives Viewed from an Evolutionary Perspective. I. Sexual Histories, Reproductive Success and Demographic Characteristics of a Random Sample of American Women." *Ethology and Sociobiology* 6: 137–54.

Europa Yearbook. 1987. London: Europa Publications.

Evans-Pritchard, Edward Evan, ed. 1965. *The Position of Women in Primitive Societies and Other Essays.* New York: Free Press.

———. 1969 [1951]. *Kinship and Marriage Among the Nuer.* Oxford: Oxford University Press.

Fader, John. "The Transitional Person: Understanding Infidelity." *Marriage Guidance,* June 1982.

Falk, Candace. 1984. *Love, Anarchy and Emma Goldman: A Biography.* New York: Holt, Rinehart & Winston.

Fausto-Sterling, Anne. 1986. *Myths of Gender.* New York: Basic Books.

Ferguson, Ann; Philipson, Ilene; Diamond, Irene; Quinby, Lee; Vance, Carole; and Snitow, Ann Barr. 1984. "Viewpoint: Forum: The Feminist Sexuality Debates." *Signs: Journal of Women in Culture and Society* 10 (1): 144–58.

Ferrier, Susan. 1986 [1818]. *Marriage.* Edited by Herbert Foltineck. Oxford: Oxford University Press.

Festinger, Leon. 1957. *A Theory of Cognitive Dissonance.* Stanford, Calif.: Stanford University Press.

Finch, Janet. 1983. *Married to the Job: Wives' Incorporation into Men's Work.* London: Allen & Unwin.

Finch, Janet; and Groves, Dulcie, eds. 1983. *A Labour of Love.* London: Routledge & Kegan Paul.

Finer, Sir Morris. 1974. *The Finer Report on One-Parent Families.* London: Command 5629, Her Majesty's Stationery Office.

Firestone, Shulamith. 1970. *The Dialectic of Sex.* New York: William Morrow.

Fisher, Elizabeth. 1979. *Woman's Creation: Sexual Evolution and the Shaping of Society.* Garden City, N.Y.: Anchor Press, Doubleday.

Fisher, Helen E. 1984. *The Sex Contract.* St. Albans, England: Paladin.

Fletcher, Joseph Francis. 1966. *Situation Ethics.* Philadelphia: Westminster Press.

Fonda, Nicky; and Moss, Peter. 1975. *Mothers in Employment.* London: Brunel University Press.

Ford, Clellan S.; and Beach, Frank A. 1952. *Patterns of Sexual Behaviour.* New York: Harper & Row.

Fortes, Meyer. 1962. *Marriage in Tribal Societies.* Cambridge, England: Cambridge University Press.

Foucault, Michel. 1973. *Birth of the Clinic: An Archaeology of Medical Perception.* New York: Pantheon.

———. 1980. *History of Sexuality,* vol. I: *An Introduction.* Originally published as *La Volonté de savoir.* Translated as *The Will to Knowledge.* New York: Vintage.

———. 1985. "The Battle for Chastity." In Phillipe Ariès and André Béjin, eds., *Western Sexuality: Practice and Precept in Past and Present Times.* Translated by Anthony Forster. Oxford: Basil Blackwell.

Fox, Robin. 1985. "The Conditions of Sexual Evolution." In Phillipe Ariès and André Béjin, eds., *Western Sexuality: Practice and Precept in Past and Present Times,* pp. 1–13. Translated by Anthony Forster. Oxford: Basil Blackwell.

Francoeur, Anna; and Francoeur, Robert. 1973. "Hot and Cool Sex—Closed and Open Marriage." In Roger W. Libby and Robert N. Whitehurst, eds., *Renovating Marriage,* pp. 30–41. Danville, Calif.: Consensus.

———. 1974. *The Future of Sex Relations.* Englewood Cliffs, N.J.: Prentice-Hall.

Franklin, Clyde W., II. 1984. *The Changing Definition of Masculinity.* New York: Plenum Press.

Franklin, Denise. 1987. "How Far is Too Far? Even 'Experts' Disagree." *Santa Cruz Sentinel*, 30 June, p. D1.

Franks, Alan. 1985. "Why More Women Aren't Fellows." *The Times* (London), 14 January.

Frazer, James. 1936. *The Golden Bough: A Study in Magic and Religion.* Pt. VIII, vol. 12: *The Magic Art*, Part I, vol. 1 and Part I, vol. 2. London: Macmillan.

Freedman, Estelle B.; and Thorne, Barrie. 1984. "Viewpoint: Introduction to Forum: The Feminist Sexuality Debates." *Signs: Journal of Women in Culture and Society* 10 (1): 142–43.

Freeman, M. 1979. "Law and Sexual Deviation." In Ismond Rosen, ed., *Sexual Deviation.* 2nd ed. Oxford: Oxford University Press.

French, Marilyn. 1977. *The Women's Room.* New York: Summit Books.

———. 1980. *The Bleeding Heart.* New York: Summit Books.

———. 1985. *Beyond Power: On Women, Men and Morals.* New York: Summit Books.

French Institute of Public Opinion. 1961. *La Française et l'amour.* Translated by Robert Laffont as *Patterns of Sex and Love: A Study of the French Woman and her Morals,* 1961. New York: Crown Publishers.

Freud, Sigmund. 1959 [1910]. "Fetishism." In *Collected Papers*, vol. 5. New York: Basic Books.

———. 1961 [1930]. *Civilization and its Discontents.* New York: W. W. Norton.

———. 1977 [1910, 1912, 1917–18]. *On Sexuality: Three Essays on the Theory of Sexuality and Other Works.* Edited by Angela L. Richards. Vol. 7 in Pelican Freud Library. Harmondsworth, England: Penguin.

Friedan, Betty. 1963. *The Feminine Mystique.* London: Victor Gollancz.

———. 1983. *The Second Stage.* Tunbridge Wells, England: Abacus Sphere.

———. 1985. "How to Get the Women's Movement Moving Again." *New York Sunday Times Magazine*, 3 November, p. 26.

Fromm, Erich. 1956. *The Art of Loving.* New York: Harper & Row.

Fullerton, Gail Putney. 1984. *Survival in Marriage.* Hinsdale, Ill.: Dryden Press.

Gagnon, John; and Simon, William. 1973. *Sexual Conduct: The Social Sources of Human Sexuality.* Chicago: Aldine.

Gamarnikow, Eva; Morgan, David; Purvis, Jane; and Taylorson, Daphne, eds. 1983. *The Public and the Private—A Selection of Papers from the 1982 British Sociological Association Conference.* London: Heinemann.

Gavron, Hannah. 1966. *The Captive Housewife.* Harmondsworth, England: Penguin.

Gebhard, Paul. 1980. "Sexuality in the Post-Kinsey Era" (Galton Lecture, 1978). In W. Armytage, R. Chester, and J. Peel, eds., *Changing Patterns in Sexual Relations*, pp. 45–57. New York: Academic Press.

Geertz, Clifford. 1965. "The Impact of the Concept of Culture on the Concept of Man." In J. R. Platt, ed., *New Views on the Nature of Man.* pp. 106–7. Chicago: University of Chicago Press.

———. 1973. *The Interpretation of Cultures.* New York: Basic Books.

Gendlin, Eugene T. 1987. "A Philosophical Critique of Narcissism." In David Michael Levin, *Pathologies of the Modern Self: Postmodern Studies on Narcissism, Schizophrenia and Depression.* New York and London: New York University Press.

General Household Survey. 1981. No. 11. London: Office of Population Censuses and Surveys.

Gerth, H. H.; and Mills, C. Wright. 1946. *From Max Weber—Essays in Sociology.* New York: Oxford University Press.

Gibran, Kahlil. 1978 [1923]. *The Prophet.* New York: Alfred A. Knopf.

Giele, Janet Z. 1980. "Adulthood as Transcendence of Age and Sex." In Neil J.

Smelser and Erik Erikson, eds., *Themes of Love and Work in Adulthood*, pp. 151–73. Cambridge, Mass.: Harvard University Press.

Gilbert, Nigel; and Abell, Peter, eds. 1983. *Accounts and Action: Survey Conferences on Sociological Theory and Methods.* Aldershot, Herts, England: Gower.

Gilligan, Carol. 1982. *In a Different Voice: Psychological Theory and Women's Development.* Cambridge, Mass.: Harvard University Press.

Glazer, Nathaniel. 1976. "Housework." *Signs: Journal of Women in Culture and Society* 1 (Summer): 905–22.

Goffman, Erving. 1971. *Relations in Public.* Harmondsworth, England: Penguin.

Goldstein, Rebecca. 1983. *The Mind-Body Problem: A Novel.* New York: Random House.

Goldstine, Daniel. 1977. *The Dance-Away Lover.* New York: William Morrow.

Goodall, Jane V. Lawick. 1968. "The Behaviour of Free-Living Chimpanzees in the Gombe Stream Reserve." *Animal Behaviour Monographs* 1: 165–311.

———. 1971. *In the Shadow of Man.* Boston: Houghton Mifflin.

Goode, William. 1959. "The Theoretical Importance of Love." *American Sociological Review* 24: 37–48.

———. 1984. "Individual Investments in Family Relationships over the Coming Decades." *Tocqueville Review, La Revue Tocqueville* 7 (1 [Spring–Summer]).

Goodman, Ellen. 1987. "Why Don't Women Politicians 'Manize'?" San Francisco *Chronicle*, 12 May, p. B7.

Goody, Jack. 1956. "A Comparative Approach to Incest and Adultery." *British Journal of Sociology* 7: 286–305.

Gorer, Geoffrey. 1971. *Sex and Marriage in England To-day.* London: Nelson.

Gouldner, Alvin. 1981. "Doubts about the Uselessness of Men and the Meaning of the Civilising Process: A Reply to de Swaan's 'The Politics of Agoraphobia.'" *Theory and Society* 10: 413–17.

Gramsci, Antonio. 1973. *Letters from Prison.* Translated by Lynne Lawner. London: Jonathan Cape.

Granada. 1984. "7-UP" and "28-UP" shown November on Channel 4. Distributed to U.S. cinemas 1985.

Greer, Germaine. 1970. *The Female Eunuch.* London: MacGibbon & Kee.

———. 1984. *Sex and Destiny.* London: Secker & Warburg.

Groslière, Jean Claude. 1976. *La Reforme du Divorce.* Paris: Sirey.

Grosskopf, Diane. 1984. *Sex and the Married Woman.* London: Columbus.

Guggenhem Museum. 1987. *Juan Miró: A Retrospective.* New Haven: Yale University Press.

Guy, Catherine; and Saunders, Stephen, eds. 1984. *Asking about Marriage.* Rugby, Warwickshire, England: National Marriage Guidance Council.

Halfpenny, Peter. 1984. "Review of Gilbert and Abell 1983." *British Journal of Sociology* 18 (1): 134.

Hall, Trish. 1987. "Infidelity and Women: Shifting Patterns." *New York Times*, 1 June, p. B8.

Hampton, Christopher. 1986. *Les Liaisons dangereuses.* London: Faber & Faber.

Hansard. 1857. London: Her Majesty's Stationery Office.

Hansen, Karen. 1987. "Feminist Conceptions of Public and Private: A Cultural Analysis." *Berkeley Journal of Sociology* 32: 105–28.

Harris, Marvin. 1974. *Cows, Pigs, Wars and Witches.* New York: Vintage.

Hart, Herbert Lionel Adolphus. 1962. *Law, Liberty and Morality: The Harry Camp Lectures at Stanford University.* Stanford, Calif.: Stanford University Press.

Hartmann, H. 1980 [1937]. *Ego Psychology and the Problem of Adaptation.* Translated by D. Rapaport. New York: International Universities Press.

Hatfield, Elaine. 1983. "What Do Women and Men Want from Love and Sex?" In Elizabeth Rice Allgeier and Naomi B. McCormick, *Changing Boundaries: Gender Roles and Sexual Behavior*, pp. 106–34. Palo Alto, Calif.: Mayfield.

Hawthorne, Nathaniel. 1963 [*c.* 1883]. *The Scarlet Letter*. New York: Holt, Rinehart, & Winston.

Haynes, Edmund Sydney Pollack. 1915. *Divorce As It Might Be*. Cambridge: W. Heffer and Sons.

Health Trends. 1982. Welsh office: Department of Health and Social Security.

Hearst, Norman; and Hulley, Stephen B. 1988. "Preventing the Heterosexual Spread of AIDS." *Journal of the American Medical Association*. 259 (16 [April]): 2428–32.

Helson, Ravenna; Mitchell, Valerie; and Moane, Geraldine. 1984. "Personality and Patterns of Adherence and Non-Adherence to the Social Clock." *Journal of Personality and Social Psychology* 46: 1079–96.

Henriques, L. Fernando. 1970. *Love in Action*. St. Albans, England: Panther.

Henwood, Melanie; Rimmer, Leslie; and Wicks, Malcolm. 1987. *Inside the Family: Changing Roles of Men and Women*. Occasional paper no. 6. London: Family Policy Studies Centre.

Herschberger, Ruth. 1970 [1948]. *Adam's Rib*. New York: Harper & Row.

Hetherington, E. Mavis. 1972. "Effects of Father Absence on Personal Development in Adolescent Daughters." *Developmental Psychology* 7 (3): 313–26.

Hewitt, Florence. 1908. "Some Sea-Dyak Tabus." *Man* 8: 186–87.

Hinde, Robert A. 1979. *Towards Understanding Relationships*. London and New York: Academic Press.

Hirst, Paul; and Woolley, Penny. 1982. *Social Relations and Human Attributes*. London: Tavistock.

Hite, Shere. 1976. *The Hite Report—A Nationwide Study of Female Sexuality*. New York: Macmillan.

———. 1978. *The Hite Report on Male Sexuality*. New York: Macmillan.

———. 1987. *Women and Love*. New York: Alfred A. Khopf.

Hochschild, Arlie. 1979. "Emotion Work, Feeling Rules and Social Structure." *American Journal of Sociology* 85: 551–75.

———. 1981. "Attending to, Codifying and Managing Feelings: Sex Differences in Love." In Laurel W. Richardson and Verta Taylor, eds., *Sex and Gender*. Wakefield, England: Heath.

———. 1983. *The Managed Heart: The Commercialization of Human Feeling*. Berkeley: University of California Press.

Hoggett, Brenda M.; and Pearl, David S. 1983. *The Family, Law and Society*. London: Butterworths.

Hoinville, G.; and Jowell, R. 1978. *Survey Research Practice*. London: Heineman Educational Books.

Hooper, Anne. 1982. "Open Space" and "Letters." *Guardian*, 8 and 22 March.

———. 1983. *The Thinking Woman's Guide to Love and Sex*. London: Robson Books.

Horney, Karen. 1967 [1928]. "The Problem of the Monogamous Ideal." In H. Kelman, ed., *Feminine Psychology*, pp. 84–98. New York: W. W. Norton.

Horstman, Allen. 1985. *Victorian Divorce*. New York: St. Martin's Press.

Howard, Philip. 1983. *A Word in Your Ear*. London: Duckworth.

Hsu, Francis, ed. 1971. "A Hypothesis on Kinship and Culture." In Francis Hsu, ed., *Kinship and Culture*, pp. 3–32. Chicago: Aldine.

Hsu, Francis. 1972 [1961]. "Kinship and Ways of Life: An Exploration." In Francis Hsu, ed., *Psychological Anthropology*, pp. 509–67. Homewood, Ill.: Dorsey.

Huber, Joan; and Spitze, Glenna. 1983. *Sex Stratification: Children, Housework and Jobs*. New York: Academic Press.

Hunt, Morton M. 1969. *The Affair: A Portrait of Extra-Marital Love in Contemporary America*. New York: World Publishing.

———. 1974. *Sexual Behavior in the 1970's*. New York: Dell Publishing.

Ickeys, William. 1985. "Sex role influences on compatibility in relationships." In W. Ickeys, ed., *Compatible and Incompatible Relationships*. New York: Springer-Verlag.

Jackson, Joseph. 1969. *The Formation and Annulment of Marriage*, 2nd. ed. London: Butterworths.

Jacques, Elliot. 1965. "Death and the Mid-Life Crisis." *International Journal of Psycho-analysis* 46 (4 October): 502–74.

Johnson, Ralph H. 1972. "Attitudes towards Extramarital Relationships." *Medical Aspects of Human Sexuality* 6 (4): 168–91.

Johnson, Robert A. 1983. *We: Understanding the Psychology of Romantic Change*. New York: Harper and Row.

Jong, Erica. 1973. *Fear of Flying*. New York: Holt, Rinehart & Winston.

Jowell, Roger; and Airey, Colin, eds. 1984. *British Social Attitudes*. Social and Community Planning Research. Aldershot, England: Gower.

Jowell, Roger; and Witherspoon, Sharon, eds. 1985. *British Social Attitudes*. Social and Community Planning Research. Aldershot, England: Gower.

Kanter, Rosabeth Moss. 1977. *Men and Women of the Corporation*. New York: Basic Books.

Kaplan, Howard B., ed. 1983. *Psychosocial Stress: Trends in Theory and Research*. New York: Academic Press.

Kardiner, Abram. 1939. *The Individual and His Society*. New York: Columbia University Press.

Keays, Sara. 1985. *A Question of Judgement*. London: Quintessential Press.

Kesey, Ken. 1962. *One Flew Over the Cuckoo's Nest*. New York: Viking Press.

Kiechel, Walter. 1984. "Beyond Sexist Management." *Fortune*, 15 October, pp. 273–74.

Kierkegaard, Sören. 1959 [1834–55]. *Journals*. London: Oxford University Press.

Kinsey, Alfred C.; Pomeroy, Wardell B.; and Martin, Clyde E. 1948. *Sexual Behavior in the Human Male*. Philadelphia: W. B. Saunders.

Kinsey, Alfred C.; Pomeroy, Wardell B.; Martin, Clyde E.; and Gebhard, Paul H. 1953. *Sexual Behavior in the Human Female*. Philadelphia: W. B. Saunders.

Koehler, Lyle. 1980. *A Search For Power—The Weaker Sex in Seventeenth-Century New England*. Urbana: University of Illinois Press.

Kohn, Melvyn; and Schooler, C. 1983. *Work and Personality: An Inquiry into the Impact of Social Stratification*. Norwood, N.J.: Ablex Publishing.

Komarovsky, Mirra. 1964. *Blue-Collar Marriage*. New York: Random House.

Korn, Francis. 1973. *Elementary Structures Revisited: Lévi-Strauss on Kinship*. Berkeley: University of California Press.

Kotarba, Joseph; and Fontana, Andrea, eds. 1984. *The Existential Self and Society*. Chicago: University of Chicago Press.

Kovel, Joel. 1976. *A Complete Guide to Therapy*. New York: Pantheon.

Kraymer, Lisa. 1979. "Work: The Intimate Environment." *Alternative Lifestyles* 1 (February): 7–32.

Kundera, Milan. 1987 [1984]. *The Unbearable Lightness of Being: A Lover's Story*. New York: Harper & Row, Perennial Library.

Laclos, Pierre Choderlos de. 1985 [1781]. *Les Liaisons dangereuses*. Translated by P. W. K. Stone. Harmondsworth, England: Penguin.

Lake, Tony; and Hills, Ann. 1979. *Affairs: The Anatomy of Extra-Marital Relations*. London: Open Books.

Lamb, Patricia Frazer; and Hohlwein, Kathryn Joyce. 1983. *Touchstones: Letters between Two Women 1953–1964*. New York: Harper & Row.

Lancaster, Jane B. 1985. "Evolutionary Perspectives on Sex Differences in the

Higher Primates." In Alice S. Rossi, ed., *Gender and the Life Course*. New York: Aldine.

Lane, Marion; and Hubbard, Ruth. 1979. "Sociobiology and Biosociality: Can Science Prove the Biological Basis of Sex Difference in Behavior?" In Ruth Hubbard and Marion Lane, eds., *Gene and Gender*. II: *Pitfalls in Research on Sex and Gender*. New York: Gordian Press.

Lasch, Christopher. 1977. *Haven in a Heartless World*. New York: Basic Books.

Laslett, Peter. 1977. *Family Life and Illicit Love in Earlier Generations*. Cambridge and New York: Cambridge University Press.

———. 1985. "Foreword." In Philippe Ariès and André Béjin, eds., *Western Sexuality: Practice and Precepts in Past and Present Times*. Oxford: Basil Blackwell.

Laws, Judith Long; and Schwartz, Pepper. 1977. *Sexual Scripts: The Social Construction of Female Sexuality*. Hinsdale, Ill.: Dryden Press.

Lawson, Annette. 1983. "On the New Freedom." *Studies in Women Abstracts*, April.

Lawson, Annette; and Ingleby, David. 1974. "Daily Routines of Pre-School Children." *Psychological Medicine* 4 (4 [November]): 399–415.

Lawson, Annette; Robinson, Ian; and Bakes, Claire. 1985. "Problems in Evaluating the Consequences of Disabling Illness: The Case of Multiple Sclerosis." (part 1: "The Postal Diary"; part 2: "The Standard Day"). *Psychological Medicine* 15: 555–79.

Lawson, Annette; and Samson, Colin. 1988. "Age, Gender and Adultery." *British Journal of Sociology* 39 (3): 408–39.

Leach, Edmund. 1961. *Rethinking Anthropology*. London School of Economics Monographs on Social Anthropology, no. 22. London: Athlone Press.

Lederer, Wolfgang. 1968. *The Fear of Women*. New York: Harcourt Brace Jovanovich.

Lees, Sue. 1986. *Losing Out: Sexuality and Adolescent Girls*. London; and Dover, N.H.: Hutchinson.

Le Roy Ladurie, E. 1978. *Montaillou-Cathars and Catholics in a French Village 1294–1324*. London: Scollar Press.

Lerner, Laurence. 1979. *Love and Marriage: Literature and Its Social Context*. London: Arnold.

Levine, Judith. 1988. "Thinking About Sex." *Tikkun, A Bimonthly Jewish Critique of Politics, Culture and Society* 3 (2): 43–45.

Levinson, Daniel J. 1978. *The Seasons of Man's Life*. New York: Alfred A. Knopf.

Lévi-Strauss, Claude. 1969. *The Elementary Structures of Kinship*. Boston: Beacon Press.

———. 1976. *Structural Anthropology*. New York: Basic Books.

Levy, Marion J. 1971. "Notes on the Hsu Hypothesis." In Francis Hsu, ed., *Kinship and Culture*, pp. 33–41. Chicago: Aldine.

Lewis, C. S. 1959 [1936]. *Allegory of Love*. London: Oxford University Press.

Lewis, Charlie; and O'Brien, Margaret, eds. 1987. *Reassessing Fatherhood*. London: Sage.

Lewis, Helen. 1976. *Psychic War in Men and Women*. New York: New York University Press.

Libby, Roger W.; and Whitehurst, Robert N. 1973. *Renovating Marriage*. Danville, Calif.: Consensus.

Lichtenstein, Helen. 1970. "Changing Implications of the Concept of Psychosexual Development." *Journal of the American Psychoanalytic Association* 18: 300–17.

Lieberman, Morton A.; Yalom, Irving D.; and Miles, Matthew B. 1973. *Encounter Groups: First Facts*. New York: Basic Books.

Liebow, Elliot. 1965. *Tally's Corner*. Boston: Little, Brown.

Life Magazine. 1987. "*Life* Polls America: Sex and the Presidency." August, pp. 70–75.

Linton, Ralph. 1974. *The Material Culture of the Marquesan Islands*. Millwood, N.Y.: Kraus Reprint.

Lodge, David. 1984. *Small World*. London: Secker & Warburg.

Lowie, R. 1933. "Marriage." *Encyclopedia of the Social Sciences*. London: Macmillan.

Lowrys, Suzanne. 1983. "The Celibate Chic." *Sunday Times* (London), 31 January.

McBride, Angela Barron. 1976. *A Married Feminist: Living with Contradiction*. New York: Harper & Row.

McBroom, Patricia. 1986. *The Third Sex: The New Professional Woman*. New York: William Morrow.

McCary, James Leslie; and Copeland, Donna R. 1976. *Modern Views of Human Sexual Behaviour*. Chicago: Science Research Associates.

Macfarlane, Alan. 1978. *The Origins of English Individualism*. Oxford: Basil Blackwell.

———. 1986. *Marriage and Love in England 1300–1840*. Oxford and New York: Basil Blackwell.

McGinnis, Tom. 1981. *More Than Just a Friend: The Joys and Disappointments of Extramarital Affairs*. Englewood Cliffs, N.J.: Prentice-Hall.

McGregor, Oliver Ross. 1957. *Divorce in England: A Centenary Study*. London: Heinemann.

McIntosh, Jim. 1977. *Communication and Awareness in a Cancer Ward*. London: Croom Helm.

MacKinnon, Catherine A. 1988. "Male Dominance and Epistemology in Law and Politics." Beatrice M. Bain Lecture, University of California at Berkeley, 29 March.

MacLean, Mavis; and Eekelaar, John. 1986. *Maintenance after Divorce*. New York: Oxford University Press.

Mair, Lucy. 1971. *Marriage*. Harmondsworth, England: Pelican Anthropology Library, Penguin.

Malinowski, Bronislaw. 1962 [1929]. *Sex, Culture and Myth*. New York: Harcourt Brace & World.

Mannheim, Karl. 1936. *Ideology and Utopia*. New York: Harcourt Brace & World.

Mansfield, Penny. 1982. "A Portrait of Contemporary Marriage: Equal Partners or Just Good Companions." In *Change in Marriage*. London: National Marriage Guidance Council.

Marcus, Stephen. 1966. *The Other Victorians*. New York: Basic Books.

Market and Opinion Research International (MORI). 1982. Survey for the *Sunday Times* (London).

Martin, David. 1967. *A Sociology of English Religion*. London: Heineman.

Martin, Jean; and Roberts, Ceridwen. 1984. *Women and Employment: A Lifetime Perspective*. London: Department of Employment and Office of Population Censuses and Surveys, Her Majesty's Stationery Office.

Martin, Mike W. 1986. *Self-Deception and Morality*. Lawrence, Kan.: University Press of Kansas.

Maslow, Abraham. 1968. *Toward a Psychology of Being*. New York: Van Nostrand.

Matza, David. 1964. *Delinquency and Drift*. New York: John Wiley.

———. 1969. *Becoming Deviant*. Englewood Cliffs, N.J.: Prentice-Hall.

Mazur, Ronald. 1973. *The New Intimacy: Open-Ended Marriage and Alternative Lifestyles*. Boston: Beacon Press.

Mead, George Herbert. 1934. *Mind, Self and Society*. Chicago: University of Chicago Press.

Medawar, Peter. 1967. *The Art of the Soluble*. London: Eyre Methuen.

Meillassoux, Claude. 1981. *Maidens, Meal, and Money*. Cambridge and New York: Cambridge University Press.

Mensch, Betty; and Freeman, Alan. 1987. "Liberation's Public/Private Split." *Tik-*

kun, a Bimonthly Jewish Critique of Politics, Culture and Society 3 (2 [March/April]):
24–30.

Miller, Arthur. 1988. *Timebends: A Life*. New York: Random House.

Miller, Jean Baker. 1986. *Toward a New Psychology of Women*. Boston: Beacon Press.

Mills, C. Wright. 1959. *The Sociological Imagination*. Harmondsworth, England:
Penguin.

Moerman, Michael. 1974. "Accomplishing Ethnicity." In Roy Turner, ed., *Ethnomethodology*, pp. 54–68. Harmondsworth, England: Penguin.

Moore, Monica; and Butler, Diana. Forthcoming. "Predictive Aspects of Non-verbal
Aspects of Courtship Behavior in Women." *Semiotica*.

More, Hannah. 1798. *Thoughts on the Importance of the Manners of the Great to General
Society*. London: Cadell.

Morgan, Robin. 1970. *Sisterhood Is Powerful*. New York: Vintage.

Morris, Lydia. 1987. "The No-Longer Working Class." *New Society* (3 April): 16–19.

Moskin, J. Robert. 1969. "The New Contraceptive Society." *Look* 33 (3 [4 February]):
50–53.

Moulton, Ruth. 1977. "Some Effects of the New Feminism." *American Journal of
Psychiatry* 1 (134 [January]): 1–6.

Mount, Ferdinand. 1982. *The Subversive Family*. London: Jonathan Cape.

Moynahan, Brian. 1987. "French Are So False at Loving." London *Sunday Times*, 31
May, p. 17.

Mueller, Gerhard. 1980. *Sexual Conduct and the Law*, 2nd ed. Dobbs Ferry, N.Y.:
Oceana.

Murdock, G. 1949. *Social Structure*. New York: Macmillan.

My Secret Life (anonymous). 1966. New York: Grove Press. First published *c.* 1867.

Myers, Lonny. 1976. "Extra-Marital Sex: Is the Neglect of Its Positive Aspects Justified?" In Wilbur W. Oaks et al., eds., *Sex and the Life Cycle*, pp. 105–15. New York:
Grune & Stratton.

Myrdal, A.; and Klein, Viola. 1956. *Women's Two Roles: Home and Work*. London:
Routledge.

Nass, Gilbert D.; Libby, Roger W.; and Fisher, Mary Pat. 1981. *Sexual Choices*. Monte-
rey, Calif.: Wadsworth.

Needham, Rodney, ed. 1971. *Rethinking Kinship and Marriage*. London: Tavistock.

Neubeck, Gerhard, ed. 1969. *Extramarital Relations*. Englewood Cliffs, N.J.: Prentice-
Hall.

Neumann, Erich. 1963. *The Great Mother: An Analysis of the Archetype*. Princeton, N.J.:
Princeton University Press.

New Woman. 1986. "Infidelity Survey." October and November.

Newson, John; and Newson, Elizabeth. 1966. *Patterns of Infant Care in an Urban Community*. Harmondsworth, England: Penguin.

Nichols, Peter. 1981. *Passion Play*. London: Eyre Methuen.

Noddings, Nell. 1984. *Caring*. Berkeley: University of California Press.

Norton, Arthur J.; and Moorman, Jeanne E. 1987. "Current Trends in Marriage
and Divorce among American Women." *Journal of Marriage and the Family* 49
(February): 3–14.

Nye, Francis Ivan; and Berardo, Felix M. 1973. *The Family: Its Structure and Interaction*. New York: Macmillan.

Nye, Francis Ivan; and Hoffman, Lois, eds. 1963. *The Employed Mother in America*.
Chicago: Rand McNally.

Oakley, Ann. 1976. *Housewife*. Harmondsworth, England: Penguin.

———. 1984. *Taking It Like a Woman*. London: Jonathan Cape.

Oaks, Wilbur W.; Melchiode, Gerald A.; and Fischer, Ilda, eds. 1976. *Sex and the Life
Cycle*. New York: Grune & Stratton.

O'Brien, Conor Cruise. 1983. "A Woman of Some Importance." _The Observer_, 16 October.

Offen, Karen. 1987. "The Theory and Practice of Feminism in Nineteenth Century Europe." In _Becoming Visible: Women in European History_. Edited by Renate Bridenthal, Claudia Koonz, and Susan Mosher Stuard. Boston: Houghton Mifflin.

Office of Population, Censuses and Surveys. 1980. "Marriage and Divorce Statistics." Series FM2, no. 7.

O'Kelly, Charlotte; and Carney, Larry. 1986. _Women and Men in Society: Crosscultural Perspectives on Gender Stratification_. Belmont, Calif.: Wadsworth.

O'Leary, Virginia. 1986. "Affect Returns to Social Psychology: A Feminist View." Address by Distinguished Publication Award Winner, Association for Women in Psychology Conference, Oakland, Calif., 8 March.

O'Leary, Virginia; Unger, Rhoda Kesler; and Wallston, Barbara Strudler. 1985. _Women, Gender and Social Psychology_. Hillsdale, N.J.: Lawrence Erlbaum.

O'Neill, Nena; and O'Neill, George. 1972. _Open Marriage: A New Life Style for Couples_. New York: M. Evans.

Oppong, Christine. 1979. "Changing Family Structure and Conjugal Love." In M. Cook and G. Wilson. _Love and Attraction_. Oxford: Pergamon.

Organization for Economic Cooperation and Development (OECD). 1980. _Women and Employment: Policies for Equal Opportunities_. Paris.

Outhwaite, R. B. 1981. _Marriage and Society_. London: Europa.

Packard, Vance. 1968. _The Sexual Wilderness: The Contemporary Upheaval in Male-Female Relationships_. New York: David McKay.

Pareto, Vilfredo. 1963 [1935]. _A Treatise on General Sociology_, vol. II: _Theory of Residues_. New York: Dover.

Philo. _The Decalogue_ 120–25. In _Works_. Cambridge, Mass.: Harvard University Press, Loeb Classical Library, 1950.

Piachaud, David. 1984. _Round about Fifty Hours a Week_. London: Child Poverty Action Group.

Pierce, Jennifer. 1987. "Toward a Sociological Understanding of Gender and Depression." Paper delivered at the University of California, Berkeley, March.

Piercy, Marge. 1976. _Woman on the Edge of Time_. New York: Alfred A. Knopf.

Pietropinto, Anthony; and Simenauer, Jacqueline. 1977. _Beyond the Male Myth: What Women Want to Know about Men's Sexuality_. New York: Times Books.

Pincus, Lily; and Dare, Christopher. 1976. _Secrets in the Family_. New York: Pantheon.

Pines, Ayala; and Aronson, Elliot. 1983. "Antecedents, Correlates and Consequences of Sexual Jealousy." _Journal of Personality_ 51 (1 [March]): 108–36.

Pinter, Harold. 1978. _Betrayal_. London: Eyre Methuen.

Platt, Jennifer. 1981. "On Interviewing One's Peers." _British Journal of Sociology_ 32 (March): 75–91.

Pleck, Joseph H., ed. 1979. "Married Men: Work and Family." Summarized by Eunice Corfman in _Families Today_. National Institute of Mental Health _Science Monographs_ 1: 387–411. U.S. Department of Health, Education and Welfare. Rockville, Md.: U.S. Government Printing Office.

———. 1986. _Working Wives, Working Husbands_. Beverly Hills, Calif.: Sage.

Pleck, Joseph H.; and Sawyer, J. 1974. _Men and Masculinity_. Englewood Cliffs, N.J.: Prentice-Hall.

Pole, David. 1961. _Conditions of a Rational Enquiry into Ethics_. London: Athlone Press.

Popeno, David. 1987. "Beyond the Nuclear Family: A Statistical Portrait of the Changing Family in Sweden." _Journal of Marriage and the Family_ 49 (February): 173–83.

Presser, Harriet. 1986. "Shift Work among American Women and Child Care." _Journal of Marriage and the Family_ 48: 551–63.

The Psychologist: The Bulletin of the British Psychological Society 1 (2 [February 1988]): 46–51. Special Issue on AIDS.

Quaife, Geoffrey Robert. 1979. *Wanton Wenches and Wayward Wives: Peasants and Illicit Sex in Early Seventeenth Century England.* New Brunswick, N.J.: Croom Helm and Rutgers University Press.

Quinn, Robert E. 1977. "Coping with Cupid: The Formation, Impact, and Management of Romantic Relationships in Organizations." *Administrative Science Quarterly* 22 (March): 30–45.

Ramey, James. 1972. "Emerging Patterns of Innovative Behaviour in Marriage." *Family Coordinator*, October.

———. 1976. *Intimate Friendships.* Englewood Cliffs, N.J.: Prentice-Hall.

Reich, Wilhelm. 1945. *The Sexual Revolution: Toward a Self-Governing Character Structure.* Translated by Theodore P. Wolfe. New York: Orgone Institute Press.

Reich, Wilhelm. 1973 [1942]. *The Function of the Orgasm: Sex and Economic Problems of Biological Energy.* Translated by Vincent R. Carfagno. New York: Farrar, Straus & Giroux.

Reisman, David. 1985. Preface to Michel Crozier, *The Trouble with America.* Berkeley: University of California Press.

Reiss, Ira. 1970. "Premarital Sex as Deviant Behavior: An Application of Current Approaches to Deviance." *American Sociological Review* 35 (1): 78–82.

———. 1960. *Premarital Sexual Standards in America.* Glencoe, Ill.: Free Press of Macmillan.

———. 1967. *The Social Context of Premarital Sexual Permissiveness.* New York: Holt, Rinehart & Winston.

———. 1980. *Family Systems in America*, 3rd ed. New York: Holt, Rinehart & Winston.

Reiss, Ira; Anderson, Ronald; and Sponaugle, R. N. 1980. "A Multivariate Model of the Determinants of Extramarital Sexual Permissiveness." *Journal of Marriage and the Family* 42 (12 [May]): 395–411.

Reskin, Barbara. 1988. "Bringing the Men Back In: Sex Differentiation and the Devaluation of Women's Work." *Gender and Society* 2 (1 [March]): 58–81.

Rheinstein, M. 1971. "Divorce Law in Sweden." In Paul Bohannan, ed., *Divorce and After*, pp. 171–204. Garden City, N.Y.: Doubleday Anchor.

Reiter, Rayna, ed. 1979. *Towards an Anthropology of Women.* New York: Monthly Review Press.

Rich, Adrienne. 1983. "Compulsory Heterosexuality and Lesbian Existence." In Ann Snitow, Christine Stansell, and Sharon Thompson, eds., *Powers of Desire: The Politics of Sexuality*, pp. 177–205. New York: New Feminist Library, Monthly Review Press.

Richardson, Laurel. 1981. *The Dynamics of Sex and Gender.* Boston: Houghton Mifflin.

———. 1985. *The New Other Woman: Contemporary Single Women in Affairs with Married Men.* New York: Free Press.

———. 1988. "Secrecy and Status: The Social Construction of Forbidden Relationships." *American Sociological Review* 53 (April): 209–19.

Richardson, Laurel (with Verta Taylor). 1983. *Feminist Frontiers: Re-thinking Sex, Gender and Society.* Reading, Mass.: Addison Wesley.

Rimmer, Leslie. 1981. *Families in Focus.* London: Study Commission on the Family.

———. 1983. "The Economics of Work and Caring." In Janet Finch and Dulcie Groves, eds., *A Labour of Love: Women Work and Caring*, pp. 131–47. London: Routledge & Kegan Paul.

Rivière, Peter. 1971. "Marriage: A Reassessment." In Rodney Needham, ed., *Rethinking Kinship and Marriage.* London: Tavistock.

Roberts, Elizabeth. 1984. *A Woman's Place.* Oxford: Basil Blackwell.

Roberts, Helen, ed. 1981. *Doing Feminist Research*. London; and Boston, Mass.: Routledge & Kegan Paul.

Robertson, Kenneth G. 1982. *Public Secrets: A Study in the Development of Government Secrecy*. New York: St. Martin's Press.

Robinson, Ian. 1983. *Discovering the Diagnosis of MS* [multiple sclerosis]. Brunel–ARMS (Action for Research in Multiple Sclerosis) Research Unit, general report no. 3.

———. 1988. "Reconstructing Lives: Living with Multiple Sclerosis." In Michael Bury and Robert Anderson, eds., *Living With Chronic Illness: The Experience of Patients and their Families*. London: Unwin Hyman.

Robinson, John P. 1977. *How Americans Use Time: A Socio-Psychological Analysis*. New York: Praeger.

Rogers, Carl R. 1961. *On Becoming a Person*. Boston: Houghton Mifflin.

———. 1972. *Becoming Partners: Marriage and Its Alternatives*. New York: Dell.

Rojek, Chris. 1983. "Review of Benson and Hughes 1983." *British Journal of Sociology* 18 (1): 129.

Roscoe, J. 1923. *The Bakitara or Banyoro*. Cambridge, England: The University Press.

Rose, Arnold, ed. 1962. *Human Behaviour and Social Processes*. London: Routledge & Kegan Paul.

Rose, Phyllis. 1984. *Parallel Lives*. London: Chatto & Windus.

Rose, Steven; Kamin Leon J.; and Lewontin, Richard C. 1984. *Not in Our Genes: Biology, Ideology and Human Nature*. Harmondsworth, England: Penguin.

Rosen, Ismond, ed. 1979. *Sexual Deviation*. Oxford: Oxford University Press.

Rosen, Richard Dean. 1978. *Psychobabble*. Hounslow, England: Wildwood House.

Ross, Ellen. 1980. " 'The Love Crisis': Couples Advice Books of the Late 1970s." *Signs* 6 (1): 109–22; and in Catharine R. Stimpson and Ethel Spector Person, eds., *Woman, Sex and Sexuality*. Chicago and London: University of Chicago Press.

Rossi, Alice S., ed. 1985. *Gender and the Life Course*. New York: Aldine.

Rothman, Ellen K. 1984. *Hands and Hearts: A History of Courtship in America*. New York: Basic Books.

Rubin, Gayle. 1975. "The Traffic in Women: Notes toward a 'Political Economy' of Sex." In Rayna Rapp Reiter, *Towards an Anthropology of Women*. New York: Monthly Review Press.

———. 1984. "Thinking Sex." In Carole Vance, ed., *Pleasure and Danger: Exploring Female Sexuality*. Boston and London: Routledge & Kegan Paul.

Rubin, Lillian. 1983. *Intimate Strangers*. New York: Harper & Row.

Ruddick, Sarah. 1982. "Maternal Thinking." In Barrie Thorne and Marilyn Yalom, eds., *Rethinking the Family: Some Feminist Questions*, pp. 76–94. New York and London: Longman.

Russell, Diana. 1986. *The Secret Trauma: Incest in the Lives of Girls and Women*. New York: Basic Books.

Safilios-Rothschild, Constantina. 1969. "Attitudes of Greek Spouses Toward Marital Infidelity." In Gerhard Neubeck, ed., *Extramarital Relations*, pp. 75–93. Englewood Cliffs, N.J.: Prentice-Hall.

Saga of Tristram and Isonde [early thirteenth-century Icelandic version] 1973. Translated by Paul Schach. Lincoln: University of Nebraska Press.

Said, Laila. 1986. *A Bridge Through Time*. New York: Summit Books.

Salaman, Edna. 1984. *The Kept Woman: Mistresses in the 1980's*. London: Orbis.

Sanday, Peggy Reeves. 1981. *Female Power and Male Dominance: On the Origins of Sexual Inequality*. Cambridge and New York: Cambridge University Press.

Sarsby, Jacqeline. 1983. *Romantic Love and Society*. New York: Penguin.

Scanzoni, John H. 1978. *Sex Roles, Women's Work and Marital Conflict*. Lexington, Mass.: Lexington Books.

Scarf, Maggie. 1987. *Intimate Partners: Patterns in Love and Marriage*. New York: Random House.

Schofield, Michael. 1973. *The Sexual Behaviour of Young Adults*. London: Lane.

———. 1976. *Promiscuity*. London: Gollancz.

Schorer, Mark. 1946. *William Blake: the Politics of Vision*. New York: Henry Holt.

Schumer, Fran R. 1982. "Is Sex Dead?" *New York Magazine*, 6 December, pp. 69–97.

Seabrook, Jeremy. 1982. *Working Class Childhood*. London: Gollancz.

Segal, Erich. 1980. *Man, Woman and Child*. London: Granada.

Sennett, Richard. 1977. *The Fall of Public Man*. New York: Alfred A. Knopf.

Sermat V.; and Smith, M. 1973. "Content Analysis of Verbal Communication in the Development of a Relationship: Conditions Affecting Self-disclosure." *Journal of Personality and Social Psychology* 26 (3): 332–46.

Shaver, P.; and Hendrick, C., eds. 1987. *Sex and Gender*. Newbury Park, Calif.: Sage.

Shepherd, Michael. 1961. "Morbid Jealousy: Some Clinical and Social Aspects of a Psychiatric Symptom." *Journal of Mental Science* 107: 687.

Sherr, Lorraine. 1988. "Has AIDS Changed Women's Attitudes to Condoms?" *The Psychologist* 1 (2): 48–49.

Shorter, Edward. 1975. *The Making of the Modern Family*. New York: Basic Books.

Shostak, Marjorie. 1983. *Nisa, the Life and Words of a !Kung Woman*. New York: Viking.

Simmel, Georg. 1902. "The Number of Members as Determining the Sociological Form of the Group." *American Journal of Sociology* 8 (1 [July]): 45–46.

———. 1950. *The Sociology of George Simmel*. Edited by Kurt H. Wolff. London: Free Press of Glencoe and Collier-Macmillan Ltd.

———. 1984. *On Women, Sexuality and Love*. Translated by Guy Oakes. New Haven: Yale University Press.

Skolnick, Arlene. 1983. *The Intimate Environment: Exploring Marriage and the Family*. Boston: Little, Brown.

Skynner, Robin; and Cleese, John. 1984. *Families and How to Survive Them*. London: Eyre Methuen.

Smelser, Neil J.; and Erikson, Erik, eds. 1980. *Themes of Work and Love in Adulthood*. Cambridge, Mass.: Harvard University Press.

Smith, Audrey D.; and Reid, William J. 1987. *Role-Sharing Marriage*. New York: Columbia University Press.

Smith, Lynn G.; and Smith, James, R., eds. 1974. *Beyond Monogamy*. Baltimore: Johns Hopkins University Press.

Snitow, Ann; Stansell, Christine; and Thompson, Sharon, eds. 1983. *Powers of Desire: The Politics of Sexuality*. New York: New Feminist Library, Monthly Review Press.

Social Trends. 1981–84. Nos. 11–14. London: Her Majesty's Stationery Office.

Spender, Dale. 1985. *Man Made Language*. London; Routledge & Kegan Paul.

Stanley, Liz; and Wise, Sue. 1983. *Breaking Out: Feminist Consciousness and Feminist Research*. London: Routledge & Kegan Paul.

Starr, Paul. 1987. "A Response to Mensch and Freeman," *Tikkun* 2 (3 [March–April]): 31–32.

Steffensen, D. 1984. "*Nelson V. Jacobsen*: A New Causation Standard for Alienation of Affection Actions." *Utah Law Review* 4: 885–900.

Sternberg, Robert. 1986. "A Triangular Theory of Love." *Psychological Review* 93 (2): 119–35.

Stewart, David. 1885. *The Law of Husband and Wife as Established by England and the United States*. San Francisco: Bancroft-Whitney.

Stimpson, Catharine R.; and Person, Ethel Spector, eds. 1980. *Women, Sex and Sexuality*. Chicago and London: University of Chicago Press.

Stone, Lawrence. 1965. *The Crisis in the Aristocracy 1558–1641*, part III: *Minds and Manners*. Oxford: Clarendon Press.

————. 1977. *The Family, Sex and Marriage in England 1500–1800*. London: Weiden-feld & Nicolson.

Stoppard, Tom. 1982. *The Real Thing*. London: Faber.

Study Commission on the Family. 1980. *Happy Families*. London.

Sutherland, Edwin Hardin; and Cressey, Donald. 1974 [1924]. *Criminology*, 9th ed. Philadelphia: Lippincott. Originally by Sutherland only.

Swidler, Ann. 1980. "Love and Work in American Culture." In Neil J. Smelser and Erik Erikson, eds., *Themes of Work and Love in Adulthood*, pp. 120–47. Cambridge, Mass.: Harvard University Press.

Szalai, A., ed. 1972. *The Uses of Time: Daily Activities of Urban and Suburban Populations in Twelve Countries*. The Hague: Mouton.

Tanner, Tony. 1979. *Adultery in the Novel: Contract and Transgression*. Baltimore: Johns Hopkins University Press.

Tavris, Carol; and Sadd, Susan. 1977. *The Redbook Report on Female Sexuality*. New York: Delacorte Press.

Temoshok, Lydia; Sweet, D.; and Zich, J. 1987. "A Three-City Comparison of the Public's Knowledge and Attitudes about AIDS." *Psychology and Health* 1: 43–60.

Thoits, Peggy. 1984. "Dimensions of Life-Events That Influence Psychosocial Distress: An Evaluation of the Literature." In H. B. Kaplan, ed., *Psychosocial Stress: Trends in Theory and Research*. New York: Academic Press.

Thomas, Keith. 1959. "The Double Standard." *Journal of the History of Ideas* 20: 195–216.

Thompson, A. P. 1984. "Extra-Marital Relations." *Journal of Marriage and the Family* 46 (1 [February]): 34–42.

Thompson, Sharon. 1984. "Search for Tomorrow: On Feminism and the Reconstruction of Teen Romance." In Carole Vance, ed., *Pleasure and Danger: Exploring Female Sexuality*, pp. 350–84. Boston and London: Routledge & Kegan Paul.

Thoreau, Henry David. 1946 [1854]. *Walden*. New York: Dodd, Mead.

Thorne, Barrie; Kramarae, Cheris; and Henley, Nancy. 1983. *Language, Gender and Society*. Rowley, Mass.: Newbury House.

Thorne, Barrie; and Yalom, Marilyn. 1982. *Rethinking the Family*. New York: Longman.

Tiefer, Leonore. 1987. "Social Constructionism and the Study of Human Sexuality." In P. Shaver and C. Hendrick, eds., *Sex and Gender*, pp. 70–94. Newbury Park, Calif.: Sage.

Toffler, Alvin. 1970. *Future Shock*. New York: Random House.

————. 1980. *The Third Wave*. New York: William Morrow.

Tolstoy, Leo. 1964 [1878]. *Anna Karenin*. Introduced by Rosemary Edmonds. Harmondsworth, England: Penguin Classics.

Toufexis, Anastasia. 1987. "Season of Autumn–Summer Love." *Time*, 30 November, p. 75.

Trimberger, Ellen Kay. 1983. "Feminism, Men, and Modern Love." In Ann Snitow, Christine Stansell, and Sharon Thompson, eds., *Powers of Desire: The Politics of Sexuality*, pp. 149–52. New York: New Feminist Library, Monthly Review Press.

Trivers, R. L. 1972. "Parental Investment and Sexual Selection." In B. H. Campbell, ed., *Sexual Selection and the Descent of Man*, pp. 136–79. Chicago: Aldine.

Trumbach, Randolph. 1978. *The Rise of the Egalitarian Family: Aristocratic Kinship and Domestic Relations in Eighteenth Century England*. London; San Francisco and New York: Academic Press.

Turner, Ralph H. 1970. *Family Interaction*. New York: John Wiley.

————. 1976. "The Real Self: From Institution to Impulse." *American Journal of Sociology* 81 (5): 989–1017.

Turner, Roy, ed. 1974. *Ethnomethodology*. Harmondsworth, England: Penguin.

Valverde, Mariana. 1987. *Sex, Power and Pleasure*. Philadelphia: New Society.

Vance, Carole, ed. 1984. *Pleasure and Danger: Exploring Female Sexuality*. Boston and London: Routledge & Kegan Paul.

Van Sommers, Peter. 1987. *Jealousy*. London: Penguin.

Vargas Llosa, Mario. 1986. *The Perpetual Orgy: Flaubert and Madame Bovary*. New York: Farrar, Straus & Giroux.

Verlet, Agnes. 1978. *Yseult et Tristan*. Paris: Librairie Editions l'Harmattan.

Viorst, Judith. 1976. *How Did I Get to be 40? and Other Atrocities*. New York: Simon & Schuster.

Voltaire 1924. *Philosophical Dictionary*. Selected and arranged by H. I. Woolf. New York: Alfred A. Knopf.

Voysey, Margaret. 1975. *A Constant Burden*. London: Routledge & Kegan Paul.

Walker, Barbara, ed. 1983. *The Women's Encyclopedia of Myth and Secrets*. New York: Harper & Row.

Walker, Kenneth M. 1957 [1940]. *The Physiology of Sex*. Harmondsworth, England: Penguin.

Wallach, Michael A.; and Wallach, Lise. 1983. *Psychology's Sanction for Selfishness*. San Francisco: W. H. Freeman.

Wallerstein, Judith; and Kelly, Joan. 1980. *Surviving the Breakup*. New York: Basic Books.

Wallerstein, Judith; and Corbin, Shauna. 1986. "Father-Child Relationships after Divorce: Child Support and Educational Opportunities." *Family Law Quarterly* 20 (2 [Summer]): 109–28.

Wall Street Journal. 1986. "My Lover, My Colleague," and "The New Double Standard." Special Supplement on Corporate Woman. 24 March, pp. 25 and 31.

Weber, Max. 1946. *From Max Weber—Essays in Sociology*. Edited by Hans H. Gerth and C. Wright Mills. New York: Oxford University Press.

———. 1958. *The Protestant Ethic and the Spirit of Capitalism*. New York: Charles Scribner.

Wedeck, Harry Ezekiel. 1975. *A Treasury of Witchcraft*. New London, Conn.: Citadel Press.

Weeks, Jeffrey. 1981. *Sex, Politics and Society: The Regulation of Sexuality since 1800*. London: Longman.

———. 1985. *Sexuality and Its Discontents: Meanings, Myths and Modern Sexualities*. London: Routledge & Kegan Paul.

———. 1986. *Sexuality*. New York: Tavistock and Ellis Horwood in association with Methuen.

Weitzman, Lenore J. 1981. *The Marriage Contract: Spouses, Lovers and the Law*. New York: Free Press.

———. 1985. *The Divorce Revolution: The Unexpected Economic and Social Consequencies for Women and Children*. New York: Free Press.

West, Candace; and Zimmerman, Don H. 1983. "Small Insults: A Study of Interruptions in Cross-Sex Conversations between Unacquainted Persons." In Barrie Thorne, Chris Kramarae, and Nancy Henley. *Language, Gender and Society*, pp. 102–17. Rowley, Mass.: Newbury House.

Westermarck, Edvard. 1921. *The Origin of Sexual Modesty*. London: The British Society for the Study of Sex Psychology, no. 8.

———. 1934a. *Three Essays on Sex and Marriage*. London: Macmillan.

———. 1934b. *The Future of Marriage in Western Civilisation*. London: Macmillan.

———. 1936. *A Short History of Marriage*. London: Macmillan.

———. 1939. *Christianity and Morals*. London: Macmillan.

White, Jerry. 1986. *The Worst Street in North London*. London: Routledge & Kegan Paul.

Whitehurst, Robert. 1969. "Extramarital Sex: Alienation or Extension of Normal

Behavior." In Gerhard Neubeck, ed., *Extramarital Relations*, pp. 129–45. Englewood Cliffs, N.J.: Prentice-Hall.

Whitelegg, Elizabeth et al., eds. 1982. *The Changing Experience of Women*. Oxford: Martin Robertson in association with the Open University.

Willmott, Peter; and Young, Michael D. 1973. *The Symmetrical Family*. London: Routledge & Kegan Paul.

Winnicott, Donald Woods. 1958. "Transitional Objects and Transitional Phenomena." *Collected Papers*. London. Tavistock.

———. 1965a. *Maturational Processes and the Facilitating Environment*. New York: International Universities Press.

———. 1965b. *The Family and Individual Development*. London: Social Science Paperbacks, Tavistock.

———. 1984. *Deprivation and Delinquency*. Edited by Clare Winnicott, Ray Shepherd, and Madeleine David. London: Tavistock.

Wolfe, Linda. 1975. *Playing Around: Women and Extramarital Sex*. New York: William Morrow.

Wolff, Kurt H., ed. 1950. *The Sociology of Georg Simmel*. London: Free Press of Glencoe and Collier-Macmillan.

Wolstenholme, G. E. W.; and Fitzsimmons, D. W., eds. 1973. "Law and Ethics of AID and Embryo Transfer." Ciba Foundation Symposium, report no. 17. Amsterdam and New York: Elsevier.

Woman's World. 1985. "Marriage To-day: Is Divorce Going Out of Date?" October, pp. 62–64.

Woo, Louise. 1986. "Women Set New Standards for Sexuality." Oakland (Calif.) *Tribune*, 6 October, pp. C1,3.

Wright, Peter. 1987. *Spycatcher*. New York: Viking Press.

Yablonsky, Lewis. 1979. *The Extra-Sex Factor*. New York: Times Books.

Yalom, Marilyn. 1985. *Maternity, Mortality and the Literature of Madness*. University Park: Pennsylvania State University Press.

Yalom, Marilyn; Estler, Suzanne; and Brewster, Wanda. 1982. "Changes in Female Sexuality: A Study of Mother/Daughter Communication and Generational Differences." *Psychology of Women Quarterly* 7 (2): 141–54.

Yankelovich, Daniel. 1981. *New Rules: Searching for Self-Fulfillment in a World Turned Upside Down*. New York: Random House.

Youngs, J. William T. 1985. *Eleanor Roosevelt: A Personal and Public Life*. Boston: Little Brown.

Zuboff, Shoshana. 1988. *In the Age of the Smart Machine: The Future of Work and Power*. New York: Basic Books.

Index